Classicism, Politics, and Kinship

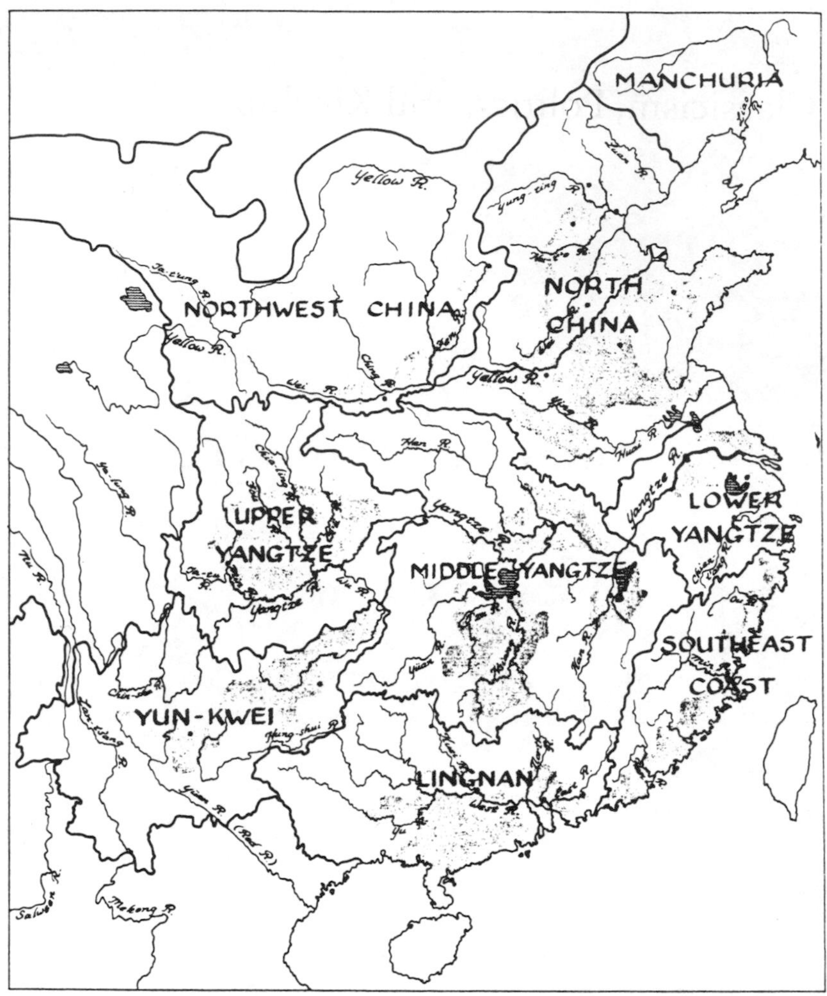

Map 1. Physiographic Macroregions of Agrarian China in Relation to Major Rivers and Showing Regional Cores

Source: G. William Skinner, ed., *The City in Late Imperial China*. Reprinted with the permission of the publishers, Stanford University Press.

Classicism, Politics, and Kinship

The Ch'ang-chou School of New Text Confucianism in Late Imperial China

Benjamin A. Elman

UNIVERSITY OF CALIFORNIA PRESS
Berkeley · Los Angeles · Oxford

University of California Press
Berkeley and Los Angeles, California

University of California Press, Ltd.
Oxford, England

Library of Congress Cataloging-in-Publication Data

Elman, Benjamin A., 1946–
Classicism, politics, and kinship: the Ch'ang-chou school of new text Confucianism in late imperial China/Benjamin A. Elman.
p. cm.
Bibliography: p.
Includes index.
ISBN 0-520-06673-1 (alk. paper)
1. Neo-Confucianism—China—Ch'ang-chou shih (Kiangsu Province, China)
2. Ch'ang-chou shih (Kiangsu Province, China)—Intellectual life. 3. Political science—China—History—19th century.
I. Title.
B5243.N4E46 1990
181'.112—dc20 89-34636
CIP

Printed in the United States of America

1 2 3 4 5 6 7 8 9

The paper used in this publication meets the minimum requirements of American National Standard for Information Sciences—Permanence of Paper for Printed Library Materials, ANSI Z39.48-1984. ♾™

In memory of Louis/Shmarral
and for Sonia/Rachel,
my father and mother.

The world fell into decay, and the Way became obscure. Perverse speech and oppressive deeds again arose. There were instances of ministers who murdered their rulers and of sons who murdered their fathers. Confucius was fearful and compiled the *Spring and Autumn Annals*. The *Annals* represents the affairs of the Son of Heaven. Therefore, Confucius said: "It will be on account of the *Annals* that people will know me. It will be due to the *Annals* that people will condemn me."

Mencius

History has a more important task than to be a handmaiden to philosophy, to recount the necessary birth of truth and values; it should become a differential knowledge of energies and failings, heights and degenerations, poisons and antidotes. Its task is to become a curative science.

Michel Foucault

Lo Ping. *Portrait of the Artist's Friend I-an* (1798). Ching Yuan Chai Collection. Courtesy of James Cahill.

CONTENTS

ILLUSTRATIONS

FIGURES

MAPS

TABLE

Errata

The images for figures 1–3 have been transposed:

The illustration for figure 1 (New Text: Clerical Script) can be found on page xxix.

The illustration for figure 2 (Large Seal Script) can be found on page xxvii.

The illustration for figure 3 (Old Text: Small Seal Script) can be found on page xxviii.

ACKNOWLEDGMENTS

Primary research for the preparation of this study was supported by many public organizations and private individuals in the United States, China, Japan, and Taiwan. First, I must thank Yang Xiangkui (Institute of History, Chinese Academy of Social Sciences, Beijing) and Tang Zhijun (Institute of History, Shanghai Academy of Social Sciences) for their kindness and help while I was researching the Ch'ang-chou New Text School in China in 1983 and 1984 under the auspices of the National Academy of Sciences, Committee for Scholarly Communication with the People's Republic of China. Many primary sources were available only in manuscript, which I was able to read in Beijing and Shanghai. My thanks to professors Yang and Tang for making these manuscripts available to me. Thanks are also due Wang Junyi of People's University and Huang Shaohai from the Shanghai Academy.

The project was initiated in Taiwan and Japan in 1982 and continued at libraries and archives in Taipei, Kyoto, and Tokyo at various times until 1984 under the sponsorship of the Foundation for Scholarly Exchange (Fulbright Foundation), the National Endowment for the Humanities, and the Pacific Cultural Foundation. In Taiwan, I was privileged to be a visiting scholar affiliated with the Institute of Modern History, Academia Sinica. In Japan, I was given a cordial welcome as a visiting professor affiliated with the Institute for Humanistic Studies of Kyoto University. In particular, professors Ono Kazuko, Hazama Naoki, and Kawata Teiichi made my stay in Japan very rewarding and fruitful. While in Taiwan, Wu Jing-jyi and Tony Wang enabled me to carry on research under ideal conditions. Others who deserve mention for their support are Hamaguchi Fujio, Shimada Kenji, Sakade Yoshinobu, Chao Chung-fu, Huang Chün-chieh, Lin Ch'ing-chang, and Ts'ai Su-erh.

I would also like to acknowledge the help of the staff of the following libraries: the Tōyō Bunko, the Naikaku Bunko, and the National Diet Library in Tokyo; the Oriental Library of the Institute for Humanistic Studies in Kyoto; the Academia Sinica, Institute of History and Philology, Fu Ssu-nien Rare Books Library, in Nankang, Taiwan; the Central Library, Rare Books Collection, in Taipei; the Beijing National Library, Rare Books Collection; the Shanghai Municipal Library; the Shanghai Academy of Social Sciences, Institute of History Library, in Xujiahui; the Suzhou Museum Archives; the Wuxi Municipal Library; the Chinese Academy of Sciences Library in Wangfujing; the Chinese Academy of Social Sciences, Institute of History Library, in Beijing; the Beijing University Library; and the People's University Library in Beijing. I regret that unsympathetic Chinese officials in the Nanjing office of the Ministry of Culture twice refused me admission to the Ch'ang-chou Municipal Library.

Many of the issues raised in this book were first presented while I was a postdoctoral fellow at the Center for Chinese Studies of the University of Michigan from 1984 until 1985. In particular, Robert Dernberger, Albert Feuerwerker, Donald Munro, Michel Oksenberg, Martin Whyte, R. Bin Wong, and Ernest Young encouraged me to complete the project. Portions of the book were presented before colleagues at Rice University, Columbia University, Harvard University, and UCLA. Thanks are due Derk Bodde, Peter Bol, Wm. Theodore de Bary, Philip Huang, Robert Hymes, Allen Matisow, Herman Ooms, Peter Reill, Philip Rieff, Richard Smith, Frederic Wakeman, Jr., and Norton Wise for their suggestions.

Susan Naquin and Nathan Sivin of the University of Pennsylvania read through the initial draft of the project, and each helped me to pare away the dross and highlight the key issues in my presentation. In addition, an anonymous reader for the University of California Press ruthlessly and yet graciously recommended essential revisions that have made the present volume much sounder and leaner. I would also like to thank the editors at U.C. Press for their efforts, particularly Sheila Levine and Betsey Scheiner. A summer Humanities Travel Grant from Rice University in 1986 and UCLA Faculty Senate Grants from 1987 to 1988 have enabled me complete revisions on schedule. Finally, my special thanks to Donald Munro, Richard Smith, and Philip Huang for the professional support I received after leaving China in the summer of 1984 still unemployed. Their confidence in my work brought to fruition the generous grants and fellowships that had made my research possible.

EXPLANATORY NOTES

1. Dates for well-known historical figures such as Confucius or Mencius have not been included unless needed for the discussion in which their names appear. Dates for all other people are given on their first appearance in each chapter. The Chinese characters for all names, book titles, and terms are included in the Bibliography or the Glossary. The Bibliography includes all primary and secondary sources cited specifically in the footnotes. Works mentioned in the text and not in the notes are not cited in the Bibliography; the Chinese characters for their titles occur in the Glossary.

2. In this volume the term *literati* refers to those select members of the Chinese gentry who through demonstrated literary qualifications on the civil service examinations maintained their status as Confucians (*Ju*) in the elite class of imperial China. Although *literati* does not express the social, economic, and political power of this group, the term suits those whose careers stressed classical scholarship and publishing. *Gentry* is used when the focus is not on examination qualifications per se but on local social and economic power, wielded by the elite as landlords, or on political power, wielded by the elite as officials in the state bureaucracy. Hence the Chuangs and Lius are examples of gentry lineages in Ch'ang-chou, whereas Chuang Ts'un-yü and Liu Feng-lu were distinguished Confucian literati from those lineages.

3. *Orthodoxy* does not refer here to a fixed set of elements in China, unchanged since antiquity. Rather, my account stresses a flexible conception of orthodoxy because different orthodoxies existed at different

levels in imperial politics and society and under different historical circumstances. New Text Confucianism was the state orthodoxy of the Former Han dynasty (206 B.C.–A.D. 8), whereas the T'ang (618–906) Confucian orthodoxy was based on Old Text versions of the Classics. Similarly, Neo-Confucianism, based on the teachings of Ch'eng I and Chu Hsi, was enshrined in the civil service examinations of the Ming (1368–1644) and Ch'ing (1644–1911) dynasties as the orthodox curriculum. Even a particular orthodoxy had distinct components. Neo-Confucianism, for example, must be disaggregated into a school of philosophy based on the moral theories of Sung (960–1279) Confucians and the state ideology, entrenched in public life during the late empire. Although related, these aspects of Neo-Confucianism are analytically distinct. *Neo-Confucian orthodoxy* will refer specifically to the imperially sanctioned Ch'eng-Chu school of interpretations of the Classics. As the bulwark of the imperial system, *orthodoxy* in the political arena refers to an ideological system of exclusion and inclusion that served the interests of those in positions of social, political, and economic power. Inherent in the term is the tension of competing orthodoxies, for example, the Sung Learning versus Han Learning debate in the eighteenth and nineteenth centuries, during which labels of heterodoxy were applied to one's opponents.

4. Confucius's role in compiling the Classics has been questioned by contemporary scholars. Because the *Spring and Autumn Annals*, one of the Five Classics, is not mentioned in Confucius's *Analects*, Herrlee Creel, among others, thinks Confucius had nothing whatsoever to do with it.[1] For our purposes, however, Creel's evidence will be bracketed, because the *Annals* remained a Classic throughout the imperial period. Even when belittled, it remained closely associated with Confucius. Most Confucians from the Han (206 B.C.–A.D. 220) through the Ch'ing dynasties regarded the *Annals* as the work of Confucius and the repository of his moral judgments concerning the past. For our discussion we will therefore reconstruct the controversies surrounding the *Annals* by granting the unproved premise that Confucius did indeed compile the text. This does not mean that we accept it. Confucians did, however, and we should understand why they accepted it in order to discover the impact of the *Annals* on the evolution of Confucianism. Göran Malmqvist, for example, contends that the *Annals* does not contain a coherent moral vision, but he admits that during the Han dynasty most

1. See Creel, *Confucius and the Chinese Way*, p. 103.

Confucians affirmed that Confucius had encoded the *Annals* with a moral system of "praise and blame."[2]

5. The use of the term *cultural resources* in chapter 1 and elsewhere is derived from Pierre Bourdieu's important notion of "symbolic capital." Although indebted to Bourdieu, my use of *resources* instead of *capital* in the Chinese case is necessary, I think, because no economic and social system comparable to capitalism in Western Europe emerged in imperial China until the late nineteenth century. Bourdieu, for example, contends that symbolic capital is a "disguised form of physical 'economic' capital."[3] Accordingly, references to cultural capital in late imperial China—despite the existence of complex markets in the Yangtze Delta, modes of cultural calculation among elites to maintain or improve their economic status, and substantial investment in education by Chinese gentry and merchants—seem anachronistic and misleading to a general reader accustomed to accounts of Western European history.

6. Mythical dates of little historical value are included in the text for reference to traditional Chinese beliefs about the chronology of antiquity and are followed by *??*. Doubtful dates that have some historical basis are followed by *?*.

7. The mythical animal known as a *lin* and mentioned in the last entry of Confucius's *Spring and Autumn Annals* has been translated into English as "unicorn," although in fact a *lin* appears to have been a fabulous beast not unlike a chimera. Because "unicorn" is the established translation, I have used it, despite its inexact correspondence to a *lin*.

2. See Malmqvist, "Studies on the Gongyang and Guuliang Commentaries I", p. 68.
3. Bourdieu, *Outline of a Theory of Practice*, p. 183.

INTRODUCTION

Historical mind-sets are difficult to gauge. Historians of modern China quickly learn, for example, that in 1898 New Text Confucianism, the first of all imperial Confucianisms, became the last stand for radical Confucians. During that fateful year the mercurial New Text advocate K'ang Yu-wei and his coterie (including Liang Ch'i-ch'ao and T'an Ssu-t'ung) came to the attention of the Kuang-hsu Emperor, who with K'ang's support initiated the eventful but abortive Hundred Days' Reform in Peking.[1] Earlier New Text scholars like Wei Yuan and Kung Tzu-chen are characterized in twentieth-century accounts of modern Chinese intellectual history as the stalking-horses for late imperial reformers. In the Hundred Days' Reform forty years after Wei Yuan's death, New Text ideas were quixotically appropriated in place of Neo-Confucian orthodoxy to legitimate imperial sovereignty and to promote extensive political reform.

The uproar over New Text Confucianism in late imperial scholarly circles has, however, led to the misrepresentation of the historical circumstances within which that movement incubated and developed. Linear accounts that organize the historical record in neat cadences from K'ang Yu-wei back to Wei Yuan and Kung Tzu-chen too often reflect unexamined assumptions about the key issues and important

1. See Liang, *Intellectual Trends in the Ch'ing Period*, pp. 85–110. For a revisionist account see Kwong, *A Mosaic of the Hundred Days*. For a discussion see T'ang and Elman, "The 1898 Reforms Revisited."

figures in modern Chinese intellectual history. A phenomenal number of books and articles have been published on K'ang, Liang, Kung, and Wei since 1900, and essays on them continue to proliferate in Chinese, Japanese, and Western scholarly journals. Although hundreds of works that touch on the nineteenth-century vicissitudes of New Text Confucianism have appeared, few scholars have explored the roots of New Text ideas in the late eighteenth century beyond some perfunctory paragraphs. The roles played by Chuang Ts'un-yü and Liu Feng-lu in the reemergence of New Text Confucianism have, when acknowledged, been conveniently subsumed within a linear historical agenda that makes 1898 the target of explanation.[2]

New Text Confucianism is unfortunately a case in point that scholarly expectations have colored scholarly research. It has long been assumed that the story of New Text Confucianism centers on K'ang Yu-wei and the 1898 reforms initiated by the Kuang-hsu Emperor. It therefore comes as a surprise that opposition between a well-placed but aging Chinese imperial grand secretary (Chuang Ts'un-yü) and a youthful Manchu palace guard (Ho-shen) who gained the ear of the Ch'ien-lung Emperor should be at the heart of the classical reemergence of New Text Confucianism in the 1780s.

Who was Chuang Ts'un-yü? Normally he appears as a curious footnote in accounts by historians who are satisfied that Wei Yuan and Kung Tzu-chen accurately represent the reformist ethos of nineteenth-century China. Who was Liu Feng-lu? Usually he is depicted in historical accounts as no more than the teacher of Wei and Kung. When the historical documents, genealogies, and manuscripts of Chuang and Liu are examined, however, a scholarly vertigo sets in. Chuang Ts'un-yü was on center stage in the political world of late imperial China. Indeed, by comparison Wei Yuan and Kung Tzu-chen were marginal figures whose historical importance has been determined largely by a consensus of twentieth-century scholars.

Furthermore, it is curious that Confucians first actively dissented from the late imperial state's orthodox raison d'être beginning in the late Ming, not after the Opium War. When New Text Confucianism reemerged in the late eighteenth century, after centuries of neglect, its advocates were retracing political agendas that had been raised and

2. An exception to this general trend is On-cho Ng's "Text in Context: *Chin-wen* Learning in Ch'ing Thought" (Ph.D. diss., University of Hawaii, 1986), which was brought to my attention after I completed a first draft of my study.

then rejected in the seventeenth century, when Manchu armies destroyed the Ming dynasty. Sixty years before Western imperialism began to transform the political, military, economic, and social institutions through which the Ch'ing (1644–1911) state legitimated itself, Confucians were already showing an interest in alternative forms of political discourse. Why?

Such dissent raises intriguing questions about the history of Confucianism and its links to the imperial state. They force us to reconsider the tensions within Confucian political culture that gave rise to dissenting movements such as the New Text reform initiative. What continuities existed in Confucian political discourse following the Western incursion? Why did New Text studies reemerge in the eighteenth century? Why was the New Text agenda first rearticulated in Ch'ang-chou Prefecture, a trading center on the Grand Canal in the prosperous Yangtze Delta (map 2)? After all, Ch'ang-chou had been the center for much of the gentry political dissent in the 1620s, which challenged the usurpation of Ming imperial power by palace eunuchs.

Accounts of the 1898 reform movement have presented New Text Confucianism as a subset of what historians considered "more important" events in late-nineteenth-century political and intellectual history. To remedy this situation, I will reevaluate the origins of the New Text revival during the Ch'ing dynasty in light of long-standing political battles to control the interpretation of the Classics in the imperial state. The reemergence of New Text Confucianism in eighteenth-century Ch'ang-chou also provides us with an interesting example of the interaction of scholarship and politics in the late empire before the advent of Western imperialism.

The origins of New Text Confucianism will tell us a great deal about long-term historical developments in late imperial China—more, in any event, than its political climax in the 1890s revealed, when K'ang Yu-wei briefly rose to national prominence in Peking. By 1899 New Text was already passé as a political force, although it remained important among intellectuals and scholars. In contrast, New Text Confucianism in eighteenth-century Ch'ang-chou reveals important features of gentry intellectual and social life. The Chuang and the Liu families, whose high social standing in Ch'ang-chou society lasted from 1450 until 1850, exemplify the interaction of classical scholarship, corporate lineages, and Confucian politics in the rise of the Ch'ang-chou school of New Text Confucianism.

I try to avoid the biases inherent in typical linear accounts of New

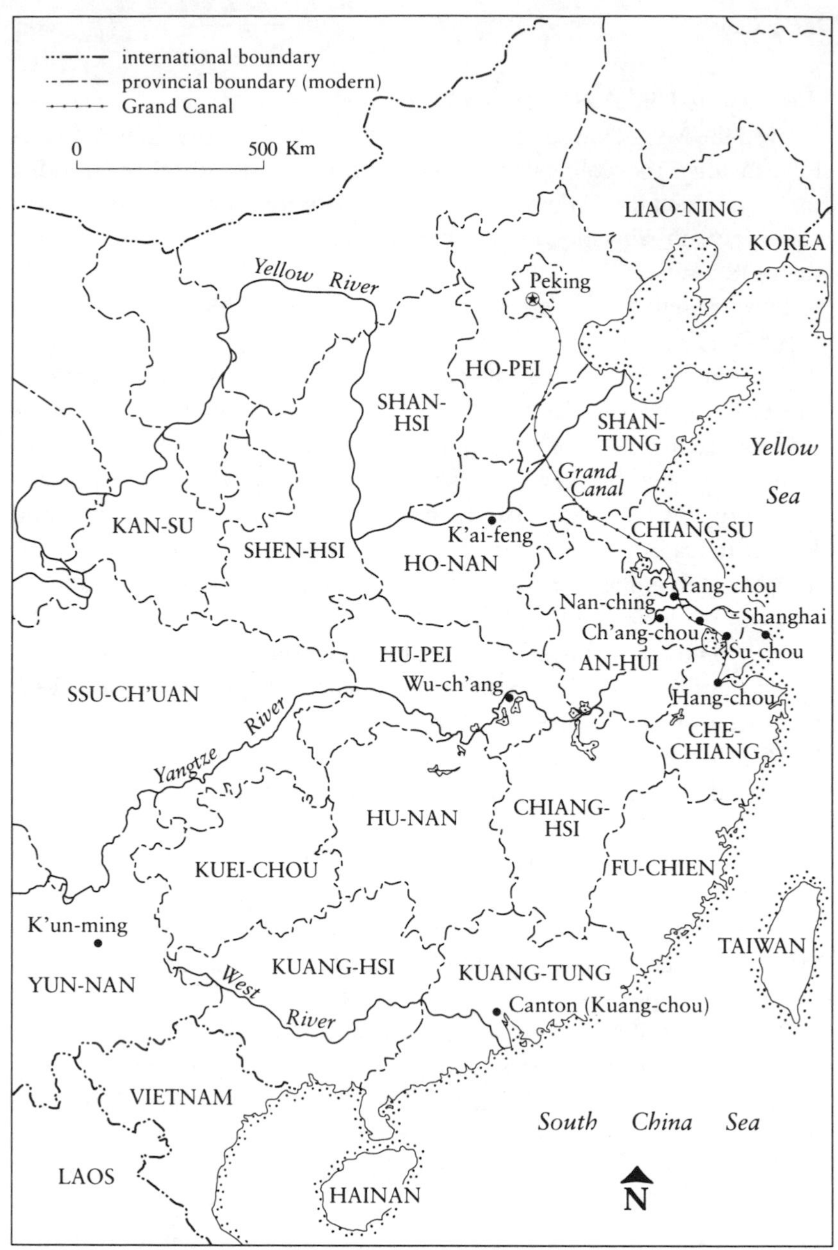

Map 2. Administrative Map of China

Source: Benjamin Elman, *From Philosophy to Philology: Intellectual and Social Aspects of Change in Late Imperial China*. Reprinted with the permission of the publishers, the Council on East Asian Studies, Harvard University. © 1984.

Text during the Ch'ing dynasty by not focusing on the achievements of Wei Yuan, Kung Tzu-chen, Liang Ch'i-ch'ao, or K'ang Yu-wei. They appear in these pages to help elucidate the accomplishments of Chuang Ts'un-yü and Liu Feng-lu. Whether this substitution of beginnings for endings will stand up over time is unclear. My aim is not to downplay the importance of New Text Confucianism in the 1898 reforms. Rather, my intent is to discover the beginnings as beginnings, without the historical teleologies commended by hindsight.

In my earlier work I have suggested that the philosophic rebellion spawned by the Ch'ing dynasty *k'ao-cheng* (evidential research, lit., "search for evidence") movement set the stage for the social and political conclusions drawn by New Text scholars. In the present work I shall try to document this claim. New Text Confucianism must be understood in light of its ties to classicism and philology, for without such an understanding, it may appear to be a peculiar Confucian aerolite that depended entirely on the nineteenth-century Western influence for its visibility.[3]

During the Ch'ing dynasty *k'ao-cheng* scholars advocated a program to reconstruct missing sources from antiquity. They first sought out T'ang (618–906) and then Later Han (25–220) sources to overcome limitations they found in Sung (960–1279) and Ming forms of Neo-Confucianism. Because Later Han classical sources were relatively unaffected by the Neo-Taoist and Buddhist notions that had influenced T'ang, Sung, and Ming Confucians, Han Confucians received increased respect and attention from textual purists in the seventeenth and eighteenth centuries.

The debate between those who favored Later Han classical scholarship (that is, Han Learning [*Han-hsueh*]) and those who adhered to the Neo-Confucian school (that is, Sung Learning [*Sung-hsueh*]) was philologically technical, but its political repercussions were considerable. Han Learning represented more than just an antiquarian quest. Its advocates cast doubt on the Confucian ideology enshrined by Manchu rulers when they legitimated imperial power. When tied to classical studies, philology thus had a political component.

Reconstruction of Han Learning during the eighteenth century

3. Levenson's account in his *Confucian China and Its Modern Fate*, vol. 1, pp. 79–94, remains the most influential interpretation of New Text Confucianism. See also Chang, *Liang Ch'i-ch'ao and Intellectual Transition*, pp. 3–34, and Philip C. C. Huang, *Liang Ch'i-ch'ao and Chinese Liberalism*, pp. 13–24. Cf. Hsiao, *Modern China and a New World*.

brought with it the discovery that Confucianism during the Later Han dynasty—when the Old Text school became, if not the dominant, at least the most influential intellectual force—differed greatly from the Confucianism of the Former Han (206 B.C.–A.D. 8), when the New Text school had been in vogue. When New Text Confucianism lost its political authority, its very existence was forgotten for fifteen hundred years.

Han Learning, strictly speaking, denotes a school of scholarship that came into fashion in Su-chou in the mid-eighteenth century. In raising the slogan of Han Learning to prominence in the Yangtze Delta, Hui Tung and his large Su-chou following actively opposed Sung Learning. They turned instead to a study of Later Han classical interpretations, especially those by Cheng Hsuan, who had successfully synthesized earlier New and Old Text doctrines. It was assumed that because such interpretations were closer to the time the Classics were compiled than T'ang and Sung sources were, they were more likely to reveal the authentic meanings of the Classics.

This rediscovery in the eighteenth century of the Old Text vs. New Text debate led some Ch'ing scholars to view the Confucian tradition in a new light. Scholars in Ch'ang-chou were the first Ch'ing literati to stress the New Text school of the Former Han dynasty. First, they turned to the New Text scholar Ho Hsiu, of the Later Han, who had been Cheng Hsuan's major rival. Ho Hsiu had defended the New Text ideas of the Former Han. After rediscovering Ho Hsiu, Ch'ing New Text scholars then returned to Tung Chung-shu's Former Han New Text orthodoxy. Accordingly, New Text learning really meant "Former Han Learning." Deep and potentially irreconcilable differences among competing orthodoxies emerged in the Han Learning agenda for classical studies. By returning to what they considered a purer form of Han Learning, New Text scholars in Ch'ang-chou touched off from within their ranks the breakup of Han Learning itself.[4]

New Text scholars, as we shall see, alleged that much of what had once been considered orthodox by Sung and Ming Neo-Confucians and Ch'ing *k'ao-cheng* scholars was in fact based on Old Text sources fabricated by Confucian scholars during the reign of the "Han usurper," Wang Mang. New Text advocates turned instead to the *Kung-yang*

4. See the comments by Wei Yuan in his "Hsu" (Introduction) to *Shu ku-wei*, pp. 1a–6b. On the New Text–Old Text debate during the Later Han dynasty see Dull, "Historical Introduction," pp. 338–411. See also Chou, *Chou Yü-t'ung hsuan-chi*, pp. 93–95.

Fig. 1. New Text: Clerical Script (*Li-shu* 隸書) during the Former Han Dynasty

Source: *Han Ts'ao Ch'üan pei* 漢曹全碑 (Han dynasty stelae of Ts'ao Ch'üan; Peking: Hsin-hua Bookstore, 1982).

commentary on Confucius's *Spring and Autumn Annals* because it was the only New Text commentary on one of the Classics that had survived intact from the Former Han dynasty. Recorded in contemporary-style script (*chin-wen*, hence "New Text" [fig. 1]), the *Kung-yang Commentary* supported the Former Han New Text school's portrayal of Confucius as a charismatic visionary and institutional reformer—an uncrowned king (*su-wang*).

Fig. 2. Large Seal (*Ta-chuan* 大篆) Script during the Western Chou Dynasty

Source: "Hsiao K'e-ting ming-wen" 小克鼎銘文 (Engraved script on the smaller K'e tripod), in *Yü-ting K'e-ting* 盂鼎克鼎 (Yü and K'e tripods; Shanghai: Shanghai Museum, 1959).

During the middle of the second century B.C., however, versions of the Classics written in pre-Han styles of calligraphy (figs. 2 and 3) were purportedly discovered in Confucius's old residence in what is today Shan-tung Province. They were subsequently placed in the imperial archives. According to Former Han accounts, these Old Text Classics were recorded in ancient script (*ku-wen*, hence "Old Text"), that is, various forms of ancient seal script (*chuan-shu*) (fig. 2) in use during the Chou dynasty (1122?–221 B.C.). Because the Old Text Classics were written in more ancient calligraphic forms (fig. 3), their defenders claimed priority for those versions over the New Text Classics. The latter were

Fig 3. Old Text: Small Seal (*Hsiao-chuan* 小篆) Script during the Ch'in and Han Dynasties

Source: *Ch'in-Han wa-tang wen-tzu* 秦漢瓦當文字 (Ch'in-Han script inscribed on palace roof-end tiles; 1878 Heng-ch'ü shu-yuan edition).

written in the Former Han contemporary-style clerical script (*li-shu*) (see fig. 1), a calligraphy instituted after the unification of writing forms and the burning of the books (*fen-shu*) during the Ch'in dynasty (221–207 B.C.) and were thus much later in origin.

Among the texts in the imperial archives was another commentary to the *Spring and Autumn Annals*, which later became known as the *Tso chuan* (*Tso Commentary*). Portraying Confucius as a respected teacher and transmitter of classical learning, rather than as a charismatic visionary, the commentary lent support to the Later Han Old Text School. After the demise of the Later Han dynasty in A.D. 220, however, the Confucian Canon was not reconstituted until the seventh century, under the T'ang. Thereafter, the *Tso Commentary* remained the orthodox guide to the *Spring and Autumn Annals* until the mid-eighteenth century, when Ch'ang-chou scholars called it into question.[5]

Han dynasty Old Text vs. New Text debates had not been limited to textual issues. Textual expertise on a particular Classic was a prerequisite for appointment as an erudite (*po-shih*) in the prestigious and politically powerful Han Imperial Academy (*T'ai-hsueh*). The latter had been formed to ensure the transmission of orthodox texts under state sponsorship. After disciples of erudites completed their course of study, they were examined and then granted government positions if they passed. In essence, this simple recruitment process was the precursor to the elaborate Confucian civil service examination system set up during the T'ang and Sung dynasties. Accordingly, classical texts and their interpretation were the basis for political loyalties in the schools system (*chia-fa*) for classical studies. When eighteenth-century Ch'ang-chou scholars reopened the New Text–Old Text controversy, they recognized they were not dealing with an idle textual issue. In fact, they were reconstructing the fortunes of an academic and, by implication, political movement that had been replaced by another.[6]

In chapters 1 and 2 I will explore the social, political, and intellectual circumstances in Ch'ang-chou Prefecture and the Yangtze Delta region during the sixteenth and seventeenth centuries. The rise to prominence of the Chuang and Liu lineages in Ch'ang-chou Prefecture during the

5. On the Old Text version of these events see Liu Hsin, "I T'ai-ch'ang po-shih shu." See also Ssu-ma Ch'ien, *Shih-chi*, vol. 10, pp. 3124–27 (*chüan* 121). See also Karlgren, *On the Tso Chuan*, and Maspero, "La composition et la date du Tso tchouan."

6. Dull, "Historical Introduction," pp. 338ff. See also Lu Yuan-chün, "Ching-hsueh chih fa-chan."

late Ming will be interpreted in light of sixteenth- and seventeenth-century gentry political dissent directed against the authoritarian imperial state.

In chapter 2 I will measure the success of the Chuangs and the Lius in civil service examinations during the Ming and Ch'ing dynasties and, in chapter 3, I will reconstruct statecraft traditions in Ch'ang-chou in an effort to understand the intellectual and social milieu from which Chuang Ts'un-yü emerged. Chuang was a distinguished scion of a powerful local lineage, which for generations placed members in the prestigious late imperial Hanlin Academy and other high government positions in Peking. A former secretary to the Ch'ien-lung Emperor, Chuang Ts'un-yü turned to the *Kung-yang Commentary* late in his official career to depict in classical garb Ho-shen's usurpation of imperial power. Ho-shen reminded late-eighteenth-century Ch'ang-chou literati of the infamous eunuch Wei Chung-hsien. In the late Ming Wei had similarly usurped power from the T'ien-ch'i Emperor and purged dissident literati who were associated with the Tung-lin Academy from nearby Wu-hsi County.

Ch'ang-chou intellectual traditions drew heavily on the statecraft formulations enunciated in the late Ming by T'ang Shun-chih. An analysis of the affinal ties between the T'angs and Chuangs reveals how T'ang Shun-chih's scholarship was emulated first by Chuang Ch'i-yuan in the late Ming and then by Chuang Ts'un-yü in the middle of the Ch'ing dynasty. The "learning of Ch'ang-chou" eventually became associated with precise scholarship and practical statecraft; the Ch'ang-chou New Text school should be seen as an outgrowth of these native currents.

In chapters 4–7 I will present the scholarly setting in which New Text Confucianism reemerged after fifteen hundred years of obscurity. My account will try to recapture the centrality of Confucian classical studies for political discourse in imperial China and the conflicting positions read into the Classics during the Ming and Ch'ing dynasties. The role of Sung Neo-Confucianism as the orthodox voice of the late imperial state permits us to weigh the political significance of recurrent classical controversies from which the New Text agenda reemerged.

Chapter 5 describes how Chuang Ts'un-yü resisted the inroads of Han Learning philology and the resulting fragmentation of the classical legacy by appealing to a holistic vision of the Classics. Chuang placed particular emphasis on the monistic cosmology of the *Change Classic* and the lessons of voluntarism encoded in the *Kung-yang Commentary*.

In chapter 6 I trace the way in which Chuang Ts'un-yü's holistic vision was advanced by his successors in the Chuang lineage. I also explain how the unraveling of Sung Learning first into Han Learning and then into New Text Confucianism tied in to Chuang Ts'un-yü's *Kung-yang* Confucianism.

In chapter 7 the official career and scholarly contributions of Liu Feng-lu are presented. If Chuang Ts'un-yü marked the reemergence of *Kung-yang* Confucianism in the eighteenth century, Liu Feng-lu in the nineteenth century linked his grandfather's *Kung-yang* theoretical vision to evidential research (*k'ao-cheng*) techniques. In Liu's hands, New Text Confucianism emerged as a sophisticated reinterpretation of Confucius's prophetic role in establishing the Classics for posterity. Moreover, Liu Feng-lu turned to *k'ao-cheng* for the epistemological leverage he needed to convince other Han Learning scholars of the dubious provenance of the Old Text Classics and the superior value of the New Text ones.

By analyzing the scope of the debate over Han Learning vs. Sung Learning among Confucian literati during the Ch'ing dynasty we can pinpoint the classical reformation represented by Chuang Ts'un-yü's turn to *Kung-yang* Confucianism and the way his legacy culminated in a recasting of the classical tradition among his immediate lineage and affines. Liu Feng-lu's articulation of a unified vision of New Text Confucianism signified the logical outcome of Chuang and Liu lineage traditions and cultural resources, which Chuang Ts'un-yü passed on to his grandson Liu Feng-lu, and which Liu then transmitted to Wei Yuan and Kung Tzu-chen.

In my concluding discussions in chapters 8 and 9 I will place the rise of New Text studies in Ch'ang-chou within a broader discussion of the unity between late imperial conceptual change, *ch'ing-i* (voices of remonstrance) political protest, and literary debate in the early nineteenth century. The reemergence of New Text Confucianism was paralleled by a revival of interest in late Ming political activism after the demise of Ho-shen. The renewed popularity of ancient New Text studies and more recent Tung-lin-style political concerns in the early nineteenth century was a twin legacy of Ch'ang-chou statecraft traditions.

Chapter 8 will refer to the underlying themes of pragmatism and realpolitik that Ch'ing dynasty New Text Confucians rediscovered while retracing the Confucian-Legalist synthesis of rituals and laws during the Former Han dynasty. In chapter 9 I will contend, following Mizoguchi Yūzō, that late Ming political activism, although defeated, was not completely eliminated. Tensions between the autocratic imperial state and local gentry interests reappeared during the late eighteenth century, when Ho-shen and his men are said to have carved out personal financial empires not seen since the appropriations of late Ming eunuchs. The Ho-shen era was a watershed for imperial politics: the classical legitimation for autocratic government weakened, and the politics of literary expression shifted decisively in favor of literati dissent.[7]

I will end by presenting the reformist sentiments of the Ch'ang-chou literatus Yun Ching, which set the political direction that New Text ideas would take after transcending their origins in Ch'ang-chou. Written between 1800 and 1809, Yun's political tracts contained formulations for institutional reform later elaborated by Wei Yuan, Kung Tzu-chen, and K'ang Yu-wei. New Text Confucianism and ancient-style prose, strands woven together by Yun Ching, symbolized the rise of gentry dissent in the early nineteenth century.

My major themes are the interaction of Confucian classical scholarship, elite kinship structures, and orthodox imperial ideology in the formation of the Ch'ang-chou New Text tradition. I hope thereby to show how the intellectual history of China can be enriched when social and political history is interwoven with the history of ideas. The Ch'ang-chou New Text school, we shall discover, represented a lineage of ideas, whose scholarly transmission depended on elite kinship ties and cultural resources within a particular social and political context. The history of ideas in Ch'ang-chou mirrored the social configurations that Confucians there unconsciously presupposed as they grappled with local and national political issues.

New Text studies became a strand in the larger web of gentry challenges to the diminishing power of the Manchu imperial court; under the additional pressures of massive peasant rebellion and Western imperialism, they culminated in the 1911 Revolution and the demise of imperial China. By 1800, then, new intellectual forces had appeared in late imperial China. Investigation of the Ch'ang-chou New Text school of Confucianism in the Yangtze Delta enables us to trace the native origins and internal mutations of one of these new strands, whose supporters were destined under the influence of Western ideas to champion a radical reworking of imperial institutions and traditional ideology.

7. Mizoguchi, "Iwayuru Tōrinha jinshin no shisō."

ONE

Schools of Scholarship and Corporate Lineages in the Yangtze Delta during the Late Empire

Intellectual historians and social historians of China have much to learn from each other. The world of ideas in Ming and Ch'ing times moved in a historical setting dominated by remarkable social and economic forces. To be sure, such forces were continuations of the economic revolution that began in the middle of the T'ang (618–906) period and climaxed in the striking urbanization under the Northern (960–1126) and Southern (1127–1279) Sung dynasties. During this period the rich delta lands of the south became China's chief granaries, and Southern literati initiated most of the great movements in art, letters, and scholarship that later dominated Ming and Ch'ing civilization.

Economic and cultural resources translated into political agendas. Seventeenth-century clashes between the Ming state and an aroused Confucian gentry led many back to the Confucian Classics to search for political remedies for excessive imperial power. In the Yangtze Delta the Tung-lin partisans of Ch'ang-chou Prefecture (Wu-hsi County) helped to lead gentry efforts to defend their interests against eunuch agents of the emperor. In the eighteenth century the Chuang and Liu lineages in Ch'ang-chou (Wu-chin County) turned to the New Text Classics for alternatives to the political status quo.

We shall discover that between 1600 and 1700 in Ch'ang-chou, the Tung-lin-style gentry alliance was replaced by another social form within which elites were mobilized: Chuang- and Liu-style lineages. Unlike contemporary Europe, where wide kinship ties were relatively unusual, elites in China were forced by historical circumstances to choose kinship strategies rather than political alliances to protect their interests. Until the nineteenth century, political dissent in China was successfully channeled away from gentry associations and controlled within kinship groups.

SCHOOLS OF SCHOLARSHIP

My earlier work focused on the Lower Yangtze River Basin—that is, the core areas of Chiang-su, Che-chiang, and An-hui provinces (map 3)—as the hub of culture, commerce, and communication in late imperial China. My regional approach to the eighteenth-century *k'ao-cheng* (evidential research) movement and its links to the emergence of an academic community devoted to precise scholarship and Han Learning both helped and hindered historical analysis. Certainly, a macrohistorical perspective permitted me to present the larger regional picture.

In the case of the Lower Yangtze Delta (map 3) such an approach brought to light the cross-fertilization of ideas and research methods among different schools of learning there. Definite unifying features in Han Learning transcended individually defined schools. Despite obvious differences in focus and interest, most schools during the Ch'ing dynasty defined themselves according to shared criteria. These criteria, based on evidential research standards of verification, in turn allowed each school to emphasize its uniqueness.[1]

A macrohistorical analysis by nature must slight lesser components that nevertheless produce important local differences. In my earlier depiction of a "Lower Yangtze academic community" devoted to evidential research, I dealt cursorily with schools of learning within that larger community. Regional subdivisions of the Lower Yangtze macroregion certainly deserve more attention. I propose to provide such attention to the social and intellectual milieu from which the Ch'ang-chou New Text School of Confucianism emerged.[2]

During the Ch'ing dynasty contemporaries themselves classified the diversity of ideas according to schools of scholarship that centered on the Yangtze Delta. School divisions were taken for granted as evidence of the filiation of scholars, who through personal or geographical association, philosophic or literary agreement, or master-disciple relations could be classed as distinct "schools of learning" (*chia-hsueh*). Such schools sometimes mirrored the "schools system" (*chia-fa*) of the Han

1. See my *Philosophy to Philology*, pp. 8–13.
2. See Skinner, *Marketing and Social Structure in Rural China.*

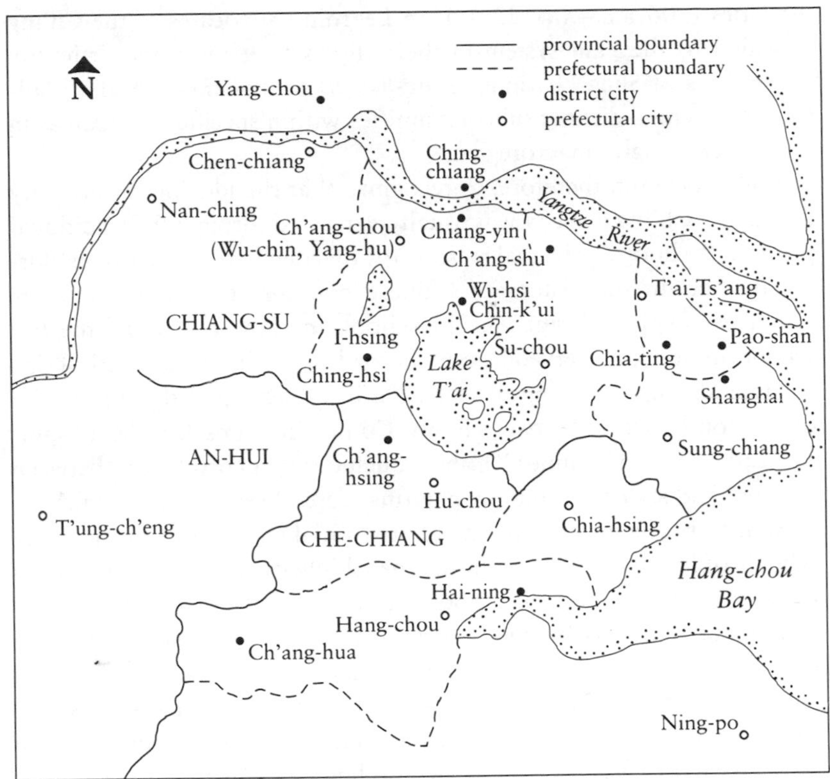
provincial boundary
prefectural boundary
district city
prefectural city
N
Yang-chou
Chen-chiang
Ching-
chiang
Nan-ching
Ch'ang-chou
(Wu-chin, Yang-hu)
Chiang-yin
Yangtze River
Ch'ang-shu
T'ai-Ts'ang
Wu-hsi
Chin-k'ui
CHIANG-SU
I-hsing
Su-chou
Chia-ting
Pao-shan
Lake
T'ai
Ching-hsi
Shanghai
AN-HUI
Ch'ang-
hsing
Sung-chiang
Hu-chou
T'ung-ch'eng
Chia-hsing
CHE-CHIANG
Hang-chou
Bay
Hai-ning
Hang-chou
Ch'ang-hua
Ning-po

Map 3. The Yangtze Delta (Chiang-nan)

dynasties (206 B.C.–A.D. 220). Han Learning advocates of the Ch'ing appealed to the Han system in their efforts to gainsay the orthodox pretensions of Sung Learning (*Sung-hsueh*) proponents. Local schools also represented distinct subcommunities within specific urban areas in the Lower Yangtze macroregion.[3]

It is important, therefore, to recognize that the ideological diversity during the Ch'ing dynasty was usually perceived through the traditional prism of "schools." The real reasons for this diversity are worth exploring further. In the history of Chinese painting, for example, James Cahill has explained that the Che school (in Hang-chou) and the Wu school (in Su-chou) served as centers for historical and theoretical discussions during the Ming dynasty. He has questioned the utility of a distinction between the two schools. Confessing himself to be a "splitter" rather than a "lumper," Cahill concludes that correlations between regional and stylistic criteria in painting were observable and real.[4]

Similar problems arise in any effort to make sense out of the many schools of learning in China during the Ch'ing dynasty. Traditional notions of a *p'ai* (faction), *chia* (school), or *chia-hsueh* are less precise than traditional scholars and modern sinologists tend to assume. In some cases, a school was little more than a vague category whose members shared a textual tradition, geographical proximity, personal association, philosophic agreement, stylistic similarities, or combinations of these. In many cases, a "school" would be defined merely to legitimate the organizations that prepared its genealogy or provided rationalizations for the focus of scholarly activities peculiar to a region.

Nathan Sivin, for example, has defined a school as the "special theories or techniques of a master, passed down through generations of disciples by personal teaching." Such a definition stresses "the intact transmission of authoritative written texts over generations, generally accompanied by personal teaching to ensure that the texts would be correctly understood so that their accurate reproduction and transmission could continue." These lineages of teaching were not fixed historical entities, however. Rather, a "school" in the latter sense represented a claim made by individuals or groups about their connections to forebears. The act of passing on the texts through personal teachings was key.[5]

3. For more detail see my "Ch'ing Dynasty 'Schools' of Scholarship."
4. Cahill, *Parting at the Shore*, pp. 135, 163.
5. Sivin, "Copernicus in China," p. 96n. See also Sivin's "Foreword," in my *Philosophy to Philology*.

We are on firmer ground, however, when "schools" refer to specific geographical areas during particular periods of time. To speak, as Chinese scholars did, of the "Su-chou," "Yang-chou," or "Ch'ang-chou" schools during the Ch'ing dynasty does not completely obviate the dangers outlined above. Such groupings can nevertheless help us to evaluate intellectual phenomena below the macroregional level.

It is interesting, for example, that in a preliminary survey of Ch'ing academic life in Yang-chou and Ch'ang-chou, the Japanese scholar Ōtani Toshio has pointed to the decisive influence of Hui-chou merchants from southeastern An-hui Province in Lower Yangtze social and cultural affairs. According to Ōtani, such commercial links provided the social background for the transmission of Hui-chou scholarship first to Yang-chou (via Tai Chen, 1724–77) and then to Ch'ang-chou (via Tai's followers). Thus, the turn to Han Learning among Ch'ang-chou literati, which we will discuss further in chapter 4, can be traced in part to the influence of both the Su-chou school of Han Learning to the south and the Yang-chou school to the north.[6]

Although it may be true that Ch'ang-chou's place in the Han Learning movement may have been derivative, such a perspective fails to explain the origins of the Ch'ang-chou New Text school, which neither Su-chou nor Yang-chou (or even Hui-chou) currents of thought ever duplicated. In fact, the commitment of Yang-chou families to Old Text traditions and of Ch'ang-chou families to New Text studies indicate that considerable tension and variation existed among Lower Yangtze schools of scholarship in the eighteenth and nineteenth centuries. Accordingly, we shall have to search for the origins of New Text Confucianism in the schools of scholarship championed by Confucian literati in Ch'ang-chou itself.[7]

The problem of what constitutes an intellectual school in China is central to our concerns. In our efforts to interweave the eighteenth-century reemergence of New Text Confucianism with the social history of Ch'ang-chou Prefecture—one of the key economic and cultural centers in the Lower Yangtze macroregion during the Ming and Ch'ing dynasties—we shall explore local differences in intellectual content and style. Three questions will be in the background of our inquiry: (1) What role did late-Ming intellectual movements in Wu-hsi County play

6. Ōtani, "Yōshū Jōshū gakujutsu kō," pp. 319–21. Hsu K'o, in his *Ch'ing-pai lei-ch'ao*, vol. 69, pp. 19–20, had earlier also noted the links between the "Ch'ang-chou school" and the "Hui-chou school."

7. Elman, "Ch'ing Dynasty 'Schools' of Scholarship," pp. 12–15.

in the intellectual life of Ch'ang-chou Prefecture? (2) Why during the Ch'ing dynasty did the mantle of scholarly leadership in Ch'ang-chou pass from Wu-hsi to scholars associated with the Chuang and Liu lineages in the prefectural capital? (3) What similarities and differences do we note between late-Ming currents in Ch'ang-chou and the rise of the New Text school there? Such questions reflect the local flavor that intellectual life could develop at prefectural and county levels within the larger academic community of the Lower Yangtze.

LINEAGES AND SCHOOLS OF SCHOLARSHIP

The tendency to concentrate on individuals in the development of Confucianism has obscured the important roles played by family and lineage in the practice of Confucian social and political values. Historians cannot isolate Chinese literati from their social setting. Nor can intellectual historians afford to neglect the complex machinery of lineage communities in Chinese society.[8] Confucian scholars did not construct a vision of their political culture *ex nihilo*. Their mentalities were imbedded in larger social structures premised on the centrality of kinship ties. The influence of large kinship groups in traditional Chinese society should not be overexaggerated, yet at the same time we would do well to bear in mind that in the day-to-day affairs of local gentry, the Confucian elite was frequently defined by kinship relations; cultural resources were focused on the formation and maintenance of lineages.

THE HUIS IN SU-CHOU

The Chuangs and Lius in Ch'ang-chou were not the only lineages whose scholarly achievements gained national prominence. The scholarly traditions of the Hui lineage were intimately tied to the emergence of Han Learning in Su-chou during the eighteenth century. Hui Tung (1697–1758) built upon the teachings of his great-grandfather Hui Yu-sheng (d. ca. 1678) and grandfather Hui Chou-t'i (fl. ca. 1691), which had been transmitted to him by his distinguished father, Hui Shih-ch'i (1671–1741). Su-chou Han Learning traditions show us how teachings, once the cultural property of a particular line within a

8. Twitchett, "A Critique," pp. 33–34.

lineage, passed into the public domain. Keeping Confucian teachings within the family line, and thus within the lineage, was a typical political strategy designed to maintain the success of a descent group in the empire-wide civil service examinations. State examinations were based solely on classical studies, so they were frequently pursued within a "lineage of teachings" based on kinship organizations. Such teachings were preserved to further the interests of the lineage in local society and in the civil service.

The Han Learning of the Huis demonstrates, however, that there was a tension between public prestige and private traditions. The exclusivity of lineage schools, for instance, could be tempered by a local tradition of scholarship. This could then enhance lineage prestige when its scholarly tradition entered the public domain. Consequently, lineage academies could fulfill exclusive and inclusive roles, depending on the cultural strategies of a particular lineage vis-à-vis surrounding society. Accordingly, both Han Learning in Su-chou and New Text Confucianism in Ch'ang-chou represented at different times the exclusive teachings of a particular lineage and the inclusive doctrines of a school of learning.

Originally from Shensi Province in the northwest, the Huis began their flight south when the Wei River valley—the heartland of Chinese civilization during the Han and T'ang dynasties—fell to Khitan invaders by 947. During the Ming dynasty the Huis settled in Su-chou, but they did not come to prominence there until the late Ming and early Ch'ing, when the scholarly achievements of Hui Wan-fang, Hui Tung's great-great-grandfather, were widely recognized.[9]

Hui Chou-t'i was the first in the Hui lineage to pass the highest level *chin-shih* (presented literatus) examinations. It was his subsequent appointment to the prestigious Hanlin Academy (*Han-lin yuan*) that moved the Huis into national prominence. His son Shih-ch'i passed the provincial examinations in 1708, and in 1709 Shih-ch'i duplicated his father's achievement by passing the *chin-shih* examination in Peking with high honors. The Hui lineage had thus placed its sons from two consecutive generations in the Hanlin Academy, which was the starting point for guaranteed official power and influence. The "Han Learning" associated with Hui Tung in Su-chou derived from scholarly traditions

9. On the Hui lineage see *Hui-shih ssu-shih ch'uan-ching t'u-ts'e*. See also Yang Ch'ao-tseng (then governor-general in Su-chou), "Chi-lu," pp. 1a–7b. Cf. Dardess, "Cheng Communal Family."

and cultural resources built up over four generations of his immediate family.[10]

Hui Tung drew on traditions of "ancient learning" (*ku-hsueh*) and "classical techniques" (*ching-shu*) transmitted within his lineage to articulate a scholarly position predicated on the superiority of Han dynasty sources over T'ang, Sung, and Ming Confucian writings. Rather than study the Four Books (a Sung-Yuan concoction associated with Sung Learning), the Huis stressed the Five Classics of antiquity in their efforts to reconstruct Han Learning. The Huis' financial success and intellectual prominence in the eighteenth century permitted Hui Tung the luxury of study and research to build a "school of learning" in Su-chou.

Despite the exclusivity of lineage schools, the success of the Hui family in influencing Su-chou scholarship illustrates that lineage traditions possessed important complementary elements of private advantage and public influence. The organizational rationale for the Su-chou "school of Han Learning" rested on teachings transmitted by the Huis to scholars and students outside of the Hui lineage who resided or studied in Su-chou. Ch'ien Ta-hsin and Wang Ming-sheng, both native sons of nearby Chia-ting, for example, were caught up in the wave of Han Learning in the 1750s when they were studying in Su-chou. They became influential *k'ao-cheng* scholars during the heyday of Han Learning in the 1780s and 1790s.

Hui Tung remained a private scholar throughout his life and worked in his Su-chou studio famous for its library. This independent scholarly tradition, financed by the Huis' earlier successes, would diverge from official standards and ultimately add to critical *k'ao-cheng* styles of classical inquiry. Hui Tung's career also suggests that during the early decades of the Ch'ien-lung Emperor's reign there was a chasm between private Han Learning and public examination studies, which remained predicated on mastery of Sung Learning.[11]

10. See Lu Chien's "Hsu" (Preface) to Hui Tung's *Chou-i shu*, p. 1b. See Bourdieu, *Theory of Practice*, pp. 171–83, for a discussion of "symbolic capital."

11. Hummel et al., *Eminent Chinese*, pp. 138, 357–58. Cf. my discussion of "professionalized scholars" in *Philosophy to Philology*, pp. 133–34. Before the abolition of the Confucian examination system in 1905, the Five Classics and Four Books were the backbone of the education system. The Five Classics were the *Change, Documents, Poetry, Rites*, and the *Spring and Autumn Annals*. A *Music Classic* had been lost in the classical period. The Four Books were the *Analects*, the *Mencius*, the "Great Learning," and the "Doctrine of the Mean."

THE WANGS AND LIUS IN YANG-CHOU

In Yang-chou the Wang and Liu lineages, much like the Huis in Su-chou, carried on traditions of Han Learning. *K'ao-cheng* studies had become important in Yang-chou during the eighteenth century initially through the efforts of Wang Mao-hung (1688–1741). The latter applied evidential research techniques to the study of Chu Hsi's (1130–1200) life and scholarship. Wang compiled a detailed chronological biography (*nien-p'u*) of Chu Hsi that cut through the hagiography that secured Chu's status as the fountain of Neo-Confucian moral philosophy. Later scholars in Yang-chou traced their studies back to Wang Mao-hung, but few actually received or continued his teachings.[12]

Yang-chou scholars were strongly influenced by Hui Tung's Su-chou school of Han Learning. Chiang Fan, for instance, studied in Su-chou under some of Hui Tung's direct disciples and was frequently sponsored by his townsman Juan Yuan, one of the great patrons of Han Learning in the late eighteenth and early nineteenth centuries. Chiang Fan, with Juan's support, subsequently compiled a controversial but authoritative genealogy of Han Learning masters entitled *Kuo-ch'ao Han-hsueh shih-ch'eng chi.*[13]

The more formative scholarly influence in Yang-chou, however, was the polymath Tai Chen and his critical approach to scholarship. Although himself a member of the southeast An-hui (*Wan-nan*) school centering on Hui-chou Prefecture, Tai lived and taught in Yang-chou from 1756 until 1762. Initially, Tai taught in the home of Wang An-kuo, who had the foresight to have his son Wang Nien-sun receive instruction from one of the future giants of the *k'ao-cheng* movement. Wang Nien-sun acquired his training in ancient phonology (*ku-yin*) and etymology (*ku-hsun*) from Tai Chen, which he then transmitted to his celebrated son Wang Yin-chih (1766–1834). Nien-sun and Yin-chih became two of the most influential Han Learning scholars during the Ch'ing dynasty, and therefore brought honor and prestige to their lineage in Yang-chou.[14]

The scientific cast to Tai Chen's *k'ao-cheng* studies was the product of Hui-chou traditions of learning. Since Mei Wen-ting (1633–1721) and the Jesuit introduction of Western science to Chinese intellectuals,

12. Liang, "Chin-tai hsueh-feng chih ti-li te fen-pu," pp. 20–21.
13. Kondo, "Ō Chū to Kokusho Jurinden kō," pp. 64–69.
14. Cf. my "Ch'ing Dynasty 'Schools' of Scholarship," pp. 12–14.

Hui-chou learning had stressed the reconstruction of classical astronomy, mathematics, and calendrical science. Going beyond Han Learning scholars (who they thought placed undue emphasis on Later Han dynasty sources as the basis for textual criticism and verification), Tai Chen and his followers developed a more impartial approach to Han materials and attempted to verify knowledge in a more formal manner. A distinguished textual scholar in his own right, Wang Chung described the Yang-chou intellectual scene: "At this time [ca. 1765], ancient learning [*ku-hsueh*] was popular [in Yang-chou]. Hui Tung of Yuan-ho [in Su-chou] and Tai Chen of Hsiu-ning [in An-hui] were admired by everyone."[15] Such scholarly currents also penetrated the Liu lineage in Yang-chou, where learned members like the Wangs began to specialize in Han Learning. Liu Wen-ch'i (1789–1865), in particular, initiated research on the *Tso Commentary* on the *Spring and Autumn Annals*, which became the pet cultural project of his line into the twentieth century, when Liu Shih-p'ei (1884–1919) gave up radical politics to devote himself to the scholarly traditions of his lineage.

By concentrating on the Old Text interpretation of the *Annals* based on the *Tso chuan*, the Lius in Yang-chou placed themselves in direct opposition to New Text views emerging in Ch'ang-chou. Liu Shih-p'ei's father, Liu Kuei-tseng, and grandfather Liu Yü-sung had continued the task of reconstructing the *Tso chuan* into the last half of the nineteenth century. They stressed the more orthodox traditions of Han Learning that upheld the priority of Later Han Confucians for interpreting the classical legacy.[16]

The scholarly disputations between Liu Shih-p'ei (Old Text) and K'ang Yu-wei (1858–1927) (New Text) in the twentieth century became famous. The roots of this confrontation between the Lius in Yang-chou (Old Text) and the Chuangs and Lius in Ch'ang-chou (New Text) have not been generally recognized. Liu Wen-ch'i had set the course in 1838 for this confrontation with his *Tso chuan chiu-shu k'ao-cheng* (Evidential analysis of ancient annotations of the *Tso Commentary*), in which he tried to reconstruct the Later Han dynasty (hence, Old Text) appearance of the *Tso chuan*. In his 1805 study entitled *Tso-shih ch'un-ch'iu k'ao-cheng* (Evidential analysis of Master Tso's *Spring and Autumn Annals*), Liu Feng-lu presented the Ch'ang-chou school's New Text position on the *Tso chuan* (see chapter 7).

15. Wang Chung, *Shu-hsueh, wai-p'ien* (outer chapters), 1.9b.

16. See Chang Po-ying's "Hsu," (Preface), p. 1a; and Hummel et al., *Eminent Chinese*, pp. 534–36.

The Lius' research project—carried on by Liu Wen-ch'i's son, Liu Yü-sung, but never completely finished even in the twentieth century—sought to dismiss post-Han interpretations, principally those of Tu Yü (222–284). They argued that these interpretations had falsely articulated "precedents" (*li*) in the *Annals* on the basis of forced inferences from the *Tso chuan*. Liu Wen-ch'i's research was mainstream Han Learning and drew on the legacy of Hui Tung and on the contributions of Chiao Hsun, who was Tai Chen's disciple in Yang-chou.[17]

In addition, Liu Wen-ch'i came out in favor of his maternal uncle Ling Shu's *Kung-yang li-shu* and Ch'en Li's *Kung-yang i-shu*. Both works were Old Text–based reconstructions of the *Kung-yang chuan* as a historical source that complemented the *Tso chuan*. Ling Shu and Ch'en Li saw historical value in the *Kung-yang Commentary* but were suspicious of the "empty speculations" (*k'ung-yen*) associated with the *Kung-yang* tradition. They attributed such speculations to the unfortunate millennial visions Ho Hsiu (129–182) had read into the text during the Later Han dynasty.[18]

At first sight, the opposition between the Lius in Yang-chou and Chuangs in Ch'ang-chou over the correct commentary on the *Spring and Autumn Annals* seems mainly intellectual, with few political overtones. In fact, however, the debate represented the clash of opinion between a Yang-chou lineage devoted to apolitical Han Learning scholarship and a lineage in Ch'ang-chou bent on preparing its sons for the political arena. Unlike the Huis and Wangs, the Chuangs would use New Text studies to voice their concern over the rising influence of apolitical *k'ao-cheng* during the last decades of the Ch'ien-lung Emperor's reign, when the dynasty was beset with what they considered unprecedented corruption and political instability. We shall discuss the Chuangs' use of New Text studies in later chapters.

THE FANGS AND YAOS IN T'UNG-CH'ENG

In addition to Su-chou and Yang-chou, the city of T'ung-ch'eng in northern An-hui Province (known as Wan-pei), also featured a distinctive school of scholarship transmitted by prominent gentry lineages, the

17. Liu Wen-ch'i, *Ch'ing-hsi chiu-wu wen-chi*, 3.9b.

18. Ibid. See also his "Hsu" (Preface) to Ch'en Li's *Chü-hsi tsa-chu*, pp. 1a–2a; and Ling Shu's *Kung-yang li-shu*, 862.15b. For a discussion, see Yang Hsiang-k'uei, "Ch'ing-tai te chin-wen ching-hsueh," 190–96. However, Ch'en Li, as we will see in chapter 7, was also influenced by Liu Feng-lu's New Text scholarship.

Fangs and the Yaos, for much of the Ming and Ch'ing dynasties. In contrast to their southern An-hui (that is, Hui-chou) contemporaries, members of the T'ung-ch'eng school of learning were famous for their influence in promoting the ancient-style prose from the T'ang and S'ung dynasties, called *ku-wen* writing, and for their partisan support of Sung dynasty Confucian moral philosophy in the late eighteenth and early nineteenth centuries.[19]

Through family traditions in literature and examination studies members of the Fang and Yao lineages provided the organizational framework and intellectual resources for articulating and passing on the orthodox teachings of the Ch'eng-Chu persuasion in T'ung-ch'eng. During the Ch'ing period, for example, fourteen Yaos and twenty-one Fangs had mastered the orthodox Chu Hsi teachings well enough to achieve *chin-shih* status. Fang lineage traditions extended back to the Ming dynasty and Fang I-chih (1611–71) among others. But later followers such as Fang Tung-shu (1772–1851) referred to Fang Pao (1668–1749) as the progenitor of an orthodox defense of Chu Hsi teachings.

Having endured, with his family, the heavy hand of the Manchu state, Fang Pao served during his last years as a spokesman for state orthodoxy. He defended the authenticity of the long-impugned Old Text *Rituals of Chou* (*Chou-li*), for example, and ridiculed those who dared label the Han Confucian Liu Hsin (45 B.C.–A.D. 23) a forger of the *Chou-li* and other Old Text Classics, a major issue in the Old Text–New Text controversy. Seeking to convert heterodox scholars (usually those who followed Han Learning) to Sung Learning, Fang Pao went so far as to claim on the occasion of the death of Li Kung's (1659–1733) eldest son that the misfortune was brought on by Li's heterodoxy and his irresponsible attacks on Chu Hsi.

In his scholarship on the *Spring and Autumn Annals*, for example, Fang Pao directly linked the literary heritage of ancient-style prose to the world-ordering commitments Confucius had enunciated in the *Annals*. Fang equated the "models and rules" (*i-fa*) that would be the hallmark of the T'ung-ch'eng school's orthodox position with the historical style of the *Annals*. The latter was encoded in literary forms of "praise and blame," which Fang Pao contended were best elaborated and developed by the *Tso chuan*. The *ku-wen* prose tradition revived by

19. Hsu K'o, *Ch'ing-pai lei-ch'ao*, vol. 69, p. 7; vol. 70, pp. 30–34.

Han Yü in the eighth century had, according to Fang, recaptured the moral power of ancient literary forms.[20]

In the late eighteenth century—in part because Fang Pao and his family were implicated in the 1711 literary inquisition and were thus uprooted from their ancestral home—the Yao lineage in T'ung-ch'eng assumed leadership of "orthodox" Confucianism through the influence of Yao Nai (1732–1815) and Yao Ying (1785–1853). Yao Nai sought to counter the compositional principles used in parallel-prose writing (*p'ien-t'i-wen*), favored by Han Learning scholars in Yang-chou and elsewhere, by championing "models and rules" preferred by writers of ancient-style prose. Yao's efforts were supported by the Yang-hu school of ancient prose in Ch'ang-chou Prefecture, with whom the T'ung-ch'eng school developed a literary rivalry. In addition, Yao Nai defended Sung Learning orthodoxy against what he considered the wayward classical studies produced by *k'ao-cheng* scholars.[21]

Likewise, Yao Ying, along with Fang Tung-shu and others associated with the T'ung-ch'eng school, felt the Han Learning movement threatened the Sung Learning orthodoxy in official life and thus public morality in private life as well. They therefore defended in passionate terms the state-sanctioned teachings of the Sung Ch'eng-Chu school. Yao Ying, for example, wrote:

> In antiquity, scholars studied the Way to rectify their minds. Today, scholars study literary composition [*wen*] to damage their minds. . . . In antiquity, scholars were intent [on following] the Way. Thus they relied on loyalty and trustworthiness to study filial piety. They studied [such ideals] in order to serve their ruler, respect their elders, and clarify rituals. Literary composition was therefore mastered in the process of study. Today, scholars are intent [only on mastering] literary composition. They seek only for fame and fortune in their studies. Thus, their literary compositions are empty.

From such lineage alignments we see that the Han Learning–Sung Learning debate was also carried on in literary fields. The predilection of Han Learning advocates for Han dynasty "parallel prose" versus the

20. *Fang Pao chi*, pp. 16–21, 58–59; and Hummel et al., *Eminent Chinese*, pp. 235–40. Fang Pao and his family were initially imprisoned and then later served either as nominal slaves to Manchu bannermen in Peking or were exiled to the northeast. See also Aoki, *Shindai bungaku hyōronshi*, pp. 518–26; Beattie, *Land and Lineage in China*, p. 51; and Ebrey, "Types of Lineages in Ch'ing China."

21. See Yao Nai's *Ku-wen tz'u lei-tsuan*; and Yao's 1796 "Hsu" (Preface), to his *Hsi-pao-hsuan chiu-ching shuo*, pp. 1a–1b. See also Yao Ying, *Tung-ming wen-chi*, 3.2b. See also Guy, *The Emperor's Four Treasuries*, pp. 140–56.

preference for T'ang-Sung "ancient-style prose" among Sung Learning scholars meant that for each side proper composition required forms of expression appropriate for the task of precise scholarship (Han Learning parallel prose) or moral-philosophical articulation (Sung Learning ancient-style prose). Lineages such as the Huis, Wangs, and Lius in Su-chou and Yang-chou thus stressed in their private schools cultural and linguistic training in writing techniques acceptable for Han Learning.

Similarly, the Fangs and Yaos in T'ung-ch'eng made ancient-style prose the vehicle for their moral-philosophical commitments. T'ung-ch'eng schoolmen saw ancient prose and moral values as inseparable and tried to effect a synthesis of moral philosophy and literary style by equating the content of Sung Learning—that is, Neo-Confucianism—with ancient-style prose as the proper vehicle for its expression.[22] Moreover, the Fangs and Yaos attacked the Han Learning emanating from Su-chou and Yang-chou as heterodox and morally bankrupt. Yao Nao in particular developed a large following in Nan-ching in the late eighteenth and early nineteenth centuries while teaching at the prestigious Chung-shan Academy. Despite his Sung Learning priorities, however, Yao Nai, as well as Yao Ying and Fang Tung-shu, had to admit the importance of *k'ao-cheng* research techniques. In his 1798 preface to Hsieh Ch'i-k'un's (1737–1802) widely acclaimed *Hsiao-hsueh k'ao* (Critique of classical philology), for example, Yao Nai appealed for a balance between Han Learning and Sung Learning in a proper Confucian education.[23]

Similar alignments occurred in Ch'ang-chou, where scholars associated with the Yang-hu school (named after a county) of ancient-style prose and the Ch'ang-chou school of *tz'u* (lyric) poetry also navigated the literary and philosophic currents separating Han Learning from Sung Learning. In both classical scholarship and traditional Chinese prose and poetry, Ch'ang-chou literati tended to be less favorably disposed to Han Learning than their peers in Su-chou and Yang-chou.

This brief sample of the cultural resources of kinship groups in late imperial China demonstrates that kinship is a unique vantage point from which to interpret the social and political dimensions in Yangtze Delta intellectual life. Before turning in chapter 2 to more detailed discussion of the Chuang and Liu lineages in Ch'ang-chou, we shall first

22. Yao Ying, *Tung-ming wen-chi*, 2.14a–14b. See Edwards, "A Classified Guide," pp. 770–88; Aoki, *Shindai bungaku hyōronshi*, pp. 526–33; and Pollard, *A Chinese Look at Literature*, pp. 140–57.

23. Yao Nai, *Hsi-pao-hsuan ch'üan-chi*, 4.22a–23b.

explore the social, political, and cultural factors that enabled kinship organizations in the Yangtze Delta to achieve prominence in local society and national affairs.[24]

LINEAGES IN LATE IMPERIAL CHINA

Individuals did not speak as individuals in Confucian China. Western historians assume the autonomy of the individual from his descent group, so it is difficult for them to understand that Confucian literati spoke as members of kinship organizations. A lineage was not an abstract social grouping. For its members it was, according to James L. Watson, "an integral part of their personal identities." Confucian moral theory added to, and was channeled by, the politics of lineage formation.[25]

It is now generally recognized that there was no uniform process of lineage formation in late imperial society. The Chuangs and the Lius in late imperial China constituted a territorial entity as well as a descent group. Both geographical and historical factors added variations to highly localized forms of kinship ties. Late imperial society was structured by political and economic forces that made descent an ideological system as well as a social fact. Elite lineages in traditional society were not passive reflections of, but rather dynamic contributors to, the political, economic, and social order.[26]

Lineages dominant in particular regions played an essential organizational role in late imperial Chinese society. With corporate property, ancestral halls, and written genealogies, they were largely a product of gentry descent-group strategies dating back to the Sung dynasty. Their social importance and increased numbers in the sixteenth century coincided with the weakening of the Ming imperial state in local society between 1400 and 1600. Corporate lineages with charitable estates occurred more frequently among gentry in local society as the forces of rural commercialization and market specialization changed the face of

24. Chia-ying Yeh Chao, "Ch'ang-chou School of *Tz'u* Criticism," pp. 151–88. I have limited mention of lineages to those given above to avoid being carried too far afield from the focus of my study.

25. Maurice Freedman, *Chinese Lineage and Society*; and James L. Watson, "Hereditary Tenancy," p. 176.

26. For a discussion see Rubie S. Watson, "Creation of a Chinese Lineage," 95–99; Pasternak, "Role of the Frontier," 551ff; Baker, *Chinese Family and Kinship*; Ahern, "Segmentation in Chinese Lineages," pp. 1–15; and Maurice Freedman, *Chinese Society*, pp. 339ff.

Lower Yangtze local society after 1400. Through a corporate estate, which united a set of component local lineages, higher-order lineages became an essential building block in local society.[27]

GENTRY SOCIETY IN THE LATE MING

Serving as state servants and local leaders, gentry became part of the machinery established by the Hung-wu Emperor (r. 1368–98) in the late fourteenth century to control the countryside. The Ming *li-chia* tax system (*li-chia* is a village/family unit of 110 households), geared to a village commodity economy, represented a compromise between the state's efforts to consolidate imperial power while relying on agrarian communities for state income. Families in each village thus assumed social and fiscal responsibilities. Every civilian household was in effect located in a hierarchy of command that empowered local elites.[28]

But imperial institutions could not keep pace with the social and economic changes in the fifteenth and sixteenth centuries, which introduced new elements into agrarian society. China's population grew from approximately 65 to 150 million between 1400 and 1600, a phenomenon accompanied by significant changes in economic conditions. The court and its bureaucracy lost control of its land and labor resources. The Ming tax system, based on fourteenth-century assumptions regarding land, population, labor service, and tax registers, quickly became anachronistic.[29]

The amount of uncollected taxes increased as lands were deserted, government lands were illegally sold on the open market, and land trusteeships (*kuei-chi*) were secretly established to take advantage of tax exemptions that favored government officials. As a consequence, even greater financial and labor service burdens were placed on taxable farm households. In the Lower Yangtze, the fraudulent registration of property under names of officials had become a pervasive practice by the late Ming. Su-chou, Hang-chou, and Ch'ang-chou prefectures were especially notorious in this regard.

27. Twitchett, "Fan Clan's Charitable Estate," pp. 97–98; and Ebrey, "Development of Kin Group Organization," pp. 53–56. For late Ming social change, see Shigeta, "Origins and Structure of Gentry Rule," pp. 337–85. See also Wiens, "Changes in the Fiscal and Rural Control Systems," pp. 53–69; Eberhard, *Social Mobility in Traditional China*, pp. 31ff; and Dennerline, "New Hua Charitable Estate," p. 53.

28. Ray Huang, *Taxation and Governmental Finance*, pp. 1–24; Huang Ch'ing-lien, "*Li-chia* System," pp. 103–155; Brook, "Ming Local Administration," pp. 29–37; and Wang Yuquan, "Ming Labor Service System," pp. 1–44.

29. Huang Ch'ing-lien, "*Li-chia* System," pp. 120–45; and Wang Yuquan, "Ming Labor Service," pp. 24–25.

Exemptions for officials became the single greatest tax loophole. Poorer households renounced their financial independence and chose to subordinate their land to influential households with a tax-exempt status—further stratifying rural society. The tax quota in the Lower Yangtze gradually shifted from government, that is, "official," land to private, or "commoner," land.[30]

The increasing monetarization of the economy in the Lower Yangtze and elsewhere also crippled the *li-chia* system by making inevitable the commutation of labor services into cash levies. The tax collection and labor service machinery of the *li-chia* system became obsolete, while absentee landlords, rural-urban migration to the cities, and secret trusteeships through official tax exemptions all increased, shattering the myth of communal solidarity in the "village/family" tax system. In the end, the state lost any capacity to regulate the economy through the tax system.[31]

During the sixteenth century the Single-Whip tax reform (*I-t'iao pien-fa*) represented the culmination of late Ming efforts to come to grips with the tax assessment crisis. This remarkable reform transferred the tax burden entirely to agricultural fields, thereby amalgamating and commuting many taxation categories. Taxes were equalized on the basis of both adult-male labor and land holdings, and in turn land and labor taxes were converted into a single payment in silver.[32]

As regional trade increased the economic functions (as opposed to political status), of market towns and cities enlarged. Market towns increased twofold between 1500 and 1800, and many village settlements in the Lower Yangtze Delta became local trading centers. The functions and activities essential to operating commercial townships within rural communities fell into the hands of local gentry. This devolution of political power from the magistrate to local gentry facilitated the dominance of the latter.[33]

30. Wiens, "Changes," pp. 61–65; Huang, *Taxation*, pp. 154–62; and Wang Yuquan, "Ming Labor Service," pp. 16–21. See also Hamashima, *Mindai Kōnan nōson shakai no kenkyū*, pp. 215–61.

31. Philip C. C. Huang, *Peasant Economy in North China*. See Wiens, "Lord and Peasant," 3–34; and Kawakatsu, *Chūgoku hōken kokka no shihai kōzō*, pp. 440–45.

32. Shigeta, *Shindai shakai keizaishi kenkyū*, pp. 155–201; Ray Huang, *Taxation*, pp. 112–33; and Yamane, "Reforms in the Service Levy System," pp. 279–310. See also Wiens, "Cotton Textile Production in Early Modern China," pp. 515–34; and Mori, "Gentry in the Ming," pp. 31–38. On cotton, see Dietrich, "Cotton Culture in Early Modern China," pp. 130ff; Nishijima, "Early Chinese Cotton Industry," p. 27; and Tanakà, "Rural Handicraft in Jiangnan," pp. 81–100.

33. Fang Xing "Economic Structure of Chinese Feudal Society," pp. 126–30; and Shih-chi Liu, "Some Reflections on Urbanization." See also Brook, "Ming Local Administration," pp. 2–3, and Brook "Merchant Network."

Larger market towns in Su-chou, Sung-chiang, and Ch'ang-chou prefectures became interlocked with rural markets in the surrounding counties. By the late Ming many Lower Yangtze market towns below the county level specialized in commerce and handicrafts. The extent to which rice land was replaced by commercial crops in the delta region can be seen in the remarkable rise of "specialized towns" (*chuan-yeh shih-chen*), in which the cultivation and manufacture of cotton, for example, tended to become separate operations, with a concomitant division of labor. Local commodity production along Lake T'ai in the Yangtze Delta quickly shifted from traditional household handicrafts of the early Ming into a kind of merchant or factory production.[34]

Silk, cotton, and rice markets emerged in specialized market towns, aided by the dense land and water routes of the Yangtze Delta. Such markets furthered the commercialization of the rural economy and spurred the cities' trading activities. Improved seeds, changing cropping patterns, and new cash crops (many from the New World) produced a doubling of grain yields as a complement to the extension of cultivated acreage between 1500 and 1800.

Commercialized handicraft production meant that changes in the rural economy would produce corresponding changes in the social order. The differentiation between urban enterprises and rural production households, which made peasant producers dependent on market forces and merchant middlemen, instituted financial relations that undercut Confucian social-moral obligations between landlord-officials and peasant-commoners in rural society.[35]

The mutual-assistance-and-support ideal of the Confucian moral economy, although unrealized, had been based on the protective (that is, favored) role played by the state and individual gentry-landlords in local society. But commercial activities drew more and more rural landlords and gentry into cities and towns, and the absentee landlordism that ensued meant diminished roles and moral prestige for gentry-landlords in village society. By 1600 market towns were populated in large part by merchants, hired laborers, and absentee gentry-landlords. Many were newcomers to late Ming urban life. Conspicuous consumption, the reduction of parochialism, and the growth of an urban culture, fre-

34. Shih-chi Liu, "Some Reflections," pp. 14–19; Wiens, "Cotton Textile Production," pp. 519–22; and Fang Xing, "Economic Structure," pp. 124–31.

35. Perkins, *Agricultural Development in China*, pp. 13–53; Ping-ti Ho, *Population of China*, p. 264; and Yeh-chien Wang, *Land Taxation in Imperial China*, p. 7.

quently described in late Ming novels, were produced by social conditions peculiar to the Lower Yangtze.[36]

Between 1400 and 1600 the complex triangular relationships among the imperial state, local gentry, and village peasants had been transformed. The retreat of the imperial bureaucracy from direct involvement in village affairs confirmed the dominance of the gentry-landlord elite in the late Ming and early Ch'ing periods, and the elite adjusted successfully to the transformation: under the umbrella of the centralized bureaucratic system, gentry-landlords in the Yangtze Delta diversified their interests into various forms of profiteering based on land rent and commercial enterprises; they also populated the state bureaucracy.

LINEAGE ORGANIZATION

In the late Ming, therefore, those gentry who organized into powerful local lineages were able to fill the power vacuum in local affairs and to maintain political and economic control over rural society. Representing social groupings that operated between the family and the county-level political system, the lineage was uniquely situated to take advantage of late Ming economic opportunities as the increasingly anachronistic *li-chia* tax system gave way to the relative autonomy of villages and gentry rule. At times lineages were formed to manage the burden of imperial land taxes. At other times, they emerged to take advantage of economic opportunities for rural handicraft industry and increased agricultural commercialization.[37]

During the late Ming and Ch'ing dynasties, precisely because imperial administration was remote, powerful lineages in the Yangtze Delta (typically organized as localized kinship groups with high degrees of internal differentiation) influenced political and economic life in their area out of proportion to their actual numbers. This development did not represent an ideal of self-government. Partial decentralization, which ensured limited village autonomy, was one of the products of the struggle between Yangtze Delta gentry and imperial interests during the

36. Wiens, "Cotton Textile Production," pp. 522–30; and Wiens, "Lord and Peasant," pp. 28–34. See also Kawakatsu, "Chūgoku kinsei toshi no shakai kōzō"; Fu I-ling, *Ming-Ch'ing nung-ts'un*; and Yeh Hsien-en, *Ming-Ch'ing Hui-chou nung-ts'un*. The level of rural surplus remains unclear. The late Ming was a watershed in the development of the Chinese novel. See Hegel, *Novel*, pp. 67–130.

37. Xu Yangjie, "Feudal Clan System," pp. 70–78. Cf. Freedman, *Study of Chinese Society*, pp. 338–39; and Freedman, *Lineage Organization*, pp. 114, 125, 138.

late Ming. Imperial power would blunt the literati parties and academies that threatened the absolutist state, but the social power of local gentry was not challenged. In the seventeenth century their local clout was redirected and redefined within powerful descent groups and affinal social and political strategies.[38]

During the Ming dynasty the breakdown of earlier sharp distinctions between landed wealth and merchant profits signaled a shift in gentry perceptions of acceptable financial resources and legitimated the involvement of degree holders and their lineages in local private economic affairs. Despite the anti-merchant biases voiced in official Confucian rhetoric, China did not have the rigid barriers between merchants and gentry that characterized early modern Europe or Tokugawa Japan (1600–1867). The Confucian order of gentry, peasants, artisans, and merchants, in that order, had long been a rhetorical ideal largely divorced from social reality. The Ch'ing dynasty "elite" was composed of both merchants and gentry.

Because the economic elite was closely linked to the gentry elite, success in one sphere frequently led to success in the other. Movement into the ranks of the literati from outside established gentry lineages took place through the accumulation of wealth derived from trade, not simply from land. A wealthy lineage relied on more than agriculture for its corporate investments. Trading, usury, and bureaucratic office each provided external sources of wealth that reinforced the local prestige of the lineage.

New corporate estates did not appear in every generation. First, a sizable profit had to be made by a prominent kinsman. Then each estate had to be managed and organized by a literate elite with the requisite legal, social, and political skills. Incorporation for the long-term management of wealth became routinized and lent form and structure to the process of amassing cultural prestige and political power for a lineage. Representing a collective structure of private interests, the corporate estate became the common denominator of elite lineage organizations and the bureaucratic rationalization of family-held concentrations of wealth.

Surpluses that quickly accumulated in the highly productive rice, sericulture, and cotton economies in the Yangtze Delta helped to orga-

38. Beattie, *Land and Lineage in China*, pp. 86–87; and Xu Yangjie, "Feudal Clan System," pp. 30–33. See also Cole, "Shaohsing," pp. 112ff; Dennerline, "New Hua Charitable Estate," pp. 26–29; Freedman, *Chinese Lineage and Society*, pp. 20–21; Rubie S. Watson, *Inequality Among Brothers*, pp. 37–38; and Hsiao, *Rural China*, p. 263.

nize corporate property and to promote the development of large descent groups. Access to land-based or trade-oriented financial resources enabled a typical lineage to maintain its ancestral halls, pay for the upkeep of its private schools, and perform the expensive rituals associated with birth, death, and marriage appropriate to its high social standing.[39]

Also representing patriarchal authority, the corporate estate was legitimated through moral claims made in the name of the lineage. Alliances with affinal relations perpetuated lineage solidarity. To be recognized by state authorities, the estate had to be endowed by lineage members to relieve needy members and to help defray ritual expenses associated with burial ceremony and marriage protocol. As a philanthropic organization, the corporate estate gained certain tax advantages and reductions and was also protected from potentially disruptive property disputes.

Although the precise legal features granting political legitimacy to such corporate estates require more focused study, it is clear that such lineage strategies mitigated the damages wrought by partible inheritance. Perhaps legally savvy elites within a well-placed lineage performed many functions for their brethren that are comparable to the evolution of legitimate fiduciary advice in modern legal efforts to maintain the wealth and prestige of elite American families. The quasi-fiduciary role of elite segments within powerful higher-order lineages meant that those closest to the sources of wealth that created the estate to begin with benefited the most from tax reductions and access to estate income.[40]

Despite its stress on kinship solidarity, then, a lineage was not an egalitarian institution that bestowed benefits or prestige equally on all its members. Those kin distinguished by wealth and genealogical connection to wealthy benefactors dominated the complex social and economic dimensions of corporate property. Descent groups were imbedded in a class-based social and political system and thus included people from every stratum of society. Members were not treated equally

39. Twitchett, "A Critique," pp. 33, 37–38, 98; and Potter, "Land and Lineage," p. 134. See also Freedman, *Lineage Organization*, pp. 53–54, 75; Rubie S. Watson, *Inequality*, pp. 4, 36–40, 53, 115, 168, 172, 174; Dennerline, "Marriage, Adoption, and Charity," pp. 201–202; Marcus, "American Family Dynasties," pp. 224–41; and Zurndorfer, "Local Lineages."

40. Marcus, "American Family Dynasties," pp. 221–23; and Hu, *Common Descent Group*, pp. 22–26; the judicial functions of a lineage are discussed in detail on pp. 53–63.

because differential conditions of economic wealth and political power gave some segments more say in lineage financial and ritual affairs, regardless of kinship, seniority, or age.

Clearly, dominant lineages had many local advantages when compared to lesser agnatic kinship groups in traditional China. Because they monopolized ties with the world beyond the locality, members of wealthy segments within a higher-order lineage served as cultural, legal, political, and economic intermediaries for poorer members of their descent group.[41]

LINEAGES AND CULTURAL RESOURCES

Granted imperial legitimacy, the social and economic strength of a lineage quickly correlated with success in the civil service examination, which in turn correlated with dominant control of local cultural resources. Lineages required literate and highly placed leaders who moved easily in elite circles and could mediate with county, provincial, and national leaders on behalf of the kin group. Economic surpluses produced by wealthy lineages, particularly in the prosperous Yangtze Delta, gave members of the rich segments better access to a classical education—fairly ensuring success on state examinations. Such success led in turn to sources of political and economic power outside the lineage. Greater educational opportunities ensured that powerful members of a dominant lineage had more knowledge of and control over the management of their lineage affairs.[42]

In order for a lineage to succeed over the long term, it needed sufficient financial resources to pay for the protracted education of its bright young male members in archaic classical Chinese. Wealth was the key to passing the formidable civil service examinations for which all talented males prepared. Students who came from a family with a strong tradition of classical scholarship thus had inherent local advantages over sons of lesser families and lineages. It was clearly more difficult for the son of a peasant or artisan to compete on equal terms with males in a lineage that already had established itself as an "official-producing group."

41. Twitchett, "A Critique," p. 38; Freedman, *Chinese Lineage and Society*, pp. 97–117; and Shang, *Chung-kuo tzu-pen chu-i kuan-hsi fa-sheng*, pp. 257ff. Cf. Dennerline, "New Hua Charitable Estate," pp. 19–70; and Dennerline, "Marriage, Adoption, and Charity," p. 204. See also Rubie S. Watson, *Inequality*, pp. 104, 117–25.

42. Bourdieu and Passeron, *Reproduction*, pp. 71–102.

Education was not simply a marker of social status. Within a broader society of illiterates and those literate only in the vernacular, those who controlled the written word in classical texts had political advantages. Compilation of genealogies, preparation of deeds, and settlements for adoption contracts and mortgages required expertise and contacts that only the elite within a descent group could provide. A cultural pattern for social climbing and entry into gentry society was readily apparent for any ambitious family on its way up the social ladder in late imperial China.[43]

Lower Yangtze merchants also became known as patrons of classical scholarship, supporting schools and academies in Su-chou, Yang-chou, and Ch'ang-chou. The result was a merging of literati and merchant social strategies and cultural interests. In late imperial China merchants in the Lower Yangtze and elsewhere were in the forefront of cultural life. It is nearly impossible, for instance, to distinguish Han Learning literati from salt merchants in the academic world of Yang-chou during the Ch'ing dynasty. The success of merchants in local society—particularly in urban centers like Ch'ang-chou, Wu-hsi, and so forth—clearly points to the correlation between profits from trade and high social status. Classical scholarship flourished as a result of merchant patronage, and books were printed and collected in larger numbers than ever before.[44]

Possession of the proper linguistic tools and educational facilities for mastering Confucian political and moral discourse was perceived as the sine qua non for long-term lineage success and prestige. Success on the imperial examinations and subsequent office-holding conferred direct power and prestige on those most closely related to the graduate and the official. But the flow of local prestige could go further afield, following diverse agnatic routes within the lineage and among affines. Lesser members could identify with, and to some degree share in, the prestige of men of their lineage or of affines.[45]

Charitable schools (*i-hsueh*) within lineages represented another example of the intermingling of charitable institutions, education, and philanthropy. Lineage-endowed schooling provided more opportunity

43. Ping-ti Ho, *Ladder of Success*. Cf. Freedman, *Lineage Organization*, p. 56; and Rubie S. Watson, *Inequality*, p. 105. See also Hu, *Common Descent Group*, pp. 64–80.

44. Ping-ti Ho, "Salt Merchants," pp. 130–68; and Ōkubo, *Min-Shin jidai shoin no kenkyū*, pp. 221–361. See also Freedman, *Lineage Organization*, pp. 58–59, 128; and Peterson, *Bitter Gourd*, pp. 67–72.

45. Bourdieu, *Theory of Practice*, pp. 159–97, esp. 165, 169–71.

for the advancement of lesser families in the lineage than would have been possible where lineages were not prominent. Corporate descent groups as a whole benefited from any degree-holding member of the lineage, no matter how humble in origins. Accordingly, the failure of families in a lineage to maintain their status as degree-holders for several generations could be offset by the academic success of other agnates or affines. The social mobility of lineages, when taken as a corporate whole, was thus distinct from that of individual families.

Lineage schools and academies (*shu-yuan*) reserved for sons of merchants became jealously guarded private possessions whereby the local elite competed with each other for social, political, and academic ascendancy. The kinship groups described earlier in this chapter began in the late Ming to concentrate on classical scholarship as a corporate strategy. As a result, they were able to set aside lineage resources to underwrite the education of male students before they took the imperial examinations and to subsidize their classical scholars after they passed these same examinations. Lineages in the Lower Yangtze provinces were best able to make these expensive long-term cultural investments.[46]

Analysis of the systems of inheritance, marriage, affinity, and education, along with land tenure and political organization, shows that powerful ideological statements were being made through elite kinship institutions. One such statement is seen in the reemergence of New Text Confucianism in Ch'ang-chou Prefecture during the Ch'ing dynasty, which was closely tied to the lineage traditions of the Chuangs and their long-standing affinal relations with the Lius. The Chuangs and Lius were able to allocate lineage resources in such a way that their prestige as a "cultured" (*wen-hua*) lineage endured for more than three centuries. Written genealogies show they were an urbanized local elite based on wealth, education, kinship, and marriage ties.[47]

Our inquiry into the Chuang and Liu lineages and their rise to prominence in Ch'ang-chou society during the Ming-Ch'ing transition period—that is, the seventeenth century—provides an interesting portrait of the cultural roles that higher-order lineages played in late impe-

46. Twitchett, "Fan Clan's Charitable Estate," pp. 122–23, Rubie S. Watson, *Inequality*, pp. 7, 98, 175; Cohen, "Lineage Development," p. 11; Freedman, *Lineage Organization*, p. 54; and Rawski, *Education and Popular Literacy*, pp. 28–32, 85–88.

47. Peterson, *Bitter Gourd*, pp. 25–35; and Ōtani, "Yōshū Jōshū gakujutsu kō," pp. 313–14, James Watson, "Chinese Kinship Reconsidered," p. 601; Marcus, "Fiduciary Role," p. 239.

rial local society. To conclude our account of the interaction between schools of learning and lineage organizations in the Yangtze Delta, we shall address the political climate within which lineages such as the Chuangs and Lius replaced associations such as the Tung-lin partisans as vehicles for gentry mobilization.

LINEAGES AND THE STATE

We normally assume that there existed an inverse correlation between the power of the state and the development of kinship groups. Certainly kinship solidarity within a lineage and potential rivalry among powerful lineages in local society were not entirely compatible with a central government. Officials, particularly the county magistrate, would often tolerate limited autonomy of kinship organizations as long as they did not directly challenge the authority of the central government in local society. Moreover, by joining with other lineages to form higher-order clans (based on real or fictional kinship), members of corporate descent groups could pressure provincial administration to protect their judicial autonomy and tax exemptions.[48]

It is interesting, however, that despite the state's isolated efforts to control recalcitrant lineages and clans, it encouraged the growth of kinship groups in local society. The famous Fan charitable estate, for example, owed its very existence from the Northern Sung on to state officials who arranged tax exemptions for their lands. Without the active support of the state, the Fan lineage, which was based on the financial resources of its tax-exempt charitable estate, would not have survived as long as it did.

The reason the state supported localized kinship groups is not difficult to understand. The Confucian persuasion, conceptualized as a social, historical, and political mentality organized around ancestor worship, encouraged kinship ties as the cultural basis for moral behavior. Kinship values of loyalty and filial piety were thought to redound to the state. Accordingly, the moral influence of a higher-order lineage as a building block in local society was thought beneficial to the state.[49]

More important, however, local lineages were a strong force for sta-

48. James L. Watson, "Chinese Kinship Reconsidered," p. 616. See also Hu, *Common Descent Group*, pp. 95–96, and Hsiao, *Rural China*, pp. 323–70.

49. Twitchett, "Documents of Clan Administration," and "Fan Clan's Charitable Estate," p. 108. See also Freedman, *Lineage Organization*, pp. 64, 114, 138.

bilizing rural society below the county magistrate's jurisdiction and thus facilitated the work of local officials. The legal-moral principle of collective responsibility in local society, moreover, applied both to the family units in the *li-chia* organizational system and to lineage groups in rural China. For tax administration and local justice, we have seen that the influence of lineage organizations frequently complemented that of the state in promoting order in village communities. Lineages—like *li-chia* appointees—served as unofficial auxiliaries for the state at or below the county level.

Lineages consequently did not develop in antagonism to the imperial state but rather evolved as a result of the interaction between state policies and social economic forces at the local level. They represented one form of social organization (based on kinship) in the larger context of nonkinship-based forms of community solidarity. Elite interests in local society were directed through organizational forms the state could accept: corporate lineages. What is remarkable about these social developments is that they were authorized by the Confucian state.[50]

FACTIONS IN SUNG-MING CONFUCIAN POLITICS

The ideology of Chinese family and lineage solidarity—which placed primary emphasis on maintaining good relations with one's agnates and affines—was easily assimilated into the broader ideology of gentry society; it also served as a defense of its role as mediator between the state and commoners. During the Ming and Ch'ing dynasties the state had no ideological problems with the principle of descent as the primary means of local organization. Such tolerance sharply contrasted with the state's unceasing opposition to the principle of nonkinship alliance through gentry associations, best represented in seventeenth-century China by the demise of the partisans associated with the Tung-lin Academy in Wu-hsi County.

Representing a late Ming convergence of Confucian moral philosophy and political activism, the Tung-lin partisans at their apogee of national influence commanded the attention of Confucians all over the Ming empire. As a Ch'ang-chou-based political faction, however, the

50. Hu, *Common Descent Group*, pp. 53–63. My interpretation of the auxiliary-to-the-state role of lineages suggests this was an unintended outgrowth of the collapse of the Ming tax system. For discussion, see Faure, *Chinese Rural Society*, pp. 12–13, 164–65, 178–79, where lineages appear as "the unintentional creation of official policies."

Tung-lin partisans, unlike kinship organizations, had few respectable precedents with which to justify their actions in a Confucian-cum-Legalist state system. In a much quoted phrase from the *Analects*, Confucius said: "I have heard that the gentleman does not show partiality." The often-cited "Great Plan" chapter of the *Documents Classic* also specified that political unity required the absence of factions (*wu-tang*).[51]

In Confucian political theory persons of equal or near-equal status who formed parties or factions (*p'eng-tang*) were typically criticized as seekers of personal profit and influence. Impartiality, was the classical ideal, and government officials followed prescribed avenues of loyal behavior based on hierarchical ties between ruler and subject. Those opposed to groups like the Tung-lin partisans were thus able to stand on the moral high ground of Confucian teaching when they accused the partisans of being devoted solely to their own profit and influence.[52]

But such literati associations had their own moral high ground. Confucians had distinguished between good and bad factions since the Sung dynasty. The statesman Fan Chung-yen (989–1052) argued: "If through friendship men should work together for the good of the state, what is the harm?" Shortly thereafter, in 1045, Ou-yang Hsiu submitted a memorial to the emperor entitled "On Factions" (*P'eng-tang lun*), which built on Fan Chung-yen's strategy of transforming factionalism into a mark of moral prestige. In order to rally support for reforms that first Fang Chung-yen and then he had advocated, and to bring supporters of the proposed reforms into the government, Ou-yang Hsiu affirmed the loyalty and public-mindedness of legitimate factions.[53]

Others were ambivalent about peer group collaboration in the form of parties or factions. A leader of more conservative gentry, Ssu-ma Kuang (1019–1086), thought factions were tinged with private interests, but he blamed their existence on the political climate produced by the ruler: "Therefore, if the imperial court has parties, then the ruler should blame himself and should not blame his groups of officials." Chu Hsi, the later voice of imperial orthodoxy, was somewhat less forgiving. In his view parties and factions were in essence "selfish" (*ssu*)

51. *Shang-shu t'ung-chien*, 24.0499; *Lun-yü yin-te*, 13/7/31; and Lau, trans., *Confucius*, p. 90. See Wakeman, "Price of Autonomy," 41ff, and Chu T'an, *Ming-chi she-tang yen-chiu*.

52. Munro, "Concept of 'Interest,'" pp. 182–83.

53. Ou-yang, *Ou-yang Wen-chung kung chi*, 3.22–23 (translated in de Bary et al., *Sources of Chinese Tradition*, pp. 391–92. See also James T. C. Liu, *Ou-yang Hsiu*, pp. 52–64; and Ono, "Tōrin tō kō (ni)," *Tōhōgakuhō* 55 (1983): 307–15.

political entities that betrayed the "public" (*kung*) Tao. Peer group associations were rejected on a priori theoretical grounds. According to Chu Hsi, they betrayed Confucian principles (*li*) of government.[54]

Nevertheless, by the middle of the sixteenth century it was not unusual for several private academies in a particular region to form an organization and to hold regular meetings to discuss educational, cultural, and political issues. Such associations were possible only through the patronage of local officials and the participation of gentry and merchants from a relatively wide surrounding region. The halls of private academies organized into these associations became stopping points and crossroads for peripatetic Confucian scholars and officials. The growth of these independent associations of private academies during the sixteenth century was viewed by many officials as a threat to the established political order.[55]

Private academies, like lineages, developed into organizations that could unify local and private involvement in cultural and political affairs. They surpassed anything comparable at the time. The Tung-lin Academy, which reappeared during the seventeenth century, was at the apex of a loose association of groups, clubs, and parties. The academy declared openly what had been brewing for more than half a century: the emergence of political organizations based on the long-term covert proliferation of private academies.[56]

The Tung-lin partisans in Ch'ang-chou predictably affirmed Ou-yang Hsiu's view of factions, implying that their position was based on a uniformity of moral views, not on private interests. Ku Hsien-ch'eng (1550–1612), for instance, distinguished between "upright men" (*cheng-jen*) and "voices of remonstrance" (*ch'ing-i*), on the one hand, and those whose partisanship was based on selfish interests, on the other. Similarly, Kao P'an-lung (1562–1626), who assumed leadership of the Tung-lin Academy in Wu-hsi after Ku's death, affirmed in unequivocal terms the useful role literati associations could play in public affairs.

Their followers appealed to an ideal of a "public-spirited party" (*kung-tang*) as the proper channel for literati involvement in national

54. Ssu-ma Kuang, *Tzu-chih t'ung-chien*, vol. 9, pp. 7899–7900. See also Chu Hsi, *Chu Wen-kung wen-chi*, 12.4b, 12.8b.

55. Meskill, "Academies and Politics," pp. 149–53.

56. Ibid., pp. 153–63; and Meskill, *Academies in Ming China*, pp. 87–96. See also Ono, "Mimmatsu no kessha ni kan suru ichi kōsatsu (jō and ge)," 45, no. 2:37–67; 45, no. 3:67–92.

politics. Unlike the "privately motivated parties" (*ssu-tang*) of the past, they claimed to be seeking an alternative that would allow men of honor to join together for the common good.[57]

THE ABORTIVENESS OF LATE MING POLITICS

For a brief period between approximately 1530 and 1630 Ming autocracy was at first quietly and then vocally threatened by elite reaction against "authoritarian Confucianism." In an era when Chinese emperors had abdicated their day-to-day involvement with affairs of state, the power vacuum created at the center was filled by contending eunuch and gentry-official factions. A devolution of local power in turn left the gentry firmly entrenched at home.

The collision course between gentry-organized private academies and central authority climaxed in the early seventeenth century, when the Tung-lin Academy in Wu-hsi joined with neighboring academies in Wu-chin and I-hsing. The resulting diffuse but still powerful Ch'ang-chou faction was able to influence imperial policy in Peking. Their power reaching a peak between 1621 and 1624, the Tung-lin partisans then suffered a series of reverses that coincided with the rise of the eunuch Wei Chung-hsien, who became the young T'ien-ch'i Emperor's (r. 1621–28) most intimate advisor. Despite their high place in the imperial court, the Tung-lin representatives were gradually undermined by Wei's faction at court and eventually dismissed from office.

The purge of Tung-lin partisans reached its apogee in the summer of 1625. Arrests and deaths by torture of Tung-lin leaders were accompanied by imperial denunciations of private academies as politically subversive organizations. Private academies throughout the empire were ordered destroyed. The halls of the Tung-lin Academy, partially destroyed in 1625, were completely torn down by imperial order in 1626. A special order was sent out from Peking to tear down all academies in Ch'ang-chou and Su-chou prefectures in particular because most were assumed to be part of the Tung-lin organizational network.

Although it was manipulated by crude politicians for their own purposes, the chief theoretical issue in 1625 was imperial prerogative versus the possibility of concerted and organized gentry involvement in politics. A century-old problem, the issue defined the threat posed by

57. Hucker, "Tung-lin Movement," p. 143; and Ono, "Tōrin tō kō (ichi)," p. 589.

private academies and associations in light of the realities of political power within an autocratic imperial state. Wei Chung-hsien's crude purge of his Tung-lin opponents mirrored a fear widely held among more cultivated Confucians that it was wrong to establish separate political organizations for the advancement of personal interests.

All factionalism was impugned and repudiated with the officially sanctioned destruction of the Tung-lin Academy. The limits of what was politically permissible in Ming political life had been reached. Factions went against the public interests, which were represented ideally by the ruler. In the national political arena at least, late Ming efforts to strengthen gentry interests had failed.[58]

But Wei Chung-hsien's uses of terror could not rein in the political forces unleashed by the Tung-lin partisans. After Wei fell into disgrace in 1627 (he subsequently committed suicide) private academies and associations emerged in full force again. Factionalism likewise reared its divisive head in the political controversies that ripped apart the last reigns of the Ming dynasty. Among the most successful and best-organized group of literati were those associated with the Fu She (Return [to Antiquity] Society) movement, which revolved around Su-chou in the 1620s and 1630s. A formidable organization dedicated to supporting its members in the factional struggles that dominated late Ming politics, the Fu She represented the largest and most sophisticated political interest group ever organized within the imperial bureaucratic structure.

With the fall of the Ming dynasty first to peasant rebels and then to Manchu conquerors, the Fu She ceased to function and Ming factionalism disappeared. Both the Tung-lin partisans and their Fu She successors had sought ways to grant the gentry scholar-official a position of political prestige. But in the end their diffuse efforts failed. Confucians of the time attributed the demise of the Ming dynasty in part to imperial despotism but blamed the debilitating factionalism even more for failing to achieve a viable consensus for gentry involvement in national politics.[59]

If gentry forces had been able to influence the provincial and national

58. Yang Ch'i, "Ming-mo Tung-lin tang yü Ch'ang-chou." See also Busch, "Tung-lin Academy." Primary sources are conveniently included in *Tung-lin shih-mo* and in Huang Tsung-hsi, *Record of Ming Scholars*, pp. 223–52. See the useful summary in Lin Li-yueh, "Ming-mo Tung-lin-p'ai te chi-ke cheng-chih kuan-nien," pp. 20–42. See also Goodrich et al., eds. *Dictionary of Ming Biography*, pp. 702–709. For a contemporary list of Tung-lin martyrs, see Chin Jih-sheng, *Sung-t'ien lu-pi*, pp. 1a–24a. Cf. *Tung-lin pieh-sheng*.

59. Atwell, "From Education to Politics."

levels through legitimate factions such as the Tung-lin Academy or Fu She, what sort of political forces would have been released in Confucian political culture? Some scholars have speculated that the late Ming drive to reform the state "showed features strikingly similar to the trend against absolute monarchy and toward parliamentary rule in the West."[60]

Ming factionalism, however, was implicated as a chief culprit in the fall of the Ming house in 1644 and in the consequent triumph of the Manchus over a native Chinese dynasty clinging to life in south China until 1662. In fact, it is doubtful that the legitimacy of Confucian parties would have been vindicated even if the Tung-lin partisans had triumphed. Fearing peasant rebellion more than Manchu occupation, gentry recognized that their social and economic privileges depended on the political power of the state, which they quickly rejoined as officials. Vigorous Ch'ing emperors soon restored imperial initiative in political affairs, making what might have been a moot point until the turmoil of the nineteenth century.

Perhaps the most novel element in this ongoing conflict was not the extremes to which imperial autocracy would go to defend itself but rather the audacity of the gentry assault. With the increase of schools and academies during the late Ming, an enlarged educated class of elites emerged. The various reformist agendas of the thousands of Confucians affiliated with the Tung-lin Academy and the Fu She crossed a treacherous boundary within Ming authoritarian government.[61]

The fruitlessness of Ming activism should be seen in light of the increasing independence of the urban order within the imperial state. Criticism of the overbearing political authority of Ming imperial institutions carried over into the early decades of the Ch'ing dynasty. This is so even though the broader political consequences of Ming activism had been successfully aborted. The startling perceptiveness of such celebrated Ming loyalists as Huang Tsung-hsi and Ku Yen-wu—if understood in the context of the disintegration of the Ming state in the seventeenth century—marked major steps forward in Chinese perceptions of the intimate relation between Confucian institutions and autocratic state power.[62]

60. Struve, "Continuity and Change," vol. 9, pt. 1.

61. On the political aspects of local Tung-lin activities see Tanaka, "Popular Uprisings," pp. 181–83. See also Dennerline, "Hsu Tu," pp. 124–25, and Tsing Yuan, "Urban Riots," pp. 296, 309.

62. Hou, "Lun Ming-Ch'ing chih chi te she-hui chieh-chi kuan-hsi ho ch'i-meng ssu-

What exactly did the Tung-lin initiative represent? Did its failure in the seventeenth century mark the decisive divergence in historical trajectories between imperial China and revolutionary Europe? Did Tung-lin activism fail because the imperial state was overly autocratic or because the Confucian political style was suicidal? For a gentry-official to remonstrate with the Ming throne was tantamount to presenting one's head on a platter. Gentry solidarity was forbidden. Martyrdom was assured. Could gentry organizations like the Tung-lin have successfully carved out a political niche in Confucian political culture? These questions immediately come to mind as we evaluate the futility of late Ming politics against the backdrop of the powerful lineages of the Yangtze Delta.[63]

LINEAGES AND POLITICAL LEGITIMACY

Modern anthropologists and sociologists have seen lineage organization as a particularistic and divisive feature of traditional Chinese society or as an impediment to community structures capable of assuming modern political form. But the Confucian state and its ideological representatives saw instead the convergence of kinship ties and community interests, which incorporated the broader egalitarian ideal of equitable distribution of wealth and resources throughout the society. In a 1736 memorial advising government support for lineages, for example, Chiang Ping, a native of Yang-hu County in Ch'ang-chou Prefecture, noted the importance of kinship solidarity in the social order:

> Mencius said: "If only everyone loved his parents and treated his elders with deference, the empire would be at peace." It is fortunate that every person has parents and elders. Through his parents and elders each person has a kinship group [*tsu*, lit., "patriline"]. The principles for having parents and elders can be extended from one family to the empire. In the past, changes in the human mind and customs have been initiated by prominent families and large kinship groups. Putting moral teachings [*chiao-hua*] into effect must begin with those of moral stature.

Chiang Ping then went on to describe the social costs when lineage solidarity broke down:

---

ch'ao te t'e-tien," 26–35. On the Tung-lin partisans, see Huang Tsung-hsi, *Ming-Ju hsueh-an*, pp. 613–42 (*chüan* 58), and Ku Ch'ing-mei, "Ch'ing-ch'u ching-shih chih hsueh yü Tung-lin hsueh-p'ai te kuan-hsi." Cf. de Bary, "Chinese Despotism." On Ku Yen-wu, see Goodrich, *Literary Inquisition*, pp. 75–76.

63. Hucker, "Confucianism."

> In recent times, there have been those literati who have performed virtuously regarding their lineage, parents, and associates. There are others, however, who know only their own personal benefit [*tzu-ssu tzu-li*]. There are even those who do not care that their wives and sons are gorging themselves with meat, while their brothers [lit., "hands and feet"] do not have enough grain to live on. Their servants ride in strong carriages or on fat horses, while their own kin and associates are starving and suffering from the cold.

Chiang's solution was to have the government encourage mutual aid and responsibility among local kinship groups so that local customs would not conflict with state interests:[64]

> If someone gives his property to the ancestral hall of a kinship group to assist members of the lineage [*tsu-jen*], the director of the local tax office should be requested to list this land separately and remove it from miscellaneous labor service requirements. At the same time, the donation should be reported to the Ministry [of Rites], Board of Ceremony for comment. Commoner and gentry lineages whose membership exceeds one thousand heads should be allowed to select publicly one careful and honest person from their lineage to act as elder and instruct and lead members of the lineage.
>
> If within three years, there is not a single case of ritual or legal infractions or of a lawsuit taken to court among the lineage members, the local prefect or magistrate should commend them with the presentation of a board containing a laudatory inscription [*pien*]. If there is no such offense or lawsuit within five years, then the governor-general and governor should commend them with the presentation of a *pien*.
>
> If during a year of famine any member of a linege can assist his kin and prevent them from scattering, the governor-general and governor should evaluate the extent of his merit and reward him either with a *pien* for encouragement or petition the government to award him an insignia of official rank.

The K'ang-hsi (r. 1662–1722) and Yung-cheng (r. 1723–35) emperors reciprocated such sentiments. They also saw in kinship a desirable framework for building stable social institutions. The second maxim of the K'ang-hsi Emperor's Sacred Edict, for example, admonished subjects "to behave with generosity to your kindred in order to demonstrate harmony and affection." In the "Amplified Instructions," the people were encouraged "to establish ancestral halls, perform sacrificial rites, set up lineage schools to teach sons and younger brothers,

64. *Huang-Ch'ing ming-ch'en tsou-i*, 23.32a–35b. I have modified the translation in Hu, *Common Descent Group*, pp. 188–89. For the Mencius quotation, see *Meng-tzu yin-te*, 28/4A/12, and Lau, trans., *Mencius*, pp. 122–23. On kinship and modernity in China, see Weber, *Religion of China*, pp. 241–42.

institute charitable estates, aid destitute kin, and revise genealogies of the kindred to bind together distant relatives."

Where gentry associations based on nonkinship ties were defined as "private" (*ssu*, that is, "selfish"), social organizations based on descent were perceived as "public" (*kung*). For example, the charitable estate enjoyed a privileged tax status in Ming-Ch'ing times because in the Confucian ideal of kinship the charitable estate symbolized the ancient goal of equitable distribution of wealth through charity, not its privatization. Consequently, as long as powerful lineage organizations operated within the limits imposed by the imperial bureaucracy, they had a strong theoretical justification for their existence, a justification upon which both state and society were agreed.[65]

This affirmation in both political and moral discourse contrasted sharply with the gentry's tenuous, uphill battle in the seventeenth century to legitimate their participation in Confucian political culture as a public-minded party or faction (*p'eng-tang*). In both official Confucian rhetoric and theory, nonagnatic political organizations were dismissed on a priori epistemological grounds as fronts for personal profit (*li*) and private interests (*ssu*).

The demise of policy-based gentry associations and the survival of kinship-based lineage organizations during the Ming-Ch'ing transition explain why higher-order lineages emerged as the mouthpieces for literati values in the Lower Yangtze. In the movement from seventeenth-century "party" (*tang*) activism among Wu-hsi's Tung-lin advocates to eighteenth-century New Text reformism in Ch'ang-chou Prefecture among the Chuangs and Lius, we note an intensification of gentry interests in principles of vertical, agnatic descent and a lessening of interest in political initiatives based on horizontal, nonkinship alliances built around parties and factions. This recasting of local authority structures in effect created new local constituencies from which the Chuang and Liu lineages in Ch'ang-chou, for example, derived their social influence and power.

Tung-lin partisans stressed alliance over kinship strategies in faction building, following precedents established during the Northern Sung dynasty. Just as Sung efforts to legitimate gentry alliances failed, only to be followed by Mongol conquest and renewed gentry reliance on kinship to protect their local interests, so too late Ming attempts to gain

65. Dennerline, "New Hua Charitable Estate," pp. 22–23, 44–45, 52–53. On the Sacred Edict, see *Ta-Ch'ing hui-tien shih-li*, 397.2b, and Hsiao, *Rural China*, pp. 348–49.

authorization for gentry associations and clubs were swept away by the Manchu invasion, whereupon elites returned once again to kinship strategies. From the early seventeenth century on clan and lineage formation increasingly became an alternative to factional alignments in Ch'ang-chou society. The futility of late Ming gentry politics and the Manchu defeat of Ming forces in the mid-seventeenth century left lineages intact. They thus became one of the most important social organizations in local society during the Ch'ing. They became imperially protected as legitimate gentry organizations once the K'ang-hsi Emperor took full control of state policy in the early Ch'ing.[66]

Identified as public institutions for charitable and philanthropic purposes, lineages had sufficient ideological leverage to escape the restraints placed on gentry alliances. Because lineages could cope organizationally with growing commercialization and social stratification—both of which increased because of late Ming population growth and rural subsistence problems—kinship organizations appeared to have superior and legitimate ways to ameliorate local poverty and hunger. Urban-based families could provide relief for poorer members of their lineage groups. In due course the Manchu triumph tipped the scale once more in favor of kinship solidarity over gentry alliance.[67]

One of the chief legacies of late Ming politics in Ch'ang-chou and elsewhere was the magnified role agnatic relations played in local society. The dominant lineages in Ch'ang-chou during the Ming-Ch'ing transition, for instance, were precisely those that rode the crest of local power through corporate lineage strategies and avoided strategies that sought local power through parties and literati associations.

Two of those lineages, the Chuangs and the Lius, successfully survived the Ming debacle. Through their internal corporate strategies and external affinal relations with each other, these two lineages transmitted their prestige in local affairs to the highest levels of imperial politics during the Ch'ing dynasty. The Ch'ang-chou New Text school accordingly provides us with a unique window on elite social and intellectual history that encompasses both the collapse of Ming political dissent and the continuation of gentry dominance in late imperial local society through kinship organizations.

66. Dennerline, pp. 24–28. See also Hymes, *Statesmen and Gentlemen*, pp. 122–23.
67. Smith, "Benevolent Societies."

TWO

The Chuang and Liu Lineages in Ch'ang-chou

Chuang Ts'un-yü's founding of the New Text school in Ch'ang-chou in the eighteenth century and the predominance of his grandson Liu Feng-lu as his chief nineteenth-century disciple suggest that the Ch'ang-chou school depended on the political and economic strength (as well as the cultural resources) of the Chuang and Liu lineages. By turning now to these prominent lineages in the Yangtze Delta, I hope first to show how they navigated the late Ming social, political, and economic changes we have discussed above.

An investigation of Ch'ang-chou elite society during the late Ming will also reveal that after Ch'ing rule brought peace and stability to the Yangtze Delta the local gentry managed not only to survive the Manchu conquest but also to prosper as never before. Our inquiry documents how ideological transformations can be embodied in particular people caught up in specific social and historical contexts. The prominence of the Chuang and Liu lineages in Ch'ang-chou society (map 4) and their ties to the rise of the Ch'ang-chou school in the late eighteenth century enables us to glimpse the social icebergs that lurked beneath intellectual life in late imperial China.

THE BEGINNINGS OF THE CHUANGS

The Chuang lineage, particularly the second branch (*erh-fen*) to which Chuang Ts'un-yü's family belonged, first came to prominence in Ch'ang-chou in the late fifteenth century. Like many other lineages south of the Yangtze River, the Chuangs traced their line back to families that migrated from north China during the great social and economic dislocations that preceded the eventual fall of the north to the Jurchen. The Chuangs had already established a beachhead in Chiang-su Province in the eleventh century. They settled in Chen-chiang, on the southern bank of the Yangtze, from where the Grand Canal continued south toward Ch'ang-chou, Su-chou, and Hang-chou.

Robert Hartwell notes that the chief indicator of the profound social changes in China from 750 to 1550 was the major demographic shifts from north to south China. In the six centuries that preceded the establishment of Ming rule in 1368, successive waves of migration had filled in the frontiers of various southern macroregions. These dynamic interregional settlements were accompanied by rapid population growth and a "filling up" of the rice-producing areas in the Yangtze Delta.[1]

As participants in these important demographic shifts, some of the Chuangs left Chen-chiang (ca. 1086–92?) and settled in Chin-t'an County, further inland and south of the Yangtze River. Such moves to hinterland counties in search of fortune were a typical migration pattern for segmented branches of core lineages. Chuang I-ssu, in the fifth generation of the Chuangs who resided in Chin-t'an, achieved distinction as prefect of Ch'ang-chou Prefecture from 1102 until 1106. Later he was appointed to the Hanlin Academy. Thereafter, segments of the Chuang lineage continued to scatter throughout the Lower Yangtze.

Initially a lesser segment that had become allied to another family in the hinterlands, the Chuangs in Ch'ang-chou were a lineage to be reckoned with by the late fifteenth century. In the eighth generation of the Chin-t'an descent group, Chuang Hsiu-chiu married into a Ch'ang-chou family, surnamed Chiang, which had no male heir. Accordingly, he took the place of a son (*chui*) for this family and moved to Ch'ang-chou. Uxorilocal marriage was a common strategy among important lineages in the Lower Yangtze since at least Sung times. The son of a family with higher social status could establish a new segment of the lineage by moving to another community and marrying the daughter of a family with no heir. But rather than carrying on the family line for the heirless family (the usual procedure in uxorilocal marriages), the son continued to use his own surname in a new community. By moving to Ch'ang-chou, Chuang Hsiu-chiu could take advantage of an entrenched

1. Hartwell, "Demographic Transformations of China," esp. pp. 391ff.

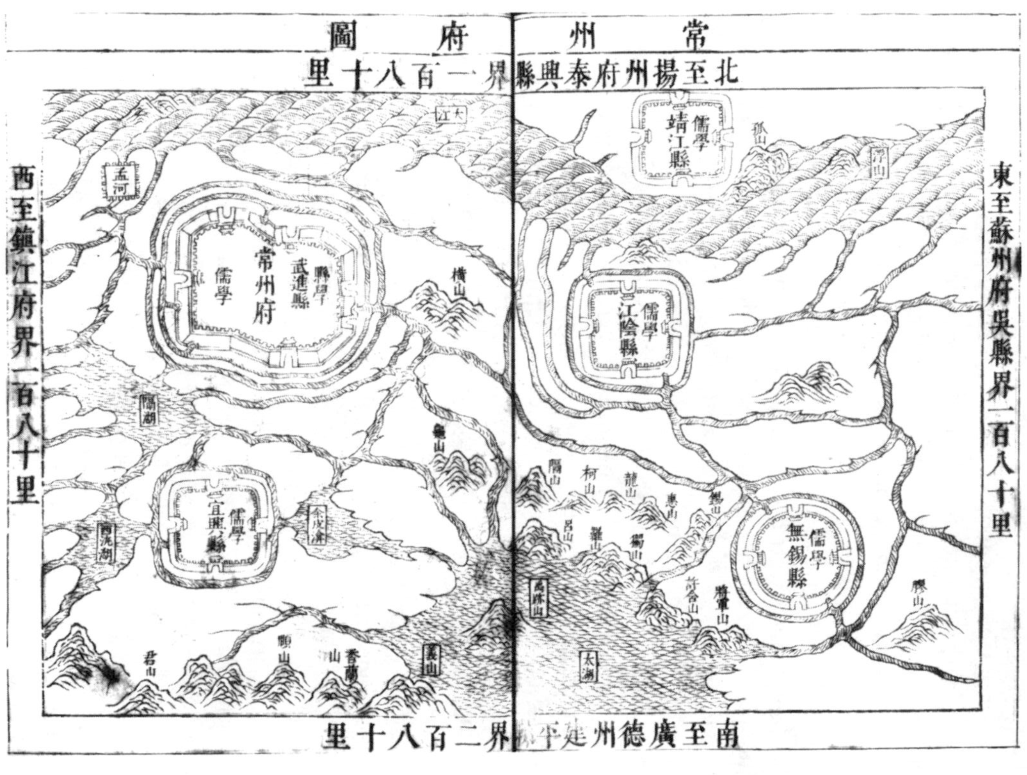

Map 4. Gazetteer Map of Ch'ang-chou Prefecture and Counties

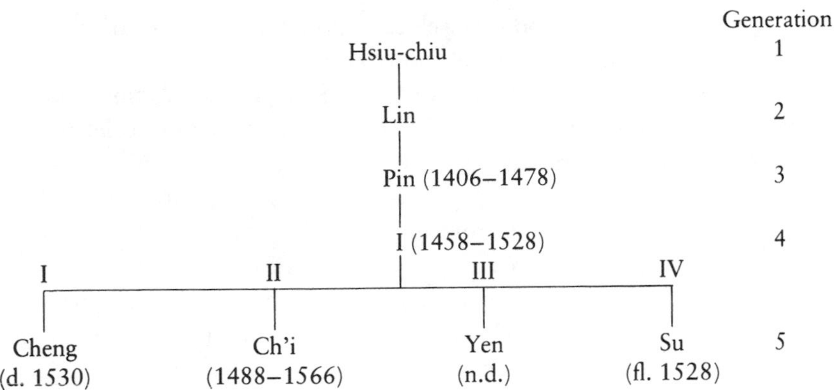

Fig. 4. Major Segments of the Chuang Lineage in Ch'ang-chou during the Ming Dynasty

family that had become fused with the Chin-t'an Chuangs. Thus, by the fifteenth century another segment of the Chuangs had come into existence, dating themselves back to Chuang Hsiu-chiu's move to Ch'ang-chou.[2]

The rise of the Ch'ang-chou Chuangs to high social standing began in the fourth generation (in Chuang Hsiu-chiu's line), when Chuang I took the *chin-shih* degree in 1496. Chuang I's academic success, and the high political office that such success brings, provided the financial resources from which four major branches in the Ch'ang-chou lineage developed (fig. 4). The second branch of the Ch'ang-chou Chuangs, who descended from Chuang I, rose to particular eminence during the Ming and Ch'ing dynasties. They were able to produce in nearly every generation a highly placed government official who owed his success to high achievement on the imperial examinations. Through marriage politics, this second branch of the Chuang lineage had established relations with other important lineages in Ch'ang-chou—a sign of the emerging status of the Chuang lineage vis-à-vis other more established lineages in the area. The

2. Ibid., pp. 405–20. On the Chuangs see *Chu-chi Chuang-shih tsung-p'u*, partially unpaginated manuscript dated 1796, 2.1a–8a, 3.1a–2b. See also *P'i-ling Chuang-shih tseng-hsiu tsu-p'u*, (1935), 12A.36a, and *Wu-chin Chuang-shih tseng-hsiu tsu-p'u* (ca. 1840), 16.25b. Uxorilocal marriage could create allies out of other powerful and wealthy families lacking a male heir. See James L. Watson, "Anthropological Overview," pp. 284–85, and Dennerline, "Marriage, Adoption, and Charity," pp. 173–74 (both articles appear in *Kinship Organization in Late Imperial China*, ed. Ebrey and Watson). Cf. Pasternak, "Uxorilocal Marriage in China," and Zurndorfer, "Local Lineages and Local Development," p. 33.

Chuangs could now define themselves within a community of prestigious affines built around strategic marriages.

The eldest daughter of Chuang Ch'i (1488–1566), for example, was married to T'ang Shun-chih (1507–60), one of the most celebrated scholar-officials of the Ming period. In addition, Chuang Ch'i's grandson, Chuang I-lin, a major patriarch in the second branch of the Chuangs, married a woman from the T'ang lineage and was intimate with T'ang Shun-chih, whose distinguished family belonged to one of the most important Ch'ang-chou lineages during the Ming dynasty. T'ang and Hsueh Ying-ch'i (1500–73) were influential in all aspects of Ch'ang-chou's cultural life and were mentors to many of the subsequent leaders of the Tung-lin movement in Wu-hsi County.[3]

T'ang Shun-chin was a leading Confucian whose interests ranged from literary pursuits to statecraft issues. He championed the role of the charitable estate in lineage organizations by appealing to the classical ideal of broadly based kinship solidarity.

> The ancients relied on kin [*tsu*, lit., "patriline"] to establish kinship groups for them. Those kinsmen who had surplus wealth then returned it to the kindred, and those who could not provide sufficiently for themselves partook of the kindred's wealth. These kinsmen treated one another as parts of a single body, like bone and sinew, hand and foot. Their resources covered all like digestive juices, overflowing into interstices, filling up only the empty places, and there was no depressed or swollen places, no excesses or deficiency. Thus, in the whole kin group there were no wealthy and no poor families. Moreover, no kin group under heaven was without a kindred, and in this way there were no wealthy or poor families in the empire. Isn't this what was meant by saying that when everyone treats relatives as relatives the empire is tranquil?[4]

As an ancient ideal, kinship solidarity had begun to fade when private interests, according to T'ang, had increasingly penetrated Chinese society:

> Only after the demise of the well-fields [*ching-t'ien*] were there means for ranking property in the village. Only after the demise of kinship regulations [*tsung-fa*] were there means for ranking by property within the kin group. At

3. *Chu-chi Chuang-shih tsung-p'u* (1796), 3.1b. See also *P'i-ling T'ang-shih chia-p'u* (1948 ed.), vol. 9, pp. 1a–1b (*Wu-fen shih-piao*), and T'ang Shun-chih, *Ching-chuan hsien-sheng wen-chi*, 15.27a–31b, for his epitaph for his wife from the Chuang lineage, who died in 1548. Cf. *P'i-ling Chuang-shih tseng-hsiu tsu-p'u* (1935), 13.4a–5b, and Goodrich et al., eds., *Dictionary of Ming Biography*, pp. 619–22, 1252–56.

4. T'ang Shun-chih, *Ching-ch'uan hsien-sheng wen-chi*, 12.24b. Cf. the translation in Dennerline, "New Hua Charitable Estate," pp. 45–47, and *Wu-hsi Chin-k'uei hsien-chih* (1881), 37.2a–3b.

> the extreme there are cases where slave boys tire of meat and gravy while kinsmen grab for the ladle. The benevolent gentleman sympathizes and thereupon makes use of his position to create charity land to succor his kin. Thus, even though there is something that the great kindred bequeaths to them, yet as charity lands are established the term "great kindred" [*ta-tsu*] is further obscured.

Ideals of ancient society, symbolized best by the well-field system canonized by Mencius, had declined to the point that T'ang Shun-chih admitted that kinship relations were by his time a pale shadow of the public-minded (*kung*) values they once stood for. T'ang understood how the forces of commercialization and market specialization had affected idealized traditional values and transformed the context within which kinship values were expressed:

> In essence, it is the case with charity land that it exists because there is a man of means, while under the kinship regulations [in antiquity] even the most valuable properties were shared. In the case of charity land, it is only the benevolent person as a part of the kin group who treats others in a public-minded manner [*hsiang-kung*], while under [ancient] kinship regulations, even where the inheritance was small and niggardly, no one could treat others sparingly. Therefore, as a model, charity land leads to narrowness and one-sidedness, whereas the kinship regulations [of antiquity] lead to equity and universality.[5]

Nevertheless, T'ang continued to advocate an emphasis on distant agnates in order to reaffirm the primacy of kinship models from antiquity. Broadly based kinship relations were at least a means to overcome the contemporary suspicion of selfishness (*ssu*), when stress was placed on household and family line and not lineage group:

> Still, since the understanding of the benevolent gentleman is already sufficient to attain this level, can the fact that no one shares his means with others really be owing to the differences between ancient and contemporary times? Might it not also be that charity land emanates from the ability of such a person to take responsibility upon himself, while [ancient] kinship regulations could only be imposed from above and never be established by joint responsibility.

Admitting the devolution of local power into the hands of gentry families and lineages, T'ang Shun-chih made the best of an irreversible process. If the communal ideals of the ancients could not be revived in contemporary sixteenth-century rural society, then well-intended

5. T'ang Shun-chih, *Ching-ch'uan hsien-sheng wen-chi*, 12.24b–25a. See also Ku Yen-wu, *Jih-chih-lu*, pp. 649–55.

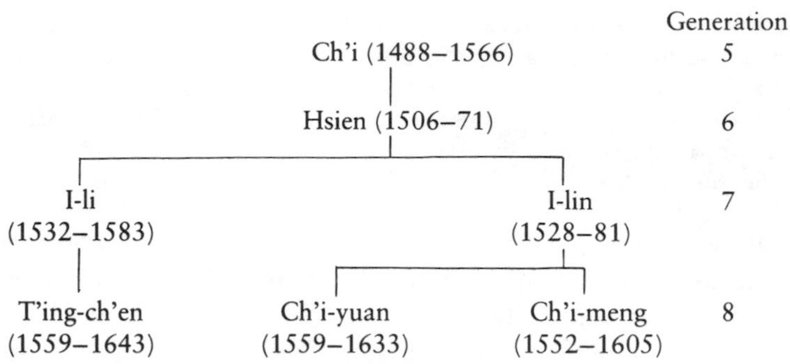

Fig. 5. Major Segments of the Second Branch of the Chuang Lineage during the Ming Dynasty

kinship groups could at least approximate the classical ideal of equitable distribution of wealth through the creation of charitable land for their kin and descendents. T'ang was not speaking as a disinterested bystander. A key figure in the T'ang lineage in Ch'ang-chou with strong affinal ties to the Chuang lineage there, T'ang's views reflected the moral high ground on which late Ming lineages in the Yangtze Delta were taking a stand.[6]

THE CHUANGS' RISE TO PROMINENCE

The Chuangs' social climbing accelerated by the late Ming. The Chuang lineage, particularly its second branch, outstripped the T'ang name in prestige and influence in Ch'ang-chou (fig. 5). An analysis of the social milieu (in which the Chuangs first married their women into more elite gentry families and then received women from other less elite lineages such as the Lius [see below] as brides for their increasingly well-placed sons) reveals how the local standing of the Chuangs increased. Such social climbing also brought with it increased educational opportunities for Chuang women, which we shall discuss below. By the eighteenth century the marriage strategies of the Ch'ang-chou Chuangs were well entrenched, as families in the lineage successfully arranged prestigious links for both its sons and daughters.

In 1580 Chuang I-lin, one of the major scions of the second branch, saw to it that a genealogy was compiled for the Chuang lineage. This

6. T'ang Shun-chih, 12.25a. See also Ebrey, "Early Stages," p. 40n.

event shows that the descent group had reached a major point in its development as a higher-order lineage. The Chuangs traced their line back to Chuang Hsiu-chiu, claiming shared estate property that had accrued through Chuang I-lin. Ancestral halls, sacrificial fields (the income from such lands financed the sacrificial rituals of ancestor worship), and updated genealogies were important elements in the development of lineage solidarity.[7]

Subsequent editions of the Chuang genealogy were compiled regularly—1611, 1651, 1699, 1761, 1801, 1838, 1883, and 1935. In addition, the Chuangs became a lineage whose most prestigious branches were urban-based, taking advantage of the city's economic and cultural advantages. The Chuangs' prestigious second branch, for example, was so urbanized that its two chief wings in Ch'ang-chou City were known as the "Eastern and Western Chuangs." Localized in Ch'ang-chou, the Chuangs could also include in their genealogy dispersed segments in nearby Lower Yangtze locales, as well as in Fu-chien and Kuang-tung.[8]

It would be inaccurate to see the emergence of the Chuangs in Ch'ang-chou simply as part of the segmentation within the kinship system, however. This perspective would overlook the historical conditions that underlay late Ming lineage formation. We need to be cognizant of the social situation within which lineages such as the Chuangs emerged. The Chuang lineage developed as part of the response of elite segments to the changing regional economy and the political turmoil surrounding the fall of the Ming dynasty. The Chuangs' successful response to these external nonkinship factors brought them increased prestige and prominence as a higher-order lineage. Just as the favorable economic climate of the late Ming encouraged lineage formation, the powerful organization the Chuangs had forged by the

7. *P'i-ling Chuang-shih tseng-hsiu tsu-p'u* (1935), 18B.36a–39a. The Chuangs developed a pattern of intermarriage with the Liu lineage in Ch'ang-chou, which we will discuss in more detail. See also, Ebrey, "Early Stages," pp. 55–56.

8. *Chu-chi Chuang-shih tsung-p'u*, 1883 printed ed. pp. 8.29a–36a. See *P'i-ling Chuang-shih tseng-hsiu tsu-p'u* (1935), pp. 1a–5b (1934 "Hsu" [Preface]), for mention of the various editions of the Chuang genealogy. See also ibid., 12A.40a, for discussion of the "Eastern and Western Chuangs." I have located and used the 1801 (through a 1796 manuscript version), 1838 (printed ca. 1840), 1883, and 1935 editions. For the urban- and rural-based Chuang lines, see *Wu-chin Chuang-shih tseng-hsiu tsu-p'u* (ca. 1840), 7.1a–2b, 8.49a–53b, 9.21a–26b, 13.1a–2b, 13.41a–43b. See in particular Chuang Ch'i-yuan's "Hsu" (Preface) to his *Ch'i-yuan chih-yen*, p. 10b. Other Chuang segments resided in Su-chou, Hang-chou, and Chia-hsing. See the ca. 1840 edition, 8.25a–41b. For Chuang segments in Fu-chien and Kuang-tung, see Chuang Yu-kung's 1761 "Hsu" (Preface) in *P'i-ling Chuang-shih tseng-hsiu tsu-p'u* (1935), pp. 2a–2b.

seventeenth century helped them to compete for land, wealth, and power in Ch'ang-chou during the Ch'ing dynasty.

Before the fall of the Ming dynasty, lineages such as the Chuangs in Wu-chin had come to grips with the need for tax reform. Affinal relations with the prestigious T'ang lineage in Wu-chin via T'ang Ho-cheng (son of T'ang Shun-chih and his Chuang wife), who was one of the Tung-lin advocates of tax reform, implies that some Ch'ang-chou lineages were predisposed to accept tax reforms that had been championed during the Ming but not enacted until the Ch'ing. The alarming extent of special tax exemptions granted in Wu-chin County had been noted in the 1605 county gazetteer compiled under T'ang Ho-cheng's direction.[9]

Beginning in the fifteenth century tax exemptions were discussed within the context of long-term changes in Wu-chin land policy. Ch'ang-chou genealogies point to the interaction of several lineage groups and suggest that some lineage members supported late Ming calls for social and tax reform. The continuity of dominant lineage groups in local society from the Ming debacle to the Manchu triumph means that some gentry had successfully identified their interests in line with local reformist programs.[10]

We see in chapter 1 that the Ming tax system was weakened by its granting of exemption to those who lived on official salaries. The burden of labor services was left squarely on the shoulders of commoners, who in addition to the land tax had to provide labor services to local officials. Tung-lin supporters in Ch'ang-chou Prefecture were acutely aware of this unfair situation. But in the sixteenth century T'ang Shun-chih, in addition to his concerns for kinship solidarity, had already prefigured the reform proposals of the Tung-lin partisans. In a letter directed to the Su-chou prefect, Wang Pei-ya, T'ang pointed to the link between secret trusteeship of land (*kuei-chi*) and tax exemptions granted to gentry:

> The practice of secret trusteeship by influential households is due to excessive exemptions granted to official households. These two ills are actually one. For example, an official who is entitled to exemptions on 1000 mou of land in a household but owns 10,000 mou, or who has no land but receives 10,000 mou under custody, will divide the 10,000 mou of land into ten

9. Kawakatsu, *Chūgoku hōken kokka no shihai kōzō*, pp. 209, 235–36, 336, 440–45. Nan-ching (Nan-chih-li) had also tried tax reform in the 1570s. For T'ang Ho-cheng's remarks see *Wu-chin hsien-chih*, preface.

10. Beattie, *Land and Lineage*.

households. Therefore, with each 1000 mou receiving exemption in a household, the whole 10,000 mou are exempted from the labor service obligation.[11]

T'ang Shun-chih's landsman and colleague Hsueh Ying-ch'i, also influential in Wu-chin County among the Tung-lin leaders, described the hardships faced by families. According to Hsueh, the labor services tax forced many of Ch'ang-chou's promising local talents to forgo their Confucian studies in order to fulfill the tax obligations incurred by their families. Many lower-level gentry-literati such as Liu Ta-chung in Wu-hsi County, among others, only made it as far as a licentiate (*sheng-yuan*, that is, license to participate in the local-level imperial examination) before the labor services tax compelled them to give up their studies. Liu Ta-chung had grown up with Hsueh Ying-ch'i and T'ang Shun-chih. But his father's early death meant that Liu was now shouldered with the sole responsibility for his mother and for performing the labor service his household owed. In his epitaph for Liu, Hsueh Ying-ch'i noted that such commitments had prevented his friend from matching the local and national acclaim garnered by friends Hsueh and T'ang.[12]

Late-sixteenth-century reform efforts in Ch'ang-chou Prefecture pivoted around the swelling inequities in local society. Labor tax obligations fell on households that could least afford them. Ch'ang-chou local leaders in the 1590s increasingly called for enaction of a system of land and labor equalization (*chün-t'ien chün-i*), a successor to piecemeal reforms in the 1570s aimed at equalizing labor service obligations of taxable households. In the face of commoner opposition to the abuse of tax exemptions gentry-officials had granted their own households, Ou-yang Tung-feng (fl. ca. 1604), prefect in Ch'ang-chou, and Hao Ching, magistrate in Chiang-yin County, unsuccessfully called on gentry to help make up for deficiencies in the labor service rolls (*t'ieh-i*). Hao Ching had been demoted to assistant magistrate in I-hsing County in Ch'ang-chou in 1599 after denouncing greedy imperial tax collectors. From 1600 to 1603 he served in Chiang-yin. We shall encounter Hao, a critic of Old Text Classics, later on. Ou-yang Tung-feng had close ties to the Tung-lin partisans in Wu-hsi and had helped protect the Lung-

11. See Wiens, "Fiscal and Rural Control Systems," pp. 61–65. See also T'ang Shun-chih, *T'ang Ching-ch'uan hsien-sheng wen-chi*, in *Ch'ang-chou hsien-che i-shu*, 10.13b–14a.

12. Hamashima, *Mindai Kōnan nōson shakai no kenkyū*, pp. 525–26. See also Hsueh Ying-ch'i, *Fang-shan Hsueh hsien-sheng ch'üan-chi*, 30.1a–3a.

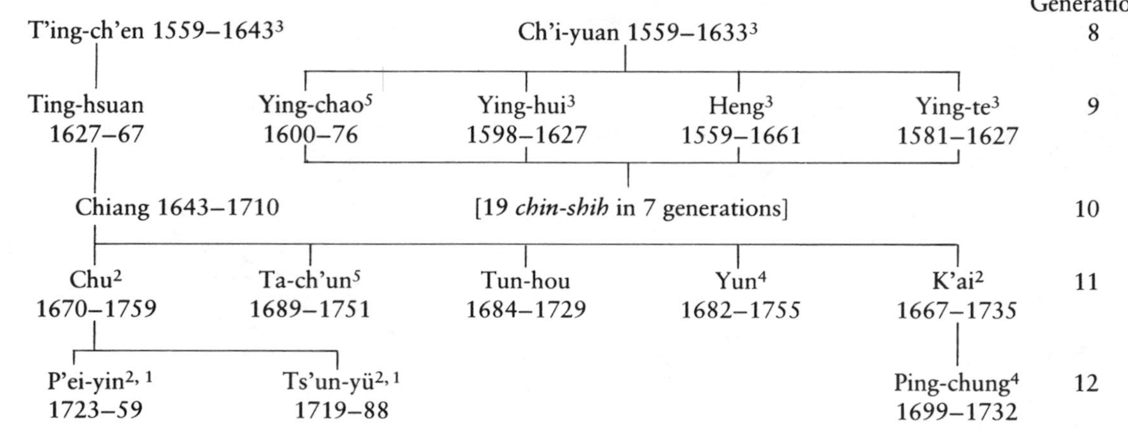

Key: [1] Grand secretary
[2] Hanlin academician
[3] *Chin-shih*
[4] *Chü-jen*
[5] *Fu-pang*: supplemental *Chü-jen*

Fig. 6. The Second Branch of the Chuangs in Ch'ang-chou during the Late Ming and Early Ch'ing

ch'eng Academy in Wu-chin from repressive government policies against private academies.

Peasant and bond servant rebellions in the Yangtze Delta, and the resulting pressure to reform, continued, however. Beginning around 1611, provincial leaders simultaneously instituted tax relief in Su-chou, Sung-chiang, and Ch'ang-chou. These were the "big three" (Su-Sung-Ch'ang) prefectures in the Lower Yangtze, where agricultural commercialization and market specialization were most advanced. These reform efforts continued into the 1630s, which indicates that there was substantial entrenched gentry opposition to any curtailment of their privileged tax status.

Provincial and county pressure to institute a system of "equal labor for equal fields" was more successful in Ch'ang-chou Prefecture than in neighboring Su-chou and Sung-chiang. Hamashima Atsutoshi attributes Ch'ang-chou's relative success to the influence of Tung-lin supporters in Wu-hsi and Wu-chin counties. The gentry landlords there, such as Ku Hsien-ch'eng and Kao P'an-lung, maintained more enlightened views than their peers elsewhere in the Yangtze Delta–Lake T'ai area. We should also recall that the leaders in the T'ang, and by implication the Chuang, lineage responded to the exploitive behavior of late Ming gentry by discouraging excesses among their kin and by putting their weight behind tax reform.[13]

Within this context, it is interesting that Chuang Ts'un-yü's great-great-great-grandfather Chuang T'ing-ch'en (fig. 6), who rose to a high position in the Ministry of Rites, had opposed proposals to establish shrines throughout China honoring Wei Chung-hsien, the eunuch-confidant of the T'ien-ch'i Emperor and archenemy of the Tung-lin school. When asked to lend his calligraphic hand to composing script for the engraved monuments of such shrines, Chuang T'ing-ch'en refused. Moreover, in his last years, just before the fall of Peking to the Manchus in 1644, T'ing-ch'en had been involved in the activities of the Lung-ch'eng Academy in Wu-chin County and the Su-chou-based Fu She movement, which had tried to keep the reformist policies and statecraft goals of the Tung-lin partisans alive.

Members of closely related lines in the Chuang lineage joined T'ing-ch'en in participating in the emerging political societies of the late Ming. Although no evidence points to the direct participation of any

13. Hamashima, *Mindai Kōnan*, pp. 434–35, 486–89, 499–501. See also Goodrich et al., eds., *Dictionary of Ming Biography*, p. 503, and Beattie, "Alternative to Resistance," p. 249. Cf. Mori, "The Gentry," pp. 49–51.

members of the Chuang lineage in the meetings of the Tung-lin partisans in Wu-hsi and elsewhere in Ch'ang-chou Prefecture (Wu-chin, 1609; I-hsing, 1610), it is clear that Chuang T'ing-ch'en and others in the lineage knew that by opposing Wei Chung-hsien and his tax extortion they were siding with the Tung-lin party in its dangerous battle with the eunuch's faction at court. Moreover, T'ing-ch'en's son and grandson (Ting-hsuan and Chiang, respectively) refused to serve the Manchu Ch'ing dynasty out of loyalty to the Ming dynasty. It was not until Chuang Chu—T'ing-ch'en's great-grandson and Chuang Ts'un-yü's father—that this segment of the second branch of the Chuang lineage reentered mainstream Confucian politics. Chuang T'ing-ch'en's opposition to Wei Chung-hsien and his participation in the Fu She become clearer when understood in the larger social milieu of Ch'ang-chou lineage relations and affinal ties.[14]

THE CHUANGS AND THE MING-CH'ING TRANSITION

The fall of the Ming dynasty to Manchu barbarians was a bitter experience for Lower Yangtze gentry, although the Manchu triumph, if anything, only enhanced what we are calling "gentry society." Once the winds of dynastic change had blown through, the demise of organizations centering on the Tung-lin and Fu She movements left lineage organizations intact as the major social mechanisms of local control. Local elites in T'ung-ch'eng, An-hui, for example, easily reestablished themselves during the Ch'ing dynasty. In fact, the dislocations wrought by the change of dynasties probably strengthened lineage organization and structure there.

Many of the large corporate lineages in eighteenth-century Kuang-tung Province came into existence only after the dislocations of the mid-seventeenth century. Rubie S. Watson has traced the elaborate "High Ch'ing" lineage organization to the era of prosperity that followed on the heels of the social turmoil of the seventeenth century. The enhanced local power of the Ch'ing elite, organized through higher-order

14. *P'i-ling Chuang-shih tseng-hsiu tsu-p'u* (1935), 12A.2a–4b. See also Wang Hsi-hsun's biography for Chuang Shu-tsu in *Ch'ieh-chu-an wen-chi*, p. 221, which links T'ing-ch'en's opposition to Wei Chung-hsien to Chuang Ts'un-yü's opposition to Ho-shen. Wang also notes that for two generations after T'ing-ch'en, his descendents did not serve the Ch'ing dynasty. On Wei and the shrines see Ulrich Mammitzsch, "Wei Chung-hsien," p. 250.

lineages, dates from, or was substantially expanded in, the late seventeenth and eighteenth centuries.[15]

The Chuang lineage as a whole showed relatively little effect from the wars and economic dislocation brought on by the fall of the south in the 1640s, when invading Manchu armies, whose ranks were swollen with Chinese mercenaries, ended the Ming dynasty. As we have seen, some Chuangs retired to private life out of loyalty to the fallen Ming house. Despite this, the Chuangs (particularly Chuang Ch'i-yuan's line [see fig. 6]) went on in the new dynasty much as they had in the old. How could the Chuangs in Ch'ang-chou have survived relatively intact during the Ming-Ch'ing transition? As in T'ung-ch'eng, An-hui, the mid-seventeenth-century tax rebellions that threatened the elite's financial privileges in Ch'ang-chou forced lineage leaders to make important strategic decisions. To ensure local order and to reestablish their local preeminence, the elite had to accede to the new central power.

Tax reform programs associated with the Single-Whip policy (discussed in chapter 1 as part of the legacy of late Ming reformism) became state policy during the early Ch'ing. Although most of the elite opposed these reform programs during the late Ming, Ch'ang-chou Prefecture, particularly Wu-chin County, had conducted some of the most progressive experiments with tax reforms. As we have seen, the power of the Tung-lin partisans in their home counties meant that in Ch'ang-chou there was a more broadly based recognition among elites that tax reform was necessary.

It is ironic that reform policies advocated in the late Ming by the Tung-lin partisans, among others, were enacted in local society by the Ch'ing dynasty. According to Kawakatsu Mamoru, the Manchus needed to stabilize grain transport to the north, increase tax resources, and come to terms with local gentry influence in order to consolidate conquered territories. The new dynasty therefore undertook various measures, including efforts to equalize land and labor taxes. In addition, in 1657 the regulations for tax exemption were changed abruptly in an effort to curb the excessive tax privileges of the gentry. This change was given political teeth in the well-publicized legal arraignments of selected Yangtze Delta gentry in 1661–62 for back taxes owed

15. For discussion of the fall of the south, see Dennerline, *Chia-ting Loyalists*. On the fall of Chiang-yin see Wakeman, "Localism and Loyalism." See also Struve, *Southern Ming*, pp. 1–14, 167–95; Rubie S. Watson, *Inequality*, pp. 6, 14, 22–24, 34–35, 174; and Beattie, *Land and Lineage*, pp. 44–48, 129, 267. Cf. Ray Huang, *Taxation*, pp. 147, 149; and Twitchett, "Fan Clan's Charitable Estate," pp. 128–29.

the state. The tax cases centered on the three prefectures of Su-chou, Sung-chiang, and Ch'ang-chou.

According to Frederic E. Wakeman, Jr., a compromise was reached between the Chinese landowning elite and the Manchu throne whereby gentry tax exemptions were restricted and Manchu military prerogatives were limited in favor of civilian rule. Reforms that a native Chinese dynasty could not push through because of local opposition were enacted by a conquering foreign dynasty. Problems pertaining to rural society were ameliorated through the force of arms.[16]

In its efforts to carry out tax reform, the Ch'ing state placed reform-minded lineages in a better position vis-à-vis their more conservative competitors to maneuver for local power and position. Lineages, for example, continued to play an important role in tax collection under Manchu rule, and the court relied on local gentry in many cases to effect the "equal service for equal fields" reforms below the county level. In return for such local support, the K'ang-hsi Emperor (r. 1661–1722) reaffirmed imperial support for lineage organizations and for the special tax status for charitable corporate estates.

It was no accident, then, that in Ch'ang-chou Prefecture the Chuang and Liu lineages became increasingly prominent in both local society and national affairs under the new dynasty. They represented local higher-order lineages that quickly renounced Ming loyalism in favor of recognizing and thereby exploiting the new social and political realities in place by the 1660s. Of course, an officially patronized elite family gained prestige within a kinship group over lower levels in its own network. In the process, kinship solidarity mitigated the taxing power of the state and helped keep landholding profitable. At the same time, traditional gentry prerogatives in local society were maintained in modified form.[17]

After the Ming debacle lineage members had to track down the lineage's scattered members and to recompile genealogies. Land left vacant had to be recovered and placed under new, more reliable management. By 1651 the Chuangs had completed the revision of their genealogy, and thereafter the most successful segments of the lineage continued their remarkable rise to local and national preeminence. The

16. Mori, "The Gentry," pp. 52–53; Kessler, *K'ang-hsi*, pp. 33–39; and Wakeman, "Seventeenth-Century Crisis," p. 16. See also Kawakatsu, *Chūgoku hōken kokka*, pp. 576–77; Beattie, "Alternative to Resistance," p. 263; and Meng, *Ming-Ch'ing-shih lun-chu chi-k'an*, pp. 434–52.

17. Hsieh, *Ming-mo Ch'ing-ch'u te hsueh-feng*, pp. 79–80, discusses the modus vivendi reached between Manchu conquerors and Chinese landowners.

Chuangs soon became an elite lineage that fully accepted and thrived under the alien central government in Peking.

Two lines within the second branch, which emanated from Chuang T'ing-ch'en and Chuang Ch'i-yuan respectively (both became *chin-shih* in 1610) became so prominent during Ch'ing times that they can only be described as a literati factory for producing *chin-shih* degree-holders (see fig. 6). Chuang Ch'i-yuan's line produced nineteen *chin-shih* in seven generations, including three of his four sons. Nearly as productive was Chuang T'ing-ch'en's line, which produced Chuang Ts'un-yü in its eighth generation (counting from Chuang Hsiu-chiu).[18]

Charitable estates remained in a privileged tax position after the tax cases of 1661–62. Lineage trusts helped keep scattered properties under unified control and protected those who shared in the trust from the inequities of the tax system. Such arrangements lasted into the middle of the eighteenth century, when abuse of lineage tax privileges again became a cause for concern. In 1756, for example, Chuang Yu-kung—then governor of Chiang-su Province in Su-chou—memorialized the throne concerning the sale of charitable estates by unscrupulous descendents. What disturbed Chuang Yu-kung was that the ideal of charitable land, which the state wholly supported, was being compromised. Chuang urged the Ch'ien-lung Emperor to harshly punish those who would manipulate lineage trusts for their private profit.[19]

Chuang Yu-kung, although not in the direct lines of descent of the four branches of the Ch'ang-chou Chuang lineage, represented a Chuang constituency in Kuang-chou that developed clan (that is, artificial kinship ties) relations with their Ch'ang-chou namesakes in the early seventeenth century. The Kuang-chou group traced its roots from southeast China (Fu-chien and Kuang-tung) back to Ch'ang-chou. By the 1750s Chuang Yu-kung and Chuang Ts'un-yü, representing their respective lineages, had reached the highest echelons of political power in the state. While Yu-kung served in Su-chou as governor (his jurisdiction included Ch'ang-chou Prefecture), Ts'un-yü in 1756 was academician of the Grand Secretariat (*nei-ko hsueh-shih*) in the inner court. The Chuangs' Ch'ang-chou genealogy was then undergoing revision for its third edition, and Chuang Ts'un-yü prevailed upon Chuang Yu-kung as a Kuang-chou namesake to contribute a preface for it.

18. *Chu-chi Chuang-shih tsung-p'u* (1883), 8.9b–10b, 8.14b–16a, 8.20b–21a.

19. Chuang Yu-kung's memorial appears in *Huang-Ch'ing ming-ch'en tsou-i*, 50.18a–21a.

Published in 1761, Yu-kung's preface appealed to kinship solidarity as the basis for social order. When seen in the context of the sale of corporate land by profit-seeking opportunists, Yu-kung's preface underscores the importance of kinship ideals to the Chuangs, as public officials and lineage members. The betrayal of such ideals, said Yu-kung, warranted harsh punishment.[20]

The emperor eventually responded to the growing exploitation of kinship privileges. In a 1764 edict, for example, he decreed that only those lineage properties with legitimate ritual and relief functions could be incorporated as trusts and receive special tax status. Efforts to close the tax loophole did not challenge the belief that charitable estates, when properly organized for the sake of kin, provided legitimate protection from the tax system. The emperor noted:

> In order to give importance to kinship groups and to cultivate affectionate feelings among their members, people established ancestral halls to perform annual sacrificial rites. If indeed these halls are located in native villages or cities inhabited by kinsmen, all of whom are blood relatives of the same lineages, [these halls] are not only permitted by law but are encouraged as constituting a good custom.[21]

The steady rise to prominence of the Chuang lineage in Ch'ang-chou provides a window on the long-term social and economic changes we have presented. Through farsighted lineage strategies, gentry interests dealt successfully both with the crises in late Ming rural society in the Yangtze Delta and with the Manchu triumph in south China in the mid-seventeenth century. The success of the Chuang lineage in surviving the Ming-Ch'ing transition and in increasing its prominence both in Ch'ang-chou and in Peking's elite bureaucratic circles during the Ch'ing dynasty suggests that kinship strategies during the seventeenth century played a significant role in defending elite interests in local society.

THE CHUANGS AS A PROFESSIONAL ELITE

During the Ch'ing dynasty the Chuang lineage became the most important intellectual force (if success is measured by achievement in the im-

20. *P'i-ling Chuang-shih tseng-hsiu tsu-p'u* (1935), pp. 2a–2b (table of contents). See also *Ch'ing-tai chih-kuan nien-piao*, vol. 2, pp. 975, 1414.

21. *Ta-Ch'ing hui-tien shih-li*, 399.3b. On the Ch'ien-lung Emperor's reaction to lineage excesses, see Hsiao, *Rural China*, pp. 348–57, where portions of the 1764 edict are translated.

perial civil service examinations) in the prefectural capital of Ch'ang-chou. For the Ch'ing period alone, the Chuang lineage had a total of ninety-seven degree holders, compared with a total of seven during the Ming dynasty. The lineage was accorded the further honor of twenty-nine *chin-shih*, compared with only six during the Ming, earning eleven places on the Hanlin Academy. Five of the latter came from Chuang Ts'un-yü's immediate family. From 1644 until 1795 a total of thirty-four Hanlin academicians came from Wu-chin County. Nine of these (26 percent) were from the Chuang lineage, and four (12 percent) from Ts'un-yü's line.[22]

In three generations, from his father to his sons, Ts'un-yü's family produced eight *chin-shih* and four *chü-jen*. In six generations, beginning in the late Ming, the line had nine *chin-shih*. Using Ping-ti Ho's figures for the total number of *chin-shih* in Ch'ang-chou Prefecture during Ch'ing times (618), we find that the Chuangs received 4.7 percent of that total. If the combined figures for Wu-chin and Yang-hu counties (the latter was separated from Wu-chin in 1724) are used (265), then the Chuang lineage accounted for more than 11 percent of the total number of *chin-shih* there during the Ch'ing dynasty.[23]

An inordinate number of this line in successive generations were appointed to the Hanlin Academy, the highest academic honor that could be conferred on successful *chin-shih* examination candidates and the ticket to high office (fig. 7). Chuang Ts'un-yü's father, Chuang Chu, and uncle Chuang K'ai were so appointed, as were Ts'un-yü and his younger brother P'ei-yin—the latter *optimus* (*chuang-yuan*) on the 1754 palace examination. Ts'un-yü had had the distinction of achieving *secundus* (*pang-yen*) on the 1745 palace examination. This remarkable run continued when Ts'un-yü's son, T'ung-min, finished near the head of the palace examination of 1772 and was also appointed to the Hanlin Academy. Another son, Hsuan-ch'en, finished high on the 1778 palace examination. Chuang P'ei-yin's son, Shu-tsu, passed the palace examination in 1780, and Ts'un-yü's great-great-great-nephew Shou-ch'i was also appointed to the Hanlin Academy in 1840.[24]

22. See *P'i-ling Chuang-shih tseng-hsiu tsu-p'u* (1935), 9.1a–8a, especially 9.19b–20a, for a list of all members of the Chuang lineage who were successful on the examination system. A list of Hanlin academicians from the lineage is also included. Cf. Lui, *Hanlin Academy*, pp. 132–33. Figures include those for Yang-hu County, which was separated from Wu-chin County in 1724.

23. Ping-ti Ho, *Ladder of Success*, pp. 247, 254.

24. On the Hanlin Academy, see Lui, *Hanlin Academy*.

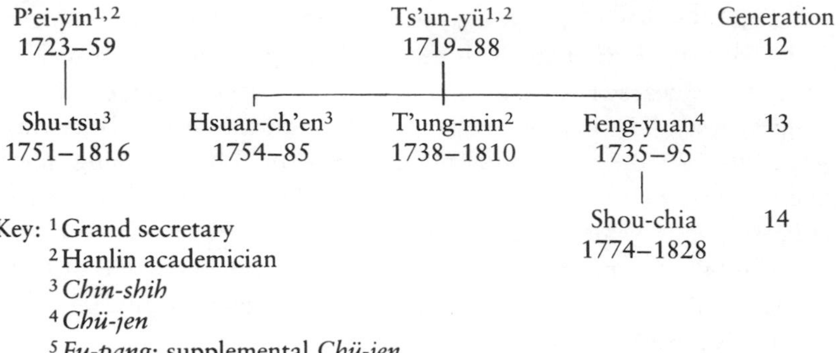

Fig. 7. Major Segments of the Second Branch of the Chuang Lineage in Ch'ang-chou during the Ch'ing Dynasty

SUCCESS IN THE IMPERIAL BUREAUCRACY

Interestingly, the Chuang's success at the Hanlin Academy became a crucial feature of their rise to national prominence. After placement in the Hanlin Academy, a member of the academy could normally expect an appointment in the Ministry of Rites as the logical next step in his career. Although the name "Ministry of Rites" sounds peripheral, in imperial China its ministers and functionaries were on center stage. The Bureau of Ceremonies, for example, was charged, as its name suggests, with all ceremonial affairs, which included administration of the National university (*Kuo-tzu chien*) system, as well as supervision of the nationwide civil service examination system from the county, prefecture, and provincial levels to the national level in Peking. Hence the Ministry of Rites controlled the imperial education system. In addition, the Bureau of Receptions (*Chu-k'e ch'ing-li-ssu*) was charged with the management of foreign relations under the traditional tributary system in effect since the Han dynasties.

In other words, the Ministry of Rites had as its portfolio two major functions of government: education and foreign affairs. Confucian classical training, inculcated through the rigorous examination system, was applied in the arena of foreign affairs. Hanlin academicians had priority in appointments dealing with these aspects of government.

By taking care of both imperial sacrifices in the Bureau of Sacrifices (*Tz'u ch'ing-li-ssu*) and imperial family matters in the Imperial Clan Court (*Tsung-jen fu*) under the Bureau of Ceremonies, the Ministry of

Rites had the further distinction of being the only ministry that was a member of the inner court of the emperor while remaining a full-fledged member of the outer court bureaucracy. It thus had access to the inner sanctum of imperial power and could effect its policies through the education bureaucracy down to all county levels outside Peking.[25]

Important members of the inner court during the Ch'ing dynasties came from the Hanlin Academy, the Grand Secretariat (*Nei-ko*), and the Grand Council (*Chün-chi-ch'u*). After the first Ming emperor Chu Yuan-chang had reduced the power of the state bureaucracy by doing away with all key leadership posts in the bureaucracy, personal secretaries to the emperor, known as "grand secretaries" (*Ta-hsueh-shih*) increasingly took on the job of coordinating and supervising the six ministries. Because it straddled the middle ground between inner and outer echelons of power, the Ministry of Rites became more and more important.

When later Ming emperors, particularly during the sixteenth and seventeenth centuries, delegated much of their authority to members of the inner court, the links between grand secretaries and the Ministry of Rites became more intimate, and produced career patterns of major political and institutional consequences, not only for the Ming but also for the Ch'ing bureaucratic system. The doyen of the Ch'ang-chou New Text school of Confucianism, Chuang Ts'un-yü, exemplified this trend in the eighteenth century. This is to say that the Ministry of Rites provided more grand secretaries than any other ministry. Close links between the Ministry of Rites and Grand Secretariat had another distinctive feature: most grand secretaries had also been members of the Hanlin Academy early in their official careers. Out of a total of 165 grand secretaries during the Ming, 124 (75 percent) had been members of the Hanlin Academy.[26]

Moreover, 109 out of these 165 grand secretaries (66 percent) had also served in the Ministry of Rites, and 93 of the latter (56 percent of 165) went directly from the Ministry of Rites to the Grand Secretariat. What we see emerging in Ming political life is the remarkable convergence of the Hanlin Academy, Ministry of Rites, and Grand Secretariat. In a typical Ming-Ch'ing bureaucratic career, then, a successful graduate (normally with high honors) of the capital examination (*chin-shih*)

25. Yun-yi Ho, *Ministry of Rites*, pp. 60–75.

26. Von der Sprenkel, "High Officials of the Ming," pp. 98–99. See also Ho, *Ministry of Rites*, p. 16, and Ku, "Career Mobility Patterns."

was first appointed to the Hanlin Academy, where he served the court as a compiler or editor, or as a personal secretary to the emperor. From there he went on to serve in a variety of possible positions but eventually became a fixture in the Ministry of Rites, often as a capital or provincial examination official supervising the examination system.

The Ministry of Rites, then, served as a springboard for promotion to the Grand Secretariat, which until the emergence of the Grand Council remained the highest advisory body in the state apparatus. Those who spoke for the state in the name of the emperor were, for the most part, the top-ranking graduates of the highest-level examinations. The latter had served initially as apprentices in the proximity of the emperor through placement in the Hanlin Academy and Ministry of Rites.[27]

CULTURAL RESOURCES AND POLITICAL PRESTIGE

Such highly placed members within the lineage meant that Ts'un-yü's family assumed a leadership role in the lineage from the late Ming until the late Ch'ing—a period of three centuries. Because only the wealthy and classically literate segments were responsible for lineage ritual and worship, ordinary members would not be directly involved in managing ancestral halls, organizing rituals, or allocating funds derived from charitable estates. The eminence of Ts'un-yü's family line thus overrode considerations of seniority. Within its own segment, Ts'un-yü's line brought its national and local prestige and influence to bear on its position as gentry spokesmen for the Chuangs in the Ch'ang-chou social and cultural world. In effect, the Chuangs became a "professional elite" of office-holding families, specializing in government service for generations.[28]

Of the four branches of Ch'ang-chou Chuangs, the second had superior prestige vis-à-vis the other three, but not seniority. The two lines emanating from Chuang T'ing-ch'en and Chuang Ch'i-yuan were clearly dominant within the second branch. When, for example, Chuang Ts'un-yü served concurrently in the Hanlin Academy, Ministry of Rites, and Grand Secretariat in the Peking imperial establishment, he became a local figure of immense prestige in his place of birth—prestige that accrued to his family, branch, and lineage in Ch'ang-chou.[29]

27. Ho, *Ministry of Rites*, pp. 16–19. See also Lui, *Hanlin Academy*, pp. 29–44.
28. Hartwell, "Demographic Transformations of China," pp. 405–25.
29. Freedman, *Lineage Organization*, pp. 67, 69; Rubie S. Watson, *Inequality*, p. 27; and James L. Watson, "Chinese Kinship Reconsidered," pp. 608–12.

The unparalleled academic success of the Chuang lineage in the imperial examination system can be directly tied to its private lineage school, known as the Tung-p'o Academy. The school was named after the great Sung dynasty Confucian and man of letters Su Shih, who had visited Ch'ang-chou during his travels through south China. Su purchased property in Ch'ang-chou and had hoped to retire there. In fact, he died in Ch'ang-chou after being recalled from exile on Hainan Island.

Success on the examination system required a classical education. A rich and prestigious lineage could nearly assure such success by pooling its resources, establishing a school, and hiring qualified teachers. Coming from a family in a lineage with a strong tradition of scholarship, coupled with sufficient financial resources to pay for the protracted education in the Confucian Classics, Chuang Ts'un-yü and his family were blessed with rare advantages.

Among elite lineages in the Lower Yangtze, however, private lineage schools were common enough. The phenomenal success of the Chuang lineage on the examinations most likely points to the quality of its private preparation course and curriculum; the Chuang lineage school was probably more rigorous and demanding than similar schools in Ch'ang-chou and elsewhere. In addition, the Chuangs had become so well placed in local and national affairs as a result of earlier examination success and affinal relations that success, tinged with favoritism, fed on success.[30]

Not only males but also females, who stood outside the patrilineal system of descent, benefited from the educational facilities provided by wealthy lineages in traditional Chinese society. Lacking freedom of movement and barred from the official examinations and any possibility of holding political office, women in scholarly families were nonetheless often well-versed in literature and the arts. The Chuang lineage in Ch'ang-chou, by way of example, was famous for its female poets.

Including women who married into the lineage, Hsu K'o has counted twenty-two female poets of note from the Chuang lineage during the Ch'ing dynasty. Among these were Chuang Ts'un-yü's second daughter and Chuang P'an-chu, who was perhaps the best-known female poet from the area in the eighteenth century. The important function of poetry and the arts in gentry cultural life allowed both men and

30. On lineage schools see Rawski, *Education and Popular Literacy*, pp. 28–32, 85–88. On Su Shih see Hatch's biography in *Sung Biographies*, vol. 2, pp. 954, 966–67.

women from prestigious lineages to spend their leisure moments in aesthetic pursuits.[31]

It was in the interest of a lineage and its long-term mobility strategies to provide facilities for the education of its talented members. Thus, the Chuangs, like most powerful lineages, guarded their scholarly traditions very carefully. Success of lineages often hinged on success in the examination system more than anything else. Philanthropic and charitable aspects of higher-order lineages, however, frequently meant that such private strategies for education were also complemented by more public-minded concerns, which derived from the public rhetoric used by kinship groups to legitimate their local activities.

For instance, outsiders such as the Han Learning scholar Hung Liang-chi were occasionally permitted, as young men, to study briefly with the Chuangs. With the death of his father, Hung, then only six years old, and his mother (née Chiang) were left very poor in Ch'ang-chou. One of his teachers at his mother's lineage school came from the Chuang lineage. In addition, Hung's mother had a sister who had married into the Chuang lineage. These links enabled Hung to study with several Chuang children his own age. So, in 1762 Hung was busy reading both the *Kung-yang* and *Ku-liang* commentaries to the *Spring and Autumn Annals* in the Chuang lineage school. Hung Liang-chi's eldest son later married a woman from the Chuang lineage, the daughter of Chuang Yun, a descendent in Chuang Ch'i-yuan's prestigious line.[32]

Another Ch'ang-chou native who benefited from Chuang lineage largesse was the *k'ao-cheng* historian Chao I. In his biography for Chuang Ch'ien written after Chao had gone on to fame and fortune in the Hanlin Academy after passing the *chin-shih* examination of 1761, Chao wrote of the help he had received from the Chuangs to further his studies. Chao I's granddaughter later married into the Chuang lineage.

Similarly, Liu Feng-lu, whose family and lineage had long been affinally tied to the Chuangs (see below), also received help in his early studies from the Chuang lineage. Because his mother, Chuang T'ai-kung, was a typically well educated Chuang woman, daughter of Chuang Ts'un-yü, Liu was permitted to study with the Chuangs. At an early age, he impressed his grandfather with his abilities in classical

31. Hsu, *Ch'ing-pai lei-ch'ao*, 70/162. See also Rubie S. Watson, *Inequality*, p. 134; Chang, "Ch'ing-tai Ch'ang-chou tz'u-p'ai yü tz'u-jen," p. 134.

32. Hung, *Hung Pei-chiang ch'üan-chi*, pp. 2b, 5a–5b. See also Hung's epitaph for his aunt in *P'i-ling Chuang-shih tseng-hsiu tsu-p'u* (1935), 13.13b–14a, in which he notes that his aunt frequently took him to the Chuang lineage school. Cf. the 1935 genealogy, ibid., 18B.38b, and 19.26, and *Chu-chi Chuang-shih tsung-p'u* (1883), 7A.17b.

studies. In this manner, the Chuang lineage could demonstrate that it was fulfilling its public obligations to the larger community while at the same time benefiting kin.[33]

Lineage schools, particularly high-powered ones, were therefore schools in both the institutional and scholarly sense. The Chuang "school" represented a tradition of learning passed down within the lineage itself by its distinguished members and examination graduates. The special theories or techniques of a master, passed down through generations of disciples by personal teaching (which usually demarcated a "school"), could take place in a conducive social and institutional setting provided by a dominant agnatic descent group. The Ch'ang-chou New Text "school" was actually an eighteenth-century version of the Chuang tradition in classical learning, a tradition that drew on the distinguished place held by the Chuang lineage in Ch'ang-chou society since the seventeenth century.

AFFINAL RELATIONS: THE LIUS AND THE CHUANGS

As formidable as the Chuang lineage had become by the eighteenth century, its strength and influence was not based on kinship solidarity alone. Marriage strategies and descent were both used by elite households to serve their larger social and political ends. Alliance with other powerful families and lineages complemented kinship solidarity. The Chuangs thus developed close external affinal ties with the Liu lineage in Ch'ang-chou. Although prominent scholar-officials often preferred to build social networks based on more than local kinship, lineage organization, particularly through affinal ties, nevertheless remained a prominent feature in elite life. In the cases of the Chuangs and Lius, we can see how broader national level networks overlapped with local level lineage organizations and their interrelation in national and local politics.[34]

Unlike the Chuangs—whose migration to the Yangtze Delta can be

33. See *P'i-ling Chuang-shih tseng-hsiu tsu-p'u* (1935), 18B.39a, and *Chu-chi Chuang-shih tsung-p'u* (1883), *ts'e* 10, pp. 25a–26b. Liu Feng-lu's mother wrote a collection of poetry and took charge of her son's early literary training. See *Wu-chin Hsi-ying Liu-shih chia-p'u* (1929), 8.14a.

34. James L. Watson, "Chinese Kinship Reconsidered," pp. 616–17. See also Ebrey, "Early Stages," p. 40n, and Hymes, "Marriage in Sung and Yuan Fu-chou," pp. 95–96 (both articles are published in Ebrey and Watson, eds., *Kinship Organization*). Hymes cautions against overly contrasting strategies of alliance and descent. Cf. Dennerline, *Chia-ting Loyalists*, pp. 104–11, 113, for different views.

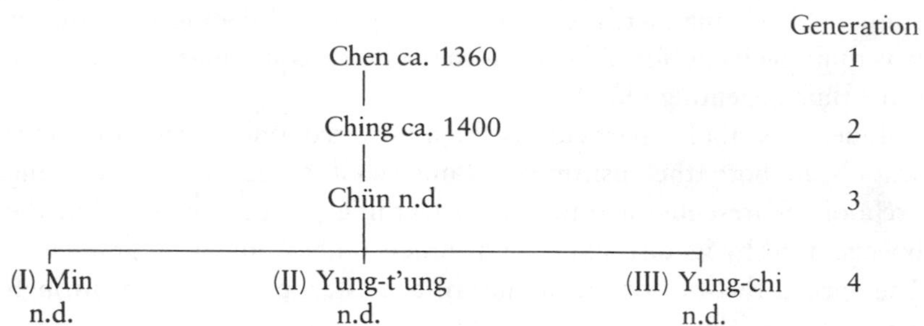

Fig. 8. Major Segments of the Liu Lineage in Ch'ang-chou during the Ming Dynasty

traced to the twelfth-century advances of the Jurchen forces in north China—the Lius traced their origins in Ch'ang-chou to the mid-fourteenth century and the social and political convulsions that overtook the Lower Yangtze when rebel forces rose against Mongol rule. Contending armies struggled against Mongol forces and among themselves for control of the lucrative resources of the Mongol empire's richest region. One of these armies, led by Chu Yuan-chang, succeeded in establishing the Ming dynasty in Nan-ching in 1368.

Liu Chen, a native of the northern town of Feng-yang in He-nan Province, arrived in Ch'ang-chou Prefecture in 1356 in the service of one of the armies allied with Chu Yuan-chang. After aiding in the pacification of Ch'ang-chou, Liu stayed on for a decade, marrying and raising a son, Liu Ching. In 1366–67, Liu Chen left Ch'ang-chou to participate in military campaigns in Shan-hsi, leaving behind his son, who remained in Ch'ang-chou and transmitted the Liu family line in local society there. Although a military epochal ancestor for the Lius, Liu Chen never returned to Ch'ang-chou. Later investigations by the Lius in Ch'ang-chou revealed that Liu Chen had established yet another Liu family in Ta-t'ung, Shan-hsi, after he left Ch'ang-chou (fig. 8).[35]

Liu Ching passed the provincial *chü-jen* examination in 1400 and served as a county magistrate during the early fifteenth century, bringing the Lius to prominence in Ch'ang-chou society. His son, Liu Chün in turn became the chief ancestor for the three major branches of the Liu lineage in Ch'ang-chou, and the lineage became increasingly important in the late Ming. By comparison to the T'ang and Chuang lineages,

35. *Wu-chin Hsi-ying Liu-shih chia-p'u* (1929), 1.13a, 3.1a, and *Hsi-ying Liu-shih chia-p'u* (1792), 2.1a–b.

however, the Lius were relative newcomers in Ch'ang-chou. They did not become prominent in elite local circles until, in the eighth and ninth generations, the first and second branches produced a distinguished crop of scholar-officials.

In the eighth generation, Liu Ch'un-jen, of the main branch (*ta-fen*), became the first of the lineage to pass the national *chin-shih* examination, finishing eighteenth in the competition of 1592. Liu Ch'un-jen's sons, along with those of his younger brother Ch'un-ching (direct ancestor of Liu Feng-lu), counted among their ranks two *chin-shih*, one *chü-jen*, and two tribute students (*kung-sheng*; nominees of local schools for advanced study and subsequent admission to the civil service). The ninth generation was conspicuous for producing three imperial censors (*yü-shih*) during the late Ming: Liu Kuang-tou (son of Liu Ch'un-ching); Liu Hsi-tso (son of Liu Ch'un-jen); and Liu Hsien-chang (son of Liu K'e-ch'ang), a member of the second branch of the lineage (fig. 9).[36]

Liu Hsien-chang, for example, had taken his *chin-shih* degree in 1637 and was politically active in the late Ming, participating in the meetings of the Fu She activists. Liu Hsi-tso, in addition to his government service, had begun a pattern of marriage alliances with the Chuangs in Ch'ang-chou by marrying his daughter to Chuang Yin (1638–78), son of Chuang Ying-chao in the prominent ninth generation of the second branch of the Chuangs (see list). Hsi-tso's younger brother, Liu Yung-tso, was among those who participated in the Tung-lin movement. The intermarriages continued as follows (generation number is in brackets):

Liu	*Chuang*
Hsi-tso's [9] daughter	m. Yin [10]
I-k'uei [10]	m. daughter of Yu-yun [10]
Lü-hsuan's [10] daughter	m. Tou-wei [12]
Yü-i's [11] mother	née Chuang
Wei-ning's [11] daughter	m. Pien [11]
Hsueh-sun [13]	m. daughter of Ch'u-pao [13]
Hsing-wei's [14] daughter	m. Fu-tan [15]

36. *Wu-chin Yang-hu hsien ho-chih* (1886), 17.44a. See also *Hsi-ying Liu-shih chia-p'u* (1876), 8.18a, 8.33a.

Lun's [14] son	m. daughter of Ts'un-yü [12]
Lun's [14] granddaughter	m. Ch'eng-sui [14]
Chung-chih's [15] granddaughter	m. Ch'ien [16]
Chao-yang's [15] daughter	m. Ch'eng [15]

Another important member of the pivotal ninth generation of the Lius (in the second branch) was Liu Han-ch'ing, who took his *chü-jen* degree in 1642 and became a *chin-shih* in 1649. Before his death, Liu Han-ch'ing compiled the first genealogical record of the Liu lineage, which was completed in 1689. Six subsequent revisions were made in 1693, 1750, 1792, 1855, 1876, and 1929. Han-ch'ing's son, Liu I-k'uei, married the eldest daughter of Chuang Yu-yun, who was Chuang Ying-chao's eldest son. We should add that Han-ch'ing's great-uncle Liu Ying-ch'ao earlier had arranged for a marriage between his eldest daughter and Chuang Heng, Chuang Ying-chao's elder brother. Thus, by the early Ch'ing dynasty, the seventh and eighth generations of the Lius and the ninth and tenth generations of the Chuangs had developed close marriage ties.[37]

Liu Kuang-tou, in the main branch of the lineage, passed the *chü-jen* examination in 1624 (fig. 10). The following year he took the *chin-shih* degree in Peking. Involved in the up and down, factional nature of late Ming politics during the Tung-lin party's efforts to gain control of the imperial bureaucracy, Liu was appointed imperial censor, subsequently dismissed, and then reappointed as censor during a period of extreme bureaucratic corruption. Kuang-tou's examination success and high office—as important as they were in promoting his official career and the fortunes of the Liu lineage during the late Ming—were overshadowed by his remarkable behavior when Manchu armies, filled with Chinese mercenaries, launched their invasion of Ch'ang-chou in 1645.[38]

As a Ming dynasty censor, Liu Kuang-tou was bound by traditions of loyalty to the dynasty he served. The generation of 1644, which witnessed the demise of a native Chinese dynasty, had an established

37. *Hsi-ying Liu-shih chia-p'u* (1792), 2.1a–13a, 4.1a–2a, 4.14a–14b; (1876), 1.36b, 2.1a–2b, 4.1a–2a; *Chu-chi Chuang-shih tsung-p'u* (1883), 5.34b, 5.43a–44b, 5.46b–47a; and *Wu-chin Chuang-shih tseng-hsiu tsu-p'u* (1840), 3.20b. See also Chuang Chu, *P'i-ling k'e-ti k'ao*, 1.17b, 8.33a. Cf. Chin Jih-sheng, *Sung-t'ien lu-pi, ts'e* 1, p. 14a; *Wu-chin Yang-hu hsien ho-chih* (1886), 24.48b–49a; and Crawford, "Juan Ta-ch'eng."

38. *Hsi-ying Liu-shih chia-p'u* (1792), 2.13a–14a. See also Crawford, "Juan Ta-ch'eng," p. 42.

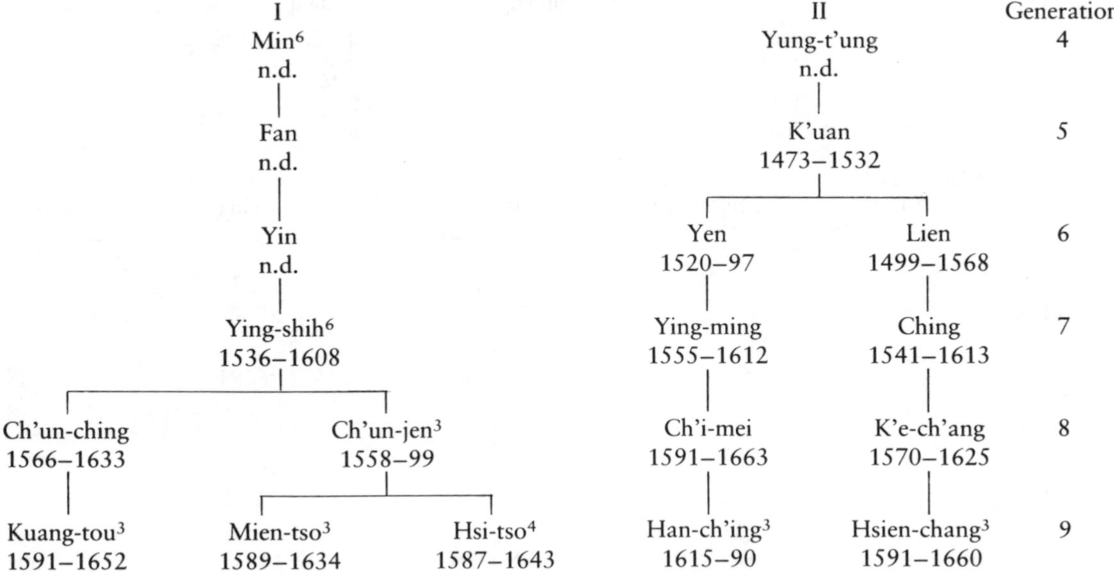

Key: [1] Grand secretary
[2] Hanlin academician
[3] *Chin-shih*
[4] *Chü-jen*
[5] *Fu-pang*: supplemental *Chü-jen*
[6] Tribute student

Fig. 9. Major Segments of the First and Second Branches of the Lius during the Ming Dynasty

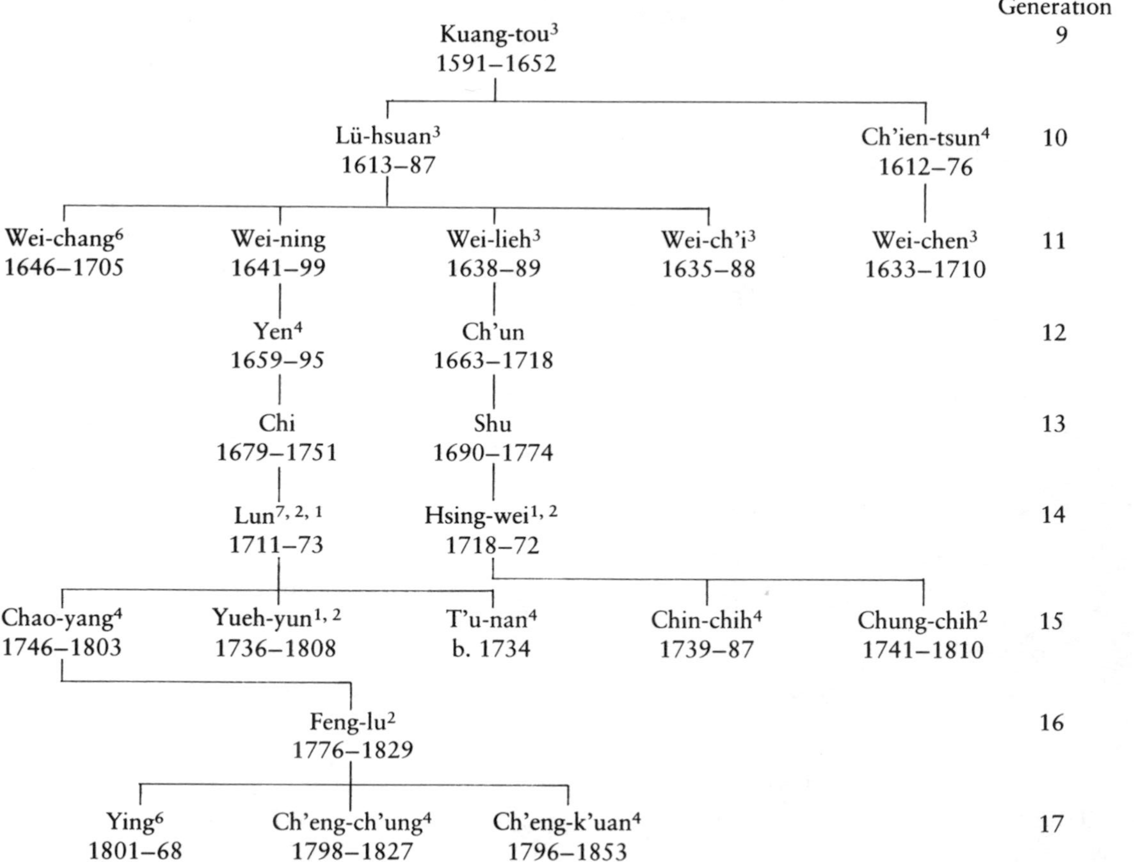
Generation
9
Kuang-tou[3]
1591–1652
10
Lü-hsuan[3]
1613–87
Ch'ien-tsun[4]
1612–76
11
Wei-chang[6]
1646–1705
Wei-ning
1641–99
Wei-lieh[3]
1638–89
Wei-ch'i[3]
1635–88
Wei-chen[3]
1633–1710
12
Yen[4]
1659–95
Ch'un
1663–1718
13
Chi
1679–1751
Shu
1690–1774
14
Lun[7, 2, 1]
1711–73
Hsing-wei[1, 2]
1718–72
15
Chao-yang[4]
1746–1803
Yueh-yun[1, 2]
1736–1808
T'u-nan[4]
b. 1734
Chin-chih[4]
1739–87
Chung-chih[2]
1741–1810
16
Feng-lu[2]
1776–1829
17
Ying[6]
1801–68
Ch'eng-ch'ung[4]
1798–1827
Ch'eng-k'uan[4]
1796–1853

Key: [1] Grand secretary
[2] Hanlin academician
[3] *Chin-shih*
[4] *Chü-jen*
[5] *Fu-pang*: supplemental *Chü-jen*
[6] Tribute student
[7] Grand counselor

Fig. 10. Major Segment of the Main Branch of the Liu Lineage during the Ch'ing Dynasty

ideology of "not being a servant of two dynasties" (*pu erh-ch'en*). This ideology forbade an official—even a subject—in one dynasty to serve in another. Ming loyalists, who remained influential for the remainder of the seventeenth century, expressed their dissent through the Confucian imperative of loyalty.[39]

In contrast to celebrated Yangtze Delta Ming loyalists such as Ku Yen-wu and Huang Tsung-hsi, however, Liu Kuang-tou was among the first Confucian officials in the Lower Yangtze to urge submission to the conquering Manchus. Unlike the grandson (Liu Ch'ao-chien) of his cousin Liu Hsi-tso, who went into seclusion after the Ming collapse in south China, Liu Kuang-tou urged the surrender of the Chiang-yin county seat in Ch'ang-chou Prefecture, which became, along with Yang-chou and Chia-ting, a symbol of Ming resistance to the invading armies. Chiang-yin loyalists chose instead to hold out. Thousands perished when mercenary armies brutally subdued and sacked the city.

Victimized by late Ming factionalism, Kuang-tou seems to have had few qualms about deserting the Ming banner. Moreover, because Ming loyalist forces labeled him a traitor after the fall of Chiang-yin, Liu was quickly appointed county magistrate in Chiang-yin by Manchu authorities in the Yangtze Delta. Later he served the new Ch'ing dynasty as pacification commissioner (*an-fu shih*) in his home area of Ch'ang-chou Prefecture. It is intriguing that Liu Kuang-tou became associated under Manchu rule with the reform policy of "equal service for equal fields" in Ch'ang-chou, a policy that late Ming reformers had been unable to implement.[40]

Whatever the ethical implications of Kuang-tou's behavior, the Liu lineage in Ch'ang-chou benefited for the duration of the Ch'ing dynasty. Liu Kuang-tou's line in the main branch of the lineage assumed central importance in lineage affairs, and in almost every succeeding generation, the Lius produced a scholar-official of national and local prominence.

Kuang-tou's son, Liu Lü-hsuan, for instance, took his provincial degree in 1642 and passed the capital examination of 1649, surviving the dynastic change barely missing a rung in the bureaucratic ladder of

39. Mote, "Confucian Eremitism."

40. See Wakeman's poignant account of Chiang-yin's fall entitled "Localism and Loyalism," pp. 43–85, esp. p. 54, for a discussion of Liu Kuang-tou. Hamashima, "Mimmatsu Nanchoku no Sō-Sō-Jō sanfu ni okeru kinden kin'eki hō," pp. 106–108, discusses tax reform efforts during the Ming-Ch'ing transition. See also *Wu-chin Yang-hu hsien ho-chih* (1886), 28B.7b, and *Hsi-ying Liu-shih chia-p'u* (1876), 2.27a. Cf. Li T'ien-yu, *Ming-mo Chiang-yin Chia-ting jen-min te k'ang-Ch'ing tou-cheng*, pp. 16–34.

success. Similarly, Liu Han-ch'ing took his *chü-jen* degree in 1642 under Ming dynasty auspices; he had few hesitations in competing, successfully, for *chin-shih* status in 1649 under Manchu jurisdiction. Liu Kuang-tou's reputation as a turncoat and his sons' examination success under two dynasties did not ruin the status of the Lius in local society either. Lü-hsuan gave the hand of his eldest daughter to Chuang Tou-wei, a member of the twelfth generation of the prominent second branch of the Chuangs and grandson of Chuang Ch'i-yuan. Although some Chuangs were Ming loyalists, such matters were of secondary importance in the advancement strategies of the Lius and Chuangs.[41]

Both the Chuangs and Lius had come through the Ming-Ch'ing transition remarkably intact and relatively unaffected by ideological commitments to the fallen Ming dynasty. Only slightly less successful than the Chuangs in the examination system, Liu Kuang-tou's line could count ten *chin-shih* from the ninth through sixteenth generations. There were an additional nine *chü-jen* graduates in generations nine through eighteen. Among these nineteen officials, the Lius could point to five Hanlin academicians, three grand secretaries, and one grand counselor (see fig. 10).

The intermarriage between the two lineages, as we have seen, was already important during the Ming-Ch'ing transition. Arranged marriages were common during the Ch'ing dynasty, no doubt in part to solidify the local position of the Chuangs and Lius as gentry who had switched rather than fought. The high incidence of such intermarriages, from the ninth to fifteenth generations of the Lius and from the tenth to the sixteenth generations of the Chuangs, signals an intimate relation of affines that carried over from Ch'ang-chou local society to the inner sanctum of imperial power in Peking.[42]

In the tenth generation, the main branch of the Liu lineage began to place sons in the upper levels of the imperial bureaucracy. Beginning with the eleventh and twelfth generations, the Lius were honored with Hanlin Academy graduates. By the fourteenth generation, the Lius had "arrived," placing sons of that generation in the Grand Council and Grand Secretariat. They reached the pinnacle of national and local prominence by the middle of the eighteenth century, coinciding almost

41. Chuang, *P'i-ling k'e-ti k'ao*, 8.7a, and *Hsi-ying Liu-shih chia-p'u* (1792), 2.13b–14a; (1876), 4.14a–14b. See also *Wu-chin Yang-hu hsien ho-chih* (1886), 24.84a–84b, *Chu-chi Chuang-shih tsung-p'u* (1883), 7.22b, and *P'i-ling Chuang-shih tseng-hsiu tsu-p'u* (1935), 1.23b, 3.25.

42. Cf. Dennerline, "Marriage, Adoption, and Charity," p. 182.

exactly with the prominence of the Chuangs. Moreover, the key players in the Lius' and Chuangs' dual rise to power had affinal ties of great strategic importance, both for career advancement and as a guarantee for future success of the lineages.[43] The role of the two families from 1740 to 1780 may be summarized as follows (generation number is in brackets):

Chuangs	*Lius*
Ts'un-yü [12] Hanlin Grand Secretariat	Yü-i [11] Grand Secretariat
P'ei-yin [12] Hanlin Grand Council	Lun [14] Hanlin Grand Secretariat Grand Council
Yu-kung (from Kuang-chou) Grand Secretariat Governor-general (Chiang-su)	Hsing-wei [14] Hanlin Grand Secretariat

Liu Yü-i, a *chin-shih* of 1712, was the first Liu from Ch'ang-chou to reach the Grand Secretariat. An eleventh-generation member of the second branch (*erh-fen*) of the Lius, Yü-i served in the Hanlin Academy, where he worked on the Neo-Confucian compendium entitled *Hsing-li ta-ch'üan* (Complete collection on nature and principle) before holding the position of assistant grand secretary from 1744 until 1748. His mother came from the Chuang lineage. Liu Lun and Liu Hsing-wei, cousins in the main branch of the lineage that traced its prominence back to Liu Kuang-tou, took their *chin-shih* degrees in 1736 and 1748 respectively.[44]

Liu Hsing-wei, whose great-grandfather Wei-lieh and great uncles Wei-ch'i and Wei-chen had all been eleventh-generation *chin-shih*, served first in the Hanlin Academy. In 1765 he served as grand secretary in the Imperial Cabinet, along with Chuang Ts'un-yü, who had been a grand secretary (in his second term) since 1762. Liu Hsing-wei's daughter was married into the Chuang lineage when she became the wife of Chuang Fu-tan, who was granted *chü-jen* status on the special

43. *Hsi-ying Liu-shih chia-p'u* (1876), 2.80a–87b.
44. *Ch'ing-tai chih-kuan nien-piao*, vol. 1, pp. 49–51, and *Wu-chin Hsi-ying Liu-shih chia-p'u* (1929), 4.16b.

examination of 1784 administered during the Ch'ien-lung Emperor's last southern tour. In addition, Hsing-wei's son, Liu Chung-chih, was admitted to the Hanlin Academy after passing the *chin-shih* examinations with honors in 1766. Chung-chih's granddaughter married Chuang Ch'ien, another in the prestigious second branch of the Chuang lineage, further cementing affinal ties between the Lius and Chuangs.[45]

Liu Lun's rise to prominence began when he finished first among more than 180 candidates on the special 1736 *po-hsueh hung-tz'u* examination ("broad scholarship and extensive words"; that is, qualifications of distinguished scholars to serve the dynasty) to commemorate the inauguration of the Ch'ien-lung Emperor's reign. Liu was subsequently appointed to the Hanlin Academy where he worked on a successive series of prestigious literary and historical projects, including compilation of the *Veritable Records* (*Shih-lu*) of the preceding K'ang-hsi Emperor.

After serving as Hanlin compiler, Liu Lun's duties shifted from scholarship to politics. He rose to the presidency of a number of ministries after his appointment to the Grand Secretariat from 1746 to 1749. Liu Yü-i was concurrently an assistant grand secretary. In 1750 Lun was promoted to the Grand Council, where he served for much of the remainder of his career. As a grand counselor, Liu Lun was involved with initial efforts in the 1750s to put down the Chin-ch'uan Rebellion.[46]

As a senior colleague of Chuang Ts'un-yü, who served as a grand secretary more or less continuously from 1755 until 1773, Liu Lun presented the Chuangs with an ideal opportunity to strengthen the marriage links between the two lineages. Thus, when Chuang Ts'un-yü's second daughter, née Chuang T'ai-kung, married Liu Lun's youngest son, Liu Chao-yang, it represented a unification of the two most important lines within two extremely powerful higher-order lineages in Ch'ang-chou. Their combined influence extended into the upper echelons of the imperial bureaucracy. For all intents and purposes, the Chuangs and the Lius, via Chuang Ts'un-yü and Liu Lun, had engineered a marriage alliance of remarkable social, political, and intellectual proportions. Liu Lun's second son, Liu Yueh-yun, himself a Hanlin

45. *Ch'ing-tai chih-kuan nien-piao*, vol. 2, p. 981. See also *Chu-chi Chuang-shih tsung-p'u* (1883), 7.36a–37b, and *P'i-ling Chuang-shih tseng-hsiu tsu-p'u* (1935), 18b.38a.

46. See the *Chuan-kao* of Liu Lun, no. 5741. See also *Hsi-ying Liu-shih chia-p'u* (1792), 2.38a–40a; (1876), 2.81a–83b. Cf. *Ch'ing-tai chih-kuan nien-piao*, vol. 1, pp. 138–41, 609–14; vol. 2, pp. 965–68.

academician and grand secretary, would later compose a preface for the 1801 Chuang genealogy.[47]

Counting the Chuangs' twelfth generation and Lius' fourteenth generation as a single one within an affinal framework, we discover, more or less contemporaneously, five Hanlin academicians, four grand secretaries (including assistants), and one grand counselor within this interlineage social formation. Chuang Ts'un-yü and his younger brother, Chuang P'ei-yin, as *secundus* (1745) and *optimus* (1754) respectively on the palace examinations, both served as personal secretaries to the Ch'ien-lung Emperor early in their careers. In overlapping periods, Chuang Ts'un-yü, Liu Lun, and Liu Hsing-wei served in the Grand Council and Grand Secretariat. All three were affinally related.

When we include the clan relations that brought Chuang Yu-kung (see above), a Cantonese and *optimus* on the 1739 palace examination, into kinship ties with the Chuangs in Ch'ang-chou through the efforts of Chuang Ts'un-yü, the picture of powerful Ch'ang-chou lineages well-positioned in mid-eighteenth-century Peking politics is even more compelling. Chuang Yu-kung had served as assistant grand secretary (1746–47), education commissioner for the Lower Yangtze region (*Chiang-nan hsueh-cheng*, 1748, 1750–51), and governor of Chiang-su (1751–56, 1758, 1762–65) and Che-chiang (1759–62) provinces.

We have noted above that Yu-kung's appointment in Su-chou as governor of Chiang-su placed Ch'ang-chou (and the Chuangs) under Chuang Yu-kung's jurisdiction. Lineage interests, cemented through clan association with Yu-kung, could be expected to further, legitimately, the Chuang's position in their home province and prefecture while Yu-kung served there. It was hardly any accident, then, that Chuang Ts'un-yü urged Yu-kung to prepare a preface (dated 1761) for the Chuang genealogy, then being revised. The 1760s and 1770s marked the height of Liu and Chuang political power in the Ch'ien-lung era. The Ho-shen era of the 1780s would force them into careful retreat.[48]

The above account situates the reemergence of New Text Confucianism in Ch'ang-chou during the late eighteenth century within the lineage structures and affinal relations we have described. Liu Chao-yang, who

47. See Freedman, *Chinese Lineage*, pp. 97–104. See also earlier citations from *P'i-ling Chuang-shih tseng-hsiu tsu-p'u* (1935), and *Hsi-ying Liu-shih chia-p'u* (1792 and 1876).

48. *Ch'ing-tai chih-kuan nien-piao*, vol. 1, pp. 138–41, 609–14, 624–32; vol. 2, pp. 974–89.

married T'ai-kung (née Chuang), finished first on the special 1784 *chü-jen* examination administered by the Ch'ien-lung Emperor on the last of his six Grand Canal tours to the Yangtze Delta. The emperor was overjoyed that the son of one of his trusted advisors had done so well. Chuang Fu-tan (see above)—who had married the daughter of Liu Hsing-wei (Chao-yang's immediate uncle)—also passed that examination.

But Liu Chao-yang declined high office and contented himself with the life of a schoolmaster. Compared with his two more distinguished elder brothers—Liu T'u-nan, a 1768 *chü-jen*, and Liu Yueh-yun, a 1766 *chin-shih*, Hanlin academician, and grand secretary—Liu Chao-yang led a scholarly life in the company of his talented wife devoted to poetry, the Classics, mathematics, and medicine. As we shall see in chapter 4, Liu's "contentment" may have been enforced. His brothers' careers in the bureaucracy were cemented before the 1780s, which witnessed the rise of Ho-shen and his corrupt followers to prominence. In 1784, therefore, Liu Chao-yang faced an uncertain political career. His influential father-in-law, Chuang Ts'un-yü, was opposed to Ho-shen but was helpless to break Ho-shen's hold over the aging emperor. His powerful father, Liu Lun, had died in 1773. The Lius and Chuangs now had to tread very carefully in the precincts of imperial power. One wrong move and the cumulative efforts of generations of Lius and Chuangs to further the interests of their kin could be undone by an unscrupulous imperial favorite.

Liu Chao-yang's son, Liu Feng-lu, first studied poetry and the Classics under his mother's direction, before continuing his classical education in the Chuang lineage school. Women had considerable influence with their sons, husbands, and fathers, and were therefore important participants in affinal relations between lineages. Liu Feng-lu's mother, for instance, brought her son to her father, Chuang Ts'un-yü, for instruction at an early age.

Under Ts'un-yü's direction, Liu studied the Classics and other ancient texts before turning to Tung Chung-shu's *Ch'un-ch'iu fan-lu* (The *Spring and Autumn Annals'* radiant dew) and the *Kung-yang Commentary* based on Ho Hsiu's annotations. From his maternal grandfather, he absorbed the "esoteric words and great principles" (*wei-yen ta-i*) that Chuang Ts'un-yü had stressed in his writings and teachings. Ts'un-yü was so pleased with the progress of his precocious grandson that when Liu was still only eleven, Chuang remarked: "this maternal grandson will be the one able to transmit my teachings." The old man, politically defeated in his last years, had toward the end turned to the New Text Classics to salvage a hope of victory over a corrupt age. His grandson would transmit the message to a post–Ho-shen age.[49]

As Chuang Ts'un-yü's major disciple, Liu Feng-lu, represented the culmination of the development of the Ch'ang-chou school. After Feng-lu, New Text Confucianism transcended its geographical origins to become a strong ideological undercurrent through the writings of Kung Tzu-chen and Wei Yuan. Both of the latter studied in Peking in the 1820s under Liu Feng-lu's direction when Liu was serving in the Ministry of Rites.[50]

In the next chapters, we shall begin to analyze the New Text ideas transmitted by Chuang Ts'un-yü and Liu Feng-lu to the Confucian academic world in the late eighteenth and early nineteenth centuries. Here, we will conclude by observing that both Ts'un-yü and Feng-lu drew on their links to the cultural resources of their lineage organizations and interlineage connections in Ch'ang-chou to learn and transmit the set of classical ideas that later would be labeled as the "Ch'ang-chou New Text school." Liu Feng-lu, accordingly, was a product of Chuang lineage traditions that crossed over to the Liu lineage through the affinal relations that had been built up since the Ming-Ch'ing transition.

Although the achievements of the Liu lineage were substantial, the Lius were at a distinct disadvantage when compared with the Chuangs. The Chuangs had a higher level of scholarly achievement, as distinct from mere success in the examination system. Although Grand Counselor Liu Lun had published on a variety of subjects, the Chuangs and their longer tradition of classical scholarship proved to be the model that Liu Feng-lu, through his mother, would choose to follow. The two grandfathers, Liu Lun and Chuang Ts'un-yü, had sired a loyal son of the Liu lineage who would transmit the teachings of the Chuangs.[51]

Consequently, the intellectual direction of the eighteenth-century revival of New Text studies in Ch'ang-chou was indebted to Chuang

49. *Hsi-ying Liu-shih chia-p'u* (1792), 2.39b; (1876), 2.81b–84a, 12.15a-18b, and *Wu-chin Hsi-ying Liu-shih chia-p'u* (1929), 12.19b. See also *Ch'ing-tai chih-kuan nien-piao*, vol. 2, pp. 997–1001, and *Wu-chin Yang-hu hsien ho-chih* (1886), A.26b–27a. Cf. Liu Feng-lu, *Liu Li-pu chi*, 10.25a–26b, on née Chuang T'ai-kung, and Dennerline, "Marriage, Adoption, and Charity," p. 182.

50. See "Shen-shou fu-chün hsing-shu," by Wang Nien-sun (1744–1832), a major figure in the Yang-chou Han Learning tradition, in *Hsi-ying Liu-shih chia-p'u* (1876), 12.55b. See also *Kung Tzu-chen nien-p'u*, p. 603, and Wang Chia-chien, *Wei Yuan nien-p'u*, pp. 30, 33n.

51. For a list of publications by members of the Liu lineage, see *Wu-chin Hsi-ying Liu-shih chia-p'u* (1929), 8.12a–14a. See also Liu Lun, *Liu Wen-ting kung chi*.

and Liu lineage traditions and their affinal relations. During his years under Chuang tutelage, Liu Feng-lu formed close friendships with his cousins Chuang Shou-chia (1774–1828) and Sung Hsiang-feng (1776–1860). Chuang Ts'un-yü's teachings were thus carried on by two grandsons, Chuang Shou-chia and Liu Feng-lu, and a nephew, Sung Hsiang-feng, son of Chuang P'ei-yin's third daughter, who had married into the Sung family in nearby Su-chou. Each went on to stress different aspects of the teachings they received, which they applied to broadening the content of New Text studies.[52]

We turn now to the rise of the New Text tradition as a product of classical teachings and statecraft ideals that represented in part the continuing legacy, however diluted, of late Ming political agendas in Ch'ang-chou within the organizational framework of kinship networks drawn around the Chuang lineage. Internal descent strategies and external affinal relations with the Lius would successfully harbor activist Confucian political values that had survived among Ch'ang-chou literati despite the Ming debacle and the Manchu triumph.

52. *Chu-chi Chuang-shih tsung-p'u* (1883), 8.30b–31a, 8.36a. See Chuang Shou-chia, *She-i-pu-i-chai i-shu*, "Shang-shu k'ao-i hsu-mu" (Preface), pp. 1a–2b, where he discusses his relationship with Liu Feng-lu; and Wang Nien-sun's biography of Feng-lu in *Hsi-ying Liu-shih chia-p'u* (1876), 12.55a–b.

THREE

Statecraft and the Origins of the Ch'ang-chou New Text School

The centrality of classical studies (*ching-hsueh*) for political discourse in imperial China cannot be overemphasized. After the formation of imperially sanctioned New Text Confucianism during the Former Han dynasty (206 B.C.–A.D. 8), politics in succeeding dynasties was usually expressed through the language of the Classics or the Dynastic Histories. Scholar-statesmen, political opportunists, and even autocrats were forced to articulate their political views through the controlled medium of state ritual, classical sanction, and historical precedent.[1]

The millennial connection between the Confucian Classics of antiquity and premodern Chinese political discourse (reactionary, moderate, or radical) suggests the power these texts had over political behavior and expression in imperial China. Perhaps the impact of charters and constitutions on modern Western political culture is analogous to the role of the Confucian Classics in traditional Chinese, Japanese, and Korean politics. The "constitutionality" of the late imperial state in China was legitimated through classical political discourse; political reformism and classical iconoclasm often went hand in hand.

A set of abstruse texts written in ancient forms of classical Chinese, the "Classics" (*ching*, lit., "warp"—hence the image of continuity) preserved the orthodox teachings and political institutions of the sage-

1. On rituals, see Wechsler, *Offerings of Jade and Silk*, and Yun-yi Ho, *Ministry of Rites*, pp. 1–35.

kings. Generation after generation, century after century, the Classics and the Histories constituted the core curriculum for all those who would participate actively in the political arena. Replaced in relative importance by the more readable Four Books (*Ssu-shu*) after the Sung dynasties (960–1279), the Classics nonetheless remained keys to advancement, fame, and power in the political arena of late imperial China.

Manipulation of the political machinery was justified through the classical values and ideals upon which the imperial state was based. Classical erudition provided Confucian officials, scholars, and students in East Asia with a set of assumptions about good and evil in government and society. If the ideals of the sage-kings were to be realized, the past had to be studied and cherished. And the legitimacy of Confucian institutions was given in the Classics.

By controlling the interpretation of the Classics, one could therefore also control the articulation of and justification for state power. Confucian scholars and officials were indispensable handmaidens of the imperial state. Setting a precedent that lasted from 1313 until 1905, Mongol rulers during the Yuan dynasty (1280–1368) installed, at the urging of their Confucian advisors, the interpretations of the great Sung philosophers Ch'eng I and Chu Hsi as the orthodox "Ch'eng-Chu" guidelines for the imperial examination system. Ming and Ch'ing emperors followed suit, similarly persuaded by their advisors that the Ch'eng-Chu school of Neo-Confucianism provided the most acceptable justification for their rule. In effect, Neo-Confucianism had "captured politics" in the late empire.[2]

Beginning in the sixteenth century, however, the Ch'eng-Chu orthodoxy was increasingly challenged. Criticism accelerated during the seventeenth and eighteenth centuries, and a tug of war ensued among Confucians over the proper evaluation of the Classics and the Four Books. The locus for the legitimation of political power remained Confucian; yet what it meant to be Confucian was called into question. The Classics were still inviolate, but they were read and interpreted with new eyes and new strategies.[3]

2. See Julia Ch'ing, "Truth and Ideology," p. 371. For a discussion see de Bary, *Neo-Confucian Orthodoxy*, pp. 1–66. On the Ch'eng-Chu school and politics, see Peter Bol, "Chu Hsi's Redefinition," pp. 151–85.

3. On the unraveling of Neo-Confucianism see my *Philosophy to Philology*.

T'ANG SHUN-CHIH AND STATECRAFT IN CH'ANG-CHOU

When compared with nearby Su-chou and Yang-chou currents of thought, the Ch'ang-chou academic environment was unique because of the statecraft concerns that dominated its classical scholarship. By "statecraft" (*ching-shih*, lit., "ordering the world"), we mean a commitment not only to a world-ordering theory to which all Confucians adhered but also to technical expertise. The latter often included astronomy for calendrical reform, hydraulics for flood control, and cartography for military purposes. Technical competence was an important part of the statecraft issues for Ch'ang-chou literati.[4]

Classical techniques (*ching-shu*) required mastery of a wide range of practical subjects. The distinctive place that statecraft thought and practice held in Ch'ang-chou literati traditions can be traced back to the sixteenth-century contributions of T'ang Shun-chih and Hsueh Ying-ch'i in local and national affairs. Ying-ch'i, a friend and Ch'ang-chou landsman of T'ang Shun-chih, had perhaps closer ties with the Tung-lin partisans in Wu-hsi than did T'ang. He had studied under Shao Pao, a teacher at the Tung-lin Academy prior to its seventeenth-century revival. The founder of the Tung-lin partisans, Ku Hsien-ch'eng, along with Hsueh Fu-chiao, Ying-ch'i's grandson, studied under Hsueh Ying-ch'i. After Ku Hsien-ch'eng and Kao P'an-lung, Fu-chiao was one of the central figures among the Tung-lin partisans, particularly in his home county of Wu-chin. Hsueh Ying-ch'i was a direct disciple of Ou-yang Te, a fervent follower of Wang Yang-ming, which places Ying-ch'i in the Yang-ming tradition.[5]

Although he had publicly censured Wang Chi, one of the most radical members of the T'ai-chou school, for his excessive liberties with Wang Yang-ming's teachings, Hsueh Ying-ch'i stoutly defended Wang Yang-ming, especially his attempt to link knowledge and action. Wang's stress on the mind was tied to practical affairs, and to what Hsueh called "holding fast to things" (*chih-shih*). The mind, when properly trained and cultivated, served as a guide for statecraft policy: "The mind that holds fast to affairs is precisely the individual's mind."[6]

4. Li Chao-lo, an expert in geography, was typical of Ch'ang-chou literati. See Chao Chen-tso's "Hsu" (Preface) in Li Chao-lo, *Yang-i-chai wen-chi*, pp. 1a–2a.

5. Huang Tsung-hsi, *Ming-Ju hsueh-an*, pp. 256ff (*chüan* 25). See also Goodrich et al., eds., *Dictionary of Ming Biographies*, pp. 703, 619–22, 1102–4.

6. Hsueh Ying-ch'i, *Fang-shan hsien-sheng wen-lu*, 3.1a–21b, 4.1b–3b. See also Busch, "Tung-lin Academy," p. 96.

Hsueh saw in Wang Yang-ming's teachings not a subjectivist escape from practical affairs (his accusation against T'ai-chou scholars), but rather the moral basis for practical concerns and statecraft policies. In a letter to T'ang Shun-chih, Ying-ch'i was critical of contemporary scholars for missing the key to Wang Yang-ming's stress on "studies of the mind" (*hsin-hsueh*). Wang's call for the unity of knowledge and action (*chih-hsing ho-i*), according to Hsueh, had been forgotten by his so-called followers who shallowly discoursed on their teacher's claim that the mind was, in its origins, neither good nor evil (*wu-shan wu-e*) and who neglected to put their ideas into practice through concern for statecraft.

Both Hsueh Ying-ch'i and T'ang Shun-chih were committed to statecraft agendas, which would significantly influence the Tung-lin partisans and continue to be an important feature in Ch'ang-chou intellectual life even after the fall of the Ming dynasty. Below, we will focus on T'ang Shun-chih's contributions to statecraft discourse in late Ming Ch'ang-chou Prefecture.[7]

A literatus who left his mark as a Confucian scholar, official, and literary stylist, T'ang Shun-chih came to immediate prominence in national and local life when he finished first on 1529 metropolitan examination at the age of twenty-two. The T'ang lineage, which traced its ancestry back to Yang-chou, had produced Hanlin Academy members during the Sung and Ming dynasties. Shun-chih's father, T'ang Yao, passed the *chü-jen* examination in 1510, and his grandfather T'ang Kuei passed the metropolitan examination in 1490. Firmly entrenched in Ch'ang-chou local society, T'ang Yao had arranged for Shun-chih to marry the daughter of Chuang Ch'i, from the increasingly prominent Chuang lineage. The biographies for both T'ang Yao and Shun-chih in the Ch'ang-chou prefectural gazetteer were posthumously prepared by the Tung-lin leader Ku Hsien-ch'eng.

T'ang Shun-chih was strongly influenced by the teachings of Wang Yang-ming, which he studied in Peking under the T'ai-chou scholar Wang Chi, whom Hsueh Ying-ch'i had attacked. Shun-chih had a stormy political career and was banished twice, although his advice was much sought after. His forced absences from the political arena allowed him to explore his statecraft interests in geometry, astronomy,

7. See Hsueh Ying-ch'i, *Fang-shan hsien-sheng wen-lu*, 5.11b–12a, 17a–18a, for Hsueh's stress on practical studies and his correspondence with T'ang Shun-chih. For Hsueh's sympathies with Lu Hsiang-shan (1139–92) and Wang Yang-ming, see ibid., 8.1a–2a, 17.14a–16b.

and military strategy. He is generally regarded as one of the most important mathematicians of his time, especially in trigonometry. His studies encompassed Islamic traditions in astromony that had been passed down in China. His second period of banishment from the imperial court allowed T'ang to develop his literary interests while living in a cottage in the hills of I-hsing County, famous for their underground caverns and scenic spots.[8]

CALENDRICAL STUDIES AND MATHEMATICS

In an effort to ground Confucian theory in affairs of state, T'ang Shun-chih appealed to his fellow literati to undertake a new regimen. In his view, the centrality of the mind for moral awakening (*pen-hsin*) was tied to the "teaching of holding fast to things" (*chih-shih chih chiao*), which was the literatus's responsibility to master. Seeking a unification of theory and practice, T'ang turned to calendrical science and mathematics. "Concrete studies" since the Yuan astronomer Kuo Shou-ching's pioneering breakthroughs had lost their vitality and became, according to T'ang, "lost learning" (*chueh-hsueh*) for the last three centuries.[9]

T'ang Shun-chih's efforts to reintegrate calendrical studies and mathematics with Confucian learning in the sixteenth century signaled a broadening of literati traditions in Ch'ang-chou, where T'ang's views were most influential. He argued his position on the basis of Neo-Confucian theory and the technical aspects of calendrical science. According to T'ang, trigonometric "calculations" (*shu*) had become totally separated from the "underlying principles" (*li*) by which one understands calendrical studies. The solution, T'ang contended, was a reintegration of "underlying principles" with trigonometric "calculations":

> One must know both calendrical principles and calculations. This is where I differ from [contemporary] Confucian students. One must know both fixed calculations [*ssu-shu*, lit., "dead calculations"] and variable calculations [*huo-shu*, lit., "living calculations"]. This is where I differ from [contemporary] officials in charge of the calendar. Principles and calculations are not

8. *Ch'ang-chou fu-chih* (1886), 23.33a. See also *P'i-ling T'ang-shih chia-p'u* (1948), "Hsu" (Preface) by T'ang Ho-cheng, pp. 1a–4a; "Wu-fen shih-piao," *ts'e* 9, pp. 1.1a–b; "Tsung-hsi shih-piao," *ts'e* 1, pp. 1a–5a; *ts'e* 19, pp. 11b, 19a–b. Cf. Goodrich et al., eds., *Dictionary of Ming Biography*, pp. 1253–54.

9. T'ang Shun-chih, *Ching-ch'uan hsien-sheng wen-chi* (1573), 6.36b–40a, 7.15a–18a.

two separate things. Calculations represent the concrete application and extension of principles. Variable calculations and fixed calculations are not two separate things [either]. Fixed calculations represent the basis for variable calculations.

Recently, I have met one or two Confucians who are still intent on numerology [*hsiang-shu chih hsueh*], but they don't have access to the intact [astronomical] tradition. Consequently, they continue to use empty speculations about heaven and earth within the scope of Confucian scholarship.[10]

T'ang held up the "six arts" (*liu-i*) of the sage-kings as the model for reintegrating Confucian theory with concrete studies. T'ang described the ancients' successful integration of calculations into the Way but contended that the link between theory (*i*, lit., "meaning") and numbers (*suan-shu*) had been severed by later Confucians who had denigrated the study of numbers as a "lesser technique" (*hsiao-tao*) not worthy of the attentions of the Confucian literatus. Instead, T'ang called for a return to the more comprehensive vision of antiquity in which the mathematical arts were accorded a deservedly prominent place.[11]

T'ang's attempts carried over from calendrical studies to Chinese mathematics, particularly early forms of trigonometry used to solve simple simultaneous equations in astronomy. In a series of essays (*lun*) on triangles and segments of a circle in geometric calculations (*chi-ho-hsueh*), T'ang clearly distinguished between new (*hsin-fa*) and old methods (*chiu-fa*) of calculation in solving equations and determining remainders. These essays preceded by a number of decades the earliest Jesuit transmission of medieval and Renaissance European science to China. T'ang's initiatives were part of what Willard Peterson has described as a larger effort among Confucians in Ming China to reform the calendar before the arrival of Jesuit missionaries. Techniques of calculation, dependent on mastery of mathematics, were part of what T'ang Shun-chih deemed essential to integrate Confucian theory with technical expertise.[12]

CLASSICAL STUDIES AND PHILOLOGY

Such concrete interests were also evident in T'ang Shun-chih's discussion of the role of theory and practice in classical studies (*ching-hsueh*). T'ang sought a similar balance between philosophical discussions of the

10. Ibid., 7.16a–17b.
11. Ibid., 7.19b–21b.
12. Ibid., 17.25b–44a. See also *Wu-chin Yang-hu hsien ho-chih* (1886), 26A.7a–8b. Cf. Peterson, "Calendar Reform."

mind (*hsin-hsueh*), popular among the Wang Yang-ming schoolmen of his day, and more precise philological studies of the Classics favored by Confucian scholars who stressed phonology (*hsing-sheng*), paleography (*wen-tzu*), and etymology (*hsun-ku*) in their scholarship. "The mind," according to T'ang, "could not be separate from the Classics, just as the Classics could not be separate from the mind." Instead, T'ang sought a philologically precise understanding of the Classics that would also "capture and illuminate the refinement and subtlety of the ancients."[13]

Evidence from the late Ming literary world suggests the existence of a close link between the training required to master the art of composing ancient-style prose (*ku-wen*) and the ability to carry out a philological examination of ancient texts. The essayist Kuei Yu-kuang, who came from nearby K'un-shan County (in Su-chou Prefecture), foreshadowed the move toward what would be called "Han Learning" (*Han-hsueh*) during the eighteenth century. The cultural agenda for the Confucian effort in the 1700s to "return to antiquity" (*fu-ku*) moved away from questions of *wen* as literary recreations of the past and toward the Classics themselves as the repository of classical models. In his discussion of the debates surrounding the Old Text and New Text portions of the *Documents Classic*, for instance, Kuei Yu-kuang demonstrated how literary interests and classical studies were becoming increasingly intertwined:

> I recalled accordingly how the documents of the sages had been preserved for ages. Many of [these documents] had been ruined, however, by several Confucians. What can be relied on to distinguish between the authentic and forged [parts] is simply the differences in phrasing [*wen-tz'u*] and style [*ko-chih*]. Later persons, although they tried to imitate [the original] with all their might, in the end they could not get it correct right down to the minutest detail. Scholars, on the basis of the phraseology, can reach the sages and not be deluded by heterodox theories.
>
> Today, the fact that the phraseology transmitted in Fu Sheng's [New Text] *Documents* and that of the [Old Text] version recovered from the wall in Confucius' house are different does not require [extensive] discrimination to understand. Formerly, Pan Ku [32–92] in the bibliography [to his *History of the Former Han Dynasty*] listed a *Documents Classic* in twenty-nine chapters and an ancient Classic in sixteen scrolls. This "ancient Classic" in Han times was earlier [known to be] a forgery [by Chang Pa (fl. ca. first century B.C.)]. It was separated from the other Classics and not mixed up with them.[14]

13. T'ang Shun-chih, *Ching-ch'uan hsien-sheng wen-chi* (1573), 10.3b–5a, 10.8b–11a, 11.34a–35b.

14. Kuei, *Kuei Chen-ch'uan hsien-sheng ch'üan-chi*, 1.15a–16a. For discussion, see

Recovery of "ancient learning" (*ku-hsueh*) for Kuei Yu-kuang meant rendering it relevant for the present. Writing about the decline of classical studies during the Ming, Kuei evoked a sense of reverence for the past, which had been lost in Ming literary production:

> Moreover, I venture to say that not until the Sung [dynasty] were classical studies greatly illumined. Today, however, all of the writings of the Sung Confucians are preserved, but why is it that there are so few who understand the Classics? The Classics are not the works of a single age; in addition, they cannot be fixed [in meaning] by the views of a single person. . . .
>
> Consequently, those who wish to understand the Classics, if they do not seek after the mind-set [*hsin*] of the sages and remain throughout in the arena of talk, if they remain fond of [disputing] similarities and [noting] differences, then the will of the sages will be even more unattainable.

What was required, according to Kuei, was a return to the broadly based "model learning" (*kuei-hsueh*) of Han dynasty Confucians.[15]

Like Kuei Yu-kuang, T'ang Shun-chih was concerned that the followers of Wang Yang-ming had misdirected Confucians away from the comprehensive studies (*po-hsueh*) that had undergirded the classical vision of statecraft. T'ang was intimate with several of the more radical "left-wing" followers of Wang Yang-ming, especially Wang Chi, and was sympathetic to the goals of the Yang-ming schoolmen. But he was also apprehensive about the Buddhist and Taoist aspects of the Yang-ming agenda. He feared that literati values, which should stress "practical application" (*shih-yung*) of Confucian theory, were increasingly being swallowed up by the passive and quiescent ideals of Buddhism and Taoism.[16]

What disturbed T'ang was the eclectic mixing of theories and values that served only to dilute the Confucian concern for practical affairs. He noted that during the last centuries of the Chou dynasty (1122?–221 B.C), for example, Confucians, Taoists, Mohists, and others had contended for intellectual hegemony. Each tradition had its own "original form" (*pen-se*), which distinguished each from the other. Such plural-

---

Chi Wen-fu, *Wan-Ming ssu-hsiang-shih lun*, pp. 98–105. A similar pattern can be observed in the emergence of "Ancient Learning" (*Kogaku*) philology in Tokugawa Japan from literary studies. See Okada, *Edo ki no Jugaku*, pp. 62–110.

15. Kuei, *Kuei Chen-ch'uan hsien-sheng ch'üan-chi*, 3.4b–5a, 1.19a. For a discussion see Lin Ch'ing-chang, "Ming-tai te Han-Sung-hsueh wen-t'i," pp. 133–50.

16. Kuei, *Kuei Chen-ch'uan hsien-sheng ch'üan-chi*, 11.5b. See T'ang Shun-chih, *Ching-ch'uan hsien-sheng wen-chi* (1573), 5.7a–10a, 17.18a–b, for T'ang Shun-chih's correspondence with Wang Chi. See also ibid., 5.18a–b, 7.10b–11a, 10.1a–3b.

ism, T'ang argued, maintained the integrity of each position; each tradition was in turn transmitted to posterity more or less intact.

Since the T'ang (618–907) and Sung dynasties, however, the integrity of the various traditions had been compromised. Literary men filled their works with esoteric discussions of "nature and external necessity" (*hsing-ming*) that brought together the various traditions of Confucianism, Taoism, and Buddhism into an undifferentiated mass of conflicting positions. In the process, the "original form" of Confucianism, that is, its statecraft agenda, had been diluted.[17]

To remedy this sorry state, T'ang Shun-chih called for a rooting out of heterodox doctrines:

> Those who in antiquity brought disorder to our Way, for the most part, came from outside of the Six Classics and Confucius. Those who later have brought disorder to our Way frequently come from the midst of the Six Classics and Confucius. . . . It has reached the point where our Confucians affirm two disparate doctrines and unite Confucianism and Buddhism as one.

Buddhism had become a fifth column in Confucianism, subverting the teachings of antiquity. A thoroughgoing purification of the classical tradition, according to T'ang Shun-chih, was as essential as a literary transformation, recapturing the Way of antiquity with ancient-style prose and transmitting it intact to posterity. Literary reform and classical purification were the key elements in T'ang's program for "returning to antiquity."[18]

Classical philology (*hsiao-hsueh*) for T'ang Shun-chih was an important corrective to the excesses of the followers of Wang Yang-ming. Like Kuei Yu-kuang, T'ang appealed to Han Confucians as the proper source for a Confucian orthodoxy. While not yet advocating a full-blown return to Han Learning, T'ang nevertheless labeled portions of the Neo-Confucian legacy as "heterodox." The turn to Han Confucians, in its initial stages, can be seen in the writings of late Ming Confucians.[19]

Nonetheless, T'ang Shun-chih, like his Tung-lin successors, held up the teachings of Ch'eng I and Chu Hsi as the orthodox interpretation of the role of the mind in Confucian discourse. T'ang's stress on Han Confucianism was made within a framework in which the centrality of Sung

17. T'ang Shun-chih, *Ching-ch'uan hsien-sheng wen-chi* (1573), 7.10b–11a.
18. Ibid., 10.1b–2b.
19. Ibid., 10.8b–11a. For a discussion see Lin Ch'ing-chang, *Ming-tai k'ao-cheng-hsueh yen-chiu*, pp. 14–35.

Learning was affirmed, while the excesses of Ming Neo-Confucians were reformed. The road back to antiquity followed literary and classical guidelines erected first by Han Confucians and then reconstructed by Sung Neo-Confucians.[20]

ANCIENT-STYLE PROSE

Along with his contemporary, Kuei Yu-kuang, T'ang Shun-chih became most famous during the sixteenth century for his advocacy of ancient-style prose, a literary style used by T'ang and others to break away from the strictly imitative techniques used by his Ming predecessors. Peter Bol had described how Confucian literati since the Northern Sung dynasty (960–1126) had defined themselves in light of cultural values that emphasized literature (*wen*) as a medium for civil, literary, and cultural learning. The *ku-wen* revival had its origins in the mid-T'ang, when Han Yü, among others, had called for revival of ancient forms of writing to counter the influence of Buddhism.

After the eleventh century, ancient-style prose became the literary vehicle for formulating literati values. To imitate antique styles, it was thought, signaled mastery of ancient wisdom and its application to the present. Consequently, ancient-style prose was both a literary and ideological movement. The wisdom of antiquity could be tapped for the present if the Confucian literatus mastered the difficult art of composing ancient-style prose.[21]

Efforts to redefine literati values during the Ming dynasty, particularly during the sixteenth century, took the form of rethinking *ku-wen*. If Confucians could overcome the strictly imitative tendencies that prevented students from discovering the interrelation of literary form and classical substance, then the spirit of antiquity could be recreated within contemporary literati life. T'ang Shun-chih observed:

> Suppose there are two people. One has a transcending mind and is said to be one who possesses an insightful eye able to encompass past and present. Even if he never held a piece of paper or a writing brush, or pored over books to learn to write, he simply relies on his own feelings or thoughts to write freely, as if composing a letter to his family. His writing may be sketchy or unrefined, but it definitely has no vulgar, worldly, hackneyed, or pedantic air. It is simply the excellent writing of the world.

20. T'ang Shun-chih, *Ching-ch'uan hsien-sheng wen-chi* (1573), 10.3b–5a.

21. Goodrich et al., eds., *Dictionary of Ming Biography*, pp. 1252–56. See also Diana Yu-shih Mei, "Han Yü"; Hartman, "Han Yü as Philosopher"; and Bol, "Culture and the Way," pp. 1–85. Cf. Ching-i Tu, "Neo-Confucianism."

> The other person remains just like a man of the world of dust. Although he singlemindedly has learned to write, and in the so-called rules and regulations of prose he is correct in every way, no matter which way he turns, what he produces is no more than the chattering of an old lady. Looking for his true spirit and eternal and ineluctable views, none are to be found. Although his prose might be artistically refined, it must be considered of inferior quality. This [difference] is what I mean by the "original form" [*pen-se*] of prose writing.

T'ang Shun-chih wrote about the disjunction between ancient models and contemporary practice evident among Ming literati. He noted that the reunification of ancients and moderns (*ku-chin*) required the individual to recognize that literary style as a means to academic success was an empty echo of the classical world. Clever stylists might at first disguise their inherently empty visions of antiquity, but the disguise would fail when the flowery prose was measured against the concrete matters of policy and practice.[22]

For T'ang Shun-chih, the cultural values of the Confucian literatus should be rooted in classical theory and practice informed by literary form and content. Heavily influenced by Wang Yang-ming and his followers in his early years, T'ang's vision of literary production focused on the application of classical values to "concrete studies" (*shih-hsueh*):

> First, you have to be intent on the concrete. Then you have concrete studies. Once you have concrete studies, then you have concrete matters. The techniques of the Way [*Tao-shu*] have not been clear in later ages. Consequently, what people have called "affairs and achievements" for the most part have been limited to what can be achieved through talent and brains and cannot do justice to [concrete matters]. . . . One must observe how ancient sages and worthies depended on themselves to effect [the Way]. Affairs and achievements were a mirror by which to measure oneself.[23]

T'ang Shun-chih's emphasis on "concrete studies" was not an idle boast. His vision of the values of the Confucian literatus included a rejection of pure theory in favor of a program that "held fast to things" (*chih-shih*) in all their complexity. He rejected "high-minded discussions of nature and external necessity" (*kao-t'an hsing-ming*), if they were removed from the concrete concerns of statecraft to which the sages had devoted themselves. Idle theory translated into empty literary

22. See T'ang Shun-chih, *Ching-ch'uan hsien-sheng wen-chi*, 7.11a, 7.25b, 11.25b–26b, 11.27a–28b.
23. Ibid., 8.7b–8a. See also 5.35b–38b.

production, which shielded the literatus from the true locus of his Confucian calling. Mere "talk" was morally suspect.[24]

CHUANG CH'I-YUAN AND THE CHUANG LEGACY IN THE LATE MING

T'ang Shun-chih cast a long shadow over Confucian literati traditions in Ch'ang-chou. His call for literary reformation and interest in reintegrating statecraft with moral cultivation influenced Ch'ien I-pen (1539–1601) and other literati who participated in the Tung-lin movement. In addition, Ming loyalist scholars such as Ku Yen-wu (1613–82) saw in T'ang Shun-chih, among others, the roots of a Confucian revival that would steer literati away from the intellectual pitfalls of the late Ming. "Concrete studies" (*shih-hsueh*) might provide a way to avoid empty metaphysical speculation.

T'ang's message was also transmitted to the Ch'ing dynasty, becoming part of the local traditions that distinguished Ch'ang-chou Prefecture from other areas in the Yangtze Delta. In the late Ming and early Ch'ing dynasties, Ch'ang-chou became a center for literary production that cut across all the major genres associated with literati culture. By the mid-eighteenth century, Ch'ang-chou was a literary and cultural center rivaling Su-chou and Yang-chou. As a literary center, Ch'ang-chou was home to literati who would distinguish themselves in all major genres of Confucian discourse.

The Yang-hu school of ancient-style prose (*ku-wen*), based in Wu-chin and Yang-hu counties, and the Ch'ang-chou school of lyric poetry (*tz'u*) were known throughout China. Together with the T'ung-ch'eng school in An-hui Province, Ch'ang-chou literary schools were the chief defenders of Sung and Ming ancient-style prose when Han Learning scholars were increasingly turning to parallel-prose styles (*p'ien-t'i-wen*) of the Han dynasties.[25]

The cultural achievements of Ch'ang-chou literati were recorded in numerous prestigious local compilations. For example, the *P'i-ling liu-i shih-ch'ao* (Specimens of poetry by Ch'ang-chou's six superior talents)—which was compiled in 1717 with the help of Chuang Ling-

24. Ibid., 6.25a–26b, 6.30b–31b.

25. Chia-ying Yeh Chao, "Ch'ang-chou School," and Pollard, *A Chinese Look at Literature*, pp. 140–57. See also T'ang Ho-cheng, "Hsu" (Preface) to *Ch'ang-chou fu-chih* (1886), pp. 9b–11b. For the impact of T'ang Shun-chih on Ku Yen-wu, see P'an Lei's "Hsu" (Preface) to the *Jih-chih lu*, pp. 1.47a–48a. On Ch'ien I-pen see *Wu-chin Yang-hu hsien ho-chih* (1886), 22.24b–25a.

yü, great-great-grandson of Chuang Ch'i-yuan—included the works of major seventeenth-century Ch'ang-chou poets, including Yun Shou-p'ing, who later became better know for his painting. In his preface to the collection, P'eng Hui-ch'i noted the importance of poetry in Ch'ang-chou and the latter's fame elsewhere. The compilation on poetry traditions in Ch'ang-chou entitled *P'i-ling pai-chia shih* included works by more than forty members of the Chuang lineage. The works of more than ten members of the Liu lineage were also included.[26]

Later compilations commemorated the three major genres in Ch'ang-chou literary circles during the eighteenth and nineteenth centuries: ancient-style prose, parallel prose, and lyric poetry. The *P'i-ling wen-lu* (Recordings of prose in Ch'ang-chou), for instance, noted the similarities and differences between the Yang-hu school of ancient-style prose and its counterpart in T'ung-ch'eng. The collection then reproduced representative prose essays by Ch'ang-chou's most prominent eighteenth- and nineteenth-century stylists: Chang Hui-yen, Yun Ching, Chao Huai-yü, Liu Feng-lu, Tung Shih-hsi, Chao Chen-tso, and several members of the Chuang lineage. The prose of Chuang Shou-ch'i (1839 *chin-shih*), the major nineteenth-century Chuang literatus in the second branch of the lineage, was given prominence.

Among the essays reproduced in the *P'i-ling wen-lu* was Tung Shih-hsi's "Chuang-shih I-shuo hsu" (Preface to Master Chuang [Ts'un-yü's] sayings on the *Change* [*Classic*]), which brought Chuang's classical scholarship to local and national prominence in the 1820s. Such evidence reveals that the Chuang lineage in Ch'ang-chou heeded T'ang Shun-chih's call for the wedding of literary interests and statecraft concerns—an appeal that carried over to the Ch'ing dynasty. T'ang's grandnephew Chuang Ch'i-yuan, a member of one of the most important lines in the second branch of the Chuang lineage, also made a name for himself in literary circles after he and his cousin Chuang T'ing-ch'en passed the 1610 metropolitan examination.[27]

THE LITERARY ACHIEVEMENTS OF CHUANG CH'I-YUAN

In the preface (ca. 1615) to Ch'i-yuan's literary works, Huang Ju-t'ing linked Chuang with Ch'ang-chou's ancient-style prose traditions estab-

26. *Wu-chin Chuang-shih tseng-hsiu tzu-p'u* (ca. 1840), 7.16a–16b. Chuang Ling-yü and Hsu Yung-hsuan, *P'i-ling liu-i shih-ch'ao*, *passim*, and the "Hsu" (Preface) by P'eng Hui-ch'i, p. 1a. See also *Wu-chin Yang-hu hsien ho-chih* (1886), 33.34a–36a, on the *P'i-ling pai-chia shih*. On Chuang traditions in poetry see *P'i-ling Chuang-shih tseng-hsiu tsu-p'u* (1935), 16.31a. Cf. Hummel et al., *Eminent Chinese*, pp. 960–61.

27. Chao Chen, *P'i-ling wen-lu*. Tung Shih-hsi's essay was included in this collection; see pp. 3.8a–9a.

lished by T'ang Shun-chih and Hsueh Ying-ch'i. Huang's account traced this *ku-wen* tradition back to Ou-yang Hsiu (1007–72) and Su Shih (1036–1101), the Northern Sung's premier practitioners of ancient-style prose. Su Shih had lived for a time in Ch'ang-chou. In fact, the Chuang lineage school was later named after Su Shih, which shows the degree to which the Chuangs consciously styled themselves as involved in literary pursuits. Late Ming members of the lineage were best known for their interests in the *Poetry Classic*.[28]

The organizational basis of the Chuang lineage was solidified by another of Chuang Ch'i-yuan's chief interests: genealogy. He helped to revise and complete the 1611 genealogy of the Chuang lineage, which his father, Chuang I-lin, had first compiled in 1580 and later ordered Ch'i-yuan to bring up to date. Chuang Ch'i-yuan also composed many of the biographies of his prominent ancestors, which were included in both the genealogy and his collected writings. Among the latter, he mentioned the close affinal ties between the T'angs and Chuangs dating to the sixteenth century. He also composed a biography of his grandmother, who had married T'ang Shun-chih, as well as a biography of his mother, who came from the T'ang lineage.[29]

In his mother's biography, Ch'i-yuan described the traditions of *li-hsueh* (studies of principles) associated with the Ch'eng-Chu school, in which the T'angs had become expert. He also described his mother's ability to transmit the teachings of T'ang Shun-chih to Ch'i-yuan and the Chuangs. Thus, one could attribute the Chuang lineage's literary traditions and interests in the teachings of Chu Hsi and other Sung-Ming Neo-Confucians directly to the affinal influence of the T'angs. Chuang Ch'i-yuan's concern for the Chuang genealogical record demonstrated that in the early seventeenth century leading members of the second branch of the lineage were aware of themselves as an important "cultural lineage" in Ch'ang-chou. Their heightened sense of establishing a scholarly tradition also dates from this time.[30]

NEO-CONFUCIAN DISCOURSE AND CATHOLICISM

Chuang Ch'i-yuan stressed the ties between what he called "true studies of principles" (*chen li-hsueh*) and broad training in astronomy,

28. Huang Ju-t'ing, "Hsu" (Preface) to Chuang Ch'i-yuan, *Ch'i-yuan chih-yen*.
29. Chuang Ch'i-yuan, *Ch'i-yuan chih-yen*, 6.49a–78b, 9.15a–b, 3.34a–38b.
30. Ibid., 9.15a–15b. Ch'i-yuan also established an ancestral hall in honor of his father.

geography, military affairs, civil institutions, and ritual matters. He also emphasized the positive role that lineages, based on agnatic solidarity, played in maintaining moral values and social order in local society. In a tribute to the "great masters of *li-hsueh* during the Ming dynasty," Ch'i-yuan singled out T'ang Shun-chih and Hsueh Ying-ch'i as loyal sons of Ch'ang-chou who had carried on the moral teachings of Ch'en Hsien-chang (1428–1500), Wang Yang-ming, and Lo Ch'in-shun (1465–1547).[31]

It is interesting that in his discussions of the Wang Yang-ming tradition, known as "studies of the mind," Chuang Ch'i-yuan subsumed it under the Ch'eng-Chu school of principle. Aware of Ming academic developments, Chuang was following T'ang Shun-chih and the Tung-lin partisans in their efforts to ameliorate the excesses of the Yang-ming schoolmen and to reintegrate Wang's contributions into the orthodox mainstream. *Li-hsueh* for Ch'i-yuan was the educational basis for distinguishing the "true Confucian" (*chen Ju*) from the false one.[32]

According to Chuang, achievements in Confucian studies should contribute to the literatus's calling as a government official. "To study," he contended, "was equivalent to government service" (*chi-shih chi-hsueh*). Moral principles completed the equation. They were the content of the literatus's preparation for public office. In his examination essays for the 1610 palace examination, Chuang continually stressed the centrality of the mind and its ties to self-cultivation as the beginning point for literati commitment to statecraft (*ching-shih*) and world ordering (*chih-kuo*). Ch'i-yuan had culled these ideals from the Four Books, the central corpus of the Ch'eng-Chu tradition.

Chuang's conception of the role of the human mind (*jen-hsin*) in Confucian moral theory included a peculiar reinterpretation of the famous *jen-hsin Tao-hsin* (human mind and moral mind) passage in the *Documents Classic*. It was a reading that neither Chu Hsi nor Wang Yang-ming had offered in their elucidation of Confucian "mental discipline" (*hsin-fa*). By the late Ming this passage had been subjected to increased scrutiny as perhaps a forged part of a chapter in the Old Text *Documents* entitled "Counsels of Yü the Great" ("Ta Yü mo"). In examination answers dealing with this famous passage, Ch'i-yuan stressed the orthodox views of "refinement" (*wei-ching*) and "singleness of purpose" (*wei-i*) to "pacify the mind" (*an-hsin*), but he never broached

31. Ibid., 3.12a–13b, 3.36a–37b.
32. Ibid., 3.34a–44b, 3.47a–48b.

the seminal issue of the "moral mind" (*Tao-hsin*), the cornerstone of the orthodox position.[33]

Moreover, in his earlier examination essays prepared for the 1606 provincial *chü-jen* degree, Chuang Ch'i-yuan paraphrased the famous eight-character passage, which, in the original, read: "The human mind is precarious; the moral mind is subtle." Chuang's version was: "The mind of the masses is precarious; the mind of the ruler on high is at peace." This was no covert effort to question, as others had, the authenticity of the distinction between the moral and human mind, but it also did not give the stock interpretations. The latter had long been part of the authoritative *Ssu-shu wu-ching ta-ch'üan* (Great compendium of the Four Books and Five Classics), which was compiled by Hanlin academicians during the reign of the Yung-lo Emperor (1403–25) in an effort to establish the orthodox basis for the examination system.[34]

In his provincial and palace examination essays, Chuang appealed to what he called the "true mind" (*chen-hsin*) as the key to Confucian moral theory and world ordering. He regarded the "mind of Heaven" (*t'ien-hsin*) and the "mind of the ruler" (*chün-hsin*) as efforts to approximate the universalist aspects of the "true mind." In the 1610 palace examination, Chuang made this claim a central point of his reply to a question oriented to policy issues (*ts'e*):

> I have heard from colleagues that the emperor in uniting and ordering the empire must have a true mind in order to rectify the great basis [*ta-pen*] [of the state]. Then he can cause his virtuous intentions to flow unobtrusively in order to preside magnanimously over the origins of order. He must have true intentions [*chen-nien*] to magnify the great uses [*ta-yung*] [of the state]. Then he can use laws and statutes to instruct silently in order to employ broadly the encompassing basis of order.

The "true mind" was the origin of world ordering and the key to the realization that "only by knowing the reason why heaven is heaven, can one know the reason why the ruler is the ruler."[35]

Chuang Ch'i-yuan's reversal of usual interpretations of the human mind vis-à-vis the moral mind, at first sight ingenious, could be seen as an idiosyncratic twist within the flowery prose of an examination essay.

33. Ibid., 4.2a–3b, 10.3a–11a, 10.12a–14a, 10.18a–19b. Cf. de Bary, *Neo-Confucian Orthodoxy*, p. 8, and my "Philosophy (*I-li*) versus Philology (*K'ao-cheng*)."

34. Chuang Ch'i-yuan, *Ch'i-yuan chih-yen*, 10.43a. See also the *Ssu-shu ta-ch'üan* for annotations to Chu Hsi's famous preface to the *Doctrine of the Mean*, pp. 1a–8a, where he explicitly addresses the orthodox position on the moral and human mind.

35. Chuang Ch'i-yuan, *Ch'i-yuan chih-yen*, 10.12a, 10.27a–29a, 11.3b, 10.3a–5b. We should note that there is no locus classicus for the phrase *chen-hsin*.

But, intriguingly, several of the key phrases in Ch'i-yuan's examination answers derived from his earlier essays on Catholicism and what he termed its ideal of the "true mind." He gleaned these views from the writings of the Jesuit Father Diego de Pantoja (d. 1618), who came to China in 1599. According to Chuang, Pantoja had outlined the main doctrines of Catholicism in a work entitled *Seven Victories* (*Ch'i-k'e*), which outlined Christian methods for guarding against the seven deadly sins.[36]

Exactly how Chuang Ch'i-yuan came into contact with Catholicism in general and Father Pantoja in particular is unclear. The influence of the Jesuits in this period was not pervasive. But a significant group of southern literati during the later Ming—including Li Chih, Hsu Kuang-ch'i (a native of Shang-hai County in nearby Su-chou Prefecture), among others—had taken Jesuit teachings very seriously, particularly in the natural sciences. Moreover, Catholic efforts to establish an equivalence between the "ruler on high" (*t'ien-chu*) in the Confucian Classics and the God of the Christians were unquestioned until Matteo Ricci's death in 1610. Ch'i-yuan came to maturity while efforts to accommodate Christianity were at their peak.[37]

Chuang's sympathetic discussion of Catholic doctrines is all the more remarkable when we consider his position in Ch'ang-chou society and within his lineage. An upholder of Confucian orthodoxy Ch'i-yuan was still able to enrich his interests in *li-hsueh* with Jesuit teachings. Remarkably, he sympathized with Pantoja's efforts to integrate the Catholic notion of a supreme deity into Confucian discussion of the Four Books and Five Classics:

> The *Analects* and *Doctrine of the Mean* discuss nature and external necessity. The *Poetry* and *Documents* [Classics] record imperial decrees. What more is there to add? People of our age all know there is a Heaven, but they do not all know the reason why Heaven is Heaven. If Heaven had no ruler, then there would only be the present moment, motionless and stagnant, dream-like without the mysterious spirit, and that's all. . . . The reason why Heaven is Heaven is because there is a ruler there. In the teaching of the Heavenly Ruler [that is, the Christian God], one stops at preserving the true

36. Ibid., 2.46b–48b. Pantoja's work, according to Chuang Ch'i-yuan, was entitled "Ch'i-k'e hsi-shu" (Western book on the seven victories). See also Liang, *Chung-kuo chin san-pai-nien hsueh-shu-shih*, pp. 31–39, and Gernet, *China and the Christian Impact*, pp. 28, 30–32.

37. See Bernard, "Philosophic Movement," for an overstated account of possible links between late Ming intellectual trends and Jesuit influence, particularly among the Tung-lin partisans. See also my *Philosophy to Philology*, pp. 47–48, 62–63, 184.

> mind, refrains from false intentions, grasps the unity of self and others, and gleans the unified origins of old and new. One must first realize that one's mind itself contains the [Heavenly] Ruler, before he can reverently worship the Heavenly Ruler [God]. This is what the Western teacher Father Pantoja has ordered.[38]

The extent of Chuang Ch'i-yuan's acceptance of Pantoja's ecumenical efforts is unclear. He did, however, praise the "seven victories" over sin as doctrinally superior to anything the Buddhists had to offer. In addition, he integrated the Catholic notion of the "true mind" and "the reason why Heaven is Heaven" into his successful essays for the 1610 palace examinations. At the very least, Chuang had elucidated the Neo-Confucian theory of mind using the Christian notion of the "true mind," not the "moral mind" (*Tao-hsin*). Interestingly, his replacement of *Tao-hsin* with *chen-hsin* did not represent a break with the orthodox tradition. In fact, neither he nor his examiners seem to have found anything controversial in his examination essays.[39]

CHUANG CH'I-YUAN'S LEGACY

Chuang Ch'i-yuan's broad-ranging interests were representative of a statecraft legacy bequeathed by T'ang Shun-chih and other late Ming Confucians. The lines of Ch'i-yuan and his cousin Chuang T'ing-ch'en would henceforth translate literary training, orthodox teachings, and precise studies in statecraft into long-term examination success and high political office for the second branch of the Chuang lineage. Three of Ch'i-yuan's sons achieved *chin-shih* status, signifying the importance of his line in the lineage during the Ming-Ch'ing transition.

Two of Chuang Ch'i-yuan's sons carried on his interests in practical affairs. Chuang Ying-ch'i (who later took the name Heng) and Ying-hui, *chin-shih* of 1643 and 1628 respectively, became involved in medical matters and military affairs, in addition to holding high office. Before serving as imperial censor, Ying-ch'i, whose wife was a Liu (see chapter 2), had been involved in medicine. In 1634, under provincial medical auspices, he reissued a Ming dynasty medical handbook on

38. Chuang Ch'i-yuan, *Chi-yuan chih-yen*, 2.47b–48b.

39. Chuang Chu, *P'i-ling k'e-ti k'ao* (1868), 8.6b. Ch'i-yuan's interests in Catholicism do not appear to have been shared by other members of the Chuang lineage, nor were his religious interests mentioned in his lineage biography or in later accounts written by prestigious descendants. Chuang Ts'un-yü writing in the 1780s, however, repeated Ch'i-yuan's inquiry into "the reason why Heaven is Heaven." See chapter 4.

children's diseases, adding relevant materials to the earlier editions, which had first been printed in 1405 and again in 1532.[40]

Chuang Ying-hui compiled a work on military history that laid out the strategic and moral basis for military success. This was an ambitious undertaking, and Ying-hui received the help of his brothers and sons in addition to that of his influential uncle Chuang T'ing-ch'en. In his preface, Ying-hui noted that his grandfather I-lin, whose wife came from the T'ang lineage, had bequeathed a family tradition of concern for Confucian technical expertise (*Ju-shu*), which he was continuing in his study of military affairs. The medical metaphor Ying-hui chose to describe the value of his military compilation echoed his brother Ying-ch'i's interests in medicine: "Use of troops by an outstanding commander is like the use of medicine by an outstanding doctor."[41]

CHUANG TS'UN-YÜ: STATECRAFT AND EXAMINATION SUCCESS

Ch'ang-chou's distinct statecraft traditions, which peaked during the late eighteenth and early nineteenth centuries, were not simply the product of the Ming debacle. The commitment of the Ch'ang-chou school to practical affairs preceded the fall of the Ming dynasty by a century and even contributed to the Tung-lin agenda in local and national affairs. As we have seen, members of the Chuang lineage were exemplars of the statecraft tradition.

During the Ch'ing dynasty, a succession of outstanding scholar-officials from the Chuang lineage studied mathematics, medicine, and geography in order to advance their careers. Since the late Ming, this tradition of statecraft had distinguished the "learning of Ch'ang-chou" (*Ch'ang-chou chih hsueh*) from Su-chou and Yang-chou. The emergence of Chuang Ts'un-yü, one of the major voices of the Chuang lineage in particular and Ch'ang-chou literati in general, must be understood in light of this unique statecraft tradition. Generations of successful officials in the Chuang lineage had bequeathed the fruits of their preparations and labors to their descendants. By the mid-eighteenth cen-

40. See Hsu Yung-hsuan, *Pu-yao hsiu-chen hsiao-erh fang-lun*, which includes a preface by Li T'ang that describes Chuang Ying-ch'i's role in reissuing this handbook on children's diseases. See also *Chu-chi Chuang-shih tsung-p'u* (1883), 1.34b–35a, and Chuang Chu, *P'i-ling k'e-ti k'ao* (1868), 8.26a.

41. See Chuang Ying-hui's "Hsu" (Preface) to *Tsuan-chi ching-wu sheng-lueh cheng-chi*, pp. 1a–3a.

tury, the Chuangs knew what was required of them to achieve success, first, on examinations and, subsequently, in official life.

Tai Wang, a follower of the Yen-li (Yen Yuan and Li Kung) school (who later turned to the New Text teachings of the Ch'ang-chou school through the influence of Chuang Ts'un-yü's grandson Liu Feng-lu), has described the early Ch'ing popularity of statecraft pragmatism in Ch'ang-chou in an influential work entitled *Yen-shih hsueh-chi* (Record of Master Yen [Yuan's] Teachings).

Tai noted that Chuang Chu, Ts'un-yü's father, had been attracted to the pragmatic teachings of Yen Yuan, which had been transmitted in the 1690s to south China by Yen's disciple Li Kung. Yun Ho-sheng, a native of Wu-chin County, met Li Kung in 1714 and thereafter strongly endorsed the teachings of Yen Yuan and Li Kung.

Yen Yuan was an influential northern Confucian scholar who, like others during the Ming-Ch'ing transition period, placed the blame for the tragic collapse of the Ming dynasty squarely on the shoulders of Chu Hsi and his school of *li-hsueh* (studies of moral principles). Yen was convinced that the Ch'eng-Chu orthodoxy, sullied by Buddhist notions, was misleading and heterodox. Emphasis on moral cultivation (*hsiu-yang*) at the expense of physical and mental training had clearly stultefied the Ming state.

A class of literati incapable of decisive pragmatic action and thought had emerged, Yen thought. Witnesses to the deficiencies of the Ming state and the failure of the Confucian elite to prevent the Manchu takeover, post-1644 literati doubted that self-cultivation alone could inspire effective statesmanship and vigorous government. Although loyal to the Ch'eng-Chu orthodoxy, Chuang Chu recognized the merit in Yen Yuan's position.[42]

Chuang Ts'un-yü was no exception to the Chuang tradition. He studied astronomy, medicine, geography, water conservation, water control, legal statutes, and mathematical calculation methods. In fact, Ts'un-yü's work entitled *Yao-shuo* (Theories of medicine) was listed in the medical section (*yao-lei*) of a bibiliography compiled by Ch'ang-chou natives directly under a similar work by T'ang Shun-chih called

42. Yen Yuan, *Ssu-shu cheng-wu*, vol. 1, p. 47. Ku Yen-wu blamed the late Ming "left-wing" school of Wang Yang-ming's thought for the intellectual disorder of the day. See Ku Yen-wu, *Jih-chih lu*, pp. 540–41. For a discussion see my "Unravelling of Neo-Confucianism," pp. 79–83. For Yen Yuan's links to Yun Ho-sheng see Tai Wang, *Yen-shih hsueh-chi*, p. 262 (*chüan* 10). See also Ōtani, "Yōshū Jōshū gakujutsu kō," pp. 325–26. For Chuang Chu's interests in *li-hsueh* see *Hsi-ying Liu-shih chia-p'u* (1876), 12.19a.

Yao-lun (On medicine). Chuang's broad education in Confucian theory and statecraft practice was good preparation for the wide range of problems he would face as an official in the imperial bureaucracy, where he would serve as director-general for astronomy and calendrical calculations and grand minister for medical services.[43]

Such preparation was also evident in the prize essays composed by Ts'un-yü's brother Chuang P'ei-yin for the 1754 metropolitan examinations. P'ei-yin's answer to the final policy question (*ts'e*), administered during the last session of the three-session examination ordeal, received highest honors. It was even included in the official report on the examination as the model answer to a question dealing with flood control of the Yellow River. Chuang P'ei-yin's answer made clear that his views of statecraft were tied to an evolutionary understanding of historical changes and the need of practical policy to keep pace with those changes. He wrote: "The [Yellow] River of today is the [Yellow] River of old, but its circumstances are different. Accordingly those who wish to control it must apply different [methods]."

P'ei-yin then traced the geographical history of the Yellow River and linked its present circumstances to the grain tribute system on the Grand Canal, which transported foodstuffs from south to north China. Solving the problems of flooding along the Yellow River was inseparable from dealing with the Grand Canal, he asserted. These were the present circumstances within which the flooding problem should be evaluated. In other words, new solutions were needed to solve old problems. Like the sages, who "could not go against the times," contemporary Confucians had to deal with the present in terms of the present: "The [Yellow] River of today can only be controlled by adjusting to its present conditions. Therefore, you cannot guarantee that it will never again overflow. . . . Those who were good at controlling the [Yellow] River simply adapted to the times and accorded with its circumstances."[44] Such appeals to "appropriate circumstances" would become a major element in nineteenth-century New Text reformism.

Returning to Chuang Ts'un-yü, we find that his broad interests were

43. Tsang Yung (1767–1811), "Li-pu shih-lang Chuang kung hsiao-chuan," 5.2a. See also *Wu-chin Chuang-shih tseng-hsiu tsu-p'u* (ca. 1840), 26.30b, and Chuang Shou-chia, "Tsung-pa" (General afterword) to Chuang Ts'un-yü's collected writings, in Shou-chia's *She-i-pu-i-chai i-shu*, pp. 38a–39b, for a discussion of Ts'un-yü's interest in mathematics and medicine. Cf. Lu Wen-ch'ao, *P'i-ling ching-chieh-chih*, section on *yao-lei* (medicine), and *Wu-chin Yang-hu hsien ho-chih*, 23.3b.

44. See Chuang P'ei-yin's examination essay in *Hui-shih lu* (1745), pp. 12b–14b, 51b–55b.

in many ways a conscious imitation of the T'ang Shun-chih legacy, which stressed the unity of Confucian theory with statecraft. In addition to his classical scholarship, to be discussed in the next chapter, Chuang also compiled a work on mathematical calculation entitled *Suan-fa yueh-yen* (Summary of calculation methods), which received notice in both the local county gazetteer and in Lu Wen-ch'ao's *P'i-ling ching-chieh chih* (Bibliography of Ch'ang-chou works). In the county gazetteer, Ts'un-yü's work was classed with T'ang Shun-chih's *Kou-ku teng liu-lun* (Six expositions of triangle measurements) as "techniques for numbers" (*shu-shu*). It was placed immediately after it, suggesting Chuang's attempt to follow up on T'ang's earlier research.

Chuang Ts'un-yü was especially drawn to T'ang Shun-chih's program for "investigating the Classics to find practical applications" (*yen-ching ch'iu shih-yung*) in the contemporary world. Li Chao-lo (1769–1849) was an important Ch'ang-chou statecraft scholar in his own right, whose interests ranged from mathematics and astronomy to historical geography, in addition to classical studies. He connected Chuang's stress on "classical techniques" (*ching-shu*) to Ch'ang-chou's late Ming Confucians, especially T'ang Shun-chih and Hsueh Ying-ch'i. Li then described Ts'un-yü "as a man representative of the fine cultural traditions of our native place [Ch'ang-chou]," claiming that his remarkable success mirrored the preeminence of the Chuangs in the imperial examination system. According to Li Chao-lo, Chuang Ts'un-yü was a product of his lineage's traditions in particular and the Ch'ang-chou heritage in general.[45]

CH'ANG-CHOU EXAMINATION SUCCESS

By the late Ming, Ch'ang-chou Prefecture had already become a highly cultured area with a dense population based on rich farmland and flourishing handicrafts. Native sons of Ch'ang-chou made up a large proportion of Ming officials from Nan-chih-li (the Southern Capital Region formed during the Ming out of Chiang-su and An-hui provinces). Roughly 10 percent of all Ming officials who hailed from Chiang-su or An-hui provinces (table 1) came from Ch'ang-chou's three major county seats—there were more than one hundred counties and departments in Nan-chih-li. Wu-chin and Wu-hsi ranked particularly high

45. Li Chao-lo, *Yang-i-chai wen-chi* (1878 ed.), 3.13b–14a. See *Wu-chin Yang-hu hsien ho-chih*, 33.5a, and Lu Wen-ch'ao, *P'i-ling ching-chieh-chih*, section on *yao-lei* (medicine).

TABLE 1. Ming Officials from Ch'ang-chou Prefecture as a Percentage of Nan-chih-li

County	No.	Pct.	Rank
Wu-chin	161	3.9	2
Wu-hsi	151	3.7	4
I-hsing	90	2.2	12
Chiang-yin	40	1.0	29
Total	442	10.8	

among the top five counties in the Southern Capital Region for production of officials during the Ming dynasty.[46]

During this time Ch'ang-chou was also "a prefecture of unusual academic success," in the words of Ping-ti Ho. With a total of 661 *chin-shih* degree holders between 1368 and 1644 (276 years), Ch'ang-chou ranked fifth in academic success in the Ming empire and second, after Su-chou, in Chiang-su. During the Ch'ing dynasty, Ch'ang-chou's ranking for total number of *chin-shih* between 1644 and 1911 (267 years) improved to fourth in the empire (again second only to Su-chou in Chiang-su); in total numbers, however, Ch'ang-chou received 618 *chin-shih* places, forty-three less than during the Ming.

The academic prestige of the southern prefectures in Chiang-su was further demonstrated by the percentage of *chin-shih* degree holders from the three prefectures of Su-chou, Ch'ang-chou, and Sung-chiang. Of the province's thirteen prefectures and departments, 77 percent of the *chin-shih* came from the southern prefectures. During the Ch'ing, *chin-shih* totals from the Su-chou, Ch'ang-chou, and Sung-chiang prefectures fell to 57.6 percent of the provincial total, but still constituted a majority. But the prestige of Su-chou and Ch'ang-chou academic traditions remained intact under the Ch'ing, despite the court's efforts to limit the academic success of Yangtze Delta literati in favor of other regions of the empire. Su-chou had forty-two of the highest ranking *chin-shih*, and Ch'ang-chou had twenty—easily the two most acclaimed prefectures in the province.[47]

Success of the Chuang lineage in placing its sons in high office should be measured in light of Ch'ang-chou's phenomenal success in the impe-

46. Parsons, "Ming Bureaucracy," p. 190.

47. Ping-ti Ho, *Ladder of Success*, pp. 246–54. See also Liu Chao-pin, *Ch'ing-tai k'e-chü*, pp. 97–99.

rial examinations during the Ming and Ch'ing dynasties. Wu-chin County, which after 1724 was divided into Wu-chin and Yang-hu counties, ranked seventh in the empire for local communities of outstanding academic success, for example. Its total of 265 *chin-shih* in the Ch'ing period was exceeded in Chiang-su Province, again, only by the three counties composing the Su-chou municipal area, which claimed 504 *chin-shih* degree holders. Wu-hsi, which included Chin-k'uei County before 1724, accounted for 163 total *chin-shih* during the Ch'ing, placing it twelfth in the empire and fifth in the province. What was interesting, however, was that Ch'ang-chou was the only prefecture with two localities, Wu-chin and Wu-hsi, that could claim such outstanding academic success.[48]

THE CHUANG LINEAGE'S EXAMINATION SUCCESS

During the sixteenth century T'ang Shun-chih and Hsueh Ying-ch'i had established influential literary precedents and statecraft studies in Ch'ang-chou. They became an important part of the Tung-lin agenda in Wu-hsi as well as a major component in the success of its partisans in using the examination system as a stepping stone to high political office. Similarly, politics, statecraft, and high academic achievement went hand-in-hand for the Chuang lineage since the late Ming, although now this took place within the framework of agnatic, not party, solidarity. The Chuangs' success in translating academic prowess into high political office was startling even by the high rates of local success we outlined above.

Tsang Yung, a Ch'ang-chou native associated with Han Learning, described the remarkable depth and breadth of Chuang's studies in his 1800 biography of Chuang Ts'un-yü. As a child, Ts'un-yü scrupulously obeyed the dictates of his family and concentrated on Chu Hsi's ideas and teachings. As he matured, Ts'un-yü dug into the "meanings of the Classics" (*ching-i*), which were essential for dealing with examination questions based on Ch'eng-Chu interpretations.[49]

Given the importance of Chu Hsi's interpretations, Chuang males studied the writings of Chu Hsi as children. Examination candidates all over the empire, however, could be expected to do the same. Even Ch'ing dynasty Han Learning scholars—who spurned Sung and Ming

48. Ping-ti Ho, *Ladder of Success*, p. 254.

49. Tsang Yung "Li-pu shih-lang Chuang kung hsiao-chuan," 5.2a. See also *Wu-chin Chuang-shih tseng-hsiu tsu-p'u* (ca. 1840), 26.30b.

scholarship in their *k'ao-cheng* studies—had to master some Sung Learning in order to pass local, provincial, and national civil service examinations. This remained true despite the new wave of empirically based textual studies sweeping through the Lower Yangtze in the eighteenth century.

In Ch'ang-chou, for example, Hung Liang-chi and Huang Ching-jen, friends since childhood, both studied at the Lung-ch'eng Academy where Han Learning was then in vogue. As Susan Mann (Jones) notes, by the mid-eighteenth century academies in Ch'ang-chou were no longer preoccupied with the Neo-Confucian philosophic and political issues that had energized them in the seventeenth century and produced an unprecedented period of statecraft interest and intellectual ferment.

Hung Liang-chi and Huang Ching-jen each passed the examination granting them local licentiate status easily enough (*sheng-yuan*; entitlement to the selection process), but both had more difficulty in passing the provincial examinations and considerably more difficulty on passing the metropolitan examinations in the capital. Meanwhile, both served on staffs of the leading national-level Han Learning scholar-officials of their day: Chu Yun and Pi Yuan. *K'ao-cheng* studies had not penetrated many of the examination questions, so their Han Learning training provided Hung and Huang with little help on higher-level imperial examinations.[50]

By way of contrast, Chuang Ts'un-yü, studying in his lineage school, had little trouble with examination hurdles. At the age of twenty-five, he took his *chü-jen* degree in the Chiang-su provincial examinations (which included An-hui candidates as well) in Su-chou in 1744. In the following year, he passed the *chin-shih* examination in Peking as *secundus* on his first try. An eighteen-year-old prodigy, his younger brother, P'ei-yin, passed the provincial examination in 1741, three years before him. P'ei-yin took longer on the capital examinations, however, not passing as *optimus* until 1754, when he was still only thirty-one.

Similarly, their father, Chuang Chu, was thirty years old when he passed the provincial examination in 1720; seven years later he received his *chin-shih* degree. Chuang Chu's elder brothers Chuang K'ai and Chuang Tun-hou also passed the *chin-shih* examination in 1713 and 1724 at the ages of forty-six and forty-two respectively. Another brother, Chuang Yun, was a *chü-jen* at age thirty-eight in the 1720

50. Susan Mann (Jones), "Hung Liang-chi," pp. 21, 34–36. On the role of patronage see my *Philosophy to Philology*, pp. 104–12.

Chiang-su provincial examinations, while Chuang Ta-ch'un's name was placed on the supplementary list of *chü-jen* (*fu-pang*) in 1729 at age forty.[51]

Ts'un-yü's eldest son F'eng-yuan took his *chü-jen* degree at age thirty in 1765. Another son, T'ung-min, passed the 1756 *chü-jen* examinations at the age of only eighteen, matching the achievement of his uncle P'ei-yin. It took him another fourteen years to receive his *chin-shih*, however. A third son, Hsuan-ch'en, received the *chü-jen* degree in 1774 at age twenty; in 1778 at the remarkable age of only twenty-four he passed the capital examination, two years younger than his father had been. For a final example, we should add that Chuang P'ei-yin's son, Shu-tsu, took the *chü-jen* degree in 1777 at age twenty-six and three years later received his *chin-shih*.

To sum up, within Chuang Ts'un-yü's immediate family, Chuang Hsuan-ch'en's rise was the most meteoric. Whatever else may have been involved in the success of the Chuangs, it is at least clear that one factor in their extraordinary ongoing examination excellence was the education they received from an early age on in their lineage school.[52]

Despite its popularity among Lower Yangtze literati, Han Learning, and its associated *k'ao-cheng* techniques, never penetrated the examination system as widely as had Sung Learning. Hence philological expertise not only did not ensure examination success but also in many cases may have precluded it. Chuang Ts'un-yü and his relatives did not deviate from the accepted path to examination success. Mastery of the Ch'eng-Chu orthodoxy was their ticket to high office. Unlike *k'ao-cheng* scholars (many of whom devoted themselves to their Han Learning academic interests and avoided or retired from government service), the Chuangs paid little heed at first to the Han Learning wave sweeping through Su-chou, Yang-chou, and even their native Ch'ang-chou.

Because it was opposed to orthodox Confucian studies, which were based on Sung Learning, Han Learning was at best on the periphery of examination studies. Its proponents were thus frequently excluded from directly holding office. The fruits of the *k'ao-cheng* agenda were specialization and professionalization of Confucian scholarly roles. Han Learning scholars attained and maintained their positions within the Lower Yangtze academic community by virtue of the protection and patronage extended by broader elite segments of Confucian official-

51. *Chu-chi Chuang-shih tsung-p'u* (1883), 8.29b–35a.
52. Ibid.

dom, persuaded that there was special value in their philological studies.[53]

The Chuang lineage in general, and Chuang Ts'un-yü in particular, opposed these new intellectual currents and affirmed instead the traditional Confucian pattern. Chuang's reputation rested on his proximity to imperial power in Peking. He was at home in the political arena. His interests in the Classics, conservative when compared to his Han Learning peers, were inseparable from his political career, whether he served as grand secretary, education commissioner, or examination supervisor (see below). Scholarship and politics were not alternatives for Chuang Ts'un-yü. The two went hand in hand. Chuang Ts'un-yü and his relatives devoted themselves to government service after undergoing academic preparation. The Chuangs prepared for the traditional Confucian vocation.[54]

CHUANG TS'UN-YÜ AS A SCHOLAR-OFFICIAL

High government office was nearly assured for Chuangs like Ts'un-yü. It was also assumed that a Chuang would aspire to nothing else. The rise of New Text Confucianism in Ch'ang-chou represents in part the story of a remarkably successful Yangtze Delta lineage whose possession of a scholarly tradition was as much a sign of its prosperity as was its possession of land, charitable estates, or financial resources. A lineage could focus on the learning of a school (*chia-hsueh*) and maintain cultural resources in the same way it owned rice fields or urban estates.[55]

We turn now to the distinguished official and scholarly career of Chuang Ts'un-yü, the Chuang lineage's most prestigious scion of the Ch'ing and representative of the Chuangs' special traditions of learning dating back to the Ming. These lineage traditions are crucial; it is there that we will locate the spiritual and eruditional resources for the political leverage that enabled a Lower Yangtze Han Chinese such as Chuang Ts'un-yü to dare practice his Confucian principles in the explosive precincts of a Manchu-dominated educational and military bureaucracy.

The origin of the New Text revival via Chuang Ts'un-yü in Ch'ang-

53. *Wu-chin Chuang-shih tseng-hsiu tsu-p'u* (ca. 1840), 26.30b. See also my *Philosophy to Philology*, pp. 67–85.

54. *Chuang-shih ching-hsueh-chia chia-chuan*, p. 2b.

55. Bourdieu, *Theory of Practice*, pp. 171–83.

chou was not purely intellectual or social. It was charged from the beginning with political overtones that translated into substantive consequences for public policy. The Chuang lineage's scholarly conservatism (radical in its political application) and its reformist statecraft were the product of a privileged Confucian education. For generations the Chuang lineage successfully translated its local scholarly prestige into national-level political power and were indelibly tied ideologically and practically to a system of power that confirmed and explained their remarkable success. They spoke for and embodied the classical voice of the past in the present.

Chuang Ts'un-yü's activism should be viewed in light of Ch'ang-chou's late Ming political legacy. New Text Confucianism, however, initially represented a lineage-based political statement in contrast to the Tung-lin "party" initiatives of the late Ming. Nevertheless, structurally, both Ch'ang-chou reform movements were similar. The usurpation of imperial power by the eunuch Wei Chung-hsien in 1625 climaxed the Tung-lin crusade in Wu-hsi. Similarly, the Ho-shen affair was the immediate occasion for Chuang Ts'un-yü's turn to New Text Confucianism. In fact, the New Text interlude was an important eighteenth-century undercurrent in Ch'ang-chou. Protected by the legitimacy of lineages in late imperial China, New Text Confucianism not only drew on seventeenth-century Tung-lin activism but also fed into the nineteenth-century mainstream of literati activism (see chapter 9).

When we ask ourselves why the New Text school emerged in Ch'ang-chou, not Su-chou or Yang-chou, we find that the Ch'ang-chou traditions of learning during the eighteenth century helped to determine how scholars would come to grips with Han Learning. Most accounts of the Ch'ang-chou school emphasize Chuang Ts'un-yü's key role in reviving interest in the *Kung-yang Commentary* and New Text Confucianism. According to members of the Ch'ang-chou New Text school, Chuang Ts'un-yü was the one who took a stand against the prevailing current in a sea of Old Text–oriented Han Learning and initiated the New Text alternative. Kung Tzu-chen wrote: "Chuang [Ts'un-yü] took scholarship as his personal responsibility, and in the process he opened the door to the complexities of Old and New [Text studies]. Over the [last] hundred years, only one man [that is, Chuang] accomplished this [feat]."[56]

56. Kung Tzu-chen, *Kung Tzu-chen ch'üan-chi*, p. 141. Wei Yuan, *Wei yuan chi*, vol. 1, p. 238, includes Wei's "Hsu" (Preface) to Chuang Ts'un-yü's collected works, which stresses Chuang's place in the emergence of New Text ideas in Ch'ang-chou.

Compared with his contemporaries in Su-chou and Yang-chou, Chuang was less concerned with textual issues than with what he considered the "esoteric words containing great principles" (*ta-i wei-yen*), which he thought were best expressed in the *Spring and Autumn Annals*:

> The *Spring and Autumn Annals* brings order to chaos. It must express this [intent] through subtlety. This [method] is known as the "rituals prohibiting what came before there were rituals." That is what is expressed throughout the *Annals*. Therefore, everything in it has [special] signifiance.
>
> The *Annals* records affairs of Heaven and man and those of inner and outer. It focuses on recording [events] to establish doctrine. Then it connects many [events] and broadly encompasses them. Accordingly, the Tao of rulership is complete within.[57]

THE HANLIN "CLUB"

These were not the idle thoughts of a marginal scholar, but the influential opinions of a highly placed national official who had the ear of the Ch'ien-lung Emperor. *Secundus* on the palace examination of 1745, Chuang Ts'un-yü followed a career pattern typical of a Hanlin academician. As we have seen in chapter 2, this pattern typically took a successful young scholar through the Hanlin Academy to the Ministry of Rites and finally to the Grand Secretariat. Members of the Hanlin Academy became in effect the emperors's private secretaries and generally advanced easily to the pinnacles of power in the bureaucracy and the inner court. Chuang's career was a model for advancement through these complementary and overlapping government bodies during the Ch'ing dynasty.

Passing the 1745 capital examinations with such high honors immediately placed Chuang in the Hanlin "club." After some initial career problems owing to his poor calligraphy, Chuang served as a Hanlin Academy advisor and personal secretary to the Ch'ien-lung Emperor in the Southern Study (*Nan shu-fang*). There he opposed efforts to excise Old Text portions of the *Documents Classic* (*Shu-ching*) from the required texts used in the imperial examinations. This intellectual stance placed Chuang directly at odds with the Han Learning mood of the mid-eighteenth century in the Lower Yangtze region. The claim that the Old Text portions of the *Documents* were forgeries from the third cen-

57. Chuang Ts'un-yü, "Ch'un-ch'iu yao-chih," pp. 1a–2a. Chuang is citing a passage on ritual by Ssu-ma Ch'ien in the latter's *Shih-chi*, vol. 5, p. 3298 (*chüan* 130).

tury A.D., and not the work of the sage-kings of antiquity, was a cause célèbre among *k'ao-cheng* scholars.[58]

THE OLD TEXT *DOCUMENTS* CONTROVERSY

Considered a complement to the *Change Classic* (*I-ching*), the *Documents Classic* was regarded by Confucian scholars in all dynasties as the most important statement, among the texts that comprised the orthodox Five Classics (*wu-ching*), of the concrete institutions and practical teachings from antiquity. The *Documents* had been venerated as a "sacred Classic" (*sheng-ching*) since the Former Han dynasty. It had been a centerpiece of the Confucian examination system from the T'ang dynasty. The *Change* and *Documents* were frequently paired and given special attention. Many contended that the *Change* reflected the "essence of the Tao" (*Tao chih t'i*) while the *Documents* contained "its practical efficacy" (*Tao chih yung*) in the world.[59]

Doubts had been expressed since the Sung dynasty concerning the provenance of the Old Text chapters of the *Documents Classic*. But it was not until Yen Jo-chü's (1636–1704) research and the definitive conclusions in his *Shang-shu ku-wen shu-cheng* (Evidential analysis of the Old Text *Documents*) that the question was considered settled. Based on Yen's demonstrations that the Old Text portion was not authentic, proposals were sent to the throne in the 1690s calling for elimination of the Old Text chapters from the official text used in the imperial examination system. The proposals were set aside.

Hui Tung (1697–1758), the doyen of Han Learning in Su-chou, renewed the attack on the Old Text chapters in the 1740s. Because Yen Jo-chü's findings were passed around only in manuscript form until 1745, Hui wrote that he did not see Yen's work until 1743. By then, Hui was already deep into his own analysis of the Old Text chapters in a work called *Ku-wen Shang-shu k'ao* (Analysis of the Old Text *Documents*). He admitted that much of Yen's work agreed with his own findings and cited Yen as an authority to corroborate textual questions

58. See *Chuan-kao*, no. 5784, of Chuang Ts'un-yü in the Palace Museum archives, Taiwan, p. 53a, for imperial criticism of Chuang's calligraphy after his appointment to the Hanlin Academy. For Chuang's position on the Old Text *Documents*, see his biography in *Wu-chin Yang-hu hsien ho-chih* (1886), 23 : 3b–4a. See also Kung Tzu-chen, *Kung Tzu-chen ch'üan-chi*, pp. 141–42. On the "Hanlin Club," see Dennerline, *Chia-ting Loyalists*, pp. 17–23.

59. Chu I-tsun, *Ching-i k'ao*, 88.6a, where the remarks of Wang Ch'ung-ch'ing are cited.

that overlapped in their research. Appending Yen Jo-chü's points of agreement, Hui noted that it had taken several centuries for suspicions concerning the Old Text *Documents* to lead anywhere conclusive.[60]

Hui Tung's Han Learning followers continued research on the Old Text chapters. Ch'ang-chou's Sun Hsing-yen, with his definitive *Shang-shu chin-ku-wen chu-shu* (Notes and annotations to the Old and New Text *Documents*), brought to completion the attack on the spurious Old Text chapters. Begun 1794 and completed in 1815, Sun's analysis of Later and Former Han sources to evaluate Old and New Text variants marked the high point of the Old Text school's prestige during the Ch'ing dynasty.

Chuang Ts'un-yü, like most of his contemporaries, had at first agreed with Yen Jo-chü's findings that the Old Text chapters were forgeries. Chuang had read Yen's study of the *Documents* early on in his classical studies. When memorials were once again sent to the emperor in 1750 to request the removal of the Old Text chapters from official use, however, Chuang thought this was going too far. His grandson, Chuang Shou-chia, wrote of Ts'un-yü's anguish over the issue in an afterword to Ts'un-yü's own study of the *Documents Classic*:

> At first Ts'un-yü also thought the New Text and Old Text [portions] were different. He taught [the text] to my late father [Chuang F'eng-yuan] and uncle [Chuang Shu-tsu] by recording the portions separately for a textbook. Later when he saw the [specially] summoned [to the capital for imperial examinations] gentlemen Yen Jo-chü's *Evidential Analysis of the Old Text Documents*, Ts'un-yü thought [Yen's] attacks and criticisms went too far. Because of these [attacks], Ts'un-yü felt the Five Classics would in the end be corrupted. Sacred teachings since the Han and T'ang [dynasties] had declined and perished. [Until now,] only the Five Classics remained reliable.[61]

Chuang was continuing a classical position that had also been defended in Ch'ang-chou by the leaders in the Tung-lin Academy. The Tung-lin leaders had affirmed the authenticity of the Old Text *Document*'s *jen-hsin Tao-hsin* passage without questions. Ku Hsien-ch'eng, for example, had accepted Chu Hsi's explanation for the distinction between the "moral and human mind." Wang Yang-ming, Ku argued, had not meant that the moral mind contained neither good nor evil.

60. See my "Philosophy versus Philology," pp. 176–77, 206–208, 211–12, and *Philosophy to Philology*, pp. 177–80, 207–212.

61. Chuang Shou-chia, *Wen-ch'ao*, pp. 34a–35b. See also *Wu-chin Yang-hu hsien ho-chih* (1886), 23.3b.

What was at issue was the unreliable nature of the human mind. Ku concluded that both Chu Hsi and Wang Yang-ming agreed on this point, although they had articulated their positions differently.[62]

There were differences of opinion among the Tung-lin partisans, however. Ch'ien I-pen, who had helped to establish the Ching-cheng-t'ang (Hall of Classical Orthodoxy) as a Tung-lin meeting place in Ch'ang-chou, saw little positive in Wang Yang-ming's position. Rejecting Wang's doctrine of *wu-shan wu-e* (nature is neither good nor evil), Ch'ien cited Mencius: "Anyone without a mind that discriminates right from wrong is not human." Similarly, Sun Shen-hsing, another Ch'ang-chou follower of Ku Hsien-ch'eng and the great-great-grandfather of the Han Learning scholar Sun Hsing-yen, chose to follow Chu Hsi, not Wang Yang-ming, on the issue of the mind. He wrote:

> The human mind and the moral mind are not two separate minds. What makes someone human is the mind. What makes the mind the mind is the Tao. Within the human mind there is only the moral mind, which [encompasses] all moral principles. It is not that outside the moral mind there exists separately a human mind [composed] of a type of material form.[63]

Given such interpretive precedents, Chuang Ts'un-yü used his high position in the Hanlin Academy and the Southern Study to defend the imperial authorization of the Old Text *Documents Classic* on the grounds that the doctrines contained in these chapters were essential for social and political order. To remove the Old Text chapters from the officially authorized Classics would, he thought, not only cast serious doubt on the entire classical legacy but would also serve to undercut the theoretical underpinnings of the Confucian state.

At the confluence of classical studies, legitimation of state power, and policy articulation, Chuang's conservative position represented his ideological solidarity with the state orthodoxy of the Ch'ing dynasty. The Han Learning threat to the Old Text Classics threatened the consensus among officials and gentry enshrined in the curriculum for the examination system. Political power and ideology, not simply philology, were at issue for Chuang Ts'un-yü.

Chuang noted that if the Old Text chapter long accepted as "Coun-

62. For Chu Hsi's position, see *Chu-tzu ta-ch'üan*, 76.21b. See Ku Hsien-ch'eng's paraphrase of Chu Hsi's position in his "Hsiao-hsin-chai cha-chi," 5.7a.

63. Sun Shen-hsing, *Hsuan-yen-chai k'un-ssu ch'ao*, 1.25a. Cf. Huang Tsung-hsi, *Ming-Ju hsueh-an*, pp. 649–51 (*chuan* 59). See also Ch'ien I-pen, *Kuei-chi*, 1.11a, and Chien I-pen, *Fan-yen*, 1.9a–9b. See *Meng-tzu yin-te*, 13/2A/6. Cf. Busch, "Tung-lin Academy," pp. 92–97, 130–31.

sels of Yü the Great" was impugned, then the cardinal doctrine of the "human mind and moral mind" (*jen-hsin Tao-hsin*) would be subverted. Also in jeopardy, according to Chuang, was the legal injunction or Kao Yao, minister to Emperor Shun (tr. r. 2255–2206?? B.C.), which stated: "Rather than put to death an innocent person, you [Shun] would rather run the risk of irregularity." These teachings, Chuang contended, depended on their classical sanction. Accordingly, on ideological grounds, Chuang Ts'un-yü attempted to set limits on the growing *k'ao-cheng* research by scholars in the Han Learning mainstream.[64]

REFORMISM IN THE EARLY CH'IEN-LUNG ERA

After leaving the Hanlin Academy, Chuang served for much of his distinguished career as an undersecretary in the Ministry of Rites. True to his career path, Chuang became a mainstay of the Grand Secretariat from 1755 until 1758, and again from 1762 to 1773. Besides other duties in the Ministry of Rites, he also served periodically as director of education (*hsueh-cheng*) in the capital region and elsewhere. Experienced and well-read, Chuang Ts'un-yü used his influence and prestige as an examination official in Shun-t'ien County (in the capital) to push through basic reforms in the imperial examination system.[65]

While education commissioner in Chih-li Province (1756–58), in the capital region, Chuang memorialized that all local-level licentiates (that is, all those permitted to take higher examinations) should register with the Ministry of Rites. The aim was to prevent irregularities and to keep substitutes from taking the examination under assumed names. The ministry was powerless to prevent cases of examination fraud, because it could not keep track of who was who and who was authorized to take the examinations administered in the north and south respectively.[66]

In addition, Chuang memorialized that the emperor should limit examination quotas for successful provincial *chü-jen* candidates in order

64. *Wu-chin Yang-hu hsien ho-chih* (1886), 23.3b–4a. See also the translation in Legge, *Shoo King*, p. 59. On the Hanlin Academy and Southern Study, see Lui, *Hanlin Academy*, pp. 31–32.

65. See *Ch'in-ting hsueh-cheng ch'üan-shu*, which Chuang Ts'un-yü helped to compile. Problems with the examinations are raised in 2.12b, 6.1a–13b, 14.1a–2b. See also *Ch'ing-tai chih-kuan nien-piao*, vol. 2, pp. 614, 624–32, 974–89; and vol. 4, pp. 2662–63, 2672.

66. *Chuan-kao* no. 5784 of Chuang Ts'un-yü, pp. 54a–54b.

to maintain control over the numbers of local degree holders. The Ch'ien-lung Emperor accepted Chuang's proposal and limited successful candidates for the *chü-jen* degree in populous provinces to one in twenty participants. Medium-sized provinces were limited to a ratio of one in fifteen, while border areas and small provinces could accept one in ten candidates. In this way, it was hoped that cases of fraud in provincial examinations could also be brought under control.[67]

Chuang Ts'un-yü's reformist mettle was severely tested, however, when he effected similar reforms in examinations in Peking for Manchu and Mongol bannermen—that is, members of the Ch'ing dynasty's standing army. In reversing the lax and corrupt administration of these examinations, Chuang precipitated a riot during the 1758 bannermen examination owing to his new, strictly enforced policies. It seems bannermen had grown accustomed to trading information in order to answer examination questions. Things had gotten so far out of control that soldiers used slips of paper and hidden notes in order to pass around information on the questions and to receive in turn information on the answers.[68]

Chuang was quickly cashiered through the efforts of T'ang Shih-ch'ang, the Han Chinese censor for the capital region. In a memorial to the Ch'ien-lung Emperor, T'ang blamed Chuang's overly strict policies for the riot. Chuang Ts'un-yü's career hung in the balance. The emperor, however, came to Chuang's rescue, after determining to his own satisfaction that the irregularities Chuang had opposed were indeed common among the bannermen taking examinations for advancement. Infuriated by the censor's unfair portrayal of Chuang Ts'un-yü's part in the incident, the Ch'ien-lung Emperor used the occasion to defend Confucian values and to admonish his Manchu entourage in Peking:

> Manchu customs until now have been sincere and simple. Followers of the Eight Banners have energetically studied their own national language [*Kuo-yü*, that is, Manchu]. They have accepted the need to focus their energy on firing [crossbows] from horseback. If they want to study the Chinese language, however, they must also devote their minds to oral recitations. [In this way] they will have the [mental] strength to take the examinations. If they cannot compose the [proper] written answers by themselves, and can only

67. Ibid., pp. 57a–58a.

68. The examination riot of 1758 is taken up in an edict preserved in the *Shang-yü tang*, pp. 038–050, under Ch'ien-lung 23, 2d month. See also *Ta-Ch'ing Kao-tsung Ch'un (Ch'ien-lung) huang-ti shih-lu*, vol. 11, pp. 8161, 8166–67, 8168, 8170. For a discussion of military examinations see Chuang Chi-fa, "Ch'ing Kao-tsung Ch'ien-lung shih-tai te hsiang-shih," 29–31.

> cheat by passing slips of paper containing the answers, or by secretly carrying notes or books into the examination room, thereby through reckless luck achieving an honored name [on the examination roll], then the time spent in studying Chinese can be seen as a deleterious means for taking laws and regulations lightly and indulging in corrupt practices. Moreover, one can question what [sort of] moral character and spiritual intent will ensue.[69]

In complete support of his former personal secretary, the emperor had those involved in the riot punished; the necessary reforms were carried out. From then on, all Manchu and Mongol bannermen above the third grade, as well as their sons and grandsons (who inherited their military positions), were required to pass written examinations in Chinese appropriate to their position. Cashiered as Chih-li education commissioner by a Han Chinese censor who had not foreseen where the Manchu emperor's wrath would fall once the facts in the case were verified, Chuang Ts'un-yü emerged from the racially charged examination incident vindicated and firmly entrenched in the Grand Secretariat.[70]

Ts'un-yü, accordingly, was a voice for the gentry-official elite at the pinnacles of the Manchu imperium. Along with Grand Counselor Liu Lun (1711–73), Chuang Ts'un-yü also exemplified the penetration of Ch'ang-chou lineages into the highest reaches of the imperial bureaucracy (see chapter 2). The Chuangs and Lius were insiders during the Ch'ien-lung Emperor's regime until the meteoric rise of the Manchu palace guard Ho-shen.

To appreciate fully the significance of Chuang Ts'un-yü's reformism in his illustrious official career, we need to understand the role Chuang's classical studies played in his perilous political postures. The rise of New Text studies in Ch'ang-chou, we shall discover, was not an isolated intellectual event. It is tied to Confucian political culture as scholar-officials like Chuang Ts'un-yü sought ways to mitigate what Ch'ang-chou literati considered the pernicious impact of Ho-shen on late-eighteenth-century political life.

CHUANG TS'UN-YÜ VS. HO-SHEN

A man of power and prestige since the 1740s, a man who had challenged the bannermen's incompetence and fraud in the Peking military

69. *Shang-yü tang*, p. 045.
70. Ibid., pp. 039, 042, 046–047.

examinations at the risk of offending his Manchu ruler, Chuang Ts'un-yü served out his last years in office in the high levels of the imperial bureaucracy; he retired in 1786. These were precisely the years when Ho-shen emerged triumphant in the state apparatus. In 1776, at age twenty-six, the handsome former guard was already in the Grand Council. By 1784 Ho-shen was concurrently an assistant grand secretary and president of the ministries of personnel and finance. In 1786 Ho-shen became a grand secretary. A confidant of the Ch'ien-lung Emperor since his service as secretary in the 1740s to the emperor in the Southern Study, Chuang Ts'un-yü was thus witness to the changes that ensued. Ho-shen is said to have cemented his position as the emperor's favorite and translated prestige into a private financial and political empire not seen since the hated eunuch factions of Wei Chung-hsien of the late Ming.[71]

In his preface to Chuang Ts'un-yü's writings on the *Change Classic*, Tung Shih-hsi, a Ch'ang-chou Han Learning scholar, described the shadow Chuang had cast during the Ch'ien-lung Emperor's reign:

> His prose was discerning yet precise, judicious yet unrestrained. The lessons [contained] are lofty and yet the meaning is close at hand. He broaches the key issue and yet does not overlook minute details. He was able to enunciate what other Confucians could not. Those who did not know him thought he represented an ancillary current within the [mainstream of] classical studies during the Ch'ien-lung era. Those who knew him thought he epitomized the grand union of classical studies during the Ch'ien-lung period.

Tung's account, about which more later, suggests that Chuang Ts'un-yü's classical scholarship should be read on many levels. Chuang's efforts to avoid the pitfalls of partisan classical debate, whether Han Learning or Sung Learning, pointed to a deeper question lurking at the heart of his classical studies and his turn to the *Kung-yang Commentary* on the *Spring and Autumn Annals* in the 1780s.[72] Like his great-great-grandfather Chuang T'ing-ch'en, who had opposed the pretentions of the eunuch Wei Chung-hsien in the 1620s, Ts'un-yü opposed Ho-shen in the 1780s. The exact form of this opposition remains murky, but we have evidence that Chuang Ts'un-yü was allied in imperial politics with the Manchu general and Grand Counselor A-kuei against Ho-shen and his group. To illustrate Chuang Ts'un-yü's

71. *Ch'ing-tai chih-kuan nien-piao*, vol. 1, p. 144 ff.
72. Tung Shih-hsi, "I-shuo hsu," pp. 3a–3b.

ties to A-kuei's faction, we have an account prepared around the year 1816 by the Yang-chou Han Learning scholar Wang Hsi-hsun, whose father, Wang Chung, was a distinguished Han Learning scholar from Yang-chou.[73]

In his biography of Ts'un-yü nephew, Chuang Shu-tsu, Wang Hsi-hsun described what had happened when Shu-tsu took the *chin-shih* examinations in Peking in 1780. Chuang P'ei-yin, Shu-tsu's father, had been *optimus* on the palace examination of 1754, and in 1745 his uncle Ts'un-yü had been *secundus*. Hence Shu-tsu had early on come to the attention of A-kuei, then a senior member of the Grand Council, through Chuang Ts'un-yü, A-kuei's friend and colleague. Because Shu-tsu was the only son of a high official, he was entitled to official status by virtue of the inheritance principle (*yin-tzu*) granting one son exemptions from normal recruitment obligations. Consequently, A-kuei had wished to bring Shu-tsu into his service. Fearing impropriety, however, Shu-tsu opted to take his chances on the *chin-shih* examinations to gain public office on his own merits.

During the 1780 palace examinations, however, Ho-shen outmaneuvered A-kuei. After the palace examination papers had been graded and were formally sent to the emperor for the final ranking of candidates, Shu-tsu's materials were deemed among the best, a ranking that would have entitled him to an immediate appointment in the Hanlin Academy. Fearing that A-kuei's influence at court would be increased by Shu-tsu's placement in the Hanlin Academy (Chuang Ts'un-yü was then the senior Chinese minister in the Ministry of Rites), Ho-shen's accomplices were able to change the rankings while the examination papers were in transit to the emperor. Chuang Shu-tsu's materials were relegated to a lower ranking, below the top ten papers, rendering him ineligible for appointment to the Hanlin Academy.[74]

Cheated out of his high ranking, Chuang Shu-tsu returned to Ch'ang-chou. On the pretext of taking care of his widowed mother (his father P'ei-yin had died in 1759), Shu-tsu turned his attention to classical scholarship. Over the next decades, as a private scholar, Chuang Shu-tsu became one of the leading voices in *k'ao-cheng* research, producing a long list of specialized philological studies, which we shall discuss in chapter 5. In addition, Shu-tsu promoted the New Text studies of his uncle.

73. Wang Hsi-hsun, *Ch'ieh-chu-an wen-chi*, pp. 221–22.
74. Ibid.

As a successful *chin-shih* graduate, Chuang Shu-tsu, despite Ho-shen's efforts, was still technically entitled to an official appointment. By the late eighteenth century, a wait of ten years for an official position as county magistrate, for example, was not unusal. Again, however, Shu-tsu ran afoul of Ho-shen. All successful *chin-shih* candidates had their names included on a list of eligible appointees used by the Grand Council in deciding appointments. Such candidates, including officials eligible for promotion to higher office, were required by this time to appear before Ho-shen to pay their respects. This ceremony included the required bows and prostrations. Chuang Shu-tsu, along with a prefect from Yun-nan Province, T'u Shen, refused to appear before Ho-shen, who used the affront as an excuse to remove Shu-tsu's name from the list. But a close personal secretary to the Ch'ien-lung Emperor, upon hearing what had happened to Shu-tsu, intervened, and Chuang's name was restored to the roster. Shu-tsu was subsequently offered official posts, but he remained adamant in his refusal to serve while Ho-shen remained in power.[75]

Imperial politics had cost Shu-tsu the official career to which members of his line in the Chuang lineage had long been accustomed. Ironically Chuang T'ing-ch'en, who had snubbed Wei Chung-hsien the way Shu-tsu snubbed Ho-shen, was honored in 1746 as an outstanding Ming dynasty official by the Ministry of Rites. Chuang Ts'un-yü was then a personal secretary to the emperor and no doubt influenced the decision. By 1780 the wheel had turned, and the Chuangs were again opposed to a usurper. Wang Hsi-hsun's account of Chuang Shu-tsu's troubles with Ho-shen was openly presented in light of his forebear's earlier opposition to the eunuch Wei Chung-hsien.[76]

This incident also helps us to better understand why Chuang Ts'un-yü's son-in-law, Liu Chao-yang retired to private life in 1784 after passing the special examination administered that year during the Ch'ien-lung Emperor's southern tour to the Yangtze Delta. Chao-yang's older brothers and illustrious father had all reached high office before Ho-shen began his meteoric rise in the palace. Like his generational counterpart in the Chuang lineage, Shu-tsu, Liu Chao-yang decided to stay out of the maelstrom of politics in the 1780s, demonstrating the better part of valor. Too much was at stake, both individually and for the Liu lineage. After Ho-shen's death in 1799, Chao-yang's

75. Ibid., pp. 222–23.
76. *Wu-chin Chuang-shih tseng-hsiu tsu-p'u* (ca. 1840), 3.25b.

son, Liu Feng-lu, continued the Liu commitment to serving in public office.

Chuang's classical scholarship, particularly his turn to the *Kung-yang Commentary*, likely represented an attempt to use the language of Confucian politics in order to create a legitimate framework for criticizing the wrongs of the late Ch'ien-lung era. Chuang Ts'un-yü's links to A-kuei and his efforts to oppose Ho-shen in the imperial court corroborate this supposition. Wei Yuan, in his 1828 preface prepared for the posthumous publication of Chuang Ts'un-yü's collected writings, referred, for example, to Chuang's sense of political impotence in the 1780s. As late as the reign of the Tao-kuang Emperor (1821–50), Wei Yuan had to be careful about his public discussions of the Ho-shen affair. Among rare unpublished manuscripts that survive in the Peking National Library, drafts of Wei Yuan's preface reveal that Wei considered excluding final remarks about Chuang Ts'un-yü that would raise the Ho-shen affair. The remarks Wei pondered read as follows:

> Master [Chuang Ts'un-yü] served as a high court official during the end of the Ch'ien-lung era at the same time as Grand Secretary Ho-shen. They did not get along and could not work together. Consequently, Chuang Ts'un-yü used the *Poetry* and *Change* [Classics] to describe the dilemmas gentlemen face in their fortunes vis-à-vis small-minded men. Throughout his writings, Chuang expressed his pent-up concerns, indulging his unending sighs of grief. In reading his works, one can sympathize with his ambitions.[77]

Wei Yuan's remarks are instructive on a number of points. Early confidants of the Ch'ien-lung Emperor were confronted during his last decades of rule with the ultimate betrayal of their efforts to serve the throne for the sake of the dynasty. Their loss of status at the court must also have stung. A-kuei's faction at court remained in the forefront of efforts to root out what they perceived as the evils unleashed by Ho-shen and his henchmen throughout the 1790s (see chapter 9). Hung Liang-chi, a Ch'ang-chou literatus affinally linked to the Chuangs and associated with A-kuei's faction moralized on the change in political atmosphere that had occurred during the Ch'ien-lung era:

> Long ago, while I was still quite young and following my grandfather and father about, whenever we saw someone in the neighborhood with the title of prefect or county magistrate, his friends and relatives would be consoling

77. The manuscripts in question are entitled *Ku-wei-t'ang wen kao*. The compilers of the *Wei Yuan chi* relied on these unpaginated draft essays for their edition. See *Wei Yuan chi*, vol. 1, pp. 236–38, for the "Hsu" (Preface) to Chuang Ts'un-yü's collected writings.

and encouraging, expressing their concern by saying, "the business of this post of his is quite complex," or "the affairs of this post are quite simple," or "this post has a reputation for being difficult to administer." I never heard them mention other things.

During the twenty- or thirty-year period after I had come of age, and before I took office, the character of public morals underwent a transformation. Now when I see someone in the neighborhood with the title of prefect or magistrate, his friends and relatives console and encourage him and likewise express their concern by saying, "the profits of this post are such and such," or "the bribes for favors you can get at this post are such and such," or "what you can profit at this post is thus and so." But they no longer consider such matters as the welfare of the people or the management of personnel.[78]

Later, in a 1799 letter addressed indirectly to the Chia-ch'ing Emperor (r. 1796–1820), and for which he almost lost his life, Hung Liang-chi alluded to "exacting standards of the previous emperor's early rule" as the ideal that the Ho-shen era had betrayed:

Why was the Ch'ien-lung Emperor, at the beginning of his reign, a worthy successor to his father [the Yung-cheng Emperor, r. 1723–35] and grandfather [the K'ang-hsi Emperor, r. 1662–1722]? Why did he surpass the other princes and win the hearts of the people like this? It is not only because the Ch'ien-lung Emperor was indeed a sage without peer, but also because the crowds of upright men who filled his court, and those around him, were all men who were not afraid to speak out in the face of opposition.[79]

According to the accounts of Wang Hsi-hsun, Wei Yuan, and Hung Liang-chi, the Chien-lung Emperor's early advisors, such as Chuang Ts'un-yü, witnessed the crumbling of moral standards during the Ho-shen era. Wei Yuan's contention, discussed above, that Chuang Ts'un-yü's opposition to Ho-shen gave his classical scholarship a certain momentum and direction is instructive on a second level. To this point, we have ascribed the eighteenth-century revival of New Text Confucianism in Ch'ang-chou to intellectual factors, chiefly the late Ming statecraft legacy. In addition, we have delineated the social dimensions of the Ch'ang-chou New Text school by stressing how New Text traditions were incubated within the Chuang and Liu lineages in gentry society. The difficulties of the Ho-shen era add yet another dimension to our understanding of the precise historical genesis of New Text Confucianism in the late eighteenth and early nineteenth centuries.

78. Hung, *Hung Pei-chiang shih-wen-chi*, vol. 1, p. 40 (*chüan* 1) and Susan Mann (Jones), "Hung Liang-chi," p. 3

79. *Pei-chuan chi*, 51.7a, and Susan Mann (Jones), "Hung Liang-chi," p. 163.

In other words, the rise of New Text Confucianism was part of an effort to ameliorate the divisive impact of the Ho-shen affair in Confucian political culture. In this effort, New Text ideas symbolized the revival of literati concern for their political fate precisely when the relations between the state and its gentry constituency were dramatically changing. Although we will describe the Ch'ien-lung–Chia-ch'ing transition in more detail later, we should observe here that Chuang Ts'un-yü's turn to *Kung-yang* Confucianism was strategic and political. The renascence of New Text Confucianism, then, was part of a larger transformation of literati perceptions regarding their personal and dynastic responsibilities—a transformation that began during the Ho-shen era. New Text Confucianism was offered as a solution to the ensuing crisis of confidence.

Chuang Ts'un-yü, as we have seen, devoted much of his career to official duties. From 1745 until 1786—the pivotal four decades of his sixty-nine years of life—Chuang served the dynasty as an influential capital official, whose prestige as imperial advisor, Hanlin academician, grand secretary, and vice-president of the Ministry of Rites filtered down to his lineage and affinal relations in Ch'ang-chou. His scholarly reputation, as we will see in the next chapter, was virtually unrecognized until the 1820s. Ts'un-yü began to receive notice only posthumously, via the writings of his grandsons, Liu Feng-lu and Chuang Shou-chia. Yet even in the 1820s it was hard to discuss the political context within which Chuang Ts'un-yü had composed his *Kung-yang* studies.

In the last years of his life, Chuang turned to classical studies and completed a series of works that initiated the revival of *Kung-yang* Confucianism, touching off a reformist line of classical discourse that would lead to the New Text Confucianism of Liu Feng-lu and the latter's more radical nineteenth-century followers. Chuang Ts'un-yü's involvement in the Ho-shen affair, consequently, enables us to perceive the political context within which the Ch'ang-chou New Text school emerged. Wei Yuan's discussion of Chuang Ts'un-yü's political impotence vis-à-vis Ho-shen in the 1780s reveals that, initially, *Kung-yang* Confucianism was a classically veiled criticism of bureaucratic corruption.

In the opening remarks for his *Ch'un-ch'iu cheng-tz'u* (Correcting terms in the *Spring and Autumn Annals*)—organized under the heading "Injunction Against Tyranny" ("Chin-pao tz'u")—Chuang described the conditions by which a "state could perish" (*wang-kuo*):

> Contention runs counter to morality. Upon the culmination of battles and wars, [a state] is weakened, never to rise again. We realize this through the unfolding of events; such events frequently recur. Knowing the past, we become enlightened about this pattern. The mind of the sages accorded with benevolence [*jen*] and no more. Benevolence is the root of humility [*jang*]. Through benevolence, profit [*li*] is eliminated. Humility is the root of rituals. Through humility, contention is eliminated. Rituals are the root of the state. Through rituals, war is eliminated. If benevolence is not earnestly practiced, then neither profit nor war can be eliminated. Without any benefits, such a course is the way [a state] perishes. . . .
>
> Doesn't the *Analects* say, "If one is guided by profit in one's actions, one will incur much ill will?" Or, "If a man is able to govern a state by observing rituals and practicing humility, what difficulties will he have [in public life]?" If good men make up a government, then for a hundred years they can triumph over cruelty and eliminate murders. If there is a king like this, then the age will become benevolent. Is this not a warning that evil must be changed to the way of good? Without benevolence and humility, then contention to see [who will] profit and [who will] lose will lead to war! Contention over right and wrong will also lead to war. [Such] evils are committed in different ways, but they all lead back to the same results: chaos![80]

In Chuang's discussion of the final "key point" (*yao-chih*) of Confucius's *Spring and Autumn Annals* Classic, his intent in turning to the *Kung-yang chuan* was clear:

> A state cannot [survive] without its exalted status and mandate [to rule from Heaven]. Without [the mandate], the ruler is a usurper. According to the meaning articulated by Master Kung-yang, there were eight cases in which those who took power were all usurpers. Ho Hsiu recorded it in his commentary. Yes! Yes! The position of ruler is what licentious men use to gain the upper hand. Therefore, the *Annals*, with regard to a time when secret dealings determine life and death, tried mightily to prevent such [usurpations of power].[81]

It is easy to understand why Chuang Ts'un-yü's classical studies were not published until the 1820s, given Ho-shen's alleged usurpation of imperial power. After all, Chuang Ts'un-yü's views also reflected his role as an important spokeman for the Chuang lineage in Ch'ang-chou, which since the early Ch'ing period had been dependent on the imperial

80. Chuang Ts'un-yü, *Ch'un-ch'iu cheng-tz'u*, 383.1a–3a. For the citations from the *Analects*, see *Lun-yü yin-te*, 6/4/12, and 6/4/13. Cf. Lau, trans., *Confucius*, p. 73.

81. Chuang, "Ch'un-ch'iu yao-chih," p. 7b. Satō Shinji mistakenly suggests that very little reformist sentiment is reflected in Chuang's writings. See Satō, "Shinchō Kuyōgakuha kō (jō)," 24–25.

power structure then in place for confirmation of its local and national prominence.

Chuang Ts'un-yü's remarks were both a harbinger of the "voices of remonstrance" (*ch'ing-i*) at the turn of the nineteenth century and an echo of his Tung-lin forbears, opposed to the tyranny of Wei Chung-hsien. Chuang Ts'un-yü's critical intent, which he enunciated through the classical repertoire available to him, had two major elements. First, we see his political intent, which forces us to reevaluate Chuang's conservative position in imperial politics. Second, we see his reformist intent, which later champions of New Text ideas such as Wei Yuan and Kung Tzu-chen read into his writings.

An aging scholar-official imbued with ideals of the Confucian vocation since childhood, Chuang Ts'un-yü "expressed his pent-up grief" through classical studies. Model precedents for a "gentleman" (*chün-tzu*) in a time when "small-minded men" (*hsiao-jen*) had the upper hand began with Confucius's life. His *Spring and Autumn Annals* stood as a record of death and destruction, a model for political criticism within which Confucius had measured his contemporaries and envisioned, according to the *Kung-yang Commentary*, a new order to come. Our discussion in the next chapters of the *Annals* and *Change Classic* as sources for an activist vision takes on added significance when understood in light of Chuang Ts'un-yü's political response to his sudden fall from favor and to the perceptible decline of the Ch'ing state.

The rise of New Text Confucianism must be understood within the larger political landscape of the decline of China's last imperial dynasty. Only then can we fully appreciate why elements of reform and later utopianism became associated with this emerging vision of Confucian regeneration and rebirth. If the Han Learning vs. Sung Learning controversy represented the intellectual limits within which New Text Confucianism was reformulated, its social and political direction was foreshadowed by the Ho-shen era and the revival of Tung-lin-style political activism in the early nineteenth century.

Beginning with chapter 4, we shall move from the social and political roots of New Text Confucianism to its strategic position in the intellectual life of eighteenth-century Ch'ang-chou. Turning from the statecraft tradition of the Chuang lineage, we shall then explore the history of Confucian classicism in Ch'ang-chou and the scope of Chuang Ts'un-yü's influence and legacy there.

FOUR

Recasting the Classical Tradition

Chuang Ts'un-yü's dramatic turn to *Kung-yang* Confucianism marked an important stage in the ongoing efforts of Ch'ing Confucians to recast the classical tradition. Han Learning savants, enamored of evidential research, had decisively challenged the state's Ch'eng-Chu orthodoxy. The Ch'ang-chou turn to New Text Confucianism continued this classical reappraisal, although the content and meaning of Han Learning was now recast in favor of reformism.

In imperial China, classical and historical studies provided frameworks for the habits, interests, and values inherited by Confucian scholar-officials. Each classical text accumulated a history of its effects and interpretations, which then became a constituent part of the state's raison d'être.[1] As state ideology during the late empire, Neo-Confucian orthodoxy represented the institutionalization of "truth." Accordingly, state authorities selected and interpreted commentaries on the Classics and Dynastic Histories that would present acceptable views of man, society, and the world and thus help to consolidate state authority. Because of the role played by the sage-kings and Confucius in articulating (through the Classics) the guidelines both for political authority and for dissent against that authority, later Confucians easily stepped into their

1. Mannheim, "Ideological and Sociological Interpretation," pp. 116–31. See also Rieff, *Triumph of the Therapeutic*, pp. 1–27. Cf. Kahn, "Education of a Prince," and Mote, "Growth of Chinese Despotism," 33–34. Mote notes that even the despotic first Ming emperor appealed to "collective goals which had to be justified in terms of values of the society."

own roles as interpreters and transmitters of these "guidelines": the classical legacy.[2]

HAN LEARNING IN CH'ANG-CHOU

Paradoxically, the rise of New Text studies was at first associated with a conservative political movement—paradoxical because New Text Confucianism is normally linked with the more radical statecraft agendas of the nineteenth century. It is true, nevertheless, that Chuang Ts'un-yü turned to New Text studies in an effort to preserve state orthodoxy, although the very effort included remarkable concessions to Han Learning. New Text interpretations of the Han dynasty Classics, it was feared, would hardly uphold the Sung Learning orthodoxy then under attack by Han Learning scholars.[3]

Because Chuang Ts'un-yü was a political creature, his interests in the Classics were inseparable from his political career. As a member of a prominent lineage and a confidant of the Manchu ruler, Chuang Ts'un-yü exemplified the scholar-official striving to uphold the Confucian consensus at the heart of the balance between national and local interests in the imperial state. Judging from Ts'un-yü's career and writings, the reemergence of New Text Confucianism in Ch'ang-chou was brought on by concerns about the traditional Confucian state and the classical articulation of political power through which its directives, laws, and rituals were legitimated. Chuang sought in the *Kung-yang Commentary* to reconfirm classical precedents for the legitimation of power, realizing that the Sung Learning rationale for the Confucian imperium was in jeopardy.[4]

Oblivious to the full radical political implications of *Kung-yang* Confucianism, Chuang essentially sought to preserve the classical legacy, regardless of the criticisms of Han Learning and *k'ao-cheng* scholarship. Institutional reformation (e.g., the examination system) was for Ts'un-yü mandated by his conservative vision whose ideals harkened to a golden past in search of a remedy for a chaotic present. The *Annals, Rituals of Chou*, and *Change Classic*, as we shall see below, provided the classical medium for this conservative articulation of power.

As we have seen, Chuang Ts'un-yü used the *Kung-yang chuan* as a

2. Julia Ching, "Truth and Ideology," p. 371. See also Pocock, *Politics, Language, and Time*, pp. 42–79.
3. See T'ang Chih-chün, "Ch'ing-tai ching chin-wen-hsueh te fu-hsing," pp. 145–56.
4. Ibid., p. 156

veiled criticism of the Ho-shen era. In this dangerous context, conservatism could have radical implications in a corrupt body politic rampant with the betrayal of classical ideals. And, indeed, this was borne out by the overt radicalism of Ts'un-yü's successors—New Text Confucians such as Wei Yuan and Kung Tzu-chen. But we should be careful to demarcate the conservative classical agenda Chuang Ts'un-yü passed on to his grandson Liu Feng-lu from the inherent radicalism that later emerged as part of the New Text agenda.

In the mid-eighteenth century a new group of Ch'ang-chou literati took form, and their influence in local and national affairs lasted into the nineteenth century. Sun Hsing-yen, great-great-grandson of the Tung-lin partisan Sun Shen-hsing (1565–1636), and Hung Liang-chi, along with friends and colleagues such as Huang Ching-jen, Chao Huai-yü, and Chao I, formed a coterie of Han Learning scholars and literary men in their native Wu-chin and Yang-hu counties. Chao Huai-yü and Hung Liang-chi were cousins and, along with Chao I, had ties to the Chuang lineage. They frequently met as an informal poetry group at the I-chou-t'ing (Pavilion for Mooring Boats) east of the city walls, as well as at the Hung-mei-ko (Hall of Red Plums). The latter, dating back to the thirteenth century under a different name, had been a popular gathering spot for Ch'ang-chou gentry since the Ming dynasty.[5]

As leading scholars in Ch'ang-chou, Sun Hsing-yen, Hung Liang-chi, and Li Chao-lo were each active participants in the turn toward Han dynasty sources and interpretations. In many ways they represented the Old Text position in Ch'ang-chou, paralleling similar intellectual and cultural currents to the north in Yang-chou and to the south in Su-chou. Han Learning had been transmitted to Ch'ang-chou in part by the Hang-chou native Lu Wen-ch'ao, a leading *k'ao-cheng* scholar, during the 1790s when he was in charge of the Lung-ch'eng Academy, the city's leading private academy. Earlier, Lu Wen-ch'ao had taught at the prestigious Chi-yang Academy in Chiang-yin County, north of the prefectural capital in Ch'ang-chou.[6]

By the eighteenth century academies in Ch'ang-chou were no longer venues for political ferment, although they remained intellectual centers

5. See Kuo Shao-yü, *Chi-nien shih-jen Huang Chung-tse*, and Wu Hsiu's "Hsu" (Preface), p. 9a. Chao Huai-yü was a nephew of the eminent historian Chao I. See Tu Wei-yun, *Chao I chuan*, pp. 121, 129. See also the epitaph for Hung Liang-chi by Wu Hsi-lin, in Hung Liang-chi, *Hung Pei-chiang ch'üan-chi, chüan* for biographies, pp. 17a–21b, and Chao Huai-yü's "Hsu" (Preface).

6. *Ch'ang-chou fu-chih* (1886), 15.13a–13b, and *Wu-chin Yang-hu hsien ho-chih*, 12.43a–46b. See also Hsu K'o, *Ch'ing-pai lei-ch'ao*, 69.4–5.

where new trends in *k'ao-cheng* scholarship were transmitted. Founded in the late Ming, the Lung-ch'eng Academy was directed by Shao Ch'i-tao when its students first studied Han Learning. Two of the most acclaimed literati who studied at Lung-ch'eng after it was rebuilt in the 1760s were Huang Ching-jen and Hung Liang-chi. Huang and Hung were childhood friends who had lived on opposite sides of the same stream and remained close colleagues thereafter.[7]

The Chi-yang Academy in Chiang-yin had been founded in the early Ch'ing period, but it did not become a Han Learning center until Lu Wen-ch'ao was appointed director in 1756. Li Chao-lo was appointed director in 1823 and remained in his post until 1840. A native of Yang-hu County, Li began his studies at Lung-ch'eng in 1789 under Lu Wen-ch'ao's tutelage. He built on typically Ch'ang-chou interests in mathematics, mathematical astronomy, and geography, which he then tied to the standard *k'ao-cheng* fields of philology and phonology. Later he became well known for his wide-ranging studies, which included major contributions in geography and local history. The New Text scholar Wei Yuan praised Li for his broadly based scholarly interests, which he attributed to the influence of Chuang Ts'un-yü and the Ch'ang-chou New Text school:

> Since the middle of the Ch'ien-lung [Emperor's reign], literati in the empire have championed Han Learning. Moreover, this [development] has been especially prominent north and south of the Yangtze River. . . . The result has been that the talented and intelligent have followed a useless path [of study]. . . . [Li Chao-lo] made no distinction between Han and Sung [Learning] in his writings, focusing only on personal achievement as the key. . . .
>
> During the Ch'ien-lung [Emperor's reign], among classical masters there was [only] Chuang Fang-ching [i.e., Ts'un-yü], who as undersecretary [in the Ministry of Rites] was able to master the great meanings [in the Classics]. . . . Both of these perceptive Confucians [i.e., Chuang and Li] arose together at the same time from Wu-chin [County in Ch'ang-chou Prefecture]. Isn't [this place] very productive? I never met Mr. Chuang, but I did meet Mr. Li. Accordingly, I have recorded [Li Chao-lo's] main teachings here.

The Chi-yang Academy remained the most prominent school in Chiang-yin until the appearance of the Nan-ch'ing Academy, which the nineteenth-century "self-strengthener" Tso Tsung-t'ang helped to establish in 1884. It is interesting that one of the major projects com-

7. Susan Mann (Jones), "Hung Liang-chi," pp. 21, 34–36.

pleted at Nan-ch'ing was an authoritative continuation, published in 1886–88, of the widely acclaimed 1827 *Huang-Ch'ing ching-chieh* (Ch'ing dynasty exegesis of the Classics). This commemoration of Han Learning carried the pedigree of evidential research from the Ch'ien-lung and Chia-ch'ing reigns into the late nineteenth century.[8]

Reflecting on the emergence of Han Learning in Ch'ang-chou, Hung Liang-chi noted:

> During the Yuan and Ming [dynasties], Confucians devoted themselves to empty and useless studies. They not only attacked but also refused to discuss the six rules [for paleography] or glossing [for etymology]. As a result, Confucian studies daily were obscured and idle talk took over. Although some could still read [classical] texts, such as Yang Shen [1488–1559] and Chu Mou-wei [d. 1624], they never went beyond idiosyncratic manipulation [of what they read]. They carelessly interpolated false materials and established notions that never could be supported.
>
> With the rise of our dynasty, solid learning first appeared. The retired scholar Ku Yen-wu [1613–82] and the summoned [for special imperial examinations] gentleman Yen Jo-chü [1636–1704] first opened the way, but all the obscure possibilities were not yet realized. By the beginning of the Ch'ien-lung Emperor's reign, the world had already benefitted from over one hundred years of peace. Brilliant and remarkably learned scholars appeared in quick succession. The erudition of the summoned gentleman Hui Tung and the compiler Tai Chen was at last sufficient to surpass the ancients.

With interests ranging from literature (*wen-chang*) to classical techniques (*ching-shu*), Ch'ang-chou scholars were also noted for their attention to New Text studies. Standing on the borderline between philosophy and philology—that is, between Sung Learning and Han Learning—Ch'ang-chou literati, as Wei Yuan noted, relied on a peculiar mixture of statecraft concern and philosophic focus. Nevertheless, the Han Learning rebellion against Sung Learning spawned in Su-chou and Yang-chou established the intellectual context for the social and political conclusions drawn by eighteenth- and nineteenth-century New Text scholars in Ch'ang-chou.[9]

The emergence of Han Learning and *k'ao-cheng* in Ch'ang-chou can be traced to Tsang Lin. His major work, *Ching-i tsa-chi* (Assorted jottings on the meanings of the Classics), has been recognized by Yen Jo-chü (a leading *k'ao-cheng* scholar during the early Ch'ing) as pivotal in overturning Sui-T'ang and Sung-Yuan-Ming interpretations and return-

8. Wei Yuan, *Ku-wei-t'ang nei-wai chi*, 4.27a–30b.

9. Hung, *Hung Pei-chiang ch'üan-chi*, 9.3a–3b. See also Su Wan-en's "Hsu" (Preface) to ibid., pp. 1a–2a.

ing to Han scholia of the Classics. In addition, Tsang wrote philological studies on New Text–Old Text issues. In a nineteenth-century essay by Lü Ching-nan entitled "Introduction to Ch'ang-chou Classical Masters during the Ch'ing Dynasty," the work of Tsang Lin is featured prominently and linked to prevailing trends of Han Learning and evidential research, known popularly as "solid studies" (*p'u-hsueh*).[10]

TSANG LIN

Tsang Lin's stress on the early sources of the Classics was noted by Ch'ien Ta-hsin, perhaps the most distinguished Han Learning scholar in the late eighteenth century:

> [Tsang Lin] took as his mission reading books to inquire into antiquity. He taught others first the *Erh-ya* [Progress toward correctness] and *Shuo-wen* [Explanation of writing] [dictionaries]. According to Tsang, if one does not understand the written graphs [in the *Shuo-wen*], how can one read books? If one does not master etymology [based on glosses in the *Erh-ya*], how can one grasp the Classics? He contended that in ordering the Classics one must give priority to the Han commentaries and T'ang subcommentaries. When Yen Jo-chü of T'ai-yuan [Shan-hsi] prefaced Tsang's book, Yen praised him for deeply illuminating the [classical] learning of the two Han dynasties [that is, Former and Later Han].

When Lu Wen-ch'ao was placed in charge of the Lung-ch'eng Academy in Ch'ang-chou (1790–96), he came to know Tsang Yung, Tsang Lin's great-great-grandson. Yung allowed Lu to see his ancestor's manuscripts and Lu Wen-ch'ao later was responsible for the republication of Tsang Lin's *Ching-i tsa-chi*. The reprint included additional prefaces by Han Learning specialists Wang Ming-sheng, Ch'ien Ta-hsin, Tuan Yü-ts'ai, and Chiang Sheng—all followers of Hui Tung's Su-chou school of Han Learning—and placed Tsang Lin firmly at the forefront of Han Learning in Ch'ang-chou.[11]

Tsang Lin's stress on Han commentaries provoked interest because he adhered to the notes and emendations of the Classics by Cheng Hsuan (A.D. 127–200). Cheng's Later Han classical views were the main pillars of the Han Learning school in Su-chou. Although he

10. In Chao Chen, *P'i-ling wen-lu*, 8.5a–10b. See Yen Jo-chü, "Yuan-hsu," pp. 1a–2b, in Tsang Lin, *Ching-i tsa-chi* (*hsu-lu*).

11. *Wu-chin Yang-hu hsien ho-chih* (1886), 26A.17a–17b. See the prefaces by Wang Ming-sheng (pp. 3a–4a), Ch'ien Ta-hsin (pp. 4a–5b), Tuan Yü-ts'ai (pp. 5b–7b), and Chiang Sheng (pp. 7b–9a), in Tsang Lin, *Ching-i tsa-chi* (*hsu-lu*), "tsa-lu," pp. 3a–9a, on which the gazetteer biography is based.

affirmed the Old Text position of the Later Han, Tsang Lin also attempted to reconstruct earlier Old Text and New Text recensions, which Cheng Hsuan had weaved together to present a comprehensive classical framework.[12]

On the *Analects*, *Poetry Classic*, and *Documents Classic*, for example, Tsang presented detailed research on the different New Text and Old Text recensions for each, arguing that both were essential for reconstructing the "schools system" (*chia-fa*, lit., "methods of the schools") for classical studies during the Former and Later Han dynasties. Tsang Lin also sought to clarify the Old and New Text traditions through his studies on the *Spring and Autumn Annals*. He shed light on differing interpretations of the *Annals* in the three orthodox Han commentaries.[13]

By focusing on the Han dynasty "schools system," Tsang Lin was among the first to reject the Sung-Ming "orthodox transmission" (*Tao-t'ung*) tradition, which had neglected Han and T'ang commentaries since the Sung Confucians. Tsang proposed that the Sung-Ming transmission be replaced by Han dynasty master-disciple transmission of interpretations of the Classics, a position that became a staple of Ch'ing dynasty Han Learning. We can therefore understand why eighteenth-century Han Learning scholars praised Tsang so highly.

In seizing upon Tsang Lin's long-overlooked classical writings, Hui Tung's Han Learning school demonstrated that Ch'ang-chou scholars could not remain isolated from the surrounding intellectual currents. Even Chuang Shu-tsu, Chuang Ts'un-yü's nephew, was involved in collating and publishing Tsang's volume on the Classics. Despite strong local traditions, Han Learning and evidential research had spilled over into Ch'ang-chou during the last half of the eighteenth century.

What went unnoticed, however, was the degree to which Tsang Lin had reopened a philological can of worms: the New Text–Old Text debate. Scholars redoubled their efforts to differentiate the Later Han Old Text and Former Han New Text "schools system" for the Han transmission of the Five Classics. The Ch'ang-chou New Text position was clearly foreshadowed by Tsang Lin in the early eighteenth century. But when his views were later championed by prestigious Han Learning scholars in Ch'ang-chou, no one was aware of the implications of the New Text–Old Text split.[14]

12. Tsang Lin, *Ching-i tsa-chi* (*hsu-lu*), "tsa-lu," 17.6a–9b.
13. Ibid., 2.10b–16b, 14.2a–5b, 21.12a–12b, 26.3a–5a.
14. Ibid., 26.13a–16a.

YANG CH'UN

Yang Ch'un, regarded as another precursor of Han Learning, is best known for his biting criticism of the *Rituals of Chou.* But the Ch'ang-chou classical scholar and Hanlin academician also wrote a number of technical essays demonstrating the inauthenticity of Old Text chapters of the *Documents Classic.* Yang was especially critical of both Cheng Hsuan, the exemplar of Ch'ing dynasty Han Learning, and K'ung Ying-ta (547–648). The latter had compiled the *Shang-shu cheng-i* (Orthodox meanings in the *Documents*) under T'ang dynasty imperial auspices in an effort to provide a definitive version of the Old Text and New Text chapters for use in the civil service examination system.[15]

Building on the earlier findings of Yen Jo-chü, Yang Ch'un employed textual, stylistic, and chronological criteria to demonstrate the spuriousness of the twenty-five Old Text chapters that suddenly "reappeared" early in the fourth century A.D. Yang also confirmed Yen's conclusion that the long-accepted K'ung An-kuo (156–74? B.C.) "Preface" (*Hsu*) to and "Commentary" (*Chuan*) on the *Documents Classic* were actually forgeries from the third century A.D.; the twenty-five Old Text chapters were also implicated. Yang went beyond Yen's analysis, however, of the implications of the forged preface.[16]

Yang's most innovative conclusion was, perhaps, his rejection of the tradition regarding the recovery of sixteen Old Text chapters from the wall of Confucius's old residence when King Kung of Lu (r. 154–127 B.C.) assumed the throne and decided to enlarge his palace. According to the *Han-shu* (History of the Former Han dynasty), the chapters were secreted away in order to escape the Ch'in (221–207 B.C.) "burning of the books." Yang argued that this tradition—supported by the "Forged K'ung An-kuo Preface" (*wei K'ung An-kuo hsu*)—was demonstrably false because other members of the K'ung family, not K'ung An-kuo (as was claimed in the forged preface), had presented the original Old Text chapters to the Han imperial court. Yen Jo-chü had already demonstrated as much, but Yang Ch'un said the discrepancy meant that the original Old Text version had not been hidden away, but instead had been preserved and protected by the K'ung lineage all along.[17]

Yang pushed these conclusions further by pointing out that later

15. Yang Ch'un, *Meng-lin-t'ang chi*, 6.6b–7a.
16. Ibid., 6.12b–13a, 6.16a–16b, 6.19b–20a. For a discussion see my *Philosophy to Philology*, pp. 177–80, 207–212.
17. Yang Ch'un, *Meng-lin-t'ang chi*, 6.16a–17b.

commentators misunderstood the *Han-shu* (History of the Former Han dynasty) accounts of the Old Text chapters. He argued that two commentators in particular, Cheng Hsuan and K'ung Ying-ta, presumed that the *Han-shu* account referred to "Old Text" and "New Text" as two separate groups of chapters. But, in fact, there was only one version of the *Documents* chapters, which was later differentiated according to calligraphy styles used in recopying this version. "New Text" versions had been recorded in the clerical script (*li-shu*), characteristic of the Former Han dynasty; the "Old Text" versions were rewritten in a seal script (*chuan-shu*) that predates the Han (see figs. 1–3).

Yang Ch'un maintained that the original "New Text" version had also been recorded in seal script (that is, "Old Text") only to be rerecorded in the clerical script. What, then, was Old Text and New Text? Yang contended that Cheng Hsuan and K'ung Ying-ta had misrepresented the true provenance of the original *Documents Classic*, thereby leading to later perversion of one of the original Five Classics. In the process, a forged version of twenty-five "Old Text" chapters had replaced the original sixteen "Old Text" chapters lost since the Later Han.[18]

Yang Ch'un's philological assault on the Old Text Classics culminated with his research on the *Chou-li* (*Rituals of Chou*), one of the Thirteen Classics since the T'ang dynasty. In a 1747 preface to his *Chou-li k'ao* (Examination of the *Rituals of Chou*), Yang noted that he had devoted more than six decades to the study of the *Chou-li* and had concluded that the work could not be traced back to the Duke of Chou (Chou-kung, tr. d. 1094 B.C.?), as claimed by Han Confucians. Instead, he tied the *Chou-li* to Shen Pu-hai's (d. 337 B.C.) more Legalist views on political statecraft. Yang dismissed the *Rituals* as a heterodox text that drew on utilitarian doctrines developed by the enemies of Confucianism during the Warring States period (403–221 B.C.). He claimed it was ludicrous to link the *Chou-li* to the sagely Duke of Chou.

In his 1818 preface for the Ch'ang-chou publication of Yang Ch'un's collected essays, Chao Huai-yü described Yang's powerful criticism of the *Rituals* and its penetration of the Confucian mainstream. According to Yang, two of the greatest calamities in Chinese history had resulted from the *Chou-li's* pernicious utilitarian and legalistic political values. Both Wang Mang's brief usurpation (A.D. 9–23) and Wang An-shih's (1021–86) Northern Sung reform program were doomed to failure,

18. Ibid., 6.14a–15a, 15a–15b.

Yang contended, because they had championed the heterodox ideas in the *Rituals of Chou.*[19]

Wang Mang and Wang An-shih had drawn a detailed bureaucratic structure of ancient provenance from the *Rituals* that justified comprehensive agrarian and bureaucratic reform. Such reform, however, stressed the priority of the state in establishing policy. Not only Wang Mang and Wang An-shih but also emperors and officials of the Ming and Ch'ing dynasties derived their rural control systems from the *Rituals.* The distinctive systems of neighborhood and village tax collection (*li-chia*) and household registration (*pao-chia*), each based on units of ten households, received their classical pedigree from the *Rituals.*[20]

Chao Huai-yü's 1818 preface also described Yang Ch'un's classical contributions during the early years of the Ch'ien-lung Emperor's reign. It was during this time that Han Learning had begun to take center stage in *k'ao-cheng* scholarship. Chao failed to anticipate that Yang had unintentionally lent support to the Ch'ang-chou New Text school's claim that New Text Confucianism was superior to the Old Text classical tradition. By challenging the authenticity of centrally important Old Text classical texts, Yang was also calling into question the legitimacy of state policy.[21]

New Text scholars in Ch'ang-chou were intimately linked to the rise of Han Learning, which, as we have seen, revived the New Text–Old Text debate. All sides of the debate focused on the Han dynasty to overcome limitations in the Sung dynasty orthodoxy. Han Learning and its offspring, New Text Confucianism, were therefore, in effect, reinvented by Lower Yangtze literati in an effort to eradicate the heterodox Taoist and Buddhist notions plaguing official Neo-Confucian ideology.

STUDIES OF THE *CHANGE CLASSIC* IN CH'ANG-CHOU

As head of the Lung-ch'eng Academy, Lu Wen-ch'ao apparently felt responsible for recording and preserving local scholarship in Ch'ang-

19. Ibid., 5.17b–23a. On Shen Pu-hai see Creel, *Shen Pu-hai*, and Chao Huai-yü, "Hsu" (Preface) to Yang's *Meng-lin-t'ang chi*, pp. 1a–3a.

20. Yang Hsiang-k'uei, *Ching-shih-chai hsueh-shu wen-chi*, pp. 149, 247–48. On the political content of the *Chou-li*, see pp. 228–76, and pp. 18–28. For Wang Mang's use of the *Chou-li* see Uno, *Chūgoku kotengaku no tenkai*, pp. 81–82.

21. Chou, *Ching chin-ku-wen hsueh*, pp. 27–36.

chou. He therefore compiled the *P'i-ling ching-chieh-chih* (Bibliography of classical works from Ch'ang-chou).[22] Lu's efforts were especially welcome in view of the prefecture's lack of an archivist. Beginning with works on the *I-ching*, Lu's bibliography traced local scholarship on the *Change Classic* back to late Ming writings by Tung-lin partisans Ch'ien I-pen and Sun Shen-hsing in Wu-chin County, as well as to Kao P'an-lung and Ku Yun-ch'eng in Wu-hsi. Ch'ien's work received particular notice in the authoritative bibliographic summary (*t'i-yao*) for the *Ssu-k'u ch'üan-shu* (Complete collection of the Four Treasuries); the editors praised Ch'ien's efforts to reconstruct the images (*hsiang*) in the *Change*.[23]

YANG FANG-TA AND YANG CH'UN

Lu Wen-ch'ao accorded Yang Ch'un and Yang Fang-ta (fl. ca. 1724) eminence of place in his section on local *I-ching* studies. Both men had achieved high public office during the early eighteenth century. Their interest in the Classics foreshadowed Hui Tung's influential application of the Han Learning agenda to *I-ching* scholarship.[24]

A specialist in *I-hsueh* (studies of the *Change Classic*), Yang Fang-ta was well-read in the Classics. Like many early Ch'ing Confucians, however, Yang had already begun to stress Han and T'ang dynasty scholia for classical studies, a perspective that drew praise from Yen Jo-chü, for example. Yang Fang-ta's movement toward Han dynasty sources, however, did not represent the irrevocable break with Sung-Ming Confucians that Hui Tung's Han Learning did.[25]

In his preface to Yang Ch'un's collected writings, discussed above, Chao Huai-yü first linked Yang to T'ang Shun-chih and late Ming traditions of ancient-style prose in Ch'ang-chou. He then claimed that Yang Ch'un's classical studies had set the stage for conclusions later drawn by Han Learning scholars in Ch'ang-chou. We have noted above that Yang Ch'un's positions lent support to the emerging New Text position in

22. Lu Wen-ch'ao's *P'i-ling ching-chieh-chih* has survived as an unpaginated manuscript in the Peking National Library. In 1859 a compilation entitled *Ch'ang-chou fu pa-i i-wen-chih* (Bibliography of the eight towns in Ch'ang-chou Prefecture) appeared. Lu also initiated this edition of shorter essays and writings by Ch'ang-chou natives to complement the first. The latter was completed by Chuang I-p'i of the Chuang lineage. See the "Hsu-lueh" (Overview) to *Ch'ang-chou fu pa-i i-wen-chih* by Chuang I-p'i, p. 1b. See also Lu Wen-ch'ao's "Hsu" (Preface) to the *P'i-ling ching-chieh-chih*, pp. 1a–1b.

23. See *Ssu-k'u-ch'üan-shu tsung-mu*, 5.14b–15b.

24. Lu, *P'i-ling ching-chieh-chih*, "I-lei" (Works on the *Change Classic*).

25. *Wu-chin Yang-hu hsien ho-chih* (1886), 23.2b–3a, 26A.24a–24b.

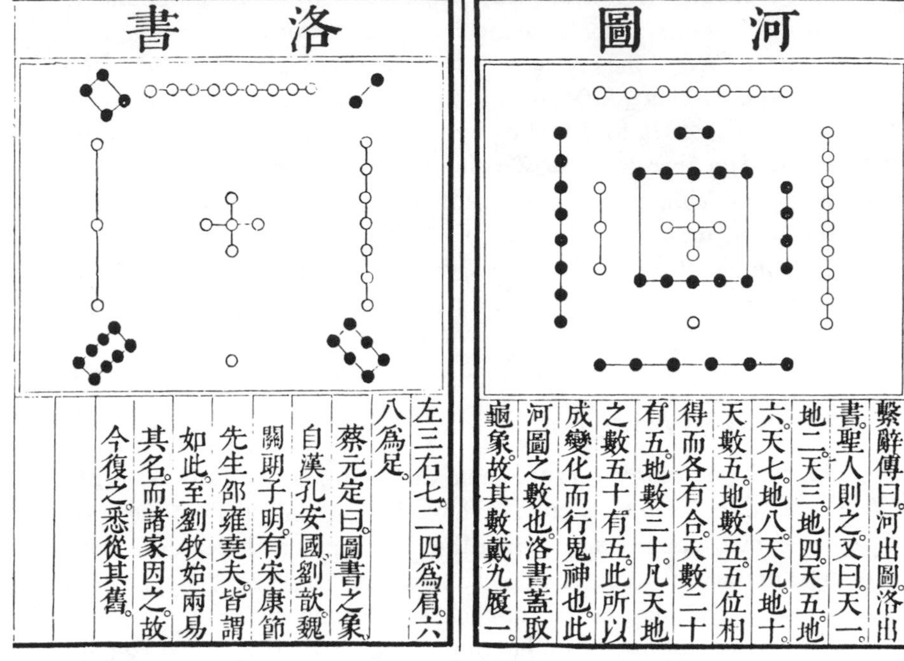

洛書
左三右七二四爲肩六
八爲足
蔡元定曰圖書之象
自漢孔安國劉歆魏
關朗子明有宋康節
先生邵雍堯夫皆謂
如此至劉牧始兩易
其名而諸家因之故
今復之悉從其舊
河圖
繫辭傳曰河出圖洛出
書聖人則之又曰天一
地二天三地四天五地
六天七地八天九地十
天數五地數五五位相
得而各有合天數二十
有五地數三十凡天地
之數五十有五此所以
成變化而行鬼神也此
河圖之數也洛書蓋取
龜象故其數戴九履一

Fig. 11. The *Ho-t'u* 河圖 (River Chart; right) and the *Lo-shu* 洛書 (Lo Writing; left)

The *Lo-shu* is a magic square in which numbers along any diagonal, line, or column add up to 15. The *Ho-t'u* is arranged so that when the central 5 and 10 are disregarded, both odd and even number sets add up to 20.

Source: Chu Hsi's *Chou-i-pen-i* 周易本義 (Original meaning of the Chou *Changes*; Taipei: Hua-lien ch'u-pan-she, 1971).

Ch'ang-chou, which was closely tied to *k'ao-cheng* research on the Old Text Classics and the doubts it threw on the Confucian Canon.[26]

COSMOGRAMS IN THE *CHANGE CLASSIC*

In their *I-hsueh*, neither Yang Fang-ta nor Yang Ch'un accepted the more radical positions of late Ming and early Ch'ing Confucians, who had exposed the Taoist provenance of certain cosmic diagrams that since the Sung dynasty had been part of the official text of the *Change Classic*. In fact, Yang Fang-ta based his own research on the nine charts in Chu Hsi's annotations of the *Change Classic*. But Yen Jo-chü's friend and colleague Hu Wei (drawing on the findings of Huang Tsung-hsi and Kuei Yu-kuang) had earlier rejected the classical antiquity of the *Ho-t'u* (River Chart) and *Lo-shu* (Lo Writing) cosmic diagrams (*t'u*) (fig. 11) in his widely read *I-t'u ming-pien* (Discerning clearly the diagrams in the *Change Classic*).

Embarrassed by the inclusion of the charts in Chu Hsi's commentary on the *Change*, Huang Tsung-hsi and others tried to play down the importance of the cosmic diagrams in that work. Huang also denied the cosmological significance of the charts and maintained instead that they were originally primitive geographical maps and charts. In his critique of their purported mystical correspondences Hu Wei demonstrated the Taoist origins and associations of the cosmic diagrams in the *I-ching*. Their heterodox origins also placed into doubt the legitimacy of Sung Confucians as transmitters of the Confucian Canon.[27]

The charts had traditionally been understood as the graphic progenitors of the primal world-ordering instruments used by the sage-kings and were thought to be linked to the eight trigrams (*pa-kua*) of the *I-ching*. According to legend, the sage-king Yü (tr. r. 2205–2197?? B.C.) was presented with two magic charts by miraculous animals after he had tamed raging floods. The River Chart was the gift of a dragon-horse that emerged from the Yellow River; the Lo Writing was presented by a turtle from the Lo River. These cosmograms were considered by Sung Confucians to be the origin of Chinese mathematics. The Han Learning attack on the authenticity of the charts thus

26. Chao Huai-yü, "Hsu" (Preface).

27. *Ssu-k'u ch'üan-shu tsung-mu*, 10.13a–14a. See also Kuei, *Kuei Chen-ch'uan hsien-sheng ch'üan-chi*, 1.20a–25a. Huang Tsung-hsi's *I-hsueh hsiang-shu lun* was another influential work in late Ming *I-ching* studies. Cf. Henderson, *Development and Decline of Chinese Cosmology*, pp. 137–73, 218–25.

struck at the heart of the Sung Learning cosmological ordering of the heavens and earth.[28]

In the process, heterodox accretions to the *Change Classic* (traced back to the Lao-Chuang [Lao-tzu and Chuang-tzu] scholar Wang Pi [226–249] after the fall of the Later Han dynasty) were increasingly subjected to critical scrutiny. Criticism of the *Ho-t'u* and *Lo-shu* became so sharp that even Ch'ing dynasty Sung Learning scholars felt compelled to dissociate themselves from the teachings of their Sung dynasty masters. By the 1780s the editors of the *Complete Collection of the Four Treasuries* could express their pride in recapturing the true face of the ancient *Change Classic* and in demystifying the more recent superstitions surrounding the Sung Learning version of the text. Hui Tung's research, according to the editors, was the epitome of Han Learning.[29]

A decisive shift in *I-hsueh* was in the making, and in the mid-eighteenth century Hui Tung emerged as the premier *I-ching* scholar of his time. His followers among the Yangtze Delta literati employed the Han Learning framework to reconstruct the "images and numbers" (*hsiang-shu*) of the *Change Classic*. The Han Learning legacy of Hui Tung captured *I-hsueh*.

HUI TUNG AND *I-HSUEH*

Hui Tung reissued a book in 1756 in an effort to counteract the heterodox Taoist doctrines that he thought Wang Pi had introduced into the interpretation of the *I-ching*. Written by the Southern Sung Confucian Wang Ying-lin (1223–96), the work was entitled *Cheng-shih Chou-i* (Master Cheng [Hsuan's] version of the Chou [dynasty] *Change* [*Classic*]). It contained some notable additions, including sources. Wang Ying-lin's pioneering *k'ao-cheng* studies were revived by a number of Ch'ing dynasty evidential research scholars. In his preface for the reissued work, Lu Chien (fl. ca. 1756) wrote:

> Cheng Hsuan's scholarship had been established in the official academy since the Han, Wei [221–280], and Six Dynasties [280–589]. For several hundred years there were no differing opinions. During the T'ang dynasty, between 627 and 649, K'ung Ying-ta composed the *Orthodox Meanings in the Five Classics*. For the *Change* [*Classic*] he relied on Wang Fu-ssu [that is, Pi]; for the *Documents* [*Classic*], he relied on K'ung An-kuo. As a result, Cheng

28. Saso, "What Is the *Ho-t'u*?" See also Needham, *Science and Civilization in China*, vol. 3, pp. 55–59.

29. *Ssu-k'u ch'üan-shu tsung-mu*, 1.1a–2a.

> [Hsuan's] meanings for these two Classics were lost. Today, the only available sources [for Cheng Hsuan's annotations] are the three *Rituals* [*Classics*] and the Mao recension of the *Poetry* [*Classic*].
>
> Until the Northern Sung, Cheng's version of the *Change* was still extant. By the Southern Sung, however, four chapters [of the latter] had already been lost. As a result Wang Ying-lin from Ling-i began to collect materials from many books in order to reconstruct Cheng [Hsuan's] version of the *Change* in one [complete] chapter.[30]

At stake in such reconstructions was the relocation of the foundation of orthodox Confucianism in the teachings of Han dynasty Confucians, thereby overturning the Sung-Ming tradition of *Tao-t'ung* (orthodox transmission). The latter stressed Confucius and Mencius but rejected Han Confucians such as Cheng Hsuan as the basis for Neo-Confucian orthodoxy. Sung Confucians had gone so far as to claim that "after the Ch'in burning of the books, [some] books nonetheless survived. As Han Confucians pored through the Classics, the Classics were lost." Hui Tung and his followers stressed the restoration of the Han dynasty transmission of classical studies through the networks of teacher-student relations within the officially sponsored Han Confucian Academy (*T'ai-hsueh*). Once the "schools system" was restored, even late writings from the Han would yield an authoritative framework for Confucian orthodoxy based on Han Learning. Lu Chien noted the importance of this strategy:

> Han Confucians when explicating the *Change Classic* all followed the schools system [*chia-fa*]. They would not dare produce works that did not follow in this line of tradition. What Wang Ying-lin has collected together still contains remnants of this system. My friend Hui Tung From Yuan-ho [that is, Su-chou] has mastered the ancient meanings and added [materials] and revisions to be combined with the sayings of the Han [Confucian Cheng Hsuan] who reached the top of Mount Sung [the highest of the Five Sacred Mountains]. As a result, Hui reissued [Wang Ying-lin's work] in three chapters [incorporating these additions].[31]

In his own major studies, entitled *I Han-hsueh* (Han Learning of the Change Classic) and *Chou-i shu* (Transmission of the Chou *Change Classic*), Hui Tung noted that the reconstruction of Han Learning

30. Lu Chien, "Hsu" (Preface) to Wang Ying-lin's *Cheng-shih Chou-i*, pp. 1a–1b. See also Hui Tung's "Hsu" (Preface) to his *I Han-hsueh*, and *Ssu-k'u ch'üan-shu tsung-mu*, 1.7a–8a.

31. Lu Chien, "Hsu," (Preface), p. 1b. See also Hsueh Ying-ch'i, *Fang-shan hsien-sheng wen-lu*, 20.7b, for the Sung attack on Han Confucian scholarship. On the Han "schools system," cf. Ebrey, "Patron-Client Relations in the Later Han."

required the recognition that much of the present classical canon was of dubious origin:

> The Six Classics were authoritatively transmitted by Confucius, burned under the Ch'in [dynasty], and retransmitted under the Han. Han Learning has been lost for a long time now. Only the *Poetry*, *Rituals*, and *Kung-yang* [*Commentary*] have remained intact. The three Mao, Cheng, and Ho traditions of the *Spring and Autumn Annals* were disordered by Mr. Tu [Yü, 222–284]. The *Documents Classic* was disordered by the forged K'ung [An-kuo] version. The *Change Classic* was disordered by Mr. Wang [Pi]. . . .
>
> Still, although Han Learning had been lost, it had not been completely lost. Only when Wang Fu-ssu [Pi] borrowed the theories of images [*hsiang*] to explicate the *Change Classic* and based them on Huang-Lao [Huang-ti (Yellow Emperor) and Lao-tzu] Taoism were the meanings taught by Han classical masters irrevocably lost.[32]

Hui Tung wanted to purify the *I-ching* of Taoist interpretations that since the Sung dynasty had replaced the Han dynasty "schools system" tradition for the transmission of the *Change*. So Hui began to compile the *Chou-i shu* to overturn Chu Hsi's *Chou-i pen-i* (Original meanings of the Chou *Change*), considered an orthodox text since the Yuan dynasty. Because Chu Hsi's version included the Taoist cosmic diagrams that Huang Tsung-hsi and Hu Wei had already called into question, as well as anachronistic metaphysical concepts such as *hsien-t'ien* (before heaven, that is, a priori) and *wu-chi* (vacuous ultimate), Hui regarded it as a continuation of Wang Pi's misguided *I-hsueh*.[33]

Hui Tung passed away before finishing the *Chou-i shu*, but his Su-chou disciple Yü Hsiao-k'o (1729–77) completed the project. In this work, Hui Tung was intent on restoring the "esoteric words" (*wei-yen*) and "great meanings" (*ta-i*) in the *Change Classic*, which would then clarify the "precedents" (*i-li*) and "models" (*i-fa*) that Han Confucians had gleaned from the *Classic*. Hui therefore made frequent use of the *Kung-yang* commentary on the *Spring and Autumn Annals* to clarify the Han dynasty version of the *I-ching*. Yang Hsiang-k'uei has recently pointed out the degree to which Hui Tung's *I-hsueh* lead him to re-evaluate the *Change Classic* in light of New Text vs. Old Text recensions.

Hui Tung's Han Learning position allowed him to move back and forth from the *Kung-yang Commentary* and the *Change Classic* because the former was one of the few Han dynasty classical commentaries to

32. Hui Tung, "Hsu."

33. Hui Tung, *I Han-hsueh*, 8.5b–6b, where Hui notes the superiority of Ch'eng I's version of the *Change* because it contains fewer Taoist accretions. See also Lu Chien's "Hsu" (Preface) to Hui Tung's *Chou-i shu*, pp. 1a–2a.

have survived in one piece after the demise of Han Confucian traditions during the T'ang and Sung. The *Kung-yang*'s authoritative presentation of "precedents" and "models" that Confucius had encoded in the *Annals* (see chapter 5) could thus be applied to Confucius's version of the *Change* as well. For Hui Tung, "the *Change* and *Annals* both represented the Way of Heaven and man" (*t'ien-jen chih tao*). The logic of Han Learning assumed the existence of an overriding classical symmetry among the texts Confucius had brought together to form the Six Classics.[34]

Hui Tung's program for Han Learning was applied to all of the surviving Five Classics and their Han commentaries. In Ch'ang-chou, the *Change Classic* and *Spring and Autumn Annals* came under close scrutiny by both Chang Hui-yen and Chuang Ts'un-yü.

CHANG HUI-YEN AND CH'ANG-CHOU *I-HSUEH*

Eleven of Chang Hui-yen's books on the *Change Classic* received mention in Lu Wen-ch'ao's Ch'ang-chou bibliography. This impressive number far surpassed mention of Chuang Ts'un-yü's work, of which only six were included. Surprisingly, Ts'un-yü was second in prominence in the *I-hsueh* bibliography. Chang Hui-yen, like many Ch'ang-chou classicists, had close ties with the Chuang lineage, especially to Chuang Chün-chia (1761–1806), Ts'un-yü's grandson. This friendship extended to Yun Ching, who prepared an epitaph for Chün-chia describing Chang Hui-yen's and Chün-chia's mutual interests in classical studies, and especially their admiration for Ts'un-yü's *I-hsueh*.[35]

The development of Han Learning *I-ching* studies in Ch'ang-chou yielded the influential studies of Chang Hui-yen, which shed much light on Chuang Ts'un-yü's interest in the *Change Classic* and its place in Chuang's classical scholarship. Su Wan-en also noted the link between Ch'ang-chou *I-hsueh* and *Kung-yang* studies, which he considered characteristic of the "learning of Ch'ang-chou":

> The learning of Ch'ang-chou moreover has become prominent within the empire. For example, Mr. Chang Hui-yen's ordering of the Cheng [Hsuan] and Yü [Fan, 172–241] versions of the *Change Classic* and Mr. Liu Feng-

34. Hui Tung, *I-li*, 137.1b. See also Yang Hsiang-k'uei, *Chung-kuo ku-tai she-hui yü ku-tai ssu-hsiang yen-chiu*, vol. 2, pp. 901–11.

35. Yun Ching, *Ta-yun shan-fang chi*, pp. 182–83 (*erh-chi, chüan* 4). See also *Chu-chi Chuang-shih tsung-p'u* (1883), 8.32a–33a, and *P'i-ling Chuang-shih tseng-hsiu tsu-p'u* (1935), 13.20b–21b.

lu's ordering of the *Kung-yang* [*Commentary*] to the *Annals* are both outstanding illustrations of a single tradition.[36]

In an 1803 preface to Chang Hui-yen's study on the *Change Classic*, Juan Yuan (speaking for the Yang-chou Han Learning tradition) described the book as a continuation of Hui Tung's efforts to reconstruct the Han dynasty appearance of the *Change Classic*. In his own preface to the work, Chang confirmed Juan's appraisal, claiming that his reconstruction of Han dynasty interpretations of the *Change* derived from Hui Tung's pioneering research on "ancient meanings" (*ku-i*).[37]

But Chang Hui-yen went beyond Hui, widening the Han Learning approach to the *Change* by including attempts to reconstruct the Hsun Shuang (128–190) and Yü Fan recensions, and not just Cheng Hsuan's version that Hui had emphasized. Chang's research on the Yü Fan recension was of particular interest. It added considerable collateral evidence on the *I-ching* during the Han period.[38]

Like Hui Tung, Chang Hui-yen was interested in reconstructing the pre–Wang Pi version of the *Change Classic* in order to recapture the thought-world of the ancients after centuries of misrepresentation. In particular, he sought to build on the seventeenth-century criticism of the cosmic diagrams associated with the *I-ching* and to reconstruct what those charts represented during classical antiquity, before they were lost and replaced by Taoist cosmograms. Theory and cosmology did not worry him, as they worried so many *k'ao-cheng* scholars, but misguided theory and heterodox cosmology did.[39]

In another work on the Chou *Change*, Chang Hui-yen demonstrated interest in Chuang Ts'un-yü's contributions to *I-hsueh*. Chang's nephew Tung Shih-hsi later composed an important preface to this work (see below). Liu Feng-lu, in his 1802 inscription for Chang Hui-yen's *Yü-shih i-yen* (Mr. Yü's comments on the *Change*), noted his close friendship with Tung Shih-hsi, who had transmitted Chang's research on the Yü Fan recension to him. An 1803 afterword by Ch'en Shan to Chang Hui-yen's *Meanings in Mr. Yü's Chou Change* described the

36. *P'i-ling ching-chieh-chih*, "I-lei." See also Su Wan-en, "Hsu" (Preface).

37. Juan Yuan, "Hsu" (Preface) to Chang Hui-yen, *Chou-i Yü-shih i*. Efforts to restore the *Poetry Classic* to its Han dynasty form had been initiated by Hui Chou-t'i, Hui Tung's grandfather. See Hui Chou-t'i's *Shih-shuo*. Hui Shih-ch'i, Hui Tung's father, initiated similar efforts on the *Spring and Autumn Annals*, which we shall discuss in the next chapter.

38. Chang Hui-yen, "Hsu" (Preface) to his *Ming-k'o wen ssu-pien*, A.18–20.

39. Tseng, "Hsu" (Preface), which describes Chang's theoretical interests. See also *Hsu-hsiu Ssu-k'u ch'üan-shu t'i-yao*, pp. 79–81.

close friendship among Tung Shih-hsi, Li Chao-lo, and Liu Feng-lu. The pervasive impact of Chang's *I-hsueh* in Ch'ang-chou occurred within a context of literati collegiality.[40]

These links between Chang Hui-yen's research and the Ch'ang-chou New Text school are further confirmed by Chang's association with other members of the Chuang lineage with whom he corresponded or for whom he composed epitaphs included in the Chuang genealogy. In fact, it was through the efforts of Tung Shih-hsi and Liu Feng-lu that Chuang Ts'un-yü, posthumously, became known outside of Ch'ang-chou for his classical scholarship. Tung Shih-hsi, in particular, helped promote Chuang's *I-hsueh*, while Liu Feng-lu championed his grandfather's *Kung-yang* teachings.[41]

In the next section, we shall discuss Chuang Ts'un-yü's studies of the *Change Classic* in light of his attempt to revive the *Kung-yang Commentary* as a classical veil for criticizing political corruption. Then, we shall return to the intellectual world of eighteenth-century Ch'ang-chou to explore the classical debate concerning the *Spring and Autumn Annals*. Chuang's appeal to a more voluntarist approach to Confucian statecraft was based, we shall see, on both the *Change Classic* and the *Spring and Autumn Annals*.

CHUANG TS'UN-YÜ AND HAN LEARNING

Lü Ching-nan's collection of essays on Ch'ang-chou classical masters, which we cited earlier, emphasized the local development of Han Learning. He conferred special honors on Tsang Lin and Yang Ch'un (whose Han Learning positions we detailed above) in addition to Chuang Ts'un-yü and his nephew Chuang Shu-tsu. Chang Hui-yen and Liu Feng-lu were also singled out. The role of Han Learning in the evolution of New Text studies becomes still clearer in light of the 1754 palace examination. Chuang Ts'un-yü's younger brother P'ei-yin

40. Chang Hui-yen, *Chou-i Yü-shih hsiao-hsi*, 3.9b, in *Chang Kao-wen ch'ien-i ch'üan-chi* and Liu Feng-lu's "Chi" (Inscription) for Chang Hui-Yen, *Yü-shih i-yen*, in *Chang Kao-wen ch'ien-i ch'üan-chi*. See also Ch'en Shan, "Hou-hsu" (Afterword).

41. *P'i-ling Chuang-shih tseng-hsiu tsu-p'u* (1935), 3.20b–21b, includes Chang Hui-yen's epitaph for Chuang Hsiang-heng (d. 1792), in the second branch of the Chuangs. See also *P'i-ling*, 13.23a–23b, for Yun Ching's epitaph for Chuang Chün-chia (d. 1783), which describes Chang Hui-yen's close relations with the deceased, and Chang Hui-yen's *Ming-k'o wen ssu-pien, erh-pien*, B.37, for Chang's correspondence with Chuang Shu-tsu, Chuang Ts'un-yü's nephew. The letter notes the close relationship between Chuang's son and his own.

achieved *optimus* that year, and among his co-examinees were three of the future leading Han Learning scholars of the Ch'ien-lung era: Ch'ien Ta-hsin, Wang Ming-sheng, and Wang Ch'ang.

As New Text scholars from Ch'ang-chou slowly but surely legitimated their positions in the Han Learning movement, Old Text scholars in Su-chou and Yang-chou were forced to come to grips with the complexity of Han Confucianism. Although loyal to the Yang-chou Han Learning tradition, Juan Yuan saw to it while governor-general in Kuang-chou that the most important writings of the Ch'ang-chou New Text scholars were included alongside those of established Old Text scholars in the *Ch'ing Exegesis of the Classics* (*Huang-Ch'ing ching-chieh*), for example. A large compendium of the best Ch'ing dynasty classical studies, issued in 1829 after four years of compiling and editing at the Hsueh-hai-t'ang Academy, this Confucian collectanea was designed as a comprehensive sourcebook of contemporary *k'ao-cheng* scholarship. We can therefore conclude that Juan and his Han Learning associates regarded the Ch'ang-chou New Text scholars as part of the Han Learning movement. Differences between New Text Confucianism of the Former Han and Old Text learning of the Later Han dynasties, however, could no longer be glossed over by an appeal to the unanimity of Han Learning.[42]

Chuang's own writings on the *Change*, *Rituals of Chou*, and *Spring and Autumn Annals* reveal, however, that despite the inroads Han Learning had made in Ch'ang-chou in the eighteenth century, the Chuang lineage was preserving its own traditions. Although Chuang Ts'un-yü could remain aloof from the more radical implications of *k'ao-cheng* scholarship, his own position on the *Kung-yang Commentary* revealed that even he was pursuing Han Learning.

In chapter 3 we describe how Chuang resisted efforts to dislodge the Old Text portion of the *Documents* from the examination system. To circumvent this perceived threat to classical orthodoxy, Chuang refused to fuel the controversy. We therefore find the patriarch of the Ch'ang-chou New Text school defending an Old Text–based examination curricula. In his own studies, entitled *Shang-shu chi-chien* (Appearance [of the Sages] in the *Documents*) and *Shang-shu shuo* (Talks on the *Documents*), Ts'un-yü stressed the "meanings and principles" in both portions of the *Documents*. In other words, he tried to redirect the Han

42. *Hsueh-hai-t'ang chih*, p. 28b. Cf. my "Hsueh-hai T'ang," pp. 62–63.

Learning threat by seeking out areas of agreement between Han and Sung Learning.[43]

In his scholarly pursuits, Chuang Ts'un-yü was concerned with "meanings and principles" (*i-li*) in classical texts. The Sung Learning flavor of Chuang's scholarship seemed for most of the late eighteenth century to be out of touch with the empirical mood of *k'ao-cheng* studies that were pervading academic circles in the Lower Yangtze. Accordingly, outside of Ch'ang-chou, Chuang was virtually unknown as a classicist. Only when Chuang's grandson Liu Feng-lu published his own classical studies, which Liu said were inspired by his grandfather, did the Lower Yangtze academic world take note of Ts'un-yü's scholarship.[44]

BELATED SCHOLARLY RECOGNITION

Forty years after Chuang's death another grandson, Chuang Shou-chia, was able to publish Chuang Ts'un-yü's studies on the *Change Classic*. They appeared in the 1828 publication of Chuang's collected writings in Kuang-chou under the title *Wei-ching-chai i-shu* (Bequeathed writings from the Studio of Appealing Classics), sponsored by then Governor-General Juan Yuan.

Liu Feng-lu and Chuang Shou-chia had hoped that their grandfather's writings would be included in the *Ch'ing Exegesis of the Classics*, which was then being compiled by Juan Yuan's staff at the Hsueh-hai-t'ang Academy in Kuang-chou. Though impressed enough with Chuang Ts'un-yü's general scholarship to publish his writings separately, Juan Yuan found those essays on the *Change Classic* in particular inappropriate for inclusion in a collectanea dedicated to the greatest Han Learning scholars of the Ch'ing period. Interestingly, Juan did include a work of Chuang's entitled the *Ch'un-ch'iu cheng-tz'u* (Correcting terms in the *Spring and Autumn Annals*).[45]

In his preface for Chuang Ts'un-yü's collected writings, Juan Yuan noted that he himself had studied under a disciple of Chuang's, who had passed his *chin-shih* examination in Peking in 1771 when Chuang

43. See Chuang Shou-chia, "Shang-shu chi-chien pa," pp. 34a–35b.

44. Elman, *Philosophy to Philology*, pp. 99–100.

45. Satō, "Shinchō Kuyōgakuha kō (jō)," pp. 20–25. See also Juan Yuan's "Hsu" (Preface) to Chuang Ts'un-yü, *Wei-ching-chai i-shu*, and my "Hsueh-hai T'ang," pp. 62–64. Juan Yuan learned of Ts'un-yü through Chuang Shu-tsu, Liu Feng-lu, and Sung Hsiang-feng.

Ts'un-yü was one of the examiners. Despite Juan's exclusion of Ts'un-yü's studies on the *I-ching* in the *Ch'ing Exegesis*, he nonetheless expressed appreciation for Chuang's efforts to avoid the partisan controversy over Han Learning vs. Sung Learning and to select the "esoteric words and great principles" of the Classics. In conversations with Juan Yuan, the examiner Li Ch'ing-ch'uan presented Chuang's scholarship as a major step forward, beyond the limitations of partisan scholarship: "[Chuang Ts'un-yü] did not specifically focus on studies of Han or Sung scholia. Instead, he alone got at the esoteric words and great principles of the sages, which were outside of the [scope of] words and graphs. This endeavor made him a great Confucian of our enlightened age."[46]

Chuang Ts'un-yü's efforts to cut through the knot of debate that separated Han from Sung Learning scholarship in the late eighteenth century was also noted by Li Chao-lo. In a biography for Chuang Shou-chia, Li described how the Chuang school of learning (*chia-hsueh*) in Ch'ang-chou had prided itself on its classical agenda: "[The Chuangs] did not distinguish Han from Sung [Learning]. They sought to encompass the sage's profundity and return to the most appropriate [teachings]."[47]

THE GULF BETWEEN OFFICIALS AND SCHOLARS

In his 1828 preface to Chuang Ts'un-yü's *I-hsueh*, Tung Shih-hsi, a follower of *I-ching* studies championed in Ch'ang-chou by the Han Learning scholar Chang Hui-yen, perceptively observed:

> The present dynasty surpasses the Sung, Yuan, and Ming in classical studies not in quantity but in quality. During the Ch'ien-lung Emperor's reign, Hui Tung and Chang Hui-yen [surpassed their predecessors] through their writings on the *Change*. Sun Hsing-yen did so on the *Documents*. On the *Poetry* [*Classic*], it was Tai Chen. On the *Record of Rites*, Chiang Yung and Chin Pang excelled. On the *Spring and Autumn Annals*, we have K'ung Kuang-sen. In philology [*hsiao-hsueh*], Tai Chen, Tuan Yü-ts'ai, and Wang Nien-sun all brilliantly wrote books [on the subject] in this single period.
>
> Their contemporary, Mr. Chuang [Ts'un-yü], because he served as under secretary in the imperial court, had not been able to make his views on classical studies known in a book. Moreover, he did not publish anything in his lifetime. His contemporaries thus had never heard of him.[48]

46. Juan Yuan, "Hsu" to Chuang, p. 1a.
47. Li Chao-lo, *Yang-i-chai wen-chi*, 12.31b–33b.
48. Tung Shih-hsi, "I-shuo hsu," vol. 1, pp. 3a–3b. For Tung's link to Chang Hui-

Tung Shih-hsi's preface explained the gulf between Chuang Ts'un-yü and the *k'ao-cheng* mainstream. His account also suggests the chasm that separated officials and Han Learning scholars in late imperial China.

Han Learning was a scholarly movement that was largely outside examination studies until the nineteenth century. Frequently insulated from directly holding office, Han Learning scholars attained and maintained their positions within the Lower Yangtze academic community by virtue of the protection and patronage of broader elite segments of Confucian officialdom persuaded of the special value of their philological studies. The Chuang lineage in general, and Chuang Ts'un-yü in particular, were part of the traditional Confucian pattern. During Chuang's lifetime, his reputation rested on his proximity to imperial power in Peking. His own students were better known in the Lower Yangtze academic world.[49]

For example, K'ung Kuang-sen, a descendant of Confucius, had studied under Chuang Ts'un-yü before studying with Tai Chen. As Tung Shih-hsi explained above, K'ung was recognized during the eighteenth century for his important contributions to the study of the *Spring and Autumn Annals*, not Chuang Ts'un-yü. K'ung Kuang-sen's *Kung-yang Ch'un-ch'iu ching-chuan t'ung-i* (Penetrating the meanings in the *Kung-yang* commentary on the *Spring and Autumn Annals* Classic) was considered the premier work in its field. It was not until much later that anyone recognized that Chuang had cut through the philological minutiae to elaborate on broader theoretical issues in Classics such as the *Change*, *Rituals of Chou*, and the *Spring and Autumn Annals*. K'ung's renown demonstrates how marginal Chuang Ts'un-yü's classical writings were in the late eighteenth century.[50]

CHUANG TS'UN-YÜ AND *I-HSUEH*

Chuang Ts'un-yü's writings on the *I-ching* were typical of his classical interests. Based in part on Chu Hsi's *I-hsueh*, his classical writings were ecumenical. Unlike Han Learning scholars who emphasized the fragmentation and historicity of the Classics, Ts'un-yü had a holistic view

---

yen see Tung's *Ch'i-wu-lun-chai wen-lu*, 1.5b–7a, and the "Chia-p'u" (Genealogy) of the Tung family, pp. 22a–22b, in Tung Shih-hsi, *Ch'i-wu-lun-chai chi*.

49. Elman, *Philosophy to Philology*, pp. 67–85.

50. *Chuang-shih ching-hsueh-chia chia-chuan*, p. 2b. See also Tung Shih-hsi, "I-shuo hsu," vol. 1, p. 3a, and Nakamura, "Kō Kōsen Shunjū Kuyō tsūgi jo ni tsuite."

of the Classics that allowed him to move freely among them as he searched for the meanings and principles enunciated by the sages. The Classics taken together were vestiges of a golden age when for the first time sages had brought order to the world. The Classics, accordingly, could be judged together and used to complement each other. In this vein, Chuang contended that the Duke of Chou and Confucius were both central to the transmission of the sagely tradition: "The Duke of Chou said it all. Confucius gave it all meaning."[51]

THE PRIORITY OF THE SAGES

For Chuang Ts'un-yü, the *Change Classic*, *Rites of Chou*, and the *Spring and Autumn Annals* all contained meanings and principles that were drawn from the teachings of the sage-kings. In a series of works on the *Change Classic*, Chuang stressed that the *I-ching* was derived directly from the age of the sage-kings, when the empire was ordered and the values of antiquity were honored. In contrast, the *Annals* of Confucius depicted the exact opposite: the total collapse of order and lack of respect for antiquity. Consequently, Ts'un-yü saw the *Change* and the *Annals* as the key Classics that embodied the disjunction of order and chaos. In addition, Chuang thought that the *Rituals of Chou*, if properly removed of its later accretions, also contained the world-ordering principles derived from the sage-kings.[52]

Chuang Ts'un-yü used the *Change Classic* to make a philosophical statement about the centrality of the sages in bringing order to the world. The *Annals* provided him with the tools to understand Confucius's message for a chaotic age. The moral was a simple one: to deal with the chaos of the contemporary world, Confucius had set his sights on the order of the sages recorded in the Classics. Describing Chuang Ts'un-yü's stress on the holistic vision of the Classics, Tung Shih-hsi wrote:

> In 1828, [Chuang Ts'un-yü's] grandson Shou-chia printed the former's *Sayings on the Change Classic* in several chapters. When completed, he informed me, and I read it over three times. It is clear that Mister Chuang Ts'un-yü deeply grasped the *Rituals of Chou*, the *Annals*, and the five-phases theories associated with astronomy and calendrical laws. In deeply grasping

51. Chuang Ts'un-yü, "Hsu Kua chuan lun," vol. 2, p. 94a. See also Tsang Yung, "Li-pu shih-lang Chuang kung hsiao-chuan," p. 2b, for a discussion of Chu Hsi's impact on Chuang Ts'un-yü's *I-hsueh*.

52. Chuang Ts'un-yü, "T'uan-chuan lun shang-p'ien," p. 2b. See also Tung Shih-hsi, "I-shuo lun."

the *Rituals of Chou*, he was able to generalize and test the names and their referents [*ming-wu*] [in the text] without becoming lost in detail. In deeply understanding the *Annals*, he was able to compare cases through the appropriate terminology, without becoming lost in trifles. In deeply understanding the five-phases theories [applied] in astronomy and calendrical laws, he was able to bring proof to bear on institutional decisions without getting lost in generalities.[53]

THE WAY OF HEAVEN

Ts'un-yü's essay on one of the appendixes to the basic text of the *I-ching* contains his clearest formulation of the Classics. Rejecting Buddhist and Taoist accretions to the interpretation of the hexagrams, Chuang began by stating the metaphysical priority of heaven in the cosmos:

> The *Change Classic* embodies the Great Ultimate. What is the Great Ultimate? It is Heaven. Nothing is prior to the beginning of Heaven. Nothing is outside the expanse of Heaven. Nothing is more revered than reverence for Heaven. There is nothing but the unity of Heaven. In terms of origin, expanse, reverence, and unity, the meaning of the [Great] Ultimate is already complete.

Chuang's vision of cosmic origins followed his rejection of the Buddho-Taoist notion that nonbeing (*wu*) had priority over being (*yu*):

> First there was Heaven and earth. Then the myriad things were born within. The sage speaks of being. He does not mention non-being. Is it conceivable that first came non-being and afterward being? The sage said that what came later depended on the reason why the myriad things were born. Is it conceivable to leap over time and say that what came after was being?[54]

If one compares Chuang Ts'un-yü's discussion of heaven with Chuang Ch'i-yuan's late Ming writings, which reveal Catholic influences (see chapter 3), one senses the same effort to grant heaven a status and priority at the heart of creation. For both Ch'i-yuan and Ts'un-yü, heaven was the reason for there being anything rather than nothing at all. Unlike Ch'i-yuan, however, Chuang Ts'un-yü questioned the usefulness of Chu Hsi's metaphysical distinction between "before heaven" (*hsien-t'ien*, that is, "a priori") and "after heaven" (*hou-t'ien*, that is, "a posteriori") as the basis for separating heaven and earth. We

53. Tung Shih-hsi, "I-shuo lun."
54. Chuang Ts'un-yü, "Hsu kua-chuan lun," p. 89a. See also his "Hsi-tz'u chuan lun," p. 87a. Cf. Iulian Shchutskii, *Researches on the I Ching*, pp. 11, 54, 169–70.

should recall that Hui Tung and other Han Learning scholars contended that such metaphysical views were heterodox theories derived from Taoism and Buddhism.

In addition, Ts'un-yü was critical of Sung Confucians who had reified heaven and earth into postcreation entities. Heaven and earth were not second-order creations, but coterminous with creation itself. Sung Confucians, according to Chuang, had carelessly incorporated Taoist notions into the Confucian Canon. The separation introduced between the Way and heaven by the Taoist philosopher Lao-tzu left heaven and earth as derivatives of the nonbeing of the Way. In spite of the influence of Han Learning on Chuang's discussion, his views of heaven were consistent in spirit with the "creator image" that Chuang Ch'i-yuan curiously ascribed to the "Heavenly ruler."[55]

For Chuang Ts'un-yü, the *Change Classic* described the heavenly formation of unchanging images (*hsiang*) and the earthly creation of changing concrete forms (*hsing*). The concatenation of images and forms marked by the eight trigrams of the *Change Classic* undergirded the world of things (*ch'i*, lit., "implements") and represented the workings of the Way through the complementary forces of yin and yang. Sages had articulated this theory of cosmological change (*pien*) by "observing the changes in yin and yang and setting up [appropriate] trigrams." Chu Hsi's *li-ch'i* dualism, based on the priority of heavenly principles (*li*) over the perceptible world (*ch'i*), was left behind.

According to Chuang, "the Way of Heaven was none other than [the operation of] yin and yang." Because later ages had forgotten that the principle of yin and yang was a theory of cosmological change and not something that inhered in things themselves, the true import of the *I-ching* had been misrepresented for centuries:

> The sages spoke of the Way; the hundred schools [of the Warring States period] ruined [their vision] by treating [the Way] as a material object. The sages spoke of spirit; the hundred schools ruined it by treating [spirit] as a thing. Didn't Confucians, by not drawing inspiration from [their] six arts and following instead the words of the hundred schools, squander things? Accordingly, that they also say that "Heaven equals the Way," and the "Way equals Heaven" is a small change from Master Lao-tzu's words, but it is still a delusion. Those who speak properly should remove the word "equal" [*chi*], and that would suffice. Sages spoke only of the "heavenly Way" [*t'ien-tao*]. . . . The separation into two heavens [that is, the Way and Heaven] is an example of a benighted vision.[56]

55. Chuang Ts'un-yü, "Hsu kua-chuan lun," pp. 89a–90b.
56. Ibid., pp. 91a–94a.

HEAVEN AND MAN: THE CASE FOR VOLUNTARISM

Such theoretical clarifications of the *Change Classic* were preliminary to Ts'un-yü's central concern, which, like that of Chuang Ch'i-yuan before him, was "the reason why Heaven is Heaven." The scope of his inquiry was now limited to the *Change Classic*, unlike Ch'i-yuan's, which extended to include Catholicism. The theory of the *I-ching* was, according to Ts'un-yü, the touchstone for understanding how to bring order to chaos (*chih-luan*):

> Those who in antiquity spoke of bringing order to chaos placed the responsibility on men. People were unable to honor with reverence the heavenly Way, and chaos was the result so that Heaven could correct them. They said that according to the heavenly Way this was what was called chaos. Those who brought on chaos to themselves did not know that they were being corrected by Heaven. Later, they realized that chaos was caused by men and not by Heaven.
>
> Those who later spoke of bringing order to chaos placed the responsibility on Heaven. Heaven gave birth to this person who created chaos. When people heard about it, they said, "this is Heaven's creating chaos." The one who created chaos did not act on his own. It is as if Heaven forced him to do it.
>
> Is chaos caused by man? Or is the responsibility instead Heaven's? These two theories are similarly doubtful but hard to illuminate. Often both are found in the empire.[57]

In trying to articulate the role of man and heaven in bringing chaos to the world, Chuang Ts'un-yü exposed in clear terms how the effort to separate the Way from heaven had led to the delusion that heaven could be singled out within the cosmos as the cause of political chaos and moral decline. This false perspective showed the pernicious influence of the Taoists, who argued that heaven and earth did not encompass the totality of the Tao. A moral surd had been introduced into man's understanding of his responsibility to bring order out of chaos, which fed into fatalistic conclusions that appropriated the *Change Classic* to blame heaven for disorder and to presume that heaven itself would restore order.[58]

Sages had provided the solution to the dilemma, Chuang contended. They had penetrated the mysteries of change and understood the conditions under which order in the world was achieved. Consequently, to bring order to chaos meant that later men had to emulate the sages both

57. Ibid., p. 94b.
58. Ibid., pp. 94b–96a.

in their wisdom and in their actions. To restore the order of antiquity one did not wait for heaven to act. Heaven was already complete.

> Moreover, when the ruler has the empire he has to be served by his ministers. Does this mean that the ruler is not sufficient to order the empire? A father has a family, but he has to be served by his sons. Does this mean that the father is not sufficient to order the family?
>
> Heaven's having to be served by sages is just like this. . . . Only the sage receives the mandate from Heaven. Heaven grants the mandate; the sage completes it.[59]

Heaven's ordering of the world was already present in the world. Sages had discovered the basis and content of the universal order of ruler/servant, father/son, husband/wife, upper/lower, and ritual/meaning that undergirded society.

According to Chuang Ts'un-yü, the lesson of the *I-ching* was that it was man's responsibility to recognize and to uphold this universal order. If chaos reigned, it was man's responsibility to restore order. This, Chuang contended, was also the lesson of Confucius's *Spring and Autumn Annals*. The "reason why Heaven is Heaven" allowed men to grasp that "the human Way is established for myriad generations, just as if it were a single day. One does not rely on the laws of a single king. One does not depend on the strength of the sages. Heaven has ordained it so." Moreover, "the sages created the *Change* [*Classic*] to provide a standard for Heaven and earth."[60]

Given the political landscape, Chuang Ts'un-yü's voluntaristic vision of man's responsibility for order in the empire represented a classical gloss on the politics of the Ho-shen era. Fatalism, whether Taoist or Confucian, would only increase the triumph of chaos in Chinese political life. Heaven had set its standards. Sages had divined them and taught them for all to know. It was up to Confucians to address the crisis. In effect, Chuang Ts'un-yü, who represented local and national interests, called for the resurgence of literati involvement in the fate of the dynasty and the restoration of order over chaos.

To wait for heaven to act in the 1780s, Chuang seemed to be saying, was to invite further disaster. Like the sages, contemporary Confucians had to take the initiative and act on their Confucian principles. For chaos to be restored to order, men must defy those who created that chaos. Chuang Ts'un-yü therefore appealed to the priority of the sages, the Way of heaven, and the voluntarism of Confucians.

59. Ibid.
60. Ibid., pp. 96b–97b.

FIVE

Chuang Ts'un-yü and *Kung-yang* Confucianism

Traditions defy categorization. J. G. A. Pocock notes that a tradition may emphasize the continuous transmission of its teachings. The normative power of past practice can direct human conceptions of reality into acceptable social and political behavior. Traditions that stress continuous transmission become normative models for action and belief.[1] But a tradition may also stress its creative and charismatic origins. The authority of the original charisma often merges with the mediating chain of transmission, and is thereby "routinized" or "abridged" into an ideology. Hence we can draw a conceptual distinction between traditions that stress the reenactment of the originating creative actions and those that represent themselves as the mere transmission of earlier creative events. But even this distinction is problematic, for transmission and charisma are usually found together. Traditions offer a variety of responses to a given situation. Every tradition is open to diverse public and private responses.

Changes in traditions closely follow the political, social, and economic changes to which they refer. The Confucian ordering of reality, like all traditions, was subject to the inherent tensions between reality and human conceptions of that reality, including perennial moral and political issues. Although governed by the politics of the Confucian state, the responses to these issues were not static. Confucian concepts, interpretations, and verbalizations—and the actions based on them—

1. Pocock, *Politics, Language, and Time*, pp. 233–72. See also Edward Shils, *Tradition*, pp. 3, 10, 54–55, and Schwartz, "Limits of 'Tradition versus Modernity.'"

changed dramatically over time. Identical terms from the Classics could mean different things to Confucians faced with different problems.[2]

As repositories of the wisdom of antiquity, the Classics of *Change*, *Documents*, *Poetry*, and *Rites* were regarded by Confucians as creations of the sage-kings. The *Spring and Autumn Annals*, accepted as the only Classic by Confucius himself, thus became the textual lens through which Confucius's vision of history was interpreted. Although all Classics eventually became embroiled in the New Text vs. Old Text controversy, the task of unraveling Confucius's legacy focused on the *Annals*.

Ch'ing dynasty New Text Confucians of the late eighteenth and early nineteenth centuries were faced with what they regarded as unprecedented problems. We can therefore understand why they would find the New Text portrait of Confucius painted by the Han Confucians Tung Chung-chu (179?–104? B.C.) and Ho Hsiu (A.D. 129–182) more to their advantage. Rather than teaching an Old Text tradition based on a chain of classical transmission, followers of the Ch'ang-chou New Text tradition stressed creative and heroic acts.[3]

As we saw in chapter 4, Chuang Ts'un-yü possessed a compelling, voluntaristic vision of human responsibility for upholding the universal standards of heaven (discovered by the sages). This vision carried over to his remarkable interpretation of the lessons Confucius had encoded in his chronicle of chaos—the *Spring and Autumn Annals*. Like the Ming dynasty Confucian Huang Tao-chou, who had been a Tung-lin partisan in the 1630s and a Ming loyalist in the 1640s, Chuang saw the *Change* and the *Annals* as complementary, embodying a unified political vision.

As with the *Change Classic*, Chuang Ts'un-yü's views on the *Annals* were little known outside his lineage or outside of Ch'ang-chou until Liu Feng-lu's (1776–1829) influential *Ch'un-ch'iu Kung-yang ching Ho-shih shih-li* (Master Ho [Hsiu's] explication of precedents in the *Kung-yang* [*Commentary*] on the *Spring and Autumn Annals Classic*), published in 1805, made it widely known that Ts'un-yü had developed his own views concerning the *Kung-yang Commentary*.

2. Pocock, *Politics, Language, and Time*, pp. 244–45. Shils, *Tradition*, p. 44, 258. For discussion, see my "Philosophy versus Philology," pp. 175–222, and "Criticism as Philosophy." See also the essays in Hobsbawm and Ranger, eds., *Invention of Tradition*.

3. Ch'ien Mu, *Liang-Han ching-hsueh chin-ku-wen p'ing-i*, pp. 235–36, 264–65, and Lu Yuan-chün, "Ching-hsueh chih fa-chan yü chin-ku-wen chih fen-ho," p. 39. For a discussion see Ku Chieh-kang, "Ch'un-ch'iu te K'ung-tzu ho Han-tai te K'ung-tzu," vol. 2, pp. 130–39. Similar tensions are apparent in the life of Jesus and in Pauline Christianity. See Pelikan, *Jesus through the Centuries*.

Chuang Ts'un-yü's return to the *Kung-yang Commentary* must be understood in light of the vicissitudes in *Ch'un-ch'iu-hsueh* (studies of the *Annals*) during earlier dynasties. I shall summarize these studies and then continue with our evaluation of the classical tradition in Ch'ang-chou. I shall also address Chuang Ts'un-yü's scholarly contributions to studies on the *Change Classic* and *Annals*. As in the case of *I-hsueh*, eighteenth-century studies of the *Annals* were influenced by the Han Learning research agenda and the application of *k'ao-cheng* methods to resolve the textual problems in interpreting it and its three orthodox commentaries.[4]

USES OF THE *ANNALS*

During the Former Han (206 B.C.–A.D. 8) heyday of New Text Confucianism, a consensus emerged that saw an implicit code of good and evil in the *Spring and Autumn Annals*, a code that Confucius had included in his chronicles of Lu. "Praise and blame" (*pao-pien*) historiography were stressed by both of the Former Han New Text *Kung-yang* and *Ku-liang* commentaries, although the former became the touchstone for New Text moral evaluation. With the eventual rise of the Old Text tradition of the Later Han (A.D. 25–220), this praise-and-blame tradition was incorporated into Old Text interpretations of the Classics as well. By the T'ang dynasty Confucians had forgotten that "praise and blame" historiography had been a New Text creation and was accepted for the most part with little questioning.

Later Confucians believed that Confucius, by assuming the historiographical prerogatives of the Chou king and speaking for him through the chronicles of Lu, had adapted each entry to express model judgments on every event and participant he recorded. The chronicles of Lu, which encompass the 254 years between 722 and 468 B.C. (when the Old Text *Tso chuan* halted), became the basis for the traditional historiography of ancient China. Tradition, classics, and historiography were indistinguishable.[5]

Praise-and-blame doctrines carried over from the *Annals* to other Classics as well. From the Han until the Sung dynasties, for example,

4. See Huang Tao-chou, "Fan-li" (statement of contents). Cf. Satō, "Shinchō Kuyōgakuha," pp. 20–25. For a discussion see my *Philosophy to Philology*, pp. 204–29.

5. For Mencius's views of the *Annals*, see *Meng-tzu yin-te*, 25/3B/9. Cf. Legge in *Four Books*, pp. 676–77, and Lau, trans., *Mencius*, p. 114. Ssu-ma Ch'ien praised the *Annals* in his *Shih-chi*, 6/1943 (*chüan* 47). Cf. Bodde's translation of Fung Yu-lan, *History of Chinese Philosophy*, vol. 1, pp. 45–46, 400–403. See also Chou Yü-t'ung, *Ching chin-ku-wen hsueh*, pp. 22–27, and Ku Chieh-kang, *Han-tai hsueh-shu-shih lueh*, pp. 62–72.

commentators read political intent into many of the poems collected in the *Poetry Classic* (*Shih-ching*). Poetic omens were first articulated in the Former Han, and during the Later Han Cheng Hsuan (127–200) drew explicit parallels between the rise and fall of a dynasty and the vicissitudes in its poetry. Society and literature reflected the same moral judgments. Constant relearning of these ancient patterns of behavior offered Confucians conceptions of the right order of society and appropriate rituals (*li*) for proper conduct in both public and private life. Images of the Confucian past, accordingly, were stereotyped and transmitted through the moral prism used by Confucius to interpret the chronicles of Lu.[6]

The bloody details of the Spring and Autumn Period were judged normatively as precedents. For both New Text and Old Text Confucians, tradition, as it was related to the venerable Confucius, became synonymous with correct historiography. Although tensions between the New Text and Old Text manipulations of the *Spring and Autumn Annals* never disappeared, the two traditions contributed in different proportions over time to political discourse in imperial China.

For instance, Tu Yü (222–284) wrote an influential work entitled *Ch'un-ch'iu shih-li* (Explications of precedents in the *Spring and Autumn Annals*). A systematic list of historical precedents, the work was based on an Old Text reading of the *Annals* drawn from the *Tso chuan*. These precedents were devised to give the *Annals* the kind of political specificity that the *Rituals of Chou* spelled out for institutions. The classification of Confucius's moral censures of historical events in the *Annals* allowed Tu Yü and his Confucian successors to categorize historical events. Forty-two general categories for precedents (e.g., legitimate political succession, proper forms for meetings and alliances, appropriate military campaigns, etc.) were used to organize the multiplicity of names and events in the *Annals*. Executive policy (*hsing-fa*) drawn on precedents in the *Annals* could now compete effectively, or be used in tandem, with the institutions of the *Rituals of Chou*. Old Text scholars by now had reinterpreted what was left of New Text Confucianism.[7]

Prior to the T'ang dynasty (when Mencius was "rediscovered" by

6. Shils, *Tradition*, pp. 54–55. See also Chia-ying Yeh Chao, "Ch'ang-chou School," p. 159, and James J. Y. Liu, *Chinese Theories*, pp. 64–65.

7. See original preface, Tu Yü, *Ch'un-ch'iu shih-li*, by Liu Fen. Ch'ang-chou New Text scholars also made extensive use of the *Chou-li*. It was not until Sung Hsiang-feng (see chapter 6) that the *Chou-li* was categorically dismissed by New Text scholars.

Han Yü) Confucius and the Duke of Chou ("Chou-K'ung") were regarded as the axis of ancient Confucianism. During the T'ang, however, Confucius and Mencius ("K'ung-Meng") became the axis. The T'ang historian Liu Chih-chi even dismissed the *Annals* as little more than a cursory chronology. For Liu, Confucius had simply edited earlier historical records with no intention of developing a systematic framework for legal and moral precedents. He questioned the usefulness of the *Kung-yang Commentary* and dismissed the "praise and blame" tradition associated with the New Text *Kung-yang* and *Ku-liang* commentaries. Instead, he favored the *Tso Commentary* because of its detailed historical information.

In many ways, Liu's approach represented a clean break with the orthodox view of Confucius and the *Annals*. Enunciated with imperial support, this orthodox view was fashioned by K'ung Ying-ta (574–648) and his staff into T'ang commentaries on the Five Classics prepared as state guidelines for the civil service examinations. Later, Tan Chu (725–70) reduced the authority of all "three [Han] commentaries" to the status of mere amplifications of orally transmitted traditions that had lost touch with the original *Annals* Classic. More radical scholars such as Chao K'uang (fl. eighth century A.D.) went further and, on the basis of technical and stylistic considerations, rejected Tso Ch'iu-ming as the author of the *Tso chuan*. Chao questioned the canonical status of the commentary.[8]

During the Northern Sung dynasty (960–1126), when Wang An-shih sought precedents for his reform party, he appealed to the *Rituals of Chou* as the classical text that contained the actualized political ideals of the sagely Duke of Chou. To lend credence to this Old Text Classic, Wang belittled Confucius's *Spring and Autumn Annals* as a useless collection of dates and names. He eliminated them as a special field of preparation for the imperial examinations, purportedly claiming the *Annals* was "worthless fragments of a government bulletin." He favored the *Rituals* because its detailed plans for government institutions justified a more assertive government—which in turn justified the stricter control and regulation of society. As an institutional reformer, Wang An-shih placed little store by the moral principles read into the *Annals*.[9]

8. Liu Chih-chi, *Shih-t'ung* (*shih-p'ing*) pp. 381–91 (*wai-p'ien* no. 5), and Inaba, "Chū-Tō, ni okeru shin Jugaku undō no ichi kōsatsu," pp. 377–403. See also Pulleyblank, "Neo-Confucianism and Neo-Legalism," pp. 88–91, and P'i Hsi-jui, *Ching-hsueh li-shih*, p. 264.

9. For Wang An-shih's remarks, see Chou Yü-t'ung's notes in P'i Hsi-jui's *Ching-*

Conservatives led by Ssu-ma Kuang (1019–86) and Su Shih (1036–1101) rejected Wang An-shih's efforts to create new and expansive institutions as politically unfeasible and classically inaccurate. They maintained that Confucius's vision of social order and the conflict between good and evil, developed in his *Annals*, were the true lessons of the Classics. In addition to proposing the reform of bureaucratic procedures, they advocated a system of moral censure that would invigorate the government and complement political reform as the key element in effective government. Moreover, many Northern Sung scholars maintained that the *Rituals of Chou* itself was a questionable text, associated with Liu Hsin's (45 B.C.–A.D. 23) dubious efforts to legitimate Wang Mang's (r. 9–23) usurpation. Some claimed that the *Chou-li* had originally had little to do with the Duke of Chou and in fact may have been first composed during the Former Han dynasty.[10]

In contrast to Wang An-shih's efforts to dismiss the *Annals*, the conservatives saw evidence in the *Annals* for classical models that lent dynastic prestige to the ruler. Following the lead of their T'ang precursors, Sung dynasty scholars of the *Annals* proposed that the "three commentaries" (*Kung-yang*, *Ku-liang*, and *Tso*) be discarded in favor of following the text of the Classic itself (*ch'i-chuan ts'ung-ching*). This approach freed T'ang and Sung scholars of the *Annals* from the classical authority of Han interpretations and permitted them to explicate the *Annals*' "general meaning" (*ta-i*). Ancient precedents were directly referred by analogy to contemporary political problems.

After the failure of the Wang An-shih's reform program, Chu Hsi and other Neo-Confucians subordinated the *Rituals of Chou* and *Annals* to the *Analects* and *Mencius*. Of the Four Books these two were said to provide a more intimate understanding of the sageliness of Confucius. Despite the Neo-Confucian stress on Confucius and Mencius, however, Chu Yuan-chang the founder of the Ming dynasty (r. 1368–98), utilized the *Rituals* to legitimate his triumph over the Mongol Yuan dynasty (1280–1368). In particular, he saw in the *Rituals* a classical basis for restoring pre-Yuan institutions, thereby affirming

hsueh li-shih, pp. 29–30, and P'i's own discussion on p. 250. Cf. James T. C. Liu, *Reform in Sung China*, pp. 30–33.

10. Uno, "Shūrai Ryū Kin gisaku setsu ni tsuite." See also Yang Hsiang-k'uei, *Ching-shih-chai*, pp. 267–74, and Yeh Kuo-liang, *Sung-jen i-ching kai-ching k'ao*, pp. 97–109. Cf. Yoshiwara, "Hoku-Sō Shunjū gaku no ichi sokumen," p. 633

through both ritualistic and political means the governmental structure of the Chou dynasty (1122?–221 B.C.). Like Wang Mang and Wang An-shih before him, Chu Yuan-chang relied on Chou models to add classical legitimacy to his dynastic policies.[11]

During the Northern and Southern (1127–1279) Sung dynasties, "honoring the ruler" (*tsun-wang*) and "driving out the barbarians" (*jang-i*) became particularly important concepts in contemporary explications of the *Annals*. Such themes were clearly a reflection of threats from northern "barbarians" that materialized with the collapse of the Northern Sung in 1126 and the formation of the Southern Sung. Until the Mongol triumph in 1280 Sung rulers and ministers remained preoccupied with the "barbarian problem."

For many Confucians, such as Ch'en Liang (1143–94), the need to drive the Jurchen from north China and to restore it to Sung dynasty rule became a political obsession during the Southern Sung. Hoyt Tillman has pointed out that traditional Confucianism played an important role in Ch'en Liang's patriotism. Ch'en invoked Confucius and his *Annals* as the proper guide for the "way of civilized people" (*jen-tao*), in contrast to that of barbarians, who violated Chinese norms for ritual, social, and ethical behavior.[12] Ch'en Liang's own sense of national peril led him to enunciate, in a particularistic fashion, the lessons Confucius had encoded in the *Annals*. According to Ch'en's reading of the *Annals*, one such lesson was that Chinese and barbarians had separate Ways (*Tao*), which should not be mixed. Accordingly, he attributed the decline of the Chou dynasty to its failure to keep barbarians out of the Chinese heartland. In Ch'en Liang's hands, the *Annals* became a handbook on barbarians.[13]

In an influential work entitled *Ch'un-ch'iu tsun-wang fa-wei* (Bringing to light the honoring of the ruler in the *Spring and Autumn Annals*), Sun Fu (992–1057) had compared the barbarian threats posed to the Sung dynasty with the chaos in the time of the *Annals*. Just as the con-

11. Ch'ien Mu, *Liang-Han ching-hsueh chin-ku-wen p'ing-i*, p. 265, and Yang Hsiang-k'uei, *Ching-shih-chai*, pp. 149, 249–51. See Chün-chieh Huang, "Old Pursuits and New Knowledge," 211–12, and Huang's "Mencian Morality." See also Kung-chuan Hsiao, *Rural China*, pp. 43–46, 569 n. 6, and Yun-yi Ho, *Ministry of Rites*, pp. 52, 63.

12. For a discussion see Ch'en Ch'ing-hsin, "Sung Ju Ch'un-ch'iu tsun-wang yao-i te fa-wei yü ch'i cheng-chih ssu-hsiang." Cf. Tillman, *Utilitarian Confucianism*, pp. 31, 108, 166–67, and Tillman, "Proto-Nationalism in Twelfth-Century China?" 403, 423.

13. Ch'en Liang, *Lung-ch'uan wen-chi*, 4.5b–6b. See Tillman, "Proto-Nationalism," pp. 410–11. See also Langlois, "*Spring and Autumn Annals* in Yuan Political Thought," pp. 124–25, and P'i Hsi-jui, *Ching-hsueh li-shih*, p. 250.

tentiousness of the feudal lords (*chu-hou*) threatened, and eventually brought down, the Chou dynasty, so the barbarian threats of the eleventh century imperiled the Sung dynasty. What was required, Sun contended, was a strengthening of the imperial institution. "Honoring the ruler" was his proposed doctrinal remedy to end the dynasty's internal divisiveness and to unite the empire.

Sun Fu also called for "driving out the barbarians." It is interesting that Sung Confucians saw in the *Annals* principles for behavior that governed relations with barbarian dynasties. The stability of the Northern Sung dynasty clearly depended on successful relations with the Khitan and Jurchen tribes, which were slowly but surely encroaching on the north China plain. Sun Fu and his followers, however, took a hard line. Contacts and alliances with the barbarians were frowned upon. They called instead for military action to attack the intruding "barbarians" and to defend the dynasty.[14]

"Imperial majesty" (*wei*), designed to overawe foreigners, was now stressed, and protonationalism became a rallying point for antibarbarian sentiments. Chinese culturalism (based on Confucian culture rather than on particularistic appeals to the dynasty) did not automatically restrict the development of nationalism in the imperial state. The ambiguities of patriotism and nationalism during the Sung dynasties permitted interesting forms of protonationalism to develop. The *Annals* provided a convenient framework for the articulation of such sentiments and for the tributary principles they required.[15]

Hu An-kuo also composed an influential commentary to the *Annals* that elaborated on Sun Fu's twin themes of "honoring the ruler" and "driving out the barbarians," which became slogans of the hard-liners on the "barbarian question." They tried to rally support around the Sung emperor and then to retake lands in north China already lost to the Khitan (Liao, 947–1125) and Jurchen (Chin, 1115–1234) dynasties. Like Sun Fu, Hu An-kuo thought the plight of the Sung dynasty was brought on by moral failure and the betrayal of values encoded in

14. Sun Fu, *Ch'un-ch'iu tsun-wang fa-wei*, 1.1a–2a, 1.13a–13b, 1.16a–16b, 2.3b, 12.8a–8b. For a discussion see Mou Jun-sun, "Liang-Sung Ch'un-ch'iu-hsueh chih chu-liu, shang," 113–15. Cf. P'i Hsi-jui, *Ching-hsueh li-shih*, pp. 250–51.

15. Tillman, "Proto-Nationalism in Twelfth-Century China?" See also Trauzettel, "Sung Patriotism." During the last years of the Tokugawa shogunate (1600–1867) in Japan, the rallying cry for dissident samurai who wished to overthrow the Tokugawa house was "*sonnō jōi*" (to revere the emperor and expel the barbarians). This explosive combination in Japan drew from Chinese historical experience and indirectly from the Sung interpretation of the *Annals*. See Najita, *Japan*, pp. 43–68, and Earl, *Emperor and Nation*, pp. 82–210.

the *Annals*. After the Spring and Autumn period, according to Hu, Chinese and barbarians had culturally mingled to the detriment of both.

The broader question of the emperor's authority and power led Hu An-kuo and others to call for revenge (*fu-ch'iu*) against the barbarians when north China fell in the twelfth century to the Jurchen, ancestors of the Manchus. Hu's patriotic reading of the *Annals* was so powerful that it inspired the young Lu Chiu-yuan (Hsiang-shan, 1139–92)—later Chu Hsi's main intellectual antagonist—to resolve at age sixteen to become a soldier and to help drive the barbarians out of the Chinese heartland in the north. Classical scholarship and protonationalism were interwoven to form an antibarbarian political position; it proved unsuccessful in the long run.

Hu An-kuo's commentary on the *Annals* became so prominent after the fall of the Sung dynasty that when Chinese Han rule was restored in 1368, it was informally known as one of the "four commentaries" (*ssu-chuan*), standing on a par with the orthodox "three commentaries" dating from the Han dynasties. Leading Confucians perceived the need for imperial authority to ensure domestic solidarity and to rally against external threats. Sung Confucians were trying to exalt imperial power, but they were not advocating its unlimited power. But their intentions belied the Legalist consequences when Yuan and Ming emperors appropriated Sung political discourse.[16]

Uses of the *Annals* carried over in the notion of legitimate succession (*cheng-t'ung*), developed during the Northern Sung. The criteria of legitimate succession began to shift from theories of yin-yang and the five evolutive phases (which Former Han New Text Confucians such as Tung Chung-shu had used in their political cosmology) to issues of moral right and political unification. Ou-yang Hsiu (1007–72) and Chu Hsi formulated a theory of legitimate succession that eventually became a prominent principle of Chinese historiography.

Ou-yang Hsiu's official histories of the T'ang dynasty and Five Dynasties period (907–60) left him sensitive to the ambiguities of writing on periods when political legitimacy was contested. He was also the first important historian of the post-T'ang period to reject earlier New Text theories that drew on the portents and the evolving configurations of the "five phases" in determining legitimate succession. Instead, Ou-

16. On Hu An-kuo's commentary see Mou Jun-sun, "Liang-Sung Ch'un-ch'iu-hsueh chih chu-liu, hsia," 170–72. See also Sung Ting-tsung, "Sung-Ju Ch'un-ch'iu jang-i shuo"; Hervouet, ed., *Sung Bibliography*, pp. 39–40; and Schirokauer, "Neo-Confucians under Attack," pp. 165–66.

yang measured degrees of political unification as the key determinant of legitimacy. His single political criterion provided a fixed and universal historiographical guideline for evaluating changes in dynasties.[17]

Ou-yang's views were fleshed out by Chu Hsi in his *Tzu-chih t'ung-chien kang-mu* (Outline of the Comprehensive Mirror for Aid in Government), published in the late twelfth century. Although Chu Hsi thought the theme of kingship in the *Annals* was more important than that of relations with barbarians, he nevertheless admitted that the *Annals* favored keeping China and the barbarians in separate inner and outer zones. In contrast to Ch'en Liang, Chu Hsi distinguished between restoring north China to Sung control and long-term revenge against the barbarians. National unity was thus a more compelling reason for addressing the barbarian menace for Chu Hsi than it was for Ch'en Liang and others, who preferred to focus on the menace.

Chu Hsi's digest, which was later further amplified, classified China's imperial regimes as either legitimate or illegitimate. Ssu-ma Kuang had explicitly refused to do so in an earlier work (on which Chu based his digest), which tells us that Chu Hsi was facing very different political pressures. Chu's classification, based on criteria of moral right and political unification, also drew on Ou-yang Hsiu's earlier intepretations of the *Kung-yang Commentary*. Ou-yang had elaborated on the theme of "magnifying universal rule" (*ta i-t'ung*), which Tung Chung-shu and Ho Hsiu had both stressed in their New Text interpretations of the *Annals*. We find here an intriguing undercurrent of normative theory in Sung political thought. It affirmed the Former Han praise-and-blame tradition of the *Spring and Autumn Annals* and employed, in circumscribed form, doctrines once associated with New Text Confucianism. Classicism was here joined with a method for using history as a policy-making guide.[18]

Issues regarding legitimate succession continued unabated during the Mongol Yuan dynasty, when protonationalism was replaced by Sung loyalism. Confucian scholars charged by the Yuan court to compile his-

17. Davis, "Historiography as Politics," 33–39. See also Hok-lam Chan, "Chinese Official Historiography," pp. 68–71.

18. See Ssu-ma Kuang's "Hsu" (Preface) to the *Tzu-chih t'ung-chien*, vol. 1, pp. 33–34, and Hok-lam Chan, p. 96. Cf. Davis, "Historiography as Politics," pp. 40–42, and Tillman, *Utilitarian Confucianism*, pp. 33–34, and Tillman, "Proto-Nationalism," p. 413. See also Hartwell, "Historical-Analogism," 690–95. Chu Hsi's digest of China's imperial regimes was based on chronicles completed in 1084 and entitled *Comprehensive Mirror for Aid in Government*. In the chronicles, Ssu-ma Kuang had used Confucius's *Annals* as a model to cover the period from the Eastern Chou (when the *Annals* left off) to the Five Dynasties.

tories of the earlier Liao, Chin, and Sung dynasties became embroiled in heated discussions over their legitimacy. Confucius's *Annals* had ordained the historiographical prerogative of the sage-king; hence all subsequent emperors compiled records of their predecessors to justify their own legitimacy.

Historiography was thus a politically charged vocation. To interpret the past (Sung, Liao, Chin) was to affirm the present (Yuan). Efforts by Confucians under Mongol rule to formulate acceptable principles for legitimate dynastic succession were further complicated by the fact that the Liao and Chin were both alien conquerors. Further, Yuan rulers, sponsors of the history projects, were not only foreign conquerors but had also destroyed a legitimate Han Chinese dynasty, the Southern Sung.

For Han Chinese, it was imperative to defend the legitimacy of the Sung, even in the face of Mongol pressure to grant the Liao and Chin dynasties legitimacy according to Confucian historiography. For its part, the Yuan government refused to accede to Chinese scholar-official demands that the Sung be accorded priority in legitimacy simply because it was a native Chinese dynasty. Debate was so intense that the writing of official histories was paralyzed, and the Yuan History Bureau became little more than a storehouse for documents.

Composed sixty years after Sung rule had been erased, Yang Wei-chen's "Polemic on Legitmate Succession" (*Cheng-t'ung pien*) reveals that the political legitimacy of pre-Yuan dynasties was very much in dispute during the Yuan. A historian with an ongoing interest in the *Spring and Autumn Annals*, Yang Wei-chen was an ardent spokesman for traditional Confucian values and defender of the Confucian historiographical tradition. His dilemma (which Richard Davis describes as the "dilemma of a Chinese proto-nationalist") centered around his efforts to demonstrate that Northern Sung legitimacy had been transmitted to the Southern Sung and then to the Yuan—a scheme that entirely bypassed the Liao and Chin as legitimate dynasties. Yang connected philosophical orthodoxy to political legitimacy through the Neo-Confucian concept of *Tao-t'ung* (legitimate succession of the Way), which had earlier been employed by Chu Hsi and his Northern Sung predecessors to affirm the true transmission of Confucian values from the time of Confucius and Mencius to the Sung dynasty.

According to this construct, China's spiritual center, and thus its political values, had followed the Northern Sung court south when the north fell to the Jurchen in 1126. Although Yang Wei-chen accepted the

Yuan as a Chinese dynasty, this flagrant display of Han chauvinism led the Yuan court to ban his essay because of its disparaging remarks about the Khitan and Jurchen "barbarians." Yang's ethnic bias aroused court indignation and the suspicion that he was implicitly criticizing the Mongols as well.[19]

When the Ming dynasty restored Han Chinese rule, the stamp of political legitimacy was withdrawn from the alien Yuan dynasty. This is seen in the work of the historian Wang Chu (fl. ca. 1521), who refuted the legitimacy of the Mongol rulers in his influential *Sung-shih chih* (Verified history of the Sung Dynasty). He accomplished this by fabricating a chronology based on Chu Yuan-chang's ancestors (Chu founded the Ming dynasty), thereby placing Chu's line in direct succession to the Sung house. Accounts of the Liao and Chin were relegated to a section entitled the "monographs on foreign nations." Ming Confucians like Wang Chu used principles enunciated in the *Spring and Autumn Annals* to reassert the supremacy of Chinese rule over all alien conquerors in China's past. "Sung loyalism" was transformed into Ming "Han chauvinism."[20]

MING-CH'ING STUDIES OF THE *ANNALS*

Some of the New Text doctrines from the *Kung-yang* and *Ku-liang* commentaries on the *Annals*, which were prepared during the Former Han dynasty, remained perennially important. For the most part, however, the *Tso chuan* was preeminent after the T'ang dynasty in establishing the historical precedents (*li*) that later Confucians had documented in the *Annals*. Consequently, the Old Text interpretations of the *Annals* were the standard for the examination system during the Ming and Ch'ing dynasties. Tu Yü's *Explication of Precedents in the Spring and Autumn Annals* was the most influential pre-T'ang reconstruction of this Old Text reading of the *Annals* because the author had harvested Old Text interpretations of the Classics from the Later Han. During the T'ang dynasty, however, Tu's book was divided up and included with other commentaries in K'ung Ying-ta's definitive *Ch'un-ch'iu cheng-i* (Orthodox meanings in the *Annals*), which was part of an extensive imperial program for classical orthodoxy in the seventh cen-

19. Hok-lam Chan, "Chinese Official Historiography," pp. 71–88, and Davis, "Historiography as Politics," pp. 45–51.
20. Hok-lam Chan, "Chinese Official Historiography," pp. 95–105.

tury. In fact, Tu Yü's book was lost as an independent work (as were many of Cheng Hsuan's writings), although his views were incorporated into the T'ang academy. Ku Yen-wu (1613–82) and Hui Tung (1697–1758) later played important roles in reconstituting Tu Yü's original work on the *Annals*.[21]

Although the Old Text views articulated by Tu Yü remained orthodox for later dynasties, there were important exceptions. Neither Wang An-shih nor Chu Hsi—major figures in Northern and Southern Sung Confucianism respectively—had placed much store by the *Spring and Autumn Annals*, believing instead that the *Rituals of Chou* was a more authoritative text. In his old age, Chu Hsi openly stated that the *Annals* was not worth studying because it offered little guidance for moral improvement, asking: "What possible relevance does it have for us?"[22]

Moreover, Ch'eng I and Chu Hsi had both expressed their doubts that the *Tso Commentary* had indeed been composed by Confucius's disciple Tso Ch'iu-ming. Ch'eng I nonetheless maintained, unlike Chu Hsi, that the *Annals* was an important world-ordering text whose historical precedents revealed "laws for a hundred ages" (see chapter 8). Confucius's *Annals* survived its Sung dynasty critics. During the Ming dynasty, doubts about its provenance were replaced by questions concerning its earlier interpretation. As in the T'ang, the three Han commentaries were again subject to critical scrutiny, particularly the derivation of historical precedents from the *Annals* enunciated in the *Tso chuan*.[23]

YANG SHEN

An eccentric Ming Confucian, Yang Shen pioneered *k'ao-cheng* studies when he was exiled to Yun-nan during the sixteenth century. In an essay entitled "Ch'un-ch'iu li" (Precedents in the *Spring and Autumn Annals*), he challenged Tu Yü's *Explication of Precedents in the Annals*. Reversing the traditional Old Text perspective, Yang contended that the *Annals* was not simply a record of historical precedents. "In the writings of the sage," he asked, "are we to assume that he first had precedents in mind and then later wrote the *Spring and Autumn Annals*?" The *Annals* was first and foremost a chronicle of historical

21. *Ssu-k'u ch'üan-shu tsung-mu*, 26.10b–14a, 28.16b–17b, 29.5a–6b, 29.31a–34a.
22. Chu Hsi, *Chu Wen-kung wen-chi, hsu-chi*, 2.6b.
23. *Erh-Ch'eng ch'üan-shu, Ho-nan Ch'eng-shih i-shu*, 15.16a–17a, and esp. 20.1a.

events, argued Yang, and only secondarily a statement of historical precedents.[24]

Appealing to a more activist and creative interpretation, Yang Shen rejected the Old Text precedents as a "fixation on the past" (*ni-ku*), which confused the letter with the spirit of antiquity: "Consequently, the sages established ritual and music as institutions. They [themselves] were not institutionalized by ritual and music. They established the law as an institution and were not institutionalized by the law."

According to Yang, Confucius had likewise created the *Annals* to record the chaotic events following the collapse of the Western Chou in 770 B.C. Confucius thereby established precedents to be mastered, but precedents were but part of the *Annals*. The Old Text position on the *Annals*—institutionalized through hundreds of historical precedents—had misrepresented Confucius's intent in composing his chronicle. Yang saw instead an appeal to the priority of voluntarism over passivity.[25]

Yang Shen's classical studies stressed the importance of recovering the Confucian legacy of the Han dynasty, which in scope and tenor was remarkably resonant with Ch'ing dynasty Han Learning:

> Someone asked Mr. Yang [Shen]: "With regard to the Classics, you choose much from Han Confucians, but do not choose from Sung Confucians. Why is that?" He answered: "When have I not selected the refined theories of Sung Confucians? One sees that Sung Confucians were mistaken in discarding Han Confucians, and using only their own views. Let me ask you: The Six Classics were completed by Confucius. The Han era was not separated from [the time of] Confucius by very long. Although the [Han] transmitters had weaknesses, their theories still contained the truth. Sung Confucians were separated from Confucius by 1500 years. Although their intelligence surpassed ordinary folks, how could they in a single morning completely discard old [Han views] and independently become enlightened through their minds?

Hui Tung could not have put it any better. In fact, Tai Chen (1724–77) later posed this exact argument. When studying the Great Learning at age ten with his teacher, Tai asked:

> How does one know in this case that these are the words of Confucius recorded by Tseng-tzu [the reputed author of the Great Learning]? Moreover, how does one know that Tseng-tzu's intentions were recorded by his followers?

24. Yang Shen, *T'ai-shih sheng-an wen-chi*, 43.12b. On Yang Shen see Lin Ch'ing-chang, *Ming-tai k'ao-cheng-hsueh yen-chiu*, pp. 36–127.

25. Yang Shen, "Su-Ju ni-ku," 68.2a–2b; see also 45.15a–17a.

> The teacher replied: "This is what the earlier Confucian Chu Hsi said in his notes."
>
> Tai Chen asked another question: "When did Chu Hsi live?" The teacher replied: "Southern Sung" [1127–1279]. Tai asked again: "When did Confucius and Tseng-tzu live?" The teacher replied: "Eastern Chou" [770–221 B.C.]. Tai asked again: "How much time separates the Chou [dynasty] from the Sung?" Reply: "About two thousand years." Tai questioned again: "Then how could Chu Hsi know that it was so?" The teacher could not reply.

This reconsideration of the "precedent tradition" concerning the *Annals* became part of the agenda to recover Han versions of the Classics. As we have seen with T'ang Shun-chih (1507–60) and Kuei Yu-kuang (1507–71), Han dynasty classicism was becoming an important undercurrent in the Neo-Confucian mainstream.[26]

CHI PEN

Chi Pen, a Che-chiang native and student of Wang Yang-ming (1472–1529), also reconsidered Tu Yü's "precedent tradition" in his influential study of the *Annals*. Entitled *Ch'un-ch'iu ssu-k'ao* (Personal study of the *Spring and Autumn Annals*), Chi's study was honored with a long and detailed preface composed by T'ang Shun-chih in 1550. According to T'ang, the strength of Chi's analysis lay in its articulation of the true standards of the sages: "The *Annals* is a work exhibiting the right and wrong of the sages and is not a work that slanders or praises. What the true Way affirms as right, the *Annals* also affirms as right. What the true Way rejects as false, the *Annals* also rejects as false."

T'ang Shun-chih observed that earlier Confucians had lost touch with Confucius's concrete message of ameliorating chaos and punishing criminals—the hallmark of the *Annals*—and instead had turned to an esoteric discussion of historical precedents for "praise and blame." Chi Pen set out to correct such errors.[27]

Chi Pen's own discussion of the *Annals* stressed the Mencian tradition that Confucius's chronicles were "the key to understanding the Way of rulership." Chi was critical of the Old Text tradition of interpretation based on the *Tso chuan* because the latter was written much later than either the *Kung-yang* or *Ku-liang* commentaries, which had been accepted in the official academy during the the early years of the

26. Ibid., 42.2a–3b. The story about Tai Chen is recounted first in Wang Ch'ang, *Ch'un-jung-t'ang chi*, 55.6b.
27. T'ang Shun-chih, "Hsu" (Preface) to Chi Pen, *Ch'un-ch'iu ssu-k'ao*.

Former Han. Chi also noted that the phraseology of the *Tso chuan* was suspiciously unlike other works predating the Warring States period (403–221 B.C.). In fact, the text of the *Tso chuan* showed a remarkable resemblance to writings from the southern feudal state of Ch'u; he concluded that Confucius's disciple Tso Ch'iu-ming, who like Confucius was from the northern state of Lu, could not have produced it. In this way, Chi Pen undercut the Old Text link between the *Tso chuan* and the *Annals*.[28]

To elucidate the "basic intent" (*pen-i*) of the *Annals*, Chi Pen followed the T'ang interpretation tradition by emphasizing the priority of the *Annals* as a Classic over its three traditional commentaries. In so doing, Chi hoped to avoid the contentious debate that had pitted the *Kung-yang* and *Ku-liang* against the *Tso chuan* as the legitimate arbiter of the *Annals'* meaning. The distinction of right from wrong, according to Chi, should proceed directly from the Classic itself—thus avoiding futile efforts to master the hundreds of praise-and-blame precedents that had been read into the *Annals* on the basis of the commentaries.[29]

In his 1557 afterword to Chi Pen's study, Wang Chiao clarified the reason for Chi's dissatisfaction with the Old Text "precedent tradition." He explained that the effort to read elaborate historical precedents (*fan-li*) into the *Annals* on the basis of Confucius's encoding "praise and blame" into the chronicles of Lu had produced a tradition classifying the *Annals* as "Confucius's book of punishments." Rather than stressing the centrality of ritual precedents, as in the other Classics, Confucians had misappropriated the *Annals* as a legal handbook of historical precedents (see chapter 8). Consequently, the *Annals*' stress on the ritual aspects of social order had been overlooked and the true mind-set of the sages (*sheng-jen chih hsin*) overturned.[30]

In his own writings on the *Spring and Autumn Annals*, T'ang Shun-chih also maintained that the tedious elucidation of precedents in the *Annals* detracted from Confucius's central concern, which was ending the chaos of his age. Mencius had been right, T'ang thought: "The *Annals* recorded the affairs of the Son of Heaven." In line with his own more practical concerns, he called the *Annals* a "book of statecraft, whose statecraft [content] revealed how to rectify chaos and crime." It

28. Chi Pen, "Hsu" (Preface) to ibid., pp. 4a–7a. See also *Meng-tzu yin-te*, 25/3B/9. Chi Pen pointed out that Chu Hsi also noted that the *Tso chuan* was a work of history linked to the state of Ch'u.

29. Chi Pen, "Hsu" (Preface), *Ch'un-ch'iu ssu-k'ao*, pp. 7a–b.

30. Wang Chiao, "Hou-hsu" (Afterword), to Chi Pen, *Ch'un-ch'iu ssu-k'ao*.

contained concrete lessons for a time of chaos and accorded with the requirements of change (*pien*).[31]

HAO CHING

Many of the issues explored by Chi Pen were continued by the Hu-kuang literatus Hao Ching. As we note earlier, Hao was an opponent of official corruption in the late sixteenth century and had become involved with the Tung-lin partisans while serving in Ch'ang-chou Prefecture as magistrate in Chiang-yin County. Hao Ching's classical scholarship is most noteworthy for its assault on the authenticity of the Old Text portions of the *Documents*. He was even critical of Chu Hsi for his superficial analysis of the problem, distraught that Chu Hsi, despite his doubts about their authenticity, could have instructed his student Ts'ai Shen to annotate the Old Text chapters of the *Documents Classic*. Hao was also angry that Chu Hsi had told his students that much of the New Text version was indecipherable, viewing this an affront to the authentic words of the sages. Through an analysis of the stylistic inconsistencies in the Old Text chapters, Hao Ching hammered yet another nail in the coffin of the Old Text *Documents*, which Yen Jo-chü acknowledged in his own analysis of the issues five decades later.[32]

Questions concerning the authenticity of the *Tso chuan* as an orthodox commentary on the *Spring and Autumn Annals* reached an interesting climax in the late Ming. Hao Ching turned his attention to this issue in a work entitled *Ch'un-ch'iu fei Tso* (The *Annals* is not linked to the *Tso chuan*), also challenging the Old Text position on the *Annals*. Only the exposés of Liu Feng-lu and K'ang Yu-wei in the nineteenth-century would surpass Hao's acerbic assault on one of the pillars of the Old Text classical tradition.

In his preface to Hao Ching's study of the *Tso chuan*, An Chieh-ch'uan noted that Hao's account represented the (then) final step in a long line of scholars dating back to the T'ang who suspected the claim that Tso Ch'iu-ming had compiled a commentary on the *Annals*. In his own 1610 preface, Hao Ching took the bull by the horns. He explained his intent was to demonstrate that Tso Ch'iu-ming had nothing to do not only with the *Tso chuan* but also with the *Annals*. Contending that

31. T'ang Shun-chih, *Ching-ch'uan hsien-sheng wen-chi* (1573), 7.2a–3a, 17.4a–6a, 17.12b.

32. Yen Jo-chü, *Shang-shu ku-wen shu-cheng*, 8.14a–18b. See also Hao Ching, "Tu-shu," p. 3b.

the *Tso chuan* had achieved such exalted status that no one dared criticize its links to Confucius's chronicles of Lu, Hao Ching explained it was his duty to defy convention in order to right the classical record.[33]

Hao traced mistaken views on the *Tso chuan* back to Ssu-ma Ch'ien (145–86? B.C.), who as grand historian in the Former Han had been the first to identify Tso Ch'iu-ming as the author of the *Tso chuan*. Pan Ku (32–92), author of the *History of the Former Han Dynasty*, and Tu Yü had carried on this tradition, and even accepted Liu Hsin's earlier claim during the Wang Mang interregnum that Tso Ch'iu-ming personally knew Confucius and had thus recorded his true intentions for the *Annals*. Hao saw them as the culprits who had "slandered the *Annals* and deluded scholars" to an unprecedented degree.

Hao wondered why, if Tso Ch'iu-ming wrote the *Tso chuan* as a result of his personal relation to Confucius, he wasn't even mentioned among the seventy disciples? Surely a disciple who had the inside story on the *Annals*—Confucius's own historical record—would have been worthy of mention. That Tso Ch'iu-ming had no relation to Confucius or the *Annals*, according to Hao Ching, was confirmed by the fact that Confucius had terminated the *Annals* with the capture of the marvelous *lin* (a one-horned doe-like animal, perhaps similar to a unicorn) in 481 B.C. (see chapter 7), whereas the *Tso chuan* went on for another thirteen years, not ending its account of the Spring and Autumn era until 468 B.C. If the *Tso chuan* were actually a commentary on the *Annals*, why this discrepancy?

In his analysis, Hao Ching said he accepted the position of New Text Confucians. During the last years of the Former Han they had opposed Liu Hsin's efforts to advance the Old Text Classics, particularly the *Tso chuan*, into the Imperial Academy. Moreover, Hao explained that his efforts were not new. Appealing to the authority of illustrious T'ang Confucians such as Han Yü, Hao concluded: "Therefore, the fact that the *Tso* [*Commentary*] is not reliable was already realized by former people. It is not just due to me." Hao was seeking to reestablish the New Text version of Confucius as an "uncrowned king" (*su-wang*), which had been "unclear" (*pu-ming*) for several dynasties because of the influence of the *Tso chuan* in *Ch'un-ch'iu-hsueh*.[34]

33. Hao Ching, "Hsu" (Preface) to his *Ch'un-ch'iu fei-Tso*. See also An Chieh-ch'uan, "Hsu" (Preface) to ibid.

34. Hao Ching, *Ch'un-ch'iu fei-Tso*, 2.29b–30b, 2.32b–33a. See also Hao, "Tu ch'un-ch'iu," pp. 2b–4b.

It would be interesting to speculate about Hao Ching's radical attack on Old Text classicism. How did the *Documents* and *Tso Commentary* relate to his checkered official career and largely unsuccessful reform efforts? Hao was not a New Text scholar, but one senses in his efforts to gainsay the orthodox Old Text position and in his anti-Sung Learning stance an inchoate appeal to a Confucianism unsullied by the values of his day. Again, classicism was not an escape from political reality but a search for the way back to ancient ideals betrayed in the present.

YAO CHI-HENG

Questions about the Old Text tradition of "precedents" in the *Spring and Autumn Annals* carried over into the Ch'ing dynasty, when the turn to Han Learning became more pronounced. Yao Chi-heng, the distinguished evidential research scholar and antiquarian, who in addition to his eradication of spurius elements from the Confucian Canon (including the Old Text *Documents*) wrote the *Ch'un-ch'iu t'ung-lun* (Penetrating discussions of the *Annals*). This work called for an impartial (that is, *k'ao-cheng*) reevaluation of the "precedent tradition" associated with the *Annals*. Citing both Chi Pen and Hao Ching as his immediate predecessors on the matter, Yao Chi-heng reopened the problem of the provenance of the *Tso chuan* as a commentary that legitimated the historical precedents encoded in the *Annals*.[35] Yao reaffirmed the priority of the *Annals* over its commentaries and changed the epistemological context in which the "right and wrong" taught by the *Annals* would be corroborated:

> Everyone has a mind that discerns right from wrong. If something is right, then the Classic makes it right. If something is wrong, then the Classic makes it wrong. There have never been two branches with regard to the scope of right and wrong. One should examine a work for its reasonableness. If the human mind is of itself the same, then there is no need to speak [of the commentary]. . . . This is why scholars should appropriately discard the commentary and follow the Classic. One cannot discard the Classic and follow the commentary.

Analysis of the Classic should be corroborated by the reasonableness of claims made for right and wrong. The commentaries, Yao maintained, had strayed from the practical concerns of right and wrong that in-

35. Yao Chi-heng, "Hsu" (Preface) to his *Ch'un-ch'iu t'ung-lun*. See also Yao "Ch'un-ch'iu lun-chih," in ibid., A.6b.

formed the *Annals* and become lost in esoteric discussions of tedious points based on its phraseology.[36]

Chief among the faults in *Ch'un-ch'iu-hsueh*, according to Yao Chi-heng, was its long-established "precedent tradition," which was purported to hold the key to the meaning of the *Annals*:

> The single graph for "precedent" [*li*] did not exist in antiquity. Later some vulgar [that is, noncanonical] graphs were converted to this graph [of *li*] to discuss the *Annals*. From the beginning this was a mistake. Moreover, how could one say that Confucius had used this single graph to compose the *Annals*? If one had forced Confucius to compose the *Annals* on the basis of a single graph [of *li*], then Confucius would not have been as ignorant as this. Accordingly, to search out the precedents he purportedly created does not agree very much with Confucius.

T'ang and Sung Confucians had erred by accepting a bogus "precedent tradition." By turning the *Annals* into a work that recorded "extraordinary affairs" (*fei-ch'ang chih shih*), Confucians had converted it into a casebook for ritual and legal transgressions (*fei-li fei-fa*), which in the end misrepresented Confucius as a Legalist (*Fa-chia*) and the *Annals* as a book of punishments (*hsing-shu*) (see chapter 8).[37]

The culpit for this misguided line of interpretation, according to Yao, was Tu Yü, whose *Explication of Precedents* was the first work to invoke the *Tso chuan* as the repository of historical precedents in the *Annals*. Moreover, Tu had prepared a commentary on the Chin dynasty legal code of A.D. 268, which had overlapped with his work on the *Annals*. At about the time Yao Chi-heng was writing, Ku Yen-wu and others were rescuing Tu Yü's work from the T'ang dynasty scissors of K'ung Ying-ta (see above). For Yao Chi-heng, unlike Ku Yen-wu, the Old Text tradition associated with the *Tso chuan* had clouded the *Annals*' true meaning: "Alas, since the single graph of *li* [precedent] appeared, the meaning of the *Annals* from the beginning has not been illuminated in the empire. The sage, basing himself on the history of Lu, composed the *Annals*. How could he have first affirmed its precedents?"

Yao demonstrated Tu Yü's errors by appending a detailed case-by-case rejection of the precedent tradition entitled "Ch'un-ch'iu wu-li hsiang-shuo" (Detailed discussion on the lack of precedents in the *Annals*) to his study of the *Annals*. In addition, Yao claimed that the effort to systematize the events in the *Annals* into precedents was untrue

36. Yao Chi-heng, "Hsu," p. 2a.
37. Ibid., pp. 2b–3a.

to history (*shih*): "History is used to record events. Events have ten thousand changes. How can precedents even things out? If it matches with this event, then it betrays that one; if it is the same as this event, then it differs from that one." History was too complicated to be reduced to a single system of precedents. Tu Yü had recognized this problem and created a special category called "changing precedents" (*pien-li*) in an effort to address it—although *pien-li* is a contradiction in terms, if a precedent really represents an unchanging historical lesson.[38]

According to Yao Chi-heng, the precedent tradition provided the theoretical basis for the praise-and-blame (*pao-pien*) tradition that had grown up around the *Annals*. Not only did Confucius have no intent to praise and blame (*wu pao-pien chih hsin*), but also the *Annals* itself included no formalized and consistent pattern for praise or blame. The Old Text precedent-based interpretation placed all the various items in the *Annals* into a straitjacketed account of good and evil that had forced history into an unchanging pattern of events.[39]

Yao exhibited a view of history that would later be championed by eighteenth-century *k'ao-cheng* historians such as Ch'ien Ta-hsin and Wang Ming-sheng. Like them, Yao appealed to the integrity of history as the complicated record of human events, not a simplistic acting out of precedents in a praise-and-blame drama: "History is used to record events. Consequently, normal and abnormal events are both recorded. If one selects only abnormal events to record, and does not record normal events, how can it be history?" In essence, Yao Chi-heng was calling for a demystification of the *Annals*, hoping to restore it to its legitimate position as a historical chronicle of the state of Lu during the decline of the Eastern Chou dynasty.[40]

To correct the prevailing precedent tradition, which had portrayed Confucius as a Legalist, Yao proposed that the *Annals* be evaluated in light of its "essential points" (*yao-chih*). Yao's use of "point" (*chih*) to replace "precedents" (*li*) represented an effort to recast the interpretation of the *Annals*. It may also represent the impact of the New Text tradition of *Ch'un-ch'iu-hsueh*, which stressed the "three classifications and nine points" (*san-k'e chiu-chih*) to clarify the *Annals* (see chapter 7).

But Yao Chi-heng discarded both the praise-and-blame tradition

38. Yao Chi-heng, *Ch'un-ch'iu t'ung-lun*, A.1a–b and "Fu" (Appendix). See also *Ssu-k'u ch'üan-shu tsung-mu*, 26.5a–6b.

39. Yao Chi-heng, *Ch'un-ch'iu t'ung-lun*, A.2a–3a.

40. Ibid., A.3a–b. On *k'ao-cheng* historiography see my *Philosophy to Philology*, pp. 70–76.

associated with the New Text commentaries (*Kung-yang* and *Ku-liang*) and the precedent tradition associated with the Old Text *Tso chuan*:

> Everyone knows that the *Kung-yang* and *Ku-liang* [commentaries] are perversions. For the moment there is no need to mention them. Few people, however, are aware of the impractical errors and perversions of Master Tso's [commentary], and thus they remain deluded. Why is this? The *Kung-yang* and *Ku-liang* [commentaries] both discuss meanings [*i*]; hence their perversions can be brought to view. Master Tso's [commentary] discusses events [*shih*]; hence its mistakes and perversions are difficult to encompass.

The locus for the interpretation of the *Annals* was in flux. It is interesting that Chuang Ts'un-yü would later entitle one of his essays *Ch'un-ch'iu yao-chih* (Essential points in the *Annals*), suggesting the influence of Yao's attack on the Old Text precedent tradition.[41]

Yao singled out the *Tso chuan* for criticism because it was the basis for the dominant precedent tradition. In partial agreement with Hao Ching's stinging rejection of the *Tso chuan*, Yao Chi-heng noted the many factual inconsistencies between the commentary and the Classic. Yao also rejected the tradition that Tso Ch'iu-ming, Confucius's reputed disciple, had composed the commentary. Although he did not go as far as Hao Ching in linking the *Tso chuan* to Liu Hsin, Yao still undercut one of the essential texts in the Old Text classical canon. Liu Feng-lu would later weave the various strands in Hao Ching's and Yao Chi-heng's criticism of the *Tso chuan* into a coherent attack on the Old Text Classics as a whole.[42]

HAN LEARNING AND THE *ANNALS*

Efforts to properly interpret the *Annals* became caught up in Han Learning currents through Hui Shih-ch'i's research on Confucius's chronicles of Lu, published in 1749 by his celebrated son Hui Tung. As we note in chapter 1, Hui family traditions were decisive in determining the prominence of Han Learning in eighteenth-century Su-chou. Hui Shih-ch'i's attempt to restore the *Annals* to its Han dynasty form in many ways served as the model for Hui Tung's later efforts to reconstruct "Han Learning on the *Change Classic*."[43]

Because the Han Learning movement in Su-chou affirmed Later Han Confucians such as Cheng Hsuan, Hsu Shen (58–147), Ma Jung (76–

41. Yao Chi-heng, *Ch'un-ch'iu t'ung-lun*, A.4a–5b, 6a–6b.
42. Ibid., A.6b–7b.
43. See Yang Ch'ao-tseng, "Pei" (Epitaph) for Hui Shih-ch'i.

166), as well as Tu Yü (men who were directly and indirectly tied to the triumph of Old Text over New Text classicism), Hui Tung and his followers viewed earlier efforts to expunge the *Tso chuan* from the classical record with disdain. In fact, the editors of the *Ssu-k'u ch'üan-shu* project in the 1780s—most of whom were mainstream Han Learning advocates—were extremely critical of Chi Pen and Hao Ching for their temerity to question the *Tso chuan*. The editors went so far as to argue that the Ming dynasty represented the lowest point in the long history of *Ch'un-ch'iu-hsueh*. At least Chi Pen's and Hao Ching's works on the *Annals* were considered important enough to be included in the Imperial Library. Yao Chi-heng's work on the matter was not even mentioned in the catalog of works on the *Annals*. From the outset of their account of the development of *Ch'un-ch'iu* studies, the *Ssu-k'u ch'üan-shu* editors made their allegiance clear: (1) Tso Ch'iu-ming had indeed compiled the *Tso chuan*, and (2) the *Tso chuan* was not only a legitimate commentary on the *Annals* but was also far superior to both the *Kung-yang* and *Ku-liang* alternatives. Han Learning had pitched its tent in Old Text classicism.[44]

A champion of Later Han sources, Hui Shih-ch'i was critical of T'ang and Sung Confucians for ignoring Han dynasty commentaries in their efforts to elucidate the *Annals*. Hui singled out Tan Chu and Chao K'uang in particular for their pernicious influence on *Annals* scholarship. What troubled him was the inability of post-T'ang Confucians to see that the *Annals* and *Rituals of Chou* were complementary Classics that together completed the classical paradigms for political and social order. Chao K'uang, for example, argued that the *Chou-li* was a later forgery; Wang An-shih asserted the *Annals* was worthless. In many ways, Shih-ch'i sought to reconstruct the Later Han version of the *Annals* while reaffirming the Old Text emphasis on the *Rituals of Chou*.[45]

Unlike Yao Chi-heng, Hui Shih-ch'i continued to accent the precedent tradition associated with the *Annals*. He continued to regard Tu Yü's *Explication of Precedents* as authoritative because it was a post–Han dynasty work chronologically close to the Han "schools system" of classical transmission. In addition, Hui's commitment to Later Han classicism led him to reaffirm the priority of the *Tso chuan* over the *Kung-yang* and *Ku-liang* commentaries for understanding the historical precedents in the *Annals*.[46]

44. *Ssu-k'u ch'üan-shu tsung-mu*, 30.11a–b, 17a–b.
45. Hui Shih-ch'i, *Pan-nung hsien-sheng ch'un-ch'iu shuo*, 7.18a–19b.
46. Ibid., 5.10a, 1.22a–22b.

According to Hui Shih-ch'i, the *Rituals of Chou* was a work of the Western Chou dynasty, while the *Annals* exemplified Eastern Chou rituals and institutions. Together they formed the basis, Hui thought, for understanding the Chou ritual traditions that Han Confucians had drawn on: "The Duke of Chou accordingly created the six records [that is, the *Rituals of Chou*], and Confucius composed the *Annals*. Both were means [to understand] completely the nature of man and things, and how to oppose a chaotic age and restore it to order."

Sung Confucians had questioned the authenticity of the *Chou-li* but, aside from Wang An-shih, had never wavered on the provenance of the *Annals*. In Hui Shih-ch'i's Han Learning study of the *Annals*, the latter was secondary to the *Rituals of Chou* in importance. The *Chou-li* was drawn from early antiquity (that is, the Western Chou), while the *Annals* came much later (that is, the Eastern Chou). The roles of the *Annals* and *Rituals* in classical discourse were thus more properly understood as complementary rather than antagonistic. Consequently, it is misleading to assume, as earlier studies have done, that the New Text school regarded Confucius alone as its model and that only the Duke of Chou was the ideal of the Old Text school.[47]

CH'UN-CH'IU-HSUEH IN CH'ANG-CHOU

In the middle of the eighteenth century, research on the *Spring and Autumn Annals* showed little unanimity on the problems of the precedent tradition and the relationship between the *Tso chuan* and the *Annals*. But by the time Chuang Ts'un-yü formulated his ideas concerning the *Kung-yang Commentary*, an influential consensus had been reached. Han Learning scholars of the Su-chou school became wedded to the Old Text traditions of the Later Han and accepted without question the precedent tradition associated with the *Annals* since Tu Yü. Moreover, they stressed the legitimacy of the *Chou-li* as an orthodox Classic. This consensus penetrated the highest levels of Confucian scholarly institutions and became the official view of the Imperial Library on *Ch'un-ch'iu-hsueh*. Both Hui Shih-ch'i and Hui Tung were praised in no uncertain terms by the editors of the *Ssu-k'u ch'üan-shu* project. Shih-ch'i was lauded for his use of the *Tso chuan* as a source; Hui Tung's efforts to reconstruct Tu Yü's annotation of the *Tso chuan* was likewise commended.[48]

47. Ibid., 8.18b–19a, 9.26a–27b. See also Karlgren, "Chou-li and Tso chuan Texts."
48. *Ssu-k'u ch'üan-shu tsung-mu*, 26.27b–28b, 26.31a–34a.

This Han Learning consensus was also influential in local scholarship. In Ch'ang-chou both Ku Tung-kao and Yang Ch'un reaffirmed the Old Text position. In a prodigious work of scholarship entitled *Ch'un-ch'iu ta-shih piao* (Table of major events in the *Spring and Autumn Annals*), the Wu-hsi scholar Ku Tung-kao brought together chronological, geographical, genealogical, and economic information, using the *Annals* as a historical source on the Eastern Chou and adding all relevant material he could find in related sources—in effect a tour de force in *k'ao-cheng* historical studies.[49]

In his preface to Ku Tung-kao's study, Yang Ch'un traced the evolution of the precedent tradition from the *Kung-yang* and *Ku-liang* commentaries to the *Tso chuan*. He claimed that the *Tso chuan* provided the most precise understanding of precedents. Tu Yü's *Explication of Precedents*, according to Yang Ch'un, represented a distillation of views that could be traced back to both the New and Old Text schools. For Yang, the strength of Ku Tung-kao's account was its success in drawing on the virtues of each of the three Han commentaries and weeding out doctrines and facts that betrayed Confucius's intent. For example, Ku's account emphasized both precedents (*li*) and meanings (*i*), suggesting to Yang Ch'un an effort to synthesize the Former Han and Later Han commentaries.[50]

In his own discussion, however, Ku Tung-kao maintained that although he used the Former Han commentaries, he had gainsaid their message. On the question of why Confucius made the capture of the mythical *lin* the final entry of the *Annals*, Ku rejected Ho Hsiu's messianic New Text theories as "lies and deceptions" (*tan-wang*). Ho Hsiu's fanciful interpretation of the *Kung-yang chuan* made Ku conclude that Confucians had misunderstood Confucius's true intent in recording the capture of the mythical *lin* (unicorn).

According to Ku Tung-kao, the sage had ended his account in 481 B.C. because in that year a vassal had not been punished for assassinating his lord. By this time, Confucius was seventy-one, and he saw no hope for ending the chaos of the age. The capture of the unicorn came at precisely this time, confirming the irrevocable decline of the Eastern Chou. Therefore, Confucius ended his chronicles. The capture of the *lin* had historical significance but, according to Ku, no transhistorical import.[51]

49. Ibid., 26.28b–30a. For a discussion see my *Philosophy to Philology*, p. 188.

50. Yang Ch'un, "Hsu" (Preface) to Ku Tung-kao, *Ch'un-ch'iu ta-shih-piao*. For Yang's own views on the *Annals* see his *Meng-lin-t'ang chi*, 5.13b–17b.

51. Ku Tung-kao, *Ch'un-ch'iu ta-shih-piao*, 42.18b–21b.

Although Yang Ch'un vigorously attacked the Old Text *Rituals of Chou* as a Legalist text in Confucian garb, he still upheld the Old Text position on the *Annals*. As yet, there was no inconsistency in such a stand. The Old Text–New Text debate had not yet been fully reconstructed, and the classical consensus seemed impervious to the full implications of growing interest in New Text sources from the Former Han dynasty. Like Yao Chi-heng, however, Yang Ch'un rejected efforts to turn the *Annals* into a simple list of historical precedents. The moral judgments encoded in the chronicles by Confucius did not have independent status: Confucius "drew on the history of Lu for meanings; he did not create the meanings all by himself."[52]

Links between Ku Tung-kao and Yang Ch'un indicate that Han Learning and its Old Text biases had powerful protagonists in Ch'ang-chou Prefecture when Chuang Ts'un-yü began to turn to New Text studies. But Chuang's new interest was rooted in the *kao-cheng* movement. Important scholars such as Yao Chi-heng—less wedded to Han Learning and more committed to impartial research methods—initiated questions about the Old Text precedents tradition by calling the *Tso chuan* into doubt as a legitimate source for interpreting the *Annals*' meaning (*i*). Even the editors of the *Ssu-k'u ch'üan-shu* admitted the chief weakness of Hui Tung's Han Learning agenda was its unquestioning adoration of antiquity (*ni-ku*).[53]

In fact, Chuang Ts'un-yü's New Text interests had been anticipated in Ch'ang-chou by Yang Fang-ta. Yang's *Ch'un-ch'iu i pu-chu* (Appended notes to the Meanings in the *Annals*) furthered the work of his mentor, the distinguished Hanlin academician Sun Chia-kan, who had contended that "the *Change*, *Poetry*, and *Annals* constituted the complete Classics of the sages." For his part, Yang Fang-ta turned his attention to the long-neglected *Kung-yang* and *Ku-liang* commentaries. In addition, he began to rely for some of his interpretations of the *Annals* on Tung Chung-shu's *Ch'un-ch'iu fan-lu* (*Spring and Autumn Annals*' radiant dew), the definitive Former Han New Text interpretation of Confucius's chronicles.[54]

Chuang Ts'un-yü, followed by his grandson Liu Feng-lu, would further clarify and enlarge on Sun's and Yang's writings. Han Learning

52. Yang Ch'un, "Ch'un-ch'iu k'ao hou-hsu" (Afterword to a study of the Annals), 5.15b–17b.

53. *Ssu-k'u ch'üan-shu tsung-mu*, 29.34a. Cf. my *Philosophy to Philology*, pp. 59–60.

54. *Ssu-k'u ch'üan-shu tsung-mu*, 31.36a–38a. The editors describe Yang as "secretly honoring Han Confucians" because he did not cite his borrowings from Tung Chung-shu. See also Lu Wen-ch'ao, *Pao-ching-t'ang wen-chi*, pp. 361–66 (*chüan* 27).

scholars, in their attempts to recover and reconstruct the original teachings of the sages, were employing the Old Text exegetical tradition of the Later Han. Continuing this scholarly enterprise, Ch'ang-chou scholars associated with the Chuangs and Lius in the late eighteenth and early nineteenth centuries began to push back the frontiers of classical learning and to focus on the Former Han dynasty as a better source for the wisdom of the sage-kings.

CHUANG TS'UN-YÜ AND THE *ANNALS*

In a series of works on the *Rituals of Chou* initiated in 1783, Chuang Ts'un-yü sought to restore that text to its original form by adding quotations and materials from other works that cited the *Rituals of Chou*. The version with which Chuang was working was severely limited as a repository of references to classical institutions. Although he made no claim that the *Rituals* was a forgery, Ts'un-yü was critical of the surviving version. In this he was corroborating suspicions dating from the Northern Sung, and most recently reiterated in Ch'ang-chou by Yang Ch'un.[55]

In keeping with his ecumenical position on the Classics, Chuang Ts'un-yü affirmed as much as possible of the classical legacy that undergirded official ideology. As with the Old Text chapters of the *Documents Classic*, Chuang saw no benefit to be had from purist efforts to rid the Confucian Canon of suspicious Classics such as the *Chou-li*. Instead, he feared the *k'ao-cheng* assault on Confucian orthodoxy might spill over into the political arena. His position on the *Annals* was syncretic, and he incorporated both New and Old Text Classics, believing them to be the core of a vision of antiquity bequeathed by the sages to the present. To verify certain points in the *Annals*, Chuang used both the *Ku-liang* and *Tso* commentaries. If he affirmed the *Kung-yang* over the *Tso* commentary, for example, it was not because he attempted to restore the New Text Classics as a whole to their Former Han position of preeminence.[56]

KUNG-YANG CONFUCIANISM

Chuang's work on the *Spring and Autumn Annals* did, however, break new ground. Although he focused on the historical "precedents" (*li*)

55. Chuang Ts'un-yü, *Chou-kuan chi*, 161.1a. See also Chuang Shou-chia, "Chou-kuan chi pa," pp. 36a–37a.
56. Li Hsin-lin, "Ch'ing-tai ching chin-wen-hsueh shu," 174.

and "meanings" (*i*) that Confucius had encoded in his chronicles of Lu from 722 to 468 B.C., Chuang followed the New Text alternative and rejected the Old Text position. According to Ts'un-yü, the *Tso chuan* was primarily a historical record. It stressed historical affairs (*shih*) in the *Annals* but went no further than elaborating the facts. To overcome the limitations of this Old Text commentary, Ts'un-yü turned to the *Kung-yang chuan*, which contained historical interpretations that, in Ts'un-yü's mind, revealed the true design for Confucius's chronicle of events.[57]

Ho Hsiu's Later Han explication of the *Kung-yang chuan* was the chief source for Chuang Ts'un-yü. Long ridiculed for his "preposterous theories" (*wu-li chih shuo*), Ho Hsiu had been Cheng Hsuan's archrival for the articulation of the Classics during the last century of the Later Han. Unlike his more famous rival, Ho Hsiu had been a staunch defender of the *Kung-yang Commentary* and New Text interpretations of the Classics. Besides composing an influential commentary to the *Kung-yang* text, Ho also penned a vitriolic trilogy attacking Cheng Hsuan's position on the *Annals*. Cheng Hsuan, an advocate of synthesizing Old Text and New Text views whenever possible, defended his position on the *Annals* in his equally stinging replies. The bone of contention in the Later Han New Text vs. Old Text controversy was the *Kung-yang chuan*.[58]

By stressing Ho Hsiu and the *Kung-yang chuan*, Chuang Ts'un-yü was unequivocally controverting his Han Learning contemporaries who had installed Cheng Hsuan as the patron saint of Han Learning. Moreover, the influential compilers of the *Ssu-k'u ch'üan-shu* had, as we have seen, established the Old Text position associated with the *Tso chuan* as the authentic representative of the Han Learning version of the *Annals*. Initially championed in Su-chou by Hui Tung in the 1750s, the Han Learning wave crested in the 1780s with the imperially sponsored enshrinement in Peking of Later Han Confucianism in the Imperial Library.[59]

To be sure, Chuang Ts'un-yü was still appealing to the authority of Han Learning with his emphasis on the *Kung-yang chuan*. But his form of Han Learning was in many ways inimical to Old Text versions domi-

57. *Ssu-k'u ch'üan-shu tsung-mu*, 26.4b–6b.

58. Ho Hsiu's trilogy is entitled *Tso-shih kao-huang* (Incurability of Master Tso), *Ku-liang fei-chi* (Disabling diseases of Ku-liang), and *Kung-yang mo-shou* (Stalwart defense of Kung-yang). For a discussion see Dull "Apocryphal Texts of the Han Dynasty," pp. 388–400.

59. *Ssu-k'u ch'üan-shu tsung-mu*, 26.1a–4b.

nant in Su-chou and Yang-chou. Because it was a Han dynasty source, Ho Hsiu's *Kung-yang chieh-ku* (Explication of the *Kung-yang Commentary*) could not be summarily dismissed by those who championed Han Learning.

If we cannot call Chuang Ts'un-yü a New Text scholar, then we can at least refer to his position on the *Annals* as the turning point in the revival of the *Kung-yang Commentary* as the key to Han Learning. Chuang's overall classical vision (which encompassed the *Change*, *Chou-li*, and *Annals*) will therefore be described as "*Kung-yang* Confucianism." Later advocates of "New Text Confucianism" such as Wei Yuan (1794–1856) maintained that Chuang Ts'un-yü was the "true Han Learning scholar" (*chen Han-hsueh che*), in contrast to his "false" contemporaries.[60]

HISTORICAL "PRECEDENTS" VS. "GUIDING POINTS"

Chuang Ts'un-yü's principal work on the *Annals* was entitled *Ch'un-ch'iu cheng-tz'u* (Correcting terms in the *Annals*), to which were appended two shorter works: *Ch'un-ch'iu chü-li* (Examples of precedents in the *Annals*) and *Ch'un-ch'iu yao-chih* (Essential points in the *Annals*). As the titles suggest, Chuang affirmed the legitimacy of the "precedent tradition" while stressing the phraseology of the *Annals* as the key to its interpretation.

Although they acknowledged the praise-and-blame legacy of the *Annals*, Chuang's works also revealed the influence of Ming-Ch'ing Confucians who had questioned Tu Yü's reading of the *Tso chuan*, which we describe above. As a result, Chuang turned away from Tu Yü's detailed list of precedents in the *Annals* and emphasized a simpler and more general list drawn from the *Kung-yang Commentary*. In addition, Ts'un-yü discussed "guiding points" (*chih*, lit., "directives") in the *Annals*. Yao Chi-heng had earlier proposed such "directives" as an appropriate alternative to "precedents" in elucidating the significance of the *Annals*.[61]

During the Former Han dynasty Tung Chung-shu enunciated "Ten Guiding Points" (*shih-chih*), upon which Yao Chi-heng and Chuang Ts'un-yü both drew. Tung wrote:

60. Wei Yuan, *Wei Yuan chi*, p. 238, includes Wei's "Hsu" (Preface) to the collected works of Chuang Ts'un-yü.

61. All these works are included in Chuang Ts'un-yü's *Wei-ching-chai i-shu*. The character that Chuang used for *chih* includes the "hand" (*shou*) radical, while the character for *chih* in Yao's "points" does not. The meanings are homologous, however.

> The *Annals* is a text covering 242 years, in which the great outline of the world and the broad changes of human events are all fully included. In summary, however, it may be reduced to Ten Guiding Points, by which [all] the events [it narrates] may be linked, and from which [all] the transforming influences [in the rule] of kings may be derived. (1) To describe the changes in human events and show what is important in them is one guiding rule. (2) To show what these changes lead to is another. (3) To utilize what leads and controls them is another. (4) To strengthen the trunk, weaken the branches, stress what is primary, and minimize what is secondary, is another. (5) To discriminate among uncertainties and differentiate what [seemingly] belong to similar categories is another. (6) To discuss the appropriate [use] of the good and talented, and differentiate them according to the abilities in which they are preeminent, is another. (7) [To show how a ruler should] cherish persons who are close to him, induce those who are distant to come near, and identify himself with the desires of his people, is another. (8) [To show how], having inherited the refinement of Chou, he is to revert to simplicity, is another. (9) [To make clear that] Heaven's starting point lies in the fact that the wood [phase] produces the fire [phase], which constitutes summer, is another. (10) And to analyze how those whom it criticizes are punished, and examine how prodigies are accordingly applied in [compliance with] Heaven's principle, is another.[62]

By stressing the "key points" of the *Annals*, Chuang was emptying the *Annals* of Old Text historical "precedents" and replacing them with New Text "meanings."

The immediate thread of Chuang Ts'un-yü's position went back further than Ming dynasty questions regarding Tu Yü's position on precedents, however. Chuang appealed to the authority of pre-Ming scholarship in an effort to turn *Ch'un-ch'iu-hsueh* in a direction he thought would get at the heart of what Confucius had encoded in the chronicles of Lu.

CHAO FANG

Chuang Ts'un-yü's *Correcting Terms in the Annals* drew heavily on the work of Chao Fang, the Yuan dynasty scholar. Chao's *Ch'un-ch'iu shu-tz'u* (Comparative phraseology of the *Annals*) had tried to delineate Confucius's systematic linguistic framework for compiling the *Annals*. According to Chao Fang, the key to unlocking the secrets of the *Annals* lay in grasping the interrelation of Confucius's use of the words and his

62. See Su Yü's (d. 1914) edition of Tung's work entitled *Ch'un-ch'iu fan-lu i-cheng*, 5.9a–9b, for Tung Chung-shu's account of the "Ten Guiding Points." Chuang and Tung use the same character for "points." Cf. Fung, *History of Chinese Philosophy*, vol. 2, p. 76.

comparative evaluation of historical events (*shu-tz'u pi-shih*), which during the Han dynasty had enabled Confucians to use the *Annals* as a legal casebook (see chapter 8).

In his preface to Chao's study, the distinguished Confucian scholar Sung Lien (1310–81) noted that Chao Fang had reopened the path to understanding the "law-models of the *Annals*" (*Ch'un-ch'iu chih fa*). In addition, by applying historical methods (*shih-fa*) to the text of the Classic (*ching-wen*), Chao Fang had recaptured the links between language and moral vision Confucius had used in his chronicles.[63]

Chao Fang was a follower of the Sung-Yuan Neo-Confucian Wu Ch'eng (1247–1331), who had attacked the authenticity of the Old Text chapters of the *Documents Classic*. Chao also studied the *Annals* under Huang Tse, who stressed the Old Text tradition of precedents based on the *Tso chuan* as interpreted by Tu Yü. In his *Ch'un-ch'iu Tso-shih chuan pu-chu* (Additional annotations to Master Tso's commentary for the *Annals*), Chao Feng pioneered efforts to restore Tu Yü's commentary to the *Tso chuan* to its original form, for it had been cut up and included piecemeal in K'ung Ying-ta's T'ang dynasty versions of the Classics and their orthodox commentaries. Ku Yen-wu and Hui Tung would later bring to completion such reconstructions of Tu Yü's commentary.[64]

The Han Learning editors of the Imperial Library catalog (completed in the 1780s) praised Chao's research as a model for *k'ao-cheng* scholarship on the *Annals*. They noted that Ming scholars had been unable to maintain Chao's high standards of research:

> His clarifications and explanations are all correct. Not only has he added to Tu [Yü's] commentary, he has also contributed to the study of the *Tso chuan*. So much so that the points left unsaid by the sage are brilliantly illuminated. Consequently, Chao Fang [has presented] impartially the theories of the schools [of thought] regarding the *Annals*.

Despite his predilection for the *Tso chuan* and Tu Yü's commentary, Chao Fang was not averse to using the *Kung-yang* and *Ku-liang* New Text commentaries to correct errors in the *Tso chuan*. By drawing on both the Old Text and New Text commentaries, Chao Fang, according

63. Sung Lien, "Hsu" (Preface) to Chao Fang, *Ch'un-ch'iu shu-tz'u*. See also Chao Fang, "Hsu" (Preface) to his *Ch'un-ch'iu shu-tz'u*, and *Hsu-hsiu Ssu-k'u ch'üan-shu t'i-yao*, vol. 2, pp. 736–37.

64. See my "Philosophy versus Philology," pp. 186–88. See also *Ssu-k'u ch'üan-shu tsung-mu*, 28.13b–18a, and Goodrich et al., eds., *Dictionary of Ming Biography*, pp. 125–27.

to the editors, had "gotten the salient points of each" and encompassed both traditions on the *Annals*.[65]

Chao Fang had made some interesting discoveries in his analysis of comparative phraseology in the *Annals*. Although he did not reject the "precedent tradition" of the *Annals*, Chao contended that earlier commentators had gotten bogged down in idle discussion of praise-and-blame and thereby missed the *Annals*' raison d'être (*shih-chung*). Even Sung Neo-Confucians, according to Chao, had failed to grasp the "esoteric points of the Five Classics" (*wu-ching wei-chih*): "Consequently, I say: If the meaning of the *Annals* is unclear, then the knowledge of scholars will be insufficient to understand the sage. As a result, they will not follow the teachings of the *Annals*." For Chao Fang, it was important to grasp correctly the teachings of the *Annals* in order "to be able to talk about the statecraft meanings of the later sage [that is, Confucius]."[66]

Interestingly, Chao was critical of the *Tso chuan* because its records of historical precedents (*shih-li*) were divorced from the meanings (*i*) around which Confucius had organized the *Annals*. Although he recognized that the New Text commentaries were strong precisely because they elucidated these "meanings," Chao was critical of the *Kung-yang* and *Ku-liang* commentaries because they failed to take into account the historicity of Confucius's chronicles. Chao's attempts to explicate the eight "general precedents" (*fan-li*) in the *Annals*, which Tu Yü had drawn from the *Tso chuan*, represented an interesting compromise position.

Some earlier commentators had rejected the notion that there were any general precedents at all. Others argued that "the *Annals* originally had no precedents." What scholars like Tu Yü had done was "to create precedents based on the traces of events" described in the *Annals*. To deflect this powerful line of criticism (which Yao Chi-heng and others would later develop further), Chao's teacher Huang Tse said: "The history of [the state of] Lu has precedents. The sacred Classics have no precedents. It is not that they lack precedents, but only that they use meanings as precedents."

Chao Fang similarly tried to escape from the polarized positions on the *Annals*. Seeing a larger pattern that encompassed both the "meanings" and "precedents" of the *Annals*, Chao insisted that the precedent

65. *Ssu-k'u ch'üan-shu tsung-mu*, 28.15a–16b.
66. Chao Fang, "Hsu" (Preface) to his *Ch'un-ch'iu shu-tz'u*.

tradition was not able to grasp the totality of Confucius's teachings. Accordingly, Chao recommended his *shu-tz'u pi-shih* approach to the *Annals* as a way to cut through the impasse while affirming the "uniform chronicles" (*t'ung-chi*) of Lu.[67]

Chao Fang's ability to transcend the debates surrounding the precedents in the *Annals* and to focus instead on the *Annals*' overall framework first impressed Mao Ch'i-ling (1623–1716). A leading protagonist in the defense of the Old Text chapters of the *Documents Classic*, Mao Ch'i-ling also compiled a work on the *Spring and Autumn Annals*, building on Chao Fang's earlier discovery of the "interrelation between Confucius' use of words and his comparative evaluation of historical events" (*shu-tz'u pi-shih*).

Using the study of ritual to decipher the *Annals*, Mao Ch'i-ling created twenty-two divisions of "meanings and precedents" (*i-li*) drawn from the comparative phraseology pioneered by Chao Fang. The editors of the Imperial Library catalog noted in their account of Mao Ch'i-ling's study that Mao had differentiated between the *Rituals of Chou* as an example of references to early Chou imperial governmental structures and the *Tso chuan* as an account of events dealing with imperial vassals (*chu-hou*). This distinction allowed Mao Ch'i-ling to affirm that the *Chou-li* provided a model of ideal government and that the *Tso chuan* was a record of institutional reform.

Witness to the travail that had befallen China after the Ming debacle, Mao Ch'i-ling feared that attacks on the Classics by Yen Jo-chü and others, if left unchallenged, would cut literati off from their classical heritage. Interestingly, his efforts to read reformist themes into the *Annals* smacked of New Text commentaries. In effect, Mao was interpreting the *Tso chuan* as a record of change, unlike the *Rituals of Chou*, which he interpreted as the unchanging essence of statecraft.[68]

A subtle shift in *Ch'un-ch'iu-hsueh* was nonetheless evident. Like Mao Ch'i-ling, Chuang Ts'un-yü would find Chao Fang's approach to the *Annals* a useful way to balance classical orthodoxy against contemporary reformism. Evading fixations on the past was no easy task. The Classics had to be freed from their post-Han shrouds. An alternative vision of the classical ordering of the world would preserve the Classics and affirm the need for change and adaptation.

67. *Ssu-k'u ch'üan-shu tsung-mu*, 28.15a–b. See also Goodrich et al., eds., *Dictionary of Ming Biography*, p. 127.
68. On Mao Ch'i-ling's position see *Ssu-k'u ch'üan-shu tsung-mu*, 29.17a–b.

GUIDING PRINCIPLES IN THE *ANNALS*

Chao Fang's study of the *Annals* appealed to a scholar-official like Chuang Ts'un-yü because he, like Chao in the fourteenth century, was trying to avoid a divisive insistence on one commentary to the *Annals* to the exclusion of the others. When it involved the *Annals*, the acrimony of the Han vs. Sung Learning debate was for the most part played out during the Ch'ing dynasty as another version of the long-standing fissure between the repressed *Kung-yang* and triumphant *Tso* commentaries. Chuang, like Chao, was seeking consensus.

In addition, Chao Fang's analysis of the *Annals*' phraseology was in tune with the *k'ao-cheng* temper of the eighteenth century. The compilers of the *Ssu-k'u ch'üan-shu* noted this with pleasure in their summaries of Chao Fang's works on the *Ch'un-ch'iu*. Such agreement was no doubt one reason for Juan Yuan's inclusion of Chuang Ts'un-yü's *Correcting Terms in the Annals* in the *Ch'ing Exegesis of the Classics*. Ts'un-yü's study could be seen as a continuation of Chao Fang's and Mao Ch'i-ling's pioneering application of linguistic criteria to Confucius's chronicles of Lu.[69]

Although Chao Fang had been ecumenical in his selection from the Old and New Text commentaries to the *Annals*, his focus had remained on Tu Yü's annotations to the *Tso chuan*. Chuang Ts'un-yü, however, focused on the New Text *Kung-yang Commentary* to clarify the phraseology of the *Annals*. In his "Examples of Precedents in the *Annals*," for instance, Chuang chose his examples exclusively from the *Kung-yang Commentary* to reconstruct the code of precedents Confucius had entered in his chronicles.

Despite his affirmation of precedents in the *Annals*, Chuang Ts'un-yü's discussion implicitly rejected the complex framework of detailed precedents that Tu Yü had "discovered" in the *Tso chuan*. In place of Tu's tedious listing of hundreds of historical events organized according to forty-two general precedents, Chuang (following the lead of Tung Chung-shu's New Text interpretation based on "Ten Guiding Points") substituted a simpler list of organizational schemes, which Confucius had used to construct the praise-and-blame phraseology of the *Annals*.[70]

Seeing a "system of meanings" (*i-fa*) in the *Annals*, which ancient-prose stylists such as Fang Pao (1668–1749) and Yao Nai (1732–1815)

69. *Ssu-k'u ch'üan-shu tsung-mu*. 28.15a–b. See also *Hsu-hsiu Ssu-k'u ch'üan-shu t'i-yao*, vol. 2, p. 736.
70. Chuang Ts'un-yü, "Ch'un-ch'iu chü-li," pp. 1a–4b.

also discerned, Ts'un-yü articulated precedents in the *Annals* in light of "Ten Guiding Principles":[71]

1. When there is no false resemblance between the noble and mean, the *Annals* uses the same title in both cases. When there is no false resemblance between good and evil, the *Annals* uses the same phrase in both cases.
2. When the *Annals* gives a detailed account without omissions, this indicates approval of correctness [of the action].
3. When one event appears twice, the first is specified in detail, while the second is generalized.
4. Once an event appears [in the record], it does not have to be repeated.
5. The *Annals* does not delay apportioning blame or criticism to condemn evil. When an incident occurs, the *Annals* does not have to first blame or renounce it in order to reveal its condemnation of evil.
6. The *Annals* blames and renounces and then condemns evil. When an incident occurs it can blame and renounce it in order to reveal the condemnation of evil.
7. The *Annals* selects the incident that warrants the most severe criticism and applies its criticisms there.
8. Blame must be placed on the most severe incidence [of evil].
9. The *Annals* criticizes the first occurrence of an incident. The *Annals* condemns the first incidence [of evil].
10. When the *Annals* repeats a key phrase, then one must scrutinize its context, because there must be something deserving praise within.

Compared with the Old Text historical precedents enumerated by Tu Yü, the precedents Chuang culled from the *Kung-yang Commentary* were general and flexible. Tu Yü's system placed the *Annals* within a tightly knit construct of specific historical classifications. Following Chao Fang, Chuang Ts'un-yü preferred a focus on judgmental language in the *Annals* rather than on the events themselves. In effect, Chuang was returning to Tung Chung-shu's interpretation of the *Annals*. Tung studied the *Annals*' "latent language" in an effort to unveil the intent

71. Ibid. See also Malmqvist, "Gongyang and Guuliang Commentaries 1," pp. 73, 77, 82, 123, 163, 168.

(*chih*) behind Confucius's listing of events in Lu from 722 to 481 B.C.

By examining the phraseology of the *Annals*, Chuang Ts'un-yü was able to reconstruct a more flexible web of "words and meanings" drawn from the more voluntarist New Text tradition. He was making the "precedent tradition"—the dominant feature of the *Tso chuan*–based Old Text position since Tu Yü—secondary to an affirmation of "essential points" (*yao-chih*) drawn from the New Text tradition of the Former Han.[72]

THE "ESSENTIAL POINTS" IN THE *ANNALS*

Chuang Ts'un-yü's use of the term "points" (*chih*) reveals a shift away from "precedents" (*li*) toward earlier traditions associated with the *Annals*. The "three classifications and nine points" (*san-k'e chiu-chih*) (which we shall discuss when we turn to Liu Feng-lu's role in the emergence of New Text Confucianism in Ch'ang-chou) had been the cornerstone of Ho Hsiu's New Text studies in the Later Han. Moreover, the word *chih* resonated powerfully with the Han legal term for "rescripts" (*chih*), used for imperial responses to memorials. In chapter 8 we shall describe how legal decisions during the Former Han dynasty had frequently been based on the *Annals* and the *Kung-yang chuan*. Ho Hsiu reaffirmed this link between legal and classical studies in his own New Text studies.[73]

In his analysis of the "essential points" (*yao-chih*) in the *Spring and Autumn Annals*, Chuang explained: "The reason why people value the *Annals* is not because it is a history that records affairs. What is not included exceeds what is. On the basis of what is not included, we know [the meaning of] what is included. On the basis of what is included, we know [the meaning of] what is not included." Hence the significance of the *Spring and Autumn Annals* lay not in the events recorded, but rather in their encoding:

> The *Annals* uses words [*tz'u*] to form images [*hsiang*]. It uses images to spell out laws [*fa*]. It speaks to later generations in the world through the sublime mind-set [*hsin*] of the sages. When looking at its words, one must use the mind-set of the sages to preserve [its images and laws]. . . . Therefore, those who are proficient in the *Annals* stop at the laws [taught by] the sages, and that's all.

72. Chuang Ts'un-yü, "Ch'un-ch'iu yao-chih," pp. 1a–11b.
73. See Vandermeersch, "Chinese Conception of the Law," p. 8.

The will (*chih*) of the sages was expressed through the chronicle of events. The events themselves were secondary, however, to their pattern. Chuang turned the Han Learning preoccupation with facts, institutions, and "names and their referents" (*ming-wu*) inside out. Han Learning scholars were, he thought, missing the forest for the trees.[74]

Confucius's holistic vision of the *Annals*, thought Chuang Ts'un-yü, could be glimpsed in Chao Fang's efforts to grasp the interrelation of the *Annals*' phraseology and its comparative evaluation of historical events (*shu-tz'u pi-shih*). Chuang wished thereby to escape from the dustbin of historical precedents that had limited Confucius's message to idle scholarly classification and tedious historical detail, which influential Confucians such as Wang An-shih and Chu Hsi had both scorned.

History was released from its fixation on "events" (*shih*) and reattached to the perennial rediscovery of "meaning" (*i*). Confucius's words (*tz'u*) were for Chuang Ts'un-yü the correct (*cheng*) route to recover the true spirit of the past. Events described in the *Annals* were in and of themselves a dead end, a representation of chaos, death, and destruction. The events pointed instead to a higher order of meaning: the vision of the sage-kings that Confucius encoded in the Classics.

In a remarkable conversion (not unlike Tai Chen's turn late in his life from precise philology to abstract theory) Chuang Ts'un-yü, who was a friend and colleague of Tai Chen, stood Han Learning and *k'ao-cheng* on its head. As in *k'ao-cheng*, "words" (*tz'u*) remained for Chuang the key to "meaning." A major research strategy of evidential research had been turned against its practitioners. Tai Chen contended in the 1770s that "through language we can penetrate the mind and will of the ancient sages and worthies." With regard to the mind and will of Confucius, Chuang Ts'un-yü argued that the *Kung-yang chuan*, not the *Tso chuan*, was the key to decoding the *Annals*.[75]

In some ways, Chuang's discussion of twenty-two "essential points" in the *Annals* overlapped with his earlier account of "precedents." His comments on each "essential point," however, clarified what Chuang considered at the heart of the *Annals*. According to Chuang, the *Annals* had been composed as a lesson for an age of chaos. As we note in chapter 4, the *Change Classic* was a record for a time of order. It represented the fountain of ancient wisdom. The *Annals* recorded the demise of the classical world. It was a call to reform the present in the name of

74. Chuang Ts'un-yü, "Ch'un-ch'iu yao-chih," pp. 1a–2a.

75. Ibid., pp. 1a–1b. See also Tai Chen, *Tai Chen wen-chi*, p. 146. Cf. my *Philosophy to Philology*, pp. 27–29.

the past (*t'o-ku kai-chih*): "The *Annals* orders chaos. It must express this [intent] through subtlety. This is what [Ssu-ma Ch'ien] meant by 'rituals prevent [improprieties] before they appear.' All entries [in the *Annals*] express [this subtlety]. That is why the *Annals* has no meaningless entries [*k'ung-yen*]." For Chuang Ts'un-yü, the *Annals*, a record of chaos, provided a schema for order. In essence, the *Annals* was united with the *Change Classic* in outlining the cosmos: "The *Annals* chronicles the affairs of Heaven and man, of inner and outer. It focuses on recording [events] in order to establish [sacred] teachings [*li-chiao*]. Then it makes many connections [between events] and broadly finds a thread [of meaning] to encompass them. Consequently, the kingly way is complete within." A unified vision underlay the historical events chronicled in the *Annals*.[76]

As a record of the state of Lu during the decline of the Chou dynasty, Confucius's *Annals*, according to Chuang, was a "reliable history" (*hsin-shih*) whose choice of entries was intended "to be preserved and transmitted for ten thousand generations so that chaos would not arise again." Old Text historiography had lost the essential message of the *Annals*. Chronology was not the central issue. Rather, the *Annals* "subordinated the consecutive recording of events to their [overall] meaning." Instead of a list of historical precedents, the *Annals* was a work "inspired with dealing with Heaven's affairs" (*chih t'ien-shih*). Within it, Confucius's "statecraft intent" (*chien ching-shih chih chih*) was disclosed.[77]

In the phraseology of the *Annals*, Chuang thought he had rediscovered the "points" (*chih*) around which the *Annals* had been constructed. For example, Chuang summarized the intent behind Confucius's numerous references to burial practices as a general statement of the classical ideal of loyalty and filial piety:

> The *Annals* gives meaning to death and burial. The sages regarded seeing off the dead as an important matter. When speaking of a ruler or a father, the reason why individual life was praised was the same reason why individual death was praised. When speaking of an official or a son, the burial of his immediate [the ruler or father], therefore, is the means by which one completed oneself. And one had to complete oneself through ritual. In this way, one reached the height of loyalty and filial piety.

76. Chuang Ts'un-yü, "Ch'un-ch'iu yao-chih," p. 2a.
77. Ibid., pp. 2b–3a.

On the frequent mention of the walling of cities and the formation of military alliances in the *Annals*, Chuang explained such entries as the "perversion of what was right" (*hsieh-cheng*). He went on:

> Each event has its counterpart. If a single meaning and a single pattern are sufficient to judge the general framework, then when the general framework cannot be ascertained, the *Annals* omits and does not record [the event]. The *Annals* is not a history of recorded events. It controls the narrative [*yueh-wen*] and enunciates meanings [*shih-i*].

Chuang, in essence, agreed with Tung Chung-shu's Former Han estimation of the *Annals*. Tung had concluded: "Such is the way in which the *Annals* respects the good and emphasizes the people. Thus, although there are several hundred instances of warfare and aggression [in its 242 years of chronicles], it records them all one by one, thereby to express sorrow at the heavy extent of their harm."[78] The applied moral message of the *Annals* differentiated it from other histories that were not Classics in the strict sense.

For Chuang Ts'un-yü the Former Han *Kung-yang chuan* and Ho Hsiu's Later Han annotations were the chief tools left from the early empire that could be used to reconstruct the Han "meaning" of the *Annals*. Chuang not only championed the *Kung-yang chuan* but also began to use the New Text commentary to explicate the other four Classics. Through these New Text accounts, the Old Text fixation on the *Tso chuan* and Tu Yü's tedious classification of precedents in the *Annals* could be superseded.[79]

Chuang left unconsidered, however, how *Kung-yang* Confucianism would later apply to New Text controversies that he himself only vaguely perceived. The conservative intent behind his emphasis in the late eighteenth century on the *Kung-yang chuan* to counter the deleterious effects of the Ho-shen era is analytically distinct from the more radical consequences of full-blown New Text Confucianism in the early nineteenth century. Chuang Ts'un-yü's intellectual formulations were designed to counter what he perceived to be the radical political implications of Han Learning, which since the 1740s seemed to threaten the orthodox underpinnings of the state.

However, Chuang was not an orthodox Sung Learning advocate

78. Ibid., pp. 4a–4b. See Su Yü, *Ch'un-ch'iu fan-lu i-cheng*, 2.2a, for Tung's remarks, and Fung, *History of Chinese Philosophy*, vol. 2, p. 77.

79. Chuang Ts'un-yü, "Ch'un-ch'iu yao-chih," p. 7b. See also Li Hsin-lin, "Ch'ing-tai ching chin-wen-hsueh shu," p. 63.

either. Chu Hsi, for example, had never used the *Spring and Autumn Annals* to advance his classical teachings and, in fact, had relegated it to secondary importance. By revealing the *Annals* as the key to Confucius's classical vision, Ts'un-yü was making an end run around Chu Hsi and reclaiming the New Text portrait of Confucius. By expressing his views through a text as unorthodox as the *Kung-yang chuan*, Chuang Ts'un-yü was effectively countering not only Han Learning but also orthodox Sung Learning as well. "True Han Learning" cut both ways. Reconstruction of Former Han New Text Confucianism would inspire Chuang's followers to challenge all post-Han political discourse based on the Old Text Classics.

Although Chuang Ts'un-yü relied on Confucian theory, the textual basis for his theory was circumscribed by Han dynasty sources. Despite his mastery as a young scholar of the Ch'eng-Chu Neo-Confucian tradition and his subsequent success in and service for the civil service examination system, Chuang recognized late in his life that a new theoretical framework was required to legitimate his opposition to Ho-shen. Chuang Ts'un-yü's importance in the reemergence of New Text Confucianism should therefore not be underestimated.

Chuang could not have foreseen that his bold initiative would eventually lead to a radical reformulation of the classical language of politics and in turn affect the legitimation of the Confucian state he was trying to preserve. But he could see that new ideas were required to defend the classical legacy. The *k'ao-cheng* dismantling of Sung Learning would, he correctly perceived, leave the state with a bankrupt ideology. This was why he defended the Old Text *Documents* and affirmed the *Rituals of Chou*. Responding to what he viewed as a moral breakdown in imperial politics, Chuang sought to authorize Confucian activism and, so, turned to the *Kung-yang* tradition for his personal moral high ground.

Ts'un-yü's conservative posture, as we discussed earlier, represented both local and national interests. The interstices of classical theory and political discourse, interesting for the history of ideas, take on added meaning when viewed in light of (1) the long-term Chuang lineage traditions in Ch'ang-chou and (2) the threat Ho-shen posed to the Chuangs' continued status as a "professional elite" in national affairs.

Ts'un-yü's turn to *Kung-yang* Confucianism is evidence of the deep inroads Han Learning had made in Ch'ang-chou society. New scholarly strategies were afoot, and the transmission of Chuang lineage traditions from Chuang Ts'un-yü to Liu Feng-lu took place within the larger context of a lineage adjusting its cultural resources and scholarly agenda from Sung Learning to Han Learning. No "secret transmission" of New Text doctrines was at work here. Chuang made a conscious decision largely based on political convictions, to turn to *Kung-yang* Confucianism. In so doing, the grand secretary transformed and redirected the scholarly traditions of his distinguished and powerful lineage.

Two grandsons, Chuang Shou-chia and Liu Feng-lu, carried on his teachings. Along with Sung Hsiang-feng, Chuang Ts'un-yü's nephew, they all studied under the auspices of the Chuang lineage, encouraged by Ts'un-yü. As we have seen, Liu Feng-lu's mother brought her son to her father for instruction at an early age. Liu studied the Classics and other ancient texts under him before turning to Tung Chung-shu's *Ch'un-ch'iu fan-lu* (*The Spring and Autumn Annals*' radiant dew) and the *Kung-yang chuan* based on Ho Hsiu's *Kung-yang chieh-ku*.

Liu Feng-lu absorbed the "esoteric words containing great principles" (*wei-yen ta-i*) that his grandfather Chuang Ts'un-yü had stressed in his classical writings and teachings. Ts'un-yü died when Liu Feng-lu was only twelve. The remainder of his education was guided by younger, but still senior, members of the Chuang lineage, whose links to Han Learning and evidential research ran deeper than they did for Ts'un-yü. Chief among Liu's mentors was Chuang Shu-tsu (1751–1816). Denied official appointment because of Ho-shen's intervention, Shu-tsu devoted himself to classical philology and New Text studies. In the hands of Liu Feng-lu, New Text Confucianism would represent the wedding of Chuang Shu-tsu's Han Learning philology and the *Kung-yang* studies of Chuang Ts'un-yü.[80]

80. *Chu-chi Chuang-shih tsung-p'u* (1883), 8.30b–31a, 8.36a. See also Wang Niensun, "Shen-shou fu-chün hsing-shu" (1876), 12.46b, and Liu's own account in his *Liu Li-pu chi* (1830 ed.), 10.25a–25b. Sung Hsiang-feng was the son of Chuang P'ei-yin's (1723–59) third daughter, who married into the Su-chou Sung family.

SIX

From Chuang Shu-tsu to Sung Hsiang-feng

CHUANG SHU-TSU

The *Kung-yang* teachings that were transmitted from Chuang Ts'un-yü to his precocious grandson Liu Feng-lu were decisively mediated by Chuang Shu-tsu. When Shu-tsu was ten years old (according to Chinese count), his father Chuang P'ei-yin passed away, in part (say the accounts) because of his excessive remorse over his own father's death that same year. Raised by his uncle Chuang Ts'un-yü, Shu-tsu nevertheless maintained his status as the eldest male in his father's immediate line. Although he distinguished himself in the *chin-shih* examinations of 1780, Shu-tsu was cheated out of a high appointment by Ho-shen's cronies because of his ties to the opposing A-kuei faction (see chapter 3). Turning chiefly to a life of scholarship, Shu-tsu served in low-level provincial and county magistracies until 1797 when at age forty-six he retired forever from public office.

Barred from the Hanlin Academy during the Ho-shen era, Chuang Shu-tsu instead became a specialist in the *k'ao-cheng* fields of paleography (*wen-tzu-hsueh*) and epigraphy (*chin-shih-hsueh*), never achieving the dizzying heights of political prestige and position enjoyed by his distinguished father and uncle, both Hanlin academicians. Shu-tsu's collected works were published posthumously in 1837. Li Chao-lo, who had been introduced to Chuang Shu-tsu's classical scholarship by Liu Feng-lu, prepared a biography and a preface for this book, heaping praise on his impartial scholarship and concern for restoring the ancient learning (*ku-hsueh*) bequeathed by the sages. In so doing, Li Chao-lo documented the importance of the Chuangs in Ch'ang-chou scholarly circles at the turn of the nineteenth century.[1]

When Chuang Ts'un-yü died in 1788, Liu Feng-lu (then twelve) continued his studies under the tutelage of Chuang Shu-tsu, together with his cousins, Chuang Shou-chia and Sung Hsiang-feng. They learned more about Chuang Ts'un-yü's *Kung-yang* teachings and were also introduced (as Chuang Shu-tsu's special protégés) to the philological techniques employed in *k'ao-cheng* studies. Although the Chuang lineage emphasized the examination-oriented Sung Learning traditions, Liu Feng-lu would develop an equal respect for Han Learning—a respect he learned from Chuang Shu-tsu. Apparently, *k'ao-cheng* studies had decisively penetrated the classical repertoire of the Chuang lineage between the line's twelfth generation of Ts'un-yü and P'ei-yin, and the thirteenth generation of Shu-tsu.[2]

Unlike his lineage forebears, for whom classical scholarship and political position were inseparable, Shu-tsu's early recourse to a life of scholarship represented—however unintentionally—the distinctive career pattern of an eighteenth-century evidential research scholar. Although *k'ao-cheng* scholars often accepted official positions, they frequently retired from office as soon as it was feasible in order to devote themselves to specialized historical and classical research. But Chuang Shu-tsu was barred from office because of political pressures, unlike Chuang Ts'un-yü, who retired from office at age sixty-seven. Shu-tsu was therefore able to spend his most productive years in private scholarship.[3]

In addition to his studies of the *Spring and Autumn Annals*, Chuang Shu-tsu wrote a number of technical Han Learning studies, including his highly praised *Mao-shih k'ao-cheng* (Evidential analysis of the Mao recension of the *Poetry Classic*) and *Shang-shu chin-ku-wen k'ao-cheng* (Evidential analysis of the New and Old Text *Documents Classic*). One of Shu-tsu's most ambitious projects was his reconstruction of Hsia (tr.

1. See the biography of Chuang Shu-tsu in *P'i-ling Chuang-shih tseng-hsiu tsu-p'u* (1935), 21.26a–26b. A longer draft biography of Chuang appears in the archives of the Palace Museum, Taipei, *Chuan-kao*, no. 4470. See also Li Chao-lo's "Hsu" (Preface) to Chuang Shu-tsu, *Chen-i-i i-shu*. For Li's biography of Chuang Shu-tsu, see Li Chao-lo, *Yang-i-chai wen-chi*, 13.5a–6b.

2. Wang Nien-sun, "Shen-shou fu-chün hsing-shu," 12.47a. See also Li Chao-lo, *Yang-i-chai wen-chi* (1852), 3.13b–14a, and Li's "Hsu" (Preface) to Chuang Shu-tsu's *Chen-i-i i-shu*. Cf. Hsu K'o, *Ch'ing-pai lei-ch'ao*, 69/28.

3. Palace Museum, Taipei, *Chuan-kao*, no. 4470, and Li Chao-lo's "Hsu" (Preface) to Chuang Shu-tsu, *Chen-i-i i-shu*. On *k'ao-cheng* career patterns, see my *Philosophy to Philology*, pp. 95–137.

2205–1766?? B.C.) and Shang (tr. 1766?–1122? B.C.) classical texts, whose importance he likened to that of the Chou dynasty (1122?–221 B.C.) legacy.

THE RECONSTRUCTION OF EARLY TEXTS

Chuang Shu-tsu brought his talents in paleography and epigraphy to bear on a series of works that unraveled the original classical text of the *Hsia-shih* (Seasonal Observances of the Hsia) from a syncretic commentary known as the "Lesser Calendar of the Hsia." The version in the *Record of Rites* (*Li-chi*) had hopelessly interpolated the original—a compendium of ancient lore dealing with astronomy, geography, animals, climate, and the calendar—with the commentary. Many scholars contended that Cheng Hsuan (127–200) and other Confucian scholars from the Han dynasties on had left the *Seasonal Observances of the Hsia* in a hopelessly mangled condition.[4] Indeed, it had been presumed that the original classical text of the *Hsia-shih* was lost, survived only by its commentary.

During the Sung dynasty Fu Sung-ch'ing argued that the text of the original work and its later commentary had been combined. Ch'ing evidential research scholars had solved a similar puzzle with the *Shui-ching chu* (Notes to the Classic of Waterways). Pi Yuan, Sun Hsing-yen, and K'ung Kuang-sen all picked up where Fu Sung-ch'ing had left off and anticipated the efforts of Chuang Shu-tsu; Liu Feng-lu would later continue where Chuang left off.[5] Eventually the "lost teachings" (*chueh-hsueh*) of the Hsia dynasty were restored through careful *k'ao-cheng* analysis. As a result, the pre-Confucius classical legacy could be pushed back to early antiquity.

As a compendium of ancient lore, the *Seasonal Observances of the Hsia* was an obvious candidate for evidential research. Chuang Shu-tsu noted:

> Confucius also ordered the *Seasonal Observances of the Hsia*. This work was drawn from writings on the four seasonal observances of the Hsia [dynasty] just as the *Spring and Autumn Annals* was drawn from the history of [the state of] Lu. The lessons of the sages are contained within in the form of "Greater and Lesser Calendars."[6]

4. Chuang Shu-tsu, "Hsu" (Preface) to the *Hsia Hsiao-cheng ching-chuan k'ao-shih*. The text of the *Hsia Hsiao-cheng* was included in the *Li-chi* classic in the edition prepared by Tai Te (fl. ca. second century B.C.).

5. Chuang Ya-chou, *Hsia Hsiao-cheng hsi-lun*, pp. 1–7. On the *Shui-ching chu* see my *Philosophy to Philology*, pp. 225–26.

6. Chuang Shu-tsu, "Hsu" (Preface) to the *Hsia Hsiao-cheng yin-tu k'ao*, pp. 5a–6a.

To recapture statecraft traditions from the Hsia would confirm, Chuang Shu-tsu thought, the precedents and lessons recorded in the *Annals*:

> Heaven has yin and yang to produce the myriad things. The production of them depends on the earth. Kingly affairs are modelled accordingly. Consequently, the stages [included in] the *Seasonal Observances of the Hsia* in general include three [levels]: (1) "Greater Calendar"; (2) "Lesser Calendar"; (3) "Kingly affairs." The "Greater Calendar" is modelled on Heaven. The "Lesser Calendar" is modelled after the earth. "Kingly affairs" are delegated to man. The heavenly way is round. The earthly way is square. The human way is benevolence [*jen*]. Benevolence is the heart of Heaven and earth. It is the height of kingly affairs.[7]

According to Chuang, study of the three commentaries on the *Seasonal Observances of the Hsia* paralleled the three commentaries on the *Annals*:

> The meanings in the *Spring and Autumn Annals* are clarified by the three commentaries. The most reliable of these is the *Kung-yang* school tradition, whose general meaning Tung Ta-chung [Chung-shu, 179?–104? B.C.] was able to encompass. Hu-wu Sheng [fl. ca. 1st century B.C.] analyzed the organization of the *Annals* and then preserved and honored the [*Kung-yang*] school tradition. Ho Shao-kung [Hsiu, 129–182] completed his *Explication* [*of the Kung-yang Commentary*] in which he rectified morality and stressed correct conduct. After this, the extremely odd meanings and strange sayings in the *Annals* all received correct [attention]. All who study the *Annals* know that the *Kung-yang* school is true [to the *Annals*]. If the *Ku-liang* [*Commentary*] cannot compare [to the *Kung-yang*], how much more so Master Tso's version, which is not [even] a commentary to the *Annals*!

For Confucius, the universal influence of benevolence—which permeated the realms of heaven, earth, and man—was the central lesson from higher antiquity, best exemplified in the *Hsia-shih* and *Kung-yang chuan*. According to Chuang Shu-tsu, these works elucidated the meanings and precedents of the Hsia dynasty that were relevant for the Chou period.[8]

OLD TEXT VS. NEW TEXT PHILOLOGY

Shu-tsu's interests in ancient history led him to reexamine the Later Han records of an academic conference held in 79 A.D. at the White Tiger Hall. The meetings were convened under imperial auspices to dis-

7. Chuang Shu-tsu, *Wen-ch'ao*, 5.7a–10a. See also Li Hsin-lin, "Ch'ing-tai ching chin-wen-hsueh shu," p. 178.
8. Chuang Shu-tsu, "Hsu" (Preface) to the *Hsia Hsiao-cheng yin-tu k'ao*, pp. 5a–5b.

cuss the New Text–Old Text controversy, which had become a prominent debate among Confucian erudites since the downfall of Wang Mang six decades earlier. Participants at the conference reaffirmed the New Text Classics as the orthodox locus of sagely teachings. Unlike an earlier conference held at Shih-ch'ü in 51 B.C. (which debated the relative merits of the *Kung-yang chuan* vs. *Ku-liang chuan* as the New Text commentaries on the *Annals*), the meetings at the White Tiger Hall displayed the characteristic respect and support of Later Han Confucians for the Old Text Classics. In fact, the record of the meetings—entitled *Po-hu t'ung-i* (Comprehensive discussions at the White Tiger Hall)—reveal that efforts were well under way in the first century A.D. to reconcile the Old Text and New Text positions.[9]

In 1777 Lu Wen-ch'ao, a major figure in the transmission of Han Learning to Ch'ang-chou, convened a meeting in Nan-ching concerning the *Po-hu t'ung-i*. He wanted to collate the most reliable edition of the White Tiger Hall discussions; Chuang Shu-tsu was one of the scholars who came. Such efforts were considered the best means to restore the classical learning of the Han dynasties to their rightful prominence in contemporary eighteenth-century academic circles. Chuang Shu-tsu's influential *Po-hu t'ung-i k'ao* (Study of the comprehensive discussions at the White Tiger Hall), published in 1784 with a preface by Lu Wen-ch'ao, was a product of the Nan-ching meeting.

Shu-tsu used his research on the White Tiger Hall meetings to elaborate on the *Kung-yang* studies his uncle Chuang Ts'un-yü had initiated. Working within a Han Learning research agenda that appeared to continue the work of Hui Tung (1697–1758) and others, Chuang Shu-tsu was in effect rewriting the history of New Text Confucianism during the Later Han. He appealed to the *Kung-yang chuan* as the accepted commentary of the day and noted that the *Tso chuan's* interpretations of the *Annals* had not been discussed at the White Tiger Hall conference. Moreover, he noted that "the teachings of the *Annals* were grasped through the interrelation between the phraseology [of the *Annals*] and its comparative evaluation of historical events [*shu-tz'u pi-shih*]." Such explicit references to his uncle's classical agenda made it clear that for Chuang Shu-tsu as for Chuang Ts'un-yü, Han Learning meant New Text learning.[10]

9. Tjan Tjoe Som, *Po Hu T'ung*. See also Hihara, "Byakko tsūgi kenkyū choron," 63–64.

10. Chuang Shu-tsu, *Po-hu t'ung-i k'ao*, pp. 1a–6a. See also the "Chiao-k'an-chi" section, ibid., 4.5a–6a.

Although he dismissed the *Tso chuan* as an irrelevant commentary on the *Spring and Autumn Annals*, Shu-tsu would later collaborate with his landsman Sun Hsing-yen on the recollation and revision of Tu Yü's famous *Explication of Precedents in the Annals*, which eighteenth-century scholars saw as the most important work from the Later Han dynasty "schools system" that preserved the teachings on the *Annals* (see chapter 5). Based on the *Yung-lo ta-tien* (Great Compendium of the Yung-lo era [1403–25]) edition, the version compiled by Chuang Shu-tsu and Sun Hsing-yen was republished in 1802 by the Imperial Printing Office (*Wu-ying-tien*). In his preface to the 1802 edition, Sun Hsing-yen noted that he and Chuang favored Tu Yü's edition because Tu "has preserved many ancient words and was unlike T'ang [Confucians] such as Tan Chu [725–70] and Chao K'uang [fl. eighth century A.D.], who had enjoyed making arbitrary interpretations and had attacked the meanings and etymologies of earlier [that is, Han dynasty] Confucians." Tu Yü's proximity to the Han Learning era made his writing an invaluable source for Ch'ing *k'ao-cheng* scholars.[11]

THE PRECURSOR OF NEW TEXT STUDIES

As a result of his contact with mainstream Han Learning scholars, Chuang Shu-tsu was not yet a vocal proponent of New Text studies, continuing to acknowledge the importance of Old Text traditions. Unlike Chuang Ts'un-yü, however, Shu-tsu placed his sympathies for New Text learning within the philological discourse of contemporary Han Learning. A scholar first, Shu-tsu differed from Ts'un-yü on the scholarly issues of the day. Therefore, the political threat Han Learning posed to the Sung Learning orthodoxy did not affect his private scholarship. But philological controversies over the Old Text–New Text debate did attract Chuang Shu-tsu's attention. In fact, he had already considered many of the philological points upon which Liu Feng-lu would later construct a consistent New Text position. His classical studies, for example, demonstrated an awareness of Liu Hsin's ominous role in promoting the Old Text Classics during the usurpation of Wang Mang. Suspicious of Liu's claim that the *Tso chuan* had originally contained many ancient forms of writing (*ku-tzu*), Shu-tsu therefore wondered why the present version had so few ancient characters. It was clear, he concluded, that the ancient version of the *Tso chuan* had been subjected

11. For Chuang Shu-tsu's contributions to Tu Yü's *Ch'un-ch'iu shih-li*, see the "Hsu" (Preface) to Tu Yü, *Ch'un-ch'iu shih-li*.

to such extensive textual changes that the present version "was not the authentic text transmitted during Han dynasty times."[12]

At first, Shu-tsu attributed the changes in the *Tso chuan* to Wei-Chin (220–316) Confucians, who had also been responsible for changing other Classics after the Later Han dynasty fell. But in his later discussions on the complementarity of classical studies and paleography, Chuang Shu-tsu would accuse Liu Hsin of interpolating the *Tso chuan*. Shu-tsu surmised that Liu did not understand the ancient seal forms of writing (*chuan-shu*) and had therefore replaced them with the more acceptable "modern" clerical script (*li-shu*). It is interesting that the initial suspicions about Liu Hsin among Ch'ang-chou scholars occurred in paleographical discussions about alternative writing forms (see figs. 1–3) during the Han dynasties.

Such issues led Shu-tsu to reconsider the textual basis for the so-called New Text *Documents Classic*. Like Yang Ch'un before him (see chapter 4), Chuang contended that *New Text* was a relative term because it came into use only after seal forms of writing had been converted to the Han dynasty clerical script. Yang Ch'un had already noted that the "New Text" classics had previously been written in ancient seal forms that antedated the third century B.C.[13]

Although he did not accuse Liu Hsin of forgery, Chuang Shu-tsu did impute some ignorance to him. The forgotten similarities between the New Text Classics and earlier seal forms of writing, for instance, suggested that Confucian scholars during Wang Mang's reign could fake the ancient seal script with relative impunity. General ignorance of these similarities allowed Liu Hsin and his followers to manipulate the texts written in ancient seal script that had survived in the imperial archives. Both the *Tso chuan* and the *I Chou-shu* (Leftover portions of the Chou *Documents*), Shu-tsu maintained, had been tampered with.

Chuang also argued that the origins of the sixteen authentic Old Text chapters of the *Documents Classic* were questionable too. He claimed that the version found by Liu Hsin and his followers in the Imperial Archives may have been altered extensively by Wang Mang's Old Text ideologues. Accordingly, it, too, hardly resembled the original version purportedly rediscovered in Confucius's former residence. In a letter to

12. Chuang Shu-tsu, *Li-tai tsai-chi tsu-cheng lu*, 1.20a.

13. Chuang Shu-tsu, *Shuo-wen ku-chou shu-cheng mu*, p. 25a. See also Chuang Shu-tsu's letter to Sung Hsiang-feng on this matter in Chuang's *Wen-ch'ao*, 6.26a–27b. Cf. Chuang Shu-tsu, *Li-tai tsai-chi tsu-cheng lu*, 1.3a–3b.

his nephew Liu Feng-lu, Shu-tsu delineated the possible ramifications of the Wang Mang era for the classical tradition: an erroneous understanding of ancient seal characters had led to the officially sanctioned establishment of a questionable series of Old Text Classics, which were translated into Han dynasty clerical script and placed in the Imperial Academy.[14] Moreover, Shu-tsu acknowledged that the twenty-five Old Text chapters of the *Documents Classic*, which appeared in the fourth century A.D., were forgeries. In his work on the *Documents*, Chuang followed the lead of the Ch'ang-chou Han Learning advocate Sun Hsing-yen. Sun used the Old Text and New Text variants of the *Documents* as the organizational basis for assembling annotations from the Han through T'ang dynasties on the authentic chapters of the classic.

Shu-tsu was integrating his own research into Han dynasty epigraphy, working from Tuan Yü-ts'ai's assertion that there were in fact *two* families of authentic texts—one New Text and the other Old. Tuan and Sun Hsing-yen regarded the Old Text recension of the *Documents* as more reliable because it was linked to the more ancient, authentic Old Text chapters said to have been rediscovered in Confucius's former home and then later lost.[15]

Although most Han Learning scholars acknowledged the spuriousness of the present twenty-five Old Text chapters, they still contended that the original sixteen Old Text chapters, long since lost, had been authentic. This was a crucial claim, for these chapters were the basis on which Tuan Yü-ts'ai and Sun Hsing-yen affirmed the priority of the authentic Old Text recension of the surviving Old and New Text chapters. But Chuang Shu-tsu, as well as the Fu-chien textual scholar Ch'en Shou-ch'i (1771–1834), were among the first to recognize the possible superiority of the New Text recension of the *Documents*. In an 1829 study on the New Text and Old Text *Documents*, Liu Feng-lu did very much what Tuan and Sun had done, but he also pushed forward Chuang Shu-tsu's analytical framework. So, instead of automatically favoring the Old Text variants, as Tuan and Sun had done, Liu held that the New Text recension was more reliable.[16]

14. For Chuang Shu-tsu's remarks on inscriptions on Han dynasty stone drums see his *Wen-ch'ao*, 5.27a–28b. On the *I Chou-shu* see *Wen-ch'ao*, 5.31a–32b. For Shu-tsu's letter to Liu Feng-lu see *Wen-ch'ao*, 6.23a–23b.

15. Chuang Shu-tsu, *Shang-shu ching-ku-wen k'ao-cheng*. For a discussion see my *Philosophy to Philology*, pp. 207–10.

16. Chuang Shu-tsu, *Shang-shu chin-ku-wen k'ao-cheng*, and Liu Feng-lu, "Hsu" (Preface) to his *Shang-shu chin-ku-wen chi-chieh*.

Once New Text scholars such as Liu Feng-lu could demonstrate that their position was based on sound philological arguments, they could apply the epistemological leverage gained thereby in order to validate the political vision of *Kung-yang* Confucianism previously enunciated by Chuang Ts'un-yü. In the process, New Text Confucianism emerged as a wedding of *Kung-yang* theory and New Text philology. As we shall see in chapter 7, Liu Feng-lu combined Ts'un-yü's theories and Shu-tsu's philological research to form a comprehensive agenda for New Text studies.[17]

CHUANG YU-K'E

Like Chuang Shu-tsu, Chuang Yu-k'e (a member of another line in the second branch of the lineage) incorporated the research techniques of technical philology (*hsiao-hsueh*) into Chuang scholarly traditions. Despite, or perhaps because of, his philological expertise, Chuang Yu-k'e was unsuccessful in the civil service examination system. He thus devoted most of his life to his research interests. His philological studies dealt with most of the issues and texts that Han Learning scholars typically investigated.[18]

The son of a poor family in his lineage, Chuang made his living as a teacher and compiler, which subsidized his years of *k'ao-cheng* research. In this, he was leading the life of a typical Han Learning scholar, who because of difficulty in obtaining examination degrees and official positions during the eighteenth and nineteenth centuries turned to teaching in order to supplement his research activities. Among his various occupations, in 1792 Yu-k'e helped to check for accuracy the thousands of volumes in the "Complete Works in the Imperial Library," which were deposited at the Wen-su ko (Pavilion of Literary Traces) in Feng-t'ien (present-day Shen-yang in Manchuria). In 1801 Chuang taught in He-fei, An-hui, where he also helped to compile the county gazetteer. During his stay there, Yu-k'e's son Chuang Hsien-nan achieved *chin-shih* status and, after the Ho-shen era, entered the Hanlin Academy in Peking.[19]

His scholarly career spanning four decades, Chuang Yu-k'e pored

17. Chou Yü-t'ung, *Ching chin-ku-wen hsueh*, pp. 28–29.

18. Chuang Yu-k'e's biography is at the Palace Museum, Taipei, *Chuan-kao*, no. 4470, under Chuang Shu-tsu. See also the "Nien-p'u" (Chronological biography) for Yu-k'e in the *P'i-ling Chuang-shih tseng-hsiu tsu-p'u* (1935), 12A.36a–39b.

19. *P'i-ling Chuang-shih tseng-hsiu tsu-p'u* (1935), 5.74.

over the Classics and produced a list of published works not matched in the Chuang lineage before or since. By the time he was fifty-five, he had already completed 500 *chüan* (scrolls, that is, text divisions) on the Classics. Although unheralded outside of Ch'ang-chou, Yu-k'e, according to his biographers, ranked with more prominent scholars such as Chang Hui-yen, Hung Liang-chi, Chuang Shu-tsu, and Yun Ching as the greatest local talents in classical studies during the Tao-kuang era (1796–1820).[20]

NEW TEXT PALEOGRAPHY

Like Chuang Shu-tsu, Yu-k'e became interested in the paleographical issues of the Old Text–New Text debate. In their correspondence, Shu-tsu marveled at Yu-k'e's broad scholarship (*po-hsueh*), praising his mastery of the *Shuo-wen chieh-tzu* (Analysis of characters as an explanation of writing) dictionary. Such careful philological research, Shu-tsu noted, enabled Chuang Yu-k'e to trace the evolution of "borrowed characters" (*chia-chieh-tzu*) during the crucial transition from Chou dynasty seal script to Han dynasty clerical forms of writing. Again, the history of writing forms was the key to understanding the distinction between Old and New Text recensions of the Classics.

Yu-k'e's most representative works concentrated on the *Change Classic* and the *Spring and Autumn Annals*. The bibiliography of the *Combined Gazetteer for Wu-chin and Yang-hu Counties*, for instance, listed five of his works on the *Change* and twelve on the *Annals*. Most were annotations of alternative recensions for these two classics, while others examined the place-names and persons mentioned in them. His *Ch'un-ch'iu hsiao-hsueh* (Philological inquiry into the *Spring and Autumn Annals*) is a representative work. Compiled in 1797 while he was teaching in Shun-te at the Lien-ch'eng Academy (in the Chih-li capital region), this study of the *Annals* was part of a larger project designed to apply rigorous *k'ao-cheng* techniques to the Five Classics and their chief commentaries.[21]

Yu-k'e's *k'ao-cheng* methods were also applied to the *Documents* and *Poetry* Classics, as well as to the *Rituals of Chou*. He produced two

20. See the "I-wen-chih" (Bibliography section) of the *Wu-chin Yang-hu hsien ho-chih* (1886), 32.4a, 32.5b, 32.7a, 32.10a–10b, for the list of Chuang Yu-k'e's published works on the Classics. See also my *Philosophy to Philology*, pp. 130–33, on the transformation of literati roles.

21. *Wu-chin Yang-hu hsien ho-chih* (1886), 32.4a, 32.10a–10b. For Chuang Shu-tsu's letter to Yu-k'e, see Chuang Shu-tsu, *Wen-ch'ao*, 6.25a–25b.

works on the *Rituals*, which Chuang Ts'un-yü praised very highly. Like Ts'un-yü, Chuang Yu-k'e was aware of the long tradition of doubt concerning the authenticity of the *Chou-li*, doubts most recently reopened in Ch'ang-chou by Yang Ch'un. Again like Ts'un-yü, however, Yu-k'e affirmed the centrality of the *Chou-li* for understanding the world-ordering institutions of antiquity. His *Chou-kuan chih-chang* (Directives and institutions in the Offices of Chou), for example, was a detailed discussion of one hundred political institutions (*tien-chang*) bequeathed by the *Rituals of Chou*.[22]

THE OLD TEXT *DOCUMENTS* CONTROVERSY

In his research on the *Documents Classic*, Yu-k'e accepted the conclusions of Yen Jo-chü and Hui Tung concerning the inauthenticity of its Old Text chapters. As a teacher and scholar of the Classics, with no ties to the political issues long associated with classical studies, Chuang Yu-k'e did not hestitate, for example, to dismiss the validity of the *jen-hsin Tao-hsin* (human and moral mind) passage in the Old Text "Counsels of Yü the Great" ("Ta Yü mo") chapter of the *Documents*. We have seen that the debate over this passage had become a cause célèbre of Han Learning. As spokesman for imperial rule in the 1740s, Chuang Ts'un-yü thought the passage essential for legitimating the political and social order. By way of contrast, however, Yu-k'e decried in typical Han Learning fashion the Buddhist doctrines that presupposed the bifurcation between the human and moral mind:

> What makes a person a person is simply his mind. The mind is equivalent to the principles of Heaven. Accordingly, it is the master of the person. Thus, all the sense organs and the body obey it. Heaven does not have two principles. A person does not have two rulers. The mind, therefore, is not two things. How can there be two names for it?
>
> When the forged Old Text *Documents* appeared, [the forger] had lifted remnants of the *Hsun-tzu* [text into the *Documents*] and thereby missed the point. . . . If Confucius and Mencius did not have this theory, how can one say that Yao [tr. r. 2356–2256?? B.C.] and Shun [tr. r. 2255–2205??] had it? When the Buddha spoke of "many minds" [*to-hsin*] and "conquering the mind" [*hsiang-fu ch'i hsin*], this is probably in agreement with the human mind passage in the [forged] Old Text *Documents*.[23]

22. *P'i-ling Chuang-shih tseng-hsiu tsu-p'u* (1935), 12A.36b. See also Chuang Yu-k'e, "Hsu" (Preface) to his *Chou-kuan chih-chang*.
23. Chuang Yu-k'e, *Chin-wen Shang-shu chi-chu*. See also Yu-k'e, *Mu-liang tsa-tsuan*, 2.9a–9b.

In the late eighteenth and early nineteenth centuries, prominent *k'ao-cheng* scholars such as Tai Chen and Juan Yuan had concluded that Neo-Confucians such as Chu Hsi and Wang Yang-ming had both been guilty of reading Buddhist doctrines into the Confucian Canon and of turning the Classics into a sourcebook for spurious metaphysical doctrines. In their discussion of other key concepts such as *jen* (benevolence), Ch'ing dynasty evidential research scholars maintained that after the fall of the Han dynasty, native traditions of "mysterious teachings" (*hsuan-hsueh*) had been mixed together with Buddhism.[24]

Later Neo-Confucians, Tai and Juan argued, had fallen under the spell of such otherworldly teachings and mistakenly incorporated them into orthodox Confucian doctrine. Buddhist penetration of Confucian teachings became a frequent theme in Han Learning criticism of the Sung Learning orthodoxy based on the Ch'eng-Chu school. Chuang Yu-k'e agreed that Buddhist doctrines must be weeded out of the Confucian Canon.[25]

Although he disagreed with Chuang Ts'un-yü on the *jen-hsin–Tao-hsin* debate, Chuang Yu-k'e nonetheless added philological precision to the emerging New Text position on the Classics. His defense of the *Rituals of Chou* shows that he still valued the Old Text tradition, as had Ts'un-yü, and did not advocate the superiority of the New Text Classics as a whole. Attacks on the Old Text chapters of the *Documents Classic* were, however, the first link in a chain of philological debate during the eighteenth century that in the nineteenth century would tie all Old Text versions of the Classics together into questionable texts. Chuang Ts'un-yü had not envisioned this possibility partly because of his political commitment to a classical ideology that legitimated the Confucian imperium and partly because of his animus toward philological research.

It was left to Chuang Yu-k'e and Shu-tsu to mine this valuable lode of Han Learning, which in the hands of Liu Feng-lu would become full-blown "New Text Confucianism." In this way, *Kung-yang* theory was combined (uncritically to be sure) for the first time with Han Learning philology. What was interesting was that members of the Chuang lineage continued to call for a more comprehensive vision of Confucianism, one that would go beyond the limited textual studies of most *k'ao-cheng* scholars.

For Chuang Yu-k'e as for Chuang Shu-tsu, the lessons bequeathed by

24. For a discussion see my "Criticism as Philosophy."
25. See, for example, Juan Yuan, *Yen-ching-shih chi*, vol. 1, pp. 213–14.

Ts'un-yü and the Chuang lineage remained important. Han Learning had to be informed by theoretical and statecraft issues and was not an end in itself. Yu-k'e wrote:

> There are many people all over the realm who read books voraciously. The only book they do not know how to read is the *Spring and Autumn Annals*. . . . I have been studying the *Annals* for over thirty years, but I [still] sigh in wonder that the meanings and principles in it are boundless. . . . [The *Annals* contains] the Tao that encompasses a thousand changes and ten thousand transformations. It never fails to amaze me that in this book I can find the essentials [of the Tao].

The Chuangs contended that without an understanding of the "esoteric principles" (*wei-li*) in the *Spring and Autumn Annals*, which informed New Text "Han Learning," the Five Classics would remain inexplicable.[26]

CHUANG SHOU-CHIA

During his years under Chuang tutelage, Liu Feng-lu formed a close relationship with his cousins Chuang Shou-chia and Sung Hsiang-feng. Each went on to stress somewhat different aspects of the teachings they received from Ts'un-yü and Shu-tsu, but they were all committed to wedding *k'ao-cheng* techniques to the more theoretical concerns of *Kung-yang* Confucianism. Li Chao-lo, a friend of both Liu Feng-lu and Chuang Shou-chia, observed that Liu continued Shu-tsu's *Kung-yang* studies while Shou-chia advanced his uncle's Han Learning interests.

Li also described the close friendship that developed between himself, Chang Hui-yen, Liu Feng-lu, Sung Hsiang-feng, and Tung Shih-hsi in Ch'ang-chou scholarly circles. They were successors to an entire generation of Han Learning scholars in Ch'ang-chou (see chapter 4) that had centered on Hung Liang-chi, Sun Hsing-yen, Chao Huai-yü, and Huang Ching-jen, among others. But between these two generations the unanimity of Han Learning was slowly eroding as the Former Han New Text vs. Later Han Old Text "schools system" was reconstructed and reevaluated.[27]

26. Chuang Yu-k'e, "Hsu" (Preface) to the *Chin-wen Shang-shu chi-chu*, and Chuang, *Mu-liang tsa-tsuan*, 1.1a. See also Chuang Shu-tsu, *Li-tai tsai-chi tsu-cheng lu*, 1.1a–21b, for the latter's contributions to this position. Cf. Chuang Shu-tsu's *Wen-ch'ao* 6.25a–25b.

27. Li Chao-lo, "Hsu" (Preface) to Chuang Shu-tsu, *Chen-i-i i-shu*, p. 2a. See also the biography of Chuang Shou-chia, included under Chuang Shu-tsu at the Palace Museum,

As a lineage member and direct follower first of Chuang Ts'un-yü and then of Chuang Shu-tsu, Chuang Shou-chia developed a position on the Classics that is representative of the learning of the Chuang tradition (*chia-hsueh*) as it entered the nineteenth century. As with Chuang Shu-tsu and Yu-k'e, Shou-chia devoted most of his career to scholarship, never achieving prominence in the examination system or in official life. His own works were left unpublished during his own lifetime because of his commitment to ensuring that Chuang Ts'un-yü's writings were finally published. When the latter was achieved in 1828, Chuang Shou-chia died at the untimely age of fifty-four.

Because of the opposition between the Chuangs and Ho-shen in the 1780s, the prominence of the Chuang lineage by the nineteenth century in fact depended more on scholarly prestige than on official position. After 1800 only two members of the lineage—Chuang Hsien-nan and Chuang Shou-ch'i—reached the Hanlin Academy, and only five passed the metropolitan examinations. This diminished success contrasted sharply with the Chuangs illustrious achievements of the eighteenth century, when seventeen lineage members achieved *chin-shih* status and seven were placed in the Hanlin Academy (see chapter 2).[28]

THE IMPORTANCE OF PALEOGRAPHY

In continuing his uncle Shu-tsu's textual scholarship, Chuang Shou-chia also emphasized the importance of paleography for classical studies. For Shou-chia, knowledge of ancient seal writing forms was essential for deriving the original, and therefore correct, meaning from the subsequent Han and T'ang dynasty writing forms. Research on the evolution of these writing forms unmasked the true distinction between Old Text and New Text. This distinction largely derived from the loss of the ancient seal versions of the Classics after the Ch'in dynasty policy of "burning of the books" between 221 and 207 B.C.

In a letter to Shou-chia, Li Chao-lo, for instance, discussed the centrality of the Ch'in-Han calligraphic transition for the study of antiquity, tying the changes in writing forms to the prominence of parallel-style prose (*p'ien-t'i-wen*) during the Han dynasty. Elsewhere,

---

Taipei, *Chuan-kao*, no. 4470, and Li Chao-lo's biography of Shou-chia in Li's *Yang-i-chai wen-chi*, 12.31b–33b.

28. *P'i-ling Chuang-shih tseng-hsiu tsu-p'u* (1935), 9.6b–8a, 9.19a, and *Wu-chin Chuang-shih tseng-hsiu tsu-p'u* (ca. 1840), 13.25a–26a. See also Li Chao-lo's preface to Chuang Shou-chia's *She-i-pu-i-chai i-shu*, pp. 1b–2a.

Li Chao-lo claimed that later terms such as "Old Text" and "ancient-style prose" represented post–T'ang dynasty coinages that misconstrued the original meaning of *ku-wen* during the Ch'in and Han dynasties. Calligraphic styles had become confused with literary styles.[29]

Writing to Shou-chia along the same lines, Chuang Shu-tsu discussed ancient large seal (*ta-chuan*) and small seal (*hsiao-chuan*) forms of writing. Noting that the latter were Ch'in dynasty precursors of the clerical script of the Han dynasties, Shu-tsu asserted that "Old Text" had emerged as a calligraphic term because of these later developments. After the appearance of Ch'in dynasty small seal script, earlier forms were designated "large seal." Similarly, after the spread of Han clerical script (so-called New Text), Ch'in dynasty small seal script was retrospectively labeled "Old Text."

Shu-tsu explained to Shou-chia that, by the Han dynasties, large seal script was for the most part lost or indecipherable. Ch'in small seal script alone was wrongly considered "Old Text" when in fact large seal forms, Shu-tsu went on, were rightly "Old Text" because of their greater antiquity. He concluded that ancient seal forms of writing contained important clues to the provenance of classical texts that had survived the disastrous Ch'in-Han transition.[30]

Chuang Shou-chia's *Shih shu-ming* (Explication of writing and names) was a preliminary history of ancient calligraphy that elaborated on the paleographic issues raised by Chuang Shu-tsu. After reviewing the early history of Chinese writing forms (which he linked to ancient cosmograms and the eight trigrams of the *Change Classic*), Shou-chia turned to the distinction between Old Text and New Text calligraphy. He argued that the distinction developed after the Chou dynasty, when ancient forms of writing had been either lost or remained indecipherable. "Old Text," then, simply referred to later antiquity and its more modern forms of calligraphy. These forms, although predating Han clerical script (called "New Text" for the first time in the second century B.C.), were not the actual forms in use during much of early antiquity.[31]

When the Old Text Classics were discovered in Confucius's former residence, they were called "tadpole-like writing" (*k'e-tou shu*) because

29. *Wu-chin Chuang-shih tseng-hsiu tsu-p'u* (ca. 1840), 22.55b. See also Li Chao-lo, *Yang-i-chai wen-chi*, 18.4b–5a, and *Li Shen-ch'i nien-p'u*, 2.7a–7b, 3.30b.

30. Chuang Shu-tsu, *Wen-ch'ao*, 6.26a–27b.

31. Chuang Shou-chia, *Shih shu-ming*, pp. 1a–6a.

the seal forms were no longer understood. Shou-chia claimed that when the latter were compared with and "translated" into the calligraphic styles of the Former Han, the older forms were lost. Owing to the intervention of Liu Hsin, Shou-chia went on, the Old Text Classics (now in their "New Text" guise thanks to scholars who never recognized the complexity of the paleographical and etymological issues) were established as the principal corpus of the Confucian Canon. The ancient seal forms for the Classics were irrevocably lost in the process. Like Shu-tsu, Shou-chia charged Liu Hsin and other Later Han Confucians with ignorance. Their emendations and interpolations of the Five Classics had created a major vacuum in the classical legacy, and as a result the original forms of the Classics had been discarded.[32]

According to Shou-chia, the role of philology in general (*hsiao-hsueh*) and paleography in particular (*wen-tzu-hsueh*) should be to recapture antiquity via the reconstruction of ancient forms of writing. In order to "return to the origins and resurrect the ancient" (*fan-pen hsiu-ku*), according to Chuang, one first had to master the history of calligraphy and the stages of written forms. Lurking within the New Text agenda for questioning the Old Text Classics lay a remarkable call to recover the "true" Old Text and to replace the false "Old Text." Paleography, accordingly, provided a key epistemological weapon in the New Text assault on Old Text. Without fully realizing it, both Chuang Shu-tsu and Shou-chia added philological ammunition to the New Text position.[33]

THE PRIORITY OF NEW TEXT

In addition to his writings on paleography, Chuang Shou-chia also prepared a work that examined "variances" in the *Documents Classic*. In his introduction, Shou-chia described how he and Liu Feng-lu had built on different but still complementary aspects of their uncle Chuang Shu-tsu's classical studies. He said that Liu stressed the *Change Classic* and *Spring and Autumn Annals*, while he himself focused on the *Poetry* and *Documents* classics. Liu Feng-lu's scholarly focus suggests his closeness to their grandfather Chuang Ts'un-yü, who also had emphasized the *Change* and *Annals*.[34]

By using a variety of sources—including epigraphical remnants of

32. Ibid., pp. 7a–10b.
33. Ibid., pp. 6a, 10b–19b.
34. Chuang Shou-chia, *Shang-shu k'ao-i hsu-mu*, p. 1a.

the Classics carved into stone during the Later Han dynasty—Chuang Shou-chia traced the surviving New Text and Old Text recensions of the authentic chapters of the *Documents* back to the different "schools system" of the Former and the Later Han dynasties. In this manner, he hoped to restore the original "Old Text" version from which both later recensions were derived. Again, the criticism of Han dynasty "Old Text" was premised on the existence of a more ancient version of "Old Text."

To supplement this strategy, Shou-chia also drew on the invaluable research of earlier *k'ao-cheng* scholars who had glossed the etymology of key words in the authentic chapters of the *Documents*. He drew on an impressive list of scholars, among whom were the major figures in Ch'ing dynasty evidential research: Yen Jo-chü, Hui Tung, Tai Chen, Ch'ien Ta-hsin, Wang Ming-sheng, Sun Hsing-yen, Tuan Yü-ts'ai, and Tsang Lin. This roll call of Ch'ing scholars suggests that Chuang Shou-chia perceived his research as a tributary of mainstream Ch'ing *k'ao-cheng* studies. Through etymology (*hsun-ku-hsueh*), another major field of philology, Shou-chia sought to restore the "general meaning" (*ta-i*) of the *Documents Classic*.[35]

Despite the influences of Han Learning, Chuang Shou-chia bent the concerns of Han Learning to accommodate the *Kung-yang* Confucianism enunciated by his grandfather, Chuang Ts'un-yü, and later reaffirmed by both Shu-tsu and Yu-k'e in a more philological form. In his collected essays, for example, Shou-chia was critical of the *Tso chuan* and especially Liu Hsin's role in establishing it as the orthodox commentary on the *Annals*. In particular, he rejected the claim that the classical precedents of the *Annals* were incorporated into the *Tso chuan*. Chuang maintained that this claim was an Old Text fabrication, which overlooked the priority of the *Kung-yang chuan* in decoding the *Annals*. Under the influence of Liu Hsin, Later Han Confucian erudites had been hoodwinked into accepting a text that was not, as claimed, a commentary to the *Annals*.[36]

Throughout his scholarly writings, then, Chuang Shou-chia affirmed the centrality of the *Kung-yang chuan* for *Ch'un-ch'iu* studies and the importance of the *Annals* for classical studies as a whole. Sung Hsiang-feng and Liu Feng-lu, as Shou-chia's relatives, classmates, and colleagues, added their own distinctive touches to the Ch'ang-chou New Text position on the Classics.

35. Ibid., pp. 1b–2b.
36. Chuang Shou-chia, *Wen-ch'ao*, pp. 9a–13b.

SUNG HSIANG-FENG

One of Chuang Shu-tsu's lesser-known students, Sung Hsiang-feng never went beyond *chü-jen* degree status, which he achieved at age twenty-four in 1800. Sung thus never held high office beyond county magistrate and is primarily remembered for his classical studies, which were closely tied to Ch'ang-chou New Text studies. According to his biographers, Hsiang-feng was a specialist in etymology (*hsun-ku ming-wu*); his research efforts included a work on the *Erh-ya* (Progress toward correctness) dictionary, the chief repository of Han dynasty glosses on the Classics.

Sung complemented his etymological interests with research aimed at reconstructing the "schools system" of the Former Han dynasty so that the original "esoteric words containing great meanings" (*wei-yen ta-i*)—by this time a code expression for New Text studies of the Former Han—would again achieve preeminence in Confucian discourse. In this effort, Sung transmitted the scholarly teachings of Chuang Ts'un-yü and Chuang Shu-tsu to students such as Tai Wang, who carried the New Text position into the late nineteenth century.[37]

"MEANINGS" IN THE *ANNALS*

Affirming the priority of *Kung-yang* Confucianism, Sung Hsiang-feng contended that "meanings" (*i*), and not "precedents" (*li*), were central in the chronicles of the *Spring and Autumn Annals*. By continuing a line of criticism on the *Annals* that dates back to the Ming dynasty, Hsiang-feng rejected as misguided Tu Yü's long-admired *Tso chuan*–based itemization of historical precedents in the *Annals* (see chapter 5). "As the list of precedents piled up," Sung claimed, "the meaning of the *Annals* became increasingly obscured, reaching the point that all understanding [of the intent of the *Annals*] was lost." Such tedious interpretations of the *Annals*, according to Sung Hsiang-feng, had led directly to calls by Sung dynasty scholars to remove the *Annals* from official authorization in the examination system. Wang An-shih had gone so far as to label the *Annals* as "irrelevant reports" (*tuan-luan ch'ao-pao*) precisely because of Tu Yü's relegation of the *Annals* to a casebook of historical precedents.[38]

37. See Sung Hsiang-feng's biography, which is kept at the Palace Museum, Taipei, under Liu Feng-lu, *Chuan-kao*, no. 4455(1). See also T'ang Chih-chün, "Ch'ing-tai Ch'ang-chou ching chin-wen hsueh-p'ai yü Wu-hsu pien-fa," pp. 73–76.

38. Sung Hsiang-feng, *P'u-hsueh-lu wen-ch'ao*, pp. 3a–3b.

The triumph of historical erudition had brought in its wake a loss of historical meaning. This emphasis on precedents in the *Annals* required a level of knowledge that, for all its precision, missed the forest for the trees. Seeking to strike a balance between classical erudition and classical meanings, Sung Hsiang-feng called for a synthesis of Han Learning philology and Sung Learning theory:

> If one orders the Classics and does not order the Histories, then one understands principles [*li*] but not affairs [*shih*]. If one orders the Histories but not the Classics, then one understands affairs but not principles. If one can unify the [two different approaches], then no harm will result from the division.
>
> In antiquity, those who studied the Classics did not drown in etymological glosses. They did not wind up in farfetched explanations. Neither were they deluded by debates and theories, nor did they get stuck in airy and distant [irrelevancies]. In this way, they knew the constant Tao of the sages and thus were outstanding scholars.
>
> The study of etymology became prominent in the Han and was completed in the T'ang. Study of theory began in the T'ang and became prominent in the Sung. Both [traditions] went a little too far, however. Etymologists, if they reach farfetched explanations, and theorists, if they wind up in airy and distant studies, must both be criticized.[39]

Sung Hsiang-feng's call for a synthesis of Han and Sung Learning was emblematic of the nineteenth-century social and political context for Confucian scholars. They were faced with questions and problems from which eighteenth-century Confucians for the most part had been spared. For instance, the introductory essay to Confucian scholarship (*Ju-lin*), included in the 1814 Wu-hsi–Chin-k'uei county gazetteer, stressed the centrality of textual studies for Confucian discourse while also calling for a balance between Sung and Han Learning approaches.

Like his Chuang lineage relatives in Ch'ang-chou, Sung called for an encompassing vision of Confucianism that would reassert the moral principles proclaimed in Confucius's *Annals*. In the Ch'ang-chou New Text agenda, *k'ao-cheng* research was informed by theoretical and ethical issues and was not an end in itself. By taking a strident position that linked scholarship to social and political order, Sung Hsiang-feng made his commitment to Confucian practice very clear: "Accordingly, if the Tao is not put into effect, then the empire will not be ordered. The blame will fall on no one else but on scholars."[40]

39. Ibid., pp. 5Aa–5Ba (original mistakes in pagination).

40. Ibid., pp. 5Ca–5Da (original mistakes in pagination). See *Wu-hsi Chin-k'uei hsien-chih*, (1814), 21.1b. See also my *Philosophy to Philology*, pp. 233–48.

New Text studies contributed to the general nineteenth-century reaction against what Ch'ang-chou scholars had long considered sterile philological studies. In addition, increased interest in the *Kung-yang Commentary* helped to stimulate a nationwide revival of the seventeenth-century statecraft orientation, which in Ch'ang-chou, the home of Tung-lin activism, had never really been lost. Ch'ang-chou's intimate links with the Tung-lin legacy in Wu-hsi and Wu-chin counties placed the Chuang and Liu lineages, among others in Ch'ang-chou, in a better position to appreciate the statecraft sensibilities of their seventeenth-century predecessors.

RECONSTRUCTING THE NEW TEXT CONFUCIUS

Both Sung Hsiang-feng and Liu Feng-lu sought to demolish the Old Text image of Confucius by reconstructing New Text interpretations of the *Analects* (*Lun-yü*). They turned from the *Kung-yang chuan* to Confucius's *Analects* to confirm their grandfather Chuang Ts'un-yü's reliance on Ho Hsiu. For Ts'un-yü, Ho Hsiu was the most dependable Later Han transmitter of the New Text "schools system." In chapter 7 we shall discuss Liu Feng-lu's reconstruction of Ho Hsiu's lost commentary on the *Analects*. But we will first evaluate Sung Hsiang-feng's parallel demonstration that the *Analects* itself was replete with doctrines that confirmed the *Kung-yang* "meanings" in the *Annals*.

Like Liu Feng-lu, Sung Hsiang-feng sought to overturn prevailing interpretations of the *Analects* that had been inspired by Old Text studies. According to Hsiang-feng, in the *Analects* Confucius had presented his views in esoteric form (*wei-yen*) for transmission by his most trusted followers. According to this point of view, the *Analects* elaborated the "great meanings" (*ta-i*) in the *Annals*. Sung used the *Analects* as collateral evidence for understanding the *Kung-yang* interpretation of the *Annals*. Controverting the traditional belief that the "esoteric words and great meanings" had been lost after the deaths of Confucius and his immediate disciples, Sung Hsiang-feng concluded:

> After Confucius perished, the "esoteric words" were still not cut off. After [his] seventy disciples passed away, the "great meanings" were still not betrayed. Confucius's intent was complete in the records of the commentaries. For hundreds and thousands of generations, [his intent] was not covered up. Its [recovery], therefore, is the duty of all who love learning and think profoundly.

The vision had not been lost; it had been whitewashed.[41]

In order to controvert the Old Text position on the *Analects* and *Annals*, both of which were based on historical accounts given in the *Tso chuan*, Sung Hsiang-feng worked from the *Kung-yang Commentary*. He asserted it was the repository of the true teachings bequeathed by Confucius himself in the *Annals* and then by his disciples in the *Analects*. Reappearing in Sung's reassessment of the *Analects* was the apocalyptic and messianic picture of Confucius dating from the Former Han. Tai Wang, Sung's student and a follower of Liu Feng-lu, described the implications of this reinterpretation of the *Annals* vis-à-vis the *Analects*:

> Confucius himself was an "uncrowned king." He wished to serve as the ruler of the empire like Yao, Shun, T'ang [r. 1766?–1744? B.C.], and Wu [r. 1122?–1116?] and to achieve [like them] an era of great peace [*t'ai-p'ing*]. Therefore, he made the "Sayings of Yao" the final chapter [of the *Analects*]. Similarly, the text of the *Spring and Autumn Annals* concluded with the lesson of the coming of the *lin* [unicorn]. It is clear that Confucius respectfully discoursed on Yao and Shun. . . . The reason for his straightforward writings [in the *Annals*], such as "the institutional reform of the three dynasties" [*san-tai kai-chih*], was to extend the lessons that Yao had enunciated.

For the Former Han Confucian Tung Chung-shu (179?–104? B.C.), the capture of the *lin* was a concrete omen of Confucius's status as an "uncrowned king." In his *Ch'un-ch'iu fan-lu* (The *Spring and Autumn Annals*' radiant dew), Tung wrote that shortly before his death in 479 B.C. Confucius had received from heaven (*t'ien*) its mandate (or decree [*ming*]):

> When Yen Yuan died, Confucius said: "Heaven has caused me this loss." When Tzu-lu died, the master said: "Heaven is cutting me off!" When a *lin* was captured in a hunt in the west, Confucius said: "My way has come to an end! My way has come to an end!" Three years later he was dead. From this [omen] we see that the sage knows the efficacy of Heaven's mandate and that there are situations in which one cannot escape one's fate.

According to Tung Chung-shu, heaven granted Confucius its mandate to correct the faults of his age and to establish the institutions of a new ruler and new dynasty. Although the mandate could not be effected during his own lifetime, Confucius was nonetheless able to speak as a ruler and to prophesize "a great unity" (*ta i-t'ung*)—that is, the Han

41. Sung Hsiang-feng, *Lun-yü shuo-i*, 398.3b.

dynasty—to come. New Text studies were moving from complicated philological debate to reaffirmation of an older vision of Confucius and of the classical legacy.[42]

Freeing the *Analects* from its Later Han Old Text interpretive moorings, Sung Hsiang-feng argued that the words of Confucius recorded by his closest disciples in the *Analects* were best evaluated in light of the "meanings" encoded in the *Annals*. In effect, Sung was grounding the interpretation of the *Analects* in the *Kung-yang* tradition of the *Annals*. The *Kung-yang Commentary* and the *Analects*, when taken together, gave overlapping clues to the holistic vision of the sage as "uncrowned king." The Old Text portrait of Confucius was pointedly redrawn in New Text strokes:

> The *Analects* represents the theories of the New Text [tradition]. New Text school members transmitted the *Annals* and *Analects* as the means to grasp the intent of the sage. As erudites, what the New Text school members transmitted was derived from [Confucius's] seventy disciples through direct transmission. Reaching back to the [Former] Han, this link had still not been broken.

Hsiang-feng argued that the direct transmission from Confucius to the officially appointed New Text erudites (via the seventy disciples) had been interrupted by the confusion brought on by the Wang Mang interregnum. Championed by Liu Hsin, the Old Text Classics briefly displaced the New Text Classics in official circles:

> Ever since the Old Text school members recovered the Classic "Offices of Chou" [*Chou-kuan*, that is, the *Chou-li*] from the wall [in Confucius's former] residence, what had been a trivial record [*mo-lu*] in the archives of the Western Han [suddenly] was attributed to the Duke of Chou [himself]. Whatever was found in the other Classics to disagree with the "Offices of Chou" was all dismissed as derivative from the Hsia and Shang dynasties. In reality, the *Annals* was finalized by Confucius. It is true to the intent of Yao, Shun, and King Wen and discoursed upon the institutions of the Three dynasties [Hsia, Shang, and Chou].[43]

Here Sung has clearly linked New Text studies to the history of skepticism concerning the provenance of the *Rituals of Chou*. And in so doing Sung brought together what had been two parallel but disparate

42. Tai Wang, *Lun-yü chu*, 20.3b. See the biography of Tai Wang, included after Liu Feng-lu and Sung Hsiang-feng at the Palace Museum, Taipei, *Chuan-kao*, no. 4455(1). See Su Yü's edition of Tung's work entitled *Ch'un-ch'iu fan-lu i-cheng*, 5.4a, 6.4b. For a discussion see Fung, *History of Chinese Philosophy*, vol. 1, pp. 71–72. Cf. Wakeman, *History and Will*, pp. 105–106.

43. Sung Hsiang-feng, *Lun-yü shuo-i*, 389.1b, 389.3a.

problems. Where Chuang Ts'un-yü in the eighteenth century had seen the *Annals* and *Chou-li* as compatible and complementary, Sung Hsing-feng in the nineteenth saw them as just the opposite. Though Yang Ch'un and others had earlier dismissed the *Rituals of Chou* as a forgery first manipulated by Wang Mang and then by Wang An-shih, they had not linked the forgery to the Old Text tradition. Although Sung pointed to Liu Hsin as the betrayer of the *Annals*, he did not accuse him of forging the *Chou-li*. Sung's contribution to the evolution of the New Text position on the *Annals* and *Chou-li* was nevertheless important.[44]

The differentiation of the Former Han from Later Han classical "schools system" now began to center on distinguishing the *Annals* from the *Rituals of Chou*. Henceforth, champions of New Text and defenders of Old Text would disentangle the two Classics from their supposed web of compatibility; two competing classical visions would now be read into the *Annals* and the *Rituals of Chou*. The questionable provenance of one of the "Nine Classics"—which according to Sung Hsiang-feng, "had no transmission of teachings"—was now used to increase the legitimacy of Confucius over the Duke of Chou and, concomitantly, of the *Annals* over the *Chou-li*. For Hsiang-feng, Later Han *chia-fa* was inferior to the tightly spun threads of transmission that bound together the "schools system" of the Former Han.[45]

NEW TEXT ESOTERICISM

Sung's reaffirmation of Confucius as an "uncrowned king" gained additional support from the efforts of his contemporaries to reconstruct the *ch'an-wei* apocrypha texts of the Former Han dynasty. During the Han New Text theory had been combined with prognostication and prophecy. An affirmation of Confucius as an "uncrowned king" was an implicit reaffirmation of Confucius as heaven's choice, in a time of chaos and decline, for receiving the mandate of heaven. Sung Hsiang-feng noted: "Contemporary rulers and officials all did not know Confucius. Only Heaven knew Confucius, causing him to receive the Mandate of Heaven as an uncrowned king." Such rhetoric was neither reducible to the rational principles of Sung Learning nor to the empirical verifications of evidential research. Instead, it harkened back to belief in the prophetic meaning of Confucius's life. The mysterious circumstances

44. Ibid., 396.3a.
45. Ibid., 389.3b–4a.

under which Confucius composed the *Annals* now competed for scholarly attention with the rational historical accounts of Confucius in the *Tso chuan*.

The capture of a marvelous creature known as a *lin*, coming as it did at the very end of the *Annals*, took on special significance for New Text scholars. The *Kung-yang Commentary* (appended as one of two orthodox New Text commentaries [the other was the *Ku-liang*] on the *Annals* during the Former Han dynasty) discussed the capture of the *lin* in apocalyptic terms:

> Why was this entry made? In order to record an extraordinary event. What was extraordinary in this? It was not an animal of the central states. Who was the one who hunted it? Someone who gathered firewood. One who gathers firewood is a man of mean position. Why does the text use the term "hunt" in this context? In order to magnify the event. Why magnify it? It was magnified on account of the capture of the *lin*. Why so? The *lin* is a benevolent [*jen*] animal. When there is a true king it appears. When there is no true king it does not appear. Someone informed [Confucius] saying: "There is a fallow-deer and it is horned!" Confucius said: "For whose sake has it come?" He turned his sleeve and wiped his face. His tears wet his robe. When Yen Yuan [Confucius's chief disciple] died, the master said: "Alas! Heaven has caused me this loss." When Tzu-lu [another disciple] died, the master said: "Alas! Heaven is cutting me off!" When a *lin* was captured in a hunt in the west, Confucius said: "My way has come to an end!"[46]

In the Han apocrypha, Confucius as uncrowned king took on touches of divinity that startle those more accustomed to conventional portrayals of the sage. In the *Apocryphal Treatise on the Spring and Autumn Annals: Expository Chart on Confucius* (*Ch'un-ch'iu-wei yen-K'ung-t'u*), he was apotheosized in the following manner:

> On Confucius' breast there was writing which said: "The act of instituting [a new dynasty] has been decided and the rule of the world has been transferred." Confucius was ten feet high and nine spans in circumference. Sitting, he was like a crouching dragon, and standing, like the Cowherd [in the sky]. As one approached him he was like the Pleiades, and as one gazed upon him, like the Ladle. Sages are not born for nothing; they must surely institute something in order to reveal the mind of Heaven. Thus, Confucius, like a wooden-tongued bell, instituted the laws for the world. . . .
>
> After the *lin* was caught, Heaven rained blood which formed into writing on the main gate [of the capital] of Lu, and which said: "Quickly prepare

46. Ibid., 389.1b, 389.13b. See *Ch'un-ch'iu ching-chuan yin-te*, 487/Ai/14. See also Malmqvist, "Gongyang and Guuliang Commentaries," p. 218, and the account by Ssu-ma Ch'ien, *Shih-chi*, vol. 6, p. 1942 (*chüan* 47), which is a summary of this position. For a discussion see Shimada, "Shinkai kakumeiki no Kōshi mondai," pp. 5–8.

> laws, for the sage Confucius will die; the Chou [ruling house], Chi, will be destroyed; a comet will appear from the east. The government of the Ch'in [dynasty, 221–207 B.C.] will arise and will suddenly destroy the literary arts. But though the written records will then be dispersed, [the teachings of] Confucius will not be interrupted."

Although the so-called superstitious elements of *ch'an-wei* apocrypha remained anathema for most Han Learning scholars, the provenance of such texts in the Former Han dynasty justified their use in reconstructing more reputable, but contemporaneous, classical writings of the Former Han. As Kondo Mitsuo explains, most *k'ao-cheng* scholars knew apocryphal texts were useful in research dealing with the Han dynasties. In fact, leading *k'ao-cheng* scholars such as Ch'ien Ta-hsin and Wang Nien-sun (1744–1832) frequently referred to apocrypha for textual corroboration. Consequently, the Han Learning legitimacy that carried over from the Later Han Old Text tradition to the New Text Classics of the Former Han also carried over to Former Han *ch'an-wei* apocryphal texts.[47]

Huang Shih, among others, made serious efforts in the nineteenth century to reconstruct the apocryphal texts in toto and to reestablish the links between the Confucian Classics and the prophecies contained in the *wei* texts. The *ch'an-wei* revival eventually transcended its limited philological purposes and influenced the less rationalistic and more messianic tendencies that characterized New Text Confucianism in the late Ch'ing, when K'ang Yu-wei and others were appealing to a more religious Confucian agenda. Philology had reopened the door to ideas and doctrines that Later Han and post-Han Confucians had long since avoided as inappropriate for serious consideration among educated Chinese.[48]

Sung Hsiang-feng's use of *Kung-yang* interpretations of the *Annals* to establish a New Text reading of the *Analects* coincided with efforts

47. Fung, *History of Chinese Philosophy*, pp. 129–30. See also Su Yü, *Ch'un-ch'iu fan-lu i-cheng*, 7.13a–14b; Dull, "Apocryphal Texts of the Han Dynasty," pp. 28–29, 524–26. The Cowherd, Pleiades, and Ladle belong to the twenty-eight constellations. The "wooden-tongued bell" is an allusion to the *Analects*. See *Lun-yü yin-te*, 5/3/24. "Destroying the literary arts" refers to the "burning of the books" carried out in 213 B.C. during the Ch'in dynasty (221–207 B.C.). Cf. Kondo, "Shinchō keigaku to isho," pp. 251–69.

48. See Harada, "Shimmatsu shisōka no isho kan," pp. 273–99. See also Li Hsin-lin, "Ch'ing-tai ching chin-wen-hsueh shu," pp. 156–57. The usual view of Old Text as "rationalistic" and New Text as "superstitious" is simplistic. Liu Hsin, for example, extensively used the apocrypha for his Old Text position, as did Cheng Hsuan during the Later Han. See Tjan Tjoe Som, *Po Hu T'ung*, vol. 1, pp. 141–54, and Yang Hsiang-k'uei, *Ching-shih-chai hsueh-shu wen-chi*, pp. 139–42.

to fill in the apocryphal elements in Han dynasty classical studies. Sung, for example, elucidated the connection between the omissions (*pu-shu*) in the *Annals* and Confucius's silence (*wu-yen*) on many issues in the *Analects*. Sung argued that the omissions and silences were evidence of the esotericism of Confucius's "subtle words" (*wei-yen*).[49]

Old Text scholars had maintained that Confucius's silence in the *Analects* on such theoretical constructs as "nature" (*hsing*) and "external necessity" (*ming*) demonstrated his aversion to pure speculation and useless discussion. In Old Text interpretations of the *Analects*, then, Confucius appeared skeptical and disinclined to theorize. This portrait of Confucius, painted with powerful rationalistic strokes, has been the most influential one in Western scholarship—so much so that Herrlee Creel and others have argued that there is no evidence to support the claim that Confucius even compiled the *Annals* because the *Analects* makes no mention of such a work. Creel carried the Old Text position further than its original proponents had intended, with Confucius emerging as an "agnostic" scholar who steered clear of superstitions.[50]

By reversing the Old Text priority, Sung Hsiang-feng made the *Analects* subject to the *Annals*. If used in conjunction with the *Analects*, the *Annals*, Sung thought, revealed that the "silence" in the former was equivalent to the "omissions" in the latter. The "subtle words" and "esoteric meanings" in the *Annals*, accordingly, could be used to understand the doctrines encoded in the *Analects*. Far from being skeptical, Confucius had presented his views in esoteric form for transmission by his most trusted disciples. Han Learning scholars, by following the Old Text tradition, had, according to Hsiang-feng, misrepresented not only the *Analects* and *Annals* but also, by implication, the Five Classics as well:

> There are those who say that Confucius did not speak of nature [*hsing*], external necessity [*ming*], or the Heavenly Way. Scholars mistakenly say that Confucius's sayings represented the unity of nature [*tzu-jan*] and the Heavenly Way. They err not merely in terms of the words and sentences, but in reality are also badly misrepresenting Confucius's intent and lessons.[51]

To demonstrate the esoteric doctrines that Confucius included in the *Annals* and his disciples recorded in the *Analects*, Sung Hsiang-feng made reference to the intellectual climate in the middle of the first mil-

49. Sung Hsiang-feng, *Lun-yü shuo-i*, 391.6a.
50. Herrlee Creel, *Confucius and the Chinese Way*, 103–104. See also Creel's "Was Confucius Agnostic?"
51. Sung Hsiang-feng, *Lun-yü shuo-i*, 391. 6a.

lennium B.C., when the two texts had been compiled. Remarkably, Sung also referred to the Taoist philosopher Lao-tzu, putatively a contemporary of Confucius, who like the sage had drawn on the naturalistic teachings of the Yellow Emperor (Huang-ti, tr. r. 2697–2597?? B.C.). Such teachings, Sung contended, were included in the *Kuei-tsang* divination texts, which furnished much of the underlying cosmology seen in the *Change Classic*. According to Hsiang-feng, Confucius's inclusion of the *Change* in his syllabus demonstrated that Confucius, like Lao-tzu, was interested in the theoretical vision bequeathed from antiquity. Therefore, Sung concluded, the "*Annals* was the locus for the esoteric words" Confucius derived from the *Change Classic*.[52]

In arguing that "the Tao of Lao-tzu and Confucius derives from a common source," Sung Hsiang-feng controverted Han Learning scholars of the Ch'ing who used Confucius's "silence" in the *Annals* in order to reject speculation in favor of moral practice. By turning Han Learning inside out, Sung could reverse the *k'ao-cheng* rejection of Sung Learning moral theory. Confucius's "silence" demonstrated the theoretical poverty of Old Text Confucianism. Sung commented on a passage in the *Analects* in which Confucius's disciple Tzu-kung said: "One can get to hear about the Master's accomplishments, but one cannot get to hear his views on human nature and the Way of Heaven." Hsiang-feng noted that the Old Text interpretation missed the point of Confucius's efforts to compile the Five Classics. The Master's teachings were confirmed, not repudiated, by his silence.[53]

Even his disciples had misunderstood Confucius's intent: "The Master said, 'I am thinking of giving up speech.' Tzu-kung said, 'If you do not speak, what would there be for us your disciples to transmit?' The Master said, 'What does Heaven ever say? Yet there are the four sea-

52. Ibid., 392.1b–3a. Cf. Shchutskii, *Researches on the I-ching*, pp. 95–98. Sung Hsiang-feng's use of Lao-tzu to demonstrate that Confucius was not an "agnostic" rationalist—at first sight eccentric—was not at all so. Wei Yuan, the New Text statecraft scholar, later reevaluated the quietistic, Buddhistic elements that had dominated Taoism since the fall of the Later Han dynasty in an effort to restore the teachings of Lao-tzu to their pre-Han naturalism and statecraft—traditions that were derived from the Yellow Emperor and encoded in the *Change*. Confucian and Taoist naturalism and statecraft, in the hands of nineteeneth-century New Text scholars, became complementary rather than antagonistic elements in New Text Confucianism. This reconstructed synthesis of ancient Confucianism and Taoism should not surprise us if we recall that the New Text Confucian orthodoxy forged by Tung Chung-shu in the Former Han represented an extraordinary confluence of Confucian, Taoist, and Legalist doctrines that formed a viable ideological legitimation for the Han Confucian state.

53. Sung Hsiang-feng, *Lun-yü shuo-i*, 391.6a–8b, 393.1a–2a. See also Lau, trans., *Confucius*, p. 70; *Lun-yü yin-te* 8/5/13.

sons going round and there are the hundred things coming into being. What does Heaven ever say?'" Sung added that Confucius meant by "giving up speech" (*wu-yen*) "esoteric words" (*wei-yen*) that transcended normal discourse. Thus, discussion of "nature" and "external necessity" were esoteric doctrines that could not be grasped in normal terms. Confucius "spoke" as Heaven "spoke"—for those who could "listen."[54]

The Taoist overtones of this remarkable passage were not missed by New Text scholars, who saw in the *Analects* confirmation of the vision of the *Annals*. As retrievers of the esoteric teachings, New Text Confucians such as Sung Hsiang-feng could claim an intimacy with the Han classical legacy. Referring to the capture of the *lin* at the close of the *Annals* and to the sense of cultural crisis in the *Analects*, Sung concluded that both texts had been encoded with "esoteric words," which, in a time of depravity and chaos, an "uncrowned king" was bequeathing to posterity. After centuries of dormancy, the voluntarist image of Confucius as sage-king was reemerging just in time for a new period of chaos.

54. Sung Hsiang-feng, *Lun-yü shuo-i*, 397.5b–6a. Cf. See also *Lun-yü yin-te*, 36/17/17, translated in Lau, *Confucius*, p. 146.

SEVEN

Liu Feng-lu and New Text Confucianism

Liu Feng-lu represents in many ways the intellectual culmination of the Ch'ang-chou New Text school. After Liu, New Text Confucianism transcended its geographical origins in Ch'ang-chou, becoming a powerful current in early-nineteenth-century intellectual circles via the writings of Kung Tzu-chen and Wei Yuan. Both of these men studied in Peking under Liu Feng-lu's direction in the 1820s, when Liu had become a celebrity in the capital.[1]

LIU FENG-LU AS AN OFFICIAL

A child prodigy who benefited greatly from the cultural resources of his two wealthy and influential lineages, Liu Feng-lu early on was considered one of the most promising talents in Ch'ang-chou, rivaled only by the slightly more senior Li Chao-lo. In due course, Liu Feng-lu and Li Chao-lo became regarded as the most exceptional local examination candidates and were known as the "two Shen" (*liang Shen*; i.e., both had *shen* as a character in their literary names) of Ch'ang-chou. A product of Ch'ang-chou Han Learning, Li Chao-lo nonetheless admired, as we have seen, the achievements of Chuang Ts'un-yü and had close ties with the Chuang lineage.

1. Wang Nien-sun, "Shen-shou fu-chün hsing-shu," 12.55b. See also Wang Chia-chien, *Wei Yuan nien-p'u*, pp. 30, 33n, and Wu Ch'ang-shou, *Ting-an hsien-sheng nien-p'u*, p. 219.

Although Liu Feng-lu did not achieve *chin-shih* status until the capital examination of 1814, his examination essays for the *chü-jen* degree in 1805 (which he prepared for the provincial examinations held in the capital rather than his own Chiang-su Province) had already caused a stir. Liu's use of *Kung-yang* interpretations to explicate the Classics "greatly astonished," said Tai Wang, "those who read over his examination materials," and Liu was treated with the respect due a national literatus. New Text had come to Peking.[2]

It of course mattered that Feng-lu possessed impeccable family and lineage credentials. His grandfathers Liu Lun and Chuang Ts'un-yü had, after all, long since left their marks on the highest levels of the Peking bureaucracy (see chapter 2). Moreover, the Liu and Chuang lineages had for generations propelled their Ch'ang-chou sons through examination success to the upper echelons of the imperial state. After the demise of Ho-shen, Liu Feng-lu continued this legacy into the nineteenth century. Appointed to the Hanlin Academy for his high standing on the 1814 palace examinations, Feng-lu quickly achieved prominence in the Ministry of Rites, a standard stepping-stone to high position in the internal politics between the inner court and outer bureaucracy (see chapter 3).[3]

Liu Feng-lu lived out what appears to have been a conventional career at the Ministry of Rites. Using his classical expertise, for example, Liu assembled proposals and precedents on the proper rituals for the sudden and unusual death of the Chia-ch'ing Emperor (r. 1796–1820), who was apparently struck by lightning. Liu also wrote a favorable opinion on a proposal from the He-nan provincial director of education, advocating that T'ang Pin be canonized in the official Confucian temple in Ch'ü-fu, Shan-tung. Then director of the Ministry of Rites, Wang T'ing-chen was pleased with Liu's advocacy of this controversial early Ch'ing Confucian, and the Tao-kuang Emperor (r. 1820–50) accepted the proposal.[4]

Using his unconventional knowledge of historical precedents, Liu Feng-lu carved out an unusual place in the foreign policy decisions of the Ministry of Rites. His knowledge of the "precedents" in the *Spring*

2. Tai Wang, "Liu hsien-sheng hsing-chuang," 1.21b–22b. See also Wang Nien-sun, "Shen-shou fu-chün hsing-shu," 12.47a; Li Chao-lo, *Yang-i-chai wen-chi* (1852), 3.13b–14a; and Li's "Hsu" (Preface) to Chuang Shu-tsu, *Chen-i-i i-shu*, Cf. Hsu K'o, *Ch'ing-pai lei-ch'ao*, 69/28. Many official families of the Yangtze Delta were able to enroll their sons for the less severe competition in the north.

3. See the *Chuan-kao*, no. 4455(1) of Liu Feng-lu at the Palace Museum, Taipei.

4. Ibid.

and Autumn Annals, for instance, proved invaluable in 1824, when a tribute mission from the recently crowned king of Vietnam and ardent sinophile Minh-mang (r. 1820–41) went awry. The Vietnamese emissary in charge of the mission objected to the language of the official rescript, which had been prepared by the Tao-kuang Emperor for transmission to the Vietnamese king. The emissary was affronted by the reference in the rescript to the Vietnamese as "outer barbarians" (*wai-i*), a term that derived from the distinction between "inner feudal lords" (*nei chu-hsia*) and "outer barbarians" (*wai i-jung*) and had been prominent during the Chou dynasty (1122?–221 B.C.). It also was a term that figured prominently in the *Kung-yang* interpretation of foreign affairs chronicled in Confucius's *Annals*.[5]

The case reveals that not only Westerners but also Asian tribute states were offended by the pejorative connotations of Confucian culturalism. A Han Chinese official serving a Manchu emperor (who represented a conquering army of barbarians), Liu Feng-lu had to tread carefully in responding to the Vietnamese objections. Like Chuang Ts'un-yü in the 1758 bannermen riot (see chapter 3), Liu Feng-lu was caught between a classical legacy based on Chinese protonationalism and the present-day political realities of barbarian rule. Ts'un-yü precipitated a riot when he demanded that Manchu and Mongol bannermen meet the same rigorous standards expected of Chinese. Liu Feng-lu was more tactful.

The Vietnamese emissary had proposed to the Ch'ing court that, instead of "outer barbarians," the Vietnamese be named "outer vassals" (*wai-fan*), a less ethnocentric nomenclature that had in fact been applied to the Mongols and Tibetans under the institutional mechanism known as the *Li-fan yuan* (Court of Colonial Affairs—that is, "office for regulating vassals of the state"). The Ch'ing court employed the *Li-fan yuan* to differentiate ethnic Chinese from Manchus and to regulate certain minorities outside the regular bureaucracy in the northern and northwestern frontiers.

Liu Feng-lu played his first classical hand carefully, observing that in the "Offices of Chou" (*Chou-kuan*, that is, the *Chou-li*) regions outside the capital region had been divided into nine areas (*chiu-fu*). The "barbarian region" (*i-fu*) was located seven thousand *li* (a Chinese "mile" approximately equal to 360 paces or .35 of an English mile) from

5. Ibid. See *Ch'un-ch'iu ching-chuan yin-te*, 239/Ch'eng 15/12 Kung, which reads: "The *Annals* [first] treats the states as inner and the feudal lords as outer. [Next] it treats the lords as inner and the barbarians as outer."

the king's area, while the "vassals' region" (*fan-fu*) was nine thousand *li* from the capital region. Liu concluded: "Consequently, vassals were distant and barbarians close." Reference to the Vietnamese as "barbarians" accordingly implied higher respect within the Chou dynasty system of foreign affairs.[6]

Next, Liu cited an etymological precedent drawn from the Later Han *Shuo-wen chieh-tzu* dictionary of paleography. Philology would corroborate diplomatic protocol. According to Liu, the ancient Chinese graphs reserved for most non-Chinese groups were composed of a classifying radical (*pu-shou*) used for words referring to "creatures" (*wu*, that is, animals such as snakes, boar, etc.). This condescending orthography was conspicuously absent in the graph *i*, used for barbarians, which followed the radicals of "great" (*ta*) and "bow" (*kung*), terms of respect for the "outer barbarians."

The clinching argument, according to Liu Feng-lu, for maintaining the use of "outer barbarians" for the Vietnamese was the far more recent policy established by the Ch'ien-lung Emperor himself. When *i* appeared in the various ancient and contemporary books the editors were collecting and collating for inclusion in the Imperial Library, the emperor issued an edict that said it was unnecessary to change the character *i* for barbarians to another more innocuous character. This edict, moreover, was promulgated at a time when one disrespectful word uttered against a Manchu or Mongol was severely punished.[7] Liu Feng-lu was discreetly pointing out that in the midst of strenuous efforts to weed out anti-Manchu sentiments in books and manuscripts as well as to trace the origins of the Manchus as a people, the Manchu emperor himself had found nothing disrespectful in the term for "barbarians."

By citing the culturalist policies whereby Manchu rulers "united six racial groups into a single state" (*liu-ho i-chia*), Liu Feng-lu brought the full weight of the long-standing late imperial barbarian-Chinese synthesis down on the Vietnamese emissary. Drawing also on the Ch'ien-lung Emperor's edict that initiated research on Manchu origins in 1777, Liu explained that the sage-king Shun (tr. r. 2255–2205?? B.C.) was called an "Eastern Barbarian" (*Tung-i chih jen*) by none other than Mencius. Moreover, Mencius went on to refer to King Wen (tr. r. 1142?–1135?), the founder of the Chou dynasty, as a "Western Barbarian" (*Hsi-i chih jen*).

6. *Chuan-kao*, no. 4455(1) of Liu Feng-lu.
7. Ibid. See also Crossley, "*Manzhou yuanliu k'ao*," 761–66.

The Ch'ien-lung Emperor had used Mencius to play down Han Chinese chauvinism. Liu Feng-lu used Mencius to gainsay the Vietnamese. If sage-kings were "barbarians," what truth could there be to the Vietnamese claim that their status in the Confucian world order was being impugned? According to the imperial account of the incident, "the Vietnamese emissary had nothing he could say in reply and retired." Such issues could not be finessed for much longer, however. The tensions between Chinese and Manchu, Confucian and foreigner, eventually exploded into the Opium War (1839–42)—a battle initiated by Great Britain for full and equal diplomatic relations with China—and the Taiping Rebellion (1850–64), an anti-Manchu peasant rebellion.[8]

Liu Feng-lu served in the Ministry of Rites for twelve years, becoming well-known for his ability "to decide problematic cases on the basis of classical meanings" (*i ching-i chueh i-shih*). Liu also used historical precedents and classical meanings in the *Annals* to decide an 1817 family succession dispute in An-hui Province and an 1824 burial controversy, applying ritual precedents to determine how the status of wives influenced family succession. In the latter, Liu cited Ho Hsiu's explication of the *Kung-yang chuan* as the authoritative basis for ascertaining proper burial attire based on the status of the deceased.[9]

Liu Feng-lu's training in *Kung-yang* Confucianism under Chuang Ts'un-yü and Chuang Shu-tsu enabled him to tap a Former Han classical tradition that, it appears, was particularly useful in solving problems in ritual protocol and legal decisions. In rediscovering that the links between Han classical studies and ritual and legal precedents could also be applied to contemporary questions, Liu Feng-lu and other New Text scholars were also reconfirming the centrality of classical studies for political discourse.[10]

LIU FENG-LU AND HAN LEARNING

Unlike his distinguished grandfathers, Liu Feng-lu became more widely recognized as a scholar than as an official. In Peking he came into contact with the leading intellectual figures of the early nineteenth century and in so doing helped to transform the Ch'ang-chou *Kung-yang* tradition into a national concern.

Liu Feng-lu's friends and acquaintances in Peking included many of

8. *Chuan-kao*, no. 4455(1), and Crossley, "*Manzhou yuanliu k'ao*," pp. 765–71. See *Meng-tzu yin-te*, 30/4B/1, and Lau, *Mencius*, p. 128.
9. Tai Wang, "Liu hsien-sheng hsing-chuang," 1.22b–25a.
10. Ibid. See also *Chuan-kao*, no. 4455(1).

the most prominent Han Learning and *k'ao-cheng* scholars of the day. In addition to close relations with Ch'ang-chou Han Learning scholars such as Li Chao-lo, Sun Hsing-yen, Yun Ching, and Chang Hui-yen, Feng-lu was also intimate with leading Han Learning patrons such as Yang-chou's Juan Yuan. Although a patron of Han Learning on a grand scale for much of his career, Juan in the 1820s had begun to take a more moderate scholarly position, which encompassed the strengths of both Han and Sung Learning.

LIU FENG-LU AND JUAN YUAN

Around 1820 Liu encouraged Juan Yuan—then a major provincial official serving as governor-general of Kuang-chou—to reissue the *Shih-san-ching chu-shu* (Commentaries and subcommentaries to the Thirteen Classics), a Sung dynasty collectanea (*ts'ung-shu*) that contained the major classical studies of the Han, T'ang, and Sung dynasties. In addition, Liu suggested that Juan compile a comprehensive collection of Ch'ing dynasty contributions to classical scholarship. The result was the 1829 publication in Kuang-chou of the *Huang-Ch'ing ching-chieh* (Ch'ing exegesis of the Classics). After four years of preparation and editing at the prestigious Hsueh-hai-t'ang Academy, the book was greeted with great acclaim in Han Learning circles in China and sent to Korea, Japan, and later the West. Designed as a continuation to the *Shih-san-ching chu-shu*, the *Huang-Ch'ing ching-chieh* represented a major tribute to the classical research of *k'ao-cheng* scholars.[11]

Juan's tribute to Ch'ing scholarship stressed the eighteenth-century Han Learning movement, which had championed the Later Han classical "schools system" of Cheng Hsuan and Hsu Shen, among others. But Liu Feng-lu prevailed upon Juan Yuan to include Ch'ing dynasty works dealing with the Former Han New Text "school system" based on Tung Chung-shu (179?–104? B.C.) and Ho Hsiu. As a result, a number of works by men connected to the Ch'ang-chou New Text tradition were reprinted in the collection: Chung Ts'un-yü's *Correcting Phrases in the Spring and Autumn Annals*; three works by K'ung Kuang-sen, including *Penetrating the Meanings in the Kung-yang Commentary to the Annals;* seven works by Liu Feng-lu, most prominently his *Master Ho Hsiu's Explications of Precedents in the Kung-yang Commentary to the Annals Classic* and the famous *Evidential Analysis of Master Tso's*

11. Wang Nien-sun, "Shen-shou fu-chün hsing-shu," 12.55a–56a. On Juan see my *Philosophy to Philology*, pp. 108–11, 124–28, 235–36.

Spring and Autumn Annals (*Tso-shih ch'un-ch'iu k'ao-cheng*); and two works by Ling Shu, a follower of Liu Feng-lu, including his *Ritual Explanations in the Kung-yang Commentary* (*Kung-yang li-shuo*).[12]

Besides associating with and patronizing scholars who studied the *Kung-yang chuan*, such as Liu Feng-lu, Juan Yuan himself developed an interest late in life in the Former Han New Text alternative to the Later Han Old Text "schools system." In an introduction to K'ung Kuang-sen's *Penetrating the Meanings*, Juan traced the transmission of *Kung-yang* studies and described their vicissitudes before their mid-Ch'ing revival. Although he pointed out four areas where K'ung's interpretation of the *Kung-yang chuan* differed from Ho Hsiu's (differences Liu Feng-lu would also stress in his own criticism of K'ung's research [see below]), Juan Yuan concluded that the *Kung-yang chuan* was superior to the *Tso chuan* in elucidating the organizing principles Confucius had subtly encoded in the *Annals*.[13]

In 1793, during his tenure as director of education in Shan-tung Province, Juan Yuan directed the rebuilding of a shrine commemorating the Later Han classicist Cheng Hsuan. This effort epitomized Juan's emphasis on Cheng Hsuan as the key figure in reconstructing the "schools system" of Han Learning. Moreover, as governor of Che-chiang Province in 1801, Juan had established the Ku-ching ching-she (Refined Study for the Glossing of the Classics) Academy in Hang-chou. He noted that the academy was named to honor the Later Han classical studies of both Cheng Hsuan and Hsu Shen, author of the *Shuo-wen chieh-tzu* dictionary.[14]

Juan Yuan established the Hsueh-hai-t'ang Academy in Kuang-chou in 1820 along the same Han Learning guidelines used for the academy in Hang-chou. But the new school—unlike the Ku-ching ching-she, which was named after Cheng Hsuan and Hsu Shen—was named in honor of the New Text scholar Ho Hsiu, who had been known honorifically as "Hsueh-hai" (Sea of learning) because of his great erudition on the Classics. We can conclude, therefore, that Chuang Ts'un-yü's rediscovery of Ho Hsiu and the *Kung-yang* tradition was by 1820 more than just a local Ch'ang-chou tradition tied to the Chuang lineage.[15]

12. See the table of contents to the *Huang-Ch'ing ching-chieh*. See also my "Hsueh-hai T'ang," 51–82.

13. Juan, *Yen-ching-shih chi*, vol. 2, pp. 222–24. See also Hou Wai-lu, *Chin-tai Chung-kuo ssu-hsiang hsueh-shuo shih*, vol. 2, p. 599.

14. Juan, *Yen-ching-shih chi*, vol. 2, p. 505.

15. See the "Hsu" (Preface) by or in behalf of Juan, *Hsueh-hai-t'ang chi*, 1st ser. 1825.

Hsu Jung, one of the eight original directors of the Hsueh-hai-t'ang, caught the symbolic significance of Juan's name for the academy. He composed the following verse in 1824 for the dedication of the academy's new buildings on Yueh-hsiu Hill:

> The Green-jade Pavilion is high and out of sight,
> Southward from the South Garden only desolate weeds.
> Of Clear Spring Refined Study no foundations remain,
> Precious Moon Tower stands alone—what sounds will follow?
>
> The roots of a hundred generations lie in past events,
> This broad mansion of a thousand rooms holds the mind of the ancients.
> We will be able to take the *Kung-yang* learning of the two Hans,
> And swiftly sweep away the superficial to reveal the Old and New.[16]

Juan Yuan had personal ties with many of the scholars associated with the Ch'ang-chou New Text tradition. Liu Feng-lu's sometime follower, Ling Shu, served late in life as Juan's assistant, also tutoring Juan's sons. Juan's close friend Ch'eng En-tse was a well-known scholar and tutored many of those involved in the New Text tradition. Ch'eng's circle of friends in Peking included Liu Feng-lu, Wei Yuan, and Kung Tzu-chen, all of whose statecraft proposals and political activities were widely admired. Such links between Han Learning and New Text scholarship in the early nineteenth century suggest that we should broaden our understanding of the Old Text–New Text controversy and be prepared to consider the manner in which the Ch'ang-chou New Text initiative entered the *k'ao-cheng* mainstream.[17]

K'AO-CHENG EPISTEMOLOGICAL LEVERAGE

Standing on the borderline between Han Learning and Sung Learning, the *Kung-yang* studies produced by Chuang and Liu scholars in Ch'ang-chou assumed national prominence through the preliminary efforts of Chuang Shu-tsu, Chuang Yu-k'e, and Chuang Shou-chia. They united Chuang Ts'un-yü's *Kung-yang* interests to Han Learning *k'ao-cheng* studies. Liu Feng-lu brought this ongoing synthesis to virtual completion. Through him, the latest philological discoveries of Han Learning were conjoined to the reconstruction of the Former Han New Text clas-

16. *Hsueh-hai-t'ang chi*, 1st ser., 16.22a–23a.

17. Ling Shu, for example, annotated Tung Chung-shu's *Ch'un-ch'iu fan-lu*, a key New Text work. See Li Hsin-lin, "Ch'ing-tai ching chin-wen-hsueh shu," pp. 81–84, and Wilhelm, "Chinese Confucianism," p. 307.

sical tradition. He also impressed the theoretical perspectives of *Kung-yang* Confucianism on leading Han Learning scholars, who began to see the import of Chuang Ts'un-yü's efforts to overcome the threatening implications of the debate between Han and Sung Learning.

Liu Feng-lu realized that the theoretical conclusions reached by Chuang Ts'un-yü and other members of the Ch'ang-chou school needed support from empirically based *k'ao-cheng* methods of demonstration. Without such support, *Kung-yang* studies lacked the epistemological leverage to be taken seriously enough to appear alongside mainstream Han Learning studies in collections such as the *Ch'ing Exegesis of the Classics*. Juan Yuan, as we saw in chapter 4, declined to include Chuang Ts'un-yü's writings on the *Change Classic* in the latter collectanea, for example, because they were not informed by *k'ao-cheng* methods. Evidential research methods were employed so widely in the eighteenth and early nineteenth centuries that the accepted forms of scholarly discourse had been transformed in epistemological terms. Works that lacked systematic methods of demonstration could no longer achieve academic respectability. This scholarly shift was as true for Han Learning as for New Text studies.

As Chuang Shu-tsu and Chuang Yu-k'e had already demonstrated, *k'ao-cheng* was no one's monopoly. Liu Feng-lu devoted considerable attention to philology and phonology to gain the respect of his Han Learning colleagues. Liu made important contributions to *k'ao-cheng* research, particularly in the field of reconstructing ancient pronunciation based on classical rhymes (*ku-yin*). When such research was allied with New Text studies, the latter acquired the epistemological leverage needed to gain scholarly credibility.[18]

LIU FENG-LU AND NEW TEXT STUDIES

Liu Feng-lu transformed *Kung-yang* Confucianism from an idiosyncratic theoretical position into a legitimate form of Han Learning. Using *k'ao-cheng* to give epistemological legitimacy to the *Kung-yang* interpretation of the Classics, Liu Feng-lu in effect opened the door for full recognition of the scope of New Text Confucianism (*chin-wen-hsueh*). Along with Sung Hsiang-feng—who raised questions concerning the authenticity of the *Rituals of Chou* in connection with doubts about the legitimacy of the Old Text Classics (see chapter 6)—Feng-lu co-opted

18. See my *Philosophy to Philology*, pp. 2–36.

the accruing philological evidence on the provenance of the Old Text portions of the *Documents Classic* and other Classics for the *Kung-yang* agenda.[19]

As the Old Text Classics increasingly became caught up in authenticity debates, the philological evidence unwittingly supplied by Han Learning scholars for more than a century became a powerful weapon in the New Text arsenal. For much of the nineteenth century, the New Text Classics enjoyed an aura of philological authenticity that contrasted sharply with the misgivings that clouded the reputations of the *Rituals of Chou*, the *Tso chuan*, and the Old Text *Documents*. Although research had by the early nineteenth century shown no unanimity on the Five Classics as a whole, the direction in *k'ao-cheng* research was evident.

In the seventeenth and eighteenth centuries, efforts to recover and reconstruct the Han Learning legacy had taken the form of a "return" (*fu-ku*) to the exegetical tradition of the Later Han "schools system." Continuing this scholarly return to the authenticated sources of the classical canon, followers of the Ch'ang-chou New Text school in the late eighteenth and early nineteenth centuries advanced the frontiers of their knowledge by focusing on the scholarship associated with the "schools system" of the Former Han dynasty as a superior source for recovering the Confucian legacy. Even the more mainstrean *k'ao-cheng* scholars who were not directly associated with the Ch'ang-chou school were moving in this direction.[20]

The Fu-chien scholar Ch'en Shou-ch'i (1771–1834) is a good example of this more general scholarly shift. A New Text philologist, Ch'en was among the first to recognize the superiority of the New Text version of the authentic chapters of the *Documents Classic* over the Old Text version. In the early part of the nineteenth century, Ch'en completed a reconstruction of the Former Han New Text commentary to the *Documents*. Such emendations of the findings of Tuan Yü-ts'ai and other Old Text supporters were continued by Ch'en Shou-ch'i's son Ch'iao-ts'ung. In addition to collating the New Text recension of the *Documents*, Chen Ch'iao-ts'ung also assembled in another work most of the conclusions reached by *k'ao-cheng* scholars concerning the Old Text *Documents* controversy in the preceding two centuries. Like Chuang Shu-tsu and Liu Feng-lu, the Ch'ens rejected the Old Text re-

19. Li Hsin-lin, "Ch'ing-tai ching chin-wen-hsueh shu," p. 186.
20. Chou Yü-t'ung, *Ching chin-ku-wen hsueh*, pp. 28–29.

cension of the *Documents* in favor of New Text variants dating from the Former Han "schools system."[21]

Philology became the means to reorder the classical legacy. Convinced of the need for an exact textual understanding of the Confucian Classics in order to reach doctrinal conclusions, *k'ao-cheng* scholars reversed earlier Sung-Ming Neo-Confucian agendas by making philology, not philosophy, the key to recovering the teachings of antiquity. Liu Feng-lu's genius lay in correctly perceiving the crucial role played by the textual criticism of the Old Text Classics. In fact, he viewed it as the philological premise for the restitution of the long-defunct New Text Classics initiated by Chuang Ts'un-yü when he turned to *Kung-yang* Confucianism. *Kung-yang* theory was now grounded on *k'ao-cheng* discourse. The joining of activist *Kung-yang* theory and intellectualist Han Learning philology would yield New Text Confucianism.[22]

As his imperial biographer explained, "Liu Feng-lu's scholarship endeavored to penetrate great meanings without overstressing the parsing of sentences and phrases [in the Classics]." Although a student of Chuang Ts'un-yü, Liu moved away from his teacher's stress on Ho Hsiu back to the Former Han New Text Confucianism of Tung Chung-shu. The unanimity of Han Learning was effectively over. Feng-lu's shift epitomized the retreat from Cheng Hsuan and the classical "schools system" of the Later Han.[23]

Liu Feng-lu perceived in the New Text concerns of the Former Han a bedrock of Confucian theory that could replace the overly philological concerns of the Later Han Old Text school. The Former Han New Text stress on theory contrasted in a fundamental way with the Later Han Old Text emphasis on philology. This contrast reaffirmed, albeit in new terms, the difference between Sung Learning moral philosophy and Han Learning *k'ao-cheng*. New Text Confucianism gave Feng-lu and others the textual means to restore the balance between theory and philology.[24]

21. Ch'en Shou-ch'i, *Tso-hai ching-pien*, A.1a–12b, A.13a–21b, A.22a–26b, A.36a–40b, for a discussion of the New Text recension of the *Documents*. See also Ch'en Ch'iao-ts'ung, *Tso-hai hsu-chi*. Cf. Liang Ch'i-ch'ao, *Intellectual Trends*, p. 90.

22. Liu Feng-lu, *Ch'un-ch'iu Kung-yang ching Ho-shih shih-li*, 1280.2b. See my "Philosophy versus Philology," pp. 211–17.

23. *Chuan-kao*, no. 4455(1), of Liu Feng-lu.

24. Tai Wang, "Liu hsien-sheng hsing-chuang," 1.26b. Liu Feng-lu stated his views in the "Hsu" (Preface) to his *Kung-yang ch'un-ch'iu Ho-shih chieh-ku ch'ien*, 1290.1a–2a.

LIU FENG-LU VS. CH'IEN TA-HSIN

Liu Feng-lu's remarkable synthesis proceeded simultaneously on a number of fronts. The central axis of his New Text synthesis was Confucius's *Spring and Autumn Annals*, which he viewed as the key to "seeking out the intent of the sages" (*sheng-jen chih chih*). Showing remarkable professional courage and intellectual integrity, he wrote an essay entitled "Discourse on the *Annals*" ("Ch'un-ch'iu lun") early in the nineteenth century that directly controverted the conclusions on the *Spring and Autumn Annals* drawn by Ch'ien Ta-hsin. The most distinguished Han Learning scholar of the Ch'ien-lung era, Ch'ien Ta-hsin was also the chief spokesman for the Su-chou Han Learning tradition after the death of Hui Tung. Just as his grandfather had opposed Su-chou and Yang-chou Han Learning currents a generation before, Liu Feng-lu, it appears, was confident enough of his roots in Chuang traditions of classical learning to challenge the giants of the *k'ao-cheng* movement.

Continuing a line of interpretation with roots in Sung dynasty skepticism, Ch'ien Ta-hsin had argued that the *Annals* "had no historiographical message" (*wu shu-fa*). Indeed, according to Ch'ien, the *Annals* contained no secret message of "praise and blame" encoded by Confucius but was simply a straightforward chronicle of events (*chih shu ch'i shih*). Ch'ien therefore contended that the *Tso chuan* was the superior commentary on the *Annals* because it added flesh to the bones of the events listed in the *Annals*. The *Kung-yang Commentary* dealt only with unverifiable and mysterious notions (*wu-wang chih shuo*) of little value in classical studies.[25]

Liu Feng-lu correctly perceived that Ch'ien Ta-hsin's efforts to define the *Annals* as a mere historical record constituted a throwback to Wang An-shih's attempt centuries earlier to dismiss the *Annals* as a useless collection of names and dates devoid of any moral message. Defending the *Kung-yang Commentary*, Liu wrote:

> [Ch'ien Ta-hsin's argument] does not prove that Kung-yang [Kao] does not compare to Master Tso, but only that the *Annals* itself does not compare with Master Tso. Master Tso gives details on affairs, but the *Annals* stresses meanings, not affairs. Master Tso never mentions precedents, but the *Annals* is filled with precedents. It does not loosely construct precedents. Instead, by

25. Ch'ien Ta-hsin, *Ch'ien-yen-t'ang wen-chi*, vol. 1, 17–22.

> emphasizing affairs, [the *Annals*] preserves only one-tenth of the hundreds and thousands [of affairs]. What is not recorded outnumbers what is recorded. Accordingly, the *Annals* does not loosely construct precedents.[26]

By accepting the superior historical status of the *Tso chuan*, Liu Feng-lu placed an enormous conceptual distance between the intent of the *Annals* as a Classic and the historical reach of the *Tso chuan* as a commentary. Ch'ien Ta-hsin and his predecessors had subsumed the *Annals* under the historical minutiae of its *Tso chuan*. By giving priority to the *Annals* as a Classic, Liu Feng-lu dismissed efforts to relegate it to the status of mere history. The debate within Han Learning over the provenance of the Classics (*ching*) vis-à-vis history (*shih*) was beginning to take shape. Liu Feng-lu made Ch'ien Ta-hsin his foil for the Old Text position and than articulated the special transhistorical status of the New Text Classics against it.

THE CLASSICS VS. HISTORY

The debate over the relationship between the Classics and Dynastic Histories became prominent in the seventeenth and eighteenth centuries. As historical studies became almost as prestigious as classical studies in the late eighteenth century, the conceptual chasm demarcating the universality of the Classics from the particularity of the Histories was called into question. The *Documents Classic* and *Spring and Autumn Annals*, for instance, were historical records derived from antiquity that had become Classics. A recurring problem was explaining the distinction between 'Classic' and 'History.'[27]

A specialist in classical and historical fields of *k'ao-cheng* research, Ch'ien Ta-hsin went further than most in his claim that, ultimately, there was no essential difference between the Classics and the Histories. This distinction had not existed in antiquity, according to Ch'ien, but had first been used in the bibliographic "four divisions" (*ssu-pu*, that is, classics, history, philosophy, literature) system of classification instituted after the fall of the Han dynasty. Consequently, Ch'ien rejected the priority accorded the Classics over the Histories in reconstructing the classical tradition. For Ch'ien, the Histories were equally important sources.[28]

26. Liu Feng-lu, "Ch'un-ch'iu lun," in *Liu Li-pu chi*, 3.17b.
27. See my *Philosophy to Philology*, pp. 72–73.
28. Ch'ien Ta-hsin, "Hsu" (Preface) to his *Nien-erh-shih k'ao-i*, p. 1.

Critical of fruitless speculation and arbitrary praise-and-blame historiography, *k'ao-cheng* historians such as Ch'ien Ta-hsin and his close confidant and brother-in-law, Wang Ming-sheng, favored application of evidential research to paint the true face of history. Wang Ming-sheng, also a follower of Su-chou Han Learning, maintained: "Discussions of praise and blame are merely empty words. The writing of history is the recording of the facts. Overall the goal is simply to ascertain the truth. Besides the facts, what more can one ask for?" Similarly, Ch'ien Ta-hsin asserted that historical facts themselves would show whom to praise and whom to blame. The process of laying blame, according to Ch'ien, should be analogous to the deliberations involved in deciding court cases. There must be no self-serving use of historical evidence to support unverifiable and mysterious theories of praise and blame drawn from the *Annals*. Ch'ien and Wang both rejected the a priori assumption that Confucius's *Annals* was the model for and embodiment of the underlying "meaning" of history.[29]

The well-known slogan "the Six Classics are all Histories," made famous in the late eighteenth century by the historian Chang Hsueh-ch'eng, should be understood in light of contributions made by *k'ao-cheng* historians such as Wang Ming-sheng and Ch'ien Ta-hsin. They set the stage for Chang Hsueh-ch'eng's dramatic conclusion, which historicized classical studies and placed the Classics unequivocally under history's purview. We should add that this demotion of the a priori status of the *Annals* at the same time threatened Confucius's status as a historian. If the *Annals* were a useless chronicle, then what of the compiler?[30]

Chang Hsueh-ch'eng, for example, argued that Confucius had been only the most important of many late Chou dynasty theorists, and Confucianism but one school among others. Confucius's role, he explained, had been limited to transmitting the teachings enunciated by the Duke of Chou centuries before. Chang's discussion of the different roles played by Confucius and the Duke of Chou revived debates concerning the priority of the *Rituals of Chou* (associated with the Duke of Chou) over the *Annals* (associated with Confucius) precisely at the time when Chuang Ts'un-yü and his Ch'ang-chou kin were developing their *Kung-yang* portrait of Confucius as a sage who used history to declare classical truths.

29. Wang Ming-sheng, "Hsu" (Preface) to *Shih-ch'i-shih shang-ch'ueh*, p. 2a. See also Ch'ien Ta-hsin, *Ch'ien-yen-t'ang wen-chi*, vol. 2, 224–25.

30. Chang Hsueh-ch'eng, *Wen-shih t'ung-i*, p. 1.

Questions about Confucius's historical pedigree revealed growing dissatisfaction in the eighteenth century with the Sung Learning version of the "orthodox transmission of the Way" (*Tao-t'ung*). Since the Sung dynasties it had stressed Confucius and Mencius as the core of the classical legacy. According to Chang Hsueh-ch'eng (who spoke unwittingly for the Old Text tradition of the Later Han when he defended the *Chou-li*), the Duke of Chou, not Confucius, had been the last of the world-ordering sages. While New Text scholars were dismantling the complementary ties between the *Annals* and the *Chou-li* by stressing the former, Old Text advocates were rending the same ties in favor of the latter. In effect, the two opposing sides were aiming for a common if still unclear result: the polarization of Han Learning traditions into New Text vs. Old Text.[31]

The revival of the unorthodox *Kung-yang* commentary to Confucius's *Annals* by Ch'ang-chou scholars suggests that opposing views concerning the historical Confucius were taking shape in the late eighteenth and early nineteenth centuries. New Text scholars deemphasized Mencius, a move that indicates their break with the Sung Learning conception of orthodoxy. For Liu Feng-lu and other New Text scholars, Confucius, not the Duke of Chou, had been the central figure.

Liu's attempts to refute Ch'ien Ta-hsin, consequently, represented more than just personal dissatisfaction with Ch'ien's position on the *Annals*. Feng-lu's criticism symbolized the reemergence of the Han dynasties' Old Text vs. New Text controversy in fully polarized form. It also represented the struggle between historicism and classicism. New Text scholars sought to save the Classics from Old Text historians without recapitulating the Sung Learning orthodoxy already bankrupt in the highest echelons of elite literati circles.

For Liu Feng-lu as for Chuang Ts'un-yü, the *Kung-yang chuan* was the central text: "I have accordingly recognized for some time that all scholars seek the [wisdom of the] sages. The Way of the sages is complete in the Five Classics, and the *Spring and Autumn Annals* is the key to the lock." Without understanding the a priori "esoteric principles" (*wei-li*) informing the *Annals*, the Five Classics, Liu maintained, would remain inexplicable, no matter how much philological research was done.[32]

31. Chang Hsueh-ch'eng, *Chang-shih i-shu*, 2.3b–4a. See also Nivison, *Chang Hsueh-ch'eng*, pp. 147–50.

32. Liu Feng-lu, "Ch'un-ch'iu lun," 3.16b–19a. See also Liu Feng-lu, *Ch'un-ch'iu Kung-yang ching Ho-shih shih-li*, 1280.2b. See Shimada, "Shinkai kakumeiki no Kōshi mondai," pp. 3–8.

LIU FENG-LU VS. K'UNG KUANG-SEN

In the second part of his essay "Discourse on the *Annals*," Liu turned to the *Kung-yang* studies of K'ung Kuang-sen, a direct descendant of Confucius who had studied briefly in the 1770s under Chuang Ts'un-yü. Although he praised K'ung for recognizing that the *Kung-yang Commentary* was intimately tied to the Han classical "schools system," Liu Feng-lu believed K'ung had misrepresented the Later Han *Kung-yang* tradition by not acknowledging Ho Hsiu as the orthodox transmitter of Former Han teachings on the *Kung-yang Commentary*. He charged that K'ung, by focusing on much later post-Han interpretations of the New Text "schools system," had missed Ho Hsiu's connection with the Former Han New Text tradition. For the Ch'ang-chou New Text scholars, Ho Hsiu represented the only surviving link to Former Han New Text teachings. The latter derived from the "schools system" of the *Annals* in the Imperial Academy when the erudites Hu-wu Sheng and Tung Chung-shu had championed the *Kung-yang chuan*.[33]

By not accepting Ho Hsiu as the legitimate transmitter of the "original meanings" (*pen-i*) in the *Annals* described by the *Kung-yang chuan* K'ung Kuang-sen had—according to Liu Feng-lu—overlooked the "bequeathed theories of earlier teachers of the *Kung-yang* and those of [Confucius's] seventy disciples." In particular, Liu asserted that K'ung had misconstrued the *san-k'e* (three classifications) and *chiu-chih* (nine points) formulations upon which the Former Han *Kung-yang* position on the *Annals* had been based. Rather than basing his theories on the orthodox commentaries—that is, the *Kung-yang* and *Ku-liang*—K'ung Kuang-sen had relied on the text of the Classic alone for his interpretation.

Moreover, instead of following reliable Later Han dynasty sources (such as Ho Hsiu's surviving writings) on the meaning of *san-k'e* and *chiu-chih*, K'ung Kuang-sen accepted unorthodox definitions which Liu Feng-lu thought betrayed the original meanings of these central terms. How ironic that this defense of Confucius by a New Text scholar, Liu Feng-lu, includes an attack on a direct descendant of the sage. Liu charged in effect that K'ung had swallowed an Old Text bill of goods that diminished Confucius's status. Ch'ang-chou New Text scholars now claimed preeminence.[34]

33. Liu Feng-lu, "Ch'un-ch'iu lun," 3.19a–19b. See also the *Chuan-kao*, no. 4455(1), of Liu Feng-lu.

34. Liu Feng-lu, "Ch'un-ch'iu lun," 3.20a.

Differences in interpretation between K'ung Kuang-sen and Liu Feng-lu were substantial and politically significant. For the "three classifications" in the *Kung-yang Commentary*, K'ung Kuang-sen gave (1) "the Way of heaven" (*t'ien-tao*), (2) "the methods of ruling" (*wang-fa*), and (3) "human sentiments" (*jen-ch'ing*). The "nine points" were organized in threes according to the "three classifications" (see list below). The Way of heaven was defined in naturalistic terms: (1) seasons, (2) the lunar month, and (3) the solar day. Methods of rulership were conceived of as (4) criticism (*chi*), (5) blame (*pien*), and (6) renunciation (*chueh*). Human sentiments were divided into (7) respect (*tsun*), (8) intimacy (*ch'in*), and (9) uprightness (*hsien*). K'ung's interpretation implied an unchanging cosmos within which constant natural, political, and moral phenomena interacted. The vision was at odds with the voluntaristic interpretations of change and reform that Tung Chung-shu and Ho Hsiu had read into the *Annals*.[35]

Although rejecting the *Tso chuan* in favor of the *Kung-yang chuan* as an acceptable commentary on the *Annals*, K'ung Kuang-sen relied in part on the Later Han Confucian Sung Chün's (fl. ca. A.D. 25–26) explication of the "nine points" and not on Ho Hsiu's. In addition, K'ung refused to accept the cyclical interpretations of the "three classifications," which both Ho Hsiu and Sung Chün had acknowledged. What disturbed K'ung about Ho Hsiu's version of the *san-k'e* and *chiu-chih* was that it contained superstitious prophecy, which Kuang-sen thought anachronistic. Confucius was a teacher not a prophet; he could not have known what the future held. To read into the *Annals* prophecies regarding the Han dynasty, according to K'ung, "had no basis in fact." K'ung thus refused to follow the Former Han version of *Kung-yang* Confucianism. He rejected Ho Hsiu's commentary because Ho had been misguided, his views not only speculative but also wildly irrational (*tsung-heng i-shuo*). They deserved, K'ung thought, the disrepute they had for centuries received.[36]

Skepticism concerning the prophetic aspects of New Text classical scholarship had been voiced in Ch'ang-chou by Tsang Lin (1650–1713) in his pioneering efforts to restore Han Learning to classical respectabil-

35. Ibid., 3.19a–19b. See also K'ung Kuang-sen, *Ch'un-ch'iu Kung-yang ching-chuan t'ung-i*, 691.1a–10a.

36. See Ojima, *Chūgoku no shakai shisō*, pp. 112–31. See also Nakamura, "Kō Kōsen Shunjū Kuyō tsūgi jo ni tsuite," pp. 892, 896, 899, 901, and *Hsu-hsiu Ssu-k'u ch'üan-shu t'i-yao*, pp. 820–22. Cf. the *Ssu-k'u ch'üan-shu* commission's ridicule of *Kung-yang* theory in *Ssu-k'u ch'üan-shu tsung-mu*, 6.1aff, and Chiang Fan, *Han-hsueh shih-ch'eng chi*, pp. 104–5.

ity (see chapter 4). The notion that the *Annals* was a repository of prophecy did not sit well with the empirical bent of the early champions of Ch'ing Han Learning. Similarly, the *k'ao-cheng* historian Ku Tung-kao (1679–1759), a native of Wu-hsi County in Ch'ang-chou, spent a lifetime reconstructing the historicity of the *Annals*; he attacked New Text advocates for their defense of superstitions that mainstream Confucians could not comprehend.[37]

Liu Feng-lu—using evidential research techniques to defuse the criticism of New Text ideas by Han Learning scholars—attacked K'ung Kuang-sen's interpretation of the "three classifications" and "nine points" because it had no basis in the Han classical "schools system" of the Former and Later Han dynasties. By disregarding Tung Chung-shu and Ho Hsiu, K'ung had avoided the inevitable conclusion that Confucius had indeed intended the apocalyptic implications captured by New Text interpretations of the Five Classics. Ho Hsiu's subcommentary on the "three classifications" and "nine points," according to Liu Feng-lu, was the true legacy of the Former Han New Text orthodoxy.

However difficult it might be for Old Text advocates to fathom, the prophecies and prognostications that were part of Tung Chung-shu's portrait of Confucius as sage and "uncrowned king" reemerged in the writings of Sung Hsiang-feng and Liu Feng-lu. Liu was integrating the Former Han vision of Confucius as larger than life, as an "uncrowned king" who had appeared "not because Heaven had wanted to save the Eastern Chou [dynasty] from chaos, but instead to mandate him through the *Annals* to save ten thousand [succeeding] generations from chaos."[38]

HO HSIU AND THE "THREE CLASSIFICATIONS"

Liu Feng-lu maintained that Ho Hsiu had been careful to transmit the interpretations of his predecessors. Ho's definitions were therefore, truer, Liu concluded, to the Former Han New Text tradition than the sources from which K'ung Kuang-sen had drawn. Liu accordingly followed Ho Hsiu on the "three classifications": (1) "the unfolding of three epochs" (*chang san-shih*), (2) "going through three periods of uni-

37. On Tsang Lin see *Hsu-hsiu Ssu-k'u ch'üan-shu t'i-yao*, vol. 2, p. 831. Cf. Ojima, *Chūgoku no shakai shisō*, pp. 113–14, and Li Hsin-lin, "Ch'ing-tai ching chin-wen-hsueh shu," pp. 183–84.

38. Liu Feng-lu, "Ch'un-ch'iu lun," 3.20a. See also Liu's *Liu Li-pu chi*, 4.35a and 4.7a–19b, for Liu's disscussion of K'ung Kuang-sen's "nine points." Cf. *Hsu-hsiu Ssu-k'u ch'üan-shu t'i-yao*, pp. 823–24.

ty" (*ts'un san-t'ung*), and (3) "differentiating the outer [barbarians] from the inner [Chinese]" (*i wai-nei*). As the following outline suggests, Ho Hsiu's position was more radical in its exposition than K'ung Kuang-sen's because, as Liu Feng-lu pointed out, Ho's interpretation elaborated a notion of cosmic and dynastic change, which Ho's predecessor Sung Chün had also accepted:

	Ho Hsiu	*Sung Chün*	*K'ung Kuang-sen*
San-k'e			
	1. Three periods of unity	Unfolding	Way of heaven
	2. Unfolding of three epochs	Unity	Methods of ruling
	3. Inner/outer	Inner/outer	Human sentiments
Chiu-chih			
	1. Chou as new dynasty	Seasons	Seasons
	2. Relegating Shang to Sung	Lunar month	Lunar month
	3. *Annals* as new king	Solar day	Solar day
	4. What was witnessed	Criticism	Criticism
	5. What was learned	Blame	Blame
	6. What was transmitted	Renunciation	Renunciation
	7. Chinese states as inner	Respect	Respect
	8. Feudal lords as outer	Intimacy	Intimacy
	9. Barbarians as outer	Uprightness	Uprightness

As an underlying theory of change and reform the "three classifications" were, in Ho Hsiu's hands, tied very closely to the "nine points" (*tsai san-k'e chih nei*). Although Sung Chün had accepted the same version for the *san-k'e* that Ho Hsiu had, he had not subsumed the "nine points" under them. For Sung, "the nine points were outside the three classifications" (*chiu-chih tsai san-k'e chih wai*). Consequently, the latter seemed to have no direct correlation to the former, a point that had permitted K'ung Kuang-sen to reject Ho's and Sung's version of the "three classifications" and yet retain Sung's "nine points" intact (see list).

Sung Chün had given priority to the "unfolding of three epochs" as the "first classification." In contrast, Ho Hsiu made "going through the three periods of unity" the "first," and relegated the "unfolding of three epochs" to the "second classification." For Ho Hsiu, "going through the three periods of unity" included "three points": (1) "making Chou the new dynasty" (*hsin-Chou*), (2) "relegating [the former Shang dynasty] to [the state of] Sung" (*Ku-Sung*), and (3) "using the *Spring and Autumn Annals* as [the basis for] establishing the new king [to come]" (*i Ch'un-ch'iu tang hsin-wang*).

Ho Hsiu's "first classification" and its "three points" implied that a mandate (*ming*) to rule had been granted to Confucius and prophetically encoded in the *Annals* "to relegate the Chou dynasty and entrust the kingship to the state of Lu" (*Ku-Chou wang-Lu*) as a harbinger of the Han dynasty unification of China. The image of Confucius as an uncrowned king of the state of Lu was clearly magnified by this conception of change and reform in the three epochs (*san-shih*) of time. In another work on Ho Hsiu, Liu Feng-lu explained:

> "To entrust the kinship to Lu" is what the *Annals* means by "using the *Spring and Autumn Annals* as [the basis for] establishing the new king [to come]." The master received the mandate to establish institutions. Thinking that it would be better to put them into effect rather than rely on empty words, [Confucius's wisdom] was broad and deep, discriminating and clear. He cited histories and records, imbuing them with the mind of a king. Mencius said "the *Annals* represents the affairs of the Son of Heaven." In establishing the models for the new king and awaiting later sages [to put them into effect], why did [Confucius] have to choose Lu? The answer is that he used the written history of Lu to avoid giving the impression that in creating institutions he was usurping the prerogatives of the ruler. Moreover, of what Confucius had known and heard, only the [affairs of] Lu were close at hand. Therefore, he chose Lu as the capital region for enunciating the basis of governance.[39]

The "unfolding of the three epochs" as the "second classification" in Ho Hsiu's interpretation overlapped with the scale of historical change enunciated in the first. The "three points" belonging to this stage were: (4) "using different terms for what [Confucius personally] witnessed" (*so-chien i-tz'u*), (5) "using different terms for what [Confucius personally] learned about" (*so-wen i-tz'u*), and (6) "using different terms for what [Confucius] had learned through transmitted records" (*so-ch'uan-wen i-tz'u*). These middle three points established that

39. Liu Feng-lu, "Ch'un-ch'iu lun," 3.20a. See also Liu's *Ch'un-ch'iu Kung-yang ching Ho-shih shih-li*, 1285.5a. See *Meng-tzu yin-te*, 25/3B/9. Liu is citing Ssu-ma Ch'ien's *Shih-chi*, vol. 10, pp. 3297–98 (*chüan* 130).

Confucius had encoded the *Annals* to differentiate the epochs of the Chou dynasty.

For the three rulers of Lu during Confucius's own lifetime (*so-chien*), the *Annals* "made its terminology esoteric" (*wei ch'i tz'u*). For the four preceding rulers Confucius had heard about (*so-wen*), the *Annals* "expressed sorrow for the calamities that had occurred" (*t'ung ch'i kuo*). Finally, for the five earliest rulers of Lu about whom Confucius had only read, the *Annals* set aside compassion and gave a dispassionate account (*sha ch'i en*). Unlike K'ung Kuang-sen, Chuang Ts'un-yü in opening remarks for his *Correcting Terms in the Annals*, for example, had already stressed the importance of the "three ages" for grasping Confucius's intent:

> [Confucius] based himself on [the reign of Duke] Ai [494–468 B.C.] and recorded events [back to the reign of Duke] Yin [722–712 B.C.]. With sympathy he pointed to [events deserving] recognition or criticism. His intentions were flexible but firm, his words were [at times] detailed [at other times] sketchy. [Yet] he did not endanger himself with his knowledge. His sense of right did not threaten his superiors. Where [punishment for] a crime had not yet been determined, his terminology served as reference. Rid of chaos and with sprouts of orderly rule, the world gradually reached [the age of] ascending peace. The twelve [reigns of the rulers of Lu] were images [of a pattern]. [The age of] great peace was brought to completion.

The unfolding of the three epochs was expressed through a "politics of language" that also implied a cosmic vision. According to Chuang Ts'un-yü and Liu Feng-lu, that vision represented a historical transition from a time of chaos (*luan*, that is, what Confucius read about), to a time of "ascending peace" (*sheng-p'ing*, that is, what Confucius heard about). These two epochs culminated in a time of "great peace" (*t'ai-p'ing*, that is, what Confucius personally saw). According to Ho Hsiu's version of the "second classification," Confucius had encoded the *Annals* with a vision of "ascending order" that would yield a "great unification" (*ta i-t'ung*).

Tung Chung-shu (upon whom Ho Hsiu's and hence Liu Feng-lu's accounts depended) had already noted that the 242 years (counting to 481 B.C.) of the *Annals* were divided into twelve generations and then subdivided into "three groups" (*san-teng*). According to the *Kung-yang Commentary*, Confucius composed the *Annals* in such a way that particular terminology was applied to each epoch, which demonstrated the historical judgment he had attached to each event. Tung Chung-shu enlarged on the *Kung-yang* view:

> The *Annals* is divided into twelve generations, which fall into three groups: those that were [personally] witnessed [by Confucius], those that he heard of [from elder contemporaries], and those that he heard of through transmitted records. Three [of these twelve generations] were [personally] witnessed, four were heard of [through oral testimony], and five were heard of through transmitted records. . . . Those that were [personally] witnessed comprise 61 years [541–480 B.C.]; that were heard of, 85 years [626–541]; and that were heard of through transmitted records, 96 years [722–626].
>
> Regarding what he witnessed, Confucius used concealing phraseology; regarding what he heard of, he expressed sorrow for calamities; regarding what he heard through transmitted records, he set his compassion aside [and wrote dispassionately]. This is in accordance with the feelings [appropriate to each situation].

On the cosmological level, Tung's theory of three epochs was embedded in a wide-reaching notion of cyclical change (*pien*), which was caused by the complementary interactions of yin and yang and correspondences with the five evolutive phases (*wu-hsing*). Political theory, the world of rulers and officials, was intertwined with cosmology, the workings of heaven. Moral philosophy of pre-Han Confucianism was wedded to the cosmological theories of nonorthodox schools prominent in intellectual life before and during the Former Han dynasty. Tung explained:

> The method of the *Annals* is to cite events of the past in order to explain those of the future. For this reason, when a phenomenon occurs in the world, look to see what comparable events are recorded in the *Annals*; find out the essential meaning of its subtleties and mysteries in order to preserve the significance of the event; and comprehend how it is classified in order to see what causes are implied. Changes wrought in Heaven and on earth, and events that affect a dynasty will then all become crystal clear, with nothing left in doubt.

Cosmological and dynastic change, in Tung Chung-shu's political theory, brought with it the need for institutional change. For each of the three epochs there was an appropriate institutional framework. Institutions like dynasties changed cyclically according to their correspondences to the five phases and yin-yang. The "three unities" (*san-t'ung*) evolved through time and space, bringing along institutional change in their wake:

> Ancient kings, after receiving [Heaven's] mandate, which made them kings [of new dynasties], changed the institutions, titles, and beginning of the year [that had been in force]. Having determined the color for clothing, they announced at the suburban sacrifices [the accession of their dynasty] to Heaven and earth and the multitude of spirits. They offered sacrifices to their

> distant and nearer ancestors, and then proclaimed [the accession of their dynasty] throughout the empire. This [proclamation] was received in their ancestral temples by the feudal lords, who then announced it to the spirits of mountains and streams. Thus there was a single rule [for all] to respond to. . . . This was the way in which Heaven's sequences were made clear.

Third and last of the "three classifications" formulated by both Ho Hsiu and Sung Chün was "differentiating outer barbarians from inner Chinese" (*i wai-nei*). But Ho Hsiu, unlike Sung Chün, set clear boundaries for the content of the last classification through the final three "points": (7) "treat the [Chinese] states as inner" (*nei ch'i kuo*), (8) "treat the various feudal lords as outer" (*wai chu-hsia*), and (9) "treat the various feudal lords as inner and the barbarians as outer" (*nei chu-hsia erh wai i-jung*).[40]

The *Annals* accordingly harbored a cultural vision of concentrically arranged internal and external groups of peoples, which carried over into the tribute system that was at the heart of the Confucian system of foreign affairs. Inner feudal states of the Chou dynasty had priority over their surrounding tribes and peripheral barbarians. This New Text view of foreign affairs had served as the underlying framework for Liu Feng-lu's resolution of the diplomatic conflict with the Vietnamese emissary, summarized above.

According to Liu, the *Annals* implied that political status was culturally, not racially, defined. The transformation from barbarian "outsider" status to Confucian "insider" status was an ongoing process of cultural assimilation based on Chinese models of imperial benevolence. Compared with the hard line taken by Northern and especially Southern Sung Confucians on relations with "outer barbarians," Liu Feng-lu's position as an official of a conquest dynasty was more accommodating.[41]

In the conclusion of his essay, "Discourse on the *Annals*," Liu Feng-lu pointed out that K'ung Kuang-sen's definitions for the "three classifications" and "nine points" lacked the dynamic vision of historical events encoded by Confucius in the *Annals*. By missing these elements in the

40. Liu Feng-lu, "Ch'un-ch'iu lun," 3.19a–19b, and *Liu Li-pu chi* 4.1a–3b. See Chuang Ts'un-yü, *Ch'un-ch'iu cheng-tz'u*, 375.1b. Cf. Li Hsin-lin, "Ch'ing-tai ching chin-wen-hsueh shu," pp. 163–66. See also Su Yü, *Ch'un-ch'iu fan-lu i-cheng*, 1.6b, 7.13a–14b; Kang Woo, *Trois Théories Politiques*, pp. 88–106, esp. 91–93; Tain, "Tung Chung-shu's System of Thought" pp. 173–75, and Fung, *History of Chinese Philosophy*, vol. 1, p. 81. For the *Kung-yang* exposition of the three epochs, see *Ch'un-ch'iu ching-chuan yin-te*, 487/Ai/14.

41. *Liu Li-pu chi*, 4.6a.

Annals, K'ung Kuang-sen had taken sides with the Old Text school despite his work on the *Kung-yang chuan*. Liu concluded: "Without the 'three classifications' and 'nine points,' there is no *Kung-yang* [*Commentary*]. Without the *Kung-yang*, there is no *Spring and Autumn Annals*. What 'esoteric words' are there then?"[42]

LIU FENG-LU ON THE *ANALECTS*

In his refutation of Ch'ien Ta-hsin and correction of K'ung Kuang-sen, Liu Feng-lu was motivated by a desire to restore a sense of grandeur to Confucius. At the same time, Liu saw in the *Kung-yang* view of the *Annals* a historical framework that would be useful in rehabilitating a holistic vision of the Classics that had been largely lost as a result of the cumulative onslaught of Han Learning. To drive home the *Kung-yang* interpretation of the *Annals*, Liu Feng-lu, like his cousin Sung Hsiang-feng, turned to Confucius's *Analects* to confirm the New Text portrait of Confucius as "uncrowned king."

In an 1802 work entitled *Lun-yü shu-Ho* (Discourse on Ho [Hsiu's commentary on the] *Analects*), Liu attempted to reconstruct Ho Hsiu's lost commentary on the *Analects*. While working on Ho's explication of the *Kung-yang Commentary*, Feng-lu had recognized the need to reconstruct the lost commentaries Ho Hsiu had prepared for the other Classics. Ho's biography in the *History of the Later Han Dynasty* (*Hou Han-shu*), Liu noted, made clear that Ho Hsiu "had meticulously studied the Six Classics, and contemporary Confucians could not compare to him." Liu realized that Ho's explication of the *Kung-yang* commentary on the *Annals* was but one piece in a much larger classical framework. Feng-lu thought Ho's notes for the *Analects* would reveal further aspects of the New Text classical legacy.[43]

In many ways, Liu was following the lead of Sung and Ming dynasty Confucians, who had made study of the Four Books (*Analects, Mencius, Great Learning,* and *Doctrine of the Mean*) a necessary complement, if not prerequisite, to understanding the nearly impenetrable Five Classics. Consequently, by using the *Analects* as a "summary of the great meanings in the Six Classics," Liu Feng-lu was applying a Sung Learning tradition to the purposes of New Text Confucianism. The

42. Liu Feng-lu, "Ch'un-ch'iu lun," 3.20a.
43. Liu Feng-lu, *Lun-yü shu-Ho*, 1298.9b–10a. The version in the *Liu Li-pu chi*, although less complete, has also been consulted.

"esoteric words" (*wei-yen*) of Confucius would be confirmed by one of the Four Books.[44]

CONFUCIUS'S SENSE OF MORAL CRISIS

In Liu Feng-lu's hands, episodes in the *Analects* took on esoteric and prophetic meanings that Old Text scholars considered unacceptable. By linking the *Annals* and the *Analects*, Liu Feng-lu, Sung Hsiang-feng, and their follower Tai Wang could now interpret Confucius's life in light of Tung Chung-shu's and Ho Hsiu's New Text portrayal of him as an uncrowned king. For example, Liu interpreted a passage in the *Analects* (dealing with Confucius's sense of cultural crisis in the sixth century B.C.) by using one of the *Kung-yang chuan's* "three classifications"—namely the theory of the "unfolding of three epochs" (*chang san-shih*). The *Analects* stated:

> The Master said, "Use your ears widely but leave out what is doubtful; repeat the rest with caution and you will make few mistakes. Use your eyes widely and leave out what is hazardous; put the rest into practice with caution and you will have few regrets. When in your speech you make few mistakes and in your action you have few regrets, an official career will follow as a matter of course."

This passage discussing "ears," "eyes," and "speech" conveniently permitted Liu Feng-lu to branch off into discussion of Confucius's historiographical designs on the history of Lu and the Chou dynasty based on the "three points": (1) what Confucius had personally seen, (2) what he had personally heard, and (3) what he had read about. The three epochs were confirmed by the *Analects*, Liu thought.[45]

Elsewhere, Liu Feng-lu used a passage in the *Analects* to illustrate Confucius's notion of dynastic change by referring to the New Text doctrine of "using the *Annals* as the basis for the establishment of the new king to come." The passage in the *Analects* read:

> Tzu-chang asked, "Can ten generations hence be known?" The Master said, "The Yin [Shang dynasty] built on the rites of the Hsia. What was added and what was omitted can be known. The Chou built on the rites of Yin. What was added and what was omitted can be known. Should there be a successor to the Chou, even a hundred generations can be known."

44. Ibid., 1298.10a.
45. Liu Feng-lu, *Lun-yü shu-Ho*, 1297.5a. See *Lun-yü yin-te*, 3/2/18, and Lau, *Confucius*, p. 65.

Liu interpreted Confucius's reply as confirmation of the vision in the *Annals* of change according to historical circumstances (see chapter 8) whereby "kingship would be entrusted to the state of Lu" (*wang-Lu*), an obilique reference to a new dynasty that would succeed the Chou. The succeeding dynasty would build on the rites of the Chou, just as the Chou had relied on its predecessor. Again, the *Analects* disclosed the prophetic nature of Confucius's classical vision.[46]

One of the key doctrines in the *Analects*, accepted by all succeeding Confucians, was the "rectification of names" (*cheng-ming*). According to Confucius, the rectification of names referred to a social order in which human behavior corresponded to clearly defined names of social and political functions. Social order demanded a one-to-one correspondence between orderly language and orderly behavior. Confucius had said: "To govern [*cheng*] is to correct [*cheng*]. If you set an example by being correct, who would dare to remain incorrect?" "To govern" and "to correct" were cognates demonstrating the moral prerequisites of political and social life.[47]

For Liu Feng-lu, the rectification of names was best exemplified in the *Annals*. As a vision of society, the *Annals* was encoded with a program of "praise and blame" that criticized the breakdown of the social order and directed attention to the hypocrisy of the feudal rulers, whose ideals were no longer grounded in actual practice. Confucius's historiographical principles in the *Annals*, according to Feng-lu, were a detailed demonstration of the "rectification of names" in the *Analects*. The centrality of ritual in social and political life was a major theme in both the *Kung-yang chuan* and the *Analects*, Liu added.[48]

VISIONS OF EPOCHAL CHANGE

As an analog in the *Analects* to the *Kung-yang* doctrine of "going through three periods of unity," Liu cited the following passage: "The Master said, 'The Chou is resplendent in culture, having before it the example of the two previous dynasties. I am for Chou.'" According to this passage, the Hsia, Shang, and Chou dynasties were models for dynastic change. Each represented a "period of unity" that gave way to its successor. Each successor, however, was indebted to its predecessor for its "cultural substance" (*wen-chih*). Confucius had enunciated in

46. Liu Feng-lu, *Lun-yü shu-Ho*, 1297.5b. See *Lun-yü yin-te*, 4/2/23.
47. *Lun-yü yin-te*, 25/13/3 and 24/12/17. See Lau, *Confucius*, pp. 115, 118.
48. Liu Feng-lu, *Lun-yü shu-Ho*, 1297.6a–6b, and *Liu Li-pu chi*, 4.8a.

both the *Analects* and the *Annals* a theme of epochal change based on dynastic cycles (*hsun-huan*) that served, according to Liu Feng-lu, as models for ten thousand generations.[49]

Liu then applied this vision of epochal change to an elaboration of Confucius's position as an "uncrowned king." Once again, the *Analects* was cited to confirm the *Kung-yang's* apocalyptic vision:

> The border official of I request an audience, saying, "I have never been denied an audience by a gentleman who has come to this place." The followers presented him. When he came out, he said, "What worry have you, gentlemen, about the loss of office? The Empire has long been without the Way. Heaven is about to use your Master as the wooden tongue for a bell."

For Liu Feng-lu, the *Analects* recorded an episode confirming that Confucius "knew that he was about to receive the mandate [to rouse the empire] and accordingly compiled the *Annals* to provide lessons for ten thousand generations." The border official at I had recognized Confucius as the "uncrowned king."[50]

This anticipation of Confucius's future in the *Analects*, Liu thought, was even more explicit in the famous passage affirming Confucius's sense of mission:

> When under siege in K'uang, the Master said, "With King Wen [founder of the Chou dynasty] dead, is not culture invested here in me? If Heaven intends culture to be destroyed, those who come after me will not be able to have any part of it. If Heaven does not intend this culture to be destroyed, then what can the men of K'uang do to me?

In this remarkable passage, Confucius acknowledges his historical mission as the successor to King Wen. The passage dovetailed with the *Kung-yang* claim that Confucius had communicated his cultural mission to his closest disciples. The Classics, then, were the textual vehicle for doctrines transmitted to posterity by disciples who had been orally initiated in the "esoteric words" and "great meanings" by Confucius himself. In other words, the *Analects* represented an oral record of esoteric teachings. Liu concluded: "Whenever the *Analects* and *Annals* mutually correspond to each other, these are all oral transmissions of the 'esoteric words' from the sage [to his disciples]. These were not included in the bamboo and silk versions [of the *Annals*]." Liu claimed

49. Liu, *Lun-yü shu-Ho*, 1297.8b. See *Lun-yü yin-te*, 5/3/14, and Lau, *Confucius*, p. 69.

50. Liu, *Lun-yü shu-Ho*, 1297.9b, and *Liu Li-pu chi*, 2.29a. See *Lun-yü yin-te*, 5/3/24, and Lau, p. 71.

that Ho Hsiu and Tung Chung-shu, by building on the *Kung-yang chuan*, were direct inheritors of this esoteric tradition.[51]

We have seen that the case for Confucius's encoding the *Annals* with his esoteric doctrines of praise and blame was argued during the Han dynasties in light of the abrupt ending to the chronicles of Lu in 481 B.C. with the capture of the *lin*. Tung Chung-shu interpreted the capture of this mythical "unicorn" as the prophetic sign that Confucius had received the mandate of heaven to rule. According to the *Kung-yang* account echoed later by Ho Hsiu and repeated in the *Household Sayings of Confucius*, the sage had himself read into the capture that all hope for the Chou kings was lost. Its mandate to rule had ended:

> A wagoner of Master Shu-sun named Tzu-ch'u-shang was gathering wood in Ta-yeh, when he came upon a *lin*. Because its left foreleg was broken, he brought it back home with him. Ch'u-shang, thinking the discovery inauspicious, threw the *lin* away outside the suburbs. He sent a messenger to inform Confucius saying: "There is a fallow-deer and it is horned. What can it be?" Confucius went to see it and said: "It is a *lin*. Why has it come? Why has it come?" He turned his sleeve and wiped his face. His tears wet his robe. When Shu-sun heard what it was, he had it brought to him. Tzu-kung [one of Confucius's disciples] asked the master why he was crying. Confucius replied: "The *lin* comes only when there is an enlightened monarch [on the throne]. Now it has come when it is not time for it to appear, and it has been injured. This is why I am so afflicted."

Liu Feng-lu found confirmation of this New Text tradition in the *Analects* as well: "The Master said, 'The phoenix [*feng-wu*] does not appear, nor does the river offer up its Chart [that is, the *Ho-t'u*]. I am done for.' "

Because the phoenix and River Chart were auspicious omens, Liu explained that Confucius's sense of hopelessness during the declining years of the Chou was a major element in both the *Annals* and *Analects*. Liu concluded:

> This saying [in the *Analects*] probably occurred after the capture of the *lin* [recorded in the *Annals*] and [before] Confucius's death. This is proof that Heaven was announcing to Confucius that he would soon perish. The Chou house would soon vanish. Sages would no longer appear. That is why Confucius said, "Why has it [the *lin*] come?" And also why he said, "My way has come to an end."

The chronology of the *Analects* and the completion of the *Annals* in

51. Liu, *Lun-yü shu-Ho*, 1297.14b, and *Liu Li-pu chi*, 2.29a. See *Lun-yü yin-te*, 16/9/5, and Lau, *Confucius*, p. 97.

481 B.C. yielded overlapping evidence that late in life Confucius had recognized in natural omens the end of an era.[52]

Ho Hsiu's versions of the *Analects* and *Annals* revealed the apocalyptic context that informed both records of the late Chou period. For Liu Feng-lu, both the *Kung-yang chuan* and the sayings recorded by Confucius's immediate disciples supplied evidence to gainsay the Old Text version of Confucius's life and his historical intent. The *Analects* belonged to the New Text tradition, Liu contended, not the Old Text: "The *Analects* represents a general statement of the great meanings in the Six Classics. It clarifies the subtle words of the *Spring and Autumn Annals*. That is why those who worked on the Old Text [versions] such as [K'ung] An-kuo [156–74? B.C.] and [Cheng] K'ang-ch'eng [i.e., Hsuan] could not master [the *Analects*]."[53]

The portrait of Confucius as a heroic sage and "uncrowned king" had reappeared in Confucian rhetoric and classical theory. Liu Feng-lu had successfully made the transition from his grandfather's diffuse commitment to the *Kung-yang* commentary to New Text Confucianism.

TAI WANG AND CH'EN LI ON CONFUCIUS

Both Tai Wang and Ch'en Li, followers of New Text Confucianism in the mid-nineteenth century, lent support to the reappraisal of Confucius's role in forging the classical vision of state and society. They accepted as accurate Liu Feng-lu's portrait of the Master. They compared the *Analects* and *Annals* topically and chronologically to add further support for the New Text position.

Tai Wang is perhaps better known for his efforts to promote the teachings of the seventeenth-century northern Yen-Li school (after Yen Yuan [1635–1704] and Li Kung [1659–1733]). But in naming his studio "Hall of the Fabulous Unicorn" (*Che-lin-t'ang*), Tai disclosed the personal importance of the *Annals'* prophetic elements—particularly the capture of the *lin*. The studio name was also the title of Tai Wang's collected writings. In following Liu Feng-lu's and Sung Hsiang-feng's efforts to tie together the *Annals* and *Analects*, Tai concentrated on the capture of the *lin* as evidence for the New Text portrayal of Confucius.[54]

52. Liu, *Lun-yü shu-Ho*, 1297.15a. See *Lun-yü yin-te*, 16/9/9, and Lau, p. 97. For the quotation see *K'ung-tzu chia-yü*, p. 42 (*chüan* 4, no. 16). See Kramers, *K'ung-tzu chia-yü*, pp. 86–94, 170–96. See also Legge, *Chinese Classics*, vol. 5, pp. 833–34.

53. Liu Feng-lu, *Lun-yü shu Ho*, in *Liu Li-pu chi*, 2.24a.

54. Tai Wang, *Che-lin-t'ang i-shu*.

To demonstrate that Confucius had received heaven's mandate, Tai cited the celebrated passage in the *Analects*: "The Master said, 'At fifteen I set my heart on learning; at thirty I took my stand; at forty I came to be free from doubts; at fifty I understood Heaven's mandate; at sixty my ear was attuned; at seventy I followed my heart's desire without overstepping the line.'" Tai Wang concluded: "As an uncrowned king, Confucius created law-models and the Five Classics to continue the law-models of Chou for another hundred generations. This is what Heaven had mandated."

Tai added that the reference in the *Analects* to Confucius (551–479 B.C.) at age seventy corresponded to the date (481 B.C.) in the *Annals* when the fabulous *lin* appeared and signaled to the Master that the Chou dynasty was coming to an end. Confucius died two years later in 479 B.C. at age seventy-two. Confucius's claim that "at seventy I followed my heart's desire without overstepping the line" was, according to Tai Wang, full of pathos and vision. A time of chaos was reaching its climax; a time of peace was at hand.[55]

By agreeing with Mencius's assessment that Confucius had compiled the *Annals* to bring order to a time of chaos, Tai Wang linked Mencius's views to the *Kung-yang Commentary*. Tai maintained that the latter was the only commentary on the *Annals* that conferred the appropriate importance to the chronicles of the state of Lu from 722 to 481 B.C. Mencius viewed the *Spring and Autumn Annals* with a seriousness generally accepted by later Confucian scholar-statesmen:

> The world fell into decay, and the Tao became obscure. Perverse speech and oppressive deeds again arose. There were instances of ministers who murdered their rulers, and of sons who murdered their fathers. Confucius was fearful and compiled the *Spring and Autumn Annals*. The *Annals* represents the affairs of the Son of Heaven [that is, the Chou dynasty king as opposed to the rulers of each feudal state]. Therefore, Confucius said: "It will be on account of the *Annals* that people will know me. It will be due to the *Annals* that people will condemn me."

Like Liu Feng-lu and Sung Hsiang-feng, Tai used the "three classifications" and "nine points" as frameworks for reevaluating the *Analects* from the *Kung-yang* point of view. The *Analects* became a window onto a New Text landscape.[56]

55. Tai Wang, *Lun-yü chu*, 2.1b. See *Lun-yü yin-te*, 2/2/4, and Lau, p. 63.

56. Tai Wang, *Lun-yü chu*, 2.1b–5a. For the quotation see *Meng-tzu yin-te*, 25/3B/9. I have modified the translation in Legge, *Four Books*, pp. 676–77. Cf. Lau, *Mencius*, p. 114.

Tai interpreted Confucius's frequent mention of the early Chou dynasty and the legacy of the Duke of Chou as evidence that the Master's vision for the future was drawn from the ideals of the past. Using the state of Lu as the focus for the chronicles in the *Annals*, Confucius, according to Tai Wang, was "entrusting the kingship to Lu" (*wang-Lu*): "Lu encompassed the rituals and music of the four dynasties [Hsia, Shang, Chou, and Lu]. Through the single transformation [from Chou to Lu], the Way can be achieved. The *Annals* accepts Lu as the ordering realm. Consequently, Confucius did not want to distance Lu [in his account]."

Confucius endeavored to make Lu the locus for understanding the principles of kingship and the restoration of ideals enunciated by the Duke of Chou. Both Liu Feng-lu and Tai Wang regarded the *Annals* as a framework for "institutionalizing laws of a new king while awaiting the appearance of later sages."[57]

The chronicles in the *Annals*, by delineating the decline of the Chou dynasty and prophesizing the rise of the Han restoration of the classical unity (*ta i-t'ung*), furnished a framework for political development through the "three unifications" (*san-t'ung*) and cosmological change through the "three epochs" (*san-shih*). Tai added:

> Confucius said if the Way of the Hsia dynasty had not been lost, then the moral power of the Shang dynasty would not have arisen. If the moral power of the Shang dynasty had not been lost, then the moral power of the Chou dynasty could not have arisen. If the moral power of the Chou dynasty had not been lost, then the *Annals* would not have appeared. Once the *Annals* appeared, gentlemen realized that the Way of the Chou had been lost.

To outline a time of chaos, Confucius had compiled the *Annals* as a critique of the contemporary world. To prophesize a time of "great peace" (*t'ai-p'ing*), Confucius had ended the *Annals* with the capture of the *lin*. According to Tai Wang, Confucius "had relied on historical records to compile the *Annals* as the proper guide of kingship."[58]

Although a follower of Liu Feng-lu on the *Kung-yang chuan*, Ch'en Li was also closely associated with the *Tso chuan* specialist Liu Wen-ch'i in Yang-chou. The latter's stress on the *Tso chuan* became a lifelong commitment and a prominent feature of the Lius' subsequent schol-

57. Tai Wang, *Lun-yü chu*, 5.1b, 7.1b, 14.6b. See also Liu Feng-lu's *Ch'un-ch'iu Kung-yang ching Ho-shih shih-li*, 1285.5a, where Liu discusses the "*wang-Lu*" intent of the *Annals*.

58. Tai Wang, *Lun-yü chu*, 2.3b, 3.3b, 11.1a, 15.2b–4a, 20.2b–3a.

arly traditions (see chapter 1). In his 1843 preface to Ch'en Li's collected works, Liu Wen-ch'i praised Ch'en's *Kung-yang* research because it drew heavily on Cheng Hsuan's Later Han classical studies. An Old Text advocate, Liu Wen-ch'i regarded Ch'en Li as superior to both K'ung Kuang-sen and Liu Feng-lu, who had blindly followed Ho Hsiu's superstitions instead of Cheng Hsuan's more reliable commentary.[59]

At first sight, Liu Wen-ch'i's claims would seem to place Ch'en Li more in the Han Learning tradition of Yang-chou than in the Ch'ang-chou New Text revival. If Wen-ch'i were right, then by relying on Cheng Hsuan for his *Kung-yang* studies Ch'en Li was in effect giving an Old Text gloss to a New Text commentary. Moreover, Ch'en had studied under the Han Learning philologist Tuan Yü-ts'ai, whose preference for Old Text recensions of the Five Classics—particularly the authentic portions of the *Documents Classic*—had been criticized by Ch'en Shou-ch'i and Liu Feng-lu. Both scholars had favored New Text recensions.

Upon careful examination, however, Liu Wen-ch'i's efforts to add an Old Text flavor to Ch'en Li's research on the *Kung-yang Commentary* were overstated. In fact, Liu Feng-lu's influence on Ch'en's scholarship went deeper than Liu Wen-ch'i supposed. Ch'en included an essay in his collected writings that explicitly stated his acceptance of Liu Feng-lu's efforts to reestablish the *Kung-yang Commentary* as the proper window through which to view the *Annals*. Entitled "The *Annals*' Theory of Entrusting the Kingship to Lu" (*Ch'un-ch'iu wang-Lu shuo*), Ch'en's essay came out in support of the New Text claim that the *Annals* had been compiled in order to establish the state of Lu as the precursor of the Han unification.[60]

By affirming Confucius as an "uncrowned king" whose *Annals* laid out the "law-models" (*fa*) for the "way of kingship" (*wang-tao*), Ch'en Li unequivocally accepted the *Kung-yang* vision of the *Annals* as first articulated by Chuang Ts'un-yü and then fleshed out by Liu Feng-lu. In Ch'en's mind, "there were no doubts concerning the New Text theory in the *Annals* of entrusting the kingship to Lu." On all of these points, Ch'en Li was affirming a key element in Ho Hsiu's explication of the *Kung-yang chuan* and rejecting Cheng Hsuan's criticism of Ho's posi-

59. Liu Wen-ch'i, "Hsu" (Preface) to Ch'en Li, *Chü-hsi tsa-chu*. See also *Chuan-kao*, no. 4455(1), of Liu Feng-lu.
60. Ch'en Li, *Chü-hsi tsa-chu*, 2.11a–12b.

tion. The capture of the *lin* in 481 B.C. represented heaven's mandate and the *Annals*' calling for a new dynasty.[61]

Following Liu Feng-lu's position, Ch'en Li rejected Old Text efforts to reduce the *Annals* to "historical records of the state of Lu" (*Lu shih-chi*). The *Annals* was more than a chronicle of events. Its "extremely unorthodox theories" (*fei-ch'ang k'e-kuai chih lun*), according to Ch'en, were a sign of the encoded design of the work. Consequently, Ch'en explicitly rejected the Old Text dismissal of Ho Hsiu's commentary. For example, in a work entitled *Kung-yang wen-ta* (Questions and answers on the *Kung-yang Commentary*), Liu Wen-ch'i's maternal uncle and mentor Ling Shu ridiculed Ho Hsiu's views as "the empty words of Han Confucians." Ling Shu, like Liu Wen-ch'i, applied Old Text criteria to the *Kung-yang* tradition. Ch'en Li gainsaid this position and argued instead that the *Annals* "illuminated the esoteric words and great meanings of Confucius's seventy disciples."[62]

Liu Feng-lu's influence on Yang-chou scholars such as Juan Yuan, Ling Shu, and Ch'en Li demonstrates the transmittal of the Ch'ang-chou New Text school to the home ground of Han Learning. Although Liu Wen-ch'i and others sought to downplay the extent of the Ch'ang-chou New Text influence in Yang-chou, it was clear that the Ch'ang-chou scholars had to be taken seriously by the Old Text camp. Subjected to Han learning influence from Yang-chou and Su-chou for much of the eighteenth century, Ch'ang-chou had by the nineteenth century turned the tables: New Text ideas were penetrating Su-chou through Sung Hsiang-feng and Yang-chou via Ch'en Li.[63]

LIU FENG-LU ON THE *TSO CHUAN*

Liu Feng-lu's efforts to restore Confucius to his proper place in the New Text scheme of things were subsequently complemented by his influential assault on the *Tso chuan*. In his controversial but highly acclaimed *Tso-shih ch'un-ch'iu k'ao-cheng* (Evidential analysis of Master Tso's *Spring and Autumn Annals*), published in 1805, Liu Feng-lu made extensive use of *k'ao-cheng* techniques to prove that the so-called *Tso Commentary* originally had not been a commentary on Confucius's *Spring and Autumn Annals*. Liu marshaled his evidence into a carefully

61. Ibid., 2.11a.
62. Ibid., 2.12a–12b. See also Ling Shu, *Kung-yang wen-ta*, 864. 15b–18b. Cf. Hummel et al., eds., *Eminent Chinese*, p. 535.
63. Li Hsin-lin, "Ch'ing-tai ching chin-wen-hsueh shu," pp. 181–87, 296.

arranged series of arguments designed to gradually expose Liu Hsin (45 B.C.–A.D. 23). Liu argued that during Wang Mang's interregnum (A.D. 9–23) Liu Hsin manipulated the *Rituals of Chou* and another text known simply as *Master Tso's Spring and Autumn Annals* (*Tso-shih ch'un-ch'iu*) in order to discredit the New Text school of the Former Han dynasty and to support Wang Mang's usurpation of power, thereby undercutting the credibility of the Old Text position.[64]

THE PROBLEM OF TSO CH'IU-MING

We have noted that attacks on the orthodoxy of the *Tso chuan* were not uncommon. Many had disagreed with Tu Yü (222–284) and Liu Chih-chi (661–721), who during the post-Han and early T'ang periods asserted that the author of the *Tso chuan*, Tso Ch'iu-ming, was a direct disciple of Confucius. Because of Tso's status as Confucius's disciple, Tu Yü and Liu Chih-chi (following Liu Hsin's lead) preferred the *Tso chuan* over the two other commentaries dating from the Former Han dynasty. T'ang commentators such as Tan Chu (725–70) and Chao K'uang (fl. ca. 8th century A.D.) had disputed such stress on the *Tso chuan*, rejecting the claim that Tso Ch'iu-ming had been its author.

Despite additional criticism during the Sung and Ming dynasties, however, the *Tso chuan* remained not only an orthodox commentary to the *Annals* but also the preferred Old Text commentary for interpreting the *Annals* and Confucius's *Analects*. Perhaps the most vitriolic criticism of the *Tso chuan* came from the late Ming Confucian Hao Ching, who was the first to suggest that the original text of the extant commentary had not been assembled to accompany and explicate Confucius's *Annals*. Rather, he contended, the *Tso chuan* had originally been a totally separate historical record, which was later "discovered" and reshaped into a commentary to the *Annals* by Liu Hsin and his followers.[65]

THE USES OF *K'AO-CHENG*

Liu Feng-lu's *Evidential Analysis of Master Tso's Spring and Autumn Annals* picked up where earlier criticism of the *Tso chuan* had left off.

64. Liu Feng-lu, *Tso-shih ch'un-ch'iu k'ao-cheng* (1805 ed.), 1.1b. Liu also linked Liu Hsin to the *Chou-kuan*. See Liu's *Chen kao-huang p'ing*, 1296.12a.

65. See Chang Hsi-t'ang's "Hsu" (Preface) to Liu Feng-lu's *Tso-shih ch'un-ch'iu k'ao-cheng* (Peking, 1932), pp. 17–22. I will refer to both the original 1805 edition and the 1932 reprint.

Unlike his predecessors, however, Liu supported his attack with empirical philological documentation, thus placing for the first time this long-standing debate directly in the *k'ao-cheng* mainstream. Ironically, Liu's models for argumentation were Yen Jo-chü's (1636–1704) influential *Evidential Analysis of the Old Text Documents* (*Shang-shu ku-wen shu-cheng*) and Hui Tung's *Examination of Old Text Documents Classic* (*Ku-wen Shang-shu k'ao*), both of which in the seventeenth and eighteenth centuries provoked heated discussion among Confucian scholars—including, as we have seen, Chuang Ts'un-yü. Liu Feng-lu's work precipitated the same sort of debate in the nineteenth century.[66]

Liu Feng-lu's use of empirical philological criteria to demonstrate the unreliability of the *Tso chuan* reveals the deep imprint left by Han Learning and its research agenda on New Text studies. Liu realized that if New Text studies lacked systematic methods of demonstration, it would not receive scholarly recognition—perhaps fearing the obscurity endured by his grandfather Chuang Ts'un-yü. The latter's scholarship, for instance, lacked the rigorous epistemological leverage that Yen Jo-chü, Hui Tung, and Tai Chen had all championed in their evidential research. Moreover, Liu had learned his research lessons from his uncle Chuang Shu-tsu very well indeed. Liu's exposé forced many scholars to reassess the reliability of the *Tso chuan* as the orthodox commentary on the *Spring and Autumn Annals*.

Liu's *Evidential Analysis of Master Tso's Spring and Autumn Annals* caused a major stir in *k'ao-cheng* circles. For example, Ch'en Li (1810–82—not to be confused with Ch'en Li from Yang-chou discussed above), a leading Cantonese Han Learning scholar, rejected Liu Feng-lu's criticism of the *Tso chuan* and Liu's reliance on Ho Hsiu's interpretations. Ch'en's attack indicated, however, that in the late nineteenth century Liu Feng-lu's thesis was still considered important enough, even in Kuang-chou, to refute.

Included in Juan Yuan's *Ch'ing Exegesis of the Classics*, the *Tso-shih ch'un-ch'iu k'ao-cheng* would eventually influence K'ang Yu-wei directly: he read the *Ch'ing Exegesis* in the 1880s. In addition, Liu Feng-lu effectively opened the door to a series of later studies by Wei Yuan, Liao P'ing (1852–1932), and K'ang Yu-wei, among others, which would link Liu Hsin to the forging of other Old Text versions of the Classics, including the Old Text *Documents* and the *Rituals of Chou*. The rise of New Text scholarship in Kuang-chou via Liao P'ing and K'ang Yu-wei in the 1890s, therefore, cannot be adequately explained without taking

66. Tai Wang, "Liu hsien-sheng hsing-chuang," 1.31b. See also *Chuan-kao*, no. 4455(1), of Liu Feng-lu.

into consideration Liu Feng-lu's research and writings on the *Tso chuan*.[67]

LIU HSIN AS MASTER FORGER

Liu Feng-lu was the first to argue and then demonstrate that Liu Hsin had manipulated a separate text entitled the *Tso-shih ch'un-ch'iu* (Master Tso's *Spring and Autumn Annals*) (mentioned by Ssu-ma Ch'ien in his *Records of the Grand Historian* [*Shih-chi*]) with the intention of overturning the *Kung-yang Commentary*. Feng-lu asserted that the *Tso chuan* was originally not a commentary to Confucius's *Annals* at all. Hao Ching had already said as much in the seventeenth century. But Liu pushed Hao's position further, accusing Liu Hsin of deliberately extracting the *Tso chuan* from a stylistically and grammatically similar "sister text" known as the *Kuo-yü* (Discourses of the States) and unscrupulously using it as an orthodox commentary to subvert the New Text Classics of the Former Han dynasty. When added to Yen Jo-chü's and Hui Tung's research on the Old Text *Documents*—a topic Liu Feng-lu himself focused on in his other research—Liu had added still more doubt concerning the troubling origins of the Old Text versions of the Classics accepted by Han Learning advocates.[68]

Liu Feng-lu boldly declared and then proved what had before only been suspected: Liu Hsin stood accused of "forgery" (*tso-wei*) and of "overturning the Five Classics and causing [succeeding] scholars to be deluded." Liu Feng-lu's tour de force proved that Liu Hsin had subverted the "*Kung-yang* tradition of meanings and precedents" in favor of the Old Text Classics. Feng-lu wrote:

> When I was twelve, I read *Master Tso's Spring and Autumn Annals* and was suspicious of the correctness of its historiographical methods [*shu-fa*] because it left out many of the "great meanings" [in the *Annals*]. I went on to read Kung-yang [Kao's] and Master Tung [Chung-shu's] accounts and realized that with regard to the *Annals* it was not a record of events. Nor was it necessary to take Master Tso's [commentary] into account in order to understand [the *Annals*].

Liu added that he had exchanged views with his cousin Sung Hsiang-feng on the matter. After Liu answered Sung's query concerning the

67. Hsu Shih-ch'ang, *Ch'ing-Ju hsueh-an*, 174.29a–32a. See also my "Hsueh-hai T'ang," pp. 51–82. Cf. Hao Chang, *Chinese Intellectuals in Crisis*, pp. 33–34.

68. Liu Feng-lu, *Tso-shih ch'un-ch'iu k'ao-cheng* (1805), 1.1a–ab, 1.8b. See Tai Wang, "Liu hsien-sheng hsing-chuang," 1.31b–32a. See also Chang Hsi-t'ang's "Hsu" (Preface) to Liu Feng-lu, *Tso-shih ch'un-ch'iu k'ao-cheng*, pp. 28–29. For later works drawing on Liu Feng-lu, see my "Hsueh-hai T'ang," pp. 65–71. Cf. Ssu-ma Ch'ien, *Shih-chi*, vol. 2, pp. 509–510 (*chüan* 14).

superiority of the *Kung-yang Commentary* to both the *Ku-liang* and *Tso* commentaries, Sung is said to have declared: "You not only are good at ordering the *Kung-yang*, but in addition you can be regarded as a loyal servant of Master Tso." By rejecting the link between the *Tso chuan* and the *Annals*, Liu Feng-lu restored the former to its proper status as an independent historical account of the Warring States period.[69]

To verify Liu Hsin's manipulation of the *Tso chuan* for Wang Mang's political purposes, Liu Feng-lu presented a case-by-case discussion of the interpolations in the *Tso chuan* that revealed Liu Hsin as a forger. Often the text suddenly stated "the gentleman says" (*chün-tzu yueh*). For Liu Feng-lu, this repeated and forced pattern revealed precisely where Liu Hsin and his followers introduced interpolations to give the text the appearance of a commentary. Feng-lu added that Chu Hsi had also suspected this forced pattern, concluding that this may have contributed to Chu's low esteem for the *Annals*.[70]

NEW TEXT AS CONFUCIAN ORTHODOXY

It is interesting that throughout his account, Liu Feng-lu cited Chu Hsi's earlier doubts about the *Annals*. Yen Jo-chü and other *k'ao-cheng* scholars frequently referred to Chu Hsi in order to give their textual criticisms orthodox support. Like them, Liu Feng-lu was drawing on the main voice of the Sung Learning orthodoxy to strengthen his side in the New Text–Old Text controversy. According to Liu, the *Tso chuan* represented a straightforward historical record that missed the moral import of the chronicles included in the *Annals*.

In contrast to the Tso account, the *Kung-yang Commentary* enunciated principles of praise and blame and affirmed proper ritual. Liu Feng-lu contended that these marked the moral vision bequeathed by Confucius to posterity. It was as if Liu Feng-lu saw in New Text Confucianism the moral strength that would overcome the corrosive effects of Old Text Han Learning and piecemeal philological studies, which by dismissing the latter as a Buddho-Taoist smokescreen had taken their toll on the moral philosophy of Sung Learning.[71]

69. Liu Feng-lu, *Tso-shih ch'un-ch'iu k'ao-cheng* (1805), 1.1b–2a. See also Ch'ien Hsuan-t'ung's "Shu-hou," (Afterword) to the 1932 reissue of Liu Feng-lu, *Tso-shih ch'un-ch'iu k'ao-cheng*, pp. 1–2.

70. Liu Feng-lu, *Tso-shih ch'un-ch'iu k'ao-cheng* (1805), 1.2b–3a.

71. Ibid., 1.4a, 4b, 1.5b. Cf. my *Philosophy to Philology*, p. 40.

For collateral evidence, Liu Feng-lu relied principally on accounts included in Ssu-ma Ch'ien's *Records of the Grand Historian*. Despite some later interpolations, the *Shih-chi* was largely a Former Han dynasty work not subject to the Old Text cloud of forgeries that plagued Later Han and T'ang dynasty classical studies. Many scholars linked Ssu-ma Ch'ien to the Former Han New Text orthodoxy because of his close contacts with his friend and colleague Tung Chung-shu. Moreover, Ssu-ma Ch'ien regarded his own historical account as a sequel to Confucius's *Annals*. In the late nineteenth and early twentieth centuries, a tug of war broke out over Ssu-ma Ch'ien, with both New Text and Old Text advocates claiming him as a partisan of their polarized positions.

In his admiring biography of Confucius, Ssu-ma Ch'ien traced the roots of the historiographical tradition directly back to judgments in the *Annals*:

> Then, utilizing historical records, [Confucius] compiled the *Annals*, going back to Duke Yin [ruler of Lu, 722–712 B.C.] and coming down to the fourteenth year of Duke Ai [481 B.C.], [a total of] twelve dukes. [In the *Annals*], he took [the state of] Lu as his standard, kept close to the Chou [dynasty], dealt with Yin [that is, the Shang dynasty] as an ancient time, and propagated [models from] the Three Dynasties. His style was concise, but his meaning rich. Thus, when the rulers of Wu and Yueh [improperly] styled themselves as "Kings," the *Annals* reproved them by giving them [their proper title of] "Viscount." And at the meeting of Chien-tu [in 632 B.C.], when the Chou King had actually been ordered to attend [by Duke Wen of Chin], the *Annals* avoided mentioning this fact by saying: "The celestial king went hunting at Ho-yang." [Confucius] offered examples of this sort to serve as rules for his own age. And if later there are kings who will draw on the intent behind the praise and blame, so that the meaning of the *Annals* becomes widely known, then rebellious subjects and criminals in the world will be seized with terror.[72]

Liu Feng-lu relied on the *Shih-chi* especially to demonstrate that the claims linking Tso Ch'iu-ming to the *Tso chuan* were patently false. Here, Feng-lu used Ssu-ma Ch'ien to prove the falseness of Liu Hsin's claim that Tso Ch'iu-ming had based his commentary directly on the Master's teachings. Because the *Shih-chi* did not mention Tso as one of Confucius's disciples—mentioning instead only a work entitled *Master Tso's Spring and Autumn Annals*, with no indication that it was a commentary to Confucius's *Annals*—Liu Feng-lu made this "argument

72. Liu Feng-lu, *Tso-shih ch'un-ch'iu k'ao-cheng* (1805), 2.1a–2b, 2b–4a. See also Ssu-ma Ch'ien, *Shih-chi*, vol. 6, p. 1943 (*chüan* 47), and Fung Yu-lan, *History of Chinese Philosophy*, vol. 1, 45–46.

based on silence" a major pillar of his *k'ao-cheng* inquiry. Later Han accounts in the *History of the Later Han Dynasty* and elsewhere were suspicious sources because, Liu said, they had unquestioningly accepted Old Text claims for the legitimacy of the *Tso chuan* fabricated after Ssu-ma Ch'ien by Liu Hsin.[73]

According to twentieth-century accounts prepared by distinguished classical scholars such as Liang Ch'i-ch'ao, Ku Chieh-kang, Chang Hsi-t'ang, and Ch'ien Hsuan-t'ung, Liu Feng-lu's *Evidential Analysis of Master Tso's Spring and Autumn Annals* stood alone alongside Yen Jo-chü's *Evidential Analysis of the Old Text Documents Classic* as seminal *k'ao-cheng* studies that prepared the way for total reconsideration of the historical status of the classical legacy after the 1911 Revolution. With the aid of their hindsight, we can properly evaluate how the doubting of antiquity in the twentieth century drew on earlier evidential research. We should add, however, that this modern result was not what Liu Feng-lu, any more than Yen Jo-chü, had intended.

Liu Feng-lu like his grandfather Chuang Ts'un-yü, could see that the fundamentalist thrust behind the Han Learning "return to the ancients" (*fu-ku*) threatened to demolish the Sung Learning orthodoxy without providing an alternative moral order and certainty. Although Liu Feng-lu's assault on the Old Text Han Learning position helped to undermine the entire Confucian legacy, his intent was actually the opposite. Liu thought that New Text teachings, drawn from Chuang Ts'un-yü's turn to *Kung-yang* Confucianism, would fill the vacuum left by eighteenth-century *k'ao-cheng*. The first of all Confucianisms, the Former Han New Text orthodoxy, would (Liu hoped) replace Later Han Old Text Han Learning.[74]

LIU FENG-LU ON HO HSIU

After using *k'ao-cheng* techniques to discredit the Old Text position on the *Annals*, Liu Feng-lu then proceeded to reconstruct the New Text theoretical position on the *Annals* and *Kung-yang Commentary*. With more precision and sophistication than that demonstrated by his predecessors, Liu rebuilt the *Kung-yang* "schools system" of Ho Hsiu, the

73. Liu Feng-lu, *Tso-shih ch'un-ch'iu k'ao-cheng*, 2.4b–7a. On Ssu-ma Ch'ien see n. 68 above.

74. Chang Hsi-t'ang's "Hsu" (Preface) to Liu Feng-lu, *Tso-shih ch'un-ch'iu k'ao-cheng*, pp. 1–56, and Ch'ien Hsuan-t'ung, "Shu-hou" (Afterward) to Liu Feng-lu, *Tso-shih ch'un-ch'iu k'ao-cheng*, pp. 1–40. For a discussion see my *Philosophy to Philology*, pp. 29–32.

only remaining reliable witness to *Kung-yang* interpretation from the Later Han. Liu's reconstruction took several forms. Reviewing the published versions of the Ho Hsiu vs. Cheng Hsuan debates of the second century A.D., Liu analyzed Cheng Hsuan's role in the eventual loss of the New Text tradition.

To champion Ho Hsiu meant in effect to attack Cheng Hsuan, the patron saint of Ch'ing dynasty Han Learning. Liu Feng-lu accordingly prepared prefaces for Ho Hsiu's critiques of the *Ku-liang* and *Tso* commentaries, to which Cheng Hsuan had written famous rejoinders. Liu's purpose was straightforward: "To spread the theories enunciated by Master Ho [Hsiu] in his *Disabling Diseases of Ku-liang* [*Ku-liang fei-chi*] and to counter the rebuttal prepared by Master Cheng [Hsuan]." In his defense of Ho Hsiu's *Incurability of Master Tso* (*Tso-shih kao-huang*), Feng-lu stressed that his aim was not to refute the historical accuracy or usefulness of the *Tso chuan*. Rather, as he wrote, "I want to restore to the *Annals* what is its due, and restore to Master Tso's account what it is due." By reopening the Ho Hsiu vs. Cheng Hsuan debate, Liu was unequivocally reasserting the priority of New Text over Old Text for the Han Learning movement.[75]

In the first of a series of works on Ho Hsiu's *Explication of the Kung-yang Commentary*, Liu Feng-lu attempted to show why Ho Hsiu's views were superior to Cheng Hsuan's. Liu concluded:

> [Cheng] K'ang-ch'eng [i.e., Hsuan] worked on all three commentaries [on the *Annals*] simultaneously. Therefore, he was not well-versed in the Classic itself. There is only one extant section one can cite from his *Expose the Defender* [that is, "expose" Ho Hsiu's defense of the *Kung-yang*], but it draws mainly from Master Tso. That Cheng's research on Mister Tung [Chung-shu] and Hu-wu Sheng was not very penetrating can be easily ascertained [from this one section].

As a contemporary scholar who "cherished the past and sought the truth" (*hao-ku ch'iu-shih*), Liu Feng-lu made clear that his dismissal of Cheng Hsuan did not overturn Han Learning but improved it. The Former Han New Text tradition, both because of its antiquity and its stress on moral theory, was superior to Cheng Hsuan's classical philology of the Later Han.[76]

After summarily dismissing the patron saint of Han Learning, Liu Feng-lu turned in 1805 to a complete articulation of Ho Hsiu's position

75. *Liu Li-pu chi*, 3.24a–25a, 3.26a–26b.

76. See Liu Feng-lu's "Hsu" (Preface) to his *Ch'un-ch'iu Kung-yang chieh-ku ch'ien*, 1290.1a. See also *Liu Li-pu chi*, 3.28b.

in Liu's provocative *Master Ho [Hsiu's] Explication of the Precedents in the Kung-yang Commentary to the Annals*. Liu saw his own efforts in light of the Han Learning agenda for research. What Hui Tung had accomplished for the reconstruction of Han dynasty *I-ching* studies (see chapter 4), Liu hoped to achieve for Han dynasty studies of the *Spring and Autumn Annals*, which meant restoring Ho Hsiu to his proper place of eminence in the "schools system" of Later Han classical studies.

Liu's stress on Ho Hsiu and the Former Han transmission of Tung Chung-shu's New Text teachings on the *Annals* was exactly parallel, Liu thought, to the success of Hui Tung and Chang Hui-yen in rescuing the *Change Classic* from its later misrepresentations, which they accomplished by stressing the *I-hsueh* of Yü Fan. In fact, Chang Hui-yen's research on the *Change* induced Liu to carry out research on the Yü Fan recension of the *Change Classic* as well. The Tung Chung-shu and Ho Hsiu axis for New Text Confucianism, Liu asserted, was also central for understanding the *I-ching*. Moreover, Liu argued the New Text doctrines presented in the *Annals* were a prerequisite for comprehending fully the *Change Classic*: "Consequently, before one can discuss the *Change*, one must first understand the *Annals*."

The *Change* encompassed ceremonies and rituals; the *Annals* used its mastery of ceremony and ritual from the "three dynasties" [Hsia, Shang, and Chou—that is, the "three unifications"] to clarify requirements of statecraft. Like his grandfather Chuang Ts'un-yü, Liu Feng-lu believed the *Annals* and *Change* were interlocking classics that opened up the thought world of the ancient sage-kings.[77]

Liu Feng-lu's use of the term *shih-li* (explication of precedents) in the title of his reconstruction of Ho Hsiu's position reveals the continuing impact of Tu Yü's precedent-based approach for interpreting the *Annals*, first seen in Tu's *Ch'un-ch'iu shih-li*. Chuang Ts'un-yü also grappled, as we have seen, with this Old Text tradition, bringing censure of Tu Yü's precedent-based analysis into the eighteenth century. Chuang made "precedents" (*li*) less important than "key points" (*yao-chih*) in his attempt to promote *Kung-yang* Confucianism. Although Liu Feng-lu consciously mimicked Tu Yü's title in that of his own study, it was clear nonetheless that "Ho Hsiu's explication of precedents"

77. Liu Feng-lu, *Ch'un-ch'iu Kung-yang ching Ho-shih shih-li*, 1280.2a–3a, 1280.9b. See also Liu Feng-lu's "Hsu" (Preface) to his *Ch'un-ch'iu Kung-yang ching Ho-shih shih-li*, pp. 2a–3a, which comes just before *chüan* 1280. On Liu's links to Chang Hui-yen's *I-hsueh*, see *Liu Li-pu chi*, 2.15a–15b, and Li Chao-lo's biography of Liu Feng-lu in Li's *Yang-i-chai wen-chi*, 14.1a–3a.

would, in Liu's account, replace the list of precedents prepared by Tu Yü. Liu put new wine in an old bottle. The "precedents-based" tradition was adapted to a New Text agenda.

Accordingly, Liu's analysis equated "precedents" (*li*) with the "three classifications" and "nine points" that Ho Hsiu had used to elucidate the *Kung-yang Commentary*. Feng-lu, following Chuang Ts'un-yü, streamlined Tu Yü's tedious list of historical precedents culled from the *Tso chuan* by drawing on New Text theory rather than Old Text historiography. Liu's work represented in part an interesting compromise between Tu Yü's precedent-based interpretation and its rejection by Confucians such as Yao Chi-heng (1647–1715?), who had questioned the appropriateness of the "precedent tradition." Among the thirty precedents assembled by Liu Feng-lu, the "three classifications" took priority. The content of precedents had changed from Old Text historiography based on the *Tso chuan* to New Text "great principles" drawn from the *Kung-yang Commentary*.[78]

On the "three periods of unity" (*san-t'ung*), for instance, Liu moved back and forth from the *Annals* to the *Change Classic* to develop his notion of a precedent. His discussion affirmed epochal change and reform of political institutions. The sages, Liu maintained, had accented statecraft concerns in their bequeathed teachings. As precedents, these concerns, Liu felt, were principally articulated in the *Annals* and *Change* classics. Political change (*pien*) was inherent in the transition from the Shang to Chou dynasties. Moreover, the *Annals* represented the third stage of that unity through the state of Lu, the harbinger for the Han unification.

As Lu's "uncrowned king," Confucius was the mouthpiece for this third stage. A "precedent" in Tu Yü's terms had implied a vision of stasis. The present was held up for comparison with the unchanging ideals of antiquity. In Liu Feng-lu's hands, this vision of antiquity as the repository for inert precedents was radically transformed. Instead, precedents became part of a vision of future change and reform. The past was held up to the present as a model of foresight and creative potential. The present became the locus for epochal change.[79]

An additional theme that Liu explored in his reconstruction of Ho Hsiu's *Kung-yang* teachings was the relation between the *Annals* and

78. See the table of contents to Liu Feng-lu's *Ch'un-ch'iu Kung-yang ching Ho-shih shih-li*.

79. Liu Feng-lu, *Ch'un-ch'iu Kung-yang ching Ho-shih shih-li*, 1280.5a–9b.

laws (*fa*). Since the Han dynasties both Confucius and the Duke of Chou had at times been perceived as lawgivers. The New Text portrait of Confucius as judge in fact complemented the Old Text portrayal in the *Rituals of Chou* of the Duke of Chou and his model authoritarian government—a portrayal dating from the early Chou dynasty. It is generally recognized that the *Rituals of Chou*, because of its textual links to pre-Han Legalist strains in administrative theory and practice, emphasized the use of laws as a system of rewards and punishments to control wayward elements in society.

The apocrypha and New Text image of Confucius as the "creator of laws," however, seems out of place, given our usual understanding of the Confucian stress on morality and ritual. Although Mencius said that Confucius had served as police commissioner in his native Lu, we normally assume that Confucius regarded law as at best a necessary evil. This conventional perspective underestimates, however, the decisive part that Legalism played in the formation of imperial Confucianism during the Former Han dynasty. The *Kung-yang Commentary* in particular paid special attention to the presence in the *Spring and Autumn Annals* of a systematic terminological and stylistic framework for making legal judgments. In chapter 8 we shall examine how Liu Feng-lu's revival of New Text Confucianism brought with it recognition of the role of the Confucian Classics in legal discourse during the Han dynasties.[80]

80. *Meng-tzu yin-te*, 48/6B/6, and Lau, *Mencius*, p. 176.

EIGHT

Legalism and New Text Confucianism

The reconstruction of *Kung-yang* Confucianism in late-eighteenth-century Ch'ang-chou brought in its wake a rediscovery of the Former Han synthesis of rituals and laws. Liu Feng-lu's research in particular revealed the link between early Confucian notions of political reform and the scope of laws and punishments in classical Legalism. The implications of this link between Legalism and *Kung-yang* Confucianism were further developed by Wei Yuan, Kung Tzu-chen, and, ultimately, late Ch'ing reformers.

LAWS AND RITUALS

Ritual beliefs and their practice were tied to everyday objectives and referents in imperial China. Rituals and their links to state laws were mutually defensible and operationally coherent within their social and political context. Brian E. McKnight notes that, "to the traditional Chinese, as to their counterparts elsewhere, the ritualized aspects of behavior were not just tasteful and aesthetically pleasing ways to perform essentially secular acts, they were essential to the efficacy of the acts."[1]

We have seen that Ssu-ma Ch'ien, grand historian during the reign of Emperor Wu (r. 140–87 B.C.) and a contemporary of Tung Chung-shu,

1. McKnight, "Specifications (*shih*) of Sung China," p. 329. See also Kertzer, *Ritual, Politics, and Power*, pp. 35–56.

modeled his own historical writings after Confucius's *Spring and Autumn Annals*. Ssu-ma Ch'ien particularly emphasized the *Annals* as the locus of correct ritual. Historiography, then, was the elucidation of proper social behavior, which Confucius had encoded as correct ritual in his *Annals*:

> I heard Master Tung [Chung-shu] say: "The way of the Chou [dynasty] declined and disappeared. When Confucius was the police commissioner of Lu, the feudal lords all maligned him, and the grandees obstructed his efforts. Confucius knew that [his] words would not be used and that the Way could not be put into practice. [Confucius] took the rights and wrongs of 242 years as the model for ceremonial behavior, by which he criticized the Son of Heaven, caused the feudal lords to retreat, and punished the grandees. All this was done to manifest the affairs of the ruler and that's all." Confucius said: "Rather than record [right and wrong] in empty words, it is better to bring [such judgments] to the level of observation through the penetrating clarity of the performance of [specific] tasks." . . .
>
> Therefore, one who has [control of] the state must understand the *Spring and Autumn Annals*. . . . The servants of the people [also] must know the *Annals*. . . . When the lessons of rituals and proper behavior are not mastered, then rulers are not [true] rulers, officials are not [true] officials, fathers are not [true] fathers, and sons are not [true] sons. . . . The affairs [recorded] in the *Annals* are the great source of rituals and proper behavior. Rituals prevent [improprieties] before they appear; laws deal with [improprieties] after the fact. It is easy to see what laws are used for, but it is hard to understand what rituals prevent from happening.[2]

Historiography reflected on and was informed by ritualized behavior. Confucian ritual was the conduct of moral theory; law was its complement when the rituals were neglected and redress was required. Law was the last resort for obtaining what could not otherwise be accomplished through ritual. Unlike Confucius in the *Annals*, Ssu-ma Ch'ien saved his moral judgments for the last sections of his chapters. But in essence he emulated Confucius's *Spring and Autumn Annals* to create his *Records of the Grand Historian*. Right acts—that is, acts based on proper ceremony and ritual—were praised; wrong acts—that is, transgressions of proper rituals—were criticized. A coherent moral worldview closely linked to ritual practice was the result.[3]

Although he championed the *Annals* and praised Tung Chung-shu as

2. Ssu-ma Ch'ien, *Shih-chi*, vol. 10, pp. 3297–98 (*chüan* 130). See Yang Hsiang-k'uei, *Ching-shih-chai*, pp. 113–38, where Yang links Ssu-ma Ch'ien to the Former Han New Text school of Tung Chung-shu. Liu Shih-p'ei (1884–1919) tied Ssu-ma Ch'ien to the Old Text position. Cf. Ojima, *Chūgoku no shakai shisō*, pp. 343–47.

3. McKnight, "Specifications (*shih*) of Sung China," p. 329, and Geertz, "Ideology as a Cultural System," p. 61.

the "great ancestor of ritual meanings," Liu Feng-lu dealt with this delicate issue of laws in the Confucian state in an intriguing way. A man who eventually became a specialist on rituals for the Ministry of Rites (see chapter 7), Liu acknowledged the efficacy of laws and their roots in the sages' teachings. In addition, he maintained that the essence of laws lay in rituals:

> Some [that is, Shao Yung, 1011–77] say the *Annals* is the "penal code of the sages." Others say "the Five Classics having the *Annals* among them is analogous to penal laws accommodating judgments and orders." Yet Master Tung [Chung-shu] of Wen-ch'eng alone referred to [the *Annals*] as the "ancestor of ritual meanings." Why is that?
>
> It is likely that rituals are the essence of punishments. If one lets loose of rituals and instead employs punishments, that means the Way has no middle ground on which to stand. Therefore, punishments are an important subclassification of rituals.[4]

Liu reduced the theoretical basis for laws to a question of ritual while affirming the use of laws themselves as a legacy of the classical tradition. Power (*ch'üan*) derived its authority and hence its legitimation from the Classics. Ritual as symbolic power had precedence over the exercise of power through laws:

> Therefore, it would be better to take the *Annals* as a means to reconstruct the rituals of the Three Dynasties than to take the *Annals* as the basis for deciding Ch'in [221–207 B.C.] and Han [dynasty] court cases. There must be some means to achieve a balance between the essence and dross and between the weighty and light [in legal judgments].

For Liu Feng-lu, justice was central to the *Spring and Autumn Annals*. Ritual remained the ideal, but laws were clearly essential in the classical ordering bequeathed by the Han state.[5]

PENAL LAW AND THE *ANNALS*

Penal law in Confucianism did not stand alone, as it had for the ancient Legalists. Formulated simply as an instrument of government, laws in pre-Han Legalism were opposed to rituals championed by Confucius and his followers. By grounding the application of law in the theory of ritual—what has been described as the "Confucianization of law"—Han Confucians fled the amoral implications of Legalism to higher

4. Liu Feng-lu, *Ch'un-ch'iu Kung-yang ching Ho-shih shih-li*, 1280.10a, 1284.1a–14a.
5. Ibid., 1284.14a–14b.

moral ground. Tension between rituals and laws in the Confucian imperium reflected an ongoing effort to close the gap between Confucian and Legalist contributions to the formation of the Confucian state and the ideology supporting its legitimacy.[6]

Ch'ing New Text scholars rediscovered that the *Annals*, particularly the *Kung-yang chuan*, were employed together in Han times to resolve the dilemma of laws versus rituals. During the Former and Later Han dynasties, historical precedents in the *Spring and Autumn Annals* were used to make legal decisions. To decide cases (*chueh-shih*) on the basis of Confucius's *Annals* meant that Han Confucians such as Tung Chung-shu had used the *Kung-yang chuan* to evaluate legal cases in their own day. It was assumed that Confucius's praise-and-blame (*pao-pien*) position encoded in the *Annals* could be utilized "to compare case decisions" (*chueh-shih pi*) and thereby to provide standards for judgments of later, analogous cases.

Serving as jurisprudential examples, the analogized (*pi*) case decisions illustrated, in Leon Vandermeersch's words, "how regulative provisions were extended to cover situations which the regulations themselves had not anticipated." When such jurisprudential precedents took on normative value and were no longer mere instances, they were referred to as *k'e* (judicial classifications). Penal law (*lü*), as we know, endured as a vital element in dynasties that succeeded the Han. Its roots went back, however, to a Legalist-Confucian synthesis that enabled Han Confucians to use the "meanings of the Classics" (*ching-i*) as the guide for legal interpretation and case analogizing.[7]

Shao Yung's famous reference to the *Annals* as the "penal code of the sages" indicates how influential the *Annals* had been in the Confucian imperium. What is interesting in light of our focus here on New Text Confucianism is the degree to which key terminology overlapped between Ho Hsiu's *san-k'e chiu-chih* (three classifications and nine points) and their corresponding use as legal expressions. In fact, the "nine points" exemplified the "three classifications" for *Kung-yang* theory in much the same way that substatutes (*t'iao-li*) stood as subdivisions of "legal classifications" (*k'e*).[8]

6. See Ch'en Huan (d. 1863), *Kung-yang i-li k'ao-cheng*, for a discussion of the link between laws and ritual. Cf. Vandermeersch, "Chinese Conception of the Law," pp. 14–15, and Ebrey, "Family in the Sung Dynasty," p. 234. Ebrey describes an adoption case during the Southern Sung that referred to the *Annals* for a precedent.

7. Vandermeersch, "Chinese Conception of the Law," pp. 17–18.

8. Chu I-tsun, *Ching-i k'ao*, 182.5a. See also Vandermeersch, "Chinese Conception of the Law," pp. 8–9.

In a Yuan dynasty analysis of the *Annals* that heavily influenced Chuang Ts'un-yü, Chao Fang described the "eight precedents" he detected in Confucius's chronicles in largely legal terms. For Chao, legal judgments and historical judgments were analogous (*pi-shih*). The first of the *Annals'* precedents in Chao's account, for example, were *ts'e-shu*, which during the Han were "imperial edicts." We might add that rescripts by the emperor (*chih*) in the Han imperial state used the same term employed by Chuang Ts'un-yü when he referred to the "key points" (*yao-chih*) in the *Annals*. The latter were also analogized from Ho Hsiu's "nine points."[9]

The influence of Legalism on Confucianism was most obvious in the Hsun-tzu (fl. ca 238 B.C.) wing of Confucianism prior to the Han, which opposed the Mencian school for its overly optimistic appraisal of human nature. Hsun-tzu's ideas exercised profound influence on the development of Legalism because two of the latter's major spokesmen, Han Fei and Li Ssu, had studied under Hsun-tzu.

Typically neglected, however, is the equally important influence Legalism had on later imperial Confucianism from the T'ang dynasty on. In fact, what T'ung-tsu Ch'ü has rightly called the "Confucianization of law" during the Han dynasties (after the Legalist excesses of the Ch'in dynasty) could just as easily be called the "Legalization of Confucianism." Legalization was most apparent in the New Text school of the Former Han. The *Kung-yang* tradition, in part, traced its lineage back to Hsun-tzu. In many respects Tung Chung-shu's legal thought represented an adaptation of Hsun-tzu's opposition to Mencius. The preeminence of law in the *Kung-yang chuan* was one end of a spectrum whose other end was the centrality of ritual.[10]

During the Former Han dynasty, New Text guidelines for "praise and blame" in the *Spring and Autumn Annals* were governed by a delicate balance between ritual (*li*) and law (*fa*). To the degree that legal judgments were interpreted on the basis of the *Annals*, these judgments were inseparable from "exemplifications of rituals." The universalism of law (its refusal to make exceptions) was tempered by the particularism of rituals (which insist on differential treatment according to personal status, relationship, and social circumstance). Judgments of

9. *Ssu-k'u ch'üan-shu tsung-mu*, 28.15a–15b. See also Li Hsin-lin, "Ch'ing-tai ching chin-wen-hsueh shu," p. 196.

10. Ch'ü, *Law and Society*, p. 278. See also Fung, *History of Chinese Philosophy*, vol. 1, pp. 279–336, and Bodde and Morris, *Law in Imperial China*, pp. 23–32. For the New Text link to Hsun-tzu see Liu Shih-p'ei, *Ch'ün-ching ta-i hsiang-t'ung lun*, pp. 21a–25b. See also Yang Hsiang-k'uei, *Ching-shih-chai hsueh-shu wen-chi*, pp. 87–97.

the *Kung-yang chuan*, for instance, were made through the formulaic expression : "This is not ritually sanctioned" (*fei li yeh*).[11]

THE *ANNALS* AND LEGAL CASES

Legalism emphasized a strictness in rewards and punishments that was easily assimilated into the *Annals'* praise-and-blame tradition. In deciding legal cases (*chueh-shih*) on the basis of precedents (*li*) in the *Annals*, Han Confucians had to employ not only the *Annals'* historiographical standards but also its behavioral standards as well. One Han casebook, now lost, was reputed to contain 13,472 cases decided according to classical precedents.

Tung Chung-shu himself produced a legal tract entitled *Kung-yang Tung Chung-shu chih-yü* (Tung Chung-shu's judgments of cases according to the *Kung-yang Commentary*), which reportedly included descriptions of 232 actual legal cases decided according to precedents in the *Annals*. Only a few of these descriptions have survived. Tung's tract was probably one of the earliest casebooks composed in imperial China and was directly linked to the Former Han New Text agenda. On one case, Tung Chung-shu observed:

> At the time, there were those who questioned the verdict saying: "A had no son. On the side of the road, he picked up the child B and raised him as his own son. When B grew up, he committed the crime of murder. The contents of the accusation [against B] included [the fact that] A had concealed B [after the crime]. What should be the judgment regarding A?"
>
> Tung Chung-shu passed judgment saying: "A had no son. He restored [B] to life and raised him [as his own son]. Although B was not A's natural son, who would think of seeing [B] as anyone but [A's] son? The *Poetry* [*Classic*] says: 'The mulberry-tree caterpillar has little ones, but the wasp raises them.' According to the intent of the *Annals*, a father must cover up for his son. A accordingly concealed B. The verdict: A does not deserve to be punished."[12]

Tung Chung-shu's use of classical precedents for legal judgments was not an isolated development. During the Former and Later Han dynas-

11. Bodde and Morris, *Law in Imperial China*, pp. 29–38.

12. Pan Ku, *Han-shu*, vol. 3, p. 1714 (*chüan* 30). For the allusion to the *Poetry Classic* see *Shih-ching yin-te*, 46/196/3. Chinese peasants believed the silkworm abandoned its young, which were then raised by wasps. Hence this expression was included in the *Poetry Classic*. See also Ch'eng Shu-te, *Chiu-ch'ao lü-k'ao*, pp. 170–77, and Shen Chi-i, *Han-lü chih-i*, 22.4a, on Han dynasty uses of the *Annals* to settle court cases. For a discussion see Hsing I-t'ien, "Ch'in-Han te lü-ling hsueh," esp. p. 66. Cf. Bodde and Morris, *Law in Imperial China*, pp. 144–45. A different but analogous case is discussed in Ebrey, "Family in the Sung Dynasty," p. 234.

ties Confucian scholars mastered both classical studies and the legal applications that derived from such studies. Han Confucians thus studied these two disciplines together for use in government appointments and careers that required both classical and legal expertise. Such renowned Later Han classicists as Ma Jung and Cheng Hsuan followed Tung Chung-shu's lead in using legal studies (*lü-ling chih hsueh*) to illuminate classical passages (*ming ching-i*). The degree to which the conjunction of classical and legal studies was required for career advancement in the Han imperial erudite system remains a problem for future research, but it is at least clear that until the Sung these two avenues of study were not independent of each other.[13]

It was assumed that Confucius's praise-and-blame position encoded in the *Annals* could be used "to make legal judgments through analogy" (*chueh-shih pi*), which would provide standards for later criminal cases. Hihara Toshikuni points out that Han Confucians made the intentions of an act the major criteria for judgment. The *Kung-yang chuan*, in evaluating Confucius's historical judgments on certain explicit political acts, focused on the intentions of the actor, not simply on the consequences of the act.[14]

For example, in the case of Duke Yin succeeding to the throne of Lu in 722 B.C., the *Kung-yang* interpretation stressed that his accession to the throne was not officially acknowledged in the *Annals*. Normally, when a ruler came to power, Confucius used the phrase "succeeded to the throne" (*chi-wei*) to acknowledge the event. But this phrase was not used for Duke Yin:

> Why does the text [of the *Annals*] not state that Duke [Yin] "succeeded to the throne"? In order to give full expression to the Duke's intention. Why so? The Duke intended to pacify the state and [eventually] restore it to Hsuan [reigned in Lu 711–694 B.C.]. Why restore it to Hsuan? Hsuan was the younger [of the two], but of nobler birth. Yin was the older, but of lower birth. The difference in their relative status was slight. People in the state did not know [whom the late Duke Hui, r. 768–723 B.C.] had elected as his [successor]. Yin was grown-up and, besides, a worthy man. The great officers brought him forward and established him as ruler.
>
> If Yin, under these circumstances had rejected [their decision to] establish him as ruler, then he would have had no assurance that Hsuan [at a later date] would be certain to be established as ruler. Furthermore, supposing that Hsuan were established as ruler, it was feared that the great officers

13. Ch'eng Shu-te, *Chiu-ch'ao lü-k'ao*, pp. 31–32, 165–70. Hsing I-t'ien, pp. 87–91, notes that the combination of legal and classical studies received less emphasis after the fall of the Han dynasty in A.D. 220. See also McKnight, "Mandarins as Legal Experts."

14. Hihara, "Shunjū Kuyōgaku no Kandai teki tenkai."

> would be unable to assist so young a ruler. Therefore, that Yin allowed himself to be established as ruler was to all intents for the sake of Hsuan.

Because Hsuan was of more noble birth than Yin, he should have taken the throne, but circumstances (Hsuan's youth) prevented proper succession. The *Kung-yang chuan*, however, covered up as much as it revealed about Duke Yin's reign. The duke remained in power for eleven years, but in 711 B.C. he was assassinated by Hsuan, who, according to the *Annals*, formally "succeeded to the throne" without waiting for Yin to abdicate in his favor. The *Kung-yang* account did not explictly implicate Hsuan in Yin's death, but the *Ku-liang Commentary* did:

> What is meant by the statement that [Duke Yin] did not choose to become duke? He intended to resign the title and hand it over to Hsuan. Was it correct to resign the title and hand it over to Hsuan? The answer is that it was not correct.The *Annals* gives full expression to a man's good qualities, but does not do so with regard to his evil qualities. Since Yin was not correct, why does the *Annals* give full expression [to his intention]? The *Annals* seeks thereby to condemn Hsuan. Why condemn Hsuan? Since Yin intended to resign [in favor of Hsuan], and Hsuan assassinated him, it is obvious that Hsuan was evil. Since Hsuan was the one who assassinated Yin, and Yin was the one who [intended to] resign [in favor of Hsuan], it is obvious that Yin was good. Because he was good, how can he [be said to] have been incorrect in this respect [of wishing to cede the throne to Hsuan]? The *Annals* values righteousness, but does not value [mere expressions of] favor. It seeks to extend the correct principles and does not seek to extend corrupt ones.[15]

Hence the *Ku-liang* account gave a different judgment on the meaning of the phrase "succeeded to the throne":

> According to the correct norm, the succession of an assassinated ruler is not indicated by the phrase "succeeded to the throne." Why is this so? The answer is that when the late Duke [Yin] did not die a natural death, his son or younger brother could not bear [to perform the ceremony of] succession. When the phrase "succeeded to the throne" is used in the case of succession of an assassinated ruler, use of this phrase indicates that the successor was an accomplice in the assassination itself. Why is this so? The answer is: when the late lord did not die a natural death, [for his successor] to take up the position in full accordance with ritual is to show lack of affection for the late lord.

15. *Ch'un-ch'iu ching-chuan yin-te*, 1/Yin 1/1 Kung, and 1/Yin 1/1 Ku. Cf. Malmqvist, "Gongyang and Guuliang Commentaries," pp. 68–69.

The *Kung-yang chuan* did refer obliquely, however, to the crime committed by Duke Hsuan in its discussion of Duke Yin's death:

> Why does the *Annals* not record the burial [of Duke Yin]? In order to commiserate with him. Why so? [He was] assassinated. Why is the burial of an assassinated lord not recorded? The *Annals* does not record the burial of an assassinated feudal lord, unless the assassin has been punished. [The *Annals* considers that unless this has been done], there are no [true] subjects and sons.[16]

Full sympathy was accorded by both the *Kung-yang* and *Ku-liang* commentaries to Yin's intention to cede his throne to Hsuan, the proper successor, when the latter was of age. In addition, the crime of murder by Hsuan, the successor, was noted. Chao Fang, a later commentator on this issue said in a work on the *Annals* admired by eighteenth-century New Text scholars that the assassination of Yin by Hsuan was a key to understanding Mencius's meaning when he wrote:

> There were instances of ministers who murdered their rulers, and of sons who murdered their fathers. Confucius was fearful and compiled the *Annals*.[17]

Niida Noboru notes that in Confucian judgments the intentions of the perpetrator of a crime were not totally divisible from its consequences. Nevertheless, good intentions, as the above case demonstrates, had precedence over even mistaken actions that resulted in horrific crimes. It was the judgment in a particular case, not the law, that determined justice. According to Tung Chung-shu, the *Annals* determined justice by elucidating the participants' intentions in each case. On another case, for example, Tung made clear the priority of good intentions over the consequences of an act:

> A is B's wife. The latter hits his [own] mother. A sees her husband hit his mother, and she kills him as punishment [for the sake of her mother-in-law]. That is similar to the act of King Wu [founder of the Chou dynasty], who killed the tyrant Chou [r. ca. 1154?–1122?, last of the Shang dynasty kings] in the name of divine vengeance.[18]

16. *Ch'un-ch'iu ching-chuan yin-te*, 23/Hsuan 1/1 Ku, and 22/Yin 11/4 Kung. Cf. Malmqvist, "Gongyang and Guuliang Commentaries," pp. 86, 94.

17. Chao Fang, *Ch'un-ch'iu shu-tz'u*, 4.11b.

18. Hihara, "Shunjū Kuyōgaku no Kandai teki tenkai," pp. 1–16. See also Huang Yuan-sheng, "Han-tai Ch'un-ch'iu che-yü chih yen-chiu," pp. 1–16, and Escarra,

Legal judgments made with reference to classical precedents (*chueh-shih pi*) constituted the body of law to be used as classical experts saw fit. By analogy, if a king could be killed for his crimes by his successors, then so could a wife justifiably kill her husband in cases where the latter failed to fulfill his filial duties to his mother. The Mencian theme of regicide could thus be applied by analogy to a family crime.

We find already in Han times a tendency to draw analogies between historical events and contemporary legal problems. Use of history as a casebook revealed the integral links between classicism, moral didacticism, and historical analogism from the early empire on. To be sure, T'ang and Sung Confucians, as Robert Hartwell points out, stressed the operation of social institutions of the more recent past. Their use of classical models from the *Annals* and *Rituals of Chou* (*Chou-li*), however, was remarkably similar in spirit, if not completely in content, to the New Text use of historical precedents for determining legal judgments during the Han dynasties.[19]

THE CLASSICS, LAW, AND NEO-CONFUCIANS

The "meanings of the Classics" (*ching-i*), especially those derived from the *Annals*, were the basis for legal interpretation not only for Han Confucians but also for later imperial Confucians. A tradition of interpretation that took the *Annals* as the "penal code of the sages" (*sheng-jen chih hsing-shu*) survived into late imperial times.[20] Ch'eng I, the eminent Neo-Confucian scholar of the Northern Sung, could write: "The Five Classics having the *Spring and Autumn Annals* among them is analogous to penal laws accommodating judgments and orders." Ch'eng I (who along with Chu Hsi became the most authoritative spokesman for the orthodox transmission of the Tao [*Tao-t'ung*] in late imperial China) affirmed the image of "Confucius the judge":

Chinese Law, pp. 383–87, and for Tung's case see Su Yü, *Ch'un-ch'iu fan-lu i-cheng*, 3.18b. Cf. Ch'eng Shu-te, *Chiu-ch'ao lü-k'ao*, pp. 230–31, 271–73, 409, for legal uses of the *Annals* through the Sui dynasty (581–618), Hulsewe, *Remnants of Han Law*, vol. 1, pp. 51–52, and Niida, *Chūgoku hōseishi kenkyū*, pp. 609–19. Niida takes issue with Hihara's portrayal of Han legal judgments based on the *Kung-yang chuan* as strictly subjective. For Hihara's reply see his "Shunjū Kuyōgaku no ronri shisō," 2–3.

19. Tillman, *Utilitarian Confucianism*, pp. 33–35, and Hartwell, "Historical-Analogism," pp. 690–727. See also Chen, "Analogy in Ch'ing Law," 213–24.

20. This was Shao Yung's position. For a survey see Chu I-tsun, *Ching-i k'ao*, 168.1a–10b.

> Confucius lived during the waning of the Chou dynasty. Fearing that sages would never again appear and that the world-ordering that was in accord with Heaven and responded to the times would not prevail again, he completed the *Spring and Autumn Annals* to proclaim the great law-models that the kings of the next hundred generations would not alter. It is something that can be described in the words "tested through the experience of the Three Kings [who founded the Hsia, Shang, and Chou dynasties] and found without error, applied before Heaven and earth and found to be without contradiction, laid before worthies without question or fear, it can wait a hundred generations for a sage to validate it."

The picture of Confucius as lawgiver was acceptable even to Sung scholars who sought a more dignified and human Confucius by stressing Old Text Classics. The painting of Confucius as teacher, while it might clash with his image as cosmological prophet or demigod, did allow for overtones of a fair and consistent judge. Ch'eng I added:

> If later kings understand the significance of the *Annals*, even though they do not possess the virture of Yü and T'ang, they can still model [their rule] on the governance of the Three Dynasties. The learning of the [*Annals*] has not been transmitted since the Ch'in [dynasty]. Regretting that the purpose of the sage may not be clear to later generations, I have written a commentary to clarify it so that later persons may understand its prose, search for its meaning, get its intent, and use it as their model. They may then revive the Three Dynasties. Although my commentary cannot reveal the full profundity of the sage, it can perhaps provide scholars with the entrance by which to pass through [to the *Annals*].

In legislating "the great law-models for governing the world" (*ching-shih chih ta-fa*), Confucius again became larger than life—a sage to emulate.[21]

The Ming dynasty Neo-Confucian Wang Yang-ming, also writing on the *Spring and Autumn Annals* Classic, later rejected Ch'eng I's efforts to read legal judgments concerning specific cases into Confucius's chronological entries—a common practice since the Han dynasty:

> Ch'eng I said: "The commentary contains cases; the Classic contains judgments." For example, in the *Annals* it is recorded that so-and-so murdered his ruler or such-and-such a feudal lord invaded such-and-such a state. It would be difficult to judge unless the facts supplied by the commentary are known.
>
> . . . [Ch'eng I] probably repeated what famous but mediocre scholars had

21. For the Sung perspective on the legal aspects see ibid., 168.3b–4b. For Ch'eng I's remarks see ibid., 182.4b–5a. See also Langlois, "Yuan Political Thought," pp. 119–31, and McKnight, "Mandarins as Legal Experts." Cf. Wing-tsit Chan, trans., *Reflections on Things at Hand*, p. 115.

said; he did not appreciate Confucius' purpose in writing the *Annals*. . . . The primary purpose of Confucius's transmitting the Six Classics was purely to rectify people's minds, to preserve heavenly principles, and to eliminate human desires.

Wang Yang-ming rejected the effort to "legalize" the *Annals* on the grounds that such efforts betrayed Confucius's intent. Laws, however clear, were definitions of crimes. Too much detail would only heighten the importance of the crime itself and lessen the moral import of the *Annals* as a guide of correct behavior. A proper Confucian, Wang Yang-ming laid out his position in a moralistic fashion:

How could [Confucius] be willing to tell people in detail all the facts [in the cases he recorded], since this would only release wicked human desires and destroy heavenly principles? That would in turn promote disorder and induce wickedness. This is the reason Mencius said, "None of the followers of Confucius spoke of the affairs of [the despots] Duke Huan [r. 685–643 B.C.] and Duke Wen [r. 636–628 B.C.], and therefore no one in later ages passed on any accounts." Such was the [intent of the] teachings of Confucius's followers.[22]

Despite Wang Yang-ming's dissenting opinions, the moral standards read into the *Annals* remained part of legal discourse through the last years of the Ch'ing dynasty. Kung Tzu-chen, one of the lesser figures in the Ch'ing New Text revival, also stressed the legalistic aspects of the *Kung-yang Commentary*, affirming in the process Tung Chung-shu's use of the *Annals* to search for legal precedents. Rituals and laws were not irrevocable opposites for many Ch'ing New Text Confucians. Kung, for example, prepared a work expressly dealing with legal interpretation and case analogizing based on the *Annals*. Entitled *Ch'un-ch'iu chueh-shih pi* (Analogous legal judgments in the *Annals*), Kung's treatise was a Ch'ing dynasty counterpart to Tung Chung-shu's Former Han legal work on the *Kung-yang Commentary*. Throughout his study, most of which has been lost, Kung Tzu-chen relied on his mentor Liu Feng-lu's explication of legal precedents based on the "three classifications" and "nine points" to present the classical moorings of penal codes.

Seeking to elicit the "eternal penal laws" (*ch'ang-lü*) encoded in the *Annals*, Kung Tzu-chen, like Liu Feng-lu, emphasized the overlap of

22. Wang Yang-ming, *Ch'uan-hsi lu*, p. 7. See the translation in Wing-tsit Chan, *Instructions for Practical Living*, pp. 20–21. See *Meng-tzu yin-te*, 1-2/1A/7, for Wang's citations from the *Mencius*.

ritual and law. Kung explained: "Some have inquired, saying, 'which is better, using rituals or using punishments?' In reply I say, 'Codes for punishments are the means by which the significance of rituals are established. Moving out of [the bounds of] rituals, one enters into the [realm of] punishments. There is no middle ground to stand on.'"

As the classical venue for "legal codes of ten thousand generations" (*wan-shih chih hsing-shu*), the *Annals*, according to Kung Tzu-chen, established legal precedents that applied to all people and all situations. In several tens of thousands of characters of text, Confucius had designated several thousand "points" (*chih*) as guidelines for legal decisions.[23]

New Text Confucians such as Liu Feng-lu and Kung Tzu-chen dressed legal codes in the ideological clothing of ritual transgressions. The aim of punishments and rituals in the end were the same: to preserve human values in the face of change. Kung argued that the major reason Confucius had prepared the *Annals* was to make the Confucian moral vision based on a hierarchy of human relations (father/son, husband/wife, etc.) appropriate to changing times. Released from a world of immutable heavenly principles depicted in Ch'eng-Chu-style Sung Learning, New Text advocates instead emphasized guiding "precedents" and key "points" in the classical order bequeathed by Confucius.[24]

Moreover, the legalistic aspects of New Text Confucianism became part of what was considered a Confucian classical education. Students at the prestigious Hsueh-hai-t'ang (Sea of Learning Hall) Academy in Kuang-chou, founded by Han Learning scholar Juan Yuan, were asked to answer the following question on an examination administered in December 1868:

> The *Kung-yang chuan-chu yin Han-lü k'ao* (Examination of citations of Han law in the notes to the *Kung-yang Commentary*) indicates that Ho Hsiu [129–182] made use of the Han dynasty laws of his time to verify his annotation of the *Kung-yang*. Examine his claims on the basis of the laws of today and extend his conclusions.[25]

One of the student answers preserved in the *Hsueh-hai-t'ang chi* shows that the standard interpretation still held that the *Annals* was the

23. See Kung Tzu-chen, *Kung Tzu-chen ch'üan-chi*, pp. 233–35.

24. See Kung Tzu-chen, *Kung Tzu-chen ch'üan-chi*, pp. 55–64, for Kung's surviving comments on legal decisions and precedents in the *Annals*.

25. Jung Chao-tsu, "Hsueh-hai-t'ang k'ao," page opposite p. 1, for the reproduction of the examination. Cf. my *Philosophy to Philology*, p. 127.

"penal code of the sages." The student, Chin Yu-chi, concluded his answer to this examination question by asserting that contemporary laws could also be analogized with precedents in the *Annals*, just as Han Confucians such as Ho Hsiu had done.[26] Such traditional views were still orthodox in a city where Western influence was most obvious and intense. Confucian conceptions of law as of 1868 still reflected an internal classical dialogue between Legalist notions and New Text compromises. The *Annals* remained a repository of legal judgments.

Liu Feng-lu's reconstruction of New Text Confucianism traced imperial Confucianism back to the Former Han dynasty, when the marriage of Confucian moral theory and Legalist political and legal institutions was consummated. Discovering the origins of this union would in the end compromise the ideals of Confucian moral philosophy as the alarming degree of the "legalization of Confucianism" was made an object of inquiry by Wei Yuan and others. In the nineteenth century Lower Yangtze centers of education were also caught up in this reevaluation. Students at the Lung-ch'eng Academy in Ch'ang-chou and the Ku-ching ching-she Academy in Hang-chou were instructed to reassess the role played by the "three classifications" and "nine points" in *Kung-yang* theory, just as students at the Hsueh-hai-t'ang in Kuang-chou wrote essays on the legal uses of the *Kung-yang Commentary*.[27]

NEW TEXT REALPOLITIK

A key doctrine in the *Kung-yang* interpretation of the *Annals* was "knowing how to weigh circumstances" (*chih-ch'üan*). Elaborating on a passage in the *Annals* that described the capture of a minister of the Duke of Cheng in 700 B.C. by the state of Sung and who was then forced to choose between participating in the overthrow of the designated Cheng heir or subjecting Cheng to an invasion by Sung forces and probable extinction, the *Kung-yang Commentary* explained why the minister Chi deserved credit for "knowing how to weigh circumstances" and for choosing the lesser of two evils:

> Who was Chi the younger? He was minister to [the state of] Cheng. Why is he not referred to by his personal name? He was worthy. In what respect was Chi the younger worthy? [The *Annals*] considers that he knew how to weigh

26. Chin Yu-chi's answer is found in *Hsueh-hai-t'ang chi*, 4th ser. (1886), 10.13a–17b.

27. Liu Feng-lu, *Liu Li-pu chi*, 4.21a–23a. See also *Ku-ching ching-she wen-chi*, pp. 79–81 (*chüan* 3), and *Lung-ch'eng shu-yuan k'e-i*, pp. 3a–5a (under 1899).

> circumstances. Under what conditions did he know to do this? In old times, [the ruler of] the state of Cheng resided in Liu. The former Earl of Cheng had gained the friendship of the Duke of K'uai. The Earl had illicit relations with the Duke's wife, and as a result the Duke took the Earl's state and moved his own state there, allowing Liu to decline. When the Duke of Chuang died and had been buried, Chi the younger was about to go and inspect Liu. On this journey he ventured in Sung. The people of Sung seized Chi saying to him, "Expel Hu and establish T'u as ruler [of Cheng] for our sake."
>
> If Chi the younger refused to obey their command, then his ruler [Hu] was bound to die, and the state [of Cheng] was bound to perish. If he obeyed their command, then his ruler would remain alive, instead of having to die, and [Chi's] state could be preserved, instead of having to perish. If things followed their course, T'u could definitely be expelled and Hu could definitely be reinstated. If this could not be achieved, then Chi would be disgraced. In this way, the state of Cheng was preserved for later ages.
>
> When men of old possessed the ability to weigh circumstances, it was exemplified by Chi the younger's ability. What is meant by weighing circumstances? To weigh circumstances means that thereby one eventually arrives at a good result, even though [initially] one has acted contrary to correct standards. As for the application of [the process of] weighing circumstances, it may not be applied in cases other than when the life [of one's ruler] or the preservation [of one's state] are at stake. There are rules governing the application of weighing circumstances. The one who practices it may suffer personal losses, but no harm must come to others. The gentleman does not kill others to save his own life, nor does he destroy [the state of] others to preserve his own state.

Such realism verged on the edge of Legalist realpolitik. Arguing that circumstances varied with the age, the Legalist philosopher cum political advisor Han Fei contended:

> Accordingly, a sage establishes policy by taking into account the quantity of things and deliberates on the vicissitudes of power. Though punishments may be light, this is not due to compassion; though penalties may be severe, this is not due to cruelty. Thus affairs change with the times, and the means for dealing with them must accord with circumstances. . . .
>
> Past and present have different customs; new and old adopt different measures. To try to use the ways of a generous and lenient government to rule the people of a critical age is like trying to drive a runaway horse without using reins or whip. This is the misfortune that ignorance invites.

Han Fei's emphasis on "according with circumstances" (*shih yü shih*) resonated with the *Kung-yang's* "knowing how to weigh circumstances" (*chih-ch'üan*). This overlap was a far cry from the strict moral formalism enshrined in the Sung Learning orthodoxy of the Ch'ing imperium, where eternal moral principles reigned supreme as the "voice of the state." The *Kung-yang's* condemnation of blind obedience to moral absolutes accented the voluntarist aspects of knowing how to act according to circumstances.[28]

Reconstruction of New Text doctrine and *Kung-yang* strains of voluntarism by Liu Feng-lu and his followers contributed to the forging of an ideological framework for statecraft reform in the early nineteenth century. *Kung-yang* forms of limited voluntarism during the Former Han dynasty had represented in part the Confucian reply to the moral relativism of Legalist theorists who were able to articulate an unfettered political agenda that supported change and reform. In their reply to the Legalists, Former Han Confucians such as Tung Chung-shu had successfully wrapped the Legalist political agenda for state power in moral clothing. The agenda for reform had crossed to the Confucian side.

Chuang Ts'un-yü, Liu Feng-lu, and other New Text scholars increasingly spoke of reform after what they considered the monstrous corruption of the Ho-shen era (which marked the transition from the eighteenth to the nineteenth century). It was no accident that their appeals—first implicit and then ever more explicit—displayed a distinctive intertwining of *Kung-yang* strands of voluntarism and Legalist-style pragmatism and statecraft. Wei Yuan, frequently accused of Legalism by his contemporaries, exemplified this evolution in literati attitudes:

> The ancients had what pertained to the ancients. To force the ancients upon the moderns is to misrepresent the moderns. To use the moderns as the standard for the ancients is to misrepresent the ancients. If one misrepresents the present, then there can be no way to order [the contemporary world]. . . .
>
> If one read the [medical] works of the Yellow Emperor and Shen Nung, and used them to kill people, one would be labelled a mediocre doctor. If one read the works of the Duke of Chou and Confucius and used them to harm the empire, would one not be labelled a mediocre Confucian? Not only would such [incompetence] bring no benefit to any particular age, but in addition it would cause people no longer to believe in the Way of the sages.[29]

Liu Feng-lu, Wei's mentor, recognized in a rudimentary way the link between New Text Confucianism and statecraft politics. And Liu's grandfather Chuang Ts'un-yü had already articulated the New Text

28. *Ch'un-ch'iu ching-chuan yin-te*, 37/Huan 11/4 Kung. See the translation (which I have modified) in Malmqvist, "Gongyang and Guuliang Commentaries," p. 106. See also *Han Fei Tzu so-yin*, p. 856. Cf. Watson, trans., *Han Fei Tzu*, pp. 99–101.

29. Liu Feng-lu, *Liu Li-pu chi*, 4.23a Cf. Grieder, *Intellectuals and the State*, pp. 114–15. See *Wei Yuan chi*, p. 48.

corollary to the *Kung-yang* notion of weighing the circumstances to interpret the past and reform the present (*t'o-ku kai-chih*). Chuang Ts'un-yü's views, however, were still tied to a conservative political position within the upper echelons of power in the Ch'ing state. His writings, moreover, did not receive public attention until four decades after his death in 1788.[30]

Liu Feng-lu's New Text synthesis provoked immediate and heated public debate after his *k'ao-cheng* studies of the Classics were published. His views could not be dismissed, however, without carefully reviewing the philological issues involved. As a result of his lineage connections and official ties in Peking, Liu had many friends in the Han Learning camp. Despite their stress on Later Han sources, they recognized the significance of Liu Feng-lu's research on the *Annals* and *Tso chuan*. Consequently, it was no accident that Juan Yuan, Liu's colleague and friend, included Liu's works in his *Ch'ing Dynasty Exegesis of the Classics*. Feng-lu's research had brought New Text Confucianism the epistemological leverage it would require in the *k'ao-cheng* climate of the time.

Liu Feng-lu's views were enlarged upon, developed, and modified by his most important disciples, notably Wei Yuan and Kung Tzu-chen. Through their efforts, New Text Confucianism became an important element in the broader call for the reform of the Ch'ing state, at a time when China was facing both foreign aggression and internal social and economic dislocation. No one could have predicted in the early nineteenth century how it would all turn out in the end, but Former Han dynasty New Text Confucianism had undoubtedly been revived by Chuang Ts'un-yü and Liu Feng-lu. It still remained for their successors to carry the *Kung-yang* alternative to its final stages of development, thereby transcending its Ch'ang-chou roots and leaving behind its origins in the Chuang and Liu lineages and their local traditions of classical learning.

With the theoretical and epistemological aspects of New Text Confucianism largely in place chiefly through the efforts of Chuang Ts'un-yü and Liu Feng-lu, nineteenth-century successors to the Ch'ang-chou New Text initiative more and more turned from "interpreting the past" (*t'o-ku*) to "reforming the present" (*kai-chih*). In the concluding portion of our account, we shall address the broader currents of moral and

30. See Wei Yuan's ca. 1830 "Liu Li-pu i-shu hsu," pp. 241–43, on Liu's "rediscovery" of the Former Han New Text tradition. See also Liu Feng-lu's "Hsu" (Preface) to Wei Yuan, *Shih ku-wei*, 9.6a–6b, for Liu's praise and support for Wei Yuan.

political crisis within which the evolution of New Text ideas enunciated by the Ch'ang-chou school took place. In the aftermath of the Ho-shen era, Confucian politics and its language of legitimation were in flux. Not since the seventeenth century had the Confucian state and its gentry-officials witnessed a revival of political activism and dissent of comparable scope and magnitude. Dramatic changes in historical context help explain how *Kung-yang* Confucianism made the jump from conservative ideology in the eighteenth century to reformist statecraft in the nineteenth.

NINE

Politics, Language, and the New Text Legacy

During the last decades of the eighteenth century the population of China reached 300 million. Such growth, accompanied by concomitant increases in gentry competition for land, education, and official status, adversely affected all Chinese. The atmosphere of corruption wrought by Ho-shen and his cronies was in fact only symptomatic of the Ch'ing state's efforts to cope with its inner decay. Internal rebellions such as the Chin-ch'uan (1770–76), Wang Lun (1774), White Lotus (1796–1805), and Eight Trigrams (1813) uprisings ended a long period of relative peace dating from the K'ang-hsi Emperor's reign (1662–1722). Dislocations in the grain tribute system along the Grand Canal, which provided south China's tax revenues to the imperial government in Peking, and corruption in the salt administration revealed the depth and pervasiveness of the problems faced by the court and bureaucracy.

With the aid of some hindsight, Confucian literati blamed such decline on the Ho-shen era, finding in Ho-shen a convenient target for gentry dissatisfaction. Literati opposition to Ho-shen by Chuang Ts'un-yü and his Ch'ang-chou followers was thus part of their larger response to the institutional problems of the late Ch'ing. Ho-shen's brief rise to power overtly jeopardized literati standards of honesty and service and covertly created the desire for reform for which New Text Confucianism stood. Blanket denunciations of Ho-shen concealed the degree to which many Confucian literati-officials had joined him in betraying orthodox political values.

Advocates of Sung Learning, Han Learning apologists, and proponents of New Text studies all recognized that an appropriate statecraft program was necessary within late imperial political culture. Given the "constitutional" framework of the Ch'ing empire, whereby the Classics remained the rhetorical guide in political matters, any reformist initiative had to find its historical precedent in the Classics.[1]

During the early decades of the nineteenth century, Confucian scholars increasingly appealed for an end to what they regarded as petty debates between Han Learning and Sung Learning partisans. Following the lead of New Text scholars such as Liu Feng-lu, Wei Yuan, and Kung Tzu-chen, many called for a comprehensive reassessment of the Confucian classical vision and its statecraft legacy. It was necessary, most thought, for scholars to come to grips again with the social, political, and economic problems at hand. The statecraft concerns once peculiar to Ch'ang-chou schoolmen were now the province of the leading scholar-statesmen of the nineteenth century.

POLITICAL CRISIS AND THE CH'IEN-LUNG TO CHIA-CH'ING TRANSITION

Political activism following China's defeat in the Opium War (1839–42) spurred renewed interest in the Tung-lin partisans, the most important instance of literati solidarity to date. The reemergence of *ch'ing-i* (voices of remonstrance, lit., "pure criticism") in the nineteenth century largely reflected changing gentry perceptions of late Ming initiatives to legitimate gentry-based politics in the imperial state. The image of the Tung-lin partisans moved from one of a "selfish" (*ssu*) political faction to that of a group of concerned literati whose aim was to address the public (*kung*) needs of their time. The abortiveness of late Ming politics (see chapter 1) was now challenged in the precincts of the late Ch'ing state.

Although it is unlikely that renewed interest in Tung-lin was touched off by Ch'ang-chou partisans, the prefecture's intimate ties to the Tung-lin legacy in Wu-hsi rendered its scholars uniquely able to appreciate their seventeenth-century predecessors. Both Tung-lin and New Text were part of a political evolution that in the nineteenth century resulted

1. Li Chao-lo, *Yang-i-chai wen-chi*, 14.1a–3a. On the complexity of the Ch'ing "decline" see Naquin, *Shantung Rebellion*, pp. 148–64. Cf. her *Millenarian Rebellion in China*.

in a remarkable transformation of literati attitudes toward political reform.[2]

Ming-style literati activism that emerged after the Opium War was preceded by a chorus of late-eighteenth-century voices critical of the political corruption of the last decades of the Ch'ien-lung Emperor's reign, known as the Ho-shen era. Members of the Chuang lineage in Ch'ang-chou were part of this chorus, particularly Chuang Ts'un-yü, who had couched his criticism, as we have seen, in the classical language of *Kung-yang* Confucianism. During the 1780s and 1790s, we should recall, the emperor had conferred great power and prestige on Ho-shen, a Manchu imperial guard.

As the emperor's favorite, Ho-shen was able to amass a personal fortune said to be second only to the imperial treasury. Eventually, factional politics reappeared on the Confucian political stage. Given the circumstances, such factions were predictable and were tolerated as long as they remained out of the public arena. Ho-shen's imperially sanctioned suicide under the Chia-ch'ing Emperor (r. 1796–1820), symbolized an important transition from the Ch'ien-lung to the Chia-ch'ing reign. But internal factional alignments within the inner and outer courts unexpectedly burst their imperial boundaries and entered the public arena.[3]

The divisive politics of the late eighteenth and early nineteenth centuries, which pivoted around Ho-shen's questionable character and purportedly despotic machinations, reveal changing literati political perceptions and intellectual interests from the final years of the Ch'ien-lung reign up to the Opium War. Controversy over Ho-shen led to the formation of covert literati alignments in the 1790s that during the early years of the Chia-ch'ing reign emerged as self-righteous "voices of remonstrance" (*ch'ing-i*). The consequent revival of interest in the Tung-lin political legacy was in part the product of contemporary events. These events produced in the minds of nineteenth-century reform-minded Confucian literati a reminder of the beleaguered status of earlier Tung-lin partisans vis-à-vis an imperial government dominated by a dangerous imperial favorite.

Tung-lin partisans had squared off against Wei Chung-hsien, who had usurped control of the imperial bureaucracy. Late-eighteenth-century Confucians faced a palace guard, Ho-shen, who had usurped

2. For the Ch'ang-chou position on the Tung-lin revival, see Polachek's *Inner Opium War*. Cf. Eastman, *Throne and Mandarins*, pp. 20–29.

3. Nivison, "Ho-shen and His Accusers," pp. 209–43.

imperial power for himself and his accomplices. Ch'ang-chou literati in particular compared Ho-shen with Wei Chung-hsien, using outraged and self-righteous rhetoric. Just as Ch'ang-chou's Chuang T'ing-ch'en discreetly snubbed Wei in the 1620s, Chuang Shu-tsu epitomized Ch'ang-chou disdain for Ho-shen (whom he dared not confront) in the 1780s. The political initiative shifted to the "voices of remonstrance."[4]

THE PROBLEM OF FACTIONS—AGAIN

Political tactics and alliances were forged during the late eighteenth century within the legal limits set by the imperial state. Like their Ming predecessors, Ch'ing emperors viewed horizontally aligned groups of gentry-officials as factions threatening the sanctity of vertical loyalties that culminated in the person of the emperor himself. The ideological constraints within Confucian political culture against gentry factions (factions = disloyalty and factions = private interests) were frequently voiced by Ch'ing emperors. In the seventeenth century Manchu emperors reaffirmed that literati factions were selfish and exclusivistic organizations that clashed with the public interests of the dynasty.

As early as 1652, licentiates (*sheng-yuan*) participating in the imperial examination system were forbidden to associate with large numbers of peers or to form alliances or join parties (*tang*). Both the Yung-cheng (r. 1723–25) and Ch'ien-lung emperors, for instance, repeatedly attacked literati factionalism, basing their objections on the ground that literati were supposed to be public protectors of the state. In their view, selfish interests of individuals organized into factions had precipitated the fall of the Ming dynasty and would similarly affect the present dynasty if factions were again allowed free rein.[5]

In an edict issued during the first year of the Yung-cheng reign (May 22, 1723), the role of literati factionalism in the Ming debacle was explicitly condemned: "Factionalism is an extremely bad pattern of behavior. At the end of the Ming, cliques were set up and plotted against each other, with the result that they all suffered injury together. This tendency has not yet been arrested." In addition to the long-standing Confucian injunction against factions, Manchu rulers invoked the Ming dynasty as a recent example of what happens when orthodox Confucian political values are overturned. Manchu emperors could, with

4. Susan Mann (Jones), "Hung Liang-chi," pp. 8–11, 85–87, 137–39.

5. See *Ta-Ch'ing Kao-tsung Ch'un-huang-ti sheng-hsun*, 192.10a–11a, and Nivison, "Ho-shen and His Accusers," pp. 223–24.

overt irony, portray themselves as protectors of Confucian political culture from the excesses of a native Chinese dynasty.[6]

The Yung-cheng Emperor was sensitive to the threat posed by factions—his insecurity most likely arising from his own faction building, undertaken in order to cement his own claim to succession in the last years of the K'ang-hsi reign. In 1724 the Yung-cheng Emperor prepared a lengthy essay entitled "On Factions" ("P'eng-tang lun") in which he disputed Ou-yang Hsiu's famous essay by the same title justifying factions. Late Ming Tung-lin and Fu She partisans had drawn considerable moral support from Ou-yang's essay. As we have seen in chapter 1, Ou-yang Hsiu's essay differentiated self-interested factions from public-minded alignments. In the process, he defended the latter as an appropriate form of literati association within the state's vertically aligned power structure.

Ou-yang's rhetoric was unsuccessfully tested by the Tung-lin partisans in the shifting political winds of the late Ming. A key element in the futility of Ming politics was the failure of public-minded factions to gain imperial legitimacy. Nevertheless, as the Yung-cheng Emperor's open and well-publicized rejoinder to the influential essay reveals, the threat of covert factions was never totally eliminated. The emperor, who succeeded his father with the help of a well-placed faction that manufactured a façade of imperial unanimity, in effect presented a position paper denying political groups even a semblance of legitimacy.[7]

Donald Munro and David Nivison observe that the Yung-cheng Emperor's essay on factions was authoritarian. Imperial interests, the emperor contended, always coincided with the greatest "public good" (*ta-kung*):

> Heaven is exalted and earth is lowly, and so the ruler and minister are differentiated. The essential duty of a minister is simply to know that he has a ruler. Then his sentiments will be firm and disciplined, and he will be able to share his ruler's likes and dislikes. This is [the meaning of] the saying "one in virtue and mind, high and low are bound together." Sometimes, however, people's minds harbor several interests, so that they cannot accept the ruler's preferences, and consequently the sentiments of superiors and inferiors become opposed and the distinction between noble and base is overturned. This is what always comes of the habit of forming cliques and factions.

6. *Ta-Ch'ing Shih-tsung Hsien-huang-ti sheng-hsun*, 19.1b, translated in Nivison, "Ho-shen and His Accusers," p. 224.

7. Munro "Concept of 'Interest' in Chinese Thought," pp. 184–86. Cf. Nivison, "Ho-shen and His Accusers," p. 225.

Factions were by their very nature opposed to the impartial standards of right and wrong that informed the public good of the state:

> The ruler fears that what he will see will not always be totally appropriate. Therefore, he opens his mind to entertain a variety of opinions. But it is necessary that all these opinions be of the utmost in rectitude. If this is so, and the ruler follows one, the choice will be directly compatible with the greatest public good. But those that move in cliques embrace biased opinions to mystify the ruler by their words. If the ruler by mistake acts on such opinion, then this will transform the ruler's intent for the greatest good into the most selfish of things.

Although the emperor's polemic is evidence of the enduring presence of factions, his essay translated official Confucian concerns into imperial policy and orthodox ideology.[8]

Similarly, the Ch'ien-lung Emperor shared earlier suspicions concerning factional groupings of officials and upheld the limits of literati presumptions in political life enunciated by his father. Nivison describes a 1781 case in which the emperor decided against the persistent requests of Ch'ien Tsai (1708–93), then under secretary of the Ministry of Rites, who had memorialized that the tomb of the sage-emperor Yao (tr. r. 2356–2255?? B.C.) be moved from its mistaken location in Shanhsi to a town in Shan-tung Province. A seemingly innocuous request. But given the umbilical cord tying Confucian orthodoxy to imperial prestige, the Ch'ien-lung Emperor saw in the bickering surrounding the case the issues that had powered earlier gentry factions opposed to the imperial will. The emperor delivered his edict with a pointed warning:

> Ch'ien Tsai is essentially a man of slow understanding, and this matter moreover is merely of archaeological importance. Therefore, we do not hold his fault to be serious. But if he were guilty of this sort of incessant bickering on administrative matters of importance, we would surely deal severely with him. At the end of the Ming, whenever some incident occurred, the hubbub among the officials filled the court. In their many litigations they made use of their public position to serve their private interests. At first, each one set up his own clique; this led to rival factions, with resulting harm to the government and a constant deterioration in the activities of the state. We cannot forbear to cite this as a pointed warning.[9]

Wary of ritual debates that had compromised the moral legitimacy of Ming imperial policy, the Ch'ien-lung Emperor even refuted the opin-

8. *Ta-Ch'ing Shih-tsung Hsien (Yung-cheng) huang-ti shih-lu*, pp. 343–44, translated in Munro, "Concept of 'Interest' in Chinese Thought," p. 185. Cf. Nivison, "Ho-shen and His Accusers," pp. 225–26.

9. *Ta-Ch'ing Kao-tsung Ch'un-huang-ti sheng-hsun*, 192.10a–11a, translated in Nivison, "Ho-shen and His Accusers," pp. 223–25.

ion of Ch'eng I (1033–1107), a linchpin of the Neo-Confucian orthodoxy to which the Ch'ing imperium subscribed. We find the emperor at odds with elements in the Neo-Confucian agenda that did not jibe with Manchu imperial prerogatives. Ch'eng I had addressed three memoranda to the throne while he was imperial tutor early in the Che-tsung Emperor's reign (1086–1100). These represented, according to Nivison, "one of the most extreme claims in Confucian literature for literati dominance over the emperor."

Ch'eng I claimed that the best rulers followed the advice of their chief advisors and that the best government existed when regents such as the Duke of Chou assisted youthful rulers and educated them in virtue. Addressing the throne, Ch'eng wrote: "Generally speaking, if in the course of a day the emperor is in the company of worthy men much of the time and is in the company of monks and concubines only a small part of the time, his character will automatically be transformed, and his virtue will become perfect." Contending that the best rulers had honored virtuous ministers, Ch'eng I concluded "the most important responsibilities in the empire are those of prime minister and imperial tutor in the Classics."[10]

The Ch'ien-lung Emperor thought Ch'eng I's views—otherwise part of the Ch'eng-Chu imperial ideology—tantamount to lèse-majesté:

> Who after all employs a prime minister if it is not the sovereign? Suppose a sovereign merely dwells in lofty seclusion, cultivating his virtue and trusting the fortunes of the empire to his chief minister rather than concerning himself with it. Then even if he is fortunate and chooses ministers like Han [Ch'i, 1008–75] and Fan [Chung-yen, 989–1052], he will not avoid contention among his high officials; and if he should be so unfortunate as to choose ministers like Wang [Tseng, d. 1038] and Lü [I-chien, d. 1044], how is the realm to escape disorder? Surely this will not do. And if a chief minister habitually thinks of the world's welfare as his own sole responsibility, as if he had no sovereign before him, his conduct would surely be intolerable.

Ch'ing emperors, like their Ming predecessors, endeavored to exalt the throne at the expense of the bureaucracy and their chief ministers. In the process, factions were self-righteously denounced.[11]

For both the Yung-cheng and Ch'ien-lung emperors, factionalism arose when scholars and officials chose to advance their selfish interests

10. In the *Erh-Ch'eng ch'üan-shu*, see *I-ch'uan wen-chi* (Complete works of the two Ch'engs, Ch'eng I's collected essays), *ts'e* 2, 2.2a–4a. Cf. Nivison, "Ho-shen and His Accusers," pp. 230–31.

11. See the Ch'ien-lung Emperor's "Shu Ch'eng I lun ching-t'ing cha-tzu hou," p. 2, translated in Nivison, "Ho-shen and His Accusers," p. 231.

through "unconstitutional" (that is, horizontally defined) peer organizations. As we have seen, this imperial position drew its ideological and epistemological strength from the long-standing rejection of organized gentry politics in the imperial state. Nivison succinctly summarizes the imperial position before the rise of nineteenth-century "voices of remonstrance" (*ch'ing-i*):

> It was never conceded that men might band together out of *disinterested* motives—to defend the state, to protect the throne, to work for common "principles." The scholar-intellectual's contribution to government, if he made any, was to be a loyal official; if he had anything to say, he was to say it directly to the throne (if he was entitled to) and was to trust the emperor's judgment. In particular he was not to question the emperor's choice of men or suggest that he was abandoning his power to others. And so while factionalism, at least of the self-serving sort which officially was all it ever was, continued in fact, the fact had to be denied: factionalism could not be conceded to exist in such an illustrious era as Ch'ien-lung, the Age of Celestial Splendor.

Remarkably, all this rhetoric did not survive the transition to the Chia-ch'ing era. The Ho-shen affair became a watershed for moves to reformulate literati prerogatives vis-à-vis the state and its imperial institutions. Tung-lin-style activism, submerged for a century and a half, reappeared as an instructive precedent rather than as evidence of selfish factionalism.[12]

LITERATI PERCEPTIONS OF HO-SHEN

Like the eunuch usurpation during the Ming, the Ho-shen affair altered Confucian discourse on gentry-official responsibilities vis-à-vis the welfare of an imperiled dynasty. For a faction to succeed in imperial politics required access to the emperor's favor. By gaining imperial support, Ho-shen could with relative impunity assemble a formidable group of supporters who were identifiable as a powerful clique in imperial and provincial politics. This unorthodox—many viewed it as illegitimate—road to power had been the key to eunuch influence for several earlier dynasties.

Opposition to Ho-shen in the 1790s, like opposition to the eunuch Wei Chung-hsien in the 1620s, brought together a disparate collection of literati and bureaucratic dissatisfaction to form a polarized faction.

12. Nivison, "Ho-shen and His Accusers," p. 232.

Behind the unified ideological façade of the Ch'ien-lung Emperor's last two decades of direct and indirect rule (he "retired" in 1795, yielding titular power to his son), covert power alignments appeared that would later emerge as overt "voices of remonstrance."[13]

In the eyes of many Chinese and Manchus, the threat that Ho-shen posed to Confucian political life and official careers conveniently exceeded the dangers of factionalism. When the ideological objections to factions were challenged in lurid literati accounts of Ho-shen's subversion of the throne for personal profit and greed, imperial bans on "factions" were portrayed as morally suspect. The Confucian opposition now held the high ground. Their "public-minded" (*kung*) duty as concerned Confucians was seen to conflict with the selfish (*ssu*) predators feeding on imperial access. The terms of discourse on political factions were slowly reversed in the 1790s.

Little actually changed until the death of the retired Ch'ien-lung Emperor in 1799. Important court officials such as Chuang Ts'un-yü, for example, could not speak out directly. Hence in the 1780s Chuang chose New Text interpretations of the *Annals*, as we have seen, to disguise his misgivings about Ho-shen. A decade later, heeding the advice of ministers who were aligned against the handsome and well-placed Manchu, the Chia-ch'ing Emperor slowly effected Ho-shen's demise. Upon taking personal command of the government, the new emperor invited all qualified officials to memorialize the throne on the problems facing the dynasty. This privilege of submitting opinions to the throne (*yen-lu*, lit., "pathway for words") signified an opening of the political process after decades of the throne's rejection of unsolicited advice.[14]

Many of Ho-shen's opponents, surprisingly, were Han Learning scholars. They rallied around the Manchu Grand Counselor A-kuei (1717–97) and Chu Kuei (1731–1807), a northern Chinese who was a friend and former tutor of the Chia-ch'ing Emperor. A-kuei was a colleague and associate of Chuang Ts'un-yü when the latter served in the Grand Secretariat a decade earlier. Chu Kuei's elder brother, Chu Yun, was a highly respected Han Learning scholar and patron of *k'ao-cheng* research. Chu Kuei—himself a supporter of Han Learning and evidential scholarship—had been recalled to Peking by his former imperial pupil to serve as head of the Board of Civil Office in the Ministry of Rites. The role of Han Learning scholars in opposing the Ho-shen fac-

13. Ibid., pp. 232–43.
14. Ibid., pp. 240–41. See also Hucker, "Confucianism and the Chinese Censorial System," pp. 182–208.

tion demonstrates a degree of political involvement that has never been associated with the *k'ao-cheng* movement. It suggests that the typical portrayal of Han Learning as apolitical philology needs to be revised substantially.[15]

Among the Han Learning antagonists Chu Kuei had assembled, Hung Liang-chi, Sun Hsing-yen, and Chang Hui-yen were Ch'ang-chou natives. The contributions of Ch'ang-chou scholarship and statecraft traditions among the Chu Kuei group should not be underestimated. Hung and Chang were closely associated with the Chuang lineage in Ch'ang-chou, for example. Given Chuang Ts'un-yü's opposition to Ho-shen in the 1780s and his association with A-kuei (whose efforts to promote the official career of Chuang's nephew Shu-tsu were sabotaged by Ho-shen [see chapter 3]), Ts'un-yü's classical studies took on special meaning for Chu Kuei's group. Two years after Ho-shen's death, for example, Chu prepared a preface for Chuang Ts'un-yü's *Correcting Terms in the Spring and Autumn Annals* that lauded the author's efforts to enunciate the *Kung-yang* vision of the *Annals*. As we have seen, the latter was encoded with anti-Ho-shen sentiment.[16]

For many among Chu Kuei's group the emperor's moves to remove Ho-shen from power did not go far enough. Although he acknowledged that many of Ho-shen's followers must have shared in crimes attributed to Ho-shen, the emperor could not allow the slightest criticism of his father, who had given Ho-shen the scope to maneuver in court. Moreover, the Chia-ch'ing Emperor wished to avoid a full-scale purge, which was the only way to weed out the Ho-shen faction. Instead, he chose to view Ho-shen as responsible for corrupting those below him. The enemy was not a faction but an individual. With Ho-shen gone, the loyalty of officials, he hoped, would return to where it belonged—the person of the emperor.

THE HUNG LIANG-CHI CASE

But the emperor's limited response to the Ho-shen subversion was challenged in late September 1799, when the Ch'ang-chou literatus Hung

15. See my *Philosophy to Philology*, pp. 13–26, 105–7. Nivison's account in his "Ho-shen and His Accusers," pp. 209–43, is filled with the names of Ho-shen antagonists who were Han Learning scholars: Chiao Hsun (1763–1820), Sun Hsing-yen (1753–1818), Hung Liang-chi (1746–1809), Wu I (1745–99), Wang Hui-tsu (1731–1807), Chang Hui-yen (1761–1802), among others.

16. Chu Kuei, "Hsu" (Preface) to Chuang Ts'un-yü, in *Ch'un-ch'iu cheng-tz'u*, pp. 1a–2a. See also Wang Hsi-hsun, *Ch'ieh-chu-an wen-chi*, pp. 203–204, 221–23, for a discussion of the opposition expressed by Chang Hui-yen and Chuang Shu-tsu to Ho-shen.

Liang-chi dramatically called for the court to address the Ho-shen era as a factional problem. Hung's veiled criticism of the throne (presented to Prince Ch'eng [1752–1823] because Hung was not entitled to address the emperor while serving as Hanlin academician) was unprecedented. Hung's passionate remonstrance with the Chia-ch'ing Emperor represented the opening salvo in the revival of literati political activism in the nineteenth century. Tung-lin-style political behavior had returned, although its fate hung in the balance as the emperor pondered his response to Hung Liang-chi's challenge. Hung's colleagues, friends, and supporters all feared that Hung's audacity would cost him his life.[17]

A protégé of the emperor's confidant Chu Kuei, Hung Liang-chi sent Chu a copy of his letter. Prince Ch'eng delivered Hung's letter at once to the emperor, who, enraged by Hung's audacity, immediately removed Hung from his Hanlin post. Angered even more by Hung Liang-chi's distributing the letter behind his back to Chu Kuei and others, the Chia-ch'ing Emperor demoted Chu Kuei, his former mentor, by three official ranks for not transmitting the copy of the letter Chu had received from Hung until the emperor called for it. The Ministry of Punishments, after convening in an emergency session with the Grand Council, recommended that Hung be decapitated for the crime of lèse-majesté. Chu Kuei's faction faced a crucial juncture. The emperor now had an opportunity, with the full ideological support of Confucian political theory, to eradicate the polarized forces that had compromised his initial policy decisions.

Susan Mann has described the furor that Hung's arrest aroused in Peking literati circles. After his incarceration, Hung Liang-chi's Ch'ang-chou landsman and cousin Chao Huai-yü—then a grand secretary in the imperial bureaucracy—visited Hung's cell the evening of his arrest. Mann poignantly describes this meeting:

> [Chao Huai-yü] walked through the cluster of guards who were still avidly comparing versions of the case, took one look at Hung (who, by this account, was seated in bonds on a straw mat), and burst into tears. Hung beckoned him inside, somehow unloosed his "bonds" and poured them each a glass of wine. Chao could not swallow. Finally, Hung said, "I have done what I did openly, before everyone. There is nothing to discuss. What are you trying to hide from me?" Chao finally burst out that he had learned a death sentence was pending. Hung took a big bite of food. Then he looked up and said, "I know I'm going to lose my head." There was a pause, and he

17. Nivison, "Ho-shen and His Accusers," pp. 240–41, and Susan Mann (Jones), "Scholasticism and Politics," 30–32.

> added, "Why should you be bitter that I am going to die this way?" And he went on eating.

Hung held the moral high ground, deliberately and openly reaffirming the right of a concerned Confucian official to remonstrate the court.[18]

As a member of a coterie of Han Learning scholars in Ch'ang-chou that had gained national prominence in the 1780s, Hung Liang-chi had been a poor outsider who had studied briefly in the Chuang lineage school as a youth (see chapter 2). His decisive letter was at first sight a radical departure from his *k'ao-cheng* studies in geography, epigraphy, and classical studies. But from the angle of Ch'ang-chou statecraft traditions—which we have studied in light of the Wu-hsi Tung-lin legacy and the Chuang and Liu lineages of Wu-chin—Hung Liang-chi's letter expressed long-latent political concerns. Political and statecraft agendas had remained an important factor in Ch'ang-chou traditions in general and among members of the Chuang and Liu lineages in particular.[19]

What prompted this sudden explosion of political concern? The eruption occurred after Ho-shen's suicide. Clearly the Ho-shen era had generated anger, frustration, and a sense of futility as the corruption of Ho-shen's henchmen and the military defeats in local rebellions rent late imperial state and society apart. Important clues to this decisive transformation in literati perception may be found in the political career of the doyen of eighteenth-century Ch'ang-chou learning, Chuang Ts'un-yü, whose turn to *Kung-yang* Confucianism signified, as we have seen, his dismay over the political corruption of the 1780s. Chuang's elucidation of the *Annals* reveals a significant shift in focus from typical Old Text erudition to a more voluntaristic Confucianism. Voluntarism and activism were derived from the *Kung-yang Commentary*, whose portrayal of Confucius as an "uncrowned king" during the declining centuries of the Chou dynasty were analogous to the declining fortunes of the Ch'ien-lung reign during the Ho-shen era.[20]

Hung Liang-chi's 1799 letter, then, like Chuang Ts'un-yü's *Kung-yang* Confucianism, was not an isolated protest appearing from nowhere. The political and social forces that had shaped Ts'un-yü's clas-

18. Susan Mann (Jones), "Hung Liang-chi," pp. 158–59. See *Pei-chuan chi*, 51.3a–3b, Li Huan, *Kuo-ch'ao ch'i-hsien lei-cheng*, 132.27a–27b, and Yun Ching, *Ta-yun shan-fang chi*, p. 163, for accounts of this episode.

19. See Susan Mann (Jones), "Scholasticism and Politics," pp. 30–33, on the problem of reconciling *k'ao-cheng* studies and political dissent in Hung's intellectual development.

20. Schwartz, "Foreword" to Liang Ch'i-ch'ao, *Intellectual Trends*, pp. xi–xxii.

sicism in the 1780s carried over into the 1790s when Hung Liang-chi challenged imperial policy and publicly represented literati activism. Two heirs of Ch'ang-chou's elite traditions had articulated intellectual and political currents at the turn of the nineteenth century that would mushroom into major movements for the remainder of the dynasty. Four decades before the Opium War, literati activism and New Text voluntarism were on the ascent.

THE LITERATI REEMERGENT

Chuang Ts'un-yü's criticism was veiled, as we have seen, in classical studies. Ts'un-yü himself did not speak out directly, no doubt because he and other officials had lost the ear of the Ch'ien-lung Emperor to Ho-shen. Chuang only witnessed Ho-shen's rise to power. Hung Liang-chi, however, protested it. It would be too much to attribute Hung's 1799 letter to the influence of Chuang Ts'un-yü's *Kung-yang* Confucianism. Yet both were products of literati debates surrounding Ho-shen's position in state politics. In addition, both Chuang and Hung drew on Ch'ang-chou traditions of statecraft and scholarship to articulate their respective positions. And Hung's relations with the Chuang lineage in Ch'ang-chou had long been intimate, going back to his childhood and continuing into his mature adult life. More a Han Learning scholar than New Text advocate, Hung Liang-chi's statecraft interests nonetheless bore the stamp of the "learning of Ch'ang-chou."[21]

Hung's letter is clearly the work of a man who lived to see the end of Ho-shen and the subsequent promise of reform under a new emperor. When the reform failed to materialize, Hung felt compelled to break the silence:

> But I am torn by an inner conflict that I cannot resolve. On the one hand I am beset by my deep devotion to my master; on the other, I dare not forget the true significance of the advice from teachers and friends. Now I am merely a Hanlin [academician]. It is not part of my duty to remonstrate. But I can think of many times, in the few years since I became an official, that I have enjoyed unusual favor in serving my country. An official does not receive such favor without repaying it. Nor would a subject dare to seem as if he had feelings that he had not voiced completely.

Hung's decision to protest as a concerned Hanlin academician may also be explained in light of efforts then underway to reconsider the

21. See Hung's exchange of scholarly views with Chuang Shu-tsu in Hung Liang-chi, *Hung Pei-chiang shih-wen chi*, vol. 1, pp. 250–51 (*chüan* 6). See also Polachek, *Inner Opium War.*

limited role of the Hanlin Academy, which had become devoid of political concerns.[22]

Yao Nai, a Sung Learning advocate distressed by the apolitical vocations of most Han Learning scholars, composed an essay entitled "On the Hanlin Academy" ("Han-lin lun"). He complained of the superficiality of the academy's purely literary concerns and its failure to encourage candor. Criticizing the Hanlin Academy's loss of its remonstrance function (*chien-shu*), which it shared in earlier dynasties with imperial censors (*yü-shih yen-kuan*), Yao Nai, perhaps mindful of Hung Liang-chi's letter to Prince Ch'eng, complained:

> For this reason, the gentleman searches after the Way. Petty men seek after [literary] techniques. The [public] responsibility of the gentleman is expressed through the Way. The responsibility of the petty man is expressed through [literary] techniques. . . . Of course, the Way is contained within [literary] technique. Yet it would be better if expressed through loyal remonstrance and public debate, which encompass the greatness of the Way. Simply to use phrases and graphs to occupy the time of a Hanlin academician only limits him to [literary] technique.

Yao pointedly added that Ming Hanlin academicians surpassed their Ch'ing counterparts as voices of remonstrance. Hung Liang-chi's 1799 letter in many ways was an early form of *ch'ing-i* protest patterns that became characteristic of nineteenth-century gentry activism.[23]

Hung Liang-chi appealed to the literatus as a concerned individual, not to any particular faction. By going it alone, Hung was able to sidestep the full force of Confucian strictures against literati cliques. His solitary stance may in part account for the Chia-ch'ing Emperor's decision to exile Hung to Chinese Turkestan instead of having him summarily executed. More important, the emperor's mercy signaled that literati dissent would be tolerated as long as it was voiced through appropriate channels.[24]

A vital precedent, imperially authorized, had been established, and Hung Liang-chi's letter became a celebrated case throughout the Ch'ing empire. Hung was treated as a hero by adoring crowds and admiring gentry he met on the way to exile in far-off I-li. The Chia-ch'ing Emperor, cognizant that an execution would unintentionally spread terror

22. *Pei-chuan chi*, 51.6b, translated in Mann (Jones), "Hung Liang-chi," p. 161.

23. Yao Nai, *Hsi-pao-hsuan ch'üan-chi*, 1.4a–5a. See Polachek, "Literati Groups." Cf. Whitbeck, "Kung Tzu-chen." For a somewhat dated discussion of *ch'ing-i* see Eastman, *Throne and Mandarins*, pp. 20–29.

24. Nivison, "Ho-shen and His Accusers," p. 242.

throughout the bureaucracy and thus prevent other officials from speaking freely and offering him needed advice, maintained that he had never considered killing Hung. In fact, he claimed he was keeping Hung's letter near his bedside as a constant reminder of a ruler's obligations in affairs of state.

In fact, the emperor pardoned Hung Liang-chi in 1800 and allowed him to return after a drought in Peking resulted in the ritual granting of amnesties to propitiate heaven. In the official pardon, the emperor publicly blamed himself for punishing a remonstrating official. Rain immediately fell, according to the imperial account, and the emperor composed a poem to commemorate the occasion, which was included in one of Hung Liang-chi's collected writings.[25]

Susan Mann observes that Hung Liang-chi regarded himself simply as an honest Confucian official in the finest tradition of official remonstrance (*yen-lu*). She adds:

> But to students of imperial power and its changes in the Ch'ing dynasty, Hung's letter marks the beginning of the shift of the balance, away from the throne and out into the ranks of the bureaucracy. For Hung's ruler not only failed to halt, but was unable to discern, the fading of imperial authority that Hung and his contemporaries had been watching for "twenty or thirty years."

By 1800 the political climate in China had changed. The Chia-ch'ing Emperor had tolerated what previous emperors—particularly the Yung-cheng and Ch'ien-lung emperors—had expressly forbidden, namely, unauthorized public censure of the throne.[26]

The Hung Liang-chi case did not legitimate factions, however. Consequently, the Chia-ch'ing Emperor's efforts to lessen the autocratic aura of the throne did not retract or even modify Confucian injunctions against collective political participation. In fact, the emperor feared that a policy of vindictiveness against the remnants of Ho-shen's cronies would revive the destructive factionalism of the late Ming. He had been lenient with Ho-shen's followers to avoid divisions at the court. Now he dealt leniently with Hung Liang-chi as well.

Tung-lin-style factionalism thus remained expressly forbidden by imperial fiat and Confucian ideology. Within a nineteenth-century imperial system caught between internal rebellion and external imperialism,

25. Susan Mann (Jones), "Hung Liang-chi," pp. 159–60. See *Ta-Ch'ing Jen-tsung Jui (Chia-ch'ing) huang-ti shih-lu*, 50.44a.

26. Susan Mann, "Hung Liang-chi," p. 160, and Nivison, "Ho-shen and His Accusers," p. 243.

however, China's lettered elite increasingly sought political legitimacy for their role in determining their fate. "Voices of remonstrance" came forth and attempted to redress literati grievances and to ameliorate the dynasty's problems. Factions and parties took shape around contemporary political, social, and economic issues.[27]

Hung Liang-chi's dramatic 1799 letter marked the first overt reemergence of gentry activism within the institutional and ideological confines of the late Ch'ing Confucian imperium. The Ch'ien-Chia transition had altered the focus of debate within which New Text Confucianism and statecraft issues would be rhetorically utilized during the nineteenth century. It was not accidental, then, that both statecraft politics and New Text theory contributed to the ideological integrity that *ch'ing-i* factions needed in order to vie for the upper hand in imperial politics and to gain the political leverage required to deal with the decay of the Ch'ing imperial state.

As the dynasty faltered, the influence of its scholar-officials grew stronger. Seeking precedents, *ch'ing-i* groups reevaluated their seventeenth-century predecessors, and the Tung-lin legacy was reopened for particular study and possible emulation. Efforts by late Ming Tung-lin activists and early Ch'ing statecraft scholars to redefine literati solidarity within the state bureaucracy were now reinterpreted as heroic examples for contemporaries to address the problems of the early nineteenth century.[28]

THE POLITICS OF LANGUAGE

Literary debate during the eighteenth and nineteenth centuries reflected changing literati values in scholarship and politics. Both Sung Learning in T'ung-ch'eng and New Text studies in Ch'ang-chou, for example, were intimately tied to revived interest in ancient-style prose (*ku-wen*) as the appropriate expression of Confucian values. The language of politics, T'ung-ch'eng and Ch'ang-chou stylists contended, was poorly served by the academic lexicon of Han Learning scholars. At issue was political conviction vs. scholarly impartiality. T'ung-ch'eng and Ch'ang-chou advocates of *ku-wen* regarded the parallel prose (*p'ien-t'i-wen*) of Han Learning and examination essays (*pa-ku-wen*) as the antithesis of Confucian ideals.

27. *Ta-Ch'ing hui-tien shih-li*, vol. 22, p. 17091, edict dated fourth Year of Chia-ch'ing. Cf. Polachek, *Inner Opium War*.

28. Whitbeck, "Kung Tzu-chen," pp. 16–17. See also Eastman, *Throne and Mandarins*, pp. 16–29, and Rankin, "'Public Opinion' and Political Power."

LITERARY GENRES

We describe earlier in this study the links between literary expression and statecraft rhetoric, specifically noting that the ancient-style-prose tradition in Ch'ang-chou dated back to T'ang Shun-chih in the late Ming. Later Ch'ang-chou literati maintained that T'ang exemplified the ideal of Confucian literary expression, "Prose is a vehicle for the Way" (*wen i tsai tao*). We find here Confucian justification for literary pursuits in which any account of moral and political ideals was tied to the narrative form used to express those ideals. Ch'ing dynasty literary men in Ch'ang-chou and T'ung-ch'eng in particular believed that Confucian values were inseparable from a certain narrative style best exemplified in the classical writings of the ancients.[29]

Differences between accounts of Confucian ideals by Sung Learning advocates and those by Han Learning advocates corresponded to disputes over what narrative form best captured the central characteristics of Confucian private and public life. It was consequently no coincidence that areas where Sung Learning traditions remained prominent (most notably in T'ung-ch'eng and Ch'ang-chou) in the eighteenth century, despite the popularity of Han Learning, were also strongholds of ancient-style prose. It is an odd paradox (or convenient sublimation) that Sung Learning, with its rhetorical denigration of the metaphysical status of human desires, would be associated with a literary genre such as *ku-wen*, in which political conviction could be expressed so directly. It is equally paradoxical that Han Learning, with its affirmation of human desires, could be tied to parallel-prose styles that favored dispassionate narrative over literary flair.[30]

When compared with their Sung-Ming Neo-Confucian predecessors, *k'ao-cheng* scholars were generally less interested in poetry. When they did write it, the verse was usually taken less seriously both by themselves and by critics. The opposite had been true in the Sung through Ming period, when T'ang dynasty poetic models were the rage. Huang Tsung-hsi and Ku Yen-wu, for instance, were important figures in early Ch'ing changes in literary criticism. Stressing classical erudition, both Huang and Ku placed classical studies (*ching-hsueh*) in a much more important position than the writing of poetry.

29. Hsu K'o, *Ch'ing-pai lei-ch'ao*, 70.31–37. See also Yeh Chia-ying Chao, "Ch'ang-chou School," pp. 153–61. On the *wen i tsai tao* ideal formulated by Chou Tun-i (1017–73), see James J. Y. Liu, *Chinese Theories of Literature*, pp. 114, 128.

30. For a discussion see MacIntyre, *After Virtue*, p. 135. See also my "Criticism as Philosophy."

Poetry, although still acceptable as an ancillary art, was considered of marginal value for the statecraft concerns that were the pillars of Confucianism. Historical and classical research, in their view, had priority. Writing in defense of his research, Ku Yen-wu explained. "The learning of a gentleman is used to illuminate the Way and is applied to save the world. If one writes nothing but poetry and [examination] essays, this indicates that one only has a petty talent for forming words in flowery ways. Of what use is it?"[31]

Eighteenth-century Han Learning scholars such as Hui Tung followed these leads, limiting their literary interests to textual annotations of poetic collections and anthologies. Applying a *k'ao-cheng* approach to poetry, Hui Tung's literary interests, according to Kondo Mitsuo, represented the kind of scholarly poetic discourse one would expect in a time when evidential research was popular.

Because academic and literary fields interacted, *k'ao-cheng* research techniques were employed to study and classify—that is, to anthologize—the poetry and prose of earlier eras. Kondo Mitsuo has argued that the triumph of evidential research in the Yangtze Delta during the eighteenth century symbolized a major transformation in poetic discourse and literary criticism. Wu Hung-i, in his recent analysis of Ch'ing poetics, also stresses the role *k'ao-cheng* scholarship played in literary criticism. In the seventeenth and eighteenth centuries an important movement in the criticism of poetic diction, phrasing, rhymes, and metrics was complemented by the establishment of a consistent theory of poetics. According to Wu, Ch'ing critics thought they had finally succeeded in identifying the phonic patterns and poetic dictions that gave poetry its aesthetic power.[32]

The appreciation of poetry among Ch'ing literati, when compared with Ming Confucians, was not overwhelming. Textual specialists such as Yen Jo-chü (despite participation in his father's poetry society), Yao Chi-heng, and Tai Chen, for example, left behind almost no poetry whatsoever. Ch'ien Ta-hsin, for instance, sought renown as a classical and historical scholar and was dismayed when he achieved fame as a

31. For Ku Yen-wu's remarks see *Ku T'ing-lin shih-wen chi*, p. 103. See Yamanoi Yū, "Kō Sōgi no gakumon," pp. 33–35, and "Ko Enbu no gakumon kan," 74–75.

32. Kondo Mitsuo, "Kei Tō to Sen Taikin," pp. 715–16, and "Kōshōgaku ni okeru bunsho hyōgen kyōri ichi shijū." "Theoretical consistency" refers to the prosodic rules for *ko-tiao* (form and style) and *shen-yun* (spirit and tone) that pervaded Ch'ing poetics. See also Wu Hung-i, *Ch'ing-tai shih-hsueh ch'u-t'an*; James J. Y. Liu, *Art of Chinese Poetry*, pp. 67–69, 77–80; and Liu, *Chinese Theories of Literature*, pp. 45, 88–97.

poet after his verse was published in literary anthologies over which he had no control.

Similarly, the historian Chang Hsueh-ch'eng (1738–1801) intentionally wrote very little poetry. He explained: "History's main concern is politics, and verse is not really of importance." Poetry, Chang thought, was at best bad prose. Chang Hsueh-ch'eng was particularly dismayed with and jealous of the popularity of what he considered to be Yuan Mei's "vulgar" poetry.[33]

Nevertheless, poetry continued to be studied and practiced by Ch'ing literati—*k'ao-cheng* scholars included. During the Ch'ing, poetry often complemented the work of the scholar. Chu I-tsun and Ch'en Wei-sung achieved considerable reputations for their influence on the revival of the difficult genre of *tz'u* (lyric poetry), in addition to their highly respected textual studies. In the late eighteenth century in Ch'en Wei-sung's native Ch'ang-chou, lyric poetry became a literati passion important enough to be recognized as the "Ch'ang-chou school" of lyric poetry.

Chao I became famous as a Ch'ang-chou stylist of *tz'u*, although his major efforts were spent in *k'ao-cheng* work on the Dynastic Histories. Likewise, Chang Hui-yen's well-known lyric poetry, which represented the pinnacle of the Ch'ang-chou school, was less important to him than his Han Learning studies of the *Change Classic* (see chapter 4). Until the nineteenth century, then, scholarship took precedence over poetry or prose, and a man's literary production was considered little more than an ornament for precise scholarship.[34]

ANCIENT-STYLE PROSE IN THE CH'IEN-CHIA TRANSITION

The T'ung-ch'eng and Yang-hu schools of ancient-style prose (the latter in Ch'ang-chou) carried literary debates into the nineteenth century, when new social and political conditions made activist Confucians seek more appealing literary vehicles for political discussion. The Han Learning vs. Sung Learning debate was frequently disguised as a literary

33. Chang Hsueh-ch'eng, *Wen-shih t'ung-i*, pp. 585–89. See Kondo, "Sen Taikin no bungaku," and "Kei Tō to Sen Taikin," pp. 705–706. See also Nivison, *Chang Hsueh-ch'eng*, pp. 134, 137, 246, and Kawata, "Shindai gakujutsu no ichi sokumen," 97–98. For Yen Jo-chü's links to his father's poetry society, known as the Wang She (Society of expectations), see Li Yuan-keng, "Wang She hsing-shih k'ao."

34. Aoki, *Shindai bungaku hyōronshi*, pp. 546–53. See also Wu Hung-i, "Ch'ang-chou-p'ai tz'u-hsueh yen-chiu," pp. 33–62, and Lung Mu-hsun, "Lun Ch'ang-chou tz'u-p'ai," 1–3, 20. On Chang Hui-yen's turn from literature to classical studies see Wang Hsi-hsun, *Ch'ieh-chu-an wen-chi*, p. 204.

quarrel. In contrast to the dispassionate genres of literary criticism and poetics associated with Han Learning, a body of critical theory on prose writing also became prominent in the late eighteenth century.

Literary critics who favored parallel-prose styles could invoke the compositional principles used in writing "eight-legged" (*pa-ku*) civil service examination essays. Li Chao-lo, a Ch'ang-chou critic of *ku-wen*, even questioned the authenticity of ancient-style prose, contending that parallel prose represented the true narrative order within which the classical vision had been articulated. Li's argument represented vintage Han Learning: because *ku-wen* was a T'ang-Sung literary form, its ties to the Han classical legacy were distant and questionable. Han Confucians had composed in parallel prose, demonstrating to Li that the latter was nearer to the time of the ancients and thus more likely to be the way the ancients expressed their views. Predilection for parallel prose among more apolitical evidential research scholars meant that reading replaced recitation. Expository prose required styles of expression that emphasized dispassionate content over emotional form.[35]

Even the T'ung-ch'eng school of ancient-style prose was influenced by these compositional principles. Literary stylists mixed their genres freely. Li Chao-lo could complain about the T'ang-Sung origins of *ku-wen*, for example, but he still became known as a master of its form. Fang Pao, the doyen of T'ung-ch'eng Sung Learning, asserted that literary composition should have "models and rules" (*i-fa*) to follow. Yao Nai, the late-eighteenth- and early-nineteenth-century spokesman for T'ung-ch'eng Sung Learning, later stipulated eight criteria for evaluating good prose writing.

Yao claimed that style should be united with content. But even he advocated proficiency in evidential studies, although only as a complement to literary training (*wen-chang*) and moral philosophy (*i-li*). Juan Yuan accused the T'ung-ch'eng scholars of stealing their compositional principles from the eight-legged essay form. Fang Pao, according to some, "used ancient-style prose for contemporary-style [examination] essays and used contemporary-style essays for ancient-style prose." Similarly, Yao Nai's examination essays were compared to his *ku-wen*.[36]

Rhetorically, however, nineteenth-century vindicators of *ku-wen* fre-

35. On the literary debate see *Li Shen-ch'i nien-p'u*, 2.7a–7b. See also Hsueh Tzu-heng, "Hsing-chuang" (Obituary for Li Chao-lo), pp. 2b–3a. Cf. Ching-i Tu, "Chinese Examination Essay."

36. Yao Nai, *Hsi-pao-hsuan ch'üan-chi*, (1984 ed.), pp. 47–48 (*chüan* 4), includes a preface for Hsieh Ch'i-k'un's (1737–1802) *Hsiao-hsueh k'ao*, a specialized reference and

quently ridiculed the eight-legged essay as a hybrid genre that had evolved from Ming dynasty literary forms. Ancient-style prose was defended as a superior genre of literati expression, especially when compared with what was considered the overly rigid and uncreative composition principles employed in examination essays (*shih-wen*, lit., "contemporary-style essays"). In the late nineteenth century *ku-wen* advocates called for an end to the "eight-legged" essays required of all examination candidates. Some Sung Learning scholars at times supported changes to an examination format that enshrined Sung Learning.[37]

Yao Nai's 1779 *Ku-wen tz'u lei-tsuan* (Classified collection of writings in ancient-style prose), for instance, comprised ancient texts that were classified into thirteen categories—e.g., critical essays, colophons, letters, epitaphs, and so forth. Yao's work served as an alternative textbook, in contrast to collections of examination essays, which brought together in convenient form many of the more polished essays written in *ku-wen*. Later, Li Chao-lo compiled his *P'ien-t'i-wen ch'ao* (Transcriptions of parallel-prose writing) to counter the popularity of Yao's collection. Genres became as much a part of Ch'ing scholarly debate as Confucian doctrine.[38]

Yao Nai's complaint about Hanlin academicians, described earlier, was that they devoted too much time to literary questions, presumably examination essays. Instead, he favored a more activist stance whereby Hanlin members would remonstrate with the throne concerning issues of state. Ancient-style prose, according to the T'ung-ch'eng partisans, was not an escape from political responsibility but, rather, served as the appropriate literary means for literati to proclaim their political opinions to the throne and others. T'ung-ch'eng stylists like Yao Nai, Yao Ying, and Fang Tung-shu saw no contradiction between political activism and proficiency in *ku-wen*. One was reflected in the other, they contended.

---

descriptive bibliography for *k'ao-cheng* studies. See also pp. 80–81 for Yao Nai's letter to Ch'in Ying (1743–1821), which discusses his efforts to balance moral philosophy, literature, and philology as complementary fields of Confucian studies. For a discussion see Wang Tse-fu, "T'ung-ch'eng-p'ai te i-fa," pp. 125–33, and Ch'iao Kuo-chang, "Lun T'ung-ch'eng-p'ai ku-wen ho Ch'ing-ch'ao te wen-hua t'ung-chih," pp. 136–37, 138–39. Cf. Pollard's discussion in his *Chinese Look at Literature*, pp. 140–57, and Leung Man-kam, "Juan Yuan," pp. 109–30.

37. Ching-i Tu, "Chinese Examination Essay," pp. 405–406. See also Ch'ien Chung-lien, "T'ung-ch'eng-p'ai ku-wen yü shih-wen te kuan-hsi wen-t'i," pp. 151–58.

38. Edwards, "Thirteen Classes of Chinese Prose," pp. 770–88. See also Chiang I-hsueh, "T'an yu-kuan T'ung-ch'eng wen-p'ai te chi-ko wen-t'i," pp. 77–87.

ACTIVISM AND LITERARY FELLOWSHIP

James Polachek has described the centrality of literary or aesthetic fellowship in forging peer group collaboration in Peking before the Opium War. Tolerance for literati remonstrances after the Chia-ch'ing Emperor's lenient treatment of Hung Liang-chi translated into the creation of numerous poetry associations in the early nineteenth century; such associations had been banned after the purge of the Tung-lin partisans in the seventeenth century. Their return to favor in the nineteenth century in turn meant that lineage strategies for local organization were no longer the only legitimate form of gentry association tolerated by the state (see chapter 1).[39]

Poetry associations, according to Polachek, "served as templates for more ambitious kinds of network-building, such as occurred when the literati mobilized for independent political action." They therefore became socially acceptable frameworks within which shared ideals "tended to draw the lettered elite into durable units of political cooperation." Consequently, the prominence of literary fellowship, when evaluated in light of earlier discussion of stylistic debates between dispassionate Han Learning scholars and politically motivated Sung Learning advocates, was not a sign of elite idleness. Rather, it symbolized the use of more activist ancient-style-prose rhetoric by literati associations. Frequently the latter opposed what they considered the apolitical stance taken by eighteenth-century Han Learning scholars.[40]

The "re-rhetorization" of stylistic expression did not produce political interest groups per se, but the formation of aesthetic fellowships did bring like-minded Confucians together into loose political alliances. As in the late Ming, such groups would eventually adopt overt political stances in the face of social, political, and military crises. Polachek shows how more vocal organizations of *ch'ing-i* ("voices of remonstrance"), so much a part of the late Ch'ing political landscape, derived from these earlier fellowships of literati. Although associations tended to reorganize literati around stylistic—that is, aesthetic—issues, they contained political overtones. We will discuss these groups below in light of the revival of interest in Tung-lin-style activism. For example, in the nineteenth century the activist image of the Ming loyalist Ku Yen-wu began to supersede his earlier reputation as a pioneer of evidential research. The literati group that coalesced in the 1830s around the Han

39. Polachek, *Inner Opium War.*
40. Ibid.

Learning scholar Chang Mu perceived in Ku's reformist intent an antidote to contemporary dynastic dislocation. In 1843 Chang Mu and his group erected a temple in Peking to pay tribute to Ku Yen-wu and thereby to justify their own political activism.[41]

Compared with the professionalized scholarly roles and apolitical associations of eighteenth-century *k'ao-cheng* scholars, nineteenth-century literary associations provided a framework for gentry political commitments. Hung Liang-chi's explosive emotionalism (*pu te i*) in his 1799 letter to Prince Ch'eng, when compared with his dispassionate philological and geographical studies, gives us a clue to the politics of language in Han vs. Sung Learning debates. In due course, the language of politics after the Ho-shen era slowly but decisively began to shift from dispassionate Han Learning classical models to politically charged themes associated with T'ung-ch'eng *ku-wen* and Ch'ang-chou New Text studies.[42]

ANCIENT-STYLE PROSE IN CH'ANG-CHOU

The Yang-hu school of ancient-style prose in Ch'ang-chou—a precursor of the literati clubs that came into vogue during the nineteenth century—comprised a diverse collection of local Confucians, for whom literary achievement went hand in hand with classical studies. Preeminent as stylists, Chang Hui-yen and Yun Ching were the mainstays of *ku-wen* in Ch'ang-chou. Their contacts with a broad range of Ch'ang-chou literati created an influential group there, which shared a feeling of literary fellowship and political concern for what they considered the deleterious effects of the Ho-shen era. The Yang-hu group, correspondingly, was broadly based enough to include Han Learning and Sung Learning within its areas of aesthetic interest.[43]

This Ch'ang-chou group of literary and political fellowship also included Chao Huai-yü, Huang Ching-jen, Hung Liang-chi, Liu Feng-lu, Chuang Shou-chia, and Li Chao-lo, who participated in the late eighteenth and the early nineteenth centuries either directly or indirectly. Along with Chang Hui-yen and Yun Ching, these men represent a notable convergence of Ch'ang-chou statecraft traditions, literary currents, and New Text studies.

41. See Kuhn, "Late Ch'ing Views," p. 15, and Guy, "Evidential Research Movement," 100.
42. Polachek, *Inner Opium War*.
43. Wilhelm, "Chinese Confucianism," pp. 309–10.

The *Kung-yang* Confucianism of Chuang Ts'un-yü and the New Text Confucianism of Liu Feng-lu were part of a more general change in literati attitudes in Ch'ang-chou toward their roles in Confucian political life. It would be too much to assert that New Text studies brought about these changes. *Kung-yang* theory confirmed, however, many of the conceptual and literary changes brought about by the debate between Sung Learning and Han Learning.[44]

As an example of the overlap between literary concerns and New Text classicism we can cite Chang Hui-yen's readiness to interpret lyric poetry as the repository of "esoteric meanings" (*wei-i*) presented by worthy men to express their hidden, critical views of contemporary events. Requiring a level of classical erudition comparable to that in parallel prose and a stylistic complexity comparable to that of ancient-style prose, lyric poetry became an appropriate poetic vehicle for literati expression of Confucian values and sentiments. Appropriating praise-and-blame theory that had long been applied to Confucius's *Spring and Autumn Annals* and *Poetry Classic*—particularly by Former Han New Text Confucians—Chang Hui-yen assumed that *tz'u* contained the same kind of indirect criticism of political affairs. Just as the *Annals* and *Poetry* classics represented, through allegorized (*pi*) prose and poetry, direct confirmation of the decline of classical values during the Eastern Chou dynasty, so too the works of lyric poets were allegorized reflections of their society. In effect, Chang Hui-yen was reading into *tz'u* what Chuang Ts'un-yü had discovered in the *Kung-yang Commentary*: the written legacy of the past provided leverage for criticizing the affairs of any age.[45]

STATECRAFT, REFORM, AND THE TUNG-LIN REVIVAL

Statecraft rhetoric was not new in the nineteenth century. Statecraft traditions dating back to the Ming dynasty had survived in Ch'ang-chou and elsewhere because elite families and lineages maintained their dual roles as officials of the empire and local leaders. The Chuangs and Lius in Ch'ang-chou were but two examples of such traditions in the Yangtze Delta. What was new in the nineteenth century, however, was

44. For Liu Feng-lu's ties to these literary currents and his involvement with other Ch'ang-chou literati see Chao Chen, *P'i-ling wen-lu*, 2.33a. See also Whitbeck, "Kung Tzu-chen," pp. 1–7.

45. Yeh Chia-ying Chao, "Ch'ang-chou School," pp. 157–62.

the overwhelming reformism of statecraft discourse. The status quo was no longer the point of departure for nineteenth-century statecraft.

Statecraft rhetoric in the Confucian lexicon was not always reformist. More often than not flood control, bandit suppression, calendar adjustment, and institutional change were seen within the general framework of daily and continual system maintenance. Too often we overlook the underlying pattern of statecraft discourse in late imperial China by automatically equating statecraft with reformism. We assume that reformist rhetoric signifies a revival of statecraft, when in fact it has been the Confucian's raison d'être since antiquity.

Those who uncritically accept the passionate calls for reform in nineteenth-century China typically assume that political statecraft had disappeared in the eighteenth century. Our account of the New Text school in eighteenth-century Ch'ang-chou demonstrates that statecraft remained an important undercurrent in Han Learning and *k'ao-cheng*. Governmental efficacy during the Ch'ien-lung Emperor's reign before the Ho-shen era, when compared to earlier dynasties, indicates that someone was fairly effectively running the empire. The political and social institutions required by a complex society in turn required bureaucratic and technical experts to preserve them. The very existence, moreover, of the Chuangs and Lius as a "professional elite" of office-holding families specializing in government service forces us to reject the notion that there was a statecraft revival in the nineteenth century.

Although Han Learning and evidential research took the brunt of nineteenth-century criticism of eighteenth-century classical scholarship for its dispassionate expression and apolitical scholarly roles, Han Learning scholars themselves had reacted against the excesses of Ho-shen's henchmen. They themselves touched off debates on the proper role of literati in political affairs. Many Confucians came to recognize that traditional stopgap measures could not solve problems of population increase, imperial corruption, and foreign imperialism. As our subsequent discussion of the Ch'ang-chou native Yun Ching will show, many Confucians in the early nineteenth century already perceived that imperial policy and institutions required a major overhaul in order to replace the outmoded forms of land and tax control then in place.[46]

The more Confucians recognized the nation's plight, the more they called for statecraft reforms. Statecraft reform thus replaced statecraft

46. On Yun Ching see Wilhelm, "Chinese Confucianism," pp. 309–10. Cf. Hartwell, "Demographic, Political, and Social Transformations of China," pp. 417ff, and Metzger, *Internal Organization of Ch'ing Bureaucracy*.

system maintenance. In due course the less reformist statecraft of the eighteenth century was overlooked in a passionate critique of everything associated with the late Ch'ien-lung reign and the Ho-shen era. New Text Confucianism was itself a product of this transition. Chuang Ts'un-yü's clarification of Confucian voluntarism in light of the *Kung-yang Commentary* was essentially conservative in intent. In the nineteenth century, however, New Text rhetoric was applied to activism and reformism.

THE TUNG-LIN REVIVAL

Emotional calls for reform of the imperial institutional structure became more frequent as the Ch'ing dynasty entered its final century of rule. Overlapping strands of classical studies, statecraft rhetoric, and literary currents in the early nineteenth century legitimated gentry participation in national political affairs. Ch'ang-chou in particular contributed to these developments.

As we have seen, Chuang Ts'un-yü's *Kung-yang* studies represented a response to the corruption of the Ho-shen era. Hung Liang-chi's controversial 1799 letter to the throne represented an overall criticism of moral laxity and literati evasion of political responsibility. In the first decade of the nineteenth century, Yun Ching commended the flexibility and adaptation that had informed the sages' handling of administrative policy. Chuang, Hung, and Yun were all products of the "learning of Ch'ang-chou."

A sense of moral crisis during the Ch'ien-Chia transition and increased tolerance for official remonstrance to the throne combined to deepen interest in earlier gentry moral protest and political criticism. Literati were now more concerned about their own abdication of political responsibility in affairs of state than with being accused of political factionalism. Of particular relevance to the "voices of remonstrance" was the precedent established by the Tung-lin partisans. According to Judith Whitbeck, "Once the efforts of the late Ming activists came to be viewed as exemplary of literati moral resolve in a time of troubles, the rationale that supported these restraints ceased to be valid, and the way was open for a revival of literati activism."[47]

Attempts to reeducate nineteenth-century Confucians about their Tung-lin predecessors placed the late Ming Tung-lin debacle in a new light. The scholar-official Wang Ch'ang (a Han Learning advocate who

47. Whitbeck, "Kung Tzu-chen," pp. 16–17, and Polachek, *Inner Opium War*.

in his student days had studied in Su-chou with Ch'ien Ta-hsin and Wang Ming-sheng) late in his life began to compile a history of the Tung-lin Academy. He conceived of the project as a first step in reviving interest in the Tung-lin legacy. Literati in Ch'ang-chou welcomed his initiative.

Both Chao Huai-yü and Li Chao-lo, each members of Ch'ang-chou literary groups, helped to reprint the works of seventeenth-century Tung-lin and Fu She activists. Wang Ch'ang similarly compiled the works of the late Ming statecraft enthusiast Ch'en Tzu-lung and compiled a chronological biography (*nien-p'u*) for him. A key figure in the Ch'ien-Chia transition in Ch'ang-chou, Li Chao-lo, prepared biographical accounts in which he lauded the moral resolve of his Tung-lin predecessors.[48]

Grandnephew of the distinguished Han Learning scholar Ch'in Hui-t'ien, Ch'in Ying (1743–1821)—a Wu-hsi native and follower of Chang Hui-yen's ancient-style prose—helped Wang Ch'ang to collect materials on the Tung-lin Academy, which Wang hoped to include in an account of all academies in the empire. Wang thought the register of academies would serve to propagate moral teachings (*ming-chiao*), championed in the late Ming by Tung-lin partisans.

Ch'in Ying also prepared a commemorative essay for the 1797–99 renovation of the Tung-lin Academy in which he stressed the importance of Wu-hsi literati in national affairs during the late Ming. The repair would, according to Ch'in, allow Tung-lin to flourish again as a center for Wu-hsi literati interests and to help Confucians escape the shackles of an education oriented simply to passing the imperial examinations. He was careful to add, however, that the harm brought by late Ming factionalism must be avoided. Writing about the Tung-lin Academy in 1799, Ch'in Ying, like Hung Liang-chi, could not openly justify political factions for literati.[49]

But in a 1795 essay that commemorated the discovery of autograph manuscripts of the Tung-lin founder Ku Hsien-ch'eng, Ch'in Ying reevaluated Ku's role in the factionalism that plagued the Ming dynasty. Noting the antifaction dictum enunciated by Confucius himself, Ch'in

48. Li Chao-lo, *Yang-i-chai wen-chi*, 10.5b, 6.1a–2b, 6.30a–32b, 7.3a–4a. See also Hummel et al., *Eminent Chinese*, pp. 102–3, 805–7.

49. See the Li Chao-lo biography in *Chuan-kao*, no. 6774(1-3), at the National Palace Museum, Taipei, and *Wei Yuan chi*, pp. 358–61. On Ch'in Ying see Hsu K'o, *Ch'ing-pai lei-ch'ao*, 70.34, and Ch'in Ying, *Hsiao-hsien shan-jen wen-chi*, 4.11a–12a, 5.40a. See also Yao Nai's letter to Ch'in Ying in Yao's *Hsi-pao-hsuan ch'üan-chi* (1984 ed.), pp. 80–81 (*chüan* 7).

Ying nonetheless praised Ku Hsien-ch'eng's efforts to infuse the Tung-lin party with "public-minded" (*kung*) concerns.

According to Ch'in Ying, Ku Hsien-ch'eng had not been guilty of organizing a political faction (*tang*). Rather, Ku had brought together a "group" (*ch'ün*, lit., "social grouping") of like-minded literati for the common good. Confucius had said: "The gentleman is conscious of his own superiority without being contentious. He comes together [*ch'ün*] with other gentlemen without forming cliques [*tang*]."[50] Ch'in Ying attempted an intriguing end run around the ideological objections to the formation of parties or factions in Confucian politics. Seeking to carve out limited space for literati "groups" to form, Ch'in cited Confucius's authorization of such "groups" to circumvent the contemporary view that "factions" were forbidden. Ch'in Ying's effort to legitimate literati groups as *ch'ün* was picked up by late Ch'ing New Text reformers such as K'ang Yu-wei and Liang Ch'i-ch'ao, who made the concept of *ch'ün* the centerpiece for their stress on political renovation.

For instance, K'ang Yu-wei, in his *Ch'ang-hsing hsueh-chi* (Notes on studies at Ch'ang-hsing), went on from where Ch'in Ying had left off to include a notion of "human community" (*ch'ün*) in his political proposals. Benevolence (*jen*) in concrete social terms was the mode in which humans associated with each other and formed communities, according to K'ang. Under the rubric of "communities," K'ang sought to legitimate gentry political organizations within the imperial system.

For his part, Liang Ch'i-ch'ao made K'ang Yu-wei's formulation of *ch'ün* (community) the centerpiece of his own emphasis on political renovation. In an essay entitled "On Community" ("Shuo-ch'ün"), Liang (as Hao Chang has perceptively observed) downplayed the moral aspects of benevolence and analyzed instead "the vital problems of political integration, political participation and legitimation, and the scope of the political community." Early-nineteenth-century Tung-lin advocates such as Ch'in Ying were Confucians who unquestioningly operated in an imperial context. But Liang Ch'i-ch'ao stepped out of that tradition, although he still carried forward concepts of political organization bequeathed by his predecessors.[51]

50. *Lun-yü yin-te*, 32/15/22, and Lau, trans., *Confucius*, p. 135. Ku Hsien-cheng's manuscripts may have emerged because of the changing political atmosphere. A member of the Ku family showed the manuscripts to Ch'in Ying.

51. Ch'in Ying, *Hsiao-hsien shan-jen wen-chi*, 6.11a. Cf. Frank Chang, *Ancestors*, pp. 322–53. See K'ang Yu-wei, *Ch'ang-hsing hsueh-chi*, pp. 9a–9b. For a discussion see Hao Chang, *Liang Ch'i-ch'ao*, pp. 45, 95–100, and Wakeman, "Price of Autonomy," pp. 64–66. See also Liang Ch'i-ch'ao, *Yin-ping-shih wen-chi*, vol. 1, pt. 2, pp. 3–4.

Ch'in Ying admitted that the Tung-lin partisans, despite their moral courage, had become embroiled in the political chaos of the late Ming. The tragedy was that Ku Hsien-ch'eng had never anticipated factional strife when he assembled his followers at the Tung-lin Academy. Reversing the long-standing view that the Tung-lin partisans helped to precipitate the factionalism that brought down the Ming dynasty, Ch'in Ying asserted that they had become entangled in political forces neither of their making nor in their control:

> Master [Ku Hsien-ch'eng] had already passed away before he could suffer the poisonous affairs that would follow. Moreover, what followed was not anything he could have foreseen. Consequently, I have often said that the Tung-lin calamity was not Master [Ku's] fault. Nor was the fall of the Ming the fault of the Tung-lin [partisans].

Ch'in's remarks reveal that the ideological premises of the imperial proscription against literati political activities were again being tested.[52]

Further interest in the Tung-lin partisans was evinced by Kuan T'ung and Fang Tung-shu in the 1820s and 1830s. Admired by Fang Tung-shu, Kuan was a proponent of statecraft initiatives in the 1820s to deal with breakdowns in administration then occurring along the Grand Canal. In an essay on changing political and social customs (*feng-su*) from the Ming to the Ch'ing dynasties, Kuang T'ung contended that the Ch'ing had gone too far in eliminating "voices of remonstrance" from the political arena. Although factionalism required drastic measures, the resulting quiescence made for a cultural environment in which no one took responsibility for needed reforms.

Cloaking his discussion of political values in an appeal for cultural change, Kuan maintained that "with regard to the ruler, officials and the people are not his bones and meat" for him to do with as he pleased. Kuan added: "There has never been a case when the customs of the empire have not changed [*pien*]. The literati of the empire make a show of calling for reform of institutions [*kai fa-tu*]. If customs do not change, then men of talent do not appear. Even with [reformed] institutions, who will put them into effect?" For Kuan T'ung, earlier dynasties perished because they were unable to keep pace with changing times. Successful dynasties were those that recognized the need to correct policy mistakes. Kuan T'ung's discussion implied that the literati were now more concerned with examination success and scholarly prestige and were thereby losing their voice in political affairs (*wu-ch'üan*). New

52. Ch'in Ying, *Hsiao-hsien shan-jen wen-chi*, 6.11a–11b.

cultural values were required that would encourage scholars and officials to deal with the problems of the age.[53]

Similarly, Fang Tung-shu, a defender of Sung Learning, acknowledged the Tung-lin partisans for their political concern and activist spirit. In a letter to Lo Yueh-ch'uan, then serving as a prefect, Fang presented his defense of Tung-lin-style activism as an antidote to the apolitical scholarly values championed by Han Learning. After introducing what was to become among Sung Learning advocates a stereotypical portrayal of Han Learning as politically uninvolved and morally unconcerned with affairs of state, Fang wrote admiringly of the statecraft concerns of late Ming Confucians, who had been devoted to practical affairs in contrast to contemporary *k'ao-cheng* bookworms.[54]

Fang's presentation sounded very much like the Ming loyalist Huang Tsung-hsi's famous mid-seventeenth-century account of the Tung-lin school:

> Today, when people talk about Tung-lin, they associate the Tung-lin party's disaster with the fate of the Ming house. So mediocre men use this as an excuse to accuse Tung-lin of causing the loss of our country to the Manchus and refer to it as the Two Parties. Even those who know better say that although many men of Tung-lin were gentlemen, the group included certain political extremists, and their associates were not all gentlemen. In the end they were no better than the partisans of the Later Han period. Alas, this is all nonsense!

Fang Tung-shu's letter to Prefect Lo contained an impassioned rejection of charges that Tung-lin activism (*Tung-lin ch'ing-i*) had been responsible for the fall of the Ming dynasty. In effect, Fang was overturning the Ch'ing dynasty consensus that factionalism precipitated by the Tung-lin partisans could be singled out as the culprit in the late Ming debacle. Refuting an "explanation that had for over a century been accepted by gentry and literati," Fang noted that, "based on his investigations," such charges against the Tung-lin activists had no foundation (*i-wei pu-ran*). He charged that the moral resolve and commitment of the partisans to mainstream Sung Learning based on the teachings of Ch'eng I and Chu Hsi had been overlooked in the haste among Chinese and Manchus in the seventeenth century to locate a scapegoat for the Ming debacle. Rhetorically, Fang asked: "Of those who at that time weakened the nation and brought its downfall, did they all come from

53. Kuan T'ung, *Yin-chi-hsuan wen-chi*, *ch'u-chi*, 4.1a–3b.
54. Fang Tung-shu, *I-wei-hsuan wen-chi*, 6.6a–9a. On Fang Tung-shu see my *Philosophy to Philology*, pp. 242–48.

the Tung-lin activists?" Of course not! According to Fang, had not the eunuchs led by Wei Chung-hsien and other imperial or gentry factions been more responsible? These latter "evil parties" (*hsieh-tang*) contrasted with the high-minded goals and moral resolve of the Tung-lin party.[55]

Supplanting the accepted wisdom concerning the fall of the Ming, Fang Tung-shu traced its decline to the national conditions (*kuo-shih*) brought on by a breakdown in political consensus in the 1620s. "We can say that those who would blame the Tung-lin [party for the Ming collapse] have not thought through the ins and outs of the matter," Fang contended. Imperial power had been delegated to unscrupulous eunuchs and officials, for which Ming emperors bore the ultimate responsibility: "If the ruler had known how to employ talent and high ministers had been public-minded and fair without private interests, then parties of like-minded individuals (*p'eng-tang*) would not have appeared." Ming despotism (*chuan-ch'üan*) had hatched factions and plots that would bring the dynasty to its knees.

According to Fang Tung-shu, "the fall of the Ming in the end had nothing to do with the 'voices of remonstrance' (*ch'ing-i*)" represented by the Tung-lin party. By undercutting the consensus concerning the Tung-lin partisans, Fang endeavored to infuse an activist spirit in his fellow literati in the hope that it would replace what he considered the amoral erudition of contemporary Han Learning scholars. Such efforts were encouraged under a broad range of rhetorical devices. Both Sung Learning and New Text Confucianism added fuel to the cause of statecraft and reform. Moreover, Fang Tung-shu's defense of the Tung-lin party presented nineteenth-century Confucians with a role model for their activities. Ideological proscriptions against factions yielded to renewed gentry activism.[56]

FROM LINEAGE DESCENT GROUPS TO GENTRY ALLIANCES

Political alliances among like-minded gentry became more defensible in the nineteenth century. The role of state ideology in channeling gentry solidarity away from horizontally aligned individuals into more acceptable organizations based on descent, (which we describe earlier)

55. Fang Tung-shu, *I-wen-hsuan wen-chi*, 6.10b–11a. For Huang Tsung-hsi's account see his *Ming-Ju hsueh-an*, pp. 613, and the translation in *Records of Ming Scholars*, pp. 223–24.

56. Fang Tung-shu, *I-wei-hsuan wen-chi*, 6.11b–15b.

weakened. This process reversed the late Ming and early Ch'ing pattern whereby kinship ties replaced nonkinship alliances as the predominant strategy for gentry mobilization. Earlier Northern Sung and late Ming efforts to legitimate gentry political organizations were repeated in the late Ch'ing.

Ch'ing-i groups in the nineteenth century increasingly represented the reemergence of gentry factions based on horizontally aligned peer groups. Descent remained an important source of gentry solidarity in local society, but in the broader provincial and national political arenas kinship strategies gradually became secondary. As in the seventeenth century, Tung-lin-style associations of concerned literati began to dominate political discussion.

Changes in New Text Confucianism during the early nineteenth century were a case in point. Protected and promoted by two powerful lineages in Ch'ang-chou, which had used descent to further their local and national interests, New Text ideas in the eighteenth century represented a local school of scholarship in which kinship ties were its raison d'être. After Liu Feng-lu, however, New Text ideas transcended their origins in the Chuang and Liu lineages. Changes in political climate meant that the *Kung-yang* agenda no longer required lineage support for survival and legitimacy. New Text ideas prospered in the nineteenth century as a vehicle for literati alliances that favored statecraft rhetoric and institutional reform.

Where lineages had once sufficed for gentry mobilization, and kinship conferred the Confucian authorization that such mobilization required, gentry were now raising their more activist political voices in Tung-lin-style literary *cum* political organizations. Reform ideology during the early nineteenth century was built around the confluence of conceptual changes and literary debates that we shall pursue in our final remarks. Changes in both the language of politics (to which the Ch'ang-chou New Text school had contributed) and the politics of language were interwoven and inseparable.[57]

THE LANGUAGE OF POLITICS

In Ch'ang-chou Prefecture, gradual changes in the language of politics were reflected by two parallel and overlapping developments. On one hand, we have the more voluntarist and reform-minded classical views

57. Cf. Harootunian, *Toward Restoration*, pp. 129–245, on the culture of politics and the politics of culture.

of the Chuang and Liu lineages, expressed through the classical writings of Chuang Ts'un-yü and Liu Feng-lu. *Kung-yang* Confucianism affirmed an image of Confucius as an activist in a time of moral and political crisis. This activist portrait emerged and became increasingly popular during the Ch'ien-Chia transition, when social and political crises were denoted as a moral crisis by Hung Liang-chi and others. The changing image of Confucius during the Ch'ing dynasty—from Sung Learning moralist to Han Learning teacher—had evolved into that of a New Text activist, corresponding closely to the conceptual and literary changes described earlier.[58]

On the other hand, these developments were contemporaneous with literary debates in Ch'ang-chou. In addition, Yang-hu County (in Ch'ang-chou Prefecture) became a center for *ku-wen* literary currents, which eventually vied with the T'ung-ch'eng school for preeminence in Ch'ing literary circles. Classical discourse and literary forms of expression complemented each other as the language of politics in the nineteenth century. This homology between classicism and literature was typified by the reformist writings of the Ch'ang-chou literatus Yun Ching.

YUN CHING

A confidant of members of the Chuang lineage, particularly close to Chuang Shu-tsu, Yun Ching is another interesting embodiment of the overlap of ancient-style prose in Ch'ang-chou and New Text studies. His use of New Text ideas will serve as a fitting conclusion to our account of the development and transformation of New Text Confucianism before the Opium War. Fifteen years before Kung Tzu-chen and Wei Yuan studied under Liu Feng-lu in Peking, statecraft reform and New Text theory had already been clearly articulated in Ch'ang-chou. In many ways, Yun Ching demonstrates that ideas enunciated by late Ch'ing reformers such as K'ang Yu-wei were not without precedent.

Well-read in the Classics and Dynastic Histories, Yun Ching never attained high office. In fact, late in his career he was impeached from his position as first-class subprefect of Nan-ch'ang Prefecture, Chiang-hsi Province, and retired from public life in 1814. Yun's family had long been known for aesthetic pursuits. A forebear, Yun Shou-p'ing, had earned his living as a painter rather than serve the conquering Manchu

58. Shimada, "Shinkai kakumeiki no Kōshi mondai," pp. 3–8.

dynasty. Ironically, Shou-p'ing became regarded as one of the great Ch'ing landscape painters. The Yun family had achieved high status during the Ming dynasty, but because of its Ming loyalism a family member never again obtained similar official prominence during the Ch'ing.[59]

In a series of eight essays entitled "Successive Reforms During the Three Dynasties" ("San-tai yin-ke lun"), Yun Ching provided a unique window on the wedding of ancient-style prose as a medium of political expression and New Text theory as a vision of institutional change. Yun Ching, for example, used the theoretical premise of progressive institutional change during the Three Dynasties to invoke the reformist spirit of the sages. For our purposes, Yun's essays epitomize the conjunction of conceptual, political, and literary themes that we have explored to this point.

Drawing on the key *Kung-yang* notion of epochal change during the Hsia (2205??–1767? B.C.), Shang (1766?–1122? B.C.)., and Chou (1122?–221 B.C.) dynasties (*san-shih*, lit., "three epochs"; see chapter 7), Yun Ching cited institutional reform (*yin-ke*) initiated by the sages to defend the notion that it was not only legitimate but also necessary for institutions to change in accord with the times. Long before K'ang Yu-wei and the impact of the West was felt, New Text Confucianism had escaped its Han Learning origins and become an overt channel for legitimating contemporary political change.[60]

THE NEW TEXT LEGACY: FROM PHILOLOGY TO POLITICS

The opening salvo in Yun Ching's series of essays demonstrated how much conceptual change had been incorporated in both the New Text and ancient-style prose agendas:

> In ordering the empire, the sages did not use excessive force to control the situation. They sought out the means to keep things within bounds and that's all. By necessity, they employed means that would accord with human feelings [*jen-ch'ing*]. Consequently, the middle way for institutions [*chung-chih*, that is, neither too autocratic nor too lenient] was the model of the sages.

59. Wilhelm, "Chinese Confucianism," p. 309, and Hummel et al., *Eminent Chinese*, pp. 959–60. See also *Wu-chin Yang-hu hsien ho-chih* (1886), 26.46a–46b. For Yun Ching's ties to members of the Chuang lineage, see Yun, *Ta-yun shan-fang chi*, pp. 182–83, 211, 226, 232.

60. Yun, *Ta-yun shan-fang chi*, pp. 4–12 (*ch'u-chi chüan* 1).

The expression "accord with human feelings" (*ho hu jen-ch'ing*) resonates with the late-eighteenth-century reevaluation of human aspirations, exemplified by Tai Chen's notion that "the sages ordered the world by giving an outlet to people's feelings." Tai Chen in the 1770s attacked what he considered the moral straitjacket of Ch'eng-Chu orthodoxy but limited his critique to scholarly issues. By Yun Ching's time the context had changed, however. Yun placed his discussion of the classical affirmation of human desires within a general discussion of political change, whereby the goal of reform was to accord with human aspirations. As a *k'ao-cheng* scholar, Tai Chen had not yet made the link between reevaluation of Neo-Confucian moral theory and institutional reform.[61]

Contrasting the sages with the rule of the five hegemons (*wu-pa*), who had usurped the kingship prerogative during the Eastern Chou dynasty, Yun Ching stressed the need for institutions that did not conflict with human feelings: "With regard to human feelings, if they do not reach extremes of indiscretion, the sages by necessity would not reject them. This was the Way of the Three Dynasties." Unfortunately, according to Yun, the "glory of early antiquity" had been lost during the era of the *Spring and Autumn Annals* (722–481 B.C.) and the Warring States period (403–221 B.C.), despite efforts during the Han dynasties to revive the sagely teachings. The institutional structure of the empire, ever since the rapacious policies of the Ch'in dynasty (221–207 B.C.), had never recaptured its earlier ideals or models. Yun Ching's intention in writing on the Three Dynasties was to clarify the legacy of the sages: "Consequently, I have discussed [the Three Dynasties] in detail, seeking out the origins of kingly government and investigating its vicissitudes in order to overturn the theories of the various Confucian erudites. I hope thereby that we can be enlightened concerning the sagely way of ordering the empire."[62]

Yun's second essay discussed ancient land policy in light of early feudal institutions, which guaranteed the people proper sustenance from the fields they cultivated. Yun Ching observed that the sages had adapted policy to changing conditions, recognizing that institutions could not remain glued to the past. As feudal institutions had become increasingly inappropriate, Yun went on, the sages had devised new

61. Ibid., "San-tai yin-ke lun i," p. 4. On Tai Chen's position see my "Criticism as Philosophy," pp. 172–75.

62. Yun, "San-tai yin-ke lun i," p. 4.

ways to solve land tenure problems that would accord with the needs of the people. Yun Ching rhetorically concluded:

> Therefore I say, even the sages would not oppose those who go beyond the middle way of government or those who are not satisfied with the middle way, as long as they do not overtly go against human sentiments. For this reason, if I am right, we can understand the means by which the Three Dynasties were at peace and well-governed for a long period. If, however, I were wrong, then the times of [the sage-kings] Yü, T'ang, Wen, and Wu would have long since been lost and forgotten. Would their sons and grandsons have had even one day of rest? [Yet, their views] hold for ten thousand generations.[63]

Flexibility was the sine qua non of proper governance of the people.

In the third essay, Yun Ching drove home his main thesis. The secret to successful government was adaptation. Blindly following the ancients was wrong. The ancients themselves had created order by according with the times: "With regard to preceding dynasties, [the sage-kings] changed what could be changed. What could not or need not be changed they preserved. That was all there was to it."

The example Yun Ching cited to verify his thesis was the well-field (*ching-t'ien*) system, a feudal model for egalitarian land tenure that was frequently invoked by Confucians from Mencius through the late empire as the ideal. Quoting the *Kung-yang Commentary*, Yun Ching argued that even this hallowed Confucian ideal had long since been deemed inappropriate because conditions no longer prevailed that would enable the system to work. To maintain the egalitarian ideals of the well-field system under conditions of empire expansion and population growth, Yun contended, required adjustments and changes to the system "to accord with the times in order to equalize human feelings" (*yin-shih i chün min-ch'ing*). Successive changes in land tenure worked out during the Hsia, Shang, and Chou dynasties served as both models and warnings. The legacy of the sage-kings was not engraved in stone.[64]

Yun Ching began to test the limits of Confucian ideals in the fourth essay. Historical realities, must take precedence over political and moral abstractions:

> The well-field system was a model that could not be discarded. Yet, in the end it was discarded. Confucians have all blamed and cursed [the Legalist]

63. Ibid., "San-tai yin-ke lun erh," pp. 5–6.
64. Ibid., "San-tai yin-ke lun san," pp. 6–7.

> Shang Yang [d. 338 B.C.] for this. Shang Yang's crime was in initiating the Ch'in [dynasty] policy of separating land into private parcels [*ch'ien-mo*], which extended from the area within the pass to the east [that is, the Wei River valley in northwest China]. Discarding the well-field system was not [Shang] Yang's crime. When a model is about to be put into practice, the sages cannot prevent it. When a model is about to be discarded, the sages cannot prevent that [either].

By rejecting the Sung Learning fixation on unalterable Confucian social and political principles, Yun Ching attempted to reintegrate institutional flexibility with Confucian statecraft. Remarkably, he cited an indirect defense of Legalism in order to gainsay the rhetoric of idealistic Confucians.

Institutions survived, according to Yun, because they accorded with the desires of the people (*yin min chih yü*). When they no longer did, they were discarded. The well-field system worked when the empire was limited in size and population. Appropriate to a small kingdom, it was impossible to put into effect when the empire grew substantially:

> For this reason, people living during the Spring and Autumn and Warring States periods could not see the benefits of the well-field system enjoyed by earlier generations. What they saw instead was how they suffered from the harm of the equal-field system. Its advantages were long since past and thus easily forgotten. Its harm was close-at-hand, and thus it was quickly gotten rid of.[65]

Institutional change occurred because of unceasing changes in the heavenly Way (*t'ien-tao*) and human affairs (*jen-shih*). In fact, the Ch'in dynasty marked the boundary between antiquity and imperial China, according to Yun Ching. Institutional changes that followed were not the work of Legalist criminals, but rather resulted from the unalterable (*pu-te pu-jan*) march of time:

> Before the Ch'in [dynasty], what was put into practice at all levels of the state and society were all institutions of the Three Dynasties. After the Ch'in, what has been put into effect at all levels of state and society are not all derived from the institutions of the Three Dynasties. The well-field system is one example. What would the sages' position be on this? I say, the sages cannot be predicted. Nevertheless, their writings all remain, and we can scrutinize and learn from them. . . .
>
> If Confucius and Mencius had been born during the time of the first emperor [of the Ch'in, that is, Shih-huang], would they necessarily have pressured the empire to revive the well-field system? Alas! This is a view that vulgar Confucians are sure to defend.

65. Ibid., "San-tai yin-ke lun ssu," pp. 7–8.

Yun Ching was broadening Confucianism to include a notion of progressive change within the empire's institutional framework.[66]

All of the first four essays in the series were composed in 1800. Nine years later Yun Ching returned to them and prepared the final four essays. In essay five Yun turned his attention to tax issues. During the Three Dynasties, he contended, land taxes were high, one in ten, but the state mobilized its resources equitably through a corvée to meet public and military requirements. After the Three Dynasties, however, land taxes were low, one in thirty, but people no longer shared equitably in their labor duties, with slaves and hired laborers performing corvée for the wealthy.

The people, happy under the equitable policies of the Three Dynasties, now succumbed to sadness and rancor. Growing social and material divisions among the people produced parasitism. Growing trade and specialization meant that more and more unproductive groups depended on less and less productive people. This dangerous development could not last for long. According to Yun Ching, the nourishing potential of heaven and earth could not support such conflicting developments.[67]

Envoking an ideal time when the people had cultivated the land of the empire as free peasants, Yun Ching then held up the present by way of contrast when only the wealthy owned land and the poor tilled the soil as tenants. An endless cycle of poverty was the product of this inequitable land system, Yun concluded. A "disease of agriculture" (*nung-ping*) was the way he described it. Yun's account of antiquity reflects more recent agricultural developments, which we trace in chapter 1. Specifically, Yun's notion of a shared corvée was a stalking-horse for the comprehensive *li-chia* land and tax system that had been pride of the first Ming emperor. The drift of peasants into tenancy after the Three Dynasties resembled late Ming social changes. It was then that the forces of commercialization and monetarization in the farm economy culminated in the Single-Whip tax reforms, effectively dismantling the labor service statutes of the tax system and forcing many peasants into tenancy and bond servant status. For Yun Ching, antiquity was a mirror for contemporary problems.

Likewise, artisans and merchants suffered from economic disloca-

66. Ibid., p. 8.
67. Ibid., "San-tai yin-ke lun wu," p. 8.

tions produced by an inequitable tax system after the Three Dynasties. Unlike today, Yun Ching explained, the sage-kings of antiquity had devised policies to increase the productivity of the four groups of people (*ssu-min*, that is, gentry, farmers, artisans, and merchants) to meet the demands of society. Because the four groups were now becoming less numerous, the needs of the larger society could no longer be met. Old social distinctions had become anachronistic. Yun proposed the following solution:

> What was the Way of the sages? In my view, they did not create difficulties for the four [groups of] people. What is the Way of not creating difficulties for the four [groups of] people? In my view, this is done by not creating difficulties for [those engaged in] farming, crafts, or commerce, but at the same time stressing no more than the supervision by the gentry.

One can see between the lines of this narrative that Yun was pointing to the growing problems of overpopulation and rural poverty that by the Chia-ch'ing Emperor's reign had become endemic. Confucians were asked to loosen their control over peasants and merchants.[68]

The sixth essay turned to the military institutions of the Three Dynasties. The Hsia, Shang, and Chou had all instituted what Yun Ching called a "commoners' army" (*min-ping*), which depended for its logistical support on an organizational infrastructure that allowed men on duty to avoid nonmilitary tasks. Off-duty soldiers provided the food, clothing, and weapons. The Chou dynasty in particular had fallen because its leaders had not maintained the organizational structures necessary for a "commoners' army."

Yun added, however, that as the size of the empire grew, small-scale local troops were no longer appropriate in major military battles. In a small kingdom, one could expect a soldier to be a farmer as well. But in later periods of large empires, this military strategy was self-defeating. Forcing military men to double as farmers led to military decline. Compelling farmers to double as soldiers led to agricultural decline. Changing conditions of warfare in an expanding empire made older organizational forms obsolete.

Yun Ching said that during the Han and T'ang (618–906) dynasties further reforms of the military system had been introduced. Confucians, using models derived from the Three Dynasties, criticized the reforms when they failed to live up to ancient ideals. According to Yun Ching,

68. Ibid., pp. 8–9.

however, this criticism was misplaced. What was important was to make changes appropriate to the present situation. A "commoners' army" should be organized in the latest and most advanced ways possible. To restrict military organization to forms appropriate to a small kingdom in ancient times would be counterproductive.[69]

Ancient administrative policies dealing with obligatory state labor service occupied Yun Ching's attention in essay 7. After discussing the myriad state-assigned labor duties during the Three Dynasties (land tax, military tax, farming tax, etc.), Yun contrasted the egalitarian ideals of the ancient system of shared local responsibilities with the inequities of later dynasties. Under the umbrella of a discussion of antiquity, Yun described the post-fifteenth-century monetarization of state labor duties, which we summarized in chapter 1. The result was the virtual disappearance of the labor service tax as a locally shared responsibility. The rich were able to hire others to take their place.

Yun Ching observed that since the middle of the T'ang dynasty, when the empire tilted economically toward the rich farmland in south China, the earlier system whereby government officials performed most state labor duties (*kuan-i*) was no longer sufficient. Population growth and the expansion of the empire during the late T'ang and Sung dynasties required labor service from the people to help keep pace with the tax and military system previously handled by officials. The Ming *li-chia* system represented for Yun Ching the bureaucratization of this long-term process, as local village leaders accepted more state responsibilities and were given official titles for their efforts. This change, Yun held, sought to address the inadequacies of earlier corvées.[70]

What was now required, Yun Ching went on, was further reform to ameliorate the inequities that had built up in the state labor service since the Sung and Ming dynasties. Labor service now fell most heavily on the shoulders of those who could least afford it, while those who could afford it were increasingly able to evade their tax responsibilities. Yun defended an evolutionary perspective on institutional reform: "There are no institutions in the empire that are [totally] without harm. There are no affairs that do not [in any way] cause unease for the people. One should select what accords with the requirements of the times and effect it in such a way that its deficiencies are lessened."

69. Ibid., "San-tai yin-ke lun liu," pp. 9–10.
70. Ibid., "San-tai yin-ke lun ch'i," pp. 10–11.

The benefits of the labor service, according to Yun, had long since been left behind: "If we realize that the labor service of officials can be lessened, then we can eliminate vexing matters. If we realize that the labor service of the people can be completely abolished, then all within the empire will be overjoyed and responsible."[71] By 1800 Confucians such as Yun Ching had recognized that the corvée was counterproductive.

In the eighth and final essay Yun Ching presented an eloquent summation of his position. The sage-kings had put in place a system of government that was still appropriate to the present, he contended, but the exact institutions and policies of that idealized system were subject to modification:

> From the above we can observe that the way the sages ordered the empire can be realized. If the gains [from government institutions] have not reached completion, then one doesn't change everything [*pu pien-fa*]. If the benefits [derived from political structures] are still incomplete, then one doesn't change [those] structures [*pu i-ch'i*]. This is common sense. . . . The way of the early kings was to make changes that accorded with the times [*yin-shih shih-pien*].

Sage-kings had bequeathed a notion of flexibility that avoided the extremes of totalistic reform or reactionary preservation.

The "middle way for institutions" (*chung-tao*) allowed the sages to navigate freely between political extremes. In conclusion, Yun Ching lashed out at Confucian ideologues and formalists who appealed to the sages for empty ideals:

> Those Confucians and erudites cannot go far enough in honoring the sages and worthies, but they have thereby ignored the general populace. They dare to follow ancient ways but are cowards when it comes to present requirements. They are earnest in believing in specialties [*chuan-men*] but are weak in examining all the possibilities. Is this sufficient to know the sages?

To counter the chaotic words (*luan-yen*) of those who had grasped only a small Old Text faction (*i-chia*) of the wisdom of the sages, Yun Ching vociferously favored a New Text Confucian statecraft agenda that emphasized pragmatism in making necessary reforms.[72]

Yun Ching's ancient-style-prose essays articulated Confucian statecraft

71. Ibid., p. 11.
72. Ibid., "San-tai yin-ke lun pa," pp. 11–12.

within an evolutionary perspective. The Three Dynasties were models (*fa*) for Confucian statecraft, not institutional icons. The well-field system, local "commoners' army," and state corvée were for Yun Ching early anachronisms that had long since proved ineffective. Yun portrayed Confucius and the sages in his essays as creative innovators who operated according to the limits placed on them by the "realities of the times" (*shih-shih*). But the portrayals were carefully modulated. A friend and frequent correspondent of the New Text scholars Chuang Shu-tsu, Liu Feng-lu, and Sung Hsiang-feng, Yun Ching expressed through his essays a vision that combined the moral ardor of ancient-style prose with New Text voluntarism. A form repopularized in the late eighteenth century for expressing Sung Learning moral philosophy was tempered by Yun Ching with an affirmation of human aspirations and the need for institutional reform. The dispassionate Han-Learning-style examination of China's institutional history was infused with statecraft concern for the present.[73]

Yun Ching's essays on the Three Dynasties were not well-researched exercises in *k'ao-cheng* erudition. They were emotional calls by an activist Confucian to find new solutions to old problems. Aroused Ch'ang-chou literati exemplified by Chuang Ts'un-yü, Hung Liang-chi, and Yun Ching were products of an economic and social crisis exacerbated by the political recriminations generated by the Ho-shen affair. Conceptual change that stemmed from Han Learning currents of thought and added epistemological leverage to dismantle the rigorous formalism of Neo-Confucian political orthodoxy neatly dovetailed with activist Tung-lin-style political rhetoric. Intellectual change spilled over into statecraft rhetoric.

Wei Yuan, Liu Feng-lu's student and follower, similarly managed a celebrated synthesis of New Text voluntarism and statecraft reform. In writings that resembled the evolutionary scheme for institutional change laid out much earlier in Yun Ching's 1800–1810 essays, Wei Yuan also discussed the irrevocability of change:

> From the Three Dynasties and before, Heaven was completely different from the Heaven of today. The earth was completely different from the earth of today. People were all different from the people of today. Moreover, things were all different from the things of today. . . .
>
> Sung Confucians only talked about the Three Dynasties. The well-field system, feudal organization, or civil service examination procedures of the

73. Ibid., "Yü Sung Yü-t'ing shu," (Letter to Sung Hsiang-feng), p. 142, and "Ta Chuang Chen-i hsien-sheng shu" (Reply to Mr. Chuang Shu-tsu's letter), p. 226.

> Three Dynasties by necessity cannot be revived. Such [talk] only allows those who are practically oriented to criticize Confucian methods for their ineffectiveness. According to the way the gentleman creates order, if it is attempted without [according with] the mind-set of the Three Dynasties and before, only vulgarity will result. Not knowing the circumstances and conditions in [changes] from the Three Dynasties to the present has produced ineffective [government]. . . .

The past, although the basis for the present, was not an eternal ideal. Just as last year's calendar does not apply to this year, so "those who speak adoringly of the past must test it in the present."[74]

Yun Ching had set New Text studies on a course that would ultimately lead to the triumph of political discourse over classical philology among late Ch'ing Confucians. Unheralded and unread in twentieth-century scholarly circles, Yun brought to virtual completion the political implications of Chuang Ts'un-yü's turn to *Kung-yang* Confucianism in the 1780s and the formation of the Ch'ang-chou New Text school. By 1810 classical scholarship and political discourse were reunited in a post-Neo-Confucian form, whose Confucian legitimacy came more and more from efforts to unify Han and Sung Learning. By rereading Yun Ching's tour de force, we can better understand the intellectual, social, and political winds of change felt by New Text Confucians thirty years before the Opium War.

74. *Wei Yuan chi*, pp. 47–49, 156–58.

Afterword

Imperial power in Ch'ing China was rarely naked. It was usually clothed in self-justifying Confucian concepts and rhetoric. Political language drawn from the Classics represented the ideological voice of the late imperial state. Through the classics, rulers, statesmen, military leaders, and local gentry tried to legitimate their monopoly over public and private institutions. Classical studies, which were institutionalized as political discourse, became a system of ideological exclusion and inclusion that delineated the raison d'être, that is, the public legitimacy, of state prerogative. Political power in the late empire was refracted through Confucian moral and political philosophy into compelling institutional and symbolic systems.

When, after 1800, the normative institutions of late imperial Chinese political culture failed to communicate morally compelling ideals, then alternative expressions of "legitimate" military and political power emerged to challenge the raison d'être of the Ch'ing state. By 1900 rebels, reformers, reactionaries, and revolutionaries competed for the reins of naked power in the name of their own ideological agendas, which they hoped to establish as normative. The stakes were very high, and millions perished as a traditional empire was replaced by a modern republic. In the course of these changes, the content and form of political discourse legitimating state power in China—the "voice of the state"—also changed dramatically. In state ideology, Western political theory—first republicanism and then Marxism—replaced Confucianism as the state's raison d'être.

Few have had a set of political values as ancient as those of the Chinese before the 1911 Revolution. Granting the appearance of Confucian "grand inquisitors," who throughout Chinese history betrayed the political ideals of the imperial state, it is remarkable that Confucian political culture (strengthened and compromised by contributions from legalism, Taoism, and Buddhism) remained intact.

Emperors, officials, scholars, and rebels came and went; socioeconomic conditions continued to change within the limits imposed by the biogeographical ecology of China. Even the state's political ideology was itself bent and refracted. What abided was the appeal to a golden past populated by sage-kings who had established acceptable guidelines for China's military, social, economic, and intellectual life. Their organizational strategies could be interpreted differently, but until 1911 they were not replaced. For two millennia, the past was the unquestioned guide for the present.

I have tried to shed light on long-overlooked links between Confucian classical discourse and political legitimation in the imperial state during a crucial transition to new forms of political discourse. We have examined the conflicting New Text vs. Old Text portraits of Confucius in order to gain a more precise and nuanced grasp of classical studies as the ideological source of the Confucian imperium's raison d'être. Our inquiry gives us a more balanced understanding of the political dimensions of intellectual change in late imperial China. Classical studies, if evaluated in a political vacuum (as is usually the case among sinologists), lose their intellectual vitality and social relevance.

The legacy of the Ch'ang-chou New Text tradition in the nineteenth century was important but not unique. Certainly New Text studies played an important role in the steady drift of gentry-officials toward new forms of political discourse to replace outmoded Neo-Confucian political values, which since the Ming dynasty had legitimated authoritarian government. Yet, by the nineteenth century Sung Learning advocates were also in the forefront of reformist politics. Social and economic pressures, coupled with population growth, placed demands on Ch'ing China that rulers and officials had never before faced.

As Yun Ching's perceptive essays on reform demonstrated, ancient ideals drawn from feudal times were already deemed unsatisfactory by New Text partisans. Alternative solutions were required. Many Confucian literati realized that the institutions enshrined in the imperial system were not inviolate. Unprecedented conditions required unprecedented solutions. To "accord with the times" became the slogan of a generation of statecraft scholars who during the early nineteenth century sought pragmatic solutions to the myriad organizational and logistical breakdowns that seemed to come all at once.

Confucian faith in the past as a guideline for the present remained intact. Increasingly, however, the past represented conflicting ideals of moral and political commitment. Institutions of the past, whether defended in Sung or Han Learning terms, were undergoing a crisis of confidence from which the imperial system would never recover. Chuang Ts'un-yü's tactical turn to the "esoteric teachings" associated with *Kung-yang* Confucianism was a pivotal event. It revealed that the crisis of confidence extended from imperial institutions to the very Confucian values he and his ancestors had served since the late Ming. Neither a marginal Confucian nor a disgruntled petty official, the Hanlin academician revealed in his scrutiny of unorthodox New Text classical texts that he had lost confidence in the Neo-Confucian lexicon, which he had mastered in his youth and defended as a young secretary to the emperor.

With hindsight, we know that in 1800 Ch'ing China was on the eve of a confrontation with Western imperialism and a rising Japan that would unleash revolutionary forces at all levels of Chinese society. Confucians like Chuang Ts'un-yü, Hung Liang-chi, and Yun Ching had already comprehended that if the Chinese empire hoped to cope successfully with its myriad problems, political reforms were required. Appeals to alternative forms of Confucianism to revamp the imperial system never succeeded, however. Reemergence of New Text Confucianism, the first of all imperial Confucianisms, coincided with the end of imperial China. Reformism, however, survived the failure of the 1898 reform movement.

Standing for new beliefs in a time of political, social, and economic turmoil, New Text Confucians championed pragmatism and the imperative of change. Recasting of Confucian tradition by the Chuangs and Lius in Ch'ang-chou also marked an initial step in emancipation from the ideological encumbrance, first, of accumulated Old Text imperial norms and ideals handed down since the Later Han dynasty and, second, from post-Sung Neo-Confucian orthodoxy. Like their Tung-lin predecessors, Ch'ang-chou New Text scholars opposed the arbitrary and oppressive political authority of the state. Unlike the Tung-lin partisans, who remained within the Neo-Confucian boundaries of political discourse, the Chuangs and Lius drew on New Text sources from the Former Han dynasty for inspiration in their ongoing efforts to express their political aspirations. Chu Hsi was left behind; Confucius reemerged as a voice for voluntarism and statecraft.

Beginning with Chuang Ts'un-yü and Liu Feng-lu, New Text Confucians appealed to a reconstruction of the past to authorize the present and to prepare for the future. Ch'ang-chou scholars had not yet reached a concept of political revolution or demonstrated a full understanding of social progress, but their New Text notions of historical change and their advocacy of practical institutional reform were important stepping-stones to an influential New Text vision of social and political transformation. K'ang Yu-wei, Liang Ch'i-ch'ao, and T'an Ssu-t'ung later elaborated on this vision in the 1890s and others thereafter.

New Text Confucianism in Ch'ang-chou was never revolutionary. Although scholars there proposed changes in the Confucian political agenda, they reaffirmed the role of classical ideals in the present. For them, Confucianism was the starting point and unquestioned constituent for new beliefs and patterns of political behavior. Their intellectual initiatives were tied to conscious and unconscious social commitments to their families and lineages, which had nurtured them and prepared them for public service. Even when iconoclastic, Ch'ang-chou scholars upheld the social status quo in which gentry-officials, organized into complex kinship and affinal alliances, continued to dominate local affairs. Their limited criticisms of state despotism offered no radical alternatives to the Confucian imperial political system or to the elitism of what we have called "gentry society."

Consequently, in addition to its intellectual legacy, the Ch'ang-chou New Text school represents an instructive example of the social and political uses of classical teachings in imperial China. Our inquiry into the eighteenth-century reemergence of New Text Confucianism in Ch'ang-chou Prefecture has documented the remarkable homology of kinship structures, classical teachings, and political agendas in gentry society. Mastery of the Confucian Classics enabled sons from elite lineages such as the Chuangs and Lius to gain admission via success on the state civil service examinations to a select world of political power and social prestige. Our study of the rise of the New Text school, accordingly, has also afforded us a unique perspective on how gentry in Ch'ang-chou weathered the great changes that occurred during the Ming and Ch'ing dynasties.

Gentry like the Chuangs and Lius were less successful, however, in navigating the fall of imperial China in our own time. When the Ch'ing dynasty formally collapsed in 1911, the demise of its imperial institutions accelerated the restructuring of the makeup and career strategies of the gentry elites who had filled those institutions. Furthermore, the fall of dynasty completed the eclipse of classical studies, which had legitimated imperial rule and the gentry monopoly on civil service examination success. The imperial state, local gentry, and Confucian ideology had evolved so closely in tandem that they were virtually inseparable. When one fell, they all fell together, bequeathing to posterity only fragments of their original political, social, and intellectual unity. Great lineages like the Chuangs and Lius in Ch'ang-chou and the schools of scholarship they spawned were no exceptions.

I have analyzed classicism, politics, and kinship in late imperial China as carefully interwoven threads, hoping to demonstrate their inseparability. The tapestry I have woven of Chinese intellectual and social history is still incomplete. Nonetheless, study of the Ch'ang-chou New Text school has revealed how elites in premodern China marshaled their cultural resources around the Confucian Classics to ensure their long-term political and social dominance. The study also demonstrates how and why Chinese scholar-officials like Chuang Ts'un-yü sometimes changed their minds about the dynasty they served and struck out in uncharted intellectual and political directions. In the final analysis, the reemergence of New Text Confucianism in late imperial China is about the power of state orthodoxy and the forms of gentry dissent, the state's intellectual hegemony and the gentry's political frailty.

APPENDIX ONE

Ch'ang-chou Administrative History

During the feudal era known as the Eastern Chou dynasty (771–221 B.C.), the area of present-day Ch'ang-chou became a county seat within the state of Wu. In the Confucian Classics, particularly the "Tributes of Yü" ("Yü-kung"; tr. reigned 2205–2198?? B.C.) chapter of the *Documents Classic*, Yang-chou, one of the nine divisions of the empire in prehistorical, traditional accounts, had included the area. But Chou dynasty historical records dated 547 B.C. mention only the city of Yen-ling (lit., "extending mound-tomb"), suggesting that the city was administratively still on the southern edge of ancient Chinese civilization. Late in the Warring States period (403–221 B.C.), the city of Yen-ling belonged at different times to the southern states of Ch'u and Yueh.[1]

After the Ch'in dynasty (221–207 B.C.) reunified the empire and established a system of prefectures (*chün*) and counties (*hsien*), Yen-ling City became part of K'uai-chi Prefecture (in present-day Che-chiang Province) with its name changed to P'i-ling (lit., "adjoining mound-tomb"). When the Han imperial system was established as a compromise between the prefectural system of the Ch'in and the feudal state system of the Chou, P'i-ling County remained part of K'uai-chi Prefecture, but within the larger administrative unit called Yang-chou. The latter unit by this time represented a geographical division in the Yang-

1. *Chiang-nan t'ung-chih* (1684), 2.22a. See also *Chiang-su ch'eng-shih li-shih ti-li*, p. 92, and *Ch'ang-chou fu-chih* (1886), 2.1a–27b.

tze Delta that was evolving from a state designation into a provincial unit, as bureaucratic density in south China increased after 200 B.C.[2]

As a result of the Han unification, P'i-ling and Wu-hsi became sister counties under a variety of prefectural divisions thereafter. During the Later Han (A.D. 25–220), for instance, P'i-ling and Wu-hsi counties were incorporated into Wu Prefecture in A.D. 129, suggesting the area was tilting increasingly toward the Su-chou region to the south. Under the succeeding Chin dynasty (265–316), however, first P'i-ling (in A.D. 281) and then I-hsing (during the Han known as Yang-hsien) became the prefectural headquarters for local government, though still within the Yang-chou regional framework. Consequently, by the fourth century A.D. P'i-ling Prefecture, now linked to Wu-chin (established in A.D. 281), Wu-hsi, and I-hsing as administrative counties within it, was the major subprovincial division in its area.[3]

Before the Sui dynasty (581–618) unification of north and south China (after three centuries of disunity), the administrative divisions in P'i-ling remained relatively stable. In A.D. 291 (some accounts give A.D. 311), however, P'i-ling's name was changed to Chin-ling (lit., "mound-grave of Chin") to avoid conflicting with the name of a lord enfeoffed in the area. The Sui dynasty subsequently restored the name to P'i-ling and, after a lapse of about two centuries, again designated Yang-chou as the equivalent of a provincial unit in the Yangtze Delta. During this period the city of Yang-chou became the premier cultural and commercial center of south China, rivaling the great cities of Ch'ang-an and Lo-yang in the traditional heartland of China along the Wei River valley in the northwest. The entire Lower Yangtze region was drawn toward Yang-chou because of its trading links to the Silk Road and because of its proximity to the north China plain. Its location north of the Yangtze River on the newly built Grand Canal made Yang-chou the key city between north and south.[4]

The Sui government created two prefectures in the P'i-ling area. In addition to P'i-ling, composed of Chin-ling (formerly Wu-chin), Wu-hsi, I-hsing, and Chiang-yin counties, the area around present-day Ch'ang-shu City was reorganized and called Ch'ang-chou Prefecture.

2. *Ch'ung-hsiu P'i-ling chih* (1483), 1.65a. See also *Chiang-su liu-shih-i hsien-chih*, p. 21, and *Chiang-su ch'eng-shih li-shih ti-li*, pp. 96–97.

3. *Chiang-nan t'ung-chih* (1684), 2.22a–22b. See also *Ch'ung-hsiu Ta-Ch'ing i-t'ung-chih*, 86.2a–4a, 72.2a. On Wu-hsi see *Wu-hsi Chin-k'ui hsien-chih* (1814), 1.1a–2b.

4. *Chiang-su ch'eng-shih li-shih ti-li*, pp. 92–93, 97–98. See also pp. 157–164, on the importance of the Grand Canal and the north-south grain tribute system for Yang-chou.

When Ch'ang-shu subsequently became a county in neighboring Su-chou Prefecture, the designation of "Ch'ang-chou" from A.D. 589 on was applied to P'i-ling. Later, however, the Sui dynasty abandoned the prefectural designation of *chou* in A.D. 607 in favor of the earlier *chün* system. The Ch'ang-chou area was again called P'i-ling Prefecture along with the four counties that had earlier been assigned to it.[5]

Chiang-yin County, which came into administrative existence in A.D. 556 under the Southern Liang dynasty (502–557), became increasingly central in the Sui and subsequent T'ang (618–906) dynasties. Its location on the southern banks of the Yangtze River gave it the only direct shipping access within Ch'ang-chou to Yang-chou trading markets on the northern edge of the great river. Chin-ling (Wu-chin) and Wu-hsi, by way of contrast, relied on the Grand Canal for indirect access via Chen-chiang to Yang-chou. As a result, trade in P'i-ling (Ch'ang-chou) increasingly went through Chiang-yin's port to Yang-chou. After holding an initial prefectural status, Chiang-yin became a county in P'i-ling in A.D. 626. Later, during the Five Dynasties period (907–960), when all of P'i-ling was reorganized under Chiang-yin prefecture (*chün*), Chiang-yin's political status reaffirmed its economic importance.[6]

During the early T'ang dynasty, in an effort to revive ancient institutions, T'ang Kao-tsu (r. 618–626) restored the name of Ch'ang-chou to the P'i-ling area. Despite a few periods of subsequent modification, Ch'ang-chou became the official administrative designation for a prefecture composed of Wu-chin (also called Lan-ling, lit., "orchid mound-grave," after being separated from Chin-ling in A.D. 686), Wu-hsi, I-hsing, Chiang-yin, and Chin-ling counties for much of the imperial period through the Yuan (1280–1368) dynasty.

As the population density of the Yangtze Delta increased dramatically in the T'ang and Sung periods, the centrality of Yang-chou in south China decreased. After the Sui dynasty it was no longer the political hub of the Lower Yangtze region, although it remained an important trading center linking the emerging southern cities of Su-chou, Nan-ching (Chin-ling), Hang-chou, and Sung-chiang to the north. Thereafter, Ch'ang-chou looked increasingly to the south (that is, Chiang-nan, lit., "south of the Yangtze"), as Su-chou and Hang-chou emerged as centers of political and economic change, change that

5. Ibid., p. 92.

6. *Ch'ung-hsiu Ta-Ch'ing i-t'ung-chih*, 86.2b–3a, and *Chiang-su liu-shih-i hsien-chih*, pp. 85–86. See also *Chiang-nan t'ung-chih*, (1684), 2.22a–22b.

accelerated during the Southern Sung dynasty (1127–1279) after the north was lost to barbarian forces.[7]

Part of Ch'ang-chou circuit (*lu*) during the Yuan dynasty, the counties of Wu-chin, Wu-hsi, I-hsing (the character for *i* was changed to avoid conflicting with the Sung ruler's name), Chiang-yin, and Chin-ling all underwent administrative changes that reflected the rise and fall of ruling Mongol forces in south China from 1280 to 1368. For a time the entire circuit was turned over to Sung-chiang Prefecture, far to the south, indicating the decline of Yuan local power in the fourteenth century. As local Chinese armies contended for the lucrative Lower Yangtze region, however, Ch'ang-chou was incorporated into Chu Yuan-chang's (1328–98) military and administrative system centering on Nan-ching, which became the capital of the Ming dynasty in 1368.

Despite some minor modifications that were later reversed, Ch'ang-chou emerged under Ming emperors as part of the Southern Metropolitan Region (*Nan-chih-li*) after the Ming capital was officially moved to Peking (the former Yuan capital) in 1421. Further administrative changes in 1471 led to the merging of Chin-ling and Wu-chin counties, and Ching-chiang County (part of Chiang-yin since the Yuan) was made a separate county. This change heightened the political importance of Wu-chin County as the venue for the prefectural government and decreased the importance of Chiang-yin, which lost administrative control over the only prefectural territory north of the Yangtze River.[8]

By the middle of the Ming period Ch'ang-chou Prefecture and its five counties of Wu-chin, Wu-hsi, I-hsing, Chiang-yin, and Ching-chiang, had evolved into a viable political and administrative framework that lasted until 1724, when further administrative changes were effected to increase bureaucratic density in the heavily populated Yangtze Delta. We should add, however, that not until 1667 was the Ming province of Chiang-nan (that is, Nan-chih-li) divided up into An-hui and Chiang-su provinces, thereby placing Ch'ang-chou within its smaller Ch'ing dynasty administrative region. For the purposes of the civil service examinations, however, An-hui and Chiang-su remained part of Chiang-nan throughout the Ch'ing.

7. Ch'ang-chou became part of the evolving geographic units that eventually became northern Che-chiang and southern Chiang-su provinces. See *Chiang-nan t'ung-chih* (1684), 2.22a–22b.

8. *Ch'ung-hsiu Ta-Ch'ing i-t'ung-chih*, 86.1a, 86.4a, *Chiang-su ch'eng-shih li-shih ti-li*, pp. 93–94, *Chiang-nan t'ung-chih* (1684), 2.23b, *Chiang-su liu-shih-i hsien-chih*, p. 91. See also *Ch'ung-hsiu P'i-ling chih* (1483) 1.66a–b. On I-hsing, see *I-hsing hsien-chih* (1869), 1.2b. Cf. *Ch'ing-ch'ao t'ung-tien*, p. 1957A (*chüan* 138).

Ch'ang-chou by the fifteenth century had evolved into a stable political and administrative entity that was no longer subject to the political, cultural, and economic dominance of Yang-chou. If anything, the prefectural capital of Ch'ang-chou and its major county centers (with the exception of Chiang-yin) were more part of the Su-chou cycle of development from the Sung period on. The three prefectures of Su-Sung-Ch'ang represented the dominance of Su-chou, Sung-chiang, and Ch'ang-chou in the Yangtze Delta during the Ming and Ch'ing dynasties.[9]

During the Ming and Ch'ing the county seat of Wu-hsi was located on the Grand Canal between the Ch'ang-chou prefectural capital in Wu-chin County thirty-five miles to the northwest and Su-chou Prefecture thirty-five miles to the southeast. Renowned as a commercial center for textiles and other products since the Sung dynasty, Wu-hsi became during the late Ming a cultural and intellectual hub whose literati rivaled those of Su-chou and Yang-chou for eminence in the Lower Yangtze region.[10]

Wu-chin County was the seat of prefectural administration in Ch'ang-chou. Altogether, the prefecture comprised five counties, four of which (Wu-chin, Wu-hsi, I-hsing, and Chiang-yin) were each important cultural and economic powers in their own right. Unlike most other prefectures, which usually favored a single, large urbanized market and political center, Ch'ang-chou was uniquely polarized north and south at the level of higher-order market towns along the Grand Canal between Wu-chin and and Wu-hsi cities. These cultural centers were in turn complemented by the next lower order of central places in Chiang-yin county on the southern side of the Yangtze River, and I-hsing, on the land route west to Che-chiang and An-hui provinces.

Within the most commercialized macroregion in late imperial China, urbanized markets in Ch'ang-chou, as in Yang-chou, Su-chou, Sung-chiang, and so forth, became a potent driving force acting on an emerging market economy in the Lower Yangtze. Wu-chin cotton and flax, Wu-hsi porcelain, and I-hsing tea and pottery became important products in China's interregional trade. Imperial orders, for example, stimulated the growth of the pottery industry in I-hsing, which along

9. *Wu-chin Yang-hu hsien ho-chih* (1886), 1.21a–b, *Chiang-su ch'eng-shih li-shih ti-li*, pp. 93, 99–100, and *Ch'ing-ch'ao t'ung-tien*, p. 2715A (*chüan* 92). On the Su-chou cycle of development see Elvin, "Market Towns and Waterways," pp. 444–47.

10. *Wu-hsi Chin-k'uei hsien-chih*, 1814: 6.16b–21a. Cf. *Ch'ung-hsiu Ta-Ch'ing i-t'ung-chih*, 89.18b, 86.5a.

with the more famous pottery and porcelain kilns in Ching-te-chen in Chiang-hsi Province, became for all intents and purposes imperially sponsored kilns.[11]

Wu-hsi and Wu-chin thus were sister cities, competing against each other economically but in tandem politically, within the complex social groups and economic relations that emerged in Ch'ang-chou prefecture. Although Wu-chin was the political center of the prefecture during the Ming and Ch'ing dynasties, Wu-hsi in the late Ming was Ch'ang-chou's cultural heart. The leading intellectual voices for Confucian orthodoxy in seventeenth-century China, for example, were those of the gentry associated with Wu-hsi's renowned Tung-lin Academy.

Trends in Wu-hsi were quickly transmitted to and adopted in Wu-chin, I-hsing, and elsewhere in the prefecture, not to mention the entire Lower Yangtze region. In the Ch'ing, however, the mantle of cultural leadership in the prefecture shifted to Ch'ang-chou. The latter was a prefectural urban center, which along with Wu-hsi rivaled the cities of Su-chou, Nan-ching, Yang-chou, and Hang-chou at the apex of the most cultured and commercialized region in China.

11. See Nishijima, "Early Chinese Cotton Industry," pp. 17–77, and Tanaka, "Rural Handicraft in Jiangnan," pp. 81–100. See also Dillon, "Jingdezhen [Ching-te-chen] as a Ming Industrial Center"; Tsing Yuan, "Porcelain Industry"; and Santangelo, "Imperial Factories of Suzhou," pp. 269–94. Cf. Zurndorfer, "Chinese Merchants," pp. 75–86, esp. p. 80.

APPENDIX TWO

The Four Branches of the Chuang Lineage in Ch'ang-chou, circa 1400–1830

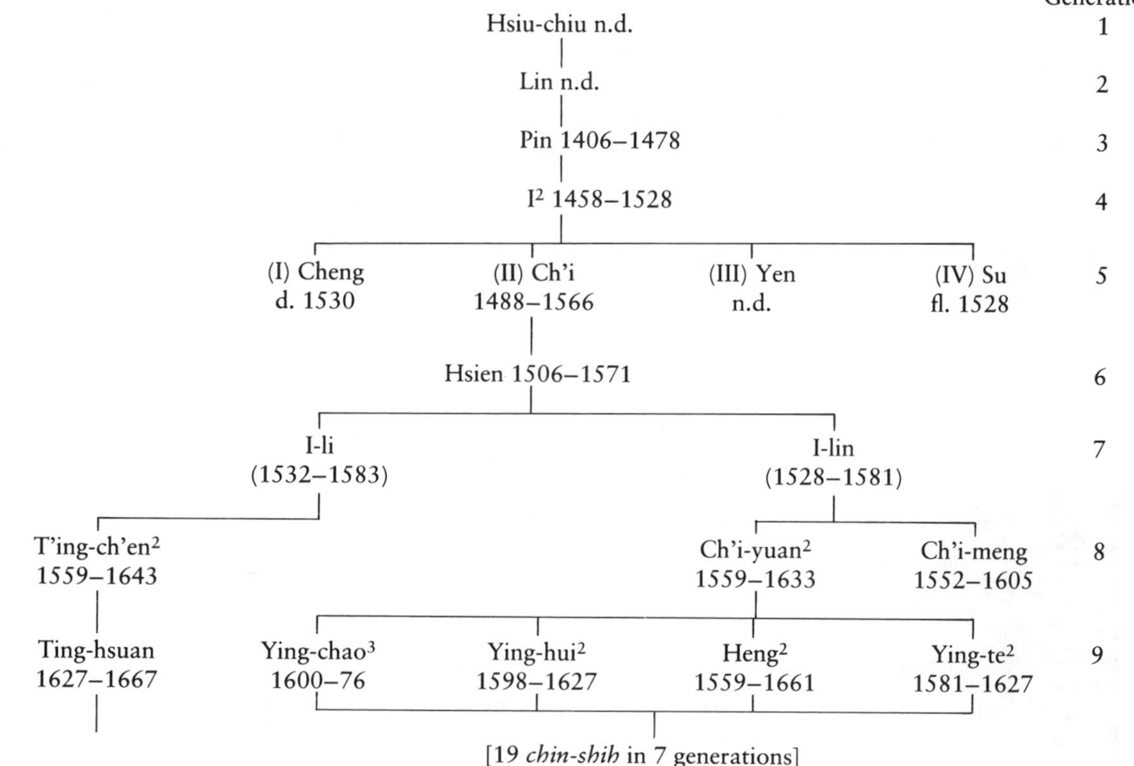
Generation
1
2
3
4
5
6
7
8
9
Hsiu-chiu n.d.
Lin n.d.
Pin 1406–1478
I2 1458–1528
(I) Cheng d. 1530
(II) Ch'i 1488–1566
(III) Yen n.d.
(IV) Su fl. 1528
Hsien 1506–1571
I-li (1532–1583)
I-lin (1528–1581)
T'ing-ch'en2 1559–1643
Ch'i-yuan2 1559–1633
Ch'i-meng 1552–1605
Ting-hsuan 1627–1667
Ying-chao3 1600–76
Ying-hui2 1598–1627
Heng2 1559–1661
Ying-te2 1581–1627
[19 *chin-shih* in 7 generations]

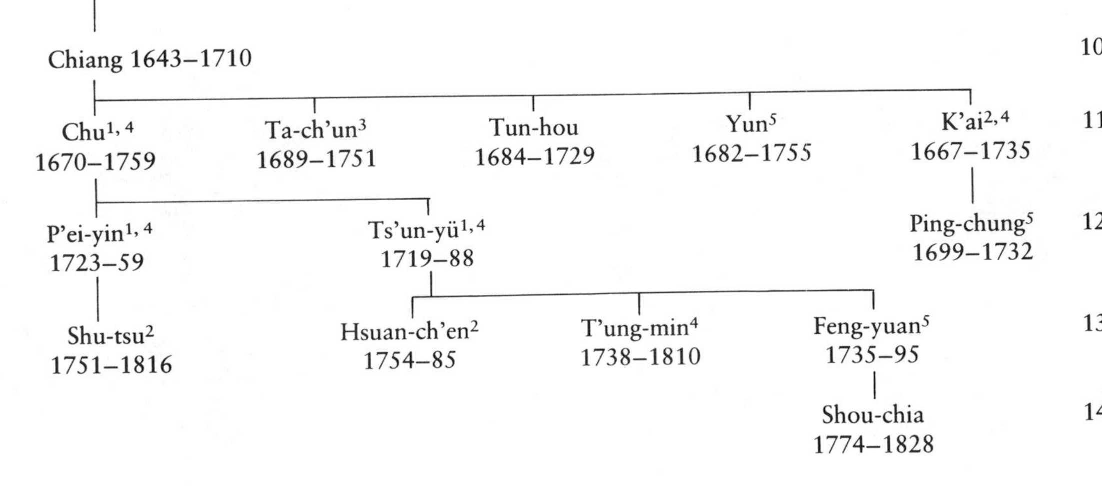

Key: [1] Grand secretary
[2] *Chin-shih*
[3] *Fu-pang*: supplemental *Chü-jen*
[4] Hanlin academician
[5] *Chü-jen*

APPENDIX THREE

The Three Branches of the Liu Lineage in Ch'ang-chou, circa 1450–1850

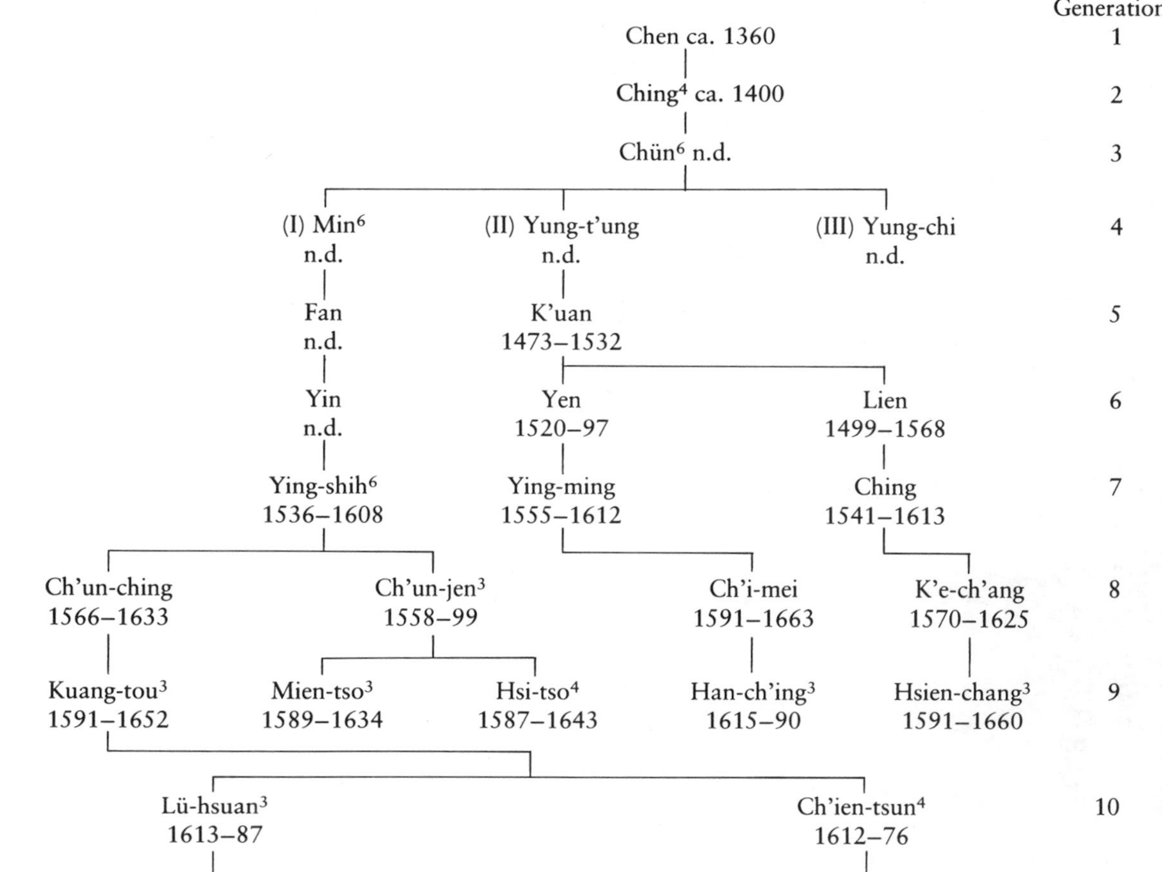
Generation
Chen ca. 1360
1
Ching[4] ca. 1400
2
Chün[6] n.d.
3
(I) Min[6] n.d.
(II) Yung-t'ung n.d.
(III) Yung-chi n.d.
4
Fan n.d.
K'uan 1473–1532
5
Yin n.d.
Yen 1520–97
Lien 1499–1568
6
Ying-shih[6] 1536–1608
Ying-ming 1555–1612
Ching 1541–1613
7
Ch'un-ching 1566–1633
Ch'un-jen[3] 1558–99
Ch'i-mei 1591–1663
K'e-ch'ang 1570–1625
8
Kuang-tou[3] 1591–1652
Mien-tso[3] 1589–1634
Hsi-tso[4] 1587–1643
Han-ch'ing[3] 1615–90
Hsien-chang[3] 1591–1660
9
Lü-hsuan[3] 1613–87
Ch'ien-tsun[4] 1612–76
10

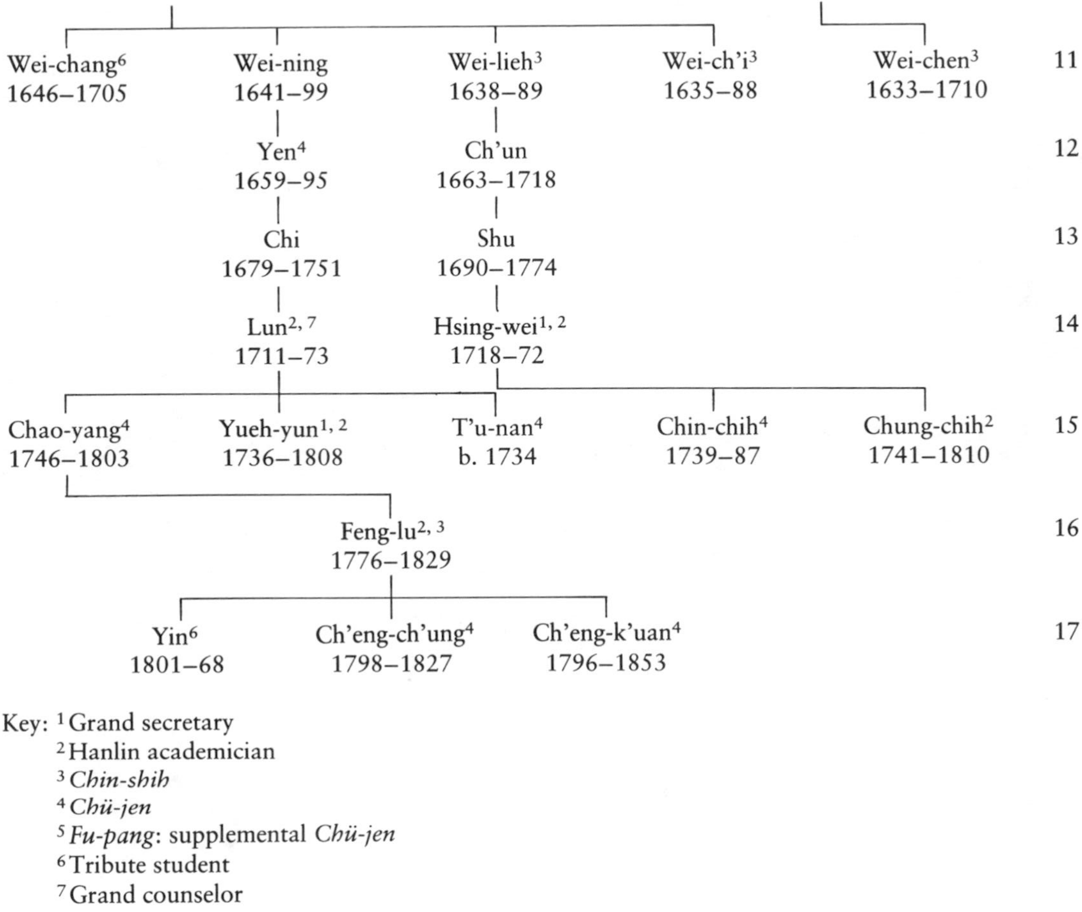

Wei-chang[6] 1646–1705
Wei-ning 1641–99
Wei-lieh[3] 1638–89
Wei-ch'i[3] 1635–88
Wei-chen[3] 1633–1710
11
Yen[4] 1659–95
Ch'un 1663–1718
12
Chi 1679–1751
Shu 1690–1774
13
Lun[2, 7] 1711–73
Hsing-wei[1, 2] 1718–72
14
Chao-yang[4] 1746–1803
Yueh-yun[1, 2] 1736–1808
T'u-nan[4] b. 1734
Chin-chih[4] 1739–87
Chung-chih[2] 1741–1810
15
Feng-lu[2, 3] 1776–1829
16
Yin[6] 1801–68
Ch'eng-ch'ung[4] 1798–1827
Ch'eng-k'uan[4] 1796–1853
17
Key: [1] Grand secretary
[2] Hanlin academician
[3] *Chin-shih*
[4] *Chü-jen*
[5] *Fu-pang*: supplemental *Chü-jen*
[6] Tribute student
[7] Grand counselor

GLOSSARY

A-kuei 阿桂
an-fu shih 按撫使
an-hsin 安心
An-hui 安徽

ch'an-wei 讖緯
Chang Hsueh-ch'eng 章學誠
Chang Hui-yen 張惠言
Chang Pa 張霸
chang san-shih 張三世
"Ch'ang" 常
Ch'ang-an 長安
Ch'ang-chou 常州
Ch'ang-chou chih-hsueh 常州之學
Ch'ang-hsing hsueh-chi 長興學紀
ch'ang-lü 常律
Chao Chen-tso 趙振祚
Chao Fang 趙汸
Chao Huai-yü 趙懷玉
Chao I 趙翼
Chao K'uang 趙匡
Che 浙
Che-chiang 浙江
chen Han-hsueh che 真漢學者
chen-hsin 真心
chen Ju 真儒
chen li-hsueh 真理學
Che-lin-t'ang 謫麐堂
chen-nien 真念
Ch'en Chen-hui 陳貞彗
Ch'en Ch'iao-ts'ung 陳喬樅
Ch'en Hsien-chang 陳獻章
Ch'en Li (1810–82) 陳澧
Ch'en Li (1809–69) 陳立
Ch'en Liang 陳亮
Ch'en Shan 陳善
Ch'en Shou-ch'i 陳壽祺
Ch'en Wei-sung 陳維崧
Cheng 鄭
cheng (governance) 政
cheng (correct, orthodox) 正
Cheng Hsuan 鄭玄
Cheng-hsueh 鄭學
Cheng-hsueh-chai 鄭學齋
cheng-jen 正人
cheng-ming 正名

Cheng-shih Chou-i 鄭氏周易
Cheng-te 正德
cheng-t'ung 正統
Cheng-t'ung p'ien 正統篇
Ch'eng 成
Ch'eng-Chu 程朱
Ch'eng En-tse 程恩澤
Ch'eng I 程頤
chi (criticism) 譏
chi (equals) 即
chi-ho-hsueh 幾何學
Chi Huan-tzu 季桓子
Chi Pen 季本
chi-shih chi-hsueh 即仕即學
Chi-tzu 季子
chi-wei 即位
Chi-yang 暨陽
Ch'i (state) 齊
ch'i (implement) 器
ch'i (energy) 氣
ch'i-chih 氣質
ch'i chih che-hsueh 氣之哲學
ch'i-chih chih hsing 氣質之性
ch'i-chuan ts'ung-ching 棄傳從經
Ch'i-k'e 七克
chia 家
chia-chieh-tzu 假借字
Chia-ching 嘉靖
Chia-ch'ing 嘉慶
chia-fa 家法
chia-hsueh 家學
Chia I 賈誼
Chia K'uei 賈逵
Chia-ting 嘉定
Chiang 將
Chiang Ching-ch'i 蔣景祁
Chiang Fan 江藩
Chiang-nan 江南
Chiang Ping 蔣炳
Chiang Sheng 江聲
Chiang-yin 江陰
Chiao Hsun 焦循
chiao-hua 教化
chien ching-shih chih chih 見經世之志
chien-shu 諫書
Ch'ien I-pen 錢一本
Ch'ien-lung 乾隆
ch'ien-ku chih sheng 前古之盛
ch'ien-mo 阡陌
Ch'ien Ta-hsin 錢大昕
Ch'ien Tsai 錢載
chih (points, rescript) 旨
chih (points) 指
chih (intent, will) 志
chih-ch'üan 知權
chih-hsing ho-i 知行合一
chih-kuo 治國
chih-luan 治亂
chih-shih 執事
chih-shih chih chiao 執事之教
chih shu ch'i shih 直書其事
chih t'ien-shih 志天事
ch'ih 恥
Chin 晉
Chin-ch'uan 金川
chin-fa 今法
Chin-ling 晉陵
"Chin-pao tz'u" 禁暴辭
chin-shih 進士
chin-shih-hsueh 金石學
Chin-t'an 金壇
chin-wen 今文
chin-wen-hsueh 今文學
Chin Yu-chi 金佑基
ch'in 親
ching 經
Ching-cheng-t'ang 經正堂
Ching-chiang 靖江

ching-hsueh 經學
ching-i 經義
Ching-i tsa-chi 經義雜記
ching-shen 精神
ching-shih (classical teacher) 經師
ching-shih (statecraft) 經世
ching-shih chih ta-fa 經世之大法
ching-shu 經術
Ching-te-chen 景德鎮
ching-t'ien 井田
hing wen 經文
ch'ing 情
ch'ing-i 清議
ch'iung-li 窮理
chiu-chih 九旨
chiu-chih tsai san-k'e chih wai 九旨在三科之外
chiu-fa 舊法
chiu-fu 九服
Chou (dynasty) 周
chou (township) 州
Chou (king) 紂
Chou Hung-mu 周洪謨
Chou-i pen-i 周易本義
Chou-i shu 周易疏
Chou-i Yü-shih hsiao-hsi 周易虞氏消息
Chou-i Yü-shih i 周易虞氏義
"Chou kuan" 周官
Chou-kuan chih-chang 周官指章
Chou Kung 周公
Chou-li 周禮
Chou-li k'ao 周禮考
chu-hou 諸侯
Chu Hsi 朱熹
Chu-k'e ch'ing-li-ssu 主客清理司
Chu Kuei 朱珪
Chu Mou-wei 朱謀㙔
Chu Yuan-chang 朱元璋
Chu Yun 朱筠
ch'ü ch'i ssu 去其私
Ch'ü-fu 曲阜
ch'ü ren-yü 去人欲
ch'ü-ssu 去私
ch'ü-ssu hsueh-li 去私學禮
chuan 篆
chuan-ch'üan 專權
chuan-men 專門
chuan-shu 篆書
chuan-yeh shih-chen 專業市鎮
chüan 卷
ch'üan 權
Chuang 莊
Chuang Cheng 莊整
Chuang Ch'eng 莊成
Chuang Ch'eng-jui 莊成蕤
Chuang Ch'eng-sui 莊成遂
Chuang Ch'i 莊齊
Chuang Ch'i-meng 莊起蒙
Chuang Ch'i-yuan 莊起元
Chuang Chiang 莊絳
Chuang Ch'ien 莊鈐
Chuang Ch'ien 莊乾
Chuang Chu 莊柱
Chuang Ch'u-pao 莊楚寶
Chuang Chün-chia 莊雋甲
Chuang Feng-yuan 莊逢原
Chuang Fu-tan 莊復旦
Chuang Heng 莊恆
Chuang Hsiang-heng 莊湘衡
Chuang Hsien 莊憲
Chuang Hsien-nan 莊詵男
Chuang Hsiu-chiu 莊秀九
Chuang Hsuan-ch'en 莊選辰
Chuang I 莊禕
Chuang I-li 莊以莅
Chuang I-lin 莊以臨
Chuang K'ai 莊楷
Chuang Lin 莊林
Chuang Ling-yü 莊令輿

Chuang P'an-chu 莊盤珠
Chuang P'ei-yin 莊培因
Chuang Pien 莊抃
Chuang Pin 莊斌
Chuang Ping-chung 莊秉中
"Chuang-shih I-shuo hsu" 莊氏易說序
Chuang-shih suan-hsueh 莊氏算學
Chuang Shou-ch'i 莊受祺
Chuang Shou-chia 莊綬甲
Chuang Shu-tsu 莊述祖
Chuang Su 莊肅
Chuang Ta-ch'un 莊大春
Chuang T'ai-kung 莊太恭
Chuang Ting-hsuan 莊鼎鉉
Chuang T'ing-chen 莊廷臣
Chuang Tou-wei 莊斗薇
Chuang Ts'un-yü 莊存與
Chuang Tun-hou 莊敦厚
Chuang T'ung-min 莊通敏
Chuang Yen 莊嚴
Chuang Yin 莊寅
Chuang Ying-chao 莊應詔
Chuang Ying-ch'i 莊應期
Chuang Ying-hui 莊應會
Chuang Ying-te 莊應德
Chuang Yu-k'e 莊有可
Chuang Yu-kung 莊有恭
Chuang Yu-yun 莊有筠
chuang-yuan 狀元
Chuang Yun 莊澐
chueh 絕
chueh-hsueh 絕學
chueh-shih 決事
chueh-shih pi 決事比
chui 贅
Ch'un-ch'iu 春秋
Ch'un-ch'iu cheng-i 春秋正義
Ch'un-ch'iu cheng-tz'u 春秋正辭
Ch'un-ch'iu chih fa 春秋之法
Ch'un-ch'iu chih shih 春秋之勢
Ch'un-ch'iu chü-li 春秋舉例
Ch'un-ch'iu fan-lu 春秋繁露
Ch'un-ch'iu fei-Tso 春秋非左
Ch'un-ch'iu hsiao-hsueh 春秋小學
Ch'un-ch'iu-hsueh 春秋學
Ch'un-ch'iu i pu-chu 春秋義補注
Ch'un-ch'iu Kung-yang ching Ho-shih shih-li 春秋公羊經何氏釋例
Ch'un-ch'iu shih-li 春秋釋例
Ch'un-ch'iu shih-tai 春秋時代
Ch'un-ch'iu shu-tz'u 春秋屬辭
Ch'un-ch'iu ssu-k'ao 春秋私考
Ch'un-ch'iu Tso-shih chuan pu-chu 春秋左氏傳補注
Ch'un-ch'iu tsun-wang fa-wei 春秋尊王發微
Ch'un-ch'iu t'ung-lun 春秋通論
Ch'un-ch'iu-wei yen-K'ung-t'u 春秋微言孔圖
"Ch'un-ch'iu wu-li hsiang-shuo" 春秋物理象說
Ch'un-ch'iu yao-chih 春秋要指
chü-jen 舉人
chün 郡
Chün-chi ch'u 軍機處
chün-hsien 郡縣
chün-hsin 君心
chün-t'ien chün-i 均田均役
chün-tzu 君子
chün-tzu yueh 君子曰
chün-yao 均徭
ch'ün 群
chung-chih 中制
Chung-shan 鐘山
chung-tao 中道
Chung-yung 中庸
Chung-yung chang-chü 中庸章句

Duke Ai 哀公
Duke Chuang 莊公
Duke Huan 桓公
Duke Hui 惠公
Duke Wen 文公
Duke Yin 隱公

Emperor Ai 哀帝
Emperor Chao 昭帝
Emperor Ch'eng 成帝
Emperor Hsuan 宣帝
Emperor Kuang-wu 光武帝
Emperor Shun 舜
Emperor Wu 武帝
erh 二
erh-fen 二分
Erh-ya 爾雅

fa 法
Fa-chia 法家
Fan 范
Fan Chung-yen 范仲淹
fan-fu 藩服
fan-li 凡例
fan-pen hsiu-ku 反本修古
fang-fa 放伐
Fang I-chih 方以智
Fang Pao 方苞
Fang Tung-shu 方東樹
Fang Ts'ung-che 方從哲
fei-ch'ang chih shih 非常之事
fei-ch'ang k'e-kuai chih lun 非常可怪之論
fei-li fei-fa 非禮非法
fei li yeh 非禮也
fen-chih 分治
fen-shu 焚書
Feng Ch'i 馮琦
feng-chien 封建
feng-su 風俗
Feng-t'ien 奉天
feng-wu 鳳物
fu 賦
Fu-chien 福建
fu-ch'iu 復仇
Fu Hsi 伏羲
fu-hsing 復性
Fu-hsing shu 復性書
fu-ku 復古
fu-pang 副榜
Fu She 復社
Fu Sheng 伏生
Fu Sung-ch'ing 傅崧卿

Han Fei 韓非
Han-hsueh 漢學
Han-hsueh shang-tui 漢學商兌
"Han-lin lun" 翰林論
Han-lin yuan 翰林院
Han-shu 漢書
Han Yü 韓愈
Hang-chou 杭州
Hao Ching 郝敬
hao-ku ch'iu-shih 好古求實
He-fei 合肥
ho-ch'ün 合群
Ho Hsiu 何休
ho hu jen-ch'ing 合乎人情
Ho Kuang 霍光
Ho-shen 和珅
ho-shih 合時
Ho-t'u 河圖
ho yü t'ien-li 合於天理
hou-t'ien 後天
Hsia 夏
Hsia Hsiao-cheng 夏小正
Hsia-shih 夏時
hsiang 象
hsiang-fu ch'i hsin 降伏其心
hsiang-jen-ou 相人偶
hsiang-kung 相公
hsiang-shu 象數

hsiang-shu chih-hsueh 象數之學
hsiao-chuan 小篆
hsiao-hsueh 小學
Hsiao-hsueh k'ao 小學考
hsiao-jen 小人
hsiao-tao 小道
hsieh-cheng 邪正
Hsieh Ch'i-k'un 謝啓昆
hsieh-sheng 諧聲
hsieh-tang 邪黨
hsieh-yü 邪欲
hsien 縣
hsien 賢
Hsien-hsien tz'u 先賢祠
hsien-t'ien 先天
Hsi-i chih jen 西夷之人
Hsin 新
hsin 心
hsin chih te 心之德
hsin-Chou 新周
hsin-fa 心法
hsin-hsueh 心學
hsin-shih 信史
hsing (form) 形
hsing (penal law) 刑
hsing-fa 行法
Hsing-li ta-ch'üan 性理大全
Hsing-li ta-ch'üan-shu 性理大全書
hsing-ming 性命
hsing shan 性善
hsing-sheng 形聲
hsing-shu 刑書
hsing-t'i 形體
hsiu-yang 修養
hsu 序
Hsu Ai 徐愛
Hsu Ching-tsung 許敬宗
Hsu Kua-chuan lun 續卦傳論
Hsu Kuang-ch'i 徐光啓
Hsu K'o 徐珂
Hsu Shen 許慎
hsuan-hsueh 玄學
hsueh-cheng 學政
Hsueh-hai-t'ang chi 學海堂集
Hsueh Ying-ch'i 薛應旂
hsun-huan 循環
hsun-ku 訓詁
hsun-ku-hsueh 訓詁學
hsun-ku ming-wu 訓詁名物
Hsun Shuang 荀爽
Hsun-tzu 荀子
Hu An-kuo 胡安國
Hu Kuang 胡廣
Hu Wei 胡渭
Hu-wu Sheng 胡毋生
Huang-Ch'ing ching-chieh 皇清經解
Huang Ching-jen 黃景仁
Huang Ju-t'ing 黃汝亭
Huang-shan 黃山
Huang Shih 黃奭
Huang-ti 黃帝
Huang Tse 黃澤
huang-ts'e 黃册
Huang Tsung-hsi 黃宗羲
Hui-chou 徽州
Hui Chou-t'i 惠週梯
Hui Shih-ch'i 惠士奇
Hui Tung 惠棟
Hui Wan-fang 惠萬方
Hui Yu-sheng 惠有聲
hui-yueh 會約
Hung-chih 弘治
"Hung-fan" 洪範
Hung Liang-chi 洪亮吉
Hung-mei-ko 紅梅閣
Hung-wu 洪武
huo-shu 活數

i (intent) 意
i (meaning) 義

i (barbarian) 夷
i (labor tax) 役
i-chia chih yen 一家之言
I-chih ch'ing-li-ssu 儀制清理司
I-ching 易經
i ching-i chueh i-shih 以經義決疑事
I Chou-shu 逸周書
I-chou-t'ing 艤舟亭
i Ch'un-ch'iu tang hsin-wang 以春秋當新王
i-fa (models and rules) 義法
I-fa (Change models) 易法
i-fu 夷服
I Han-hsueh 易漢學
I-hsing 宜興
I-hsueh 易學
I-hsueh hsiang-shu lun 易學象數論
i i-chien sha-jen 以意見殺人
i-kung mieh-ssu 以公滅私
I-li (left-over chapters of rites) 逸禮
i-li (meanings and principles) 義理
I-li (Change precedents) 易例
i-t'iao pien-fa 一條辮法
I-t'u ming-pien 易圖明辯
i wai-nei 異外內
i-wei pu-ran 以爲不然
I-wen-chih 藝文志

jang 讓
jang-i 攘夷
jen 仁
jen chih hsin 人之心
jen-ch'ing 人情
jen-hsin Tao-hsin 人心道心
jen-lun 人倫
jen-shih 人事
jen-tao 人道
jen-yü 人欲
Ju 儒
Ju-lin 儒林
Ju-shu 儒術
Juan Yuan 阮元
Jung 戎

kai-chih 改制
kai fa-tu 改法度
K'ang-hsi 康熙
K'ang Yu-wei 康有爲
Kao P'an-lung 高攀龍
kao-t'an hsing-ming 高談性命
Kao-tsung 高宗
Kao Yao 皋陶
k'ao-cheng 考證
k'ao-cheng-hsueh 考證學
k'e 科
K'e-tou shu 蝌斗書
King Kung of Lu 魯恭王
King Wu 武王
ko-chih 格質
Kou-ku teng liu-lun 勾股等六論
ko-wu 格物
kowtow 磕頭
ku-chin 古今
ku-Chou wang-Lu 故周王魯
Ku Hsien-ch'eng 顧賢成
ku-hsueh 古學
ku-hsun 古訓
Ku-liang chuan 穀梁傳
Ku-liang fei-chi 穀梁非疾
ku-i 古義
ku-Sung 故宋
Ku Tung-kao 顧棟高
ku-tzu 古字
ku-tz'u 古辭
ku-wen 古文
Ku-wen Shang-shu k'ao 古文尚書考

Ku-wen tz'u lei-tsuan 古文辭類纂
Ku Yen-wu 顧炎武
ku-yin 古音
Ku Yun-ch'eng 顧允成
kuan-hsueh 官學
kuan-i 官役
Kuan T'ung 管同
Kuang-chou 廣州
Kuang-hsu 光緒
Kuang-tung 廣東
K'uang Heng 匡衡
kuei-chi (date) 癸巳
kuei-chi (secret land trusteeship) 詭寄
kuei-hsueh 規學
Kuei-tsang 歸藏
Kuei Yu-kuang 歸有光
K'un-chih chi 困知記
kung (bow) 弓
kung (public) 公
kung-fu 工夫
kung-hsin 公心
kung-li 公理
kung-lun 公論
kung-sheng 貢生
kung shih-fei 公是非
kung-tang 公黨
Kung Tzu-chen 龔自珍
Kung-yang chieh-ku 公羊解詁
Kung-yang chuan 公羊傳
Kung-yang Ch'un-ch'iu ching-chuan t'ung-i 公羊春秋經傳通義
Kung-yang ch'un-ch'iu lun 公羊春秋論
Kung-yang chuan-chu yin Han-lü k'ao 公羊傳注引漢律考
Kung-yang i-shu 公羊義疏
Kung-yang li-shu 公羊禮疏
Kung-yang mo-shou 公羊墨守
Kung-yang Tung Chung-shu chih-yü 公羊董仲舒治獄
K'ung An-kuo 孔安國
K'ung Kuang 孔光
K'ung Kuang-sen 孔廣森
k'ung-li 空理
"K'ung-Meng" 孔孟
K'ung-tzu chia-yü 孔子家語
k'ung-wen 空文
k'ung-yen 空言
k'ung-yen ch'iung-li 空言窮理
K'ung Ying-ta 孔穎達
Kuo-ch'ao Ch'ang-chou p'ien-t'i-wen lu 國朝常州駢體文錄
Kuo-chao Ch'ang-chou tz'u-lu 國朝常州辭錄
Kuo-ch'ao Han-hsueh shih-ch'eng chi 國朝漢學師承記
kuo-shih 國勢
Kuo Shou-ching 郭守敬
Kuo-tzu chien 國子監
Kuo-yü 國語

Lan-ling 蘭陵
Lao-Chuang 老莊
Lao-tzu 老子
li (rites) 禮
li (principle) 理
li (clerical script) 隸
Li (king) 厲
Li Chao-lo 李兆洛
Li-chi 禮記
li-chia 里甲
li-chiao 禮教
Li Chih 李贄
Li Ch'ing-ch'uan 李晴川
Li-fan yuan 理藩院
li-hsueh 理學
li-i chih hsing 禮義之性
li-kuan 理官

Li Kung 李塨
Li Po 李白
Li-pu 禮部
li-shu 隸書
Li Ssu 李斯
Li T'ang 李棠
Liang Ch'i-ch'ao 梁啓超
Liang-Han 兩漢
liang-min 良民
liang Shen 兩申
Liao P'ing 廖平
Lien-ch'eng 蓮誠
lin 麟
Ling Shu 凌曙
Liu 劉
Liu Chao-yang 劉召揚
Liu Ch'ao-chien 劉朝鑒
Liu Chen 劉真
Liu Ch'eng-ch'ung 劉承寵
Liu Ch'eng-k'uan 劉承寬
Liu Chi 劉機
Liu Ch'i-mei 劉啓美
Liu Ch'ien-tsun 劉謙尊
Liu Chih-chi 劉知幾
Liu Chin-chih 劉謹之
Liu Ching 劉敬
Liu Ching 劉京
Liu Chün 劉俊
Liu Ch'un 劉淳
Liu Ch'un-ching 劉純敬
Liu Ch'un-jen 劉純仁
Liu Chung-chih 劉種之
Liu Fan 劉璠
Liu Feng-lu 劉逢祿
Liu Han-ch'ing 劉漢卿
Liu Ho 劉賀
liu-ho i-chia 六合一家
Liu Hsi-tso 劉熙祚
Liu Hsiang 劉向
Liu Hsien-chang 劉憲章
Liu Hsin 劉歆
Liu Hsing-wei 劉星煒
Liu Hsueh-sun 劉學遜
liu-i 六藝
Liu I-k'uei 劉一夔
Liu K'e-ch'ang 劉克昌
Liu Kuang-tou 劉光斗
Liu Kuei-tseng 劉貴曾
Liu K'uan 劉冠
Liu Lien 劉奩
Liu Lü-hsuan 劉履旋
Liu Lun 劉綸
Liu Mien-tso 劉綿祚
Liu Min 劉敏
Liu Ming-tso 劉明祚
Liu San-wu 劉三吾
Liu Shih-p'ei 劉師培
liu-shu 六書
Liu Shu 劉樞
Liu Ta-chung 劉大中
Liu Tsung-yuan 柳宗元
Liu T'u-nan 劉圖南
Liu Wei-chang 劉維章
Liu Wei-chen 劉維禎
Liu Wei-ch'i 劉維祺
Liu Wei-lieh 劉維烈
Liu Wei-ning 劉維寧
Liu Wen-ch'i 劉文淇
Liu Yen 劉奄
Liu Yen 劉演
Liu Yin 劉崟
Liu Ying 劉瀛
Liu Ying-ch'ao 劉應朝
Liu Ying-ming 劉應明
Liu Ying-shih 劉應時
Liu Yü-i 劉于義
Liu Yü-sung 劉毓崧
Liu Yueh-yun 劉躍云
Liu Yung-chi 劉永紀
Liu Yung-tso 劉永祚

Liu Yung-t'ung 劉永童
Lo Ch'in-shun 羅欽順
Lo-shu 洛書
Lo-yang 洛陽
Lo Yueh-ch'uan 羅月川
Lu (state) 魯
lu (circuit) 路
Lu Chiu-yuan 陸九淵
Lu Hsiang-shan 陸象山
Lu shih-chi 魯史記
Lu Wen-ch'ao 盧文弨
lü 律
Lü Ching-nan 呂景楠
lü-ling chih hsueh 律令之學
luan 亂
luan-yen 亂言
lun 論
"Lun cheng p'ien" 論政篇
Lun-yü 論語
Lun-yü shu-Ho 論語述何
Lung-ch'eng 龍城

Ma Jung 馬融
Man-chou yuan-liu k'ao 滿州源流考
Mao Ch'i-ling 毛奇齡
Mao-shih k'ao-cheng 毛詩考證
Mei Sheng 梅乘
Mei Tsu 梅鷟
Mei Wen-ting 梅文鼎
Meng-tzu 孟子
Meng-tzu chieh-wen 孟子節文
min-ch'üan 民權
min-ping 民兵
ming 命
ming-chia 名家
ming-chiao 名教
ming ching-i 明經義
Ming-i tai-fang lu 明夷待訪錄
Ming-ju hsueh-an 明儒學案
ming-pien 明辨
Ming-shih 明史
Ming-t'ang 明堂
Ming-tao 明道
ming-wu 名物
mo-lu 末錄
Mo-tzu 墨子
mu-lu 目錄
mu-yu 幕友

Nan-chih-li 南直隸
Nan-ching 南京
Nan-ch'ing 南菁
Nan shu-fang 南書房
nei ch'i kuo 內其國
nei ch'i kuo erh wai chu-hsia 內其國而外諸夏
nei chu-hsia 內諸夏
nei chu-hsia erh wai i-jung 內諸夏而外夷戎
Nei-ko 內閣
Nei-ko hsueh-shih 內閣學士
neng 能
ni-ku 泥古
nien-p'u 年譜
nu-p'u 奴僕
nung-ping 農病

Ou-yang Hsiu 歐陽修
Ou-yang Te 歐陽德
Ou-yang Tung-feng 歐陽東鳳

pa 霸
pa-i ming-tu 八邑名都
pa-ku-wen 八股文
pa-kua 八卦
p'ai 派
Pan Ku 班固
pang-yen 榜眼
p'ang-cheng 旁徵

pao-chia 保甲
pao-pien 褒貶
pei-chi 碑記
pen-hsin 本心
pen-i (original meanings) 本義
pen-i (original intent) 本意
pen-se 本色
pen-t'i 本體
P'eng Hui-ch'i 彭會淇
p'eng-tang 朋黨
"P'eng-tang lun" 朋黨論
pi 比
pi-chen 必真
pi-shih 比事
Pi Yuan 畢沅
P'i-ling 毗陵
P'i-ling chih 毗陵志
P'i-ling ching-chieh chih 毗陵經籍志
P'i-ling liu-i shih-ch'ao 毗陵六逸詩鈔
P'i-ling pai-chia shih 毗陵百家詩
P'i-ling wen-lu 毗陵文錄
pien (change) 變
pien (blame) 貶
pien (compile, chapter) 編
pien-fa 變法
pien-li 變例
p'ien-t'i-wen 駢體文
P'ien-t'i-wen ch'ao 駢體文鈔
p'ing-teng 平等
po-hsueh 博學
po-hsueh hung-tz'u 博學鴻詞
Po-hu t'ung-i 白虎通義
Po-hu t'ung-i k'ao 白虎通義考
po-shih 博士
pu erh-ch'en 不二臣
pu-i 布衣
pu i-ch'i 不易器
pu-ming 不明
pu pien-fa 不變法
pu-shou 部首
pu-shu 不書
pu-te i 不得已
pu-te pu-jan 不得不然
pu-yen 不言
p'u-hsueh 樸學

san-kang 三綱
san-k'e 三科
san-k'e chiu-chih 三科九旨
san-shih 三世
san-tai kai-chih 三代改制
"San-tai yin-ke lun" 三代因革論
san-teng 三等
san-t'ung 三統
sha ch'i en 殺其恩
Shan-hsi 山西
shan-jang 禪讓
Shang 商
Shang-shu cheng-i 尚書正義
Shang-shu chin-ku-wen chu-shu 尚書今古文注疏
Shang-shu chin-ku-wen k'ao-cheng 尚書今古文考證
Shang-shu k'ao-i 尚書考義
Shang-shu ku-wen shu-cheng 尚書古文疏證
Shang-shu-sheng 尚書省
Shao Ch'i-tao 邵齊燾
she 社
shen (spirit) 神
Shen (name) 申
shen (self) 身
Shen Pu-hai 申不害
shen-ssu 深思
shen-wen 慎問
sheng (sage) 聖
sheng (conquer) 勝
sheng-ching 聖經

sheng-jen chih chih 聖人之志
sheng-jen chih hsin 聖人之心
sheng-jen chih hsing-shu 聖人之刑書
sheng-p'ing 升平
sheng-yuan 生員
shih (affairs) 事
shih (history) 史
Shih-chi 史記
shih-chih 十指
Shih ching 詩經
shih-chung 始終
shih-fa 史法
shih-hsueh 實學
shih-i 示義
Shih ku-wei 詩古微
shih-li 史例
Shih-lu 實錄
Shih-san-ching chiao-k'an-chi 十三經校勘記
Shih-san-ching chu-shu 十三經注疏
shih-shih 實事
shih-shih ch'iu-shih 實事求是
Shih shu-ming 釋書名
shih-wen 時文
shih yü shih 適於事
shih-yung 實用
shou 手
shu (numbers) 數
shu (compassion) 恕
Shu-ching 書經
shu-fa 書法
shu-shu 數術
shu-tz'u pi-shih 屬辭比事
shu-yuan 書院
Shui-ching chu 水經注
Shun 舜
Shuo-wen 說文
Shuo-wen chieh-tzu 說文解字
so-chien 所見
so-ch'uan-wen 所傳聞
so-wen 所聞
so-chien i-tz'u 所見異辭
so-ch'uan-wen i-tz'u 所傳聞異辭
so-wen i-tz'u 所聞異辭
sonnō jōi 尊皇攘夷
ssu 私
ssu-chuan 四傳
Ssu-k'u ch'üan-shu 四庫全書
Ssu-ma Ch'ien 司馬遷
Ssu-ma Hsiang-ju 司馬相如
Ssu-ma Kuang 司馬光
Ssu-ma T'an 司馬談
ssu-min 四民
ssu-pu 四部
ssu-shu (dead calculations) 死術
Ssu-shu (Four Books) 四書
Ssu-shu ta-ch'üan 四書大全
Ssu-shu wu-ching ta-ch'üan 四書五經大全
ssu-tang 私黨
ssu-yü 私欲
"Su" 蘇
Su-chou 蘇州
Su Shih 蘇軾
Su-Sung-Ch'ang 蘇松常
Su Wan-en 蘇完恩
su-wang 素王
Suan-fa yueh-yen 算法約言
suan-shu 算數
Sun Chia-kan 孫嘉淦
Sun Fu 孫復
Sun Hsing-yen 孫星衍
Sun Shen-hsing 孫愼行
"Sung" 松
Sung-chiang 松江
Sung Hsiang-feng 宋翔鳳
Sung-hsueh 宋學
Sung-shih chih 宋史質

ta 大
ta-chuan 大篆
ta-fen 大分
Ta-hsueh-shih 大學士
ta-i 大義
ta i-t'ung 大一統
ta-kung 大公
ta-pen 大本
ta-ssu 大私
Ta-Tai li-chi 大戴禮記
ta-tsu 大族
ta-t'ung 大同
ta-yeh 大業
ta-yung 大用
"Ta Yü mo" 大禹謨
Tai Chen 戴震
Taiping 太平
Tai Te 戴德
Tai Tung-yuan 戴東原
Tai Wang 戴望
T'ai-chou 泰州
T'ai-hsueh 太學
t'ai-p'ing 太平
T'ai-yuan 太原
Tan Chu 啖助
tan-wang 誕妄
T'an Ssu-t'ung 譚嗣同
tang (party, faction) 黨
T'ang (dynasty) 唐
T'ang Ho-cheng 唐鶴徵
T'ang Kao-tsu 唐高祖
T'ang Kuei 唐貴
T'ang Pin 唐斌
T'ang Shih-ch'ang 唐世昌
T'ang Shun-chih 唐順之
T'ang-Sung 唐宋
T'ang Yao 唐瑤
Tao 道
Tao chih t'i 道之體
Tao chih yung 道之用
Tao-hsin 道心
Tao-kuang 道光
Tao-shu 道術
Tao-t'ung 道統
tao wen-hsueh 道問學
t'i 體
t'i-yao 提要
t'iao-li 條例
t'ieh-i 貼役
tien-chang 典章
tien-hu 田戶
t'ien 天
T'ien-ch'i 天啓
t'ien-chu 天主
t'ien-hsia wei-kung 天下爲公
t'ien-hsin 天心
t'ien-jen chih tao 天人之道
t'ien-li 天理
t'ien-li chih cheng 天理之正
T'ien-ning-ssu 天寧寺
t'ien-shang wu-erh 天上無二
t'ien-tao 天道
t'ien-tzu 天子
to-hsin 多心
t'o-ku kai-chih 托古改制
tsai san-k'e chih nei 在三科之內
Ts'ai Shen 蔡沈
Tsang Lin 臧琳
Tsang Yung 臧庸
Tseng Kung 曾鞏
Tseng Ying 曾櫻
ts'e 策
ts'e-shu 筞書
tso-chin yu-ku 左今右古
Tso Ch'iu-ming 左丘明
Tso chuan 左傳
Tso chuan chiu-shu k'ao-cheng 左傳舊疏考證
Tso-shih ch'un-ch'iu k'ao-cheng 左氏春秋考證

Tso-shih kao-huang 左氏膏肓
Tso Tsung-t'ang 左宗棠
tso-wei 作僞
Tsou Yang 鄒陽
tsu 族
tsui 罪
tsu-jen 族人
tsun 尊
tsun te-hsing 尊德性
tsun-wang 尊王
ts'un san-t'ung 存三統
tsung-fa 宗法
tsung-heng i-shuo 縱橫異說
Tsung-jen fu 宗人府
"Tsung-pa" 總跋
Tsung-pu 綜部
ts'ung-shu 叢書
Tu Fu 杜甫
tu-hsing 獨行
Tu Yü 杜預
T'u Shen 屠紳
tuan-luan ch'ao-pao 段爛朝報
Tuan Yü-ts'ai 段玉裁
Tung Chung-shu 董仲舒
Tung-i chih jen 東夷之人
Tung-lin 東林
Tung-p'o 東坡
Tung Shih-hsi 董士錫
Tung-tzu ch'un-ch'iu fa-wei 董子春秋發微
T'ung-ch'eng 桐城
t'ung-chi 統紀
t'ung ch'i kuo 痛其禍
t'ung san-t'ung 通三統
T'ung-tien 通典
Tzu-chih t'ung-chien kang-mu 資治通鑒綱目
tzu-jan 自然
Tzu-kung 子貢
Tzu-lu 子路
tzu-ssu tzu-li 自私自利
tz'u 辭
Tz'u ch'ing-li-ssu 祠淸理司
Tz'u-yuan 辭源

wai chu-hsia 外諸夏
wai-fan 外藩
wai-i 外夷
wai i-jung 外夷戎
Wan-li 萬歷
Wan-nan 皖南
Wan-pei 皖北
wan-shih chih hsing-shu 萬世之刑書
wang 王
Wang An-kuo 王安國
Wang An-shih 王安石
Wang Ch'ang 王昶
Wang Chi 王畿
Wang Chiao 王交
Wang Chu 王洙
Wang Chung 汪中
Wang Ch'ung-ch'ing 王崇慶
wang-fa 王法
Wang Fu-chih 王夫之
Wang Fu-ssu 王輔嗣
Wang Hsi-hsun 王喜荀
Wang Ken 王根
wang-kuo 亡國
wang-Lu 王魯
Wang Lun 王倫
Wang Mang 王莽
Wang Mao-hung 王懋竑
Wang Ming-sheng 王鳴盛
Wang Nien-sun 王念孫
Wang Pei-ya 王北厓
Wang Pi 王弼
Wang Su 王肅
wang-tao 王道
Wang T'ing-chen 王廷珍

Wang Yang-ming 王陽明
Wang Yin-chih 王引之
Wang Ying-lin 王應麟
Wei (state) 魏
wei (esoteric, subtle) 微
wei (forgery) 僞
wei (majesty) 威
wei ch'i tz'u 微其辭
wei-ching (tranquillity) 惟精
wei-ching (forged classic) 僞經
Wei Chung-hsien 魏忠賢
wei-i 惟一
wei-li 微理
wei K'ung An-kuo hsu 僞孔安國序
wei-yen 微言
wei-yen ta-i 微言大義
Wei Yuan 魏源
Wen 文
wen-chang 文章
wen-chih 文質
wen-hua 文化
wen i tsai tao 文以載道
Wen-su ko 文溯閣
wen-tzu 文字
wen-tzu-hsueh 文字學
wen-tz'u 文辭
Wen-Wu 文武
wo-shen 我身
wu (things, referents) 物
Wu (state) 吳
wu (non-being) 無
Wu Ch'eng 吳澄
wu-chi 無極
wu-chi wu-jen 無己無人
Wu-chin 武進
wu-ching 五經
Wu-ching cheng-i 五經正義
Wu-ching po-shih 五經博士
Wu-ching ssu-shu ta-ch'üan 五經四書大全
wu-ching wei-chih 五經微指
wu-ch'üan 無權
Wu-hsi 無錫
wu-hsing 五行
wu i-tz'u 無異辭
wu-li chih shuo 無理之說
wu-pa 五霸
wu pao-pien chih hsin 無褒貶之心
wu-shan wu-e 無善無惡
wu-shu-fa 無書法
wu-ssu 無私
wu-tang 無黨
Wu-ti (emperor) 武帝
wu-ti (Five emperors) 五帝
wu-wang chih shu 誣罔之書
wu-yen 無言
Wu-ying-tien 武英殿
wu-yü 無欲

Ya 牙
Yang-chou 揚州
Yang Ch'un 楊椿
Yang Fang-ta 楊方達
Yang-hsien 陽羨
Yang-hu 陽湖
Yang Shen 楊慎
Yang Wei-chen 楊維楨
Yao 堯
Yao Chi-heng 姚際恆
yao-chih 要指
yao-lei 藥類
Yao-lun 藥論
Yao Nai 姚鼐
Yao-shuo 藥說
Yao Ying 姚瑩
yen-ching ch'iu shih-yung 研經求實用
Yen Jo-chü 閻若璩
Yen-ling 延陵

yen-lu 言路
Yen-shih hsueh-chi 顏氏學記
Yen Yuan 顏淵
Yen Yuan 顏元
Yin 隱
yin-jen 因仁
yin jen-ch'ing 因人情
yin-ke 因革
yin min chih yü 因民之欲
yin-shih i chün min-ch'ing 因時以均民情
yin-shih shih-pien 因時適變
yin-tzu 蔭子
yin-tz'u 淫祠
yin-yang 陰陽
Yu (king) 幽
yu (being) 有
yü 諭
Yü Fan 虞翻
Yü Hsiao-k'o 余蕭客
"Yü-kung" 禹貢
yü-shih 御史
Yü-shih i-yen 虞氏易言
yü-shih yen-kuan 御史言官
Yueh (state) 越
yueh (control) 約
yueh-chih i li 約之以禮
yueh-wen 約文
Yun Ching 惲敬
Yun Ho-sheng 惲鶴生
Yun-nan 雲南
Yun Shou-p'ing 惲壽平
yung 用
Yung-cheng 雍正
yung-fa 用法
Yung-lo 永樂

BIBLIOGRAPHY

Ahern, Emily M. *Chinese Ritual and Politics*. Cambridge: Cambridge University Press, 1981.

———. "Segmentation in Chinese Lineages: A View through Written Genealogies." *American Ethnologist* 3 (1976): 1–15.

An Chieh-ch'uan 安皆川. "Hsu" 序 (Preface) to Hao Ching, *Ch'un-ch'iu fei-Tso*. In *Hu-pei ts'ung-shu*. 1891.

Aoki Masaru 青木正兒. *Shindai bungaku hyōronshi* 清代文学評論史 (History of Ch'ing literary criticism). In *Aoki Masaru zenshū* 全集 (Complete works of Aoki Masaru). Tokyo: Kyoritsusha, 1969.

Atwell, William S. "From Education to Politics: The Fu She." In Wm. Theodore de Bary, ed., *The Unfolding of Neo-Confucianism*. New York: Columbia University Press, 1975.

Baker, Hugh. *Chinese Family and Kinship*. London: Macmillan, 1979.

Beattie, Hilary. "The Alternative to Resistance: The Case of T'ung-ch'eng." In Jonathan Spence and John Wills, eds., *From Ming to Ch'ing: Conquest, Region, and Continuity in Seventeenth-Century China*. New Haven: Yale University Press, 1979.

———. *Land and Lineage in China: A Study of T'ung-ch'eng County, Anhui, in the Ming and Ch'ing Dynasties*. Cambridge: Cambridge University Press, 1979.

Bernard, Henry S. J. "Whence the Philosophic Movement at the Close of the Ming (1580–1640)?" *Bulletin of the Catholic University of Peking* 8 (1931): 67–73.

Bodde, Derk, and Clarence Morris. *Law in Imperial China*. Philadelphia: University of Pennsylvania Press, 1973.

Bol, Peter. "Chu Hsi's Redefinition of Literati Learning." In Wm. Theodore de Bary and John Chaffee, eds., *Neo-Confucian Education: The Formative Stage*. Berkeley: University of California Press, 1989.

———. "Culture and the Way in Eleventh-Century China." Ph.D. diss., Princeton University, 1982.

Bourdieu, Pierre. *Outline of a Theory of Practice*. Translated by Richard Nice. Cambridge: Cambridge University Press, 1977.

Bourdieu, Pierre, and Jean-Claude Passeron. *Reproduction in Education, Society, and Culture*. Translated by Richard Nice. Beverly Hills, Calif.: Sage Publications, 1977.

Brook, Timothy. "The Merchant Network in Sixteenth-Century China." *Journal of the Economic and Social History of the Orient* 24, no. 2 (1981): 165–85.

———. "The Spatial Structure of Ming Local Administration." *Late Imperial China* 6, no. 1 (June 1985): 1–55.

Busch, Heinrich. "The Tung-lin Academy and Its Political and Philosophical Significance." *Monumenta Serica* 14 (1949–55): 1–163.

Cahill, James. *Parting at the Shore: Chinese Painting of the Early and Middle Ming Dynasty, 1368–1580*. New York: Weatherhill, 1978.

Chan, Hok-lam. "Chinese Official Historiography at the Yuan Court: The Composition of the Liao, Chin, and Sung Histories." In John D. Langlois, Jr., ed., *China under Mongol Rule*. Princeton: Princeton University Press, 1981.

Chan, Wing-tsit, trans. *Instructions for Practical Living and Other Neo-Confucian Writings by Wang Yang-ming*. New York: Columbia University Press, 1963.

———, trans. *Reflections on Things at Hand: The Neo-Confucian Anthology Compiled by Chu Hsi and Lü Tsu-ch'ien*. New York: Columbia University Press, 1967.

Chang, Frank. *Ancestors: 900 Years in the Life of a Chinese Family*. New York: Morrow and Co., 1988.

Chang, Hao. *Chinese Intellectuals in Crisis: Search for Order and Meaning, 1890–1911*. Berkeley: University of California Press, 1987.

———. *Liang Ch'i-ch'ao and Intellectual Transition in China*. Cambridge: Harvard University Press, 1971.

———. "On the *Ching-shih* Ideal in Neo-Confucianism." *Ch'ing-shih wen-t'i* 3, no. 1 (Nov. 1974).

Chang Hsi-t'ang 張西堂. "Hsu" 序 (Preface) to Liu Feng-lu's *Tso-shih ch'un-ch'iu k'ao-cheng*. Compiled by Ku Chieh-kang. Peking, 1932.

Chang Hsueh-ch'eng 章學誠. *Chang-shih i-shu* 章氏遺書 (Bequeathed works of Chang Hsueh-ch'eng). Shanghai: Commercial Press, 1936.

———. *Wen-shih t'ung-i* 文史通義 (General meaning of literature and history). Taipei: Han-shang Press, 1973.

Chang Hui-yen 張惠言. *Chang Kao-wen ch'ien-i ch'üan-chi*. 張皋文箋易詮集 (Arranged collection of Chang Hui-yen's Change Classic notations). Yang-i-chai edition. Ca. 1820.

———. *Ming-k'o wen ssu-pien* 茗柯文四編 (Four chapters of Chang Hui-yen's essays). *Ssu-pu ts'ung-k'an erh-pien* edition. Shanghai: Commercial Press, 1934–35.

Chang K'o 張珂. "Ch'ing-tai Ch'ang-chou tz'u-p'ai yü tz'u-jen" 清代常州

詞派與詞人 (The Ch'ing dynasty Ch'ang-chou school of lyric poetry and poets). *Ch'ang-chou ku-chin* 常州古今 (Ch'ang-chou old and new) 1 (1980).

Chang Po-ying 張伯英. "Hsu" 序 (Preface) to Liu Shih-p'ei, *Tso-an chi*. Peking: Hsiu-pien-t'ang, 1928.

Ch'ang-chou fu-chih 常州府志 (Gazetteer of Ch'ang-chou prefecture). 1618 edition.

Ch'ang-chou fu-chih 常州府志 (Gazetteer of Ch'ang-chou prefecture). 1695 edition.

Ch'ang-chou fu-chih 常州府志 (Gazetteer of Ch'ang-chou prefecture). 1886 edition.

Ch'ang-chou fu-chih hsu-chi 常州府志續集 (Continuation of the gazetteer of Ch'ang-chou prefecture). 1513 edition.

Chao Chen 趙震. *P'i-ling wen-lu* 毘陵文錄 (Records of prose in Ch'ang-chou). Ch'ang-chou: Hua-hsin shu-she, 1931.

Chao Chen-tso 趙振祚. "Hsu" 序 (Preface) to Li Chao-lo's *Yang-i-chai wen-chi*. 1852.

Chao, Chia-ying Yeh. "The Ch'ang-chou School of *Tz'u* Criticism." In Adele Austin Rickett, ed., *Chinese Approaches to Literature from Confucius to Liang Ch'i-ch'ao*. Princeton: Princeton University Press, 1978.

Chao Fang 趙汸. *Ch'un-ch'iu shu-tz'u* 春秋屬辭 (Comparative phraseology of the Spring and Autumn Annals). In *T'ung-chih-t'ang ching-chieh*. 1676. Reprint. Kuang-chou: Yueh-tung, 1873.

Chao Huai-yü 趙懷玉. "Hsu" 序 (Preface) to Chuang K'ai 莊楷, "Liao-yuan shan-fang shih-chi" 蓼原山房詩集 (Collection of poetry from the Mountain Hut on Liao-yuan Mountain). Manuscript. Ca. 1875–1908.

———. "Hsu" 序 (Preface) to Yang Ch'un, *Meng-lin-t'ang chi*. Ch'ang-chou: Hung-mei-ko, ca. 1822.

———. *I-yu-sheng-chai wen-ch'ao* 亦有生齋文鈔 (Transcribed essays from the Pavilion of Another Life). 1819 edition.

Ch'en Ch'iao-ts'ung 陳喬樅. *Tso-hai hsu-chi* 左海續集 (Continuation to the collection of Ch'en Shou-ch'i). 1846 edition.

Ch'en Ch'ing-hsin 陳慶新. "Sung Ju Ch'un-ch'iu tsun-wang yao-i te fa-wei yü ch'i cheng-chih ssu-hsiang" 宋儒春秋尊王要義的發微與其政治思想 (Propagation of the key meaning to honor the ruler in the Spring and Autumn Annals by Sung Confucians and their political thought). *Hsin-Ya hsueh-pao* 新亞學報 1A (Dec. 1971): 269–368.

Chen, Fu-mei Chang. "On Analogy in Ch'ing Law." *Harvard Journal of Asiatic Studies* 30 (1970): 212–24.

Ch'en Huan 陳奐. *Kung-yang i-li k'ao-cheng* 公羊逸禮考徵 (Examination and verification of leftover rituals in the Kung-yang Commentary). *Ts'ung-shu chi-ch'eng* first collection. Shanghai: Commercial Press, 1935–37.

Ch'en Li 陳立. *Chü-hsi tsa-chu* 句溪雜著 (Various writings by Ch'en Li). 1843 edition.

Ch'en Liang 陳亮. *Lung-ch'uan wen-chi* 龍川文集 (Collected essays of Ch'en Liang). *Ssu-pu pei-yao* edition. Shanghai: Chung-hua Bookstore, 1927–35.

Ch'en Shan 陳善. "Hou-hsu" 後序 (Afterword), to Chang Hui-yen's *Chou-i Yü-shih i* 周易虞氏義 (Meanings in Mister Yü [Fan's] Chou [dynasty]

Change [Classic]. In Chang Hui-yen, *Chang Kao-wen ch'ien-i ch'üan-chi*. Yang-i-chai edition. Ca. 1820.

Ch'en Shou-ch'i 陳壽祺. *Tso-hai ching-pien* 左海經辨 (Classical disputations by Ch'en Shou-ch'i). 1823 edition.

Ch'en Wei-sung 陳維崧. *Hu-hai-lou ch'üan-chi*. 湖海樓全集 (Complete collection from the Pavilion of Lakes and Seas). Hao-jan-t'ang edition. 1795.

Ch'eng I 程頤. *Ho-nan Ch'eng-shih i-shu* 河南程氏遺書 (Bequeathed writings of Ch'eng I). In *Erh-Ch'eng ch'üan-shu*. Shanghai, 1927–35.

Ch'eng Shu-te 程樹德. *Chiu-ch'ao lü-k'ao* 九朝律考 (Study of law during nine dynasties). Shanghai: Commercial Press, 1955.

Chi Pen 季本. *Ch'un-ch'iu ssu-k'ao* 春秋私考 (Personal study of the Spring and Autumn Annals). Ca. 1557 edition.

Chi Wen-fu 嵇文甫. *Wan-Ming ssu-hsiang-shih lun* 晚明思想史論 (On late-Ming intellectual history). Ch'ung-ch'ing: Commercial Press, 1944.

Chiang Ching-ch'i 蔣景祁. "Hsu" 序 (Preface) to Ch'en Wei-sung, *Hu-hai-lou ch'üan-chi*. Hao-jan-t'ang edition. 1795.

———. "Hsu" 序 (Preface) to Ch'en Wei-sung, *Li-t'i wen-yuan* 儷體文原 (Original essays by Ch'en Wei-sung). In Ch'en Wei-sung, *Hu-hai-lou ch'üan-chi*. Hao-jan-t'ang edition. 1795.

Chiang Fan 江藩. *Han-hsueh shih-ch'eng chi* 漢學師承記 (Record of Han Learning masters). Shanghai: Shanghai Bookstore, 1983.

Chiang I-hsueh 蔣逸雪. "T'an yu-kuan T'ung-ch'eng wen-p'ai te chi-ko wen-t'i" 談有關桐城文派的幾個問題 (Discussion of some questions concerning the T'ung-ch'eng literary school). In *T'ung-ch'eng-p'ai yen-chiu lun-wen-chi*. He-fei: An-hui People's Press, 1963.

Chiang-nan t'ung-chih 江南通志 (General gazetteer of Chiang-nan). 1684 edition.

Chiang-su ch'eng-shih li-shih ti-li 江蘇城市歷史地理 (Historical geography of Chiang-su cities). Nan-ching: Chiang-su Society and Technology Press, 1982.

Chiang-su liu-shih-i hsien-chih 江蘇六十一縣志 (Gazetteers of sixty-one Chiang-su counties). Shanghai: Commercial Press, 1937.

Ch'iao Kuo-chang 喬國章. "Lun T'ung-ch'eng-p'ai ku-wen ho Ch'ing-ch'ao te wen-hua t'ung-chih" 論桐城派古文和清朝的文化統治 (On the ancient-style prose of the T'ung-ch'eng school and Ch'ing dynasty cultural control). In *T'ung-ch'eng-p'ai yen-chiu lun-wen chi*. He-fei: An-hui People's Press, 1963.

Ch'ien Chung-lien 錢仲聯. "T'ung-ch'eng-p'ai ku-wen yü shih-wen te kuan-hsi wen-t'i" 桐城派古文與時文的關係問題 (Concerning the question of the relation between ancient-style prose of the T'ung-ch'eng school and contemporary-style [examination] essays). In *T'ung-ch'eng-p'ai yen-chiu lun-wen chi*. He-fei: An-hui People's Press, 1963.

Ch'ien Hsuan-t'ung 錢玄同. "Shu-hou" 書後 (Afterword) to Liu Feng-lu, *Tso-shih ch'un-ch'iu k'ao-cheng*. Compiled by Ku Chieh-kang. Peking, 1932.

Ch'ien I-pen 錢一本. *Fan-yen* 範衍 (Exposition of models). Ca. 1606 edition.

———. *Kuei-chi* 龜記 (Records on tortoise shells). Ca. 1613 edition.

Ch'ien-lung 乾隆 Emperor. "Shu Ch'eng I lun ching-t'ing cha-tzu hou 書程頤論經筵劄子後 (Afterword to On Ch'eng I's Discussion as Imperial

Tutor in Classical Studies). In Ch'ien Mu, "Tzu-hsu" 自序 (Personal preface) to his *Chung-kuo chin san-pai-nien hsueh-shu-shih*. 2 vols. Taipei: Commercial Press, 1972.

Ch'ien Mu 錢穆. *Chung-kuo chin san-pai-nien hsueh-shu shih* 中國近三百年學術史 (Intellectual history of China in the last three hundred years). 2 vols. Taipei: Commercial Press, 1972.

———. *Liang-Han ching-hsueh chin-ku-wen p'ing-i* 兩漢經學今古文評議 (Criticism of New and Old Text classical studies during the two Han dynasties). Taipei: San-min Bookstore, 1971.

Ch'ien Ta-hsin 錢大昕. *Ch'ien-yen-t'ang wen-chi* 潛研堂文集 (Collected essays of the Hall of Subtle Research). *Kuo-hsueh chi-pen ts'ung-shu* edition. 8 vols. Taipei, 1968.

———. "Hsu" 序 (Preface) to his *Nien-erh-shih k'ao-i* 廿二史考異 (Examination of variances in the Twenty-two Dynastic Histories). Shanghai: Commercial Press, 1968.

Chin Jih-sheng 金日升. *Sung-t'ien lu-pi* 頌天臚筆 (Display of writings in praise of heaven). 1633 edition.

Ch'in Ying 秦瀛. *Hsiao-hsien shan-jen wen-chi* 小峴山人文集 (Collected writings from a mountain recluse). Yü-hsi ts'ao-t'ang edition. 1817.

Ching, Julia. "Truth and Ideology: The Confucian Way (Tao) and Its Transmission (Tao-t'ung)." *Journal of the History of Ideas* 35, no. 3 (July–Sept. 1974): 371–88.

Ch'ing-ch'ao t'ung-tien 清朝通典 (Complete institutions of the Ch'ing dynasty). Shanghai: Commercial Press, 1936.

Ch'ing-shih lieh-chuan 清史列傳. (Collection of biographies in the History of the Ch'ing). Taipei: Chung-hua Bookstore, 1962.

Ch'ing-tai chih-kuan nien-piao 清代職官年表 (Chronological table for holders of government positions during the Ch'ing dynasty). Compiled by Ch'ien Shih-fu 錢實甫. 4 vols. Peking: Chung-hua Bookstore, 1980.

Ch'in-ting hsueh-cheng ch'üan-shu 欽定學政全書 (Imperially sponsored collection of writings by education commissioners). Ca. 1773 edition.

Chou Yü-t'ung 周予同. *Ching chin-ku-wen hsueh* 經今古文學 (Study of the New and Old Text Classics). Taipei: Commercial Press, 1967.

———. *Chou Yü-t'ung ching-hsueh-shih lun-chu hsuan-chi* 經學史論著選集 (Selected essays on the History of Classical Studies by Chou Yü-t'ung). Shanghai: People's Press, 1983.

"Chu-chi Chuang-shih tsung-p'u" 諸暨莊氏宗譜 (Genealogy of the Chuang lineage in Chu-chi). Ch'ang-chou. Partially unpaginated manuscript. 1796.

Chu-chi Chuang-shih tsung-p'u 諸暨莊氏宗譜 (Genealogy of the Chuang lineage in Chū-chi). Printed edition. Ch'ang-chou, 1883.

Chu Hsi 朱熹. *Chu-tzu ta-ch'üan* 朱子大全 (Master Chu [Hsi's] Great Compendium). *Ssu-pu ts'ung-k'an* edition. Shanghai: Commercial Press, 1920–22.

———. *Chu-tzu ta-ch'üan* 朱子大全 (Master Chu [Hsi's] Great Compendium). *Ssu-pu pei-yao* edition. Shanghai: Chung-hua Bookstore, 1927–35.

———. *Chu-tzu yü-lei* 朱子語類 (Conversations with Master Chu [Hsi] classified topically). 1473. Reprint. Taipei: Cheng-chung Bookstore.

———. *Chu Wen-kung wen-chi* 朱文公文集 (Chu Hsi's collected essays). *Ssu-*

pu ts'ung-k'an photolithograph of Ming edition. Ca. 1522–66. Shanghai: Commercial Press, 1934–35.

———. *Chung-yung chang-chü* 中庸章句 (Parsing of phrases and sentences in the Doctrine of the Mean). Ming edition. Reprint. Taipei: Commercial Press, 1980.

Chu I-tsun 朱彝尊. *Ching-i k'ao* 經義考 (Analysis of meanings in the Classics). Shanghai: Chung-hua Press, 1927–35.

Chu Kuei 朱珪. "Hsu" 序 (Preface) to Chuang Ts'un-yü, *Ch'un-ch'iu cheng-tz'u*. In *Huang-Ch'ing ching-chieh*. Kuang-chou: Hsueh-hai-t'ang, 1860.

Chu T'an 朱倓. *Ming-chi she-tang yen-chiu* 明季社黨研究 (Research on Ming dynasty societies and parties). Ch'ung-ch'ing: Commercial Press, 1945.

Ch'ü, T'ung-tsu. *Law and Society in Traditional China*. Paris: Mouton and Co., 1961.

"Chuan-kao" 傳稿 (Draft biography) of Chuang Shu-tsu. No. 4470. Palace Museum, Taipei.

"Chuan-kao" 傳稿 (Draft biography) of Chuang Ts'un-yü. No. 5784. Palace Museum, Taiwan.

"Chuan-kao" 傳稿 (Draft biography) of Chuang Yu-k'e (under Chuang Shu-tsu). No. 4470. Palace Museum, Taiwan.

"Chuan-kao" 傳稿 (Draft biography) of Li Chao-lo. No. 6774(1–3). Palace Museum, Taiwan.

"Chuan-kao" 傳稿 (Draft biography) of Liu Feng-lu. No. 4455(1). Palace Museum, Taiwan.

"Chuan-kao" 傳稿 (Draft biography) of Liu Lun. No. 5741. Palace Museum, Taiwan.

"Chuan-kao" 傳稿 (Draft biography) of Sung Hsiang-feng (under Liu Feng-lu). No. 4455(1). Palace Museum, Taipei.

"Chuan-kao" 傳稿 (Draft biography) of Tai Wang (under Liu Feng-lu). No. 4455(1). Palace Museum, Taipei.

Chuang Chi-fa 莊吉發. "Ch'ing Kao-tsung Ch'ien-lung shih-tai te hsiang-shih" 清高宗乾隆時代的鄉試 (Provincial examinations during the reign period of the Ch'ien-lung Emperor of the Ch'ing dynasty). *Ta-lu tsa-chih* 大陸雜誌 52, no. 4 (Dec. 1975).

Chuang Ch'i-yuan 莊起元. *Ch'i-yuan chih-yen* 漆園卮言 (Words for quickly adapting to change from Chuang-tzu's garden). Ca. 1615 edition.

Chuang Chu 莊柱. *P'i-ling k'e-ti k'ao* 毘陵科第考 (Record of examination success in Ch'ang-chou). 1868 edition.

Chuang I-p'i 莊翊毘. "Hsu-lueh" 敍略 (Overview) to Lu Wen-ch'ao, *Ch'ang-chou fu pa-i i-wen-chih*, completed by Chuang I-p'i. N.d.

Chuang Ling-yü 莊令輿 and Hsu Yung-hsuan 徐永宣. *P'i-ling liu-i shih-ch'ao* 毘陵六逸詩鈔 (Specimens of poetry by Ch'ang-chou's six superior talents). Ca. 1717.

Chuang P'ei-yin 莊培因. "Ts'e" 策 (Policy examination essay). In *Hui-shih lu* 會試錄 (Record of the metropolitan examination). 1754. Preserved in the No.1 Historical Archives in Peking.

"Chuang-shih ching-hsueh-chia chia-chuan" 莊氏經學家家傳 (Biographies of classical scholars from the Chuang lineage). Unpaginated manuscript. N.d.

Chuang Shou-chia 莊綬甲. "Chou-kuan chi pa" 周官記跋 (Afterword to

[Chuang Ts'un-yü's] Notes on the Offices of Chou). In Chuang Shou-chia, *She-i-pu-i-chai i-shu*. Ca. 1838.

———. "Shang-shu chi-chien pa" 尙書旣見跋 (Postscript to [Chuang Ts'un-yü's] Appearance [of the sages] in the Documents Classic). In Chuang Shou-chia, *She-i-pu-i-chai i-shu*. Ca. 1838.

———. "Shang-shu k'ao-i hsu-mu" 尙書考異敍目 (Preface and contents for the Examination of Variances in the Documents Classic). In Chuang Shou-chia, *She-i-pu-i-chai i-shu*. Ca. 1838.

———. *She-i-pu-i-chai i-shu* 拾遺補藝齋遺書 (Bequeathed writings from the Study for Picking Up Where Others Have Left Off). Ca. 1838 edition.

———. *Shih shu-ming* 釋書名 (Explication of writing and names). In Chuang Shou-chia, *She-i-pu-i-chai i-shu*. Ca. 1838 edition.

———. *Wen-ch'ao* 文鈔 (Essays of Chuang Shou-chia). In Chuang Shou-chia, *She-i-pu-i-chai i-shu*. Ca. 1838 edition.

Chuang Shu-tsu 莊述祖. *Chen-i-i i-shu* 珍藝宧遺書 (Bequeathed writings of Chuang Shu-tsu). Ch'ang-chou, 1809 edition.

———. "Hsu" 序 (Preface) to the *Hsia Hsiao-cheng ching-chuan k'ao-shih* 夏小正經傳考釋 (Examination and explanation of the Hsia Classic and Lesser Calendar Commentary). In Chuang Shu-tsu, *Chen-i-i i-shu*. Ch'ang-chou, 1809.

———. "Hsu" 序 (Preface) to the *Hsia Hsiao-cheng yin-tu k'ao* 夏小正音讀考 (Examination of the readings of sounds in the Lesser Calendar Commentary to the Hsia Classic). In Chuang Shu-tsu, *Chen-i-i i-shu*. Ch'ang-chou, 1809.

———. "Hsu" 序 (Preface) to Tu Yü, *Ch'un-ch'iu shih-li*. Peking: Imperial Printing Office, 1802.

———. *Li-tai tsai-chi tsu-cheng lu* 歷代載籍足徵錄 (Record of sufficient evidence for works recorded during historical dynasties). In Chuang Shu-tsu, *Chen-i-i i-shu*. Ch'ang-chou, 1809.

———. *Po-hu t'ung-i k'ao* 白虎通義考 (Study of the Comprehensive Discussions in the White Tiger Hall). 1784 edition.

———. *Shang-shu chin-ku-wen k'ao-cheng* 尙書今古文考證 (Evidential analysis of the New and Old Text Documents Classic). In Chuang Shu-tsu, *Chen-i-i i-shu*. Ch'ang-chou, 1809.

———. *Shuo-wen ku-chou shu-cheng mu* 說文古籒疏證目 (Catalog of evidence for annotation of ancient large seal script in the Explanation of Writing). In Chuang Shu-tsu, *Chen-i-i i-shu*. Ch'ang-chou, 1809.

———. *Wen-ch'ao* 文鈔 (Essays of Chuang Shu-tsu). In Chuang Shu-tsu, *Chen-i-i i-shu*. Ch'ang-chou, 1809.

Chuang Ts'un-yü 莊存與. *Chou-kuan chi* 周官記 (Notes to the Offices of Chou). In *Huang-Ch'ing ching-chieh hsu-pien*. Chiang-yin: Nan-ch'ing Academy, 1888.

———. *Ch'un-ch'iu cheng-tz'u* 春秋正辭 (Correcting terms in the Spring and Autumn Annals). In *Huang-Ch'ing ching-chieh*. Kuang-chou: Hsueh-hai-t'ang, 1860.

———. "Ch'un-ch'iu chü-li" 春秋舉例 (Examples of precedents in the Spring and Autumn Annals). In Chuang Ts'un-yü, *Wei-ching-chai i-shu*. Yang-hu, 1882.

———. "Ch'un-ch'iu yao-chih" 春秋要指 (Essential points in the Spring and

Autumn Annals). In Chuang Ts'un-yü, *Wei-ching-chai i-shu*. Yang-hu, 1882.

———. "Hsi-tz'u chuan lun" 繫辭傳論 (On the tradition of aphorisms). In Chuang Ts'un-yü, *Wei-ching-chai i-shu*. Yang-hu, 1882.

———. "Hsu kua-chuan lun" 序卦傳論 (Treatise on the sequence of the hexagrams). In Chuang Ts'un-yü, *Wei-ching-chai i-shu*. Yang-hu, 1882.

———. "T'uan-chuan lun shang-p'ien" 彖傳論上篇 (On the decision chapter, part 1). In Chuang Ts'un-yü, *Wei-ching-chai i-shu*. Yang-hu, 1882.

———. *Wei-ching-chai i-shu* 味經齋遺書 (Bequeathed writings from the Study of Appealing Classics). Yang-hu, 1882 edition.

Chuang Ya-chou 莊雅州. *Hsia Hsiao-cheng hsi-lun* 夏小正析論 (Exhaustive inquiry into the Hsia Lesser Calendar). Taipei: Wen-shih-che Press, 1985.

Chuang Ying-hui 莊應會. "Hsu" 序 (Preface) to the *Tsuan-chi ching-wu sheng-lueh cheng-chi* 纂輯經武勝略正集 (Compilation of the orthodox collection for planning and operating successful military strategies). Late Ming edition.

Chuang Yu-k'e 莊有可. "Chin-wen Shang-shu chi-chu" 今文尚書集注 (Collected notes to the New Text Documents Classic). Manuscript. Ca. 1794.

———. "Hsu" 序 (Preface) to his *Chou-kuan chih-chang* 周官指掌 (Directives and institutions in the Offices of Chou). Nan-yin edition. 1829.

———. *Mu-liang tsa-tsuan* 慕良雜纂. (Miscellaneous collection in adoration of goodness). In his *Chuang Ta-chiu hsien-sheng i-chu* 莊大久先生遺著 (Bequeathed works of Chuang Yu-k'e). Ch'ang-chou, 1930.

Ch'un-ch'iu ching-chuan yin-te 春秋經傳引得 (Concordance to the Spring and Autumn Annals Classic and its commentaries). Reprint. Taipei: Ch'eng-wen, 1966.

Ch'un-ch'iu Kung-yang chuan 春秋公羊傳 (The Kung-yang Commentary to the Spring and Autumn Annals). Taipei: Hsin-hsing Bookstore, 1974.

Ch'ung-hsiu P'i-ling chih 重修毘陵志 (Revised gazetteer of P'i-ling [Ch'ang-chou]). 1483 edition.

Ch'ung-hsiu Ta-Ch'ing i-t'ung-chih 重修大清一統志 (Revised edition of the comprehensive gazetteer of the great Ch'ing). 1820 edition.

Cohen, Myron. "Lineage Development and the Family in China." 1983. Draft.

Cole, James. "Shaohsing: Studies in Ch'ing Social History." Ph.D. diss., Stanford University, 1975.

Crawford, Robert. "The Biography of Juan Ta-ch'eng." *Chinese Culture* 6 (1965): 28–105.

Creel, Herrlee G. *Confucius and the Chinese Way*. New York: Harper and Row, 1960.

———. *Shen Pu-hai*. Chicago: University of Chicago Press, 1974.

———. "Was Confucius Agnostic?" *T'oung Pao* 29 (1932): 55–99.

Crossley, Pamela. "*Manzhou yuanliu k'ao* and Formalization of the Manchu Heritage." *Journal of Asian Studies* 46, no. 4 (Nov. 1987): 761–90.

Dardess, John W. *Confucianism and Autocracy*. Stanford: Stanford University Press, 1983.

———. "The Cheng Communal Family: Social Organization and Neo-Confucianism in Yuan and Early Ming China." *Harvard Journal of Asiatic Studies* 34 (1974): 7–53.

Davis, Richard L. "Historiography as Politics in Yang Wei-chen's 'Polemic on Legitimate Succession.'" *T'oung Pao* 69, nos. 1–3 (1983): 33–72.

de Bary, Wm. Theodore. "Chinese Despotism and the Confucian Ideal: A Seventeenth-Century View." In John K. Fairbank, ed., *Chinese Thought and Institutions*. Chicago: University of Chicago Press, 1957.

———. *Neo-Confucian Orthodoxy and the Learning of the Heart-and-Mind.* New York: Columbia University Press, 1981.

———, ed. *Sources of Chinese Tradition*, vol. 1. New York: Columbia University Press, 1964.

———, ed. *The Unfolding of Neo-Confucianism.* New York: Columbia University Press, 1975.

Dennerline, Jerry. "Hsu Tu and the Lesson of Nanking: Political Integration and the Local Defense in Chiang-nan, 1634–1645." In Jonathan Spence and John Wills, Jr., eds., *From Ming to Ch'ing: Conquest, Region, and Continuity in Seventeenth-Century China*. New Haven: Yale University Press, 1979.

———. "Marriage, Adoption, and Charity in the Development of Lineages in Wu-hsi from Sung to Ch'ing." In Patricia Buckley Ebrey and James L. Watson, eds., *Kinship Organization in Late Imperial China, 1000–1940.* Berkeley: University of California Press, 1986.

———. *The Chia-ting Loyalists: Confucian Leadership and Social Change in Seventeenth-Century China.* New Haven: Yale University Press, 1981.

———. "The New Hua Charitable Estate and Local-level Leadership in Wuxi County at the End of the Qing." *Select Papers from the Center for Far Eastern Studies* (University of Chicago) 4 (1979–80): 19–70.

Dictionary of Ming Biography. L. C. Goodrich et al., eds. 2 vols. New York: Columbia University Press, 1976.

Dietrich, Craig. "Cotton Culture and Manufacture in Early Modern China." In W. E. Willmont, ed., *Economic Organization in Chinese Society*. Stanford: Stanford University Press, 1972.

Dillon, Michael. "Jingdezhen [Ching-te-chen] as a Ming Industrial Center." *Ming Studies* 6 (Spring 1978): 37–44.

Dubs, Homer, trans. *The History of the Former Han Dynasty*, by Pan Ku. 3 vols. Baltimore: Waverly Press, 1955.

Dull, Jack. "A Historical Introduction to the Apocryphal (Ch'an-wei) Texts of the Han Dynasty." Ph.D. diss., University of Washington, 1966.

Earl, David M. *Emperor and Nation in Japan: Political Thinkers of the Tokugawa Period*. Seattle: University of Washington Press, 1964.

Eastman, Lloyd. *Throne and Mandarins: China's Search for a Policy during the Sino-French Controversy, 1880–1885*. Cambridge: Harvard University Press, 1967.

Eberhard, Wolfram. *Social Mobility in Traditional China*. Leiden: E. J. Brill, 1962.

Ebrey, Patricia Buckley. "Conceptions of the Family in the Sung Dynasty." *Journal of Asian Studies* 43, no. 2 (Feb. 1984): 219–43.

———. "The Early Stages in the Development of Kin Group Organization." In Ebrey and James L. Watson, eds., *Kinship Organization in Late Imperial*

China, 1000–1940. Berkeley: University of California Press, 1986.
———. "Patron-Client Relations in the Later Han." *Journal of the American Oriental Society* 103, no. 3 (1983): 533–42.
———. "Types of Lineages in Ch'ing China: A Re-examination of the Chang Lineage of T'ung-ch'eng." *Ch'ing-shih wen-t'i* 4, no. 9 (June 1983): 1–20.
Ebrey, Patricia Buckley, and James L. Watson, eds. *Kinship Organization in Late Imperial China, 1000–1940*. Berkeley: University of California Press, 1986.
Edwards, E. D. "A Classified Guide to Thirteen Classes of Chinese Prose." *Bulletin of the School of Oriental and African Studies* 12 (1948): 770–88.
Elman, Benjamin. "Ch'ing Dynasty 'Schools' of Scholarship." *Ch'ing-shih wen-t'i* 4, no. 6 (Dec. 1979): 51–82.
———. "Criticism as Philosophy: Conceptual Change in Ch'ing Dynasty Evidential Research." *Tsing Hua Journal of Chinese Studies*, n.s., 17 (1985): 165–98.
———. *From Philosophy to Philology: Social and Intellectual Aspects of Change in Late Imperial China*. Cambridge: Harvard University Council on East Asian Studies, 1984.
———. "The Hsueh-hai T'ang and the Rise of New Text Scholarship in Canton." *Ch'ing-shih wen-t'i* 4, no. 2 (Dec. 1979): 51–82.
———. "Philosophy (*I-li*) versus Philology (*K'ao-cheng*): The *Jen-hsin Tao-hsin* Debate." *T'oung Pao* 59, nos. 4–5 (1983): 175–222.
———. "The Relevance of Sung Learning in the Late Ch'ing: Wei Yuan and the *Huang-ch'ao ching-shih wen-pien*." *Late Imperial China* 9, no. 2 (Dec. 1988): 1–28.
———. "The Unravelling of Neo-Confucianism: From Philosophy to Philology in Late Imperial China." *Tsing Hua Journal of Chinese Studies*, n.s., 15 (1983): 67–89.
Elvin, Mark. "Market Towns and Waterways: The County of Shang-hai from 1480 to 1910." In G. William Skinner, ed., *The City in Late Imperial China*. Stanford: Stanford University Press, 1977.
Erh-Ch'eng ch'üan-shu 二程全書 (Complete writings of Ch'eng Hao and Ch'eng I). *Ssu-pu pei-yao* edition. Shanghai: Chung-hua Bookstore, 1927–35.
Escarra, Jean. *Chinese Law*. Translated by Gertrude Browne. Seattle: University of Washington Press, 1936.
Fang Pao 方苞. *Fang Pao chi* 集 (Collected writings of Fang Pao). Shanghai: Rare Books Press, 1983.
Fang Tung-shu. *I-wei-hsuan wen-chi* 儀衛軒文集 (Collected writings from the studio of Fang Tung-shu). An-hui edition. 1868.
Fang Xing. "The Economic Structure of Chinese Feudal Society and Seeds of Capitalism." *Social Science in China* 2, no. 4 (1981).
Faure, David. *The Structure of Chinese Rural Society*. New York: Oxford University Press, 1986.
Freedman, Maurice. *Chinese Lineage and Society: Fukien and Kwangtung*. London: Athlone Press, 1966.

———. *Lineage Organization in Southeastern China*. New York: Humanities Press, 1965.

———. *The Study of Chinese Society*. Edited by G. William Skinner. Stanford: Stanford University Press, 1979.

Fu I-ling 傅衣凌. *Ming-Ch'ing nung-ts'un she-hui ching-chi* 明清農村社會經濟 (Village society and economy in the Ming and Ch'ing). Peking: San-lien Bookstore, 1961.

Fung Yu-lan. *History of Chinese Philosophy*. Translated by Derk Bodde. 2 vols. Princeton: Princeton University Press, 1952–53.

Geertz, Clifford. "Ideology as a Cultural System." In David Apter, ed., *Ideology and Discontent*. New York: Free Press, 1964.

Gernet, Jacques. *China and the Christian Impact*. Translated by Janet Lloyd. Cambridge: Cambridge University Press, 1985.

Goodrich, L. C. *The Literary Inquisition of Ch'ien-lung*. Baltimore: Waverly Press, 1935.

Grieder, Jerome. *Intellectuals and the State in Modern China*. New York: Free Press, 1981.

Grimm, Tilemann. "State and Power in Juxtaposition: An Assessment of Ming Despotism." In Stuart R. Schram, ed., *The Scope of State Power in China*. London: School of Oriental and African Studies, 1985.

Grove, Linda, and Christian Daniels, eds. *State and Society in China: Japanese Perspectives on Ming-Qing Social and Economic History*. Tokyo: Tokyo University Press, 1984.

Guy, R. Kent. "The Development of the Evidential Research Movement: Ku Yen-wu and the Ssu-k'u ch'üan-shu." *Tsing Hua Journal of Chinese Studies*, n.s., 16 (1984): 97–118.

———. *The Emperor's Four Treasuries. Scholars and the State in the Late Ch'ien-lung Era*. Cambridge: Harvard University Council on East Asian Studies, 1987.

Hamashima Atsutoshi 濱島敦俊. "Mimmatsu Nanchoku no Sō-Sō-Jō sanfu ni okeru kinden kin'eki hō" 明末南直の蘇松常三府における均田均役法 (The equal service for equal land law in the three prefectures of Su-chou, Sung-chiang, and Ch'ang-chou in the southern capital region during the late Ming). *Tōyō gakuhō* 東洋學報 57, nos. 3–4 (Mar. 1976): 81–115.

———. *Mindai Kōnan nōson shakai no kenkyū* 明代江南農村社會の研究(Research on rural society in Chiang-nan during the Ming dynasty). Tokyo: Tokyo University Press, 1982.

Han Fei Tzu so-yin 韓非子索引 (Index to Han Fei Tzu). Peking: Chung-hua Bookstore, 1982.

Hao Ching 郝敬. *Ch'un-ch'iu chih-chieh* 春秋直解 (Straight explanations for the Spring and Autumn Annals). Nan-ch'ien ch'iu-ch'ien edition. N.d.

———. *Ch'un-ch'iu fei-Tso* 春秋非左 (The Spring and Autumn Annals is not linked to the Tso Commentary). In *Hu-pei ts'ung-shu* 湖北叢書(Collectanea of Hu-pei). 1891.

———. "Tu ch'un-ch'iu" 讀春秋 (Reading the Spring and Autumn Annals). In Hao's *Ch'un-ch'iu chih-chieh*. Nan-ch'ien ch'iu-ch'ien edition. N.d.

———. "Tu-shu" 讀書 (Reading the Documents). In Hao's *Shang-shu pien-chieh* 尚書辨解 (Analysis of scholia to the Documents). In *Hu-pei ts'ung-shu* 湖北叢書 (Collectanea of Hu-pei). 1891 edition.

Harada Masaota 原田正己. "Shimmatsu shisōka no isho kan" 清末思想家の緯書觀 (Late Ch'ing thinkers' perspectives on the apocrypha). In Yasui Kōzan, ed., *Shin'i shisō no sōgō teki kenkyū*. Tokyo: Kokusho kankōkai, 1984.

Harootunian, H. D., *Toward Restoration: The Growth of Political Consciousness in Tokugawa Japan*. Berkeley: University of California Press, 1970.

Hartman, Charles. "Han Yü as Philosopher: The Evidence from the *Lun Yü Pi-chieh*." *Tsing Hua Journal of Chinese Studies*, n.s., 16, nos. 1 and 2 (Dec. 1984): 57–94.

Hartwell, Robert. "Demographic, Political, and Social Transformations of China, 750–1550." *Harvard Journal of Asiatic Studies* 42, no. 2 (1982): 365–426.

———. "Historical-Analogism, Public Policy, and Social Science in Eleventh- and Twelfth-Century China." *American Historical Review* 76, no. 3 (June 1971): 690–727.

Hatch, George. "Biography of Su Shih." In *Sung Biographies*. 2 vols. Wiesbaden: Franz Steiner Verlag, 1976.

Hegel, Robert. *The Novel in Seventeenth-Century China*. New York: Columbia University Press, 1981.

Henderson, John. *The Development and Decline of Chinese Cosmology*. New York: Columbia University Press, 1984.

Hervouet, Yves, ed. A *Sung Bibliography*. Hong Kong: Chinese University Press, 1978.

Hihara Toshikuni 日原利國. "Byakko tsūgi kenkyū choron" 白虎通義研究緒論 (Introductory research on the White Tiger Hall Discussions). *Nihon Chūgoku gakkai hō* 日本中國學會報 14 (1962): 63–78.

———. "Shunjū Kuyōgaku no Kandai teki tenkai" 春秋公羊學の漢代的展開 (Han dynasty development of *Kung-yang* studies pertaining to the Spring and Autumn Annals). *Nihon Chūgoku gakkai hō* 日本中國學會報 12 (1960): 1–16.

———. "Shunjū Kuyōgaku no ronri shisō" 春秋公羊學の論理思想 (Ethical values in the Kung-yang studies of the Spring and Autumn Annals). *Tōyōshi kenkyū* 東洋史研究 23, no. 3 (Dec. 1964): 237–76.

Ho, Ping-ti. *The Ladder of Success in Imperial China*. New York: Wiley and Sons, 1962.

———. "The Salt Merchants of Yang-chou." *Harvard Journal of Asiatic Studies* 17 (1954): 130–68.

———. *Studies on the Population of China, 1368–1953*. Cambridge: Harvard University Press, 1959.

Ho, Yun-yi. "Ideological Implications of Ming Sacrifices in Early Ming." *Ming Studies* 6 (Spring 1978): 55–67.

———. *The Minstry of Rites and Suburban Sacrifices in Early Ming*. Taipei: Shuang-yeh Bookstore, 1980.

Hobsbawm, Eric, and Terence Ranger, eds. *The Invention of Tradition*. Cambridge: Cambridge University Press, 1984.

Hou Wai-lu 侯外廬. *Chin-tai Chung-kuo ssu-hsiang hsueh-shuo shih* 近代中國思想學說史 (History of modern Chinese thought and theories). 2 vols. Shanghai: Shanghai Bookstore, 1947.

———. "Lun Ming-Ch'ing chih chi te she-hui chieh-chi kuan-hsi ho ch'i-meng ssu-ch'ao te t'e-tien" 論明清之季的社會階級關係和啓蒙思潮的特點 (Special characteristics of enlightened thought and social class relations in the Ming-Ch'ing era). *Hsin chien-she* 新建設 May 1955: 26–35.

Hsi-ying Liu-shih chia-p'u 西營劉氏家譜 (Genealogy of the Liu lineage in Hsi-ying). Ch'ang-chou, 1792 and 1876 editions.

Hsiao, Kung Chuan. "Legalism and Autocracy in Traditional China." *Tsing Hua Journal of Chinese Studies*, n.s., 4, no. 2 (Feb. 1964): 108–21.

———. *A Modern China and a New World: K'ang Yu-wei, Reformer and Utopian, 1858–1927*. Seattle: University of Washington Press, 1975.

———. *Rural China: Imperial Control in the Nineteenth Century*. Seattle: University of Washington Press, 1967.

Hsieh Ch'i-k'un 謝啓昆. *Hsiao-hsueh k'ao* 小學考 (Critique of classical philology). Reprint. Taipei: Kuang-wen, 1969.

Hsieh Kuo-chen. *Ming-mo Ch'ing-ch'u te hsueh-feng* 明末清初的學風 (Scholarly currents in the late Ming and early Ch'ing). Peking: People's Press, 1982.

Hsing I-t'ien 邢義田. "Ch'in-Han te lü-ling hsueh" 秦漢的律令學 (Legal studies in the Ch'in-Han period). *Li-shih yü-yen yen-chiu-so chi-k'an* 歷史語言研究所集刊 (Academia Sinica, Taiwan) 54, no. 4 (Dec. 1984): 51–101.

Hsu Ch'ien-hsueh 徐乾學. "Hsu" 序 (Preface) to Ch'en Wei-sung, *Hu-hai-lou ch'üan-chi*. Hao-jan-t'ang edition. 1795.

Hsu Fu-kuan 徐復觀, *Liang-Han ssu-hsiang-shih* 兩漢思想史 (Intellectual history of the two Han dynasties). Hong Kong: Chinese University, 1975.

Hsu K'o 徐珂. *Ch'ing-pai lei-ch'ao* 清稗類鈔 (Classified jottings on Ch'ing dynasty unofficial history). Shanghai: Commercial Press, 1920.

Hsu Shih-ch'ang 徐世昌. *Ch'ing-Ju hsueh-an* 清儒學案. (Studies of Ch'ing dynasty Confucians). 10 vols. Taipei: World Bookstore, 1966.

Hsu Yung-hsuan 徐用宣. *Pu-yao hsiu-chen hsiao-erh yung fang-lun* 補要袖珍小兒用方論 (Critical additions to the Handbook on Children's Diseases). Ca. 1634 edition.

Hsueh Tzu-heng 薛子衡. "Hsing-chuang" 行狀 (Obituary for Li Chao-lo). In Li Chao-lo, *Yang-i-chai wen-chi*. 1852 edition.

Hsueh Ying-ch'i 薛應旂. *Fang-shan hsien-sheng wen-lu* 房山先生文錄 (Recorded writings of Hsueh Ying-ch'i). Su-chou edition, 1553.

———. *Fang-shan Hsueh hsien-sheng ch'üan-chi* 房山薛先生全集 (Complete collection of Hsueh Ying-ch'i's writings). Ca. 1556 edition.

Hsueh-hai-t'ang chi 學海堂集 (Collected writings from the Hsueh-hai Academy). Compiled by Juan Yuan 阮元 et al. Canton: Hsueh-hai-t'ang, 4 series, 1825–86.

Hsueh-hai-t'ang chih 學海堂志 (Gazetteer of the Hsueh-hai Academy). Compiled by Lin Po-t'ung 林伯桐 et al. Hong Kong: Tung-Ya hsueh-she, 1964.

Hsu-hsiu Ssu-k'u ch'üan-shu t'i-yao 續修四庫全書提要 (Continuation to the Outlines of the Complete Collection of the Four Treasuries). Taipei: Commercial Press, 1972.

Hu, Hsien Chin. *The Common Descent Group in China and Its Functions*. New York: Viking Fund, 1948.

Huang Ch'ing-lien. "The *Li-chia* System in Ming Times and Its Operation in Ying-t'ien Prefecture." *Bulletin of the Institute of History and Philology* (Academia Sinica, Taiwan) 54 (1983): 103–55.

Huang, Chün-chieh. "Mencian Morality in a Political Form: Chao Ch'i's *Commentary on the Mencius* and Its Place in Later Han Scholarship." *Han-hsueh yen-chiu* 漢學研究 1, no. 1 (June 1983): 219–58.

———. "The Synthesis of Old Pursuits and New Knowledge: Chu Hsi's Interpretation of Mencian Morality." *Hsin-Ya hsueh-shu chi-k'an* 新亞學術集刊 3 (1982): 197–222.

Huang Ju-t'ing 黃汝亭. "Hsu" 序 (Preface). In Chuang Ch'i-yuan, *Ch'i-yuan chih-yen*. Ca. 1615.

Huang, Philip C. C. *Liang Ch'i-ch'ao and Modern Chinese Liberalism*. Seattle: University of Washington Press, 1972.

———. *The Peasant Economy and Social Change in North China*. Stanford: Stanford University Press, 1985.

Huang, Ray. *Taxation and Governmental Finance in Sixteenth-Century Ming China*. Cambridge: Cambridge University Press, 1974.

Huang Tao-chou 黃道周. "Fan-li" 凡例 (Statement of contents) for his *I-hsiang cheng* 易象正 (Corrections on the images in the Change Classic). In Huang's *Shih-chai hsien-sheng ching-chuan chiu-chung* 石齋先生經傳九種 (Nine kinds of works by Mister Huang Tao-chou on the Classics and commentaries). 1693 edition.

Huang Tsung-hsi 黃宗羲. *Ming-Ju hsueh-an* 明儒學案 (The Record of Ming scholars). Taipei: World Bookstore, 1973.

———. *The Record of Ming Scholars*. Edited by Julia Ching. Honolulu: University of Hawaii Press, 1987.

Huang Yuan-sheng 黃源盛. "Han-tai ch'un-ch'iu che-yü chih yen-chiu" 漢代春秋折獄之研究(Research on legal judgments based on the Spring and Autumn Annals during the Han dynasty). M.A. thesis, Chung-hsing University (Taipei), 1982.

Huang-Ch'ing ching-chieh 皇清經解 (Ch'ing dynasty exegesis of the Classics). Compiled by Juan Yuan 阮元 et al. Kuang-chou: Hsueh-hai-t'ang, 1860.

Huang-Ch'ing ching-chieh hsu-pien 皇清經解續編 (Ch'ing dynasty exegesis of the Classics, supplement). Compiled by Wang Hsien-ch'ien 王先謙 et al. Chiang-yin: Nan-ch'ing Academy, 1888.

Huang-Ch'ing ming-ch'en tsou-i 皇清名臣奏議 (Memorials of famous Ch'ing officials). Ca. 1796–1820 edition.

Hucker, Charles O. "Confucianism and the Chinese Censorial System." In David S. Nivison and Arthur Wright, eds., *Confucianism in Action*. Stanford: Stanford University Press, 1969.

———. *The Traditional Chinese State in Ming Times (1368–1644)*. Tucson: University of Arizona Press, 1961.

———. "The Tung-lin Movement of the Late Ming Period." In John K. Fairbank, ed., *Chinese Thought and Institutions*. Chicago: University of Chicago Press, 1973.

——— ed. *Chinese Government in Ming Times: Seven Studies*. New York: Columbia University Press, 1969.

Hui Chou-t'i 惠周惕. *Shih-shuo* 詩說 (Sayings on the Poetry Classic). Ca. 1812 edition.

Hui Shih-ch'i 惠士奇. *Pan-nung hsien-sheng Ch'un-ch'iu shuo* 半農先生春秋說 (Theories on the Spring and Autumn Annals of Mr. Hui Shih-ch'i). Huang-chou shu-shih edition. Compiled by Hui Tung. 1749.

Hui Tung 惠棟. *Chou-i shu* 周易述 (Transmission of the Chou Change). In Hui Tung, *I Han-hsueh*. Sung-chün-t'ang edition. Ca. 1825.

———. "Hsu" 序 (Preface) to his *I Han-hsueh*. Sung-chün-t'ang edition. Ca. 1825.

———. *I Han-hsueh* 易漢學 (Han Learning of the Change [Classic]). Sung-chün-t'ang edition. Ca. 1825.

———. *I-li* 易例 (Precedents in the Change [Classic]). In *Huang-Ch'ing ching-chieh hsu-pien*. Chiang-yin: Nan-ch'ing Academy, 1888.

Hui-shih lu 會試錄 (Record of metropolitan civil service examinations). Preserved in the No. 1 Historical Archives in Peking.

"Hui-shih ssu-shih ch'uan-ching t'u-ts'e" 惠氏四世傳經圖册 (Records of the transmission of classical learning through four generations of the Hui lineage). Su-chou, ca. 1904. Unpaginated manuscript.

Hulsewe, A. F. P. *Remnants of Han Law*, vol. 1. Leiden: E. J. Brill, 1955.

Hummel, Arthur, ed. *Eminent Chinese of the Ch'ing Period*. Reprint. Taipei: Ch'eng-wen Bookstore, 1972.

Hung Liang-chi 洪亮吉. *Hung Pei-chiang ch'üan-chi* 洪北江全集 (Complete collection of Hung Liang-chi). 1877 Shou-ching-t'ang edition.

———. *Hung Pei-chiang shih-wen-chi* 洪北江詩文集 (Collected poetry and essays of Hung Liang-chi). 2 vols. Taipei: World Bookstore, 1983.

———. "Nien-p'u" 年譜 (Chronological biography). In *Hung Pei-chiang ch'üan-chi*. 1877 Shou-ching-t'ang edition.

Hymes, Robert. "Marriage, Kin Groups, and the Localist Strategy in Sung and Yuan Fu-chou." In Patricia Buckley Ebrey and James L. Watson, eds., *Kinship Organization in Late Imperial China*. Berkeley: University of California Press, 1986.

———. *Statesmen and Gentlemen: The Elite of Fu-chou, Chiang-hsi, In Northern and Southern Sung*. Cambridge: Cambridge University Press, 1987.

I-hsing hsien-chih 宜興縣志 (Gazetteer of I-hsing county). 1869 edition.

Inaba Ichirō 稲葉一郎. "Chū-Tō ni okeru shin Jugaku undō no ichi kōsatsu" 中唐における新儒學運動の一考察 (Overview of the Neo-Confucian movement in the mid-T'ang period). In *Chūgoku chūseishi kenkyū: Rikuchō Sui Tō no shakai to bunka* 中國中世史研究六朝隋唐の社會と文化 (Research on Chinese medieval history. Society and culture during the Six Dynasties, Sui, and T'ang periods). Tokyo: Tokaido University Press, 1970.

Juan Yuan 阮元. "Hsu" 序 (Preface) to Chang Hui-yen, *Chou-i Yü-shih i* 周易虞氏易 (Meanings in Mr. Yü [Fan's] Chou [dynasty] Change [Classic]).

In Chang Hui-yen, *Chang Kao-wen ch'ien-i ch'üan-chi*. Yang-i-chai edition. ca. 1820.

———. "Hsu" 序 (Preface) to Chuang Ts'un-yü, *Wei-ching-chai i-shu*. Yang-hu, 1882.

———. *Yen-ching-shih chi* 揅經室集 (Collection from the Studio for the Investigation of Classics). 3 vols. Taipei: World Bookstore, 1964.

Jung Chao-tsu 容肇祖. "Hsueh-hai-t'ang k'ao" 學海堂考 (Study of the Hsueh-hai Academy). *Ling-nan hsueh-pao* 嶺南學報 3, no. 4 (June 1934): 1–147.

Kahn, Harold. "The Education of a Prince: The Emperor Learns His Roles." In Albert Feuerwerker et al., eds., *Approaches to Modern Chinese History*. Berkeley: University of California Press, 1967.

K'ang Yu-wei 康有為. *Ch'ang-hsing hsueh-chi* 長興學記 (Notes on studies at Ch'ang-hsing). Kuang-chou, 1891.

———. *Hsin-hsueh wei-ching k'ao* 新學偽經考 (Study of forged Classics in Hsin [dynasty] scholarship). Taipei: World Bookstore, 1962.

Karlgren, Bernhard. *On the Authenticity and Nature of the Tso chuan*. Goteborg: Hogskolas arsskrift, 1926.

———. "The Early History of the Chou-li and Tso chuan Texts." *Bulletin of the Museum of Far Eastern Antiquities*, 3 (1931): 1–59.

Kawakatsu Mamoru 川勝守. *Chūgoku hōken kokka no shihai kōzō* 中國封建國家の支配構造 (Elite structure of the Chinese feudal state). Tokyo University Press, 1980.

———. "Chūgoku kinsei toshi no shakai kōzō: Mimmatsu Shinsho Kōnan shi ni tsuite" 中國近世都市の社會構造明末清初江南都市について (Social structure in early modern Chinese cities: concerning late Ming and early Ch'ing cities in Chiang-nan). *Shichō* 史潮, n.s., 6 (Nov. 1979): 65–90.

Kawata Teiichi 河田悌一. "Shindai gakujutsu no ichi sokumen" 清代學術の一側面 (Sidelights on scholarship in the Ch'ing period). *Tōhōgaku* 東方學 57 (Jan. 1979): 84–105.

Kertzer, David. *Ritual, Politics, and Power*. New Haven: Yale University Press, 1988.

Kessler, Lawrence. *K'ang-hsi and the Consolidation of Ch'ing Rule, 1661–1684*. Chicago: University of Chicago Press, 1976.

Kondo Mitsuo 近藤光男. "Kei Tō to Sen Taikin" 惠棟と錢大昕 (Hui Tung and Ch'ien Ta-hsin). In *Yoshikawa hakusei taikyū kinen Chūgoku bungaku ronshū* 吉川博士退休紀念中國文學論集 (Studies in Chinese literature dedicated to Dr. Yoshikawa [Kōjirō] on his retirement). Tokyo: Chikuma Bookstore, 1968.

———. "Kōshōgaku ni okeru bunshō hyōgen kyōrei ichi shijū" 考證學における文章表現舉例一詩注 (An example from poetry commentaries of textual and expressive analysis in evidential research studies). *Yūdō* 有瞳 2 (1973): 43–49.

———. "Ō Chū to Kokusho Jurinden kō" 汪中と國史儒林傳稿 (Wang Chung and the draft biographies of Confucians in Ch'ing history). *Jimbun kagaku ronshū* 人文科學論集 3 (1964): 64–69.

———. "Sen Taikin no bungaku" 錢大昕の文學 (Ch'ien Ta-hsin's literature). *Tōkyō Shinagaku hō* 東京支那學報 7 (1961): 25–28.

———. "Shinchō keigaku to isho" 清朝經學と緯書 (Ch'ing dynasty classical studies and the apocryphal books). In Yasui Kōzan, ed., *Shin'i shisō no sōgō teki kenkyū*. Tokyo: Kokusho kankōkai, 1984.

Kramers, R. P. *K'ung-tzu chia-yü: The School Sayings of Confucius*. Leiden: E.J. Brill, 1950.

Ku Chieh-kang 顧頡剛. "Ch'un-ch'iu te K'ung-tzu ho Han-tai te K'ung-tzu" 春秋的孔子和漢代的孔子 (Confucius of the Spring and Autumn period versus the Confucius of the Han period). In Ku Chieh-kang et al., *Ku-shih pien* 古史辨 (Debates on ancient history). 7 vols. Peking and Shanghai: Chih-ch'eng Press, 1926–41.

———. *Han-tai hsueh-shu-shih lueh* 漢代學術史略 (Summary of Han dynasty intellectual history). Taipei: Ch'i-yeh Bookstore, 1972.

Ku Ch'ing-mei 古清美. "Ch'ing-ch'u ching-shih chih hsueh yü Tung-lin hsueh-p'ai te kuan-hsi" 清初經世之學與東林學派的關係 (Early Ch'ing statecraft studies and their relation to the Tung-lin school). *K'ung-Meng yueh-k'an* 孔孟月刊 24, no. 3 (Nov. 1985): 44–51.

Ku Hsien-ch'eng 顧憲成. *Ching-kao ts'ang-kao* 涇皐藏稿 (Collected drafts of Ku Hsien-ch'eng). Wan-li reign, Ming dynasty edition.

———. "Hsiao-hsin-chai cha-chi" 小心齋劄記 (Random notes from the Pavilion of Watchfulness). In Ku Hsien-ch'eng, *Ku Tuan-wen kung i-shu*. K'ang-hsi reign, Ch'ing dynasty edition.

———. *Ku Tuan-wen kung i-shu* 顧端文公遺書 (Bequeathed writings of Ku Hsien-ch'eng). K'ang-hsi reign, Ch'ing dynasty edition.

Ku Hung-ting. "Upward Career Mobility Patterns of High-Ranking Officials in Ch'ing China, 1730–1796." *Papers on Far Eastern History* (Australia) 29 (1984): 45–66.

Ku Tung-kao 顧東高. *Ch'un-ch'iu ta-shih-piao* 春秋大事表 (Table of major events in the Spring and Autumn Annals). Shang-chih-t'ang edition. 1873.

Ku Yen-wu 顧炎武. *Jih-chih lu* 日知錄 (Record of knowledge gained day by day). Taipei: P'ing-p'ing Press, 1974.

———. *Ku T'ing-lin shih-wen chi* 顧亭林詩文集 (Collected essays and poetry of Ku Yen-wu). Hong Kong: Chung-hua Bookstore, 1976.

Kuan T'ung 管同. *Yin-chi-hsuan wen-chi* 因寄軒文集 (Collected writings from the studio of Kuan T'ung). 1833 edition.

Ku-ching ching-she wen-chi 詁經精舍文集 (Collected essays from the Ku-ching ching-she Academy). Edited by Juan Yuan 阮元 et al. Taipei: Commercial Press, 1966.

Kuei Yu-kuang 歸有光. *Kuei Chen-ch'uan hsien-sheng ch'üan-chi* 歸震川先生全集 (Complete collection of Kuei Yu-kuang). Ca. 1575 edition.

Kuhn, Philip. "Late Ch'ing Views of the Polity." In *Proceedings of the NEH Modern China Project* (edited by Tang Tsou), 2 (1981): 1–18.

K'ung Kuang-sen 孔廣森. "Hsu" (Preface) to his *Ch'un-ch'iu Kung-yang ching-chuan t'ung-i* 春秋公羊經傳通義 (Penetrating the meanings in the Kung-yang Commentary to the Spring and Autumn Annals Classic). In *Huang-Ch'ing ching-chieh*. Kuang-chou: Hsueh-hai-t'ang, 1860.

Kung Tzu-chen 龔自珍. *Kung Tzu-chen ch'üan-chi* 全集 (Complete writings of Kung Tzu-chen). Shanghai: Shanghai People's Press, 1975.

Kung Tzu-chen nien-p'u 龔自珍年譜 (Chronological biography of Kung Tzu-chen). In Kung Tzu-chen, *Kung Tzu-chen ch'üan-chi*. Shanghai: Shanghai People's Press, 1975.

K'ung-tzu chia-yü 孔子家語 (Household sayings of Confucius). Taipei: World Bookstore, 1972.

Kuo Shao-yü 郭紹虞. *Chi-nien shih-jen Huang Chung-tse* 紀念詩人黃仲則 (Commemorating the poet Huang Ching-jen). Shanghai: Hsueh-lin Press, 1983.

Kuo-ch'ao Ch'ang-chou tz'u-lu 國朝常州詞錄 (Record of lyric poetry in Ch'ang-chou during the Ch'ing dynasty). 1896 edition.

Kwong, Luke S. K. *A Mosaic of the Hundred Days: Personalities, Politics, and Ideas of 1898*. Cambridge: Harvard University Council on East Asian Studies, 1984.

Langlois, John D., Jr. "Law, Statecraft, and *The Spring and Autumn Annals* in Yuan Political Thought." In Hok-lam Chan and Wm. Theodore de Bary, eds., *Yuan Thought: Chinese Thought and Religion under the Mongols*. New York: Columbia University Press, 1982.

Lau, D. C., trans. *Confucius: The Analects*. New York: Penguin Books, 1979.

———, trans. *Mencius*. New York: Penguin Books, 1976.

Legge, James, trans. *The Chinese Classics*, vol. 5: *The Ch'un Ts'ew with the Tso Chuan*. Reprint. Taipei: Wen-shih-che Press, 1971.

———, trans. *The Four Books*. Reprint. New York: Paragon, 1966.

———, trans. *The Shoo King*. Reprint. Taipei: Wen-shih-che Press, 1972.

Leung Man-kam. "Juan Yuan (1764–1849): The Life, Works, and Career of a Chinese Scholar-Bureaucrat." Ph.D. diss., University of Hawaii, 1977.

Levenson, Joseph. *Confucian China and Its Modern Fate: A Trilogy*. 3 vols. Berkeley: University of California Press. 1969.

Li Chao-lo 李兆洛. "Hsu" 序 (Preface) to Chuang Shu-tsu, *Chen-i-i i-shu*. Ch'ang-chou, 1809.

———. *Yang-i-chai wen-chi* 養義齋文集 (Collected essays from the Studio for Nurturing Wholeness). 1852 and 1878 editions.

Li Hsin-lin 李新霖. "Ch'ing-tai ching chin-wen-hsueh shu" 清代經今文學述 (On Ch'ing dynasty New Text studies). *Kuo-wen yen-chiu-so chi-k'an* 國文研究所季刊 (Taiwan) 22 (1978): 113–311.

Li Huan 李桓. *Kuo-ch'ao ch'i-hsien lei-cheng* 國朝耆獻類徵 (Biographies of Ch'ing venerables and worthies arranged by categories). Hsiang-yin, n.d.

Li Shen-ch'i nien-p'u 李申耆年譜 (Chronological biography of Li Chao-lo). Nan-lin Liu-shih Chia-yeh-t'ang edition. Ca. 1831.

Li T'ien-yu 李天佑. *Ming-mo Chiang-yin Chia-ting jen-min te k'ang-Ch'ing tou-cheng* 明末江陰嘉定人民的抗清鬥爭 (Popular struggles against the Ch'ing in Chiang-yin and Chia-ting during the late Ming). Shanghai: People's Press, 1955.

Li Yuan-keng 李元庚. "Wang she hsing-shih k'ao" 望社姓氏考 (Studies of the participants in the Society of Expectations). *Kuo-ts'ui hsueh-pao* 國粹學報 71 (Sept. 1910); *shih-p'ien wai* 史篇外 (articles on history, outer section).

Liang Ch'i-ch'ao 梁啟超. "Chin-tai hsueh-feng chih ti-li te fen-pu" 近代學風之地理的分佈 (Geographical distribution of scholarly currents in modern times). In *Yin-ping-shih chuan-chi* 飲冰室專集 (Collected works from the Ice-Drinker's Studio). Taipei: Chung-hua Bookstore, 1972.

———. *Chung-kuo chin san-pai-nien hsueh-shu-shih* 中國近三百年學術史 (Intellectual history of China in the last three hundred years). Taipei: Chung-hua Bookstore, 1955.

———. *Intellectual Trends in the Ch'ing Period*. Translated by Immanual Hsu. Cambridge: Harvard University Press, 1959.

———. *Yin-ping-shih wen-chi* 飲冰室文集 (Collected writings from the Ice-Drinker's Studio). 8 vols. Taipei: Chung-hua Bookstore, 1970.

Li-chi chin-chu chin-i 禮記今註今譯 (Modern notes and translations for the *Record of Rites*). Annotated by Wang Meng-ou 王夢鷗. 2 vols. Taipei: Commercial Press, 1974.

Lin Ch'ing-chang 林慶彰. *Ming-tai k'ao-cheng-hsueh yen-chiu* 明代考證學研究 (Study of Ming dynasty evidential research). Taipei: Student Bookstore, 1984.

———. "Ming-tai te Han-Sung-hsueh wen-t'i" 明代的漢宋學問題 (The question of Han and Sung Learning during the Ming period). *Tung-wu wen-shih hsueh-pao* 東吳文史學報 (Taiwan) 5 (Aug. 1986): 133–50.

Lin Li-yueh 林麗月. "Ming-mo Tung-lin-p'ai te chi-ke cheng-chih kuan-nien" 明末東林派的幾個政治觀念 (Some political concepts of the Tung-lin faction in the late Ming). *Kuo-li T'ai-wan shih-fan ta-hsueh li-shih hsueh-pao* 國立臺灣師範大學歷史學報 11 (1983): 20–42.

Ling Shu 凌曙. *Kung-yang li-shu* 公羊禮疏 (Annotations on ritual in the *Kung-yang Commentary*). In *Huang-Ch'ing ching-chieh hsu-pien*. Chiang-yin: Nan-ch'ing Academy, 1888.

———. *Kung-yang wen-ta* 公羊問答 (Questions and answers on the Kung-yang Commentary). In *Huang-Ch'ing ching-chieh hsu-pien*. Chiang-yin: Nan-ch'ing Academy, 1888.

Li-tai chih-kuan piao 歷代職官表 (Chronological tables of institutions and offices). Hong Kong: Wen-yueh Press, n.d.

Liu Chao-pin 劉兆濱. *Ch'ing-tai k'e-chü* 清代科舉 (Examination system during the Ch'ing period). Taipei: Tung-ta Books, 1979.

Liu Chih-chi 劉知幾. *Shih-t'ung (shih-p'ing)* 史通(釋評) ([Elucidations and criticisms of Liu Chih-chi's] *Historical Penetrations*). Taipei: Hua-shih Press, 1975.

Liu Fen 劉賁. "Hsu" 序 (Preface) to Tu Yü, *Ch'un-ch'iu shih-li*. Taipei: Chung-hua Bookstore, 1970.

Liu Feng-lu 劉逢祿. *Chen kao-huang p'ing* 箴膏肓評 (Criticism of [Cheng Hsuan's] Revitalize the Incurable). In *Huang-Ch'ing ching-chieh*. Kuang-chou: Hsueh-hai-t'ang, 1860.

———. "Chi" 記 (Inscription) for Chang Hui-yen, *Yü-shih i-yen* 虞氏易言 (Mr. Yü [Fan's] comments on the Change). In Chang Hui-yen, *Chang Kao-wen ch'ien-i ch'üan-chi*. Yang-i-chai edition. Ca. 1820.

———. *Ch'un-ch'iu Kung-yang ching Ho-shih shih-li* 春秋公羊經何氏釋例 (Master Ho [Hsiu's] explication of the precedents in the Kung-yang Commentary to the Spring and Autumn Annals). In *Huang-Ch'ing ching-chieh*. Kuang-chou: Hsueh-hai-t'ang, 1860.

———. "Ch'un-ch'iu lun" 春秋論 (Discourse on the Spring and Autumn Annals). In Liu Feng-lu, *Liu Li-pu chi*. 1827 edition.

———. "Hsu" 序 (Preface) to his *Kung-yang ch'un-ch'iu Ho-shih chieh-ku ch'ien* 公羊春秋何氏解詁箋 (Elucidations to Master Ho [Hsiu's] Explications of the Kung-yang Commentary to the Spring and Autumn Annals). In *Huang-Ch'ing ching-chieh*. Kuang-chou: Hsueh-hai-t'ang, 1860.

———. "Hsu" 序 (Preface) to his *Shang-shu chin-ku-wen chi-chieh* 尚書今古文集解 (Collected notes to the New and Old Text Documents). Taipei: Commercial Press, 1977.

———. "Hsu" 序 (Preface) to Wei Yuan's *Shih ku-wei* 詩古微 (Ancient Subtleties of the Poetry Classic). In Liu Feng-lu, *Liu Li-pu chi*. 1827 edition.

———. *Liu Li-pu chi* 劉禮部集 (Collected writings of Liu Feng-lu). 1827 edition.

———. *Lun-yü shu-Ho* 論語述何 (Discourse on Ho [Hsiu's version of] the Analects). In *Huang-Ch'ing ching-chieh*. Kuang-chou: Hsueh-hai-t'ang, 1860.

———. *Tso-shih ch'un-ch'iu k'ao-cheng* 左氏春秋考證 (Evidential analysis of Master Tso's Spring and Autumn Annals). 1805 edition.

———. *Tso-shih ch'un-ch'iu k'ao-cheng* 左氏春秋考證 (Evidential analysis of Master Tso's Spring and Autumn Annals). Compiled by Ku Chieh-kang 顧頡剛. Peking, 1932 edition.

Liu Hsin 劉歆. "I T'ai-ch'ang po-shih shu" 移太常博士書 (Letter to the Erudite of the Chamberlain for Ceremonies [in the Imperial Academy]). In *Han-shu* 漢書 (History of the Former Han dynasty), by Pan Ku 班固. 7 vols. Taipei: Shih-hsueh ch'u-pan-she, 1974.

Liu I-cheng 柳詒徵. "Chiang-su shu-yuan chih ch'u-kao" 江蘇書院志初稿 (Preliminary draft of a gazetteer for Chiang-su academies). *Kuo-hsueh t'u-shu-kuan nien-k'an* 國學圖書館年刊 4 (1931): 1–112.

Liu, James J. Y. *The Art of Chinese Poetry*. Chicago: University of Chicago Press, 1962.

———. *Chinese Theories of Literature*. Chicago: University of Chicago Press, 1975.

Liu, James T. C. *Ou-yang Hsiu: An Eleventh-Century Neo-Confucianist*. Stanford: Stanford University Press, 1967.

———. *Reform in Sung China*. Cambridge: Harvard East Asian Center, 1959.

Liu Lun 劉綸. *Liu Wen-ting kung chi* 劉文定公集 (Collected writings of Count Liu Lun). Yung-ch'u-t'ang edition. 1772.

Liu, Shih-chi. "Some Reflections on Urbanization and the Historical Development of Merchant Towns in the Lower Yangtze Region, ca. 1500–1900." *The American Asian Review* 2, no. 1 (Spring 1984): 1–27.

Liu Shih-p'ei 劉師培. *Ch'ün-ching ta-i hsiang-t'ung lun* 群經大義相通論 (Essays on the mutual similarities in general meaning among the several Classics). Taipei: Citizen's Press, 1959.

———. "Han-Sung i-li-hsueh i-t'ung lun" 漢宋義理學異同論 (Similarities and differences in Han versus Sung studies of meanings and principles). In his *Liu Shen-shu hsien-sheng i-shu*. Ning-wu, 1934.

———. *Liu Shen-shu hsien-sheng i-shu* 劉申叔先生遺書 (Bequeathed works of Liu Shih-p'ei). Ning-wu, 1934 edition.

———. *Tso-an chi* 左盦集 (Collection from the Left Cloister). Peking: Hsiu-pien-t'ang, 1928.

Liu Wen-ch'i 劉文淇. *Ch'ing-hsi chiu-wu wen-chi* 清溪舊屋文集 (Collected essays from the Old Room by the Blue-green Stream). 1883 edition.

———. "Hsu" 序 (Preface) to Ch'en Li, *Chü-hsi tsa-chu*. 1843.

Lu Chien 盧見. "Hsu" 序 (Preface) to Wang Ying-lin 王應麟, *Cheng-shih Chou-i* 鄭氏周易 (Master Cheng [Hsuan's] Chou [dynasty] version of the Change [Classic]). Reissued by Ya-yü-t'ang, 1756.

———. "Hsu" 序 (Preface) to Hui Tung's *Chou-i shu*. In Hui Tung, *I Han-hsueh*. Sun-chün-t'ang, ca. 1825.

Lü Tsung-li 呂宗力. "Wei-shu yü Hsi-Han chin-wen ching-hsueh" 緯書與西漢今文經學 (Apocryphal texts and Former Han New Text classical studies). In Yasui Kōzan, ed., *Shin'i shisō no sōgō teki kenkyū*. Tokyo: Kokusho kankōkai, 1984.

Lu Wen-ch'ao 盧文弨. *Ch'ang-chou fu pa-i i-wen-chih* 常州府八邑藝文志 (Bibliography of the eight towns in Ch'ang-chou prefecture). Completed by Chuang I-p'i 莊翊昆. N.d.

———. *Pao-ching-t'ang wen-chi* 抱經堂文集 (Collected essays from the Hall for Cherishing the Classics). Shanghai: Commercial Press, 1937.

———. *P'i-ling ching-chieh-chih* 毘陵經解志 (Bibliography of Ch'ang-chou works). N.d.

Lu Yuan-chün 盧元駿. "Ching-hsueh chih fa-chan yü chin-ku-wen chih fen-ho" 經學之發展與今古文之分合 (Development of classical studies and the split between New Text and Old Text Confucianism). *K'ung-Meng yueh-k'an* 孔孟月刊 15, no. 4 (Dec. 1976): 35–43.

Lui, Adam Y. C. *The Hanlin Academy: Training Ground for the Ambitious, 1644–1850*. Hamden, Conn.: Shoe String Press, Archon Books, 1981.

Lun Ming 倫明. "Hsu-shu-lou tu-shu chi" 續書樓讀書記 (Reading notes from the Pavilion of Continuous Books). *Yen-ching hsueh-pao* 燕京學報, o.s., 3 (1928): 457–511.

Lung-ch'eng shu-yuan k'e-i 龍城書院科藝 (Instruction at the Lung-ch'eng Academy). Compiled by Hua Mu 華繆. 1901 edition.

Lung Mu-hsun 龍沐勛. "Lun Ch'ang-chou tz'u-p'ai" 論常州詞派 (On the Ch'ang-chou school of lyric poetry). *T'ung-sheng* 同聲 1, no. 10 (Sept. 1941): 1–20.

Lun-yü yin-te 論語引得 (Concordance to the *Analects*). Reprint. Taipei: Ch'eng-wen, 1966.

Maclntyre, Alasdair. *After Virtue: A Study in Moral Theory*. Notre Dame, Ind.: University of Notre Dame Press, 1981.

McKnight, Brian. "Mandarins as Legal Experts: Professional Learning in Sung China." In Wm. Theodore de Bary and John Chaffee, eds., *Neo-Confucian Education: The Formative Period*. Berkeley: University of California Press, 1989.

———. "Patterns of Law and Patterns of Thought: Notes on the Specifications (*shih*) of Sung China." *Journal of the American Oriental Society* 102, no. 2 (April–June 1982): 323–31.

Malmqvist, Göran. "Studies on the Gongyang and Guuliang Commentaries I." *Bulletin of the Museum of Far Eastern Antiquities* 43 (1971): 67–222.

Mammitzsch, Ulrich. "Wei Chung-hsien (1568–1628): A Reappraisal of the Eunuch and the Factional Strife at the Late Ming Court." Ph.D. diss., University of Hawaii, 1968.

Mann (Jones), Susan. "Hung Liang-chi (1746–1809): The Perception and Articulation of Political Problems in Late Eighteenth Century China." Ph.D. diss., Stanford University, 1972.

———. "Scholasticism and Politics in Late Eighteenth Century China." *Ch'ing-shih wen-t'i* 3, no. 4 (Dec, 1975): 28–49.

Mannheim, Karl. "The Ideological and Sociological Interpretation of Intellectual Phenomena." In Kurt Wolff, ed., *From Karl Mannheim*. New York: Oxford University Press, 1971.

Marcus, George E. "The Fiduciary Role in American Family Dynasties and Their Institutional Legacy." In his *Elites: Ethnographic Issues*. Albuquerque: University of New Mexico Press, 1983.

Maspero, Henri. "La composition et la date du Tso tchouan." *Mélanges chinois et buddhiques* 1 (1931–32): 137–215.

Mei, Diana Yu-shih. "Han Yü as a *Ku-wen* Stylist." *Tsing Hua Journal of Chinese Studies*, n.s., 7, no. 1 (August 1968): 143–208.

Meng Sen 孟森. *Ming-Ch'ing-shih lun-chu chi-k'an* 明清史論著集刊 (Collection of articles on Ming-Ch'ing history). Taipei: World Bookstore, 1965.

Meng-tzu chi-chu ta-ch'üan 孟子集注大全 (Complete collection for the Collected Notes to Mencius [by Chu Hsi]). In Hu Kuang 胡廣 et al., comps., *Ssu-shu ta-ch'üan* 四書大全 (Complete collection of the Four Books). Peking: Wen-yuan ko, 1776.

Meng-tzu yin-te 孟子引得 (Concordance to Mencius). Peking: Harvard-Yenching Institute, 1941.

Meskill, John. "Academies and Politics in the Ming Dynasty." In Charles O. Hucker, ed., *Chinese Government in Ming Times: Seven Studies*. New York: Columbia University Press, 1969.

———. *Academies in Ming China: A Historical Essay*. Tucson: University of Arizona Press, 1982.

Metzger, Thomas. *The Internal Organization of Ch'ing Bureaucracy*. Cambridge: Harvard University Press, 1973.

Ming-shih 明史 (Ming history). Taipei: Ting-wen Bookstore, 1982.

Mizoguchi Yūzō 溝口雄三. *Chūgoku sen kindai shisō no kussetsu to tenkai* 中國前近代思想の屈折と展開 (The refraction and development of Chinese early modern thought). Tokyo: Tokyo University Press, 1980.

———. "Iwayuru Tōrinha jinshi no shisō" いわゆる東林派人士の思想 (The thought of the members of the so-called Tung-lin faction). *Tōyō bunka kenkyūjo kiyō* 東洋文化研究所紀要, 75 (Mar. 1978): 111–341.

Mori, Masao. "The Gentry in the Ming." *Acta Asiatica* 36 (1979): 31–38.

Mote, F.W. "Confucian Eremitism in the Yuan Period." In Arthur Wright, ed., *The Confucian Persuasion*. Stanford: Stanford University Press, 1960.

———. "The Growth of Chinese Despotism." *Oriens Extremus* 8, no. 1 (Aug. 1961): 1–41.

Mou Jun-sun 牟潤孫. "Liang-Sung ch'un-ch'iu-hsueh chih chu-liu, shang hsia" 兩宋春秋學之主流, 上、下 (Main currents in studies of the Spring and Autumn Annals during the two Sung dynasties, parts 1 and 2). *Ta-lu tsa-chih* 大陸雜誌 5, no. 4 (Aug. 1952): 113–15; no. 5 (Sept. 1952) 170–72.

Munro, Donald. "The Concept of 'Interest' in Chinese Thought." *Journal of the History of Ideas* 41, no. 2 (Apr.–June 1980): 179–87.

———. *Images of Human Nature: A Sung Portrait.* Princeton: Princeton University Press, 1988.

Najita, Tetsuo. *Japan: Intellectual Foundations of Modern Japanese Politics.* Chicago: University of Chicago Press, 1980.

Nakamura Shun'ya 中村俊也. "Kō Kōsen Shunjū Kuyō tsūgi jo ni tsuite" 孔廣森の春秋公羊通義敍について (Concerning K'ung Kuang-sen's Preface to his Penetrating the Meanings in the Kung-yang [Commentary] to the Spring and Autumn Annals). *Chūgoku bunshitetsu ronshū* 中國文史哲論集 (Tokyo) 1979: 891–902.

Naquin, Susan. *Millenarian Rebellion in China: The Eight Trigrams Uprising of 1813.* New Haven: Yale University Press, 1976.

———. *Shantung Rebellion: The Wang Lun Uprising of 1774.* New Haven: Yale University Press, 1981.

Needham, Joseph. *Science and Civilization in China.* 6 vols. Cambridge: Cambridge University Press, 1954–.

Niida Noboru 仁井田陞. *Chūgoku hōseishi kenkyū* 中國法制史研究 (Study of Chinese legal history). Tokyo: Tokyo University Press, 1964.

Nishijima, Sadao. "The Formation of the Early Chinese Cotton Industry." Translated by Linda Grove. In Grove and Christian Daniels, eds., *State and Society in China: Japanese Perspectives on Ming-Qing Social and Economic History.* Tokyo: Tokyo University Press, 1984.

Nivison, David S. "Ho-shen and His Accusers: Ideology and Political Behavior in the Eighteenth Century." In Nivison and Arthur Wright, eds., *Confucianism in Action.* Stanford: Stanford University Press, 1969.

———. *The Life and Thought of Chang Hsueh-ch'eng (1738–1801).* Stanford: Stanford University Press, 1966.

Ojima Sukema 小島祐馬. *Chūgoku no shakai shisō* 中國の社會思想 (Social Thought in China). Tokyo: Chikuma Bookstore, 1967.

Okada Takehiko. *Edo ki no Jugaku* 江戶期の儒學 (Confucian studies during the Edo Era). Tokyo: Kikuragesha, 1982.

Ōkubo Eiko 大久保英子. *Min-Shin jidai shoin no kenkyū* 明清時代書院の研究 (Research on academies in the Ming-Ch'ing period). Tokyo: Kokusho kankōkai, 1976.

Ono Kazuko 小野和子. "Mimmatsu no kessha ni kan suru ichi kōsatsu (jō, ge)" 明末の結社に関する一考察, 上、下 (Overview of late Ming societies and clubs, parts 1 and 2). *Shirin* 史林 45, no. 2 (Mar. 1962): 37–67; 45, no. 3 (May 1962): 67–92.

———. "Tōrin tō kō (ichi, ni)" 東林黨考, 一、二 (Study of the Tung-lin party, parts 1 and 2). *Tōhōgakuhō* 東方學報 52 (1980): 563–94; 55 (1983): 307–15.

Ōtani Toshio 大谷敏夫. "Yōshū Jōshū gakujutsu kō" 揚州常州學術考 (Inquiry into Yang-chou and Ch'ang-chou Scholarship). In Ono Kazuko 小野和子, ed., *Min-Shin jidai no seiji to shakai* 明清時代の政治と社會 (Society and politics during the Ming-Ch'ing period). Kyoto: Kyoto University Institute for Humanistic Studies, 1983.

Ou-yang Hsiu 歐陽修. *Ou-yang Wen-chung kung chi* 歐陽文忠公集 (Collected writings of Ou-yang Hsiu). Taipei: Commercial Press, 1967.

Pan Ku 班固. *Han-shu* 漢書 (History of the Former Han dynasty). 7 vols. Taipei: Shih-hsueh ch'u-pan-she, 1974.

P'an Lei 潘耒. "Hsu" 序 (Preface) to the *Jih-chih lu* 日知錄 (Record of knowledge gained day by day). In Wei Yuan 魏源, ed., *Huang-ch'ao ching-shih wen-pien*. 1827 edition.

Parsons, James. "The Ming Bureaucracy: Aspects of Background Forces." In Charles O. Hucker, ed., *Chinese Government in Ming Times: Seven Studies*. New York: Columbia University Press, 1969.

Pasternak, Burton. "On the Causes and Demographic Consequences of Uxorilocal Marriage in China." In Susan B. Hanley and Arthur P. Wolf, eds., *Family and Population in East Asian History*. Stanford: Stanford University Press, 1985.

———. "The Role of the Frontier in Chinese Lineage Development." *Journal of Asian Studies* 28 (1969): 551–61.

Pei-chuan chi 碑傳集 (Collection of epitaph biographies). Compiled by Ch'ien I-chi 錢儀吉. 1893 edition.

Pelikan, Jaroslav. *Jesus through the Centuries: His Place in the History of Culture*. New Haven: Yale University Press, 1985.

Perkins, Dwight. *Agricultural Development in China, 1368–1968*. Chicago: Aldine,1969.

Peterson, Willard. *Bitter Gourd: Fang I-chih and the Impetus for Intellectual Change*. New Haven: Yale University Press, 1979.

———. "Calendar Reform Prior to the Arrival of Missionaries at the Ming Court." *Ming Studies* 21 (Spring 1986): 45–61.

P'i Hsi-jui 皮錫瑞. *Ching-hsueh li-shih* 經學歷史 (History of classical studies). Hong Kong: Chung-hua Bookstore, 1961.

P'i-ling Chuang-shih tseng-hsiu tsu-p'u 毘陵莊氏增修族譜 (Revised genealogy of the Chuang lineage in Ch'ang-chou). Ch'ang-chou, 1935 edition.

P'i-ling Chuang-shih tsu-p'u 毘陵莊氏族譜 (Genealogy of the Chuang lineage in Ch'ang-chou). 1875 edition.

P'i-ling T'ang-shih chia-p'u 毘陵唐氏家譜 (Genealogy of the T'ang lineage in Ch'ang-chou). Ch'ang-chou, 1948 edition.

Pocock, J. G. A. *Politics, Language, and Time: Essays on Political Thought and History*. New York: Atheneum, 1971.

Polachek, James. "The Inner Opium War." Draft. 1983.

———. "Literati Groups and Group Politics in Nineteenth-Century China." Ph.D. diss., University of California, Berkeley, 1977.

Pollard, David. *A Chinese Look at Literature: The Literary Values of Chou Tso-jen in Relation to the Tradition*. Berkeley: University of California Press, 1973.

Potter, Jack. "Land and Lineage in Traditional China." In Maurice Freedman, ed., *Family and Kinship in Chinese Society*. Stanford: Stanford University Press, 1970.

Pulleyblank, Edwin. "Neo-Confucianism and Neo-Legalism in T'ang Intellectual Life, 755–805." In Arthur Wright, ed., *The Confucian Persuasion*. Stanford: Stanford University Press, 1960.

Rankin, Mary. "'Public Opinion' and Political Power: *Qingyi* in Late Nineteenth-Century China." *Journal of Asian Studies* 41, no. 3 (May 1982): 453–84.

Rawski, Evelyn. *Education and Popular Literacy in Ch'ing China*. Ann Arbor: University of Michigan, Center for Chinese Studies, 1979.

Rieff, Philip. *The Triumph of the Therapeutic*. New York: Harper and Row, 1968.

Santangelo, Paolo. "The Imperial Factories of Suzhou." In Stuart R. Schram, ed., *The Scope of State Power in China*. London: School of Oriental and African Studies, 1985.

Sariti, Anthony W. "Monarchy, Bureaucracy, and Absolutism in the Political Thought of Ssu-ma Kuang." *Journal of Asian Studies* 32, no. 1 (Nov. 1972): 53–76.

Saso, Michael. "What is the *Ho-t'u*?" *History of Religions* 17, nos. 3 and 4 (Feb.–May 1978): 399–416.

Satō Shinji 佐藤震二. "Shinchō Kuyōgakuha kō (jō)" 清朝公羊學派考,上 (Study of the Ch'ing dynasty Kung-yang School, part 1). *Kyūshū Chūgoku gakkai hō* 九州中國學會報 19 (1973): 20–25.

Schirokauer, Conrad. "Neo-Confucians under Attack: The Condemnation of *Wei-hsueh*." In John Haeger, ed., *Crisis and Prosperity in Sung China*. Tucson: University of Arizona Press, 1975.

Schwartz, Benjamin I. "Foreword" to Liang Ch'i-ch'ao, *Intellectual Trends in the Ch'ing Period*. Translated by Immanual Hsu. Cambridge: Harvard University Press, 1959.

———. "The Limits of 'Tradition versus Modernity' as Categories of Explanation: The Case of the Chinese Intellectuals." *Daedalus* (Spring 1972): 71–88.

Shang Yueh 尙鉞. *Chung-kuo tzu-pen chu-i kuan-hsi fa-sheng chi yen-pien te ch'u-pu yen-chiu* 中國資本主義關係發生及演變的初步研究 (Preliminary studies on the development of relations of production in Chinese capitalism). Peking: San-lien Bookstore, 1956.

Shang-shu t'ung-chien 尙書通檢 (Concordance to the Documents Classic). Peking: Harvard-Yenching Institute, 1936.

Shang-yü tang 上諭檔 (Imperial edict record book). Ch'ing dynasty archives preserved in the Palace Museum, Taipei.

Shao I-ch'en 邵懿辰. *Pān-yen-lu i-wen* 半巖廬遺文 (Bequeathed essays from the Hut in Half a Cave). 1862 edition.

Shchutskii, Iulian. *Researches on the I Ching*. Princeton: Princeton University Press, 1979.

Shen Chi-i 沈寄簃. *Han-lü chih-i* 漢律摭遺 (Collection of extant materials on Han legal statutes). Reprint. Taipei: Ting-wen Bookstore, n.d.

Shigeta Atsushi 重田德. "The Origins and Structure of Gentry Rule." Translated by Christian Daniels. In Linda Grove and Daniels, eds., *State and Society in China: Japanese Perspectives on Ming-Qing Social and Economic History*. Tokyo: Tokyo University Press, 1984.

———. *Shindai shakai keizaishi kenkyū* 清代社會經濟史研究 (Studies in the socioeconomic history of the Ch'ing dynasty). Tokyo: Iwanami Bookstore, 1975.

Shih, Vincent. *The Taiping Ideology*. Seattle: University of Washington Press, 1972.

Shih-ching yin-te 詩經引得 (Index to the Poetry Classic). Reprint. Taipei: Ch'eng-wen Bookstore, 1972.

Shih-san-ching chu-shu 十三經注疏 (Notes and commentaries to the Thirteen Classics). 1797. Reprint. Taipei: Hsin wen-feng Press, n.d.

Shils, Edward. *Tradition*. Chicago: University of Chicago Press, 1981.

Shimada Kenji 島田虔次. *Chūgoku ni okeru kindai shii no zasetsu* 中国における近代思惟の挫折 (The frustration of modern thought in China). Tokyo: Chikuma Bookstore, 1970.

———. "Shinkai kakumeiki no Kōshi mondai" 辛亥革命期の孔子問題 (The question of Confucius in the 1911 revolution). In Onogawa Hidemi 小野川秀美 and Shimada, eds., *Shinkai kakumei no kenkyū* 辛亥革命の研究 (Research on the 1911 Revolution). Tokyo: Chikuma Bookstore, 1978.

Sivin, Nathan. "Copernicus in China." In *Colloquia Copernica II: Études sur l'audience de la théorie héliocentrique*. Warsaw: Union Internationale d' Historie et Philosophie des Sciences, 1973.

———. "Foreword" to Benjamin A. Elman, *From Philosophy to Philology: Social and Intellectual Aspects of Change in Late Imperial China*. Cambridge: Harvard University Council on East Asian Studies. 1984.

Skinner, G. William. *Marketing and Social Structure in Rural China*. Tucson: University of Arizona Press, n.d. Reprinted from the *Journal of Asian Studies* 24, no. 1 (Nov. 1964): 3–43; no. 2 (Feb. 1965): 195–228; no. 3 (May 1965): 363–99.

———. "Mobility Strategies in Late Imperial China: A Regional Systems Analysis." In Carol Smith, ed., *Regional Analysis, Vol. 1: Economic Systems*. New York: Academic Press, 1976.

Smith, Joanna Handlin. "Benevolent Societies: The Reshaping of Charity during the Late Ming and Early Ch'ing." *Journal of Asian Studies* 46, no. 2 (May 1987): 309–31.

Ssu-k'u ch'üan-shu tsung-mu 四庫全書總目 (Catalog of the Complete Collection of the Four Treasuries). Reprint. Compiled by Chi Yun 紀昀 et al. Taipei: I-wen, 1974.

Ssu-ma Ch'ien 司馬遷. *Shih-chi* 史記 (Records of the Grand Historian). 10 vols. Peking: Chung-hua Bookstore, 1972.

Ssu-ma Kuang 司馬光. *Tzu-chih t'ung-chien* 資治通鑑 (Comprehensive mirror for aid in government). 11 vols. Taipei: Hung-shih Press, 1980.

Ssu-shu ta-ch'üan 四書大全 (Complete collection of the Four Books). Wen-yuan-k'o edition. Peking, 1776.

Struve, Lynn. "Continuity and Change in Early Ch'ing Thought." In *Cambridge History of China*, vol. 9, part 1. Cambridge: Cambridge University Press, forthcoming.

———. *The Southern Ming, 1644–1662*. New Haven: Yale University Press, 1984.

he Fabulous Horned Uni-

888 edition.
d of Master Yen [Yuan]).

ught: Its Sources and Its
rsity of California, Los

the Sixteenth and Seven-
n Grove and Christian
Perspectives on Ming-
University Press, 1984.
ng chin-wen hsueh-p'ai
法(The Ch'ing dynasty
). In his *Wu-hsu pien-fa*
the history of the 1898

" 清代經今文學的復興
'ing dynasty). *Chung-*

Reforms Revisited: A
dred Days: Personali-
8, no. 1 (June 1987):

g-chou fu-chih. 1886

en-chi 荊川先生文集
lition.
Collected writings of

o. Ca. 1557 edition.
先生文集 (Collected
u hsien-che i-shu
ou thinkers). 1876–

n-t'i-wen lu 國朝
ng-chou during the

hina? The Case of
no. 2 (December

to Chu Hsi. Cam-
, 1982.
sion in the White

Chinese National-
China. Tucson:

Hung Pei-chiang

'ang ch'ung-k'an
om the Hall for
hiang ch'üan-chi.

ofs of meanings in
diant Dew). 1910.

In *T'ung-chih-t'ang*
873.
玄晏齋困思抄 (Tran-
Profound Quietude).

sbaden: Franz Steiner

idation of meanings in
en. Chiang-yin: Nan-

essays from the Hut of

Ch'un-ch'iu shu-tz'u. In
uang-chou: Yueh-tung,

i shuo" 宋儒春秋攘夷說
barians in the Spring and
h-pao 成功大學學報 18

statutes and precedents in
1908.
shih-lu 大淸仁宗睿(嘉慶)
'ing Chia-ch'ing Emperor).

ti shih-lu 大淸高宗純(乾隆)
g Ch'ien-lung Emperor). Re-
1964.
大淸高宗純皇帝聖訓 (Sacred
r). Peking, n.d.
g-ti shih-lu 大淸世宗憲(雍正)
ing Yung-cheng Emperor). Re-

n 大淸世宗憲皇帝聖訓 (Sacred
ror). Peking, n.d.
Chen's collected essays). Hong

g" 劉先生行狀 (Chronicle of ac-
. In Tai Wang, *Che-lin-t'ang i-chi*

謫麐堂遺集 (Collected writings from the Hall of
corn). 1875 edition.

———. *Lun-yü chu* 論語注 (Notes to the Analects).

———. *Yen-shih hsueh-chi* 顏氏學記 (Scholarly reco
Reprint. Taipei: World Bookstore, 1980.

Tain, Tzey-yueh. "Tung Chung-shu's System of Tho
Influence on Han Scholars." Ph.D. diss., Unive
Angeles, 1974.

Tanaka, Masatoshi. "Rural Handicraft in Jiangnan in
teenth Centuries." Translated by Linda Grove.
Daniels, ed., *State and Society in China: Japanes
Qing Social and Economic History*. Tokyo: Tokyo

T'ang Chih-chün 湯志鈞. "Ch'ing-tai Ch'ang-chou ch
yü Wu-hsu pien-fa" 清代常州經今文學派與戊戌變
Ch'ang-chou New Text school and the 1898 reforms
shih lun-ts'ung 戊戌變法史論叢 (Collected essays on
Reforms). Hong Kong: Ch'ung-wen Bookstore, 197

———. "Ch'ing-tai ching chin-wen-hsueh te fu-hsing
(The revival of New Text classical studies in the C
kuo-shih yen-chiu 中國史研究 3 (1980): 145–56.

T'ang Chih-chün and Benjamin A. Elman. "The 1898
Review of Luke S. K. Kwong's *A Mosaic of the Hu
ties, Politics, and Ideas of 1898*." *Late Imperial Chin
205–13.

T'ang Ho-cheng 唐鶴徵. "Hsu" 序 (Preface) to *Ch'an
edition.

T'ang Shun-chih 唐順之. *Ching-ch'uan hsien-sheng w
(Collected writings of Mr. [T'ang] Shun-chih). 1549 e

———. *Ching-chuan hsien-sheng wen-chi* 荆川先生文集
Mister [T'ang] Shun-chih). 1573 edition.

———. "Hsu" 序 (Preface) to Chi Pen, *Ch'un-ch'iu ssu-k'

———. *T'ang Ching-ch'uan hsien-sheng wen-chi* 唐荆川
essays of Mr. T'ang Shun-chih). In *Ch'ang-ch
常州先哲遺書 (Bequeathed writings of earlier Ch'ang-c
97. Reprint. Taipei: I-wen Publishing House, 1971.

T'ao Chün-hsuan 陶濬宣. *Kuo-ch'ao Ch'ang-chou p'i
常州駢體文錄* (Record of parallel prose essays in Ch'a
Ch'ing dynasty). Ca. 1890 edition.

Tillman, Hoyt. "Proto-Nationalism in Twelfth-Century C
Ch'en Liang." *Harvard Journal of Asiatic Studies* 39
1979): 403–28.

———. *Utilitarian Confucianism: Ch'en Liang's Challenge*
bridge: Harvard University Council on East Asian Studie

Tjan Tjoe Som. *Po Hu T'ung. The Comprehensive Discus
Tiger Hall*. 2 vols. Leiden: E. J. Brill, 1949–52.

Trauzettel, Rolf. "Sung Patriotism as a First Step Toward
ism." In John Haeger, ed., *Crisis and Prosperity in Sun
University of Arizona Press, 1978.

Tsang Lin 臧琳, *Ching-i tsa-chi (hsu-lu)* 經義雜記(敍錄) ([Writings from the] Jottings on the meaning of the Classics). Compiled by Tsang Yung 臧庸 et al. In *Pai-ching-t'ang ts'ung-shu* 拜經堂叢書 (Collectanea from the Hall of Reverence for the Classics). Wu-chin edition. 1799.

Tsang Yung 臧庸. "Li-pu shih-lang Chuang kung hsiao-chuan" 禮部侍郎莊公小傳 (Brief biography of the Undersecretary in the Board of Rites Master Chuang [Ts'un-yü]). In *Pai-ching-t'ang wen-chi* 拜經堂文集 (Collected writings from the Hall of Reverence for the Classics). Photolithograph of an unpaginated manuscript. Taipei, 1930.

Tseng Kuo-fan 曾國藩. "Hsu" 序 (Preface) to Chang Hui-yen, *Ming-k'o wen ssu-pien. Ssu-pu ts'ung-k'an erh-p'ien* edition. Shanghai, 1934–35.

Tu, Ching-i. "The Chinese Examination Essay: Some Literary Considerations." *Monumenta Serica* 31 (1974–75): 393–406.

———. "Neo-Confucianism and Literary Criticism in Ming China: The Case of T'ang Shun-chih (1507–1560)." Paper presented at the Fourth Quadrennial International Comparative Literature Conference, Tanshui, Taiwan, Aug. 1983.

Tu Wei-yun 杜維運. *Chao I chuan* 趙翼傳 (Biography of Chao I). Taipei: Shih-pao wen-hua Press, 1983.

Tu Yü 杜預. *Ch'un-ch'iu shih-li* 春秋釋例 (Explanation of precedents in the Spring and Autumn Annals). Taipei: Chung-hua Bookstore, 1970.

———. *Ch'un-ch'iu shih-li* (Explanation of precedents in the Spring and Autumn Annals). Peking: Imperial Printing Office, 1802.

Tung Shi-hsi 董士錫. "Chia-p'u" 家譜 (Genealogy [of the Tung family]). In his *Ch'i-wu-lun-chai chi* 齊物論齋集 (Collection from the Studio for Making Things Equal). N.d.

———. "Ch'i-wu-lun-chai wen-lu" 齊物論齋文錄 (Records and writings from the Studio for Making Things Equal). Manuscript copy. Ca. 1843.

———. "I-shuo hsu" 易說序 (Preface to [Chuang Ts'un-yü's] Sayings on the Changes). In Chuang Ts'un-yü, *Wei-ching-chai i-shu*. Yang-hu, 1882.

T'ung-ch'eng-p'ai yen-chiu lun-wen-chi. 桐城派研究論文集 (Collected research essays on the T'ung-ch'eng school). He-fei: An-hui People's Press, 1963.

T'ung-chih-t'ang ching-chieh 通志堂經解 (T'ung-chih Hall's exegesis of the Classics). 1676. Reprint. Kuang-chou: Yueh-tung, 1873.

"Tung-lin pieh-sheng" 東林別乘 (Separate records of Tung-lin). Kuang-chou: 1958. Transcribed list from an old manuscript in the provincial Chung-shan Library.

Tung-lin shih-mo 東林始末 (Beginning and end of the Tung-lin partisans). Shanghai: Shanghai Bookstore, 1982.

Tung-lin shu-yuan chih 東林書院志 (Gazetteer of the Tung-lin Academy). 1733 edition.

Twitchett, Denis. "Comment on J. L. Watson's Article." *China Quarterly* 92 (1982): 623–27.

———. "A Critique of Some Recent Studies of Modern Chinese Social-Economic History." *Transactions of the International Conference of Orientalists in Japan* 10 (1965): 33–39, 154–72.

———. "Documents of Clan Administration: I, the Rules of Administration of the Charitable Estate of the Fan Clan." *Asia Major* 8 (1960-61): 1–35.

———. "The Fan Clan's Charitiable Estate, 1050–1760." In David S. Nivison and Arthur Wright, eds., *Confucianism in Action*. Stanford: Stanford University Press, 1959.

Uno Seiichi 宇野精一. *Chūgoku kotengaku no tenkai* 中国古典学の展開 (The development of classical studies in China). Tokyo: Hokuryūkan, 1949.

———. "Shūrai Ryū Kin gisaku setsu ni tsuite" 周禮劉歆偽作說について (On the theory that Liu Hsin forged the Rituals of Chou). *Tō-A ronsō* 東亞論叢 5 (1941): 237–73.

Vandermeersch, Leon. "An Enquiry into the Chinese Conception of the Law." In Stuart R. Schram, ed., *The Scope of State Power in China*. London: School of Oriental and African Studies, 1985.

von der Sprenkel, Otto Berkelbach. "High Officials of the Ming: A Note on the Ch'i Ch'ing Nien Piao of the Ming History." *Bulletin of the School of Oriental and African Studies* 14 (1952): 83–114.

Wakeman, Frederic, Jr. "China and the Seventeenth-Century Crisis." *Late Imperial China* 7, no. 1 (June 1986): 1–16.

———. *History and Will: Philosophical Perspectives of Mao Tse-tung's Thought*. Berkeley: University of California Press, 1973.

———. "Localism and Loyalism during the Ch'ing Conquest of Kiangnan: The Tragedy of Chiang-yin." In Wakeman and Carolyn Grant, eds., *Conflict and Control in Late Imperial China*. Berkeley: University of California Press, 1975.

———. "The *Huang-ch'ao ching-shih wen-pien*." *Ch'ing-shih wen-t'i* 1, no. 10 (1969): 8–22.

———. "The Price of Autonomy: Intellectuals in Ming and Ch'ing Politics." *Daedalus* 101, no. 2 (1972): 35–70.

Wang Ch'ang 王昶. *Ch'un-jung-t'ang chi* 春融堂集 (Collection from the Hall of Cheerful Spring). Meng-hsia-chüan shu-nan shu-she edition. 1807.

Wang Chia-chien 王家儉. *Wei Yuan nien-p'u* 魏源年譜 (Chronological biography of Wei Yuan). Taipei: Academia Sinica, 1967.

Wang Chiao 王交. "Hou-hsu" 後序 (Afterword) to Chi Pen, *Ch'un-ch'iu ssu-k'ao*. Ca. 1557.

Wang Chung 汪中. *Shu-hsueh* 述學. (Discourses on learning). Reprint. Taipei: Kuang-wen Bookstore, 1970.

Wang Hsi-hsun 汪喜荀. *Ch'ieh-chu-an wen-chi* 且住菴文集 (Collected essays from the Hut for Stopping). Taipei: World Bookstore, 1971.

Wang Ming-sheng 王鳴盛. "Hsu" 序 (Preface) to his *Shih-ch'i-shih shang-ch'ueh* 十七史商榷 (Critical study of the Seventeen Dynastic Histories). Reprint. Taipei: Kuang-wen Bookstore, 1960.

Wang Nien-sun 王念孫. "Shen-shou fu-chün hsing-shu" 申受府君行述 (Obituary for Liu Feng-lu). In *Hsi-ying Liu-shih chia-p'u*. 1876 edition.

Wang Tse-fu 王澤浦. "T'ung-ch'eng-p'ai te i-fa" 桐城派的義法 (Models and rules of the T'ung-ch'eng school). In *T'ung-ch'eng-p'ai yen-chiu lun-wen chi*. He-fei: An-hui People's Press, 1963.

Wang Yang-ming 王陽明. *Ch'uan-hsi lu* 傳習錄 (Record of transmitted cultivation). In his *Wang Yang-ming ch'üan-chi* 全集 (Complete works of Wang Yang-ming). Taipei: K'ao-cheng Press, 1973.

———. *Wang Yang-ming ch'üan-chi* 全集 (Complete works of Wang Yang-ming). Hong Kong: Kuang-chi Bookstore, 1959.

Wang, Yeh-chien. *Land Taxation in Imperial China, 1750–1911*. Cambridge: Harvard University Press, 1973.

Wang Yuquan. "Some Salient Features of the Ming Labor Service System." *Ming Studies* 21 (Spring 1986): 1–44.

Watson, Burton, trans. *Han Fei Tzu*. New York: Columbia University Press, 1964.

———, trans. *Records of the Grand Historian of China*. 2 vols. New York: Columbia University Press, 1971.

Watson, James L. "Anthropological Overview: The Development of Chinese Kin Groups." In Patricia Buckley Ebrey and James L. Watson, eds., *Kinship Organization in Late Imperial China, 1000–1940*. Berkeley: University of California Press, 1986.

———. "Chinese Kinship Reconsidered: Anthropological Perspectives on Historical Research." *China Quarterly* 92 (1982): 589–622.

———. "Hereditary Tenancy and Corporate Landlordism in Traditional China: A Case Study." *Modern Asian Studies* 11, no. 2 (1977): 161–82.

Watson, Rubie S. "The Creation of a Chinese Lineage: The Teng of Ha Tsuen, 1669–1751." *Modern Asian Studies* 16, no. 1 (1982): 69–100.

———. *Inequality among Brothers: Class and Kinship in South China*. Cambridge: Cambridge University Press, 1985.

Watt, John. *The District Magistrate in Late Imperial China*. New York: Columbia University Press, 1972.

Weber, Max. *The Religion of China*. Translated by Hans Gerth. New York: Macmillan, 1954.

Wechsler, Howard. *Offerings of Jade and Silk: Ritual and Symbol in the Legitimation of the T'ang Dynasty*. New Haven: Yale University Press, 1985.

Wei Yuan 魏源. *Ku-wei-t'ang nei-wai chi* 古微堂內外集 (Inner and outer collection of writings from the Hall of Ancient Subtleties). Reprint. Taipei: Wen-hai Press, 1966.

———. "Ku-wei-t'ang wen-kao" 古微堂文稿 (Draft essays from the Hall of Ancient Subtlety). Manuscripts in the Peking National Library Rare Books Collection. N.d.

———. *Lao-tzu pen-i* 老子本義 (Original meanings in Lao-tzu). T'ung-lu edition. 1900.

———. "Liu Li-pu i-shu hsu" 劉禮部遺書序 (Preface for the bequeathed writings of Liu Feng-lu). In *Wei Yuan chi*. 2 vols. Peking: Chung-hua Bookstore, 1976.

———. *Shu ku-wei* 書古微 (Ancient Subtleties of the Documents Classic). 1878 edition.

———. *Wei Yuan chi* 魏源集 (Collected writings of Wei Yuan). 2 vols. Peking: Chung-hua Bookstore, 1976.

———, ed. *Huang-ch'ao ching-shih wen-pien* 皇朝經世文編 (Collected writings on statecraft from the Ch'ing dynasty). 1827 and 1873. Reprint. Taipei: World Bookstore, 1964.

Weng Fang-kang 翁方綱. *Fu-ch'u-chai wen-chi* 復初齋文集 (Collected writings from the Studio of Return to Beginnings). 1877 edition.

Whitbeck, Judith. "Kung Tzu-chen and the Redirection of Literati Commitment in Early Nineteeth-Century China." *Ch'ing-shih wen-t'i* 4, no. 10 (Dec. 1983): 1–32.

Wiens, Mi Chu. "Changes in the Fiscal and Rural Control Systems in the Fourteenth and Fifteenth Centuries." *Ming Studies* 3 (Fall 1976): 53–69.

———. "Cotton Textile Production and Rural Social Transformation in Early Modern China." *Journal of the Institute of Chinese Studies of the Chinese University of Hong Kong* 7, no. 2 (1974): 515–34.

———. "Lord and Peasant. The Sixteenth to the Eighteenth Century." *Modern China* 6, no. 1 (Jan. 1980): 3–34.

Wilhelm, Hellmut. "Chinese Confucianism on the Eve of the Great Encounter." In Marius Jansen, ed., *Changing Japanese Attitudes toward Modernization*. Princeton: Princeton University Press, 1965.

Woo, Kang. *Les Trois Théories Politiques du Tch'ouen-chou interprétés par Tong Tchong-chou d'aprés les principes de l'école de Kong-yang*. Paris: Librairie Ernest Leroux, 1932.

Wu Ch'ang-shou 吳昌綬. *Ting-an hsien-sheng nien-p'u* 定盦先生年譜 (Chronological biography of Kung Tzu-chen). In *Kung Ting-an (Tzu-chen) yen-chiu* 龔定盦(自珍)研究 (Research on Kung Tzu-chen). Compiled by Chu Chieh-ch'in 朱傑勤. Hong Kong: Ch'ung-wen Bookstore, 1971.

Wu Hsiu 吳修. "Hsu" 序 (Preface) to Huang Ching-jen 黃景仁, *Liang-tang-hsuan shih-ch'ao* 兩當軒詩鈔 (Writings and poetry from the Study of Double Appropriateness). 1858 edition.

Wu Hung-i 吳宏一. "Ch'ang-chou-p'ai tz'u-hsueh yen-chiu" 常州派詞學研究 (Research on the lyric poetry studies of the Ch'ang-chou school). M.A. thesis, National Taiwan University, 1970.

———. *Ch'ing-tai shih-hsueh ch'u-t'an* 清代詩學初談 (Preliminary analysis of poetry studies in the Ch'ing period). Taipei: Mu-t'ung Press, 1977.

Wu-chin Chuang-shih tseng-hsiu tsu-p'u 武進莊氏增修族譜 (Revised genealogy of the Chuang lineage in Wu-chin). Ca. 1840 edition.

Wu-chin hsien-chih 武進縣志 (Gazetteer of Wu-chin county). 1605 edition.

Wu-chin Hsi-ying Liu-shih chia-p'u 武進西營劉氏家譜 (Genealogy of the Liu lineage from Hsi-ying in Wu-chin). Ch'ang-chou, 1929 edition.

Wu-chin T'ien-ning-ssu chih 武進天寧寺志 (Gazetteer of the Temple of Heavenly Repose in Wu-chin). Taipei: Chung-hua ta-tien Printing Co., 1973.

Wu-chin Yang-hu hsien ho-chih 武進陽湖縣合志 (Gazetteer of Wu-chin and Yang-hu counties). 1886 edition.

Wu-hsi Chin-k'uei hsien-chih 無錫金匱縣志 (Gazetteer of Wu-hsi and Chin-k'uei counties). 1814 edition.

Xu Yangjie. "The Feudal Clan System Inherited from the Song and Ming Periods." *Social Sciences in China* 3 (1980): 29–82.

Yamane, Yukio. "Reforms in the Service Levy System in the Fifteenth and Sixteenth Centuries." Translated by Helen Dunston. In Linda Grove and Christian Daniels, eds., *State and Society in China: Japanese Perspectives on*

Ming-Qing Social and Economic History. Tokyo: Tokyo University Press, 1984.

Yamanoi Yū 山井湧. "Ko Enbu no gakumon kan" 顧炎武の學問觀 (Ku Yen-wu's scholarly position). *Chūō daigaku bungakubu kiyō* 中央大学文学部紀要 35 (1964): 67–93.

———. "Kō Sōgi no gakumon" 黃宗羲の學問 (Huang Tsung-hsi's scholarship). *Tōkyō Shingaku hō* 東京支那學報 3 (1957): 31–50.

Yang Ch'ao-tseng 楊超曾. "Chi-lu" 紀錄 (Record). In Hui Shih-ch'i's *Pan-nung hsien-sheng ch'un-ch'iu shuo*, compiled by Hui Tung. Huang-chou shu-shih edition, 1749.

———. "Pei" 碑 (Epitaph) for Hui Shih-ch'i. In Hui Shih-ch'i, *Pan-nung hsien-sheng ch'un-ch'iu shuo*, compiled by Hui Tung. Huang-chou shu-shih edition, 1749.

Yang Ch'i 羊淇. "Ming-mo Tung-lin tang yü Ch'ang-chou" 明末東林黨與常州 (Ch'ang-chou and the late Ming Tung-lin party). *Ch'ang-chou ku-chin* 常州古今 2 (1981): 201–20.

Yang Ch'un 楊椿. "Ch'un-ch'iu k'ao hou-hsu" 春秋考後序 (Afterword to a study of the Spring and Autumn Annals). In Yang Ch'un, *Meng-lin-t'ang chi*. Ch'ang-chou: Hung-mei-ko, ca. 1822.

———. "Hsu" 序 (Preface) to Ku Tung-kao, *Ch'un-ch'iu ta-shih-piao*. Shang-chih-t'ang edition, 1873.

———. *Meng-lin-t'ang chi* 孟鄰堂集 (Collection from the Hall of Proximity to Mencius). Ch'ang-chou: Hung-mei-ko, ca. 1822.

Yang Hsiang-k'uei 楊向奎. *Ching-shih-chai hsueh-shu wen-chi* 經史齋學術文集 (Collected essays from the Studio of the Classics and Histories). Shanghai: Shanghai People's Press, 1983.

———. "Ch'ing-tai te chin-wen ching-hsueh" 清代的今文經學 (Ch'ing dynasty New Text classical studies). *Ch'ing-shih lun-ts'ung* 清史論叢 (Peking) 1 (1979): 177–209.

———. *Chung-kuo ku-tai she-hui yü ku-tai ssu-hsiang yen-chiu* 中國古代社會與古代思想研究 (Study of ancient Chinese society and thought). 2 vols. Shanghai: Hsin-hua Bookstore, 1964.

Yang Shen 楊慎. "Su-Ju ni-ku" 俗儒泥古 (Backward Confucians' fixation on the past). In Yang Shen, *T'ai-shih sheng-an wen-chi*. Ts'ai Ju-hsien edition. 1582.

———. *T'ai-shih sheng-an wen-chi* 太史升庵文集 (Collected essays from the Small Cottage Ascending to the Grand Historian). Ts'ai Ju-hsien edition. 1582.

Yao Chi-heng 姚際恆. "Ch'un-sh'iu lun-chih" 春秋論旨 (Discussions on points in the Spring and Autumn Annals). In his *Ch'un-ch'iu t'ung-lun*. Ch'ing manuscript; 1707 preface. Preserved in the Peking National Library.

———. "Ch'un-ch'iu t'ung-lun" 春秋通論 (Penetrating discussions of the Spring and Autumn Annals). Ch'ing manuscript; 1707 preface. Preserved in the Peking National Library.

Yao Nai 姚鼐. *Hsi-pao-hsuan chiu-ching shuo* 惜抱軒九經說 (Sayings on the Nine Classics from the Study of Cherishing and Protecting). N.d.

———. *Hsi-pao-hsuan ch'üan-chi* 惜抱軒全集 (Complete collection from the Studio of Sparing Aspirations). Chiao-ching shan-fang edition. Shanghai, 1907.

———. *Hsi-pao-hsuan ch'üan-chi* 惜抱軒全集 (Complete collection from the Studio of Sparing Aspirations). Taipei: World Bookstore, 1984.

———. *Ku-wen tz'u lei-tsuan* 古文辭類纂 (Classified collection of ancient prose phrases). Ca. 1820.

Yao Ying 姚瑩. *Tung-ming wen-chi* 東溟文集 (Collected essays of Yao Ying). An-fu edition. 1867.

Yasui Kōzan 安居香山, ed. *Shin'i shisō no sōgō teki kenkyū* 讖緯思想の綜合的研究 (Synthesis of apocryphal thought). Tokyo: Kokusho kankōkai, 1984.

Yeh Hsien-en 葉顯恩. *Ming-Ch'ing Hui-chou nung-ts'un she-hui yü tien-p'u chih* 明清徽州農村社會與佃僕制 (Tenancy and rural society in Hui-chou during the Ming and Ch'ing). Ho-fei: An-hui People's Press, 1983.

Yeh Kuo-liang 葉國良. *Sung-jen i-ching kai-ching k'ao* 宋人疑經改經考 (Study of Sung doubts and emendations of the Classics). Taipei: National Taiwan University, 1980.

Yen Jo-chü 閻若璩. *Shang-shu ku-wen shu-cheng* 尚書古文疏證 (Evidential analysis of the Old Text Documents). In *Huang-Ch'ing ching-chieh hsu-pien*. Chiang-yin: Nan-ch'ing Academy, 1888.

———. "Yuan-hsu" 原序 (Original preface) to Tsang Lin, *Ching-i tsa-chi*. Compiled by Tsang Yung et al. In *Pai-ching-t'ang ts'ung-shu*. Wu-chin edition, 1799.

Yen Yuan 顏元. *Ssu-shu cheng-wu* 四書正誤 (Correction of errors on the Four Books). In Yen Yuan and Li Kung, *Yen-Li ts'ung-shu*. Reprint. Taipei: Kuang-wen Bookstore, 1965.

Yen-Li ts'ung-shu 顏李叢書 (Collectanea of Yen Yuan and Li Kung). Reprint. Taipei: Kuang-wen Bookstore, 1965.

Yoshiwara Fumiaki 吉原文昭 "Hoku-Sō Shunjū gaku no ichi sokumen" 北宋春秋学の一側面 (A perspective on studies of the Spring and Autumn Annals during the Northern Sung period). In *Chūgoku tetsugaku shi no tembō to mosaku* 中国哲学史の展望と摸索 (Prospects and directions in the history of Chinese philosophy). Tokyo: Sōbunsha, 1976.

Yuan, Tsing. "The Porcelain Industry at Ching-te-chen, 1550–1700." *Ming Studies* 6 (Spring 1978): 45–53.

———. "Urban Riots and Disturbances." In Jonathan Spence and John Wills, eds., *From Ming To Ch'ing: Conquest, Region, and Continuity in Seventeenth-Century China*. New Haven: Yale University Press, 1979.

Yun Ching 惲敬. *Ta-yun shan-fang chi* 大雲山房集 (Collection from the mountain hut on Great Cloud Mountain). Taipei: World Bookstore, 1964.

Zito, Angela R. "Re-presenting Sacrifice: Cosmology and the Editing of Texts." *Ch'ing-shih wen-t'i* 5, no. 2 (Dec. 1984): 47–74.

Zurndorfer, Harriet. "Chinese Merchants and Commerce in Sixteenth Century China." In Wilt Idema, ed., *Leiden Studies in Sinology*. Leiden: E. J. Brill, 1981.

———. "Local Lineages and Local Development: A Case Study of the Fan Lineage, Hsiu-ning *hsien*, Hui-chou, 800–1500." *T'oung Pao* 70 (1984): 18–59.

———. "Violence and Political Protest in Ming and Ch'ing China." *International Review of Social History* 28 (1983): 304–19.

INDEX